School Counseling for the Twenty-First Century

FOURTH EDITION

School Counseling for the Twenty-First Century

Stanley B. Baker
North Carolina State University

Edwin R. Gerler, Jr.
North Carolina State University

PEARSON

Merrill
Prentice Hall

Upper Saddle River, New Jersey
Columbus, Ohio

Library of Congress Cataloging-in-Publication Data

Baker, Stanley B.
    School counseling for the twenty-first century/Stanley B. Baker, Edwin R. Gerler, Jr.—4th ed.
       p. cm.
    Includes bibliographical references and index.
    ISBN 0-13-049485-2 (casebound)
    1. Student counselors—Training of—United States. 2. Educational counseling—United
States. I. Title: School counseling for the 21st century. II. Gerler, Edwin R. III. Title.

LB1731.75.B35 2004
   371.4—dc21   2003048717

Vice President and Executive Publisher:
  Jeffery W. Johnston
Publisher: Kevin M. Davis
Editorial Assistant: Autumn Crisp
Production Editor: Mary Harlan
Production Coordinator: Thistle Hill
  Publishing Services
Design Coordinator: Diane Lorenzo
Photo Coordinator: Kathy Kirkland

Text Design and Illustrations:
  The GTS Companies/York, PA Campus
Cover Design: Jeff Vanik
Cover Image: SuperStock
Production Manager: Laura Messerly
Director of Marketing: Ann Castel Davis
Marketing Manager: Amy June
Marketing Coordinator: Tyra Poole

This book was set in OrigGarmnd BT by *The GTS Companies*/York, PA Campus. It was printed and bound by R. R. Donnelley & Sons Company. The cover was printed by The Lehigh Press, Inc.

Photo Credits: Stanley B. Baker, pp. 1, 56, 90, 325, 362; Scott Cunningham/Merrill, pp. 116, 166, 191, 206, 225; George Dodson/PH College, p. 357; Kevin Fitzsimons/Merrill, p. 43; Edwin R. Gerler, Jr., pp. 28, 30, 94; Jean Greenwald/Merrill, p. 77; Mary Hagler/Merrill, p. 120; David Mager/Pearson Learning, p. 314; Anthony Magnacca/Merrill, pp. 35, 45, 58, 129, 152, 161, 180, 227, 237, 267, 295, 311, 318; Pearson Learning, p. 321; Barbara Schwartz/Merrill, pp. 285, 339; Anne Vega/Merrill, pp. 176, 201, 249, 254, 304; Tom Watson/Merrill, p. 220; Todd Yarrington/Merrill, p. 98, 352.

Pearson Education Ltd.
Pearson Education Singapore Pte. Ltd.
Pearson Education Canada, Ltd.
Pearson Education–Japan

Pearson Education Australia Pty. Limited
Pearson Education North Asia Ltd.
Pearson Educación de Mexico, S.A. de C.V.
Pearson Education Malaysia Pte. Ltd.

10 9 8 7 6 5 4 3 2 1
ISBN 0-13-049485-2

To our wives and best friends—
Mary Esther Clark Baker
Muffin Padgett Gerler

PREFACE

The foundation for the fourth edition of *School Counseling for the Twenty-First Century* was built for us in the late 1960s and early 1970s when—as a high school counselor (Stan Baker) in Janesville, Wisconsin, and as an elementary school counselor (Ed Gerler) in Millville, Pennsylvania—we experienced the daily challenges of working with students, teachers, and parents. Racial upheaval and the Vietnam War created the headlines of that era and changed the lives of us all. Affective Education and Career Education were among the tasks mandated for school counselors of that time. Memories linger of carrying a large video camera, with cords dragging along the floor of a barn, to record a career education lesson on the work of a dairy farmer. Technology has evolved, but cultural, racial, and international tensions continue in our twenty-first century world. School counselors have new mandates and new technologies to apply, but face many of the same challenges that existed when we began our work in Janesville and Millville.

Educators across the world need to prepare a diverse citizenry to function cooperatively in a high-tech, competitive, global economy and to be well-adjusted enough to cope with its changes and challenges. The fourth edition of *School Counseling for the Twenty-First Century* takes advantage of ever-changing computer and Internet technology to prepare school counselors for helping students meet the (new and old) academic, social, psychological, and economic challenges of a complex, diverse world.

This new edition of our book features online lessons that help professors and graduate students to reflect on the content of each chapter. The online lessons also encourage professors, graduate students, and practitioners to generate ideas for an emerging School Counseling Activities Network (SCAN)—www.scan21st.com—an Internet site devoted to the invention of online materials and strategies for helping young people meet some of the challenges they face. In association with the book and online lessons, SCAN is designed to bring the graduate school classroom and the practice of school counseling into closer harmony.

The content of *School Counseling for the Twenty-First Century* has evolved in the following ways. A new opening chapter introduces readers to the school counseling profession. The introduction in chapter 1 highlights three current initiatives that may influence the school counseling profession: the American School Counselor Association's National Model for School Counseling Programs, the Education Trust's National School Counselor Training Initiative, and the School–Community Collaboration Model. The remainder of the book presents competencies for school counselors within the context of these initiatives, with a new emphasis on competencies in advocacy, leadership, and collaboration. Chapter 2 explores a balanced approach to school counseling, which is the book's theme. Chapter 3 examines the legal and ethical responsibilities of school counselors. Chapters 4 through 13 focus on important competencies for school counselors in the following areas: prevention, individual and group counseling, consulting, referral and coordination, disseminating information, helping students make transitions, assessment, advocacy, leadership, and accountability. The final chapter helps counselors reflect on their futures as professional counselors in schools.

Each chapter begins with a vignette—bringing the work of school counselors to life—to motivate serious study of subject matter important to counseling in schools. Equally compelling are the many counseling examples and activities, presented in the text and in the online assignments, that make conceptual material understandable and relevant to school counseling practice.

Our schools need excellent counseling programs. The school counseling profession is challenged to define and enunciate its priorities clearly as social changes and socioeconomic pressures influence the changing directions of both public and private schools. The next generation of counselors has an opportunity to make significant contributions to the responses the schools make to these demands. The fourth edition of *School Counseling for the Twenty-First Century* was developed with these demands and challenges in mind. The book and its online affiliates are designed primarily for courses in which graduate students are introduced to, and socialized for, the school counseling profession. The material presented is also a useful source of information for students in school administration and introductory counseling courses, as well as a resource for professional school counselors in the process of self-renewal.

The final chapter of *School Counseling for the Twenty-First Century* begins with a testimonial we heard from a school counselor (now retired) who reflected on his career with these words:

> I have been a school counselor for 35 years. As I reflect on my years in counseling, I realize that I could not have chosen a better, more rewarding career for myself.

Our goal in writing this book and in developing its online materials was to help prepare a new generation of school counselors for rewarding careers.

To professors who adopt this textbook: Please contact Kevin Davis at Prentice Hall for a copy of the Instructor's Manual—Kevin_Davis@Prenhall.com

ACKNOWLEDGMENTS

The authors wish to thank the following reviewers for their helpful comments and suggestions: Susan Norris Huss, Bowling Green State University; Jean Peterson, Purdue University; Tarrell Portman, University of Iowa; Deborah Rifenbary-Murphy, University of New Mexico; and Thomas A. Wood, University of Texas at El Paso.

DISCOVER THE COMPANION WEBSITE ACCOMPANYING THIS BOOK

THE PRENTICE HALL COMPANION WEBSITE: A VIRTUAL LEARNING ENVIRONMENT

Technology is a constantly growing and changing aspect of our field that is creating a need for content and resources. To address this emerging need, Prentice Hall has developed an online learning environment for students and professors alike—Companion Websites—to support our textbooks.

In creating a Companion Website, our goal is to build on and enhance what the textbook already offers. For this reason, the content for each user-friendly website is organized by chapter and provides the professor and student with a variety of meaningful resources.

For the Professor—

Every Companion Website integrates **Syllabus Manager**™, an online syllabus creation and management utility.

- **Syllabus Manager**™ provides you, the instructor, with an easy, step-by-step process to create and revise syllabi, with direct links into Companion Website and other online content without having to learn HTML.
- Students may logon to your syllabus during any study session. All they need to know is the web address for the Companion Website and the password you've assigned to your syllabus.
- After you have created a syllabus using **Syllabus Manager**™, students may enter the syllabus for their course section from any point in the Companion Website.
- Clicking on a date, the student is shown the list of activities for the assignment. The activities for each assignment are linked directly to actual content, saving time for students.
- Adding assignments consists of clicking on the desired due date, then filling in the details of the assignment—name of the assignment, instructions, and whether it is a one-time or repeating assignment.
- In addition, links to other activities can be created easily. If the activity is online, a URL can be entered in the space provided, and it will be linked automatically in the final syllabus.

- Your completed syllabus is hosted on our servers, allowing convenient updates from any computer on the Internet. Changes you make to your syllabus are immediately available to your students at their next logon.

For the Student—

Common Companion Website features for students include:

- **Chapter Objectives**—Outline key concepts from the text.
- **Interactive Self-quizzes**—Complete with hints and automatic grading that provide immediate feedback for students. After students submit their answers for the interactive self-quizzes, the Companion Website **Results Reporter** computes a percentage grade, provides a graphic representation of how many questions were answered correctly and incorrectly, and gives a question-by-question analysis of the quiz. Students are given the option to send their quiz to up to four email addresses (professor, teaching assistant, study partner, etc.).
- **Web Destinations**—Links to www sites that relate to chapter content.
- **Message Board**—Virtual bulletin board to post or respond to questions or comments from a national audience.

To take advantage of the many available resources, please visit the *School Counseling for the Twenty-First Century,* Third Edition, Companion Website at

www.prenhall.com/baker

BRIEF CONTENTS

CONTENTS

CHAPTER 8
Helping Students Acquire and Process Information   201

CHAPTER 9
Providing Transition Assistance in School Counseling   225

CHAPTER 1

Emergence of the School Counseling Profession

Goal: To introduce readers to the school counseling profession, provide a historical survey of the profession's development, cite current challenges to the profession, present initiatives designed to meet the challenges and move school counseling into the mainstream of school reform, and present our ideas for technology-enhanced learning that will complement this text.

During our years as counselor educators, we have listened to hundreds of graduate students discuss why they want to become school counselors. We have heard stories like these:

I have been a math teacher for 5 years. Kids are unable to concentrate on learning math because they have so many problems at home. I want to see if I can help some of these kids.

I had a very difficult childhood. No one paid much attention to me—not even my parents. After they were divorced, things at my house got worse, and I had to raise myself. My years in high school were terrible; no one cared what I did or how I lived. I want to make sure kids can deal with broken homes and parents who don't care.

My father was an alcoholic. He was killed in an automobile accident when I was 14 years old. It was a relief to have him out of my life. My mother did her very best to be a good parent after he died, but she couldn't afford to give us very much. She had to work all the time just to provide us with food and a place to live. I want to help children—like my mother helped my brother and sister and me.

I tried to be a teacher, but I couldn't manage 30 students at a time in class. I think if I can be with one or two students at a time, I can really help them.

People always come to me with their problems. Everyone says I should be a counselor because I am so kind and listen so well. Our schools really need people who like to listen; so, I want to try to be a counselor who really listens to what children have to say.

I came to the United States when I was 10 years old. Because I could only speak Spanish, I got bad grades in school, and everyone made fun of the way I talked. I'd like to make sure Mexican kids are treated better in school.

Individuals give many other reasons for wanting to join the school counseling profession. In this chapter we help aspiring counselors understand the school counseling profession and the challenges they face in preparing to become outstanding counseling professionals in the schools. This textbook is unique in that it is the foundation for an evolving online network, the School Counseling Activities Network (www.scan21st.com), whereby graduate students, their professors, and practicing school counselors can work together to bring the graduate classroom and the practice of school counseling into closer harmony. We are excited about the prospects for this network and about working with school counseling graduate students, counselor educators, and professional school counselors across the world. We hope this network will bring the perspectives of many cultures to the practice of school counseling. We describe the potential for this network later in chapter 1.

Each chapter of this textbook is supplemented by online lessons that encourage professors and graduate students to reflect on the material presented in print and to generate ideas for the School Counseling Activities Network (www.scan21st.com). The online lessons appear at http://www.prenhall.com/baker.

INTRODUCTION

We believe that school counseling is a noble profession and that school counselors, in their own way, are as important in schools as are teachers and administrators. We also believe that it is imperative that twenty-first century school counselors are:

(a) competent in the several functions surveyed in this text to the extent that their various publics are clearly aware of that competence; (b) open to and appreciative of all students and concerned advocates for the welfare and accomplishments of all students; (c) able to provide leadership in school counseling program development and delivery and in responding to the broad goals of education; and (d) open to the contributions that can be made by community agencies, families, volunteers, and other willing entities toward enhancing student welfare and academic accomplishments.

PROFESSIONALS WITH MIXED ALLEGIANCES

Ascribing Professional Status to School Counselors

Are school counselors professionals? If they are professionals, what defines them as such? *Professional* is a term used frequently and somewhat loosely in American society because it seems to create an aura of respectability. Some individuals do not deserve that respectability, whereas others truly do. Some professionals assume the respectability and accompanying status without giving much thought to the real meaning of the word *professional* and to the responsibilities it implies. Others know full well the responsibilities associated with being a professional. Ideally, all professionals would fit into the latter category.

A *profession* is a vocation requiring special knowledge or education in some department of learning or science; a *professional* is one belonging to a learned or skilled profession; and *professionalism* is the character, spirit, or methods of a professional or the standing, practice, or methods of a professional as distinguished from an amateur, according to the *American College Dictionary.* If school counselors are professionals, then school counseling is a vocation requiring special knowledge or education in some department of learning or science. What is the department of learning or science from which school counselors receive their special knowledge? This is a somewhat difficult question to answer. The historical information presented later in this chapter reveals that guidance, from which school counseling evolved, had several influences, including vocational guidance, psychometrics, mental health, and clinical psychology. The evolution of school counseling as a profession has not been clear-cut or even. When addressing this problem for guidance professionals, including school counselors, psychologists, and social workers, Shaw (1973) refers to the behavioral sciences as the department of learning from which knowledge is derived. In elaborating on this position, he says this:

> Guidance has a rich and meaningful heritage from a variety of disciplines, a fact that has had both a positive and negative impact on the development of the guidance professions. On the positive side of the ledger guidance workers have been blessed with a breadth of outlook and skills that few other professions can claim. On the debit side the very diversity of its background coupled with economic, social, and political pressures has made it difficult for guidance specialists to develop an identity, a focus, or a clearly established set of purposes. This ambivalence about their goals has resulted in an over-concern with roles and functions that in turn has failed to lead to an identity. (p. 28)

Here Shaw informs us that school counselors enjoy many different disciplines that serve as the departments of learning on which the profession is founded. He also points out that this diversity, in conjunction with historical events affected by economic, social, and political pressures, has caused the profession difficulties in establishing an identity. The behavioral science disciplines from which counselor education has formulated its knowledge base include anthropology, economics, psychology, and sociology, among others, with psychology perhaps dominant. School counselors, like other professionals, apply principles from their foundational disciplines to carry out the responsibilities assigned and ascribed to them. Therefore, they are applied anthropologists, economists, psychologists, and sociologists, as well as applied behavioral scientists.

School counseling is a part of two larger applied professions: counseling and education. These broader fields draw from the behavioral sciences, too. They have developed their own knowledge bases. Both have influenced school counseling. Finally, school counseling has been developing its own knowledge base over the years, which also influences practicing and emerging school counseling professionals. Consequently, school counseling is a profession with the behavioral sciences and the applied fields of counseling and education as its foundational departments of learning, and a profession in the process of developing its own knowledge base.

Drawing on the work of Barber (1965) and Greenwood (1957), Herr and Cramer (1987) suggest additional criteria for attributing professional status to a vocation. In summary, those criteria are:

- The members have a service orientation (they are educated to serve community rather than self-interests).
- The degree of self-control is high (practitioner behaviors are regulated via community sanctions, ethical codes, and the like).
- Systems of rewards (monetary and honorary) are included that not only are symbols of work-related achievements but also are ends in themselves.
- A professional culture is perpetrated via consistent training programs.

It is the authors' contention that school counselors have a service orientation, are regulated by community sanctions and ethical codes, derive their monetary and honorary rewards from work-related achievements, and have consistent training programs. Therefore, the evidence indicates that school counseling is a profession and that school counselors are professionals who should be expected to behave in a professional manner.

Competing Professional Loyalties

A common practice among professionals is to band together in professional associations or societies. There are a number of reasons for doing so. Among the more prominent are unity, status, influence, services, standards and guidelines, continuing education opportunities, self-regulation, and economic enhancement. School counselors, as members of the broader professional fields of education and counseling, find themselves encouraged to join professional societies in both fields. The choices are difficult because each offers different advantages, and membership in both is more expensive than in one. This is an important issue for school counselors, many of whom earn relatively modest salaries, compared with members of other professional groups.

Opportunities in the Field of Education. The major general educational professional organization to which school counselors belong is the National Education Association (NEA), which is subdivided into state, regional, and local organizations. Administrators, teachers, school counselors, college professors, and other people with an interest in education are welcome as members. It is a relatively large professional society that provides all the benefits for its members cited previously. At the national and state levels, the NEA and its state divisions have a significant impact on legislation and executive-level policy making. At the community level, NEA local chapters are often recognized by school boards as the bargaining units for their members. In this regard, the NEA, which is a professional organization, takes on the attributes of a union, making it unique as a professional organization. In other communities, the bargaining unit is the American Federation of Teachers (AFT), a true labor union affiliated with the American Federation of Labor.

The economic services the NEA and AFT provide their members are perhaps the main reason school counselors join either organization. In many instances, it is expected or required that all members of the bargaining unit belong to the local, regional, state, and national organizations. Dues may be deducted from one's wages by arrangement with the school district. When there is a choice, not to join may place one in a potentially unpopular minority position—deemed willing to benefit from the efforts of the organization but too selfish to support it. This is a very compelling argument to join the entire set of organizations. Dues for the package of memberships usually amount to several hundred dollars; they can be more than $1,000 per year in urban and suburban areas where salaries and benefits are greater.

Although NEA or AFT membership has benefits for school counselors, some of them are limited. Status as an educator is shared with all members. Within the educational community, school counselors are several steps down the hierarchy, just as they are in most schools. In addition, they are a relatively small subgroup within the organization, compared to teachers. Therefore, school counselors have little influence on policy making, and few services are directed toward the special needs of school counselors. In fact, school counselors are members of an organization that includes other professionals—administrators—who assign duties to school counselors that sometimes make it difficult for them to achieve the goals of their professional training. The largest subgroup of professionals in these organizations—teachers—includes some who hold school counselors in contempt and low esteem.

Ethical codes, publications, and conference programs reflect the responsibilities and interests of the broad field of education and the guildlike issues of professionals rightly concerned about their economic welfare. All these issues are important to school counselors because they work in the same environment as their colleagues, yet few of these presentations are specific to the responsibilities and interests of school counselors.

Belonging to a general educational professional organization such as the NEA provides school counselors with several of the advantages associated with membership in such organizations. Chief among these advantages for school counselors is economic enhancement, an important consideration that explains why most school counselors belong to the NEA or AFT. For those school counselors desiring to fulfill higher order professional needs, professional organizations in the broad field of counseling have more to offer than those in education. Unfortunately, professional counseling organizations have little or nothing to offer that matches the effect of the educational profession's unions on salaries and benefits.

Opportunities in the Field of Counseling. In 1952, four independent professional organizations in the broad field of counseling joined forces to create an umbrella association in which all four maintained their identity and autonomy but through which they worked together to achieve higher levels of professionalism. The umbrella organization was known as the American Personnel and Guidance Association (APGA); the groups that joined together to found the APGA were the National Vocational Guidance Association (NVGA), the American College Personnel Association (ACPA), the National Association for Guidance Supervisors and Counselor Trainers (NAGSCT), and the Student Personnel Association for Teacher Education (SPATE). Within a year, the American School Counselor Association (ASCA) joined the original four APGA divisions. In analyzing the original structure of the APGA, Super (1953) referred to the ACPA, SPATE, and ASCA as institutionally oriented divisions because they represented the interests of persons employed as personnel workers in the colleges and schools. The NVGA was viewed as an interest division because members working in a variety of institutions could share a common interest in vocational guidance problems, principles, procedures, and programs. The NAGSCT was seen as a functional or job-oriented division because its members were interested in the supervision and training of school counselors. In the beginning, the APGA was a counseling organization whose members were employed mainly in educational settings, including school counseling.

The APGA grew in size and gradually incorporated divisions representing counseling professionals from a broader range of institutional settings (rehabilitation counselors, employment counselors, public offender counselors, mental health counselors, and military counselors) and interest areas (assessment in counseling, marriage and family counseling, multicultural concerns, religious and value issues, and group work). State and regional branches of the APGA and its divisions were created, too. The APGA changed its name to the American Association for Counseling and Development (AACD) in 1983 to reflect more accurately the goals and membership of the organization. Some of the original divisions had changed their names earlier or did so in the 1980s for similar reasons. The National Vocational Guidance Association became the National Career Development Association (NCDA), the National Association for Guidance Supervisors and Counselor Trainers became the Association for Counselor Education and Supervision (ACES), and the Student Personnel Association for Teacher Education became the Association for Humanistic Education and Development (AHEAD).

By the 1980s, the AACD had become the primary general professional association for counselors, including school counselors. At that time, the membership of the AACD was more than 50,000, with the ASCA having perhaps 8,000 or 9,000 members. Not as large and influential as the NEA or AFT, the AACD had nevertheless become influential in its own right, and its influence was focused on the needs and services of counselors.

In 1992, the AACD changed its name to the American Counseling Association (ACA), once again stating that the change more accurately reflected the organization's goals and membership. Not all members and divisions agreed with this viewpoint, and one of the founding divisions, the ACPA, withdrew from the association, believing that its goals and mission were no longer compatible with those of the ACA. Many in the ASCA became dissatisfied with their relationship with the ACA during the 1990s, leading to consideration of withdrawing from the ACA as well. A compromise relationship was arranged between the ASCA and ACA, and although the ASCA remains a division of the ACA, it is more autonomous than was previously the case (i.e., the ASCA handles its own membership functions).

The ACA and ASCA offer professional services that respond to the higher-order needs of school counselors better than either the NEA or AFT has been able to do. Among those services are codes of ethics and policy statements specifically directed to counselors or school counselors and developed by counseling colleagues; training standards for counselors; accreditation for counselors; conferences and workshops directed primarily to the needs of counselors; placement services; lobbying for legislation that enhances the counseling profession; and publications and media directed toward counseling audiences. Members of the ACA receive the newsletter *Counseling Today* and the professional journal *Journal of Counseling & Development.* Members of the ASCA receive the newsletter *The ASCA Counselor* and the journal *Professional School Counseling.* These benefits are covered by a member's dues. The journals provide more substantive, discursive, and empirical content for counseling professionals than do the journals of the NEA.

The ACA and its divisions have been responsible for two initiatives that, although currently autonomous from the professional organizations, provide important influences on professional counseling. They are the Council for the Accreditation of Counseling and Related Educational Programs (CACREP) and the National Board for Certified Counselors (NBCC). CACREP provides the counseling profession with what are currently the highest standards for accrediting training programs, and the NBCC provides national credentials, both generic and specific, for professional counselors.

From its beginnings in the early 1980s, CACREP grew in size and influence. By 1992, 195 programs in 72 institutions were accredited (Kandor & Bobby, 1992). The *CACREP Accreditation Manual* (CACREP, 2001) covers such general areas as program objectives and curriculum, faculty and staff, and program evaluation for master's and doctoral training programs and specific standards for programs in community counseling/gerontological counseling, marriage and family counseling/therapy, mental health counseling, school counseling, and college counseling. For example, the standard for clinical instruction in a CACREP-accredited school counseling training program is a 600-clock-hour internship performed under the supervision of a certified school counselor in a school setting. Of the 600 hours, 240 clock hours are to be of direct service (e.g., individual counseling, group work, developmental classroom guidance, consultation).

What does CACREP mean to school counselors in training? CACREP training standards are being adopted by or may be adopted by state departments of education/public instruction as the minimum standards for certification/licensure. Individuals graduating from training programs that are not CACREP accredited or CACREP-like (meeting the standards without being accredited) may find it increasingly difficult to compete in the marketplace or to move across state boundaries and get certified or licensed. Since 1990, the ACA, ACES, and ASCA have been working on a plan to improve school counseling by seeking uniformity in training and state certification/licensure using the CACREP standards as their criterion (Cecil, 1990). While these efforts are still in process, it seems important for students who are selecting training programs to be aware of CACREP standards and their potential impact and for faculty members in training programs that are not CACREP accredited or CACREP-like to think about their current position and future plans carefully.

How does the NBCC affect school counselors in training? A National Certified Counselor (NCC) is one who has graduated from a CACREP-accredited training program or who has successfully completed 2 years of documented, approved, supervised work experience after graduating from a program not accredited by CACREP and passed the NBCC certification examination (National Counselor Examination). Individuals holding NCC status have documented evidence of achieving the training and testing standards established by CACREP and the NBCC, and some prospective employers use or may use this as a minimum selection criterion. In addition to the generic examination, the NBCC offers specialty area examinations for individuals who have successfully completed the generic examination. Among the specialty area examinations is the National Certified School Counselor (NCSC), which is a symbol of competence important in school counseling. As we enter the twenty-first century, state certification or licensure is the most important credential for school counselors. What influence the NCC and NCSC will have on the criteria set by state departments of education/public instruction in the future is unknown. The authors' opinion is that the influence will increase, making it more important to possess these national certificates, especially if one wishes to have job mobility over time.

Although unable to provide the economic clout that the NEA and AFT do, the ACA and ASCA offer services that appeal to the higher-order needs of professionals and that are not provided by the NEA and AFT. Because membership in the NEA or AFT is semi-voluntary and relatively expensive, the decision to join the ACA and ASCA and many of the other divisions is affected by the fact that one may have already paid dues to one professional organization; the dues for a counseling professional organization, though considerably less, have to be taken from what is left over for discretionary expenses. Under these circumstances, allegiance to a professional counseling organization such as the ACA or ASCA occurs less often for school counselors than it otherwise might. Consequently, the membership of the ASCA is much smaller than it could be. Individuals who join at a lower cost while graduate students sometimes drop out because the dues go up as they become working professionals and are faced with joining a bargaining unit (Herr, 1985). Others may not find jobs in the field immediately and allow their memberships to lapse. They may or may not join later.

The preferred scenario would be for school counselors to belong to important professional organizations in the fields of both education and counseling. Economic realities give the advantage to professional organizations in the field of education. This creates a situation in which many school counselors have no direct affiliation with a professional counseling organization. Individually, they suffer because they become isolated professionally and are less likely to behave according to the standards of their counseling profession. The counselors, their consumers, and the profession suffer as a result. Collectively, school counseling suffers because only a fraction of its members shares in the unity and influence a professional organization can achieve. The ACA and ASCA are less influential than they might be because of this lack of membership. This unfortunate circumstance is an ongoing problem the profession is challenged to address if school counseling is to survive and blossom. If the competition for professional loyalties is resolved successfully, other issues remain for school counseling to address.

THE IMPORTANCE OF TEACHING EXPERIENCE

In the early years of the profession, virtually all school counselors came from the teaching ranks. School systems and counselor educators preferred it that way. Therefore, a teaching certificate or license and one to two years of successful teaching experience became requirements for school counselor licensure or certification across the states. Changing times and circumstances led to expansion of eligibility for licensure/certification to individuals outside the teaching profession on a state-by-state basis. Concern over whether these newcomers would know how to function in schools was often alleviated by school-based internships during their training programs. These changes were accompanied by controversy over whether teaching experience should be required. This led to a spate of studies in the 1960s and 1970s.

In a review of these studies, Baker (1994) reported:

> When effectiveness of counselors was operationalized as characteristics that are important to counseling relationships, the data sometimes indicated that teaching experience could be detrimental, or there were no differences among counselors. There were no findings indicating that those lacking teaching experience might have difficulty in counseling relationships. When the dependent measures represented effectiveness as a school counselor, broad "guidance" skills, and attitudes, the findings seemed to suggest that there were no differences, or they were limited to a short period of time when counselors without teaching experience were adjusting to the school systems. (p. 321)

The controversy seemed dormant during the 1980s and then heated up again as echo baby boomers increased school enrollments significantly and fewer and fewer teachers indicated interest in becoming school counselors. As states that still held to the teaching experience requirement removed it or felt pressure to do so, more research on the topic was published.

Olson and Allen (1993) found that principals discovered no differences between high school and elementary school counselors with and without teaching experience. There were perceived differences at the middle school level on three of the 13 functions covered in the study. In a study of the perceptions of counselor educators, Smith, Crutchfield, and Culbreth (2001) found that many more of today's counselor educators, as opposed to those 35 years ago, believe that teaching experience, although potentially helpful, is not necessary for success in school counseling.

In the most recent study of which we are aware, Peterson, Goodman, and Keller (2002) compared former school counseling interns with and without teaching experience via an in-depth analysis of their responses to four open-ended questions across 16 categories of school counselor functions. The four questions focused on their recollections of the greatest challenges and difficulties, what they wished they had known, what they appreciated about the training, and what they appreciated about themselves. Peterson et al. (2002) found that all interns experienced significant adjustments during the first two years of employment as school counselors, and the adjustments of former teachers differed from those of non-teachers. This study seems to shed light on the controversy because it points out that former teachers, as well as those without teaching experience, face challenges when beginning careers as school counselors.

Documents dating back over 30 years highlight challenges faced by counselors when adapting to the school culture because they did not come up through the teaching ranks and learn about the folkways and mores (Baker, 1994). Peterson et al. (2002) discovered that, even though teachers knew the folkways and mores of teaching, being a school counselor introduced them to new roles in the established folkways and mores. For example, former teachers had to cope with (a) having to earn credibility all over again; (b) being on the receiving end of negative comments from teachers about the credibility and effectiveness of counselors; (c) learning to adjust to fragmented, disjointed days and lack of closure; (d) having no break or preparation periods; (e) needing to be less directive and content oriented; (f) feeling unfamiliar with age levels other than those previously taught; and (g) lacking a clear place in the school hierarchy.

Thus, the evidence indicates that all school counseling students have adjustments to make when starting careers as school counselors. In our opinion, regulations that restrict the school counseling profession to only former teachers are outdated and uninformed. The profession and those whom it serves will benefit from access to all caring and competent prospects. Enlightened counselor education training programs will realize that comprehensive internship experiences, such as those recommended by the Council for the Accreditation of Counseling and Related Educational Programs (CACREP), are important in the preparation of all trainees, not just those who do not have teaching experience.

HISTORICAL OVERVIEW

Pioneers

Seen as a "series of learning experiences complementing the existing curriculum" (Aubrey, 1977, p. 289), guidance first appeared in the schools like any other subject. Guidance had a curriculum, the goals of which evolved from the social reform movements of the late nineteenth and early twentieth centuries. Guidance teachers also sought to have a positive impact on the moral development of their charges. One such program was established by Jesse B. Davis, a high-school principal in Grand Rapids, Michigan, who, in 1907, had one period per week set aside in English composition classes for vocational and moral guidance. The goals for this early guidance curriculum were to help high-school students better understand their own characters, emulate good role models, and develop into socially responsible workers.

What we think of currently as school counseling did not begin with a formal design consisting of established goals, assumptions, and functions. It evolved to what it is today. Davis and other pioneers were responding to local needs. His ideas led to a school guidance curriculum. Others, like David S. Hill, Anna Y. Reed, and Eli W. Weaver, founded their guidance services on different ideas, such as making students employable, helping them find suitable employment, and responding to their individual differences (Rockwell & Rothney, 1961). Additional influences outside education were integrated into the structure of guidance and gradually reshaped its features. For example, those involved in the vocational guidance movement created an interest in assessing individual differences and making personal, educational, and vocational decisions based on the resulting data. What have become known as the psychometric and mental health movements also had an impact on the guidance movement.

Vocational Guidance Movement

Near the end of a long career as a social reformer, Frank Parsons (1909) in 1908 established a Vocation Bureau in Boston, the purpose of which was to provide vocational guidance for out-of-school youths. Parsons believed that individuals must have dependable information about occupations and about themselves in order to make good occupational choices. He also believed that the role of the vocational counselor was to make such information available and to help individuals comprehend and use it.

At about the same time, programs that would later be categorized together as representing vocational guidance were being introduced in a few metropolitan school districts. Some universities offered courses in vocations, and the federal government passed legislation that subsidized vocational education and teacher training (e.g., the Smith-Hughes Act of 1917; the George-Reed Act of 1919). Yet, in the first quarter of the twentieth century, the influence of vocational guidance on school guidance was minimal, there were no accredited training programs, and there were no widely accepted theoretical underpinnings (Aubrey, 1977).

Psychometric Movement

A series of events in the first quarter of the twentieth century led to the use of psychometric principles and techniques in applied settings. Psychometric principles, such as reliability theory and test validity, as well as techniques for standardizing psychometric instruments and making them precise, had previously been used by academicians and researchers to enhance their scholarly efforts. In 1905, Alfred Binet and his colleague T. Simon developed a scale to measure mental ability in order to help the school system in Paris, France, classify students for educational instruction. Binet's scale popularized the idea of using psychometrics to solve practical problems and was the forerunner of modern intelligence testing.

In response to the federal government's need to classify millions of young men eligible for the military when the United States entered World War I in 1917, several eminent psychologists produced a group-administered intelligence test. The success of the military use of the tests, known as Army Alpha (paper-and-pencil administration) and Beta (performance administration), popularized the idea of using group testing in education. In addition, vocational guidance workers found testing attractive as an apparently scientific means of determining a person's interests, strengths, and limitations.

Psychometrics offered school guidance not only the tools for assessment but also corresponding respectability because the tools seemed so precise and scientific. Psychometrics emphasized objectivity, individual differences, prediction, classification, and placement. With these emphases came tendencies for some school guidance workers to engage in testing and telling—relying on testing and information giving as the basis for guidance. As was the case with vocational guidance, because no uniform national guidance program existed, some were more influenced than others by the psychometric movement.

Mental Health Movement

Several parallel movements in the early part of the twentieth century ushered in what has been called the mental health movement. In 1908, Clifford Beers, a former mental patient, published a book called *A Mind That Found Itself*, which brought about reforms in the treatment of mental illness and fostered widespread interest in mental hygiene and the early identification and treatment of mental illness. Sigmund Freud's psychoanalytic ideas focusing on the importance of individual development and the influence of the mind on one's mental health became popular in the treatment of mental health problems and in mental health studies. These activities led to a newfound interest in the importance of the formative years as the foundation of personality and development. This interest in the promotion of healthy individual adjustment eventually influenced early school guidance workers.

Emergence of a School Guidance Profession

In the 1920s and 1930s, the number of guidance specialists in the schools increased, although no widely accepted standards for training or practice existed. School administrators, circumstances, and the training and beliefs of the specialists combined to influence the philosophies and practices in those early school guidance programs. Often, the secondary-school guidance programs that emerged in the 1920s were imitations of college student personnel programs that emphasized discipline and attendance (Gibson & Mitchell, 1981). Like college and university deans of students, high-school guidance counselors acquired some administrative responsibilities and often concerned themselves with remedial goals. One outcome was that guidance counselors became responsive to the day-to-day wishes of their school administrators and were more and more likely to be identified with them (Shaw, 1973).

The advent of compulsory school attendance and the influence of the vocational guidance and mental health movements helped shape school guidance in the direction of a specialty. Compulsory school attendance increased the number of students who were unsure about their future plans and who had difficulty adjusting to the school environment. Proctor (1925) advocated guidance as a means of helping students cope with life forces by providing help in the selection of school subjects, extracurricular activities, colleges, and vocational schools. Through the end of World War II in 1945, school guidance was characterized by a relatively narrow focus on vocational guidance, adjustment to one's environment, and accompanying administrative duties. Between 1924 and 1946, four states required guidance counselors to have special certificates

(Smith, 1955), indicating that school guidance was largely a function of local influences. In the few instances where guidance was offered at the elementary-school level, it was most often a transplanted version of the secondary-school program (Zaccaria, 1969).

What emerged as the dominant school guidance model in the 1930s and early 1940s has been labeled *trait and factor*, or directive, guidance (Aubrey, 1977). Publications by E. G. Williamson (1950; Williamson & Darley, 1937) had considerable influence at this time. Williamson promoted enhancing normal adjustment, helping individuals set goals and overcome obstacles to those goals, and assisting individuals to achieve satisfying lifestyles. Influenced by the medical model for treating individuals, Williamson recommended that counseling competencies include analysis, synthesis, diagnosis, prognosis, counseling, and follow-up (Ewing, 1975; Smith, 1955). Techniques were suggested for forcing conformity, changing the environment, selecting the appropriate environment, teaching needed skills, and changing attitudes (Williamson, 1950). The descriptor *trait and factor* was applied to these techniques because diagnostic data derived from standardized tests and case studies emphasizing individual differences were used to advise students about vocational and adjustment issues.

The directive approach to guidance eventually proved to be too narrow in the changing times following World War II. Aubrey (1977) thought the changes were influenced by an increasing desire for personal freedom and autonomy. Into this setting came Carl Rogers (1942, 1951, 1961), whose nonmedical approach to counseling had an impact on the field unlike the work of any person before him. His ideas transferred the focus of counseling away from problems and onto the individuals receiving counseling. Rogers emphasized the counseling relationship and climate. His general goal was to help individuals grow so that they might resolve their own problems and have the strength to function effectively.

Individual counseling had gradually emerged as the dominant guidance function in the 1930s and 1940s. The changing social environment after World War II and the addition of Rogers's ideas led Smith (1955) to conclude a decade later that counseling had become the central secondary-school guidance function, with all other functions in supplementary roles. Smith observed that the nondirective and directive approaches each had proponents, as did an eclectic approach that occupied the middle of the road but was more directive in practice. Rogers's influence had moved school counselors away from being highly directive toward being eclectic. In addition, group counseling was emerging as a relatively new idea with some merit for school counseling (Smith, 1955).

The creation of the American Personnel and Guidance Association in 1952 (now the American Counseling Association, ACA), the passage of the National Defense Education Act in 1958, and the increased school enrollments caused by the baby boomers born after World War II all caused the training of school counselors to become more standardized and increased their number in the 1960s. This was the boom era in school counseling, and Rogers's theory and techniques dominated the training programs and practices of school counselors.

Two divisions of the American Personnel and Guidance Association (APGA)— the American School Counselor Association (ASCA) and the Association for Counselor Education and Supervision (ACES)—led the way to developing and promoting standards for the training of school counselors that strongly emphasized counseling theory and practicum training. Practicum training often focused on the development of skills for one-to-one counseling relationships and occurred at the end of the training program, leaving the impression that the counseling function was very important. Although the standards tended to fortify the importance of counseling, other functions, such as record keeping, information dissemination, placement, follow-up, and evaluation, were also identified as important. In addition, uniformity was introduced to collegiate training programs and state certification standards. In the years after World War II and into the 1960s, the remaining states adopted certification standards for school counselors. In 1957, the ASCA, recognizing a need, initiated a study on elementary-school counseling.

The National Defense Education Act of 1958 (NDEA) was passed after the Soviets successfully launched the space satellite named *Sputnik* in 1957. On the basis of this perceived threat of Soviet educational superiority and the subsequent desire to identify academically talented students and guide them into careers in strategic fields, the NDEA provided federal funds to the states for the enhancement of school counseling programs and to colleges and universities to update working school counselors and train new ones. Even though the primary purpose of the funding was rather narrow, the funding was used to achieve goals of a much broader scope. New and improved counselor education programs proliferated. The demand for graduates was immense because of the need for counselors to serve the growing number of students in the schools as a result of the bulge in the birth rate after World War II.

In 1959, James B. Conant recommended a ratio of one full-time high-school counselor for every 200 to 300 students in his widely read book *The American High School Today*. Conant's focus on the importance of guidance helped create an impression that all high-school students should have access to school counselors. The following year, the 1960 White House Conference on Children and Youth emphasized the importance of extending counseling services to preadolescents. Consultants to the U.S. secretary of health, education, and welfare recommended that the NDEA be extended to elementary schools. The 1964 amendments to the NDEA gave impetus to elementary-school counseling by providing funds for training to extend the search for talent to elementary schools. This instigated a period of debate over models for elementary-school guidance that extended into the 1970s.

In *The Counselor in a Changing World*, 60,000 copies of which were printed between 1962 and 1966, C. Gilbert Wrenn chided secondary-school guidance counselors for having allowed themselves to become narrowly focused on the remedial needs of a few students. He recommended that the newly evolving population of elementary-school counselors learn from the mistaken decision by secondary-school counselors to build crisis-oriented programs and instead emphasize responding to the developmental needs of the total range of students in their programs. Wrenn's advocacy of developmental rather than remedial goals for elementary- and secondary-school guidance came at a time when others were voicing similar opinions. Dinkmeyer (1967) advocated helping children to know, understand, and accept themselves. Also emphasizing the importance of promoting positive individual growth and development, Zaccaria (1969) pointed out that the emphasis of developmental guidance should be on preventing problems. Writing that the major emphasis among authorities publishing papers and books about guidance programs seemed to be on a developmental approach, Shaw (1973) concluded that the term *developmental guidance* was being used so globally that it had yet to be defined precisely. As the 1970s approached, the number of school counseling professionals being trained and employed had grown significantly, elementary-school counseling was emerging and seeking an identity, and the traditional service delivery model was being challenged.

After the Boom

An era of declining enrollments in the schools and economic problems across the nation led to reductions in personnel in numerous school districts during the 1970s and into the 1980s. Many school counseling positions were eliminated, significantly fewer jobs were available for newly trained school counselors, and the thrust for elementary-school guidance programs initiated in the 1960s was muted. At the same time, several themes about the appropriate roles for school counselors were championed. Influenced by the turbulent 1960s and the problems of the inner-city schools, Menacker (1974, 1976) called for counselors working in metropolitan areas to become more active in the schools and communities and to rely more on the fields of sociology, political science, and economics than on psychology for helping models. The developmental guidance approach was also gaining momentum at this time. One reason for this momentum was the compatibility of the idea with elementary-school guidance. The enhancement of self-understanding and adjustment and the importance of consulting and collaboration for elementary-school counselors were already emphasized. A second reason for the momentum was the interest generated by career education proponents. Emphasizing the importance of work and careers to healthy human adjustment, career education advocates recommended integrating general and vocational education, instruction, and guidance around a career development theme from kindergarten through the 12th grade (Hoyt, Evans, Mackin, & Mangum, 1974). Some federal funds were made available for career education programming in basic education during the 1970s. A third reason was the attention given to psychological education after Mosher and Sprinthall (1970) introduced psychologically based curriculum interventions for counselors to offer students in an effort to persuade guidance programs to help the schools focus more on personal development.

Shaw (1973) advocated what Zaccaria (1969) classified as a *services approach* to guidance. Shaw believed that guidance programs should be founded on clearly stated goals and objectives. He also believed that guidance workers should be able to provide a set of functions as needed, depending on where guidance goals belonged on a continuum ranging from primary prevention to diagnosis and therapy. The functions, or services, included counseling, consultation, testing, curriculum development, provision of information, in-service training, use of records, articulation, referral, and evaluation and research. Others, like Keat (1974), advocated eclectic models. Keat's eclecticism, designed for elementary-school counselors, was summarized in a blended set of roles. Group and individual counseling, collaboration and consultation with teachers, and coordination with school district and community resources were taken from the recommendations of professional organizations (American Personnel and Guidance Association, 1969); communication with children and adults and offering an effective

Table 1.1
Highlights of the evolution of school counseling in the twentieth century.

Date	Event
1905	Binet and Simon develop mental ability scale.
1907	Jesse B. Davis conducts guidance classes in Grand Rapids, Michigan.
1908	Frank Parsons establishes Vocation Bureau in Boston.
1908	Clifford Beers publishes *A Mind That Found Itself.*
1917	Army Alpha and Beta developed.
1920	Sigmund Freud's ideas begin to influence mental health professionals.
1920–1930	Number of school guidance specialists increases in this decade. No widely accepted training or practice standards.
1924	State certification of guidance counselors begins.
1925	Proctor advocates guidance program to help students make educational and vocational choices.
1937	Williamson and Darley publish *Student Personnel Work: An Outline of Clinical Procedures* and begin *trait and factor* approach.
1942	Carl Rogers publishes *Counseling and Psychotherapy* and begins the era of individual counseling.
1945	Changing social environment after World War II and influence of Rogers's writings cause counseling to become the dominant school guidance service.
1952	American Personnel and Guidance Association created.
1953	American School Counselors Association joins the American Personnel and Guidance Association.
1958	National Defense Education Act (NDEA) passed.
1959	Conant publishes *The American High School Today.*
1960	Beginning of a boom decade in school guidance and counseling and in counselor education.
1962	C. Gilbert Wrenn publishes *The Counselor in a Changing World.*
1964	NDEA amended to provide funds for enhancing elementary-school guidance.
1970	Beginning of a decade of declining enrollments in the schools and corresponding reductions in school counselors.
1970	Mosher and Sprinthall introduce their Deliberate Psychological Education curriculum.
1974	Hoyt, Evans, Mackin, and Mangum include guidance in the career education theme.
1976	Menacker publishes *Toward a Theory of Activist Guidance.*
1985	American Personnel and Guidance Association changes its name to the American Association for Counseling and Development (AACD).
1987	AACD task force on school counseling as a profession at risk publishes its report.
1988	Gysbers and Henderson publish *Developing and Managing Your School Guidance Program.*
1990	Interdivisional task force (AACD, ACES, ASCA) begins working on plans to improve school counseling.
1991	"Multiculturalism as a Fourth Force in Counseling" is introduced in a special issue of the AACD journal.

1992	ASCA publishes *Children Are Our Future, School Counseling 2000.*
1992	American Association for Counseling and Development changes its name to the American Counseling Association (ACA).
1993	ASCA, ACA, and others reintroduce the Elementary School Counseling Demonstration Act.
1996	Beginning of effects of baby boom echo generation.
1996	Alger report indicates that youths' perception of school counseling is improving.
1997	ASCA proposes *The National Standards for School Counseling Programs.*
1997	DeWitt Wallace Reader's Digest Fund provides the Education Trust with funding to initiate a transformation of school counseling.
1998	Strong U.S. economy indicates potential for enhanced educational expenditures and an improving employment market.
1999–2000	Funding achieved for the Elementary and Secondary School Counseling Demonstration Program under the Elementary and Secondary Education Act.
2000	Application of school-community collaboration model selected by U.S. Department of Education as one of 22 outstanding model schools are encouraged to support.
2001	No Child Left Behind initiative becomes legislation (PL 107-110).
2002	ASCA presents the National Model for School Counseling Programs.
2002	The Education Trust receives funds from Met Life for the National School Counselor Training Initiative.

curriculum were borrowed from Stamm and Nissman (1971); and fostering child growth and development and teaching coping behaviors were added to the set by Keat.

In an increasing number of states, counseling students who had no teaching experience were trained and certified, creating greater diversity among the new generation of school counselors. At this time, school counseling was still a field without a central unifying theme. It was, in fact, experiencing an increasing number of themes, all having varying degrees of influence across training programs and among counselors. The newer activist, developmental, service-oriented, and eclectic themes mixed with remnants of the trait and factor, adjustment, administrative, and counseling themes that were still very much alive. In times of job shortages and threats to existing jobs, school counseling was at a loss to define itself uniformly. The winds of change led the American Personnel and Guidance Association (APGA) to rename itself the American Association for Counseling and Development (AACD) in the mid-1980s and to the American Counseling Association (ACA) in the early 1990s. Divisions and state organizations followed suit or had already initiated similar changes (Herr, 1985). Officially, the words *guidance* and then *development* had become archaic. The term *counseling* now represented the goals of the organized members of the profession more accurately. Table 1.1 presents a summary of many of these important events in chronological order.

Challenges

Generally, basic education and school counseling have been bombarded by a range of challenges that, when evaluated closely, seem to place increasing responsibility on elementary-, middle-, and secondary-school educators to respond to the nation's problems and to prepare future generations of students to cope with economic competitors. These challenges include demands that the school curriculum be made more rigorous, drug abuse be prevented, drug users be treated and rehabilitated, exceptional students and culturally different populations be integrated and their differences appreciated, dropout rates be reduced, children of working parents be cared for, students be prepared for more complex and challenging jobs, gender equity be promoted, and local and state taxes for supporting the schools be reduced or maintained at existing levels.

Depicting school counseling as a profession at risk, a task force constituted by the AACD in 1987 pointed out that standards varied widely across the 333 training programs in the United States and that only 70 programs had been accredited by the Council for the Accreditation of Counseling and Related Educational Programs (CACREP), which had existed since 1981. In addition, the task force reported that standards for certifying counselors varied widely across the United States and that, as individual members of the task force, they had mixed feelings about whether school counseling was truly a profession.

Data from a U.S. Department of Education survey of 333 heads of public high-school guidance programs suggested that school counseling faced significant challenges as the twentieth century entered its last decade (Moles, 1991). The survey data indicated that, on average, counselors in these schools spent 16% of their time on various nonguidance activities; the average ratio of students to counselors was 350 to 1 (250 to 1 is recommended; College Board, 1986); 41% of schools had no guidance-related courses or units (proactive programming); and students who continued their education beyond high school received considerably more career planning assistance from counselors than did those who ended their formal education with high school. These findings indicated that school counseling services may have been unbalanced, unevenly provided, and diluted by intrusive nonguidance responsibilities and large caseloads.

Competitors have appeared from several arenas, none apparently because of a desire to replace school counselors. Instead, more global issues seem to underscore the situations that lead to competition. Some competitors are hired to replace or supplement counselors, performing some functions traditionally in the domain of school counselors. Roberts, Coursol, and Morotti (1997) described circumstances in Minnesota that led to employment of school social workers because school districts could use federal special education funds to pay their salaries. In an article on privatization of school counseling functions, Dykeman (1995) identified six approaches that vary according to whether the school and the school counseling programs are partially or completely privatized and whether the contractors are nonprofit or for-profit entities. Thus, some privatization schemes lead to replacing school counselors, whereas others lead to sharing caseloads. Among the issues that privatization creates are job erosion, unequal pay scales, caseload inequity, insufficient supervision, and decreased confidentiality. The school counseling profession is also challenged by competitors that provide other services. For example, some school systems faced with limited funds may hire reading specialists in place of school counselors to meet the demand for improved academic performance of students, concluding that even though both programs are worthwhile, one is more important at the moment and both cannot be afforded at once.

From within the general field of counseling came a call for multicultural competence (American Association for Counseling and Development, 1991). Professional counselors are challenged to (a) know about and be able to establish relationships with individuals in all cultural groups (Westbrook & Sedlacek, 1991); (b) be able to conceptualize client concerns from their perspective or worldview (Ibrahim, 1991); and (c) provide proactive programming that is culturally sensitive (Dobbins & Skillings, 1991). Knowledge of differing worldviews is incomplete unless accompanied by corresponding knowledge of one's own feelings, thoughts, and experiences, according to Speight, Myers, Cox, and Highlen (1991).

President Bush's No Child Left Behind initiative is, according to Herr (2002), the latest national educational reform movement, and the school counseling profession finds itself assessing its role—collectively and individually. "Each time there is a change of national presidential administrations, there is likely to be a proposed shift in the emphasis that national policy and practice should address, creating a constant process of 'starting over,' looking for new solutions to enduring problems" (Herr, 2002, p. 220). Herr's paper was among several articles published in the April 2002 issue of *Professional School Counseling*, the goal of which was to address the role of school counseling in the latest school reform movement. Herr carefully addresses school reform from a historical perspective and presents viewpoints on why previous reform movements have had limited success. One is left with the belief that school counselors need to be careful not to become caught up in reform efforts that focus only on restructuring schools via increased academic rigor. That school counselors and school reform should also focus on alleviating the circumstances that prevent some children and youths from being successful in school seems clear.

Information from the U.S. Department of Education indicates that school enrollment will increase dramatically at some levels of education and in some regions of the nation over the decade of approximately 1996–1997 through 2006–2007. The impact of this *baby boom echo generation* will be felt the most in high schools (15% enrollment increases) and in the southern and western parts of the country (Goetz, 1997; Morrissey, 1996). Although at lower levels, the increases will also occur in the middle and elementary schools and in other regions of the United States. These demographics indicate that this decade of transition from one century to the next will present opportunities and challenges ranging from increased employment for school counselors to larger caseloads than were previously experienced.

Four possible causes of the rising enrollment are: (a) many baby boomers delayed marriage and childbearing, (b) more children enrolled in preschools and are remaining in school to get diplomas, (c) birth rates are high among ethnic minority populations, and (d) immigration to the United States increased. The latter two factors indicate an increased need for multicultural counseling competence. The twenty-first century schools are likely to be in settings where school counselors and their student clients have increasingly diverse cultural and economic backgrounds. Therefore, counselors will be challenged to focus on clients' presenting problems while also being comfortable exploring cultural and dispositional sources of resistance to the helping process (Coleman, 1995). School counselors will also be challenged to respond to competing individual and community needs. As an example of this dual challenge, Coleman (1995) cites a hypothetical case of a counselor seeking to help clients who perform less well on college and university admissions tests. The hypothetical counselor contacts colleges to inquire about admissions policies that do not discriminate (individual needs) and joins others in an effort to lobby for culturally sensitive admissions tests (community needs).

The 1990s were good times in the United States economically. Unfortunately, a variety of circumstances, such as increasing enrollments coupled with decreasing revenues, led to an economic downturn beginning in 2000–2001 that continues to the present. Historically, school counseling has been affected negatively by such economic developments through reductions in staff and declining opportunities for graduates of counselor education programs. This phenomenon may occur again during the early years of the twenty-first century.

Several themes seem to emerge from these challenges. First, external circumstances such as growing enrollments and decreasing revenues indicate that school counselors will be challenged to demonstrate their worth and cost-effectiveness in the schools. Second, national, state, and local governments recognize the importance of education in the future health of the nation and are concerned about viable outcomes and accountability. Third, these circumstances lead to national school reform efforts, such as Bush's No Child Left Behind initiative. Fourth, as was the case in early school reform efforts, school counseling has not been included as an important participant in the reform's response. Fifth, there is widespread belief that many school counseling programs have been and remain marginalized ancillary services that are endangered in economic hard times (ASCA, 1996; Baker, 2001; Campbell & Dahir, 1997; House & Hayes, 2002). Sixth, without a designed program, a clear mission, and an identified role or vision, counselors will continue to function at the discretion of others (Borders & Drury, 1992; Gysbers & Henderson, 2000; House & Hayes, 2002; Paisley & Borders, 1995). Seventh, a well-conceived effort by school counselors to address the needs of all students seems to be essential for the future good health of individual school counselors, school counseling programs, and the school counseling profession.

Responding to the Challenges

The ASCA, ACA, and other sister professional organizations reintroduced the Elementary School Counseling Demonstration Act (ESCDA) in 1993. Their activity had potential for responding constructively to the challenges just listed. The prospective legislation called for funding to schools proposing promising and innovative approaches to expanding elementary-school counseling programs. Included among the criteria for funding programs under the legislation were recommendations that school counselors work cooperatively with school psychologists and social workers in integrated teams, that student-to-counselor ratios be not more than 250 to 1, that 85% of the team members' time be devoted to providing direct services with no more than 15% devoted to administrative tasks, and that the program be developmental and preventive.

Working cooperatively, ACA, ASCA, the National Association of School Psychologists, the National Association of Social Workers, the American Psychological Association, and the School Social Work Association of America convinced Congress to reauthorize/rewrite the ESCDA as part of a larger Elementary and

Secondary Education Act (ESEA) bill and to fund it as part of an appropriations bill in 1998 (Urbaniak, 2000). Funding victories were accomplished in 1999 and 2000 (Urbaniak, 2000). Since 2000, school counselors, school psychologists, school social workers and other interested professionals have worked independently and through respective professional organizations to enhance the ESCDA/ESEA legislation (e.g., provide for counseling programs in secondary schools), get ESEA authorized, and acquire funding.

Harris-Aikens (2001) reported that Congress was considering versions of a bill to fund ESEA, one of which might change it to the Elementary and Secondary School Counseling Improvement Act, and support was coming in part because of concerns related to preventing violence in schools. In May 2002, an ASCA legislative alert enlisted the responses of members in an attempt to support an effort by Representatives Langevin (D-RI), Roukema (R-NJ), Hooley (D-OR), Evans (D-IL), and Baird (D-WA) to acquire appropriations of $75 million for the Elementary and Secondary School Counseling Program (ESCCP) as a part of the No Child Left Behind (NCLB) Act (P.L. 107–110). The ESCCP component of the NCLB Act is designed to establish comprehensive school counseling programs in which elementary- and secondary-school counselors, school psychologists, school social workers, child and adolescent psychiatrists, and other qualified psychologists can work together. A funding trigger requires that federal support for the program exceed $40 million in order for secondary schools to benefit. The counseling professional organizations have been working hard to respond to current challenges by seeking recognition of the important role of school counselors in responding to school-related problems and corresponding fiscal support to enhance school counseling programs.

Reports by Lapan, Gysbers, and Sun (1997); Neukrug, Barr, Hoffman, and Kaplan (1993); and Sink and MacDonald (1999) indicated that the number of states adopting comprehensive guidance programs had been increasing steadily. This development suggested a growing awareness of, and appreciation for, the concept of guidance for everyone and corresponding emphases on planned, sequential, and flexible guidance curricula integrated into the general curriculum. In turn, de-emphasis of the importance of administrative and clerical-centered response modes is suggested.

Evidence that school counseling has been effective to some extent was provided by data from *The Mood of American Youth*, a report published by the Horatio Alger Association of Distinguished Americans in 1996. It was reported that contemporary students appear to have a higher opinion of their school counselors than was the case in 1983 ("Alger Report," 1996).

A concerted effort to enhance the multicultural counseling competence of counselors in general and school counselors in particular has been under way for more than a decade. In 1991, the Association for Multicultural Counseling and Development (AMCD) approved a rationale for multicultural counseling that led to a proposed set of multicultural competencies (Sue, Arredondo, & McDavis, 1992). Although these and other efforts appear to have had an effective impact, both evidence and opinion suggest that the goals have yet to be achieved (Nuttal, Webber, & Sanchez, 1996). Counselor education programs are challenged to continue transforming their curricula to integrate multicultural perspectives, and professional counselors are challenged to become culturally competent counselors.

In an attempt to respond to Goals 2000: The Educate America Act (EAA) of 1994, the ASCA adopted *School Counseling 2000*, a set of goals for school counseling derived from the six broad goals for achieving success in American education in the EAA. The general theme of the school counseling goals is to work directly and collaboratively with students, parents, teachers, community members, and employers to develop policies and programs that address the challenging problems that have been widely identified.

Consequently, the ASCA governing board committed to developing national standards for school counseling programs (Dahir, 2001). The National Standards for School Counseling Programs (Campbell & Dahir, 1997) were completed in 1997. The standards are designed to (a) shift the focus from counselors to school counseling programs, (b) create a framework for a national school counseling program model, (c) establish school counseling as an integral part of the academic mission of the schools, (d) lead to equal access to school counseling services for all students, (e) highlight the key ingredients of developmental school counseling, (f) identify the knowledge and skills to which all students should have access from comprehensive school counseling programs, and (g) ensure that comprehensive school counseling programs are delivered in a systematic manner (Dahir, 1997). Emphasis is on the role of counseling in student achievement, on collaboration with teachers and school administrators toward helping students be successful in school, and on program content standards that specify what students should know and be able to do (Dahir, 2001).

An analysis of survey data from more than 2,000 members of ASCA led to the conclusion that the content of school programs focuses on academic development, career development, and personal-social development (Dahir, 2001). Key components of the National Standards for School Counseling Programs are found in Appendix A. As presented in Appendix A, there are nine national standards, three in each of the content areas listed earlier in this paragraph. The academic development standards focus on implementing programs and strategies that maximize student learning. Dahir (2001) points out that, in this way, the National Standards correspond to the school reform agenda.

The goal of the career development component of the National Standards is to guide school counselors toward helping students make transitions from grade to grade, from school to post-secondary education, and from school to the world of work. The personal-social component standards are designed to assist counselors in developing personal and social growth-producing experiences that lead to a successful transition to adulthood. These personal-social development experiences should also contribute to achieving the academic and career success goals. The competencies found in the National Standards are viewed as resources for counselors to use in developing program strategies and measurable criteria for assessing outcomes and achieving accountability (Dahir, 2001).

Dahir (2001) states: "More than 400 schools or districts throughout the 50 states have established comprehensive school counseling programs based on the National Standards with full statewide adoption currently under way in Delaware and New Jersey" (p. 325). Further, she notes that the Standards have been supported or endorsed by the ACA, the American College Testing Program (ACT), the Association for Career and Technical Education, the Association for Counselor Education and Supervision, the College Board, the CACREP, the National Alliance of Business, the National Association of Elementary Principals, the National Association of Secondary School Principals, the NBCC, the National Association of College Admissions Counseling, the National Career Development Association, and the National Parent Teachers Association. Finally, Dahir notes that 69% of the counselor education programs were using the Standards in some way (Perusse, Goodnough, & Noel, 2000), and some of the programs funded by the Education Trust (1997) initiative were using the Standards in pre- and in-service professional development programming (House & Martin, 1998).

Schmidt and Ciechalski (2001) compared the ASCA National Standards to those of the school social work, school nursing, and school psychology professions and concluded that a major difference in the ASCA Standards is that they do not address criteria for training school counselors, program management, ethical practice, legal parameters, and responsibilities of employers. They express concern about failure to address the unique preparation school counselors will have that makes them indispensable in the educational process depicted in the Standards. To develop specific standards for practicing school counselors, they believe this question must be addressed: "If no school counselors were employed, could teachers and other school personnel help students meet the standards that have been developed?" (p. 332).

Three well-articulated conceptualizations of how school counseling can be structured in order to be effective for all students were underway before Bush's No Child Left Behind initiative was proposed. They now seem to be the best visions the profession has to offer for school counseling in the twenty-first century. Although their origins and primary thrusts differ, they have much in common. For example, they all stress: (a) the importance of school counseling being an integral part of the educational program rather than a set of ancillary services, (b) leadership by school counselors directed toward enhancing the academic achievement of all students, (c) advocacy for students and families, (d) collaboration within and outside the schools, and (e) school counselors being well positioned to proactively play a significant role in the current school reform initiative.

Here, we provide a survey of each initiative and demonstrate how the basic competencies for school counseling presented in chapters 4 through 13 are universal and lend themselves to preparing school counselors to carry out the goals, roles, and functions of each of these initiatives as well as others. We do not promote one initiative over any of the others. As individuals who do not have a vested interest in any of the three initiatives, we believe that they have more to offer collectively than any one does individually. For example, the National Model for School Counseling Programs appears to emphasize a broad range of school counseling functions within a clearly defined program and also emphasizes school counselors being leaders in their schools and in responding to school reform initiatives. It also presents competencies devoted to enhancing student academic, career, and personal-social development directed toward success in school and life; the National School Counselor Training Initiative tends to emphasize leadership and advocacy functions for school counselors and presents a mission that all students have access to and success in a rigorous academic curriculum in order to be successful in their lives; and the School-Community Collaboration Model emphasizes the collaboration function for school counselors while following a mission to meet the social, emotional, and health needs of all students so they can be successful in school.

The National Model for Comprehensive School Counseling Programs.

The National Model is sponsored by the ASCA and incorporates the ASCA National Standards for School Counseling Programs (Campbell & Dahir, 1997). Details about the National Standards were provided earlier in this chapter and additional information is found in Appendix A. The process of developing this model began in 2001 and continues today (Bowers, Hatch, & Schwallie-Giddis, 2001; Hatch & Bowers, 2002). The general goal is that comprehensive school counseling must be integral to student academic achievement and must help set high standards for student achievement. It is believed that school counselors must be trained to inform administrators of the contributions they plan to make rather than asking them what to do.

It is also believed that the National Model maximizes the full potential of the National Standards and reflects the current education reform movements, including Bush's No Child Left Behind initiative. In so doing, the National Model incorporates school counseling standards and competencies for all students. The National Standards serve as a foundation for the National Model and lead to an organized, planned, sequential, and flexible school counseling program. Interventions will be intentional and designed to meet the needs of all students. A primary objective of intentional planning will be to close the gap between academically disadvantaged students and their advantaged peers.

The National Model is perceived as a flexible template that individual school districts can use to create programs that reflect their own needs and accountability expectations. The components of the model include, but are not limited to (a) the ASCA National Standards; (b) implementation of a district-wide delivery system that includes a guidance curriculum, individual planning, responsive services, and system support; (c) a management system that ensures that programs are based on student needs; (d) a data-driven evaluation system; (e) intentional services for academically underperforming students; and (f) infusion of systemic change, leadership, and advocacy throughout all components. The National Model was tested by seven school districts in Riverside, California, in 2001 and reviewed by school counseling leaders. For further information see www.SchoolCounselor.org.

The ASCA National Standards are viewed as complementing the comprehensive school guidance and counseling program concept, and the ASCA National Model is strongly influenced by that concept as well. Sink and McDonald (1998) reported that 35 state departments of education or school counseling associations have promoted the implementation of comprehensive school counseling models. Herr (2001) believes the concept, originally depicted as comprehensive guidance programs, has its roots in the 1960s when a systems approach in guidance was being advocated. The concept of planned, comprehensive, systematic guidance programs emerged in the 1980s and has received support from national professional associations, such as the ASCA, and from federal legislation, such as the Carl D. Perkins Vocational Education Act of 1984 and the School to Work Opportunities Act of 1994 (Herr, 2001).

Currently, many advocates are voicing their support of this concept in the professional literature, and we have selected Gysbers and Henderson (2000) to represent them here. According to Gysbers and Henderson (2001), a comprehensive guidance and counseling program consists of three elements: content, organizational framework, and resources. Content refers to the competencies students achieve through participation in components of a comprehensive guidance and counseling program.

The organizational framework consists of a K–12 curriculum of guidance activities designed to help students achieve the competencies. For example, the curriculum might include a classroom guidance program designed to help students investigate the world of work, acquire a better understanding of themselves in the world of work, and eventually make wise career decisions.

Furthermore, the organizational framework includes delivery modes for the organized curriculum such as classroom and school-wide activities and individual planning. Individual planning is a comprehensive process designed to help students learn about themselves and plan accordingly, and it calls upon counselors to possess appraisal, advisement, placement, and follow-up competencies. The organizational framework also includes services needed to respond to student problems that deter academic, career, and personal-social development. These services are identified as personal counseling, diagnostic and remediation activities, consultation, and referral. Finally, it is important not to overlook the necessity for an ongoing support system consisting of (a) program evaluation leading to continued program development, (b) continuous professional development of school counselors, (c) public relations thrusts to keep all stakeholders informed, (d) service on advisory boards, (e) community outreach, and (f) continuous program planning and management.

The resource element of a comprehensive program refers to the importance of human, financial, and political resources. School counselors, teachers, administrators, parents, students, community members, and business and labor persons all have important contributions to make in a comprehensive guidance and counseling program. Adequate financial support is needed as well. Finally, political resources need to be mobilized appropriately in order to achieve full endorsement by school district boards of education. Gysbers and Henderson (2001) believe that: "The program's organizational structure not only provides the means and a common language for ensuring guidance for all students and counseling for students that need it, it also provides a foundation for the accountable use of an ever-broadening spectrum of resources" (p. 256). Finally, Gysbers and Henderson (2001) view the comprehensive school guidance and counseling program approach as the best vehicle for achieving the convergence of the currently incongruent goals of providing an academically rigorous education while including all students.

The National School Counselor Training Initiative.

Supported by a 1996 grant from the DeWitt Wallace Reader's Digest Fund, the National Education Trust set out to bring about dramatic changes in the training of school counselors in order to transform school counseling by causing school counselors to become more responsive to student needs (Guerra, 1998). Six counselor education programs were selected to receive funding for developing model school counseling training programs. Advocates of the Trust's initiative believe that the programs for training school counselors must change if there are to be constructive changes in school counseling (Sears & Granello, 2002). New funding from the Met Life Foundation allowed the Education Trust to initiate the National School Counselor Training Initiative (Stone & House, 2002). This funding allows the Education Trust to deliver workshops to school counselors and administrators that focus on transforming the work of counselors. For more information, contact rhouse@edtrust.org.

An underlying theme of this initiative is that school counselors need to be integral participants in closing the gap between poor students and students of color and their more advantaged peers (House & Hayes, 2002). Therefore, school counselors must believe that all students can achieve at a high level and act accordingly. House and Hayes believe school counselors are in the best position to assess their schools for barriers to academic success for all students and to use that information to be advocates for equity and entitlement. While not negating the importance of traditional school counselor roles such as counselor, coordinator, and consultant, this initiative emphasizes the roles of leader, advocate, and collaborator. According to Sears and Granello (2002), the traditional roles, and their corresponding skills, remain necessary yet are no longer sufficient for school counselors to be effective in today's schools.

School counselors attempting to achieve the goals of this initiative will develop, coordinate, and implement well-articulated developmental counseling programs with attention to equity, access, and support services (House & Hayes, 2002). These programs will be designed to improve the learning success of all students, especially those who experience difficulty in rigorous academic programs. School counselors will provide leadership and collaborate in building teams of students, professional and support staff members, parents, and individuals in the community in order to accomplish a communitywide effort to achieve the goals of educational reform.

If school counselors proactively emphasize and implement the educational leader, advocate, and collaborator roles and are successful, then they will move school counseling from the periphery to a central position in the schools (Education Trust, 1997; House & Hayes, 2002). In so doing, they will make a significant contribution to closing the achievement gap between poor students and students of color and their more advantaged peers.

House and Hayes (2002) offer examples of how school counselors can take advantage of their unique position in the schools in order to achieve the goals of this initiative. These proactive leaders can present themselves to the students as caring and committed adult advocates and mentors. They are in a position to determine what barriers to academic success exist in their schools and communities and to engage in proactive efforts to alleviate them through leadership, advocacy, and collaboration. In so doing, they will be at the forefront of promoting high expectations and standards.

The School-Community Collaboration Model.

A basic principle of this initiative is that external barriers—such as poverty, violence, gangs, drugs, language and culture differences, and inadequate health care—lead to emotional, behavior, and learning problems in schools (Adelman & Taylor, 2002). Unless these are addressed successfully, efforts to leave no student behind academically will fail. This approach seems to respond to the criticism Herr (2002) shared about previous school reform movements having a focus that was too narrow.

In recent years, several writers in the counseling profession have published articles promoting this approach (Green & Keys, 2001; Hobbs & Collison, 1995; Keys & Bemak, 1997; Keys, Bemak, & Lockhart, 1998). Adelman and Taylor reported that various forms of school-community collaboration have been tested. Although these programs had limited focus and ran into many challenges, Adelman and Taylor believe there is sufficient inferential evidence that these programs can be successful and cost-effective over time.

Adelman and Taylor believe that few schools currently have the resources needed and that educational reform has ignored the importance of reforming and restructuring the work of those school professionals who are responsible for psychosocial and health programs. They recommend that new strategies for coordinating, integrating, and redeploying resources should be implemented in order to increase the comprehensiveness of school-based responses to social, emotional, and physical health problems.

The proposed model espouses the following recommendations. First, since student problems are usually complex in terms of causes and needed interventions, a comprehensive, multifaceted continuum of braided interventions is needed. These braided interventions would employ strategies that may be categorized as primary prevention, early identification and treatment, and treatment of severe and chronic problems. Second, efforts must be linked to the basic mission of schools: to educate children and youths. Therefore, "the current emphasis on improving instruction and school management should also include a comprehensive component for addressing barriers to learning" (Adelman & Taylor, 2002, p. 242).

Six arenas are offered through which coordination and eventually integration of a myriad of school and community resources might be achieved. They are all focused on addressing barriers to learning and enhancing healthy development in the school sites: (a) increase the effectiveness of classroom instruction; (b) support students and families in coping with a variety of transitions; (c) help families to become involved successfully in the education of their children; (d) provide a systematic program for crisis assistance and prevention; (e) integrate and personalize social, mental health, and physical health assistance for students and their families; and (f) create and maintain collaborative connections with public and private agencies, higher education, business and professional organizations, churches, and volunteer organizations.

Adelman and Taylor (2002) recommend trying to achieve school-community collaboration at the school and neighborhood levels first and then pursuing central restructuring thereafter. They believe that, if school counselors engage in school-community collaboration endeavors, "the roles of school counselors as advocates, catalysts, brokers, leaders, and facilitators of systemic reform will expand in order to engage in an increasingly wide array of activity to promote academic achievement and healthy development and address barriers to student learning" (p. 244).

Adoptions of the model have occurred in the California Department of Education, the Los Angeles Unified School District, and the Hawaii Department of Education. The New American Schools Urban Learning Center, an application of this approach, has been selected by the U.S. Department of Education as one of 22 outstanding models schools are encouraged to adopt.

Critics of this initiative might note that the emphasis on academic rigor may overlook two important concepts. First, there may be evidence that, even with all barriers removed, some individuals are not suited genetically or in their attitudes for rigorous academic curricula or a college education. Second, the seemingly narrow focus on preparation for college ignores the ideas that education should be preparation for work and that there is dignity in all work.

These initiatives seem to offer considerable promise for enhancing the school counseling profession, making it part of the mainstream of education, providing recommendations for the competencies school counselors need to be successful in the twenty-first century, and ensuring comprehensive and helpful interventions for the nation's students. In another publication, one of us shared an opinion that, historically, ideas that were introduced from the top down did not seem to take hold at the grassroots level of school counseling (Baker, 2001). Time will tell with these initiatives. Those promoting them seem to be willing to undertake the hard work necessary for achieving understanding and approval at the grassroots levels. We hope that they are all successful in some way and that the good that each has to offer may find its way into a mixture of all three initiatives.

Should these initiatives not succeed in achieving their important goals, the ASCA, the Association for Counselor Education and Supervision (ACES), and the ACA, through their efforts to serve school counselors in particular and counselors in general, probably remain the organizations best positioned to help counselors respond to current and future challenges. As has been demonstrated, they offer potential for counselors to respond collectively to the challenges that face the nation, the schools, and the profession. School counselors, in turn, are challenged to become members of one or more of these organizations to strengthen them and to work within them.

The Council for the Accreditation of Counseling and Related Educational Programs (CACREP) provides a vehicle for uniformity in training standards. In that

All school counseling students have adjustments to make when starting careers as school counselors.

vein, in 1990 an interdivisional task force representing the ACES, ACA, and ASCA began planning to improve school counseling. Specifically, the task force recommended uniform state certification/licensure standards and adoption of CACREP standards as minimum requirements for certification/licensure as a school counselor. The task force was thus attempting to enhance the preparation of school counselors (Cecil, 1990). Their goals have not yet been fully achieved. Seem (2002) depicts program accreditation as "a hallmark for defining a profession. . . . Its accreditation standards are the major reference for defining what is known as the counseling core" (p. 7).

HOW SCHOOL COUNSELORS ENHANCE THE ACADEMIC MISSION OF THE SCHOOL

Most school counselors believe that human learning is the product of development in a variety of areas. Carl Rogers, Rudolph Dreikurs, and William Glasser are among the counseling theorists whose writing has helped school counselors and others in education to understand that learning involves more than cognitive activity, that education involves emotional, social, and other factors as well.

The affective domain of human existence encompasses the whole range of human feelings and emotions, including feelings about self, fear, anxiety, joy, and many others. This domain is important in the learning process. No one more clearly spelled out the relationships between emotions and learning than did Brown (1971) in his book *Human Teaching for Human Learning: An Introduction to Confluent Education*. He noted that "the relationship between intellect and affect is indestructibly symbiotic . . . it is the passion of the scholar that makes for truly great scholarship" (p. 11). Brown's view about the coming together of the affective and cognitive domains, however, is only one of many attempts at explaining the role of emotions and feelings in learning. The whole notion of affective education, which gained popularity in the late 1960s and early 1970s, reflects the importance with which many educators regard the affective domain.

The most studied and discussed aspect of the affective domain is self-concept (that is, how students view themselves). Many other affective variables, such as anxiety, motivation, and interest, also influence learning. As is the case with self-concept, the degree to which these factors affect learning is uncertain. Factors of this kind cannot be neglected in the classroom if learning opportunities are to be maximized.

HOW SCHOOL COUNSELORS USE NETWORKING TECHNOLOGY

The evolving School Counseling Activities Network (www.scan21st.com) associated with this textbook encourages the invention of online projects focused on helping students succeed in school. An example is the online program *Succeeding in School* (Gerler, 2001), designed to help students focus on behaviors, attitudes, and human relations skills that lead to improved academic achievement. Graduate students and school counselors are invited to use and to contribute lessons to the topics covered in this program. The Internet address for *Succeeding in School* is http://genesislight.com/web%20files/index.htm.

The initial research on a paper-and-pencil version of this program was conducted with 900 children across North Carolina and produced promising results (Gerler & Anderson, 1986). Several subsequent studies have been conducted (Gerler, 1990; Gerler, Drew, & Mohr, 1990; Gerler & Herndon, 1993), including one in Long Beach, California, that found statistically significant improvement in children's math achievement as a result of participation in the program (Lee, 1993). The current Internet version of the program allows upper elementary and middle-school students to complete interactive program activities online and also allows students to complete pre- and post-program measures of school success online. This feature encourages studies of the program across the United States and elsewhere. The online version of *Succeeding in School* incorporates ten sections: Models of Success, Being Comfortable in School, Being Responsible in School, Listening in School, Asking for Help in School,

One of the features of this book is access to online lessons.

Improving at School, Cooperating with Peers, Cooperating with Teachers, The Bright Side of School, and The Bright Side of Me. An outline of each section appears in Appendix B.

The paper-and-pencil version of the *Succeeding in School* program has been shown to have important effects on the educational process in elementary and middle schools. The School Counseling Activities Network (www.scan21st.com) will offer counselor educators, graduate students, and school counselors the opportunity to coordinate their efforts in implementing and testing *Succeeding in School* as well as in creating new approaches toward enhancing students' performance in school.

INTRODUCTION TO THE WEBSITE FOR *SCHOOL COUNSELING FOR THE TWENTY-FIRST CENTURY*

One of the special features of this textbook is the opportunity to access online lessons and information associated with each chapter in the text. These lessons allow professors and graduate students to reflect on the material presented in print and to generate ideas for the School Counseling Activities Network (www.scan21st.com). The online lessons appear at the following Internet address: http://www.prenhall.com/baker.

SUGGESTED ACTIVITIES

1. Debate the merits of joining or not joining a professional organization.
2. Debate the merits of joining the NEA, ACA, or ASCA.
3. Debate the merits of becoming a licensed professional counselor (LPC).
4. Review several issues of the *Journal of Counseling & Development*, *Professional School Counseling*, *Counseling Today*, and the *ASCA Counselor* and assess the value of their information.
5. Discuss the merits of the following statements:
   a. School counseling was not born; it evolved.
   b. The greatest periods of growth and support for guidance have occurred when the federal government was responding to a national crisis.
6. Ask the counselor educator responsible for coordinating your program to elaborate on the most important influences during her or his master's and doctoral training programs.
7. Go to the online School Counseling Activities Network (www.scan21st.com) to participate in online counseling exercises.

REFERENCES

Adelman, H. S., & Taylor, L. (2002). School counselors and school reform: New directions. *Professional School Counseling, 5*, 238–248.

Alger Report indicates youth perceptions of school counselors improving. (1996). *ASCA Counselor, 34*(2), 11.

American Association for Counseling and Development (AACD). (1991). *Special issue:*

Multiculturalism as a fourth force in counseling. Alexandria, VA: Author.

American Personnel and Guidance Association (APGA). (1969). *The elementary school counselor in today's schools.* Washington, DC: Author.

American School Counselor Association. (1996). *School counseling legislation: Elementary and Secondary Act (ESEA).* Alexandria, VA: Author.

Aubrey, R. F. (1977). Historical development of guidance and counseling and implications for the future. *Personnel and Guidance Journal, 55,* 288–295.

Baker, S. B. (1994). Mandatory teaching experience for school counselors: An impediment to uniform certification standards for school counselors. *Counselor Education and Supervision, 33,* 314–326.

Baker, S. B. (2001). Reflections on forty years in the school counseling profession: Is the glass half full or half empty? *Professional School Counseling, 54,* 75–83.

Barber, B. (1965). Some problems in the sociology of a profession. In K. S. Lynn (Ed.), *Professions in America.* Boston: Houghton Mifflin.

Beers, C. (1908). *A mind that found itself.* New York: Longmans Green.

Borders, D. L., & Drury, R. D. (1992). Comprehensive school counseling programs: A review for policy makers and practitioners. *Journal of Counseling and Development, 70,* 487–498.

Bowers, J., Hatch, T., & Schwallie-Giddis, P. (2001, September–October). The brain storm. *ASCA Counselor,* 17–18.

Brown, G. I. (1971). *Human teaching for human learning: An introduction to confluent education.* New York: Viking.

Campbell, C. A., & Dahir, C. A. (1997). Sharing the vision: The national standards for school counseling programs. Alexandria, VA: American School Counseling Association.

Cecil, J. H. (1990). Interdivisional task force on school counseling. *ACES Spectrum, 50*(4), 3–4.

Coleman, H. K. L. (1995). Cultural factors and the counseling process: Implications for school counselors. *School Counselor, 42,* 180–185.

College Board. (1986). *Keeping the options open— Recommendations: Final report of the Commission on Precollege Guidance and Counseling.* New York: College Entrance Examination Board.

Conant, J. B. (1959). *The American high school today.* New York: McGraw-Hill.

Council for the Accreditation of Counseling and Related Educational Programs (CACREP) (2001). *CACREP accreditation manual.* Alexandria, VA: Author.

Dahir, C. (1997). National standards for school counseling programs: A pathway to excellence. *ASCA Counselor, 35*(2), 11.

Dahir, C. (2001). The national standards for school counseling programs: Development and implementation. *Professional School Counseling, 4,* 320–327.

Dinkmeyer, D. (1967). Elementary school guidance and the classroom teacher. *Elementary School Guidance and Counseling, 1,* 15–26.

Dobbins, J. E., & Skillings, J. H. (1991). The utility of race labeling in understanding cultural identity: A conceptual tool for the social science practitioner. *Journal of Counseling & Development, 70,* 37–44.

Durbin, D. M. (1982). Multimodal group sessions to enhance self-concept. *Elementary School Guidance and Counseling, 16,* 288–295.

Dykeman, C. (1995). The privatization of school counseling. *School Counselor, 43,* 29–34.

Education Trust. (1997). *Working definition of school counseling.* Washington, DC: Author.

Ewing, D. B. (1975). Direct from Minnesota—E. G. Williamson. *Personnel and Guidance Journal, 54,* 78–87.

Gerler, E. R. (1990). Children's success in school: Collaborative research among counselors, supervisors, and counselor educators. *Elementary School Guidance and Counseling, 25,* 64–71.

Gerler, E. R. (2001). *Succeeding in School.* Available: http://genesislight.com/web%20files/.

Gerler, E. R., & Anderson, R. F. (1986). The effects of classroom guidance on children's success in school. *Journal of Counseling and Development, 65,* 78–81.

Gerler, E. R., & Herndon, E. (1993). Learning how to succeed academically in middle school. *Elementary School Guidance and Counseling, 27,* 186–197.

Gerler, E. R., Drew, N. S., & Mohr, P. (1990). Succeeding in middle school: A multimodal approach. *Elementary School Guidance and Counseling, 24,* 263–271.

Gibson, R. L., & Mitchell, M. H. (1981). *Introduction to guidance.* New York: Macmillan.

Goetz, B. (1997). School enrollment to hit all time high. *Counseling Today, 40*(4), 12.

Green, A., & Keys, S. (2001). Expanding the developmental school counseling paradigm: Meeting the needs of the 21st century student. *Professional School Counseling, 5,* 84–95.

Greenwood, E. (1957). Attributes of a profession. *Social Work, 2,* 45–55.

Guerra, P. (1998). Revamping school counselor education: The DeWitt Wallace Reader's Digest Fund. *Counseling Today, 40*(8), 19, 36.

Gysbers, N. C., & Henderson, P. (2000). *Developing and managing your school guidance program* (3rd ed.). Alexandria, VA: American Association for Counseling and Development.

Gysbers, N. C., & Henderson, P. (2001). Comprehensive guidance and counseling programs: A rich history and a bright future. *Professional School Counseling, 4*, 246–256.

Harris-Aikens, D. (2001, September–October). Legislators continue fight for school counselor funding. *ASCA School Counselor,* 5.

Hatch, T., & Bowers, J. (2002, May–June). The block to build on. *ASCA Counselor,* 13–17.

Herr, E. L. (1985). AACD: An association committed to unity through diversity. *Journal of Counseling & Development, 63*, 395–404.

Herr, E. L. (2001). The impact of national policies, economics, and school reform on comprehensive guidance programs. *Professional School Counseling, 4*, 236–245.

Herr, E. L. (2002). School reform and perspectives on the role of school counselors: A century of proposals for change. *Professional School Counseling, 5*, 220–234.

Herr, E. L., & Cramer, S. G. (1987). *Controversies in the mental health professions.* Muncie, IN: Accelerated Development.

Hobbs, B., & Collison, B. (1995). School-community collaboration: Implications for school counselors. *School Counselor, 43*, 58–65.

House, R. M., & Hayes, R. L. (2002). School counselors: Becoming key players in school reform. *Professional School Counseling, 5*, 249–256.

House, R. M., & Martin, P. (1998). Advocating for better futures for all students: A new vision for school counselors. *Education, 119*, 284–291.

Hoyt, K. B., Evans, R. N., Mackin, E. F., & Mangum, G. L. (1974). *Career education: What is it and how to do it* (2nd ed.). Salt Lake City, UT: Olympus.

Ibrahim, F. A. (1991). Contribution of cultural worldview to generic counseling and development. *Journal of Counseling & Development, 70*, 13–19.

Kandor, J. R., & Bobby, C. L. (1992). Introduction to a special feature. *Journal of Counseling & Development, 70*, 666.

Keat, D. B. (1974). *Fundamentals of child counseling.* Boston: Houghton Mifflin.

Keys, S. G., & Bemak, F. (1997). School-family-community linked services: A school counseling role for changing times. *School Counselor, 44*, 255–263.

Keys, S. G., Bemak, F., & Lockhart, E. (1998). Transforming school counseling to meet the mental health needs of at-risk youth. *Journal of Counseling & Development, 76*, 381–388.

Lapan, R. T., Gysbers, N. C., & Sun, Y. (1997). The impact of more fully implemented guidance programs on the school experiences of high school students: A statewide evaluation study. *Journal of Counseling & Development, 75*, 292–302.

Lee, R. S. (1993). Learning how to succeed academically in middle school. *Elementary School Guidance and Counseling, 27*, 163–171.

Menacker, J. (1974). *Vitalizing guidance in urban schools.* New York: Dodd, Mead.

Menacker, J. (1976). Toward a theory of activist guidance. *Personnel and Guidance Journal, 54*, 318–321.

Moles, O. C. (1991). Guidance programs in American high schools: A descriptive portrait. *School Counselor, 38*, 163–177.

Morrissey, M. (1996). The baby boom echo generation: Ready or not, here it comes. *Counseling Today, 39*(6), 1, 6, 8.

Mosher, R. L., & Sprinthall, N. A. (1970). Psychological education in secondary schools: A program to promote individual and human development. *American Psychologist, 25*, 911–924.

Neukrug, E. S., Barr, C. G., Hoffman, L. R., & Kaplan, L. S. (1993). Developmental counseling and guidance: A model for use in your school. *School Counselor, 40*, 356–362.

Nuttal, E. V., Webber, J. J., & Sanchez, W. (1996). MCT theory and implications for training. In D. W. Sue, A. E. Ivey, & P. B. Pedersen (Eds.), *A theory of multicultural counseling and therapy* (pp. 123–138). Pacific Grove, CA: Brooks/Cole.

Olson, M. J., & Allen, D. N. (1993). Principals' perceptions of the effectiveness of school counselors with and without teaching experience. *Counselor Education and Supervision, 33*, 10–21.

Paisley, P. O., & Borders, D. L. (1995). School counseling: An evolving specialty. *Journal of Counseling and Development, 74*, 150–153.

Parsons, F. (1909). *Choosing a vocation.* Boston: Houghton Mifflin.

Perusse, R., Goodnough, G., & Noel, D. (2000, March). *What school counselors need to know, what counselor educators need to teach.* Paper presented at the annual meeting of the American Counseling Association, Washington, DC.

Peterson, J., Goodman, R., & Keller, T. (2002, October). *A comparison of school counseling students with and without teaching background.* Paper presented at the Association for Counselor Education and Supervision Convention, Park City, UT.

Proctor, W. (1925). *Educational and vocational guidance: A consideration of guidance as it relates to all of the essential activities of life.* Boston: Houghton Mifflin.

Roberts, W. B., Jr., Coursol, D. H., & Morotti, A. A. (1997). Chief school administrators' perceptions of professional school counselors on measures of employability in Minnesota. *School Counselor, 44,* 280–287.

Rockwell, P. J., & Rothney, J. W. M. (1961). Some ideas of pioneers in the guidance movement. *Personnel and Guidance Journal, 11,* 34–39.

Rogers, C. R. (1942). *Counseling and psychotherapy.* Boston: Houghton Mifflin.

Rogers, C. R. (1951). *Client-centered therapy.* Boston: Houghton Mifflin.

Rogers, C. R. (1961). *On becoming a person.* Boston: Houghton Mifflin.

Schmidt, J. J., & Ciechalski, J. C. (2001). School counseling standards: A summary and comparison with other student services' standards. *Professional School Counseling, 4,* 328–333.

Sears, S. J., & Granello, D. H. (2002). School counseling now and in the future: A reaction. *Professional School Counseling, 5,* 164–171.

Seem, S. (2002, April). Accreditation makes counselors strong. *Counseling Today,* 7.

Shaw, M. C. (1973). *School guidance systems.* Boston: Houghton Mifflin.

Sink, C. A., & MacDonald, G. (1998). The status of comprehensive guidance and counseling in the United States. *Professional School Counseling, 2,* 88–89.

Smith, G. E. (1955). *Counseling in the secondary school.* New York: Macmillan.

Smith, S. L., Crutchfield, L. B., & Culbreth, J. R. (2001). Teaching experience for school counselors: Counselor educators' perceptions. *Professional School Counseling, 4,* 216–228.

Speight, S. L., Myers, L. J., Cox, C. I., & Highlen, P. S. (1991). A redefinition of multicultural counseling. *Journal of Counseling & Development, 70,* 29–36.

Stamm, M. L., & Nissman, D. (1971). *New dimensions in elementary guidance.* New York: Richards Rosen Press.

Stone, C., & House, R. (2002, May–June). Train the trainers program transform school counselors. *ASCA Counselor,* 20–21.

Sue, D. W., Arredondo, P., & McDavis, R. J. (1992). Multicultural competencies/standards: A pressing need. *Journal of Counseling & Development, 70,* 477–486.

Urbaniak, J. (2000, September). The ESCDA battle. *Counseling Today,* 18.

Westbrook, S. D., & Sedlacek, W. E. (1991). Forty years of using labels to communicate about nontraditional students: Does it help or hurt? *Journal of Counseling & Development, 70,* 20–28.

Williamson, E. G. (1950). *Counseling adolescents.* New York: McGraw-Hill.

Williamson, E. G., & Darley, J. G. (1937). *Student personnel work: An outline of clinical procedures.* New York: McGraw-Hill.

Wrenn, C. G. (1962). *The counselor in a changing world.* Washington, DC: American Personnel and Guidance Association.

Zaccaria, J. (1969). *Approaches to guidance in contemporary education.* Scranton, PA: International Textbook.

CHAPTER 2

A Balanced Approach to School Counseling

Goal: To promote comprehensive, balanced K–12 school counseling programs conducted by counselors capable of meeting both remedial and developmental goals for children and adolescents living in a pluralistic society.

School counselors often reflect on the large responsibilities they encounter daily and over the course of a school year. Here are samples of what they say:

We ought to work with children in kindergarten and the early grades to prevent problem classroom behaviors. If we wait until later, the reinforcement and rewards for acceptable behaviors don't work very well.

Counselors must help school bus drivers to improve behavior on buses. Students go crazy on the bus first thing in the morning, and it continues for the rest of the school day. Improving bus behavior might prevent accidents, too.

I just got out of graduate school and learned all I could about behavior modification. I now know it sounds better in textbooks than it works. There must be a better way to change behavior in schools.

I think parents and teachers need to listen more carefully to one another. We need more parent and teacher groups that teach communication skills. There would be fewer misunderstandings.

Counselors need to listen with more empathy to the kids who fail all the time. Most of us did not have many failures in school. After all, we got through grad school. I've tried to imagine what it would be like to be in a place where I fail all the time.

Fighting is always a problem at school. Counselors need to find ways to cut down on this problem. Racial tension continues to cause a lot of fighting in and out of school.

Career education is so important. We need to help students use their imaginations to think about life after school. Students who have hope for the future will probably be better students.

School counseling offers professionals a wide choice of options for improving life at school among students, parents, teachers, and school administrators. Counselors need to explore a balanced approach to their work and to consider how to establish priorities.

INTRODUCTION

In the twenty-first century, school counselors will probably be more effective if they are able to provide proactive programs that meet and enhance developmental needs, as well as to react to demands for interventions when required. They will be challenged to meet the needs of individuals having different worldviews, as well as the needs of those sharing the same worldview. Wide-ranging needs and demands will require flexibility and a capacity for counselors to be proactive in providing services that enhance the personal and cognitive development of their student clients, help them acquire useful coping skills, and aid them in becoming multiculturally competent.

Current circumstances in the nation's schools and projections of socioeconomic conditions that will affect the schools seem to demand systematic school counseling programs designed to respond to the developmental needs of students in elementary, middle, and secondary schools. Proactive programming designed to enhance student developmental transitions and reactive interventions that help students who are in danger of arrested development are both important and needed today. The importance of both proactive and reactive program goals is the foundation of the concept depicted as a balanced approach in this textbook. Therefore, a balanced approach implies that school counselors are capable of providing both high-quality proactive programs based on perceived developmental needs of students and counseling interventions in response to threats to successful student development. Examples of proactive curriculum programming goals are enhancing self-esteem, acquiring important social skills, and improving needed coping skills. Counseling intervention goals are usually individual in nature, though occasionally they are used with small groups. Examples are helping a student or students overcome career planning indecisiveness, decide how to cope with peer pressure to engage in substance abuse behaviors, and survive an abusive home environment.

A succinct description of the philosophy on which balanced school counseling programs are founded is presented in the introduction to the Wake County, North Carolina, schools' *Comprehensive Guidance Program:*

> Schools are a microcosm of society reflecting a culture characterized by diversity, complexity, and changing values in the home, school, and community. Today's society affects our students in ways that can impact achievement. . . . Our school system supports a developmental, balanced approach to school guidance and counseling. Classroom guidance, small group and individual counseling, parent involvement, and other activities continue to be the focus of the plan. In addition, current needs may dictate that school counselors respond in new roles such as staff developer or case manager. School counselors will assess the needs of the school, will create and implement a balanced guidance program that addresses those needs, and will continuously evaluate the outcomes. (Wake County Schools, 1993)

An equally succinct philosophy is found in the Waynesboro, Pennsylvania, Area School District, which is smaller and more rural than the Wake County system:

> We believe the school guidance and counseling program must balance traditional and remedial services with a program that systematically and sequentially addresses the educational, career, personal, and social needs of students from K–12. We further believe the entire school community and community at large must play a significant and active role in the overall development of every student. (Waynesboro Area School District, n.d., p. 2)

We believe that the competencies presented in chapters 4 through 13 of this book are important ingredients of the preparation school counselors need to function successfully in balanced programs and provide leadership in developing and advocating such programs. We also believe that each of the competencies is an important component in all of the three current initiatives presented in chapter 1. That is, they are advocated by spokespersons for the National Model for School Counseling Programs sponsored by the ASCA, the National School Counselor Training Initiative sponsored by the Education Trust, and the School-Community Collaboration Model. We will attempt to point out these relationships at the beginning of chapters 4 through 13.

Readers may have noticed that the terms *guidance* and *school counseling* seemed to be used interchangeably in chapter 1. *Guidance* was the earlier label used. *Guidance counselor* followed. *Guidance* is a generic term covering all the functions in which school counselors may engage. Counseling is one of those functions. Others include consulting and assessing. The current preference of the profession is to use one of the functions, counseling, as the generic term as well. Therefore, *school counseling* is preferred to *guidance counseling*. Both *school counseling* and *guidance* are used to refer to essentially the same activities in this textbook because *guidance* has not been completely purged from the professional vernacular. An example of this is the popularity of the developmental guidance programs that were introduced in chapter 1.

WHAT IS A BALANCED APPROACH?

Current conditions appear to demand a balanced approach to school counseling. In the first years of the twenty-first century, Americans are confronted with pervasive and traumatic social problems that it is hoped, and perhaps expected, the schools will help prevent in order to improve the probability that students will be successful in school as well as in life. Problems at the top of the list are child abuse, AIDS, substance abuse, adolescent suicide, teenage pregnancy, unemployment, underemployment, and violence. At the same time the schools address prevention, they cannot ignore individuals who are at risk, suffering these and other maladies or recovering from actual and borderline encounters. Their cases, and many less serious yet reasonable demands for treatment or remedial interventions, demonstrate the importance of responding to existing problems. A balanced school counseling program, then, is one in which importance is attributed equally to prevention *and* intervention goals. *Prevention* as used here refers to school counseling functions based on systematic proactive planning, such as designing a program to teach middle-school students coping skills to help them resist peer pressure to engage in substance abuse. *Intervention* is used to label school counseling functions—such as crisis, brief individual, and group counseling—for individuals who are referred or who refer themselves for assistance and to whom counselors respond reactively to help resolve the presenting issues.

Over the years, several terms with similar meanings have evolved in the field of guidance and counseling. Some people use *developmental* instead of *prevention* because the former implies enhancing individual development and the latter implies preventing problems. This textbook uses *prevention,* programming designed to both prevent problems and enhance individual development. For example, a prevention program for teaching assertiveness skills may help some participants resist attempts by peers to promote substance abuse and help other participants cope better with typical developmental tasks such as making friends. Some people use *remediation* rather than *treatment* because the latter seems too clinical and the former seems more appropriate for school counseling that occurs in an educational setting. This textbook uses *intervention*, which includes remediation *and* treatment as well as early identification in which interventions occur before negative influences necessitate remediation or treatment. In the various forms of intervention, counselors are reacting to requests for help. They are behaving proactively when engaged in prevention programming.

Many school counseling programs are not balanced (Moles, 1991). The scale is tipped toward intervention. What appear to be several reasons for this condition were documented in chapter 1: First is the trait and factor, or directive, approach. Second is the student-centered, or nondirective, approach to helping individuals adjust, make decisions, and cope with their problems. Third is the influence of school administrators, school boards, teachers, parents, students, and legislators whose expectations are for intervention responses, placing counselors in a reactive role. As demands increase and counselors become proficient in their responses, thereby increasing their clientele and the demand, little time and energy remain for anything else. Yet, many students demand little or nothing because they and their families see the services as restricted to those in trouble or to administrative functions such as scheduling, discipline, and supervision.

In addition, the nature of school organization works against prevention programming, especially in secondary schools. Students are in classrooms receiving subject matter instruction most of the day. Therefore, counselors learn to work around scheduled academic classes in secondary schools. Thus, it is much easier for counselors to meet with individuals during study halls or other times outside academic scheduling in secondary schools than it is for them to initiate group programs with prevention goals in the academic schedule or in the classes of like-minded teaching colleagues. The structure of elementary schools, not having study halls but having intact classrooms, gives counselors at that level more opportunities to achieve prevention goals in collaboration with like-minded teaching colleagues.

Although reacting to problems is indeed challenging, it does not require as much advance planning as preventing problems. Counselors enhance their knowledge when the problems they encounter demand that they do so, but essentially they respond as needed. In contrast, prevention requires a proactive approach. To initiate prevention programs, counselors have to engage in considerable preliminary activities before implementation. Given a high demand for intervening for various problems, few counselors have the time and energy for developing lesson plans, finding periods in the master schedule for their offerings, recruiting participants and collegial collaborators, preparing teaching aids, and practicing their presentations. Loss of skills and lack of knowledge may also be factors. Prevention programming requires pedagogical skills. Many people have been trained to be counselors, with interviewing skills honed and developed, often at the expense of their teaching competencies. In some cases, counselors have never been trained for teaching. In addition, some counselors trained in programs that finely tune their therapeutic skills learn little about prevention and developmental guidance programs reported in the professional literature.

A PROPOSAL FOR ACHIEVING BALANCE

Advocacy of a balanced approach is an initial step. Suggesting ways to achieve it is the next step. What follows is a plan for achieving balance between intervention and prevention goals in school counseling.

Managing Intervention Demands

Because demands for intervention are more pervasive than demands for prevention, counselors are challenged to control intervention responses to initiate needed prevention programming. School counselors are usually unable to provide intervention services for all students. This is so, in part, because of available time, limitations of competence and expertise, and simply the lack of demand for interventions from some individuals.

School counselors benefit from prioritizing their intervention responses whenever possible. Figure 2.1 provides a paradigm that may be useful to counselors who, when

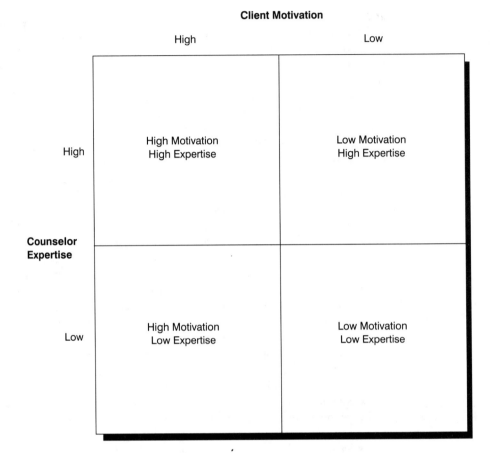

Client Motivation

	High	Low
High	High Motivation High Expertise	Low Motivation High Expertise
Low	High Motivation Low Expertise	Low Motivation Low Expertise

Counselor Expertise

Figure 2.1
A decision-making aid for prioritizing school counseling interventions.

thinking through the prioritizing process, need a system to help them in making decisions. This system is taken from the triage approach to emergency medicine, in which decisions are made about whom to treat first in an emergency on the basis of which patients seem to have the highest probability of responding successfully to treatment. School counselors are in a position to behave in a similar manner. As they explore and clarify student client needs via referral information or through the early stages of one-to-one counseling, they have an opportunity to ascertain causes for those symptoms and to hypothesize about possible intervention strategies, as well as the potential duration of an intervention and probability of success.

With information about what intervention individual clients need and the probability for success, counselors trying to prioritize their intervention responses may decide how to respond on the basis of the client's motivation to succeed and the counselor's ability to provide the needed intervention. The implication is that all prospective student clients will receive some attention. Large caseloads, however, often force counselors into prioritizing their responses to requests for help. Thus, this decision-making plan has two dimensions: levels of client motivation and degrees of counselor expertise. Assuming the range of high to low levels of each attribute, it appears that the easiest decisions are represented by two of the quadrants in Figure 2.1. On the one hand, when counselor expertise and client motivation are high (the top left quadrant), counselors can decide to proceed and expect that the probability for success is good. On the other hand, when counselor expertise and client motivation are low (the bottom right quadrant), the recommendation is to consider postponing interventions until one or both factors change and/or a referral can be made to someone with sufficient expertise and perhaps more time to work with such difficult cases.

The remaining two quadrants in Figure 2.1 represent more difficult and less clear-cut decisions. When client motivation is high but counselor expertise low, counselors may be able to change the situation by enhancing their expertise. They may also be able to make successful referrals because of the client's high motivation. The latter choice, of course, will be less time-consuming if the counselor desires to find more time for other endeavors, such as prevention programming. The fourth quadrant, in which counselor expertise is high but client motivation is low, is not unlike situations in which both expertise and motivation are low. The crucial factor seems to be low client motivation. As in cases in which both expertise and motivation are low, it appears that postponing an intervention until client motivation changes and/or until referral can be made to others who are willing and have more time is usually the best decision.

Clearly, plans like this require flexibility to make decisions occasionally when the odds for success seem low. That should always be the counselor's prerogative. The primary reason for using this or any other plan should always be kept in mind: prioritizing intervention demands to have time to implement prevention programming and achieve a balanced counseling program.

A hypothetical application follows: Several secondary-school teachers independently refer a male adolescent student to his assigned adviser and school counselor—a typical practice in secondary schools. The presenting problems are poor academic performance, an uncooperative attitude, and a general disinterest in school. The adolescent is too young to withdraw from school but seemingly has dropped out psychologically. The assigned adviser is a woman who, when interviewing the student, notices that he seems uneasy with her and is unresponsive to any attempts she makes to establish a working alliance. On the basis of the small amount of information presented, it appears that the client's motivation is low. If the counselor believes that she has a chance to reach the client, she may attempt to do so, but the chance for success is diminished by the client's attitude and may be reduced by the counselor's gender, personality characteristics, counseling style, or competence. This appears to be a case in which the counselor will be challenged to determine whether it is best to refer the student to another counselor or to terminate the counseling process if the client is not responsive relatively soon in the intervention process.

Success in implementing this or any other program depends on informing and convincing others of its purpose and merit. Unless school boards, school administrators, teachers, and parents understand and accept the principle and the plan, implementing it successfully will be extremely difficult, if not impossible. Therefore, counselors have to believe in their plan and be able to sell it convincingly and diplomatically. To do so, in addition to having a workable plan for controlling counseling interventions, school counselors must present an equally sound plan for prevention programming. This process will call upon counselors to possess the leadership and advocacy skills highlighted by proponents of the National Model for School Counseling Programs and the National School Counselor Training Initiative.

Programming for Prevention

Presenting a plan for prevention programming must have several important initial conditions. First, a school environment in which administrators view teachers and counselors as unique, yet equally important, professionals is essential. Second, participants should understand at the outset that a balanced program is a basic goal. Third, all individuals who influence the counselors' role should understand what prevention means.

The first of these conditions, though very important, is somewhat beyond the purview of this book. On the one hand, if not treated as equal to the teachers, counselors will have a difficult time. On the other hand, the balanced program advocated here may help bring about desired changes in administrative attitudes. The second condition, the goal of a balanced program, has already been addressed. Therefore, let's look at ways to help influential individuals understand the meaning of prevention.

The word *prevention* means different things to different people. For instance, the general population longs to have such pervasive problems as AIDS, violence, adolescent suicide, substance abuse, unemployment, and teenage pregnancy prevented and all students successful academically and in life. That is certainly a tall order and one that creates great expectations. These expectations have led to identification of students needing intervention responses. Therefore, the public demands prevention, and rightly so. Unfortunately, AIDS, violence, suicide, substance abuse, unemployment, and teenage pregnancy are actually outcomes, the causes of which are varied and subtle. Therefore, planning to prevent any one of those negative outcomes before it occurs is very difficult.

The public also associates some positive or developmental outcomes—such as social skills competence, appropriate assertiveness, multicultural competence, self-esteem, good self-concept, and academic success—with prevention programming. When this is the case, it is hoped and perhaps expected that planned prevention programming will cause the participants to have enhanced social skills, appropriate assertiveness, multicultural competence, greater self-esteem, improved self-concepts, or good grades. Although these appear to be agreeable and important outcomes, the words represent very general concepts that beg to be made specific and measurable enough to serve as criteria for prevention programming efforts: Programmers need to be able to associate content with identifiable outcomes. These conditions suggest challenges for prevention programmers, who must develop programs with specific activities that lead to measurable outcomes. Thus, the best thing programmers can do to prevent pervasive problems such as adolescent suicide while enhancing the desired personal qualities is to demonstrate a logical connection between their prevention programs and the desired outcomes. For example, many children who learn to cope better with anxiety, communicate better with their peers, understand the features of their developmental stages, and become more assertive when faced with peer pressure are less likely to abuse drugs and more likely to feel good about themselves. The success of such prevention programs may have to be shown simply by competence or knowledge (Durlak, 1983).

Thus, participants need to demonstrate that they have become more assertive and less anxious or that they have learned information about developmental stages. From these demonstrations, it will have to be assumed that participants are better prepared to cope and less likely to succumb to problem behavior because it is impossible to measure whether something was prevented.

In addition to helping influential people become aware of misperceptions about prevention, it is important to help them understand what prevention is. Shaw and Goodyear (1984) provide a definition that is both applicable to school settings and generalizable to other situations. It focuses chiefly on primary prevention. Taken in part from Cowen (1982), their definition is as follows:

> It must be group—or mass—rather than individually oriented (even though some of its activities may involve individual contacts). It must have a before-the-fact quality, i.e., be targeted to groups not yet experiencing significant maladjustment (even though they may, because of their life situations or recent experiences, be at risk for such outcomes). It must be intentional, i.e., rest on a solid knowledge-base suggesting the program holds potential for either improving psychological health or preventing maladaptation. School learning problems and behavior problems that contribute to school learning problems are also appropriate targets for primary prevention activities. (Shaw & Goodyear, 1984, p. 444)

Primary prevention programs are designed to help all children and adolescents cope better with the developmental tasks they must face. Some children and adolescents are

School counselors benefit from prioritizing their intervention responses.

more vulnerable to life's challenges and are more at risk for trouble. They can be helped with prevention programming, too. In these cases, at-risk children can be identified and offered prevention programming targeted to them specifically. An example is to offer assertiveness training to preteens and young teenagers who are likely to have difficulty resisting peer pressure to participate in substance-abusing behaviors. Such services may also be offered on a one-to-one basis. This form of early efforts to keep small or potential problems from becoming more serious is classified as *secondary prevention* (Shaw, 1973). The term *tertiary prevention* is confusing because in this case the word *prevention* is associated with what are essentially remedial intervention goals. In tertiary prevention, one-to-one and group counseling are used to treat individuals already experiencing problems, to prevent those problems from getting worse, to prevent relapses, and to help resolve the problems (Shaw, 1973). Providing aftercare for adolescents who have returned to school from a temporary sojourn in a drug treatment facility is an example of tertiary prevention that is also part of the intervention function of school counseling. Prevention programming may be designed to reach all students before problems exist or to reach at-risk students before remediation is necessary. In this textbook, primary and secondary prevention are treated globally as prevention.

Individuals who influence the counselor's role must understand that major features of prevention programs are the group delivery mode and the intention to help students become better prepared to cope with future events, including developmental tasks. Such influential people must also realize that the goal of prevention is to enhance individual development. Understanding this, these individuals will probably entertain suggestions for reducing counselor time devoted to intervention and administration and for initiating prevention programming into the regular classroom schedule. Beyond a general understanding of prevention, individuals who influence the counselor's role also need information concerning what specifically can be accomplished through prevention programs and how those programs might be implemented.

Intended to address the concerns of counselors who want to achieve program balance through an increasing emphasis on prevention programming, the foregoing information is not meant as a call for eliminating the equally important intervention services that school counselors are expected to provide. As stated previously, the goal is balanced programs. Achieving suitable balance requires a commitment to be informed, organized, systematic, and diplomatic.

Going Upstream

Here is a paraphrase of a metaphor sometimes used to support prevention activities: Once upon a time, two people were strolling along a stream and enjoying the scenery when suddenly another person appeared in the stream, struggling to keep from drowning. The two strollers jumped in immediately and saved the struggling individual. No sooner had they accomplished this then another struggling person appeared, and another, and another, and another. As the two rescuers struggled to save as many of the increasingly larger group of unfortunates as they could, the task became more and more hopeless. Suddenly, one of the two rescuers went to the shore and ran upstream. In response to the other's inquiry about what was going on, the person running upstream said, "I'm going to find out who's throwing all these people into the stream" (Shaw, 1973).

The metaphor supports prevention. To achieve the advocated balance between prevention and intervention, some counselors will remain downstream to rescue potential drowning victims, whereas others will go upstream to reduce the number of individuals in need of rescuing. Notice that the word *reduce* is used instead of *eliminate*. It is important to realize that the current state of the art of school counseling is such that, whether the focus is on intervention or prevention, success cannot be predicted in absolute terms. Counselors can provide successful interventions for some clients, and their prevention programs will be more successful for some individuals than for others. A balanced approach combining careful intervention and prevention has promise for more success than either approach alone because successful prevention programming reduces the need for interventions, and the existence of a complementary intervention thrust provides help for those for whom prevention programming is not enough.

INGREDIENTS OF A BALANCED SCHOOL COUNSELING PROGRAM

Prevention

Primary Prevention.   Simply stated, primary prevention activities meet anticipated developmental needs before those needs occur. For example, elementary-school counselors, anticipating that children will eventually encounter circumstances that challenge their values and attitudes, may attempt to prepare children for those challenges by offering programs to help children explore their feelings, become more aware of their feelings, and have greater confidence in their ability to understand others.

Primary prevention programs are designed to help all children and adolescents.

Secondary-school counselors, recognizing that adolescence is accompanied by enhanced cognitive development and limited experience, which can lead to immature, self-defeating thoughts about oneself and the environment, may provide programs designed to help adolescents learn how to cope with self-defeating thoughts. For example, adolescents may be taught to recognize such self-defeating thoughts as "If I ask for help, the teacher will think I am dumb." These adolescents can be taught to recognize the self-defeating thoughts for what they are and to replace them with such self-enhancing thoughts as "If I ask for help, I can learn what I need to know and therefore do better on the test." This is a productive way to cope with such challenges to clear thinking common during adolescence.

Primary prevention can also be carried out through the design of educational placement services. Knowing that high-school students need information in order to make important decisions, counselors can establish distribution systems through which all students have access to information well in advance of their need to use it. In the preceding examples, counselors planned and delivered systematic, proactive programs designed to be available to all students to prepare them to cope with developmental challenges. Because the programs were delivered in advance of problems and were available to all students, they are classified as primary prevention programs because they were offered to all students, irrespective of whether or not they had presenting problems, to prepare them for the challenge.

Secondary Prevention.   A program reported by Horan and Williams (1982) provides a good example of secondary prevention. To prevent substance abuse, junior-high-school students were taught to be more assertive in resisting peer pressure to engage in substance-abusing behaviors. This program differs from primary prevention in that the participants were selected from a general student population because they had received low scores on self-report measures of self-assertiveness. Thus, they were categorized as being more at risk of succumbing to such pressure than their peers. Secondary prevention programs may have content that is similar to, or different from, the content of primary prevention programs. The goals are different in that secondary prevention programs and treatments are focused on a selected segment, rather than on the total population. The selected clientele are those persons who are the most susceptible, or at-risk, segment of the population. If they are identified and the program is presented proactively, it is a secondary prevention program. If the selected clientele are identified because they have experienced problems, however, then the response, whether in a group or one-to-one mode, is a form of intervention best described as *early identification and treatment* (Shaw, 1973). Secondary prevention programs are designed for a select rather than general population of students, and they are proactive.

Intervention

Early Identification and Treatment.   Intervention differs from prevention in that it is reactive, rather than proactive, and is offered only to those referred for interventions, rather than to the entire population. *Early identification and treatment* is a phrase that describes the situation of at-risk individuals experiencing a problem or deficit that has not yet overwhelmed them, although they do need individualized help. The following simulations are examples of early identification and treatment cases. The majority of intervention cases with which school counselors work probably fall into this category.

- An elementary-school counselor is working with a child who has been disruptive in class. The short-term goal in this case is to help the child learn better ways to gain attention; the long-term goal is to prevent the child from becoming alienated, labeled negatively by teachers, or academically deficient.
- A middle-school counselor uses teacher-to-parent progress reports as a means of identifying students at risk of failing courses. On finding those who want assistance and for whom learning or behavioral deficits can be identified, the counselor reaches out to them in an effort to provide individual or possibly group counseling interventions that will help them. The purpose of an intervention is to help these students pass their courses and learn more appropriate or new, more useful behaviors. Over the long term, it is hoped that what was learned or changed will generalize to other challenging situations and that the recipients will have enhanced self-esteem because of their accomplishments.
- At the secondary-school level, a counselor who provides an empathic, facilitative relationship for youths experiencing grief over the loss of a loved one or the failure of a friendship may be able to prevent the impact of such experiences from being overwhelming. The immediate goal is to prevent self-deprecating or self-abusive (e.g., suicidal) responses. The long-term goal is that students will not only come to terms with the immediate incapacitating experience but also generalize the accomplishments of that struggle to similar challenges in the future.

Remedial Intervention.   Individuals needing remedial interventions are those with a history of chronic or borderline-chronic maladaptive thoughts and behaviors. Examples are the child who is known to be a school phobic, the adolescent who is or has been addicted to drugs or alcohol, and the chronic truant. These individuals usually represent a relatively small percentage of the total school population but may make up a substantial portion of the population in some individual schools or districts (e.g., inner-city schools). Yet, they require disproportionately more time per individual than do those receiving prevention and early identification and treatment services. Many of these situations would probably be classified in the Low Motivation–Low Expertise category in Figure 2.1 because of students' maladaptive attitudes and the limited knowledge and training most school counselors have for working with them. Students who fall within the remedial intervention category represent a small but hardcore segment of the school population, and school counselors are challenged to consider them among the potential recipients of their services in a balanced counseling program. Suggested approaches for helping those whose needs are within the expertise of school counselors are presented in chapters 5 and 6. Those who cannot be helped directly may be assisted through intelligent referrals, the subject of chapter 7.

Conclusion

Although prevention and intervention differ by definition, secondary prevention and early identification and treatment are found in an overlapping region. In the world of school counseling practitioners, this overlap should not matter. Prevention and intervention also differ with respect to the ratio of counselor time spent per client. Prevention programs are economical in this regard because counselors are able to serve several individuals at once through group activities. Interventions, in contrast, are often delivered on a one-to-one basis, although small-group counseling may be offered to individuals with similar needs and a willingness to share their problems with peers. Multiple one-to-one or small-group counseling sessions are usually required to achieve intervention goals. Therefore, if cost-effectiveness is the primary accountability criterion, prevention services are certainly more cost-effective than intervention services. Using cost-effectiveness as the sole criterion for judging a school counseling program is a mistake, however, because prevention programming will then dominate, and those needing interventions will go underserved and cause unrest. A balanced program serves both predicted and remedial developmental needs; an unbalanced program ignores an important needs area. A balanced counseling program serves all students at all grade levels, responding systematically to the developmental needs of children and adolescents.

EXAMPLES OF BALANCED PROGRAMS

The following sections describe two programs with their own economic, social, cultural, and geographic contexts. They are presented as examples of how a program may be balanced, rather than as the best way to operate a guidance program.

Essential Guidance Program, Wake County, North Carolina

The Essential Guidance Program is a product of the Wake County, North Carolina, School District's *Comprehensive Guidance Program*. A description of Wake County's *Comprehensive Guidance Program,* quoted earlier in this chapter, states a belief in the importance of a balanced program that addresses a broad range of student developmental needs.

Components of the Program.   Specific program components are based on goals that are organized into the following three areas.

1. **Academic Development Goals**

    *   *Planning and Programming:* The counselor acts as a liaison between home, school, and community in designing programs based on need.
    *   *Facilitating Instruction Based on Student Needs:* The counselor provides instructional consultation through screening, assessment, and interpretation of student academic records as an advocate for the whole child.
    *   *Intervention:* The counselor provides interventions on school adjustment issues related to the academic success of the student.
    *   *Assessment:* The counselor evaluates guidance program effectiveness related to student academic success on an ongoing basis through formal and/or informal means.

2. **Life Skill and Career Development Goals**

  - *Planning and Programming:* The counselor facilitates the integration of career awareness and life skills development into the curriculum.
  - *Facilitating Instruction Based on Student Needs:* The counselor coordinates and assesses enrichment opportunities in the area of life and career development.
  - *Intervention:* The counselor provides and/or coordinates career or life skills interventions related to the future success of the student.
  - *Assessment:* The counselor evaluates guidance program effectiveness related to career awareness and life skills development on an ongoing basis through formal and/or informal means.

3. **Personal/Social Development**

  - *Planning and Programming:* The counselor functions as a positive force in the school, helping create a climate in which all students' personal and developmental needs are addressed. The counselor involves school personnel, parents, and the community in this process.
  - *Facilitating Instruction Based on Student Needs:* The counselor provides consultation in the use of effective strategies in response to student needs as they relate to personal success.
  - *Intervention:* The counselor provides and coordinates interventions on personal and social issues affecting the well-being of the student.
  - *Assessment:* The counselor evaluates guidance program effectiveness related to personal and social success on an ongoing basis through formal and/or informal means.

Specific prevention programs and counseling interventions are planned components of the guidance program across elementary, middle, and secondary schools. In addition to the planned components, counselors have the latitude to initiate other programs and interventions. The components are categorized as being for all students, for students with special needs, and for parents.

All Students.   These components of the Essential Guidance Program are delivered through topics to be developed in classroom guidance and developmental conferences. These topics are planned from kindergarten through 12th grade on the basis of the theme How to Be Successful in School, with ingredients of that theme added each year (e.g., Cooperation—Working in Groups in 1st grade; Transition to Sixth Grade in 5th grade; and Emphasis on Decision Making, College and Career Planning, Résumé Writing, and Interviewing in 11th grade). Developmental individual or small-group conferences for all students are scheduled during 5th, 6th, 8th, 9th, 10th, 11th, and 12th grades. From 8th through 12th grade, there are themes for the conferences (e.g., 4-year plans in 8th grade and credit checking for graduation requirements with postsecondary career planning in 11th grade).

Students with Special Needs.   Individual and small-group counseling is available to elementary-, middle-, and secondary-school students. Individual counseling interventions are available to referred students on an as-needed basis from kindergarten through 12th grade, and at-risk students are identified and monitored with appropriate interventions from grades 6 through 12. Small-group counseling is provided on an as-needed basis in the following content areas:

- *Kindergarten Through 5th grade:* Divorce and Separation, Newcomers, and Grief and Loss
- *Sixth Through 8th grades:* Divorce and Separation, Grief and Loss, Newcomers, Assertiveness, Study Skills, and Focus on Opportunity
- *Ninth Through 12th grades:* Test Taking/Study Skills, Interview Skills, Divorce and Separation, Grief and Loss, and Forum for Opportunity

Parents.   Parents are served through developmental conferences and group meetings and concerns-based conferences. Developmental conferences and group meetings are offered in kindergarten through 5th grade on how to have a successful child in school (kindergarten) and parent education (kindergarten through fifth grade). Additional developmental conferences and group meetings are programmed for parents of students in grades 6 (How to Help Your Child Be Successful), 7 (Communication Skills), 8 (High School Planning), 9 (How to Help Your Child Be Successful in High School), 11 (Postsecondary Educational and Career Planning), and 12 (Financial Aid Planning). Concerns-based conferences are offered in elementary, middle, and secondary schools on an as-needed basis, depending on referrals from teachers, principals, and counselors. In addition, conferences are held with parents of 3rd graders who are thought to be at-risk students, and these conferences are provided again for parents of students in grades 6 through 12.

An analysis of the Wake County Essential Guidance Program indicates that it provides a balanced program, identifying the components that may be included in such a comprehensive guidance program. It is comprehensive, developmental, and designed to provide a balance between responses to prevention and counseling intervention goals.

Comprehensive Guidance Plan, Waynesboro, Pennsylvania

Guidance Curriculum.   This component of the Waynesboro Area School District's plan consists of structured developmental experiences presented systematically through classroom and group activities from kindergarten through 12th grade. The goals of the guidance component are to give all students knowledge of normal growth, to promote positive mental health, and to assist in the acquisition of useful life skills. The guidance curriculum is delivered through activities taught by counselors, by counselors and teachers in teams, and by counselors consulting with teachers. The guidance centers, classrooms, and other school facilities are used, and parent involvement is encouraged.

Individual Planning.   The goals of the individual planning component are to help all students plan, monitor, and manage their own learning and personal and career development. These activities are counselor planned and directed and are delivered primarily on an individual basis or in small groups. Strategies include individual appraisal/screening and individual advisement to assess needs, abilities, interests, skills, and achievement for developing long-range goals and assisting students in home-to-school, school-to-school, school-to-work, and school-to-additional-education-and-training transitions.

Responsive Services.   Designed to meet the immediate needs and concerns of specific students, although available to all students, responsive services are often student initiated. Consultation, personal counseling, and crisis counseling provided by trained professional school counselors are available to students, and referrals are made when appropriate.

System Support.   Management activities that maintain and enhance the total guidance program are carried out through the following processes: Counselors regularly engage in professional development; the guidance staff and community are kept up to date about the program; teachers, administrators, and other professional staff members are provided information, support, and feedback; counselors serve on curriculum and community advisory boards; counselors visit local businesses, industries, and social service agencies periodically; counselors fulfill responsibilities as members of their school faculties; and the guidance program is continuously evaluated and developed.

DIRECT AND INDIRECT PROGRAMMING

In most instances, the demands on, and expectations of, school counselors challenge or exceed their ability to respond in a manner that results in all their clientele receiving desired responses all the time. The somewhat open-ended nature of the school counselor's role and the relatively small size of counseling staffs create settings in which a systematic and careful approach is necessary both for effective programming and for protecting the mental health of the counselors themselves.

This textbook is designed to help counselors become systematic and organized. An important step in that direction is to understand that all programming need not be direct to be effective. Direct programming is provided when counselors interact with the people they are helping; indirect programming is provided when counselors influence or serve third parties such as teachers, parents, and principals, who, in turn, interact with the person being helped. A balanced counseling program may include both direct and indirect programming.

Prevention offers a vehicle for both direct and indirect programming. On the one hand, counselors may offer prevention programs directly by designing the programs and leading the groups. On the other hand, counselors may offer prevention programs indirectly by helping classroom teachers design and/or deliver prevention programs.

Direct and indirect options are available in interventions, too. The traditional one-to-one counseling relationship is a common example of direct intervention: Counselors meet directly with clients to help them in making decisions, resolving problems, changing their behaviors, or changing environmental circumstances. Consultation relationships, in contrast, are indirect interventions: Counselors help clients through others who have responsible relationships directly with the clients (e.g., a counselor helps a teacher design and implement a plan for helping a child interact more successfully with classmates).

A careful analysis of the National Model for School Counseling Programs, the National School Counselor Training Initiative, and the School-Community Collaboration Model that were presented in chapter 1 indicates that all three advocate a blend of direct and indirect programming. Otherwise, it would be impossible for school counselors to meet the goals of any of the three initiatives.

Realizing the importance of direct and indirect helping leads counselors to more efficient programming than would occur with an overreliance on one type. Balanced programs require balanced counselors who envision a place for both direct and indirect helping in their plans and who are able to provide both kinds.

BENEFICIARIES OF A BALANCED PROGRAM

School counseling programs exist to help a clientele ranging from kindergarten through senior high-school students (K–12). Although not all school systems have K–12 counseling programs, professional counseling associations and state departments of education recognize the importance of continuous, developmental programming and have designed training programs and developed certification criteria accordingly. In balanced, comprehensive programming, K–12 counseling programs will be designed around developmental concepts and organized so that all activities are coordinated across administrative levels (elementary, middle, junior high, and senior high). Conversely, allowing elementary, middle, junior-high, and senior-high school units to develop their own programs independently may lead to duplicated and disjointed programs, lost opportunities, elitism, and estrangement among counselors in the different units, as well as to negative opinions by parents, teachers, and administrators.

Much has been discovered and written about human development, but there is still much to learn. Generally, writers view human development as a somewhat linear process. For the sake of clarity, categories or stages of development across what is essentially a continuous life span are identified. Age groupings or ranges, often called *stages,* are the most common categories. Scholarly studies reveal common variables shared by those within a particular developmental stage (e.g., physical changes, cognitive changes, societal expectations). Finding that differences exist among individuals within any stage (e.g., adolescence), developmentalists assume that those differences are distributed normally. Thus, characteristics of the average members of a developmental stage are depicted as typical, although experts fully realize that variation occurs within the group. For example, if hypothetically the available data about the height of 12-year-old boys indicate that the average height is 5 feet, boys around that height will be considered normal for 12-year-olds even though some are as short as 4 feet and some as tall as 6 feet. Not all 12-year-old boys will be at the average or "normal" height, nor should they be expected to be. The range of heights for 12-year-old boys provides information about the distribution of their heights and indicates that most of them are around 5 feet tall.

Counselors who understand the attributes of developmental stages and the concepts of normality and variability can have a better sense of what to expect of children or adolescents in any particular age-group. Powers, Hauser, and Kilner (1989) suggest that individual differences may vary dramatically, not only within a developmental sphere but also across spheres. For example, a child may have average height, above-average intelligence, and below-average social skills, compared with others in his or her age-group. Therefore, practitioners are encouraged to assess the performances and experiences of individuals within each developmental sphere, rather than try to impose global developmental expectations.

Erikson's (1963) Eight Stages of Man is one developmental theory with credibility among educators and psychologists, and it is offered as the foundation for several suggestions on how counselors may use developmental theory in their prevention and intervention programming efforts. Figure 2.2 presents a summary of Erikson's developmental stages.

Note: The titles stated as adversarial relationships represent desired general goals for the stages. The first term identifies the positive goal of the stage; the second labels negative outcomes that may occur if individuals fail to achieve the desired positive goal. Such failure may lead to unresolved issues that interfere with healthy ego development.

I. **Trust versus Basic Mistrust (Infancy)**
   The infant learns to trust adults as well as to be alone at different times.

II. **Autonomy versus Shame and Doubt (Early Childhood)**
   The child begins to assume some responsibility for basic behavior (e.g., bowel control) and gains confidence in self.

III. **Initiative versus Guilt (Late Childhood)**
   The child begins to take initiative, particularly in terms of becoming educated.

IV. **Industry versus Inferiority (Early Adolescence)**
   The individual begins to acquire a basic skill related to achieving economic independence.

V. **Identity versus Role Confusion (Adolescence)**
   The individual must have achieved a separate identity based on an understanding of personal strengths and weaknesses.

VI. **Intimacy versus Isolation (Early Adulthood)**
   The individual begins to reach out to members of the opposite sex and develops close relationships.

VII. **Generativity versus Stagnation (Middle Adulthood)**
   Individuals assume responsibility for others through their contribution to society and their children.

VIII. **Ego Integrity versus Despair (Maturity)**
   Individuals recognize the inevitability of death and gain a sense of quality in their lives.

Figure 2.2
Erikson's eight stages of man.

Source: Data from *Childhood and Society,* by E. H. Erikson, 1963, New York: Norton.

School counselors, when developing prevention programs for secondary-school students or intervening with those who are experiencing parental conflicts, may base their programs or interventions on Erikson's principle for the adolescent stage—that is, an individual's need to achieve a separate identity based on understanding both strengths and weaknesses. Yet, these counselors, though making the best assumption at the outset, are also challenged to be aware that some members of their prevention groups and some clients receiving interventions may be struggling with tasks or expectations associated with earlier Eriksonian stages (e.g., failure to learn basic reading and writing skills from Stage III) or may have achieved identity successfully and be working on challenges associated with the next Eriksonian stage (developing close relationships from Stage VI).

Although a widely respected theory of ego identity development, Erikson's position seems to be more applicable to contemporary White male rather than female development or to the development of persons of color. Josselson (1987) offers an explanation of the identity development of women that seems to reflect contemporary circumstances, the central theme of which is commitment to self-in-relation, rather than to an independent self. Josselson's position is also restricted—to White, college-age women. Support for Josselson's position is found in Gilligan's (1982) emphasis on interconnections and relationships in the identity development of women. Although not proposing her own developmental stages, Gilligan suggests that women may fuse Erikson's identity (Stage V) and intimacy (Stage VI) stages.

People of color may be dealing with issues related to their racial status that influence their development differently. Helms (1995) believes that people of color in the United States have acquired and internalized racism that may cause them to have to cope with such issues as devaluing their own race, being confused about their racial identity, and learning to embrace their own culture while attempting to achieve a positive racial identity. These issues, coupled with the general issues offered by Erikson's model, indicate that children and youth of color may have additional developmental challenges.

School counselors are challenged to be aware of the values and assumptions that influence development differentially across the various worldviews that are represented in our multicultural society. Failing to do so may lead to what Sue (1992) describes as cultural oppression—that is, imposing one's values on culturally different student clients.

Acknowledging developmental changes and stages while recognizing the existence of individual and worldview differences within stages and across spheres enhances the balanced counseling program concept. In a comprehensive counseling program, counselors work cooperatively across grade levels to provide direct and indirect prevention and intervention programming appropriate for the developmental needs of average students while remaining cognizant of the possibility of developmental and cultural variations among individuals.

SUMMARY

In this chapter the authors advocate a set of school counseling functions designed to provide both prevention programs and intervention responses systematically. This balanced approach to school counseling seems appropriate for meeting the current and future developmental needs of the student clientele that school counselors serve.

Chapters 4 through 13 will focus on specific competencies that are needed in a balanced program. In chapter 3, we will enter the realm of legal and ethical matters that influence all components of a balanced program.

SUGGESTED ACTIVITIES

1. Analyze the counselor education program where you are being trained or were trained in terms of its balance between emphases on intervention responses and prevention programming.
2. Discuss the claim that prevention programming and intervention responses are both manifestations of developmental guidance.
3. Establish teams and debate prevention versus intervention goals as dominant themes of your school counseling program.
4. Take inventory of cases with which you and your colleagues are familiar and categorize them according to the system presented in Figure 2.1. Then, determine how those cases might have been handled differently if the suggestions for implementing the system had been followed.
5. Debate the merits of the theme presented in this chapter: School counseling programs should have a *balance* between intervention and prevention.
6. Critique the Wake County, North Carolina, Essential Guidance Program and the Waynesboro, Pennsylvania, Area School District Comprehensive Guidance Plan as comprehensive, balanced guidance programs.
7. Go to the online School Counseling Activities Network (www.scan21st.com) to review online programs for prevention and intervention.

REFERENCES

Cowen, E. L. (1982). Primary prevention research: Barriers, needs, and opportunities. *Journal of Primary Prevention, 2,* 131–137.

Durlak, J. A. (1983). Social problem solving as a primary prevention strategy. In R. D. Felner, L. A. Jason, J. N. Moritsuga, & S. S. Farber (Eds.), *Preventive psychology: Theory, research, and practice* (pp. 31–48). New York: Pergamon.

Erikson, E. H. (1963). *Childhood and society* (2nd ed.). New York: Norton.

Gilligan, C. (1982). *In a different voice.* Cambridge, MA: Harvard University Press.

Helms, J. E. (1995). An update of Helms's white and people of color racial identity models. In J. G. Ponteroto, J. M. Casas, L. A. Suzuki, & C. M. Alexander (Eds.), *Handbook of multicultural counseling* (pp. 181–198). Thousand Oaks, CA: Sage.

Horan, J. J., & Williams, J. (1982). Longitudinal study of assertion training as a drug abuse prevention strategy. *American Educational Research Journal, 19,* 341–351.

Josselson, R. (1987). *Finding herself: Pathways to identity development in women.* San Francisco: Jossey-Bass.

Moles, O. C. (1991). Guidance programs in American high schools: A descriptive portrait. *School Counselor, 38,* 163–177.

Powers, S. I., Hauser, S. T., & Kilner, L. A. (1989). Adolescent mental health. *American Psychologist, 44,* 200–208.

Shaw, M. C. (1973). *School guidance systems.* Boston: Houghton Mifflin.

Shaw, M. C., & Goodyear, R. K. (1984). Introduction to the special issue on primary prevention. *Personnel and Guidance Journal, 62,* 444–445.

Sue, D. W. (1992). The challenge of multiculturalism: The road less traveled. *American Counselor, 1,* 6–14.

Wake County Schools. (1993). *Wake County Schools comprehensive guidance program.* Raleigh, NC: Wake County School System.

Waynesboro Area School District. (n.d.). *Comprehensive guidance plan.* Waynesboro, PA: Author.

CHAPTER 3

Legal and Ethical Responsibilities in School Counseling

Goal: To establish the importance of legal codes and ethical standards in school counseling.

An elementary school counselor we know asked permission from a parent to do play therapy with a first grader who was having many behavior and social problems at school. The counselor received permission to conduct the therapy sessions and to videotape the sessions for professional review. The sessions proceeded well, and the child progressed to the point that no further sessions were needed; his behavior improved noticeably, and he got along better with other kids in first grade.

The child's mother was astounded by her son's progress and complimented the counselor repeatedly for the successful treatment. The mother and the school counselor became good friends as a result of their mutual concerns with this boy. A few weeks after the play therapy sessions ended, the mother said that she was curious about why the sessions had been so effective. She asked to borrow some of the videotapes of her child's therapy sessions; she wanted to see what had transpired in the sessions.

What should school counselors do in situations like this one? What legal and ethical challenges do counselors face regularly as part of their professional lives?

THE IMPORTANCE OF LEGAL AND ETHICAL RESPONSIBILITIES IN SCHOOL COUNSELING

School counselors are employed in positions of public trust. Parents in particular and communities in general entrust counselors and their professional colleagues with the education and care of their children. The general expectations of that trust are that counselors and their colleagues will obey the laws and regulations that relate to their activities and abide by the ethical guidelines of their professions. State departments of education establish standards that determine the minimum competencies that counselors and their professional colleagues must meet to be eligible for employment in the schools. The standards usually include expectations that counselors and their professional colleagues be familiar with pertinent legal codes and concepts, governmental regulations, and ethical standards. Therefore, at the level of basic counseling training, school counselors are challenged to become grounded in these important competencies and to adopt the appropriate frame of mind toward legal and ethical responsibilities. "Appropriate frame of mind" means simply that school counselors recognize the responsibilities they have assumed, strive to acquire the requisite knowledge, and endeavor to act responsibly and in good faith. These concerns are important in all facets of a balanced approach to school counseling.

Herlihy and Remley (2001) depict laws as the "musts" components in our professional behavior. Laws "dictate the minimum standards of behavior that society will tolerate" (p. 71). On the other hand, Herlihy and Remley depict ethics as the "shoulds" of our professional behavior. Ethics "represent the ideals or aspirations of the counseling profession" (p. 71).

Legal Concepts

Each state has its own laws, and new laws continue to be passed as legislators deem necessary. Some laws have a direct influence on school counselors, and counselors need to be familiar with those laws. For instance, in Pennsylvania, Act 287 requires that no school counselor who has acquired information from students in confidence shall be compelled or allowed to disclose that information in legal or governmental proceedings without the student's consent or the consent of the parent or guardian if the student is under the age of 18. This act does not supersede counselors' responsibility to report evidence of child abuse or neglect, as stated in Act 239. Obviously, all school counselors in Pennsylvania should understand the meaning of these two legislative acts.

Parental consent is required if a student is under 18 years of age.

Legal concepts are operationalized in specific pieces of legislation. For instance, Pennsylvania's Act 287 operationalized the concept of privileged communication. School counselors can become familiar with some important legal concepts before learning the specific laws that operationalize them. Pertinent examples are negligence, malpractice, libel, and slander. Counselors and their consumers are served best if knowledge about such important legal concepts is part of the school counselor's basic education. To assist readers, a glossary of the relevant technical terms used in this chapter is presented in Figure 3.1.

Governmental Regulations

State and local governing agencies, in their responsibility to care for and educate children and adolescents, may enact regulations to which professionals under their jurisdiction must conform. Such regulations are usually printed and distributed to affected professionals. Some states, for example, have a regulation that all school districts must have a student record keeping system approved by the state department of education and that that system must have printed guidelines for all staff members to follow. Following are examples of local school district regulations:

- All professional staff members must sign a form when seeking access to individual students' cumulative records.
- All instances of suspected child abuse and neglect must be reported to the building principal.

Most regulations have merit and provide guidance for professionals.

Abuse: The infliction by other than accidental means of physical harm upon a body of a child, continued psychological damage, or denial of emotional needs (American School Counselor Association, 1988).

Civil liability: The condition of being available, subject, exposed, or open to legal proceedings connected with the private rights of individuals.

Confidentiality: A situation in which one has been entrusted with the secrets or private affairs of another.

Criminal liability: The condition of being subject, exposed, or open to legal proceedings for which punishment is prescribed by law.

Defamation: An act that injures someone's reputation without foundation.

Duty to warn/protect: When a professional has a special relationship with a client and that individual's conduct needs to be controlled, the professional has a duty to act in a manner that protects the client and/or warns foreseeable victims of the client's actions (Gehring, 1982).

Ethical standards: The rules of practice set forth by a profession. Such standards tend to be general and idealistic, seldom answering specific questions for the practitioner (Remley, 1985, p. 181).

Laws: The standards of behavior a society demands of its members. Laws set forth the rights of citizens and usually define minimal acceptable behavior rather than idealized expectations (Remley, 1985, p. 181).

Libel: Words written, printed, or published, in any form other than speech or gestures, that maliciously or damagingly misrepresent.

Malpractice: Improper treatment or action of a client by a professional from neglect, reprehensible ignorance, or with criminal intent.

Mandated reporter: Those required by law (i.e., teachers, counselors, and school administrators) to report suspected child abuse immediately. Suspicions are sufficient grounds. Investigation is the domain of others.

Neglect: The failure to provide necessary food, care, clothing, shelter, supervision, or medical attention for a child (American School Counselor Association, 1988).

Negligence: The failure to exercise the degree of care that the law requires, under the circumstances, for the protection of the interests of other persons who may be injuriously affected by the lack of such care.

Privileged communication: If an interaction is designated as privileged communication under the law, a judge may not force the professional involved to disclose what was said by a client in an interview (Remley, 1985, p. 184).

Reasonableness and good faith: Criteria used by the courts to judge the conduct of professionals. Was the conduct what a reasonably prudent adult might do under similar circumstances, and was the action clearly for the benefit of the child and the employing entity (Pietrofesa & Vriend, 1971)?

Sexual abuse: Any act or acts involving sexual molestation or exploration, including but not limited to rape, carnal knowledge, sodomy, and unnatural sexual practices (American School Counselor Association, 1988).

Slander: Spoken statements that are malicious, false, and defamatory.

Figure 3.1
Glossary of terms.

Ethical Standards

Professional groups provide their members codes of ethics that serve as standards for their behavior. The groups have established standards for several reasons (Van Hoose & Kottler, 1978). First, they are supposed to provide autonomy from governmental regulation and interference by serving as a basis for self-regulation. Second, ethical codes provide behavioral standards for members of a professional group. Third, the codes protect members of the public by providing for their welfare, and protect the professionals by providing guidelines that serve as criteria for judging their actions if individuals sue them for malpractice.

The ethical codes best designed to serve school counselors are the *Code of Ethics and Standards of Practice* of the American Counseling Association (ACA, 1995) and the "Ethical Standards for School Counselors" of the American School Counselor Association (ASCA, 1992). (Copies of these codes are provided in Appendixes C and D, respectively.) Although very useful, ethical standards have limitations. One is that some legal and ethical issues are not addressed by the codes because of changing times, recent legal precedents, and the inability of the codes to cover every possible situation. Ethical codes are primarily reactive, evolving from previous practices and problems. Recognizing the limitations of ethical standards, Talbutt (1981) recommends that counselors supplement them by keeping up with state and local legislation, reading professional journals for up-to-date information on legal and ethical issues, and seeking advice from other professionals such as attorneys, counselor educators, supervisors, and colleagues. Although limited in their coverage, ethical codes are the best source of criteria for appropriate professional behaviors.

THE IMPORTANCE OF LEGAL AND ETHICAL RESPONSIBILITIES IN A BALANCED SCHOOL COUNSELING PROGRAM

The responsibility for acting in an ethical, law-abiding manner permeates all of the competencies in a balanced program. That is, school counselors are governed by legal and ethical responsibilities in all of their roles and functions. The codes of ethics provide guidelines for performing the competencies presented in chapters 4 through 13. In addition, all of the concepts and competencies highlighted in the three initiatives presented in chapter 1 are influenced by legal and ethical responsibilities, and those who promote the initiatives have taken this into account.

PERTINENT LEGAL CODES AND CONCEPTS

Federal Legislation

Title IX. Known by its full name as Title IX of the Education Amendment Acts of 1972, this legislation prohibits discrimination on the basis of gender by any institution receiving federal funds in any form. Regulated through the U.S. Department of Education, a specific section (45 C.F.R. 586.36) prohibits discrimination on the basis of gender in counseling or guidance of students. In general, this legislation reminds school counselors not to treat children and adolescents of one gender differently than the other in ways that place them at a disadvantage. It provides legal sanctions that support the gender equity principles.

Several potential manifestations of gender discrimination exist in school counseling. One that has received considerable attention is the way standardized tests and information are used in career and educational planning. For example, older interest inventories that restricted young women to considering only the limited range of careers traditionally occupied by women have been changed. School counselors are challenged to be aware of the issues and of the choices available to all standardized-test takers when using interest inventories. Whenever standardized tests or norms are separated by gender, the potential for discrimination exists. Whether discrimination always occurs is less certain.

Title II of the Education Amendment Acts of 1976 (20 U.S.C. 2301–2461).
Title II provides amendments to the Vocational Education Act. According to this legislation, states must draw up plans to ensure equal access to vocational education for both men and women in order to receive funds under the Vocational Education Act. State vocational education agency coordinators are to review these plans to ensure that men and women are provided equal opportunities in school career counseling. Title II also mandates equal opportunity.

The Family Educational Rights and Privacy Act of 1974 (PL 93-380).
Referred to as FERPA or the Buckley Amendment (after the late Senator James Buckley of New York, who sponsored it), the act was designed as a means of restoring parental rights and protecting privacy. FERPA has four major parts. Part I states that federal funds will be denied to any educational institution that prevents authorized access to school records by students who are over 18 years of age or by parents of students who are under 18 years of age. When such a request is made, the authorized student or parents are to be allowed to inspect the student's entire educational record. However, the school is allowed up to 45 days to comply with such a request.

Part II of FERPA states that parental consent, if a student is under 18 years of age, or the student's consent, if the student is over 18 years of age, is required before a student undergoes medical, psychological, or psychiatric examination, testing, or treatment or participates in any school program designed to affect or change the personal behavior or values of a student. This part of FERPA, of course, has implications for many activities included within the realm of the prevention programming described in chapter 4.

Part III forbids the schools to allow any individuals other than those directly involved in the student's education to have access to the records or to any information from the records without written consent of the student, if over 18 years of age, or the parent, if the student is under 18 years of age. Some exceptions to this section are stated later.

Part IV of FERPA states that the secretary of Health, Education, and Welfare is required to develop regulations to ensure the privacy of students with regard to federally sponsored surveys (Connors, 1979; Wilhelm & Case, 1975). Because FERPA was rather quickly developed and passed into law, some basic implementation questions about it confronted confused school officials in the mid-1970s. This situation ushered in a series of amendments and guidelines, the intent of which was to clarify the implementation problems. In December 1974, a "Joint Statement in Explanation of the Buckley/Pell Amendment" was published in the *Congressional Record* (1974). The purpose of this statement was to remedy certain omissions in the provisions of the existing law and to clarify other provisions that were subject to extensive concern. Several important points from this statement are as follows:

1. FERPA applies only to those programs delegated for administration to the commissioner of education.
2. *Education records* are defined as those records and materials directly related to students that are maintained by a school or one of its agents.
3. Private notes or confidential notes are exempt, provided they are not revealed to another qualified person.
4. Certain law enforcement records are excluded.
5. FERPA does not alter the confidentiality of communications otherwise protected by law.
6. Hearing procedures are to be developed by local school districts.
7. Wherever possible, actual documents are to be shared. When this is not possible, an accurate summary or interpretation is necessary.
8. The federal government will withdraw federal funds from violating or nonconforming schools.
9. Exceptions to the need-for-written-consent requirement for allowing access to information are: state and local officials where state laws are more liberal than FERPA, organizations giving entrance or selection examinations, accrediting agencies, parents of students over 18 years of age if the students are still dependent according to the Internal Revenue Service, and in cases of health and safety emergencies.

Another clarification appeared in the *Federal Register* of January 6, 1975. This statement clarified the relationship between the institution's right to destroy records and the individual's right to have access to the records. Eligible students or their parents are to be granted access to information in the records if said information was in the records when the request was made. If a request for information in a student's records is pending, the institution is not allowed to destroy any such information until after the requesting student or parent has had access to it. When no such requests have been made, institutions do have the right to destroy information in student records unless otherwise forbidden to do so by law. The long-range effect of FERPA has been to encourage institutions to keep and use fewer records than in the past (Wilhelm & Case, 1975).

Connors (1979) surmised that defamation suits can be filed against people whose comments in the records are deemed libelous by students or parents who have gained access to the records. Although the law is not retroactive before January 1, 1975, the statute of limitations starts when a comment is discovered, rather than when it was written. Thus, since passage of the so-called Buckley Amendment, it has become more important to give careful consideration to entries one places in student records. Connors recommends that subjective notations such as "Johnny is a cheat" be avoided.

Anything that is entered should be stated objectively—for example, "Johnny has been observed copying answers from his neighbor's test paper on 10 different occasions this year." Even objective statements such as this one may be unwise, in Connors's opinion. Perhaps the best protection against defamation suits is to enter no descriptive statements whatsoever into student records.

Legal Concepts

Privileged Communication. A legal responsibility mandated by state codes, *privileged communication* is a client's right to have prior confidences to certain professionals maintained during legal proceedings. Some states have granted it to school counselors; others have not. Sheeley and Herlihy (1988) reported that, in 20 states, interaction between school counselors and clients had been designated as privileged communication. For example, Pennsylvania mandates that school counselors are required to maintain client confidences during legal proceedings unless requested to disclose that information by their clients or by the parents of their clients if the clients are under 18 years of age. Privileged communication is not extended to instances of suspected child abuse.

Privileged communication legislation mandates that counselors follow the ethical principle of maintaining confidentiality in specific instances—that is, during legal proceedings. Although privileged communication assists school counselors in their efforts to maintain client confidentiality and recognizes their confidences as being as important as those of medical doctors, lawyers, psychologists, and the clergy, the primary purpose of the legislation is to protect clients. Boyd and Heinsen (1971) pointed out that counselors should be aware that, even under legislation granting privileged communication, there are certain exceptions, such as these:

- If a counselor has knowledge of an intended or future crime or fraud, privileged communication cannot be used as a reason for failing to disclose this information.
- Because privileged communication is granted to the client and not to the counselor, a counselor can be forced to share information received in confidence if the client waives such protection rights.
- If a client admits participation in an illegal act, the counselor may be required to report that information when asked to testify in a court of law.
- Counselors can be asked to testify in court as expert witnesses. In that capacity, counselors can be required to reveal some information through direct or hypothetical questions.

According to Glosoff, Herlihy, and Spence (2000), it is very difficult to list general exceptions to privileged communication such as those attributed to Boyd and Heinsen. This difficulty arises because provisions for privileged communications may be buried in state statutes, each state has its own statutes, and statutes are being modified continually. An exhaustive, yet admittedly incomplete, computerized search by Glosoff et al. (2000) led to their presentation of a matrix of exceptions to privileged communication by states and the District of Columbia. Nine categories of exceptions were found across the 50 states and the District of Columbia. The list includes all professional counselor categories and is not restricted to school counselors. Listed in the order of most to least often found, they are: (a) when there is a dispute between the client and a counselor, (b) when the client raises the issue of mental condition in a court proceeding (e.g., insanity defense and claim of emotional damage), (c) when the client's condition poses a danger to self and others, (d) child abuse or neglect, (e) knowledge that a client is contemplating commission of a crime, (f) information from court-ordered psychological examinations provided by counselors, (g) when counselors wish to participate in the involuntary hospitalization of clients, (h) knowledge that a client has been a victim of a crime, and (i) harm to vulnerable adults (e.g., disabled or institutionalized).

Most instances that require school counselors to testify in court involve abuse or custody cases (Anderson, n.d.). Being informed and prepared is important. Discussions with parents or lawyers who may want a counselor to testify will help determine whether a court appearance is necessary. Reasons for not testifying include having limited information to offer and having several individuals who can provide similar testimony. A counselor should consider several important guidelines if testifying in court: (a) Remember that a school counselor is a licensed or certified educator, and limit comments to facts about what students are doing in school; (b) remember that attributions about the causes of behaviors are in the domain of licensed psychologists and other professionals qualified to assess behavior; (c) review relevant information and check the facts without violating confidentiality; and (d) review and bring pertinent factual data and refer to them as needed when testifying (Anderson, n.d.). It is recommended that counselors withhold their confidential notes unless required to share them. Notes should not be destroyed after a request has been made, and they may be entered into the record if presented. The content of personal notes and how long they should be kept are covered in the record-keeping section of this chapter.

Malpractice and Negligence. Counselors, like others in the helping professions, may be subjected to charges of malpractice or negligence. *Malpractice* refers to practices that are outside a professional's training or ability and that result in damage to the recipient of those services—for example, a school counselor recommends or gives medicines or drugs to a client, causing deleterious results. *Negligence* is a breach of legal duty, or a failure, resulting in damage to a client, to perform acts that are part of the professional's obligation—for example, a school counselor fails to report evidence of child abuse.

Stone (2002) reported two instances where school counselors were embroiled in negligence cases. One case was a suit charging negligence in academic advising (*Sain v. Cedar Rapids Community School District*, 2001), and the second involved a suit alleging negligence in abortion counseling (*Arnold v. Board of Education of Escambia County*, 1989). A careful study of both cases indicates that the school counselors involved were attempting to be advocates for their clients and believed they were acting in good faith. In the first case, the majority of the Iowa Supreme Court ruled in favor of the plaintiff, stating that "negligent misrepresentation may be applied to the school counselor–student relationship when erroneous advice means a student loses a lucrative scholarship" (Stone, 2002, p. 30). The court also cautioned that "the ruling should have limited effect as negligent representation is confined to students whose reliance on information is reasonable" (Stone, 2002, p. 31).

In the latter case, the ruling was in favor of the defendants. The trial court concluded that the students had not been coerced by the principal and school counselor. Although negligence was not proven in this case, Stone (2002) points out that: "The question remains: May counselors be held liable for giving abortion advice to pregnant minors?" (p. 33). Stone recommends avoiding referrals to birth control clinics and never taking students to facilities where medical procedures are to take place.

Readers may be wondering what to do. Our best advice is to be well informed about one's legal and ethical responsibilities and to act in good faith. In those rare cases when school counselors are sued for malpractice or negligence, the courts are likely to use the concept of whether the counselor acted in good faith as the criterion for determining guilt or innocence. The concept of *acting in good faith* is based on the principle of using the ethical standards of one's profession as a criterion for making a legal determination. Therefore, school counselors will be judged by the ethical codes of the professional organizations to which they belong or could belong. If, according to the best interpretation of the ethical standards, a counselor acted appropriately, he or she can be judged as having acted in good faith and will likely be cleared of the charges. Knowing whether one is acting in good faith may be a difficult undertaking, however. Accomplishing that goal will be enhanced if school counselors do the following:

- Belong to a professional organization, know its ethical codes, and abide by them.
- Know the relevant state codes and the local board of education regulations and abide by them.
- Know the local school policies and abide by them.
- Develop departmental policies.
- Develop personal working policies based on knowledge of relevant developmental issues, parental rights, diversity issues, and personal values.

Child Abuse.   All states and the federal government have passed legislation to stop child abuse. The state codes and regulations have several common ingredients, among which are child protective services agencies, procedures for reporting and investigating child abuse, penalties for abuse and for failing to report it, a toll-free telephone system for anonymously reporting suspected abuse, and designations of certain professionals as mandated reporters. School counselors are usually included among those professionals designated as mandated reporters. Forty-six states have included school counselors, according to Camblin and Prout (1983). Although it is clear that child abuse is abhorrent, the signs of abuse are much less clear in some instances. Therefore, the mandate to report child abuse becomes less clear when counselors and their professional colleagues attempt to recognize and report it. According to Remley (1985), many states that require disclosing suspected child abuse fail to define clearly what it is. Remley (1992) also points out that although some states specifically note that child abuse must be reported no matter how much time has elapsed since it occurred, many states do not make the time frame clear, leaving it to individuals and the courts to determine how much should be reported. To help readers respond to

Figure 3.2

Signs of child abuse and neglect.

Source: Data from "The School Counselor and Child Abuse/Neglect Prevention," by the American School Counselor Association, 1988, *Elementary School Guidance and Counseling, 22,* pp. 261–263.

Examples of Child Abuse

1. Extensive bruises or patterns of bruises.
2. Burns or burn patterns.
3. Lacerations, welts, or abrasions.
4. Injuries inconsistent with information offered.
5. Sexual abuse.
6. Emotional disturbances caused by continuous friction in the home, marital discord, or mentally ill parents.

Examples of Neglect

1. Malnourished, ill-clad, dirty, without proper shelter or sleeping arrangements, lacking appropriate health care.
2. Unattended, lacking appropriate health care.
3. Ill and lacking essential medical attention.
4. Irregular/illegal absences from school.
5. Exploited, overworked.
6. Lacking essential psychological/emotional nurturance.
7. Abandonment.

---

this challenge, Figure 3.2 presents a suggested set of signs of child abuse, and Figure 3.3 offers suggested steps in the reporting process.

Abuse can include a variety of acts. Included among those acts listed in the professional literature are inadequate supervision that leads to failure of the child to thrive, emotional neglect, abandonment, psychological bullying by classmates (Neese, 1989), physical abuse (often the easiest to detect), verbal abuse, and sexual abuse or molestation. Sexual abuse encompasses a variety of acts, including using children in pornographic films. Mandated reporters are immune from civil or criminal liability in all 50 states and the District of Columbia if they have reported in good faith (Camblin & Prout, 1983). They may be fined for knowingly failing to report suspected child abuse. Civil or criminal liability should occur only for knowingly making false accusations (Knapp, 1983). For one reason or another, most cases of child abuse go unreported (Camblin & Prout, 1983). From a Kentucky survey of elementary- and middle-school counselors, Wilson, Thomas, and Schuette (1983) concluded that the majority of respondents thought that the problem was more serious elsewhere than in their communities and believed that they were aware of the signs of abuse. Overall, the respondents reported a low incidence of actually reporting child abuse. These findings leave several questions: Is relatively little abuse going on with children and adolescents in the United States? Are counselors and other mandated reporters missing or overlooking the signs of abuse, or are the signs too subtle or hidden to uncover in many cases? Are school counselors trained sufficiently to discover abuse and report it?

Concern about doing something in advance of discovering and treating child abuse that has already occurred led to an increase in systematic prevention efforts. Wilson et

Figure 3.3

Suggested steps for a school district employee in reporting child abuse.

1. Report suspected cases of child abuse to the building principal immediately; that is, children under age 18 who exhibit evidence of serious physical or mental injury not explained by the available medical history as being accidental; sexual abuse or serious physical neglect, if injury, abuse, or neglect has been caused by the acts or omissions of the child's parents or by a person responsible for the child's welfare.

2. Each building principal will designate a person to act in his or her stead when unavailable.

3. The principal may wish to form a team of consultants with whom to confer (e.g., school nurse, home and school visitor, counselor) before making an oral report to public welfare service representatives. This should be done within 24 hours of the first report.

4. It is not the responsibility of the reporter to prove abuse or neglect. Reports must be made in good faith, however.

5. Any person willfully failing to report suspected abuse may be subjected to school board disciplinary action.

al. (1983) view prevention efforts by counselors as part of their proactive child advocate role. The most popular target group for prevention programming, particularly regarding sexual abuse, is children (Eisenberg & O'Dell, 1988; Hitchcock & Young, 1986; Vernon & Hay, 1988). Parents and teachers have also been targeted for prevention programming but on a smaller scale (Allsopp & Prosen, 1988; Downing, 1982; Tennant, 1988). Repucci and Haugaard (1989) report that prevention programs targeting children include teaching all or part of the following coping skills: acquiring a broadened awareness of who potential abusers may be; learning that children have the right to control access to their own bodies; learning varieties of good, bad, and confusing forms of being touched; learning action steps to take in bad situations; knowing what secrets not to keep; understanding that children are not at fault for sexual abuse; and learning to tell trusted adults about abusers and to keep telling until something is done.

The few reported programs targeting parents seem to devote attention to helping them identify the signs of abuse, react in a constructive manner when noticing signs or being informed of abusive acts, and learn ways to educate their children for prevention (Repucci & Haugaard, 1989). Parents Anonymous (PA) represents a form of tertiary prevention for parents who are known and admitted abusers. Organized along the lines of Alcoholics Anonymous, PA meets the needs of some parents. More is needed, according to Post-Kammer (1988), who recommends that one area of need is helping PA members have a better understanding of child development. PA serves as a possible referral source for school counselors. Not much has been reported about prevention training for teachers either. Such training programs can focus on increased awareness and understanding through content, including information about offenders, current legislation, reporting procedures, and available community resources (Allsopp &

Prosen, 1988). Preventive teacher training seems to be an important topic for counselor-led in-service programming.

Repucci and Haugaard (1989) note some problems across all prevention efforts. Overall, they decided there is not enough scientific evidence that the efforts are successful or that more good than harm is being done. Assumptions that they think remain untested are these:

- One set of coping skills is appropriate for children of all age levels and for coping with all forms of sexual abuse (Repucci and Haugaard think there is a lack of consensus on what child sexual abuse is).
- Children will be able to translate knowledge into positive action (researchers think that many who are involved in prevention programming do not appreciate the process a child must go through to repel abuse and the complexity of reporting it).
- The positive effects of prevention efforts outweigh the negative ones.

Possible negative effects include undue anxiety and discomfort with nonsexual physical touching. Repucci and Haugaard also note that prevention programs are limited in many school districts to focusing on recognition and reporting of abusive acts because of the restrictions on providing helpful information about sex caused by conservative views on sex education. Although an apparently good idea, much seems yet to be accomplished before prevention efforts achieve the desired goals.

Libel, Slander, and Defamation.   *Libel* is a legal term referring to false statements that are published and bring about hatred, disgrace, ridicule, or contempt toward the individual about whom they are written. *Slander,* also a legal term, refers to verbally communicated statements that have the same results. In civil suits, plaintiffs must prove that damages in the form of defamation—an injured reputation—resulted. Historically, the number of such civil cases against counselors has been small. Nevertheless, some counseling duties and functions have the potential for making counselors vulnerable. Talbutt (1983a) cites sharing standardized test scores over the telephone, telling bystanders about students' grades, and relaying information to third parties about clients when there is no clear obligation to do so as three questionable behaviors that could lead to charges of defamation. Also, parents or students may take action over comments in students' cumulative records they deem to be inflammatory (Connors, 1979). It is also conceivable that information counselors share with colleges, universities, and prospective employers in confidence via recommendations can find its way back to the subjects of the comments and, if viewed as defamatory, lead to civil suits.

Washington (1973) pointed out that anyone can sue another person but, in so doing, is not guaranteed recovery of damages. Suits, whether won or lost by the plaintiffs, have the potential for causing counselors considerable stress and mental anguish, public embarrassment, and possible financial losses associated with defending themselves if the individuals and school districts do not have sufficient insurance. It is recommended that school counselors carry liability insurance. Regardless of insurance, it behooves counselors to be prudent about what they write and say about their charges. This, of course, is also an ethical recommendation.

Several recommendations, if followed, may help counselors minimize the chance of being sued for libel or slander and reduce the probability of the plaintiff recovering damages if a suit does occur. As recommended by Connors (1979), subjective notations need not be entered in student records, or anywhere else, for that matter. Connors goes so far as to recommend no descriptive statements whatsoever, even if they are objective. Washington (1973) recommends determining the inquirer's need to know any information before sharing it. For example, in the potentially libelous or slanderous cases cited earlier, the need of the person requesting standardized test scores over the telephone to know the desired data can be assessed by acquiring written permission from the individual whose scores are desired, and bystanders by definition have no responsible need to know information about clients.

In some instances, determining the need to know is relatively easy. For example, students who plan to matriculate to post-high-school educational institutions usually must submit transcripts and letters of recommendation; in doing so, they grant permission to representatives of their high schools, often counselors, to transmit the information and recommendations. The need to know is clear. The need to know is less clear when some of the same institutions ask questions about the character of students and request narrative evaluations. Exactly what they need to know is left to the respondents to determine; the need to know is relatively unclear.

What to do? With regard to determining the need to know, it seems logical to question the motives behind the request, to predict what will be done with the information, and to understand how that response will affect the client whose information is being shared. With regard to what to do, one is expected to act in good faith, according to the ethical principles of one's profession. Believing what one is saying or writing is also important. Knowing it is true is even better because truth is an important criterion in civil cases. Report objectively and factually (Talbutt, 1983b), but as Connors (1979) warns, some things might best be left unsaid, even objectively (e.g., accusatory statements). Bronner (1998) reports that school counselors are caught between college admissions officers desiring to ensure campus safety and avoid liability for student violence and parents who do not want details of disciplinary problems their children had to ruin their chance of getting into college. Both parties may be more determined than ever to protect their constituencies. A personal guideline of the authors has been to say and write only things that are true and favorable about clients unless there is a clear and imminent danger to themselves or others. If there is not much true and favorable to write in a recommendation about a client, then the brevity of the recommendation may speak for itself. Another option is to refuse the request for a recommendation.

Unclear Areas. Desiring to know what to do legally and ethically is a meritorious goal, as is acting responsibly. Yet, efforts to understand what to do sometimes lead to "mixed messages," leaving one unclear about what responsible behavior is. Some areas covered by the concepts of *duty to warn* and *duty to protect* are chief among the unclear legal areas with which counselors must grapple. The concepts of duty to warn and duty to protect have been highlighted by prominent court decisions (e.g., *Tarasoff v. Regents of the University of California*, 1976), which focused on concern about warning potential victims of violent behavior. In school settings, the concepts might also be applied to cases of advising minors without parental consent (e.g., providing information about abortions) and cases of suicide (counselors' apparent knowledge of the student's desire to harm him- or herself).

Tarasoff occurred in California during the mid-1970s, and the decision set off a tidal wave of concern and uncertainty across many levels of helping professionals in the country. In this case, a client informed a psychologist of his intention to kill another individual. Care was taken to commit and confine the client for observation, and the campus police were notified of his stated intentions. He was released after appearing rational and promising to stay away from the individual whose life he had threatened. The psychologist had not warned the intended victim, who was out of the country at the time, or her parents. The client went to her residence and killed her after her arrival home. The courts ruled the therapist and institution in error because there was a foreseeable victim and a duty to warn the victim or her parents. In courts that follow the reasoning of this case, mental health workers will be expected to warn people who have a special relationship with the dangerous person, as well as to warn the intended victim of that person (Gehring, 1982).

Because the *Tarasoff* case occurred in California, its results are not binding elsewhere. Courts in other states, however, may use that case as a precedent for similar decisions. Some states have not adopted the "Tarasoff doctrine" (Herlihy & Remley, 2001). In some decisions in other states, the courts have interpreted similar situations differently. For instance, in North Carolina (*Currie v. United States,* 1986), an employee, while he was in therapy, threatened to kill unspecified coworkers. Subsequently, he did indeed enter the workplace and kill a coworker. The court created what was called the *psychotherapist judgment rule* (PJR), in which it refused to allow liability for simple errors in judgment in commitment decisions. The therapist had consulted with several colleagues before deciding not to commit the client ("Therapists Bear a Duty," 1987). Clearly, this case differs from *Tarasoff* in that the intended victim was unspecified, and as it was reported, the client had threatened the therapist, too. Despite these differences, mental health professionals working with clients who pose a threat to themselves or to others or who indicate a disposition toward child abuse should be prepared to report to the proper authorities and to potential victims ("Legal Considerations," 1983).

Writing from his experience as a lawyer to an audience of clinical psychologists, Monahan (1993) offers guidelines for limiting exposure to duty to warn liability. Although the package of recommendations contains entries that are perhaps more extreme than most school counselors require, they provide food for thought:

- Know how to assess client risk, make a real effort to do so thoroughly, and communicate that information to those responsible for making final decisions.
- Have a risk-management plan in place (prepare for the few exceptions in advance with a plan for monitoring and managing individuals who may endanger themselves or others).
- Document information received and actions taken. According to Monahan (1993, p. 246), "It would be an exaggeration to state that in a tort case what is not in the written record does not exist—but not much of an exaggeration." He recommends noting three things: the source of the information, the content, and the date.

- Written policies or guidelines that have been externally reviewed by experienced clinicians and lawyers should be in place, and the staff should receive training about using the guidelines. Compliance with the guidelines should be audited, and forms developed or revised to "prompt and record the actions contemplated by the policy statement" (p. 247).
- If something goes wrong, one can control the damage by relying on the truth and remaining silent publicly when experiencing doubts about one's decisions from the vantage point of hindsight.

Advising minors without parental consent is a particularly unclear area that each counselor needs to investigate. From an ethical standpoint, adherence to the principle of confidentiality usually leads counselors to keep in confidence what minors say during counseling sessions. An example of a troublesome topic held in confidence is knowledge of pregnancy, including the client's planned responses such as abortion, and the counselor's sharing of information about the possible options, including abortion. This has been and continues to be a legal minefield because statutes vary from state to state, as do decisions in court cases, and the national conflict between right-to-life and pro-choice supporters promises to lead to more changes in the future. In this example, Talbutt's (1983b) conservative advice is that counselors encourage students to discuss pregnancies with their parents and that counselors stay within the confines of their professional training or skill—a response with which not all counselors agree. According to Hopkins and Anderson (1990, p. 33), "counselors are generally free to inform clients of the availability of birth control methods without fear of legal liability and to refer clients to family planning or health clinics for more information." Hopkins and Anderson go on to point out the distinction between providing information and imposing one's own views on a minor client, particularly one who is already pregnant. Additional important information in this domain is that states may regulate the performance of abortions, parents of unmarried pregnant minors may have some rights to know about and consent to an abortion, and physicians are recognized as qualified to provide pregnant women information and decision-making advice about abortions. Kiselica (1996) offers suggestions for counselors. Helping clarify confusion about legalities and being advocates on behalf of the clients' legal rights are important ways that counselors can help. Beyond the legal issues, counselors may also be able to provide emotional support and decision-making counseling that includes accurate information. Chapter 5 introduces decision-making counseling.

Because the resolutions of issues in this section are unclear, advice is scarce and conflicting. Two suggestions that have merit are (a) to have policy statements for crises and challenging situations that will guide individual counselors and help others determine whether the counselor acted in good faith (Lawrence & Kurpius, 2000; Monahan, 1993) and (b) to keep proper notes about one's actions and decisions in order to support one's claims if ever called into court or some other formal proceeding (Lawrence & Kurpius, 2000; Monahan, 1993; "Therapists Bear a Duty," 1987).

Most Frequently Reported Legal Issues. Hermann (2002) surveyed 273 members of the American School Counselor Association (ASCA) who were school counselors, using the Legal Issues in Counseling Survey. The most frequently reported legal issues over the past 12 months, ranked in order of frequency, were as follows: (a) determining whether a client was suicidal (90% of sample; 76% two or more times), (b) determining whether to report suspected child abuse (89% of sample; 74% two or more times), (c) determining whether a client posed a danger to others (73% of sample; 51% two or more times), (d) being pressured to verbally reveal confidential information (51% of sample; 34% two or more times), and (e) clients expressing dissatisfaction with counseling services (42% of sample; 19% two or more times).

Hermann (2002) also inquired about the participants' perceptions of how prepared to respond to the respective legal issues they thought they were. The same five legal issues that were presented above are presented with the percentage in parentheses of the participants who believed they were well prepared to respond: (a) determining whether a client was suicidal (72%), (b) determining whether to report suspected child abuse (91%), (c) determining whether a client posed a danger to others (63%), (d) being pressured to verbally reveal confidential information (57%), and (e) clients expressing dissatisfaction with counseling services (48%).

It is not surprising that reporting child abuse ranks highest given the explicit mandates found in all of the state statutes. The legal issues with lower percentages of perceived preparedness seem to fall into a rank ordering according to the severity of complications that can be encountered. For example, the professional literature is replete with checklists to be used when assessing suicide ideation, and suicide ideation is often clearly recognized. On the other hand, pressure to reveal confidential information can occur in different ways, and there are no common guidelines for dealing with these requests. This issue, as well as discerning danger to others and client dissatisfaction, may manifest themselves in more subtle, unclear ways.

Two other legal issues that occurred less often in the survey yielded higher percentages of feeling unprepared. Of the sample, 54% felt unprepared to respond to a subpoena to appear as a witness in a legal proceeding, and 22% believed they were not prepared for being asked to turn over confidential records. These two legal issues were encountered less often than the other five. Therefore, participants, having less experience and perhaps less preparation, felt less well prepared.

It appears as if experience is the best way to prepare for responding to legal issues. Actual experience is one way to address this challenge; however, real-life experiences of this nature are few and far between. The challenges can also be addressed proactively by covertly and overtly simulating what one would do if presented with each of these legal challenges and basing the rehearsed simulations on a thorough study of the relevant professional literature.

ETHICAL RESPONSIBILITIES

American Counseling Association Standards

The American Counseling Association (ACA) published a revised *Code of Ethics and Standards of Practice* in late 1995. (Appendix C contains the text of the revision. See also www.counseling.org/resources/ethics.htm.) The code has eight major sections: The Counseling Relationship; Confidentiality; Professional Responsibility; Relationships

With Other Professionals; Evaluation, Assessment, and Interpretation; Teaching, Training, and Supervision; Research and Publication; and Resolving Ethical Issues. They are followed by a set of Standards of Practice—minimal behavior statements of the code. This section of this chapter highlights the parts of the code that are most relevant to school counselors.

Preamble. This introduction to the code ends with this caveat: "All members of the American Counseling Association (ACA) are required to adhere to the Code of Ethics and Standards of Practice." Because school counselors who are members of the American School Counselor Association (ASCA) may also belong to the ACA, school counselors are subject to the codes and standards of both professional organizations.

The Counseling Relationship. Dealing with practices and procedures of individual or group counseling or both, this section focuses on such matters as client welfare, respecting diversity, client rights, clients served by others, personal needs and values, dual relationships, sexual intimacies with clients, multiple clients, group work, fees and bartering, termination and referral, and computer technology.

Confidentiality. Confidentiality being a key ethical principle for counselors, this section covers right to privacy, groups and families, minor or incompetent clients, records, research and training, and consultation. The assumption of confidentiality is a foundation for the counseling, consulting, assessment, transition, and record-keeping functions. It is the foundation for the trust that helps individuals share intimate information with counselors truthfully. Although school counselors have an ethical responsibility to their clients, they also have a legal responsibility to the parents of minor clients; this can sometimes lead to decision-making dilemmas. As Huey (1986) points out, ethical codes do not recommend violating the law. At the same time, Huey cites advice from Corey, Corey, and Callanan (1984) recommending that counselors not become hamstrung by legal concerns to the point they become ineffective. No one seems to have a definitive answer about this issue. Most counselors will not want to lose the power to help individuals that confidentiality offers. Therefore, it appears that they will have to deal with the legal ramifications on a case-by-case basis, checking applicable state laws in the process.

Zingaro (1983) provides an example of a case in which a counselor faces this dilemma:

> A child may ask to talk to you about a problem, such as how to get along with a new stepparent. After discussing the child's concern, you arrange a time to meet at a later date. The following day one of the child's parents calls you to ask about the content of your counseling session. It seems obvious from the questions that the parent is aware of some of the issues that you discussed with the child. Would you disclose information that you received from the child with the parent? What would be the effects on the child, parents, and you if you comply with the parent's request? If the child's self-referral is viewed as a step toward autonomy and independence in solving his or her problems, have you handicapped the child's efforts? Would these questions be answered differently if the parent had asked you to speak with his or her child and then asked about the content of your counseling session? (p. 262)

Professional Responsibility. In this section, matters such as knowledge of standards, professional competence, advertising and soliciting clients, credentials, public responsibility, and responsibility to other professionals are covered. Among the components important to school counselors are the emphases on monitoring one's effectiveness, consulting with other professionals about ethical questions and professional practice, keeping current, and representing one's credentials appropriately.

Relationships With Other Professionals. This section contains important standards about relationships with employers and employees (e.g., evaluation, discrimination, sexual relationships) and additional information about consultation, fees for referral, and subcontractor arrangements that may be of more interest to counselors in agencies or in private practice.

Evaluation, Assessment, and Interpretation. As the title implies, this section is devoted to concerns about the use of test and non-test appraisal techniques. Among the specific standards are statements concerning the importance of being competent to use and interpret standardized tests, providing informed consent to clients, releasing information to competent professionals, making proper diagnoses of mental disorders, selecting tests carefully, providing appropriate testing conditions, recognizing the need for caution in testing because of diversity issues, scoring and interpreting tests appropriately, keeping tests secure, avoiding use of obsolete tests and outdated data, and using appropriate procedures when constructing tests. (You should recognize a strong relationship between the standards in this section of the code and the information in chapter 10 of this book.)

Teaching, Training, and Supervision. This section is of more interest to trainers of school counselors than to school counselors. The standards herein focus on counselor educators and trainers, counselor education and training programs, and students and supervisees. The way the standards influence the training of school counselors may influence the direction of the profession throughout the twenty-first century.

Research and Publication. Probably of less interest and use to most school counselors than other sections of the code, this section points out that all participants in a research study must be told which information can be shared without affecting the study and that they must be given the opportunity to decide whether to participate. This is referred to as *informed consent.* In addition, the identity of the participants must be disguised when reporting results or making original data available, results reflecting unfavorably on the schools or other vested interests must not be withheld, and agreements to cooperate in research projects imply a responsibility to do so punctually and completely.

Resolving Ethical Issues. The standards in this section admonish counselors to know the Code of Ethics and Standards of Practice thoroughly, to respond to suspected violations appropriately, and to cooperate with ethics committees.

American School Counselor Association Ethical Standards

"Ethical Standards for School Counselors" (ASCA, 1992) in many ways reflects the standards of the ACA code and standards while also presenting issues in a manner recognizing the unique preparation and work settings of school counselors. This can be seen when comparing the ASCA standards in Appendix D with the ACA code and standards. The first section is entitled Responsibilities to Students and includes emphases on informed consent, keeping up to date, avoiding dual relationships, making appropriate referrals, confidentiality, duty to warn, and appropriate use of tests. The second section, Responsibilities to Parents, discusses informed consent for parents, confidentiality, and sensitivity to family issues. The third section, Responsibilities to Colleagues and Professional Associates, deals with such matters as cooperative relationships with faculty, staff, and administration and appropriate referrals. A fourth section, "Responsibilities to the School and Community," deals with standards for protecting the school's mission, personnel, and property and assisting in the development of school programs and services. The remaining three sections are Responsibilities to Self, Responsibility to the Profession, and Maintenance of Standards. This last section includes a statement that links the ASCA standards to the code and standards of the ACA.

Avoiding Ethical Violations

The most logical recommendation for avoiding ethical violations is that counselors be familiar with the codes and continually aware of their ramifications—always employing an ethical mind-set—without being debilitated by reactionary fears of accusations of wrongdoing. Be alert, yet not fearful. DePauw (1986) offers useful guidance for avoiding ethical violations via a timeline for organizing one's thoughts ethically. Users of DePauw's timeline can recognize ethical considerations that are relevant to phases in the counseling relationship. Four phases are addressed in the timeline: initiation, counseling, crisis, and termination.

Initiation. A major consideration relevant to school counselors in the initiation phase of the counseling relationship is that of assessing the client's needs and determining whether one is qualified to be of service. Related to this appropriateness issue is whether the prospective client may be seeing another professional helper, such as a psychologist or psychiatrist. If this is the case and if the school counselor has determined him- or herself to be an appropriate helper, the client may have to choose between helpers, negotiate with the school counselor a way to inform the other helper, or seek approval for concurrent counseling. One example is partial referrals, which are described in chapter 7.

Nevertheless, both the ACA (A.1. Client Welfare; A.3. Client Rights; A.8. Multiple Clients; B.3. Minor or Incompetent Clients) and the ASCA (responsibilities to students; responsibilities to parents) codes of ethics are clear in stating that informed consent is expected for clients and their parents. Kaplan (1996, p. 3C) offers the following analogy:

Imagine the following scenario: *a person with whom you've had a slight acquaintance comes up to you and insists that they can help you with your problems.*

However, they will not tell you how they are going to help you, what will be done with the information you provide, who will be told that you are being helped, or the possibilities of what may go wrong if you allow yourself to be helped. The next thing you hear this person saying is: "relax and tell me your deepest, darkest secrets."

To meet the spirit of the informed consent expectation, counselors must provide enough information to ensure an informed choice (Kaplan, 1996). Traditionally, school counselors, because of the nature of their work, have not emphasized informed consent as much as counselors and therapists in other settings. Prospective clients are often children and adolescents, and it is not always clear when talking with school-age students in a private or semiprivate setting that a request for counseling services has occurred. To launch into an informed consent explanation at this point could be counterproductive, overwhelming students and causing them to back off or possibly not return, not wanting to be labeled as "needing a shrink."

Because verbal statements may be misunderstood and because offering informed consent in the presence of a prospective client may be problematic, the best approach is probably to have a blanket informed consent form for all parents/guardians and students to sign when students are enrolled in school, keeping the form on file while they are in attendance. What should the informed consent form contain? Kaplan (1996), borrowing from private practitioners, offers a comprehensive approach, suggesting that the consent form might contain (a) the counselor's theoretical framework and treatment approach, (b) a section on confidentiality, (c) the counselor's educational background and training, (d) rules about appointments, (e) session charges and program fees (if appropriate), and (f) an acknowledgment sheet to be signed by the students and parents/guardians.

O'Connor, Plante, and Refvem (1998) offer a less comprehensive approach, a 1-page counseling consent form containing (a) the name of the school district and the title of the form, (b) an explanation (e.g., "Counseling services are offered to all students in ____ county. Any parent may withhold consent by checking in front of the specific service and then signing and dating the form. Please return this form to the counseling office by ____. Permission is presumed if this form is not returned."), (c) options to check off or not (e.g., group counseling, individual counseling of more than two sessions, individual nonmandated testing, and referrals—community services or medical), and (d) an acknowledgment section for signatures and dates. Glosoff and Pate (2002) provide additional important advice regarding informed consent. They recommend that school counselors treat informed consent as an ongoing process rather than attempting to address all of it at the beginning of the helping relationship.

Counseling.   Chief among the ethical considerations during ongoing counseling are confidentiality, consultation, and record keeping. Beyond informing clients about confidentiality, counselors also consider what is confidential and what is not. Certainly, it would be imprudent and inaccurate to inform clients that everything they say is confidential and then not to act accordingly. If counselors are aware of the limitations to confidentiality, such as child abuse, threats to others, and admission of a crime, they will be prepared to respond immediately when those exceptions occur.

Being aware and able to respond proactively enhances the chance that making exceptions to the confidentiality principle will not ruin one's relationship with the client and one's reputation among prospective clients.

An awareness of ethical responsibilities will help counselors in determining ways to seek consultation without violating confidentiality or placing consultants in an awkward position. One way to accomplish this is to use hypothetical information. This allows counselors to maintain anonymity for clients while acquiring helpful assistance. As the counseling phases progress, counselors will decide what will be recorded in cumulative files and private case notes. Useful guidelines for record keeping in greater depth appear later in this chapter.

Crises. Prominent among the crises for which ethical guidance can be given are threats to oneself and to others. When threats to oneself (e.g., suicide ideation) occur, counselors must assume responsibility for the client's welfare after carefully determining how serious the threats are. DePauw (1986) thinks that an open discussion of the counselor's concerns with an accompanying attempt to involve the client in the decision-making process enhances the chance of voluntary cooperation.

The parameters of the school counselor's ethical duty to warn others when clients threaten others have been presented in the section of this chapter entitled "Unclear Areas." Although it is usually clear that threats are occurring, it is less clear what to do about them. DePauw (1986) recommends having contingency plans derived from

The assumption of confidentiality is the foundation for the trust that helps individuals share intimate information.

consulting with informed specialists such as attorneys, psychiatrists, and law enforcement officials.

The following list of possible ingredients of a contingency plan is taken from Sheeley and Herlihy's (1989) guidelines for counseling practice related to duty-to-warn-and-protect issues associated with counseling suicidal clients:

- Know the privileged communication or confidentiality laws in the state where one is employed.
- Keep abreast of related court decisions.
- Communicate the need for related school board policies.
- Develop policy handbooks and ask parents to confirm that they received the materials.
- Circulate descriptions and explanations of the confidentiality principle.
- Encourage students and parents to sign waivers allowing counselors to disclose certain kinds of specified information that is confided during counseling.
- Keep good notes and records.
- Consult with professional peers when in doubt about client assessments and treatments.
- Know a lawyer to contact for legal assistance.
- Know the status of the insurance liability coverage plan the school district has, and have an additional personal liability insurance policy. The ACA and the ASCA make this coverage available to their members.

Evidence or suspicion of child abuse is a third ethical crisis area, and mandated reporting is also backed by legal statutes. As is true in cases of threats of suicide, counselors must decide how much to explain to clients in advance of making a report. The challenge here is to conform with the law while also trying to help and protect the client.

Termination. Two ethical concerns associated with termination are (a) the responsibility to determine whether a counseling relationship is still productive and (b) the decision to submit one's work for review and evaluation. Application of the former concern may lead to a decision to refer. Therefore, one is obligated ethically to know referral sources and to make appropriate referral suggestions. More information on this subject is found in chapter 7. The concept of submitting one's work for review and evaluation may be interpreted as an ethical responsibility to engage in evaluation associated with one's counseling services. Thus, the advocacy of accountability made in chapter 13 has an ethical foundation.

Ethical Multicultural Counseling

Standard A.2.a. of the ACA code of ethics provides a statement of nondiscrimination, and Standard A.2.b. indicates that counselors will respect individual differences by attempting to understand the diverse cultural backgrounds of their clients. The ASCA ethical standards state: "Each person has the right to respect and dignity as a unique human being and to counseling services without prejudice as to person, character, belief, or practice." Thus, the ethical codes seem to indicate that failure to consider a client's culture(s) may very well be unethical.

Much of what is being written about the application of ethics to multicultural counseling is at a somewhat abstract level. For example, Pedersen (1997), believing that the current ethical codes are derived from a western cultural perspective that emphasizes relativism and absolutism, recommends an approach that can fit different cultural contexts. In addition, LaFromboise, Foster, and James (1996) encourage consideration for viewing ethical decisions from both a care perspective (emphasis on relationships) and a justice perspective (social contract emphasis).

At a more practical level, LaFromboise et al. (1996) make several recommendations, taken from their review of the professional literature, that may be considered guidelines for ethical multicultural counseling.

- Consider the client's unique frame of reference and personal history. This is consistent with Herring's (1997) synergistic counseling approach.
- Provide the necessary information for informed choices. This includes a treatment plan with alternative intervention methods (e.g., traditional healers) and consideration of potential outcomes with regard to one's family and community.
- Take an activist stance when it appears necessary to protect clients from pathological systems (see reference to Menacker, 1976, in chapter 11).

Making Good Ethical Decisions

Although the codes of ethics are indeed comprehensive, the standards sometimes are in conflict with each other, and they may not be specific enough to give individual counselors definitive answers to ethical dilemmas they may encounter. Therefore, the process used to make ethics decisions is very important. Nassar-McMillan and Post (1998) provide a useful sequential scheme for making ethics decisions that evolves as follows: (a) Identify the dilemma; (b) identify and clarify one's values about the issue; (c) refer to the appropriate code of ethics; (d) determine the nature and dimensions of the dilemma with regard to the following principles: autonomy (fostering client self-determination), nonmalfeasance (do no harm), beneficence (promote good mental health), justice, and fidelity (be faithful, keep promises); (e) generate potential courses of action; (f) consider possible consequences of all options; (g) evaluate the potential effects of what appears to be the best option (e.g., How would you feel if the decision were published in a newspaper? Would you recommend this option to others or want to have it done to you? How do you feel about this option instinctively?); and (h) implement a course of action. A case study by Fielstein (1996) is abstracted in the following paragraph, and the Nassar-McMillan and Post ethics decision-making scheme is applied to it.

One morning, a high-school counselor was informed by the principal that a 15-year-old student came to school apparently intoxicated. The student was acting confused and appeared to have alcohol on his breath. The school nurse was not available to ascertain the student's condition, and the student was uncooperative about revealing the causes. As per school policy, the counselor called the student's parents to inform them of what had transpired. The student's grandparent answered the telephone, informed the counselor that the parents were out of town, and behaved in an indifferent manner, apparently not wanting to become involved.

1. *Identify the dilemma.* What should the counselor do since the parents are not at home and the grandparent seems indifferent?

2. *Identify and clarify one's values about the issue.* Possible thoughts the counselor may experience are as follows: (a) The student needs help, and his welfare must be protected; (b) this is a discipline problem, so why am I saddled with it? (c) the student has behaved foolishly, is uncooperative, and now we have to clean up the mess; (d) I have to do the right thing here, or else I could get into trouble; (e) the rules should be followed to the letter, and let the chips fall where they may; and (f) I know this person and really feel a need to help in some way. *To the reader:* What thoughts come to your mind about this situation?

3. *Refer to the appropriate code of ethics.* In the ACA code, Standard B.3. states: "When counseling clients who are minors or individuals who are unable to give voluntary, informed consent, parents or guardians may be included in the counseling process as appropriate. Counselors act in the best interests of clients and take measures to safeguard confidentiality. (See A.3.c.)." Standard B.1.c. states: "The general requirement that counselors keep information confidential does not apply when disclosure is required to prevent clear and imminent danger to the client or others or when legal requirements demand that confidential information be revealed."

4. *Determine the nature and dimensions of the dilemma.* It appears as if nonmalfeasance, beneficence, and justice are important principles to consider in this instance. The decision seems to require an option that allows the counselor to promote good mental health, do no harm, and be just.

5. *Generate potential courses of action.* Possible options that come to mind are as follows: (a) Inform the principal that it is not a counseling function but rather is a discipline problem, (b) keep the student in school under the watchful care of a responsible person until the parents can come to the school, (c) ask the grandparent to come to school to pick up the student and take him home, (d) contact social services for advice and possible help, and (e) let the student sleep it off in the nurse's office and then go to class. *To the reader:* What options other than these come to your mind?

6. *Consider possible consequences of all options, evaluate potential effects of what appears to be the best option, and implement a course of action.* Readers are invited to complete the decision-making process independently and to evaluate the process as well.

The decision made in the Fielstein (1996) scenario was to persuade the grandparent to come to school to pick up the student and take him home. It was argued that the school carried out its responsibilities by turning the minor student over to a guardian and that the student's welfare was protected. Even though the counselor in the scenario believed that the best ethics decision had been made, concerns lingered, among which were: not feeling comfortable about leaving the student with the grandparent, not knowing the severity of the condition of the student, and being unsure whether the student would receive appropriate supervision at home. These concerns point out that a decision-making scheme, though a helpful approach, is no guarantee of 100% foolproof decisions. Counselors are challenged to do their best under the circumstances, attempting to act in an ethical manner and seeking informed consultation whenever possible.

The decision-making scheme presented above is but one model among several others presented in the professional literature. Cottone and Claus (2000) identify nine other stepwise "practice-based" models for making ethical decisions in their literature review and recommend caution regarding all of them. Their recommendation for caution is derived from an apparent paucity of empirical research supporting the effectiveness of the practice-based models and lack of attention to "underlying philosophical or theoretical tenets" (p. 281). They conclude that any of the several practice-based models may be effective in particular settings with specific clients, and according to a particular standard of practice. None has been proven superior to others or universally effective.

Believing that the practice-based models rely too much on promoting an individual or intrapsychic process, Cottone (2001) offers an approach that introduces an interactive decision-making process. He believes that ethical decisions involve negotiating, consensualizing, and arbitrating (when necessary) with others. In doing so, counselors are guided by social and cultural factors.

Cottone (2001) presents a case of a 12-year-old girl who has been receiving counseling based on the consent of her grandparent who, as it turns out, is not the legal guardian. The ethical dilemma is that technically there is no informed consent to counsel the child, yet, the counselor has an ethical responsibility to the child. The subsequent interactive decision-making process involves: (a) consulting with an administrator who insists upon appropriate informed consent, (b) attempting unsuccessfully to negotiate receipt of informed consent from the legal guardian/mother, (c) consulting with colleagues in an effort to find a solution, (d) achieving consensus with the grandparent to have her get the legal guardian to sign a consent form, and (e) waiting while the grandparent uses arbitration to get the mother's support. Cottone states:

> Professionals are less vulnerable to ethical challenges if they are linked to a rich professional culture, which is not supportive of a breach of ethical standards. When concerns arise at critical moments of professional practice, the social constructivist obtains information from those involved, assesses the nature of relationships operating at the moment, consults valued colleagues and professional expert opinion (including ethical codes), negotiates when necessary, and responds in a way that allows for a reasonable consensus. (2001, p. 45)

As was the case with the practice-based models, Cottone's (2001) social constructivist model is also without empirical support. Until such support is available, counselors can benefit from both approaches. The practice-based models provide recommendations for steps to undertake in defining the problem and alternatives, and the social constructivist model offers a more sophisticated and complete approach to resolving ethical dilemmas.

KEEPING GOOD STUDENT RECORDS:
A MERGING OF LEGAL AND ETHICAL CODES

School record keeping in the United States can be traced back to the 1820s and 1830s (Kazalunas, 1977). The original purposes of record keeping seem to have been to certify student enrollment and attendance and to recognize levels of accomplishment (Fischer & Sorenson, 1996). Heayn and Jacobs (1967) point out that as the schools became more committed to the "whole child" concept, the cumulative record folder became more than an academic record; it became a humanistic document. The cumulative record files are now repositories for a variety of information about students.

A very significant development in the arena of student record keeping was the passage of the Family Educational Rights and Privacy Act of 1974 (FERPA). Details about FERPA were presented in an earlier section of this chapter.

The FERPA legislation provides specific legal guidelines for student record keeping. The ACA Code of Ethics and Standards of Practice provide guidelines, too, including clarification of the differences between confidential records and public records, a caveat to share appropriate information with those who have the right to know it, and instruction about appropriate procedures for transmitting and releasing information to third parties.

FERPA and Codes of Ethics

McGuire and Borowy (1978) insist that some confidential information typically included in student records was excluded from coverage under the Buckley Amendment. This exception hinges on the purpose or use of the information, rather than on the nature of its content. In their opinion, information obtained solely for the purpose of providing professional and diagnostic services to children is to remain confidential, on the assumption that the information has not been shared with anyone else, including fellow professionals. If it has been shared with anyone, it is no longer confidential.

Prior to the passage of PL 93-380, counselors had no guidelines other than ethical codes to use when faced with requests for information that challenged the principle of confidentiality. Such requests, for instance, may have been made by school administrators, school boards, or other persons of authority. PL 93-380 supplements the existing codes of ethical standards. Better definitions of appropriate counselor behaviors are provided through this union of law and ethics (Getson & Schweid, 1976).

Getson and Schweid (1976) offer suggestions for alleviating potential conflicts between PL 93-380 and codes of ethical standards:

- Purge files of information predating PL 93-380 that would violate students' rights of privacy.
- Remove all information that might be misinterpreted by nonprofessionals.
- Initiate a policy that allows parental review of only those records that are not a threat to client welfare.
- Be sure students are aware of the limits of privacy that exist in a counseling relationship because of parental rights to review student records.

- Make a personal study of the possibility of conflicts between PL 93-380 and the counselor's professional code of ethics.

Developing a Systematic Plan for Collection, Maintenance, and Dissemination of School Records

Guided by ethical standards to take care in record-keeping matters and mandated to engage in certain record-keeping procedures by PL 93-380, school counselors needed ideas for conducting the collection, maintenance, and dissemination of school records in a systematic manner. Into this setting came the Russell Sage Foundation (1970) guidelines, which became the foremost source of ideas for systematizing school record keeping. For example, in Pennsylvania, detailed school record-keeping systems were mandated by the state's department of education in 1976, and the Russell Sage guidelines were used as the criteria for judging the acceptability of each school district's submitted plan.

Several useful ideas are found in the Russell Sage guidelines. First, they cover the collection of data in which the distinction between individual and representational (parents' legally elected or appointed representatives) consent is discussed. Second, a useful and important system for categorizing data is given. It can be summarized as follows.

Category A Data. In this category are the minimum personal data necessary for operation of the education system. Examples are names, addresses, birth dates, and grades. This information is to be maintained perpetually.

Category B Data. This category includes verified information of clear importance but not absolutely necessary to the school in helping the child or in protecting others. Examples are scores on standardized intelligence tests, aptitude tests, and interest inventories; family background; and systematic teacher ratings. It is recommended that parents be informed periodically of the content of these records and of their right of access to the content. It is also recommended that Category B data be destroyed, or only maintained under conditions of anonymity, after a student leaves school.

Category C Data. Potentially useful data that are primarily time-bound to the immediate present are assigned to this category. Examples are legal or clinical findings, personality test results, and unevaluated reports of teachers or counselors. It is recommended that these data be destroyed as soon as their usefulness is ended, unless it is reasonable to transfer them to Category B.

Confidential Data. Any records or notes that are to be kept confidential should be located in the counselor's personal files, rather than in the cumulative records.

Implementing a Record-Keeping System

In a position statement on guidance services made at the time Pennsylvania was mandating detailed record-keeping systems, the Pennsylvania Department of Education (1977) made two useful records maintenance suggestions. First, a school district's record-keeping policies should allow for the retention of information necessary to permit full counseling, referral, and placement services in the years following a student's departure from school. This recommendation will have an important influence on what information is maintained in Category A after a student departs from school. Second, a centrally located storage facility should be established in order to allow easy access to records for those who have a legitimate interest in them. At the same time, provisions must be made for security against unauthorized use and accidental dissemination of information in student records.

In the same document, the Pennsylvania Department of Education (1977) offered useful advice (heavily influenced by the Russell Sage guidelines) for administering the record-keeping system:

- The mechanical aspects of record collection, maintenance, security, and dissemination should be handled by the clerical and/or paraprofessional staff under the supervision of the chief school administrator or that administrator's delegate. (In many instances, that authority is delegated to a school counselor.)
- Each school district should have a committee made up of staff members (instructional, pupil personnel, and administrative), parents, and students that is charged with deciding what information is to be collected and maintained for students' school records.
- The counselor's primary concern and involvement in the area of student records should be to participate with the others listed in the preceding paragraph to determine the content of records and to interpret and apply that content in the education of the student.
- The director of guidance should be responsible for establishing procedures for carrying out the school policy on records.

How involved school counselors are in the school's record-keeping system varies across districts. Certainly, they will keep and handle student records. It is assumed that most counselors will have their own confidential file notes and that they will have to conform to legal codes, ethical guidelines, and local policies when using the cumulative files. Some additional options counselors will not control because they are imposed. Those options include being the person to whom responsibility for administering the record-keeping system has been delegated, serving on the committee that determines what information should be collected and maintained, helping others be better informed through in-service training efforts, and interpreting contents to laypeople when needed. Burky and Childers (1976) offer a good general principle for counselors: Counselors should model behavior displaying their belief in the paramount rights of individuals.

Sources of Ethics Consultation

American School Counselor Association
- Members may call either 800/306-4722 or 703/683-1619 and will receive consultation from the appropriate person at ASCA headquarters or be referred to the chair of the ASCA ethics committee.

- See "Common Ethical and Legal Concerns of School Counselors," an informational brochure produced by ASCA.
- See "Doing the Right Thing: Ethics and the Professional School Counselor," an ethics packet produced by the ASCA ethics committee (1996–1997).

American Counseling Association

- Members may call either 800/347-6647 or 703/823-9800 and will be referred to a staff member for consultation.
- See Herlihy, B., & Corey, G., (1996), *ACA Ethical Standards Casebook* (5th ed.), published by the ACA.

National Board for Certified Counselors

- Counselors certified by the board who call 910/547–0607 will be referred to the ethics officer.

SUGGESTED ACTIVITIES

1. Review your knowledge of state and local legislation relative to counseling.
2. If you do not already have an informed consent statement, develop one. Have your statement critiqued by your instructor, colleagues, and prospective clients.
3. Set up two plans for training teachers to use the record-keeping system appropriately. Have one plan in a group in-service format and the other in a programmed format for self-instruction.
*4. Develop a plan of action for responding to the following legal/ethical challenge:

    An 18-year-old female high-school student has left home. Suspecting that the reasons for her leaving may be explained in the young woman's records, one of her parents calls the school counseling office and asks to see the records. Meanwhile, the young woman has decided to withdraw from school and also requests to see her records. She wants them purged of personal information. Two weeks later, the police call the guidance office for access to the young woman's file during a routine investigation. A prospective employer also calls the guidance office and requests the young woman's IQ score or equivalent information for assistance in making a decision about hiring her.

*5. Answer each of the following true-or-false questions on the basis of the ACA *Code of Ethics* and *Standards of Practice*.
    a. Ethical standards are statements of philosophy.
    b. When a member of the ACA accepts employment in a school, he or she accepts the institution's policies.
    c. In a counseling relationship, an ACA member's primary obligation is to the public welfare.
    d. It is inappropriate to continue a counseling relationship with a client who is involved in counseling or therapy with another professional.
    e. It is unethical to admit failure or inability to be of assistance to a client.
    f. Explaining to a prospective client the conditions under which the counseling service is being offered at or before entrance into the counseling relationship is essential.

    g. A school counselor can ethically charge a fee for counseling services that clients are entitled to as students.

    h. Unethical behavior by a fellow professional is the responsibility of an ACA member.

*6. Discuss the following cases, using the ethical standards in Appendixes C and D for guidance. The cases are taken from "An Ethics Quiz for School Counselors" (Huey, Salo, & Fox, 1995). Determine whether you agree (A) or disagree (D) with the counselor's decision in each case, and place the corresponding letter in the blanks:

    _____ a. A group member became very upset and wanted to leave after several members ganged up on her in a vicious verbal attack. The counselor physically barred the sobbing girl from leaving and told her that she must learn to handle conflicts within the group.

    _____ b. A counselor self-described his dislike of a new technology as "computer phobia." As part of the school's counseling program, all ninth-grade students were required to use a newly purchased computerized interest inventory. The counselor joked that he was "not sure that he could even turn the machine on" and left the students to themselves "because they were better with computers anyway."

    _____ c. As part of an ongoing peer program to assist students in being better able to help their peers with personal concerns, the counselor scheduled regular supervision sessions. Even though the peer helpers were well trained and had not had any problems, the counselor felt an obligation to check in with them.

    _____ d. A male counselor refused to close his door when counseling teenage girls, even when requested by students who were emotionally upset. A female colleague believed the counselor was unnecessarily cautious and unethical in not providing the privacy needed by clients. The colleague decided to speak to the counselor to be sure he was aware of his responsibilities.

    _____ e. A counselor strongly disliked a particular student assigned to his caseload and found himself distracted by negative feelings every time he saw the student. Despite good faith attempts to change his feelings, the counselor still disliked the student and subsequently referred the student to another counselor.

    _____ f. The parents of a sophomore who was having academic problems told the counselor they were going to transfer their son to a private school the next school year. The student loved his current school and was very involved in extracurricular activities. The parents would not reconsider and asked the counselor not to tell their son about the plans. When advising the student about his academic course work for the next year, the counselor was careful not to reveal the parents' plans.

7. Go to the following Internet site: www.scan21st.com. Discuss some of the ethical and legal issues that might arise from online programs featured at this site.

*Note that suggested and keyed responses for the activities above are found in the instructor's manual.

REFERENCES

Allsopp, A., & Prosen, S. (1988). Teacher reactions to a child sexual abuse training program. *Elementary School Guidance and Counseling, 22,* 299–305.

American Counseling Association (ACA). (1995). *Code of ethics and standards of practice.* Alexandria, VA: Author.

American School Counselor Association (ASCA). (1988). ASCA position statement: The school counselor and child abuse/neglect prevention. *Elementary School Guidance and Counseling, 22,* 261–263.

American School Counselor Association (ASCA). (1992). Ethical standards for school counselors. *School Counselor, 40,* 84–88.

Anderson, R. F. (n.d.). *Counselors going to court.* Unpublished paper, Wake County, North Carolina, Public Schools.

Arnold v. Board of Education of Escambia County, 880 F.2d 305 (Alabama 1989). Bellotti v. Baird, 443 U.S. 622 (1979).

Boyd, R. E., & Heinsen, R. D. (1971). Problems of privileged communication. *Personnel and Guidance Journal, 50,* 276–279.

Bronner, E. (1998, March 14). Guidance counselors fearful of litigation. *The News & Observer,* p. 12A.

Burky, W. D., & Childers, J. H., Jr. (1976). Buckley Amendment: Focus on a professional dilemma. *School Counselor, 23,* 162–164.

Camblin, L. D., Jr., & Prout, H. T. (1983). School counselors and the reporting of child abuse. *School Counselor, 30,* 358–367.

Congressional Record (120-S21487, daily edition, December 13, 1974). Joint statement in explanation of the Buckley/Pell Amendment, Washington, DC: Government Printing Office.

Connors, E. T. (1979). *Student discipline and the law.* Bloomington, IN: Phi Delta Kappa Foundation.

Corey, G., Corey, M. S., & Callanan, P. (1984). *Issues and ethics in the helping professions* (2nd ed.). Monterey, CA: Brooks/Cole.

Cottone, R. R. (2001). A social constructivism model of ethical decision making in counseling. *Journal of Counseling & Development, 90,* 39–45.

Cottone, R. R., & Claus, R. E. (2000). Ethical decision-making models: A review of the literature. *Journal of Counseling & Development, 78,* 275–283.

Currie v. United States, 644 F Supp. 1074 (N.C., 1986).

DePauw, M. E. (1986). Avoiding ethical violations: A timeline perspective for individual counseling.

Journal of Counseling & Development, 64, 303–305.

Downing, C. J. (1982). Parent support groups to prevent child abuse. *Elementary School Guidance and Counseling, 17,* 119–124.

Eisenberg, S., & O'Dell, E. (1988). Teaching children to trust in a nontrusting world. *Elementary School Guidance and Counseling, 22,* 264–267.

Fielstein, L. L. (1996). Case study 12: Ensuring a student's welfare. In B. Herlihy & G. Corey (Eds.), *ACA ethical standards casebook* (5th ed., pp. 248–250). Alexandria, VA: American Counseling Association.

Fischer, L., & Sorenson, G. P. (1996). *School law for counselors, psychologists, and social workers* (3rd ed.). New York: Longman.

Gehring, D. C. (1982). The counselor's "duty to warn." *Personnel and Guidance Journal, 61,* 208–210.

Getson, R., & Schweid, R. (1976). School counselors and the Buckley Amendment—Ethical standards squeeze. *School Counselor, 24,* 56–58.

Glosoff, H. L., Herlihy, B., & Spence, E. B. (2000). Privileged communication and the counselor-client relationship. *Journal of Counseling & Development, 78,* 454–462.

Glosoff, H. L., & Pate, R. H., Jr. (2002). Privacy and confidentiality in school counseling. *Professional School Counseling, 6,* 20–27.

Heayn, M. H., & Jacobs, H. L. (1967). Safeguarding student records. *Personnel and Guidance Journal, 46,* 63–67.

Herlihy, B., & Remley, T. P. (2001). Legal and ethical challenges. In D. C. Locke, J. E. Myers, & E. L. Herr (Eds.), *The handbook of counseling* (pp. 69–89). Thousand Oaks, CA: Sage.

Hermann, M. A. (2002). A study of legal issues encountered by school counselors and perceptions of their preparedness to respond to legal challenges. *Professional School Counseling, 6,* 12–19.

Herring, R. D. (1997). *Multicultural counseling in schools: A synergistic approach.* Alexandria, VA: American Counseling Association.

Hitchcock, R. A., & Young, D. (1986). Prevention of sexual assault: A curriculum for elementary school counselors. *Elementary School Guidance and Counseling, 20,* 201–207.

Hopkins, B. R., & Anderson, B. S. (1990). *The counselor and the law.* Alexandria, VA: American Association for Counseling and Development.

Huey, W. C. (1986). Ethical concerns in school counseling. *Journal of Counseling & Development, 64,* 321–322.

Huey, W. C., Salo, M. M., & Fox, R. W. (1995). An ethics quiz for school counselors. *School Counselor, 42,* 393–398.

Kaplan, D. M. (1996). Developing an informed consent brochure for secondary students: *All about ASCA membership.* Alexandria, VA: American School Counselor Association.

Kazalunas, J. R. (1977). Conscience, the law, and practical requirements of the Buckley Amendment. *School Counselor, 24,* 243–247.

Kiselica, M. S. (1996). Legal issues in abortion counseling with adolescents. *ASCA Counselor, 33*(4), 1.

Knapp, S. (1983). Counselor liability to report child abuse. *Elementary School Guidance and Counseling, 17,* 177–179.

LaFromboise, T. D., Foster, S., & James, A. (1996). Ethics in multicultural counseling. In P. B. Pedersen, J. G. Draguns, W. J. Lonner, & J. E. Trimble (Eds.), *Counseling across cultures* (4th ed., pp. 47–72). Thousand Oaks, CA: Sage.

Lawrence, G., & Kurpius, S. E. R. (2000). Legal and ethical issues involved when counseling minors in nonschool settings. *Journal of Counseling & Development, 78,* 130–136.

Legal considerations should not shape clinical decisions, seminar told. (1983, July 6). *Mental Health Reports,* pp. 7–8.

McGuire, J. M., & Borowy, T. D. (1978). Confidentiality and the Buckley/Pell Amendment: Ethical and legal considerations for counselors. *Personnel and Guidance Journal, 56,* 554–557.

Menacker, J. (1976). Toward a theory of activist guidance. *Personnel and Guidance Journal, 54,* 318–321.

Monahan, J. (1993). Limiting therapist exposure to *Tarasoff* liability. *American Psychologist, 48,* 242–250.

Nassar-McMillan, S., & Post, P. (1998, March). *Ethics reconsidered.* A program presented at the annual meeting of the North Carolina Counseling Association, Chapel Hill.

Neese, L. A. (1989). Psychological maltreatment in school: Emerging issues for counselors. *Elementary School Guidance and Counseling, 23,* 194–200.

O'Connor, K., Plante, J., & Refvem, J. (1998, March). *Parental consent and the school counselor.* Poster session presented at the annual meeting of the North Carolina Counseling Association, Chapel Hill.

Pedersen, P. B. (1997). *Culture-centered counseling interventions: Striving for accuracy.* Thousand Oaks, CA: Sage.

Pennsylvania Department of Education. (1977). *Guidance services in Pennsylvania: Position statement.* Harrisburg: Author.

Pietrofesa, J. J., & Vriend, J. (1971). *The school counselor as a professional.* Itasca, IL: F. E. Peacock.

Post-Kammer, P. (1988). Effectiveness of Parents Anonymous in reducing child abuse. *School Counselor, 35,* 337–342.

Remley, T. P., Jr. (1985). The law and ethical practices in elementary and middle schools. *Elementary School Guidance and Counseling, 19,* 181–189.

Remley, T. P., Jr. (1992). How much record keeping is enough? *American Counselor, 1,* 31–33.

Repucci, N. D., & Haugaard, J. J. (1989). Prevention of child sexual abuse. *American Psychologist, 44,* 1266–1275.

Russell Sage Foundation. (1970). *Guidelines for the collection, maintenance, and dissemination of pupil records.* Hartford, CT: Author.

Sain v. Cedar Rapids Community School District, 626 N.W.2d 115 (Iowa 2001).

Sheeley, V. L., & Herlihy, B. (1988). Privileged communication in schools and counseling: Status update. In W. C. Huey & T. P. Remley, Jr. (Eds.), *Ethical and legal issues in school counseling* (pp. 85–92). Alexandria, VA: American Association for Counseling and Development.

Sheeley, V. L., & Herlihy, B. (1989). Counseling suicidal teens: A duty to warn and protect. *School Counselor, 37,* 89–97.

Stone, C. (2002). Negligence in academic advising and abortion counseling: Courts rulings and implications. *Professional School Counseling, 6,* 28–35.

Talbutt, L. C. (1981). Ethical standards: Assets and limitations. *Personnel and Guidance Journal, 60,* 110–112.

Talbutt, L. C. (1983a). The counselor and testing: Some legal concerns. *School Counselor, 30,* 245–250.

Talbutt, L. C. (1983b). Current legal trends regarding abortions for minors: A dilemma for counselors. *School Counselor, 31,* 120–124.

Tarasoff v. Regents of the University of California, 551 p. 2nd 334 (California, 1976).

Tennant, C. G. (1988). Preventive sexual abuse programs: Problems and possibilities. *Elementary School Guidance and Counseling, 23,* 48–53.

Therapists bear a duty to commit, says U.S. district court judge. (1987). *Mental Health Law Reporter,* pp. 4–5. (sample issue)

Van Hoose, W. H., & Kottler, J. (1978). *Ethical and legal issues in counseling and psychotherapy.* San Francisco: Jossey-Bass.

Vernon, A., & Hay, J. (1988). A preventive approach to child sexual abuse. *Elementary School Guidance and Counseling, 22,* 306–312.

Washington, P. H. (1973). In-loco-parentis and student records in shared responsibility situations. In T. E. Long & G. R. Hudson (Eds.), *Shared responsibility in student record keeping and dissemination* (pp. 27–40). State College, PA: Counselor Education Press.

Wilhelm, C. D., & Case, M. (1975). Telling it like it is: Improving school records. *School Counselor, 23,* 84–90.

Wilson, J., Thomas, D., & Schuette, L. (1983). Survey of counselors on identifying and reporting cases of child abuse. *School Counselor, 30,* 299–305.

Zingaro, J. (1983). Confidentiality: To tell or not to tell. *Elementary School Guidance and Counseling, 17,* 261–267.

CHAPTER 4

Prevention Programming in School Counseling

Goals: To offer evidence of the importance of developmentally appropriate prevention programming, propose basic competencies for proactive prevention programming, and provide examples.

The Cornish Test of Insanity comprised a sink, a tap of running water, a bucket, and a ladle. The bucket was placed under the tap of running water, and the subject was asked to bail the water out of the bucket with the ladle. If the subject continued to bail without paying some attention to reducing or preventing the flow of water into the pail, he or she was judged to be mentally incompetent. (Morgan & Jackson, 1980, p. 99)

We have had many opportunities to hear school counselors discuss their hopes and aspirations for preventive programming in classrooms. The following account from an elementary-school counselor is among the most poignant we have heard:

> *I meet with small groups of children every week, giving them an opportunity to discuss their feelings about many aspects of their lives. These groups help the children to feel welcome at school and to know the benefits of self-disclosure and listening. Recently, while discussing the topic "the saddest thing that ever happened to me," a fourth-grade girl reluctantly raised her hand. When I looked toward her, she brought her hand down quickly. She seldom said anything in the group and generally appeared shy and reserved in social situations. Several other youngsters contributed to the group topic before her hand went up again. I looked toward her, and she lowered her hand. Two other members of the group spoke. Her hand went up again and remained up this time. I called on her. She spoke with great care: "The saddest thing I ever saw was my grandfather hanging from a rope in our barn." She had been holding this in for weeks and finally felt trusting enough to share this traumatic experience from her life. She was relieved. I invited her to meet with me later to discuss this matter with me.*

The flow of problems to counselors' offices can never be reduced unless counselors plan and implement preventive counseling programs. It is not surprising, therefore, that school counselors devote a major portion of their time and effort to preventing the onset of emotional problems in children. In cooperation with teachers, counselors conduct classroom programs that include listening activities and other techniques that are designed to help children (a) feel worthy as persons and as students, (b) recognize their feelings about themselves and about learning, and (c) feel comfortable about expressing these feelings openly and honestly.

DEMAND FOR PREVENTION PROGRAMMING IN SCHOOLS

In chapter 2, we advocated school counseling programs that are balanced between intervention responses and proactive prevention programming. Proactive prevention programming is the mainstay of the prevention function and is pedagogical in nature. The word *pedagogical* identifies these activities because they are primarily instructional; *pedagogics* is the "art, science, or profession of teaching" (*Merriam-Webster's Collegiate Dictionary*, 1998, p. 856). Although pedagogics is seldom associated with counselor education, there is no denying that school counselors engage in instructional or pedagogical activities when delivering many group programs. Many terms label these programs: classroom guidance, group guidance, guidance teaching, developmental guidance, guidance-related courses or units, and wellness programs. This textbook uses the term *proactive prevention programming*. We use this term because it allows us to present a set of pedagogical competencies that are needed to deliver classroom guidance, group guidance, developmental guidance, or any such school counselor program that is pedagogical in nature. The word *proactive* indicates that the activities involved are anticipatory. *Prevention* indicates that the goals are to prevent problems and enhance human development. The word *programming* indicates that the process involves systematically arranging a sequence of intentional applications based on goals and objectives derived from an underlying conceptual rationale. School counselors are challenged to be competent teachers/pedagogues in order to offer proactive prevention programs. Providing a balanced school counseling program seems to require competence as teachers.

The American School Counselor Association uses the term *developmental guidance* when referring to proactive prevention programming. Excerpts from its 1978 position statement (reviewed and revised in 1984) on developmental guidance indicate that, aside from differing semantics, the association seems to agree that proactive prevention programming is an important school counseling function:

> Developmental guidance should be an integral part of every school counseling program and be incorporated into the role and function of every school counselor. During recent years a number of counselor educators and school counselors have advanced the proposition that counseling can and should be more proactive and preventive in its focus and more developmental in its content and process.... Developmental guidance is a reaffirmation and actualization of the belief that guidance is for all students and that its purpose is to maximally facilitate personal development.... The program should be systematic, sequential, and comprehensive.... The program should be jointly founded upon developmental psychology, educational psychology, and counseling methodology. (n.d., p. 33)

The public hopes to have pervasive social and personal problems prevented. Childhood and adolescence are opportune times to prevent many problems. Therefore, the school years are an excellent time for programs designed to help children and adolescents get the most out of their school experience and cope better with life's challenges. This is also a good time to identify at-risk individuals and to prevent them from being overwhelmed by the problems they are at risk of experiencing. Proactive prevention programming usually has several common features: It is structured, planned in advance, presented in a group format, and led by individuals working from a predetermined plan.

Many school counselors enter the field with degrees in education and with teaching experience. Traditional counselor education programs are designed to provide them additional competencies such as counseling and assessing skills. School counseling trainees, however, increasingly come from fields outside education, especially in states that do not require teaching experience as a prerequisite for school counseling certification or licensure. Because these individuals are not trained in pedagogics, it is important to train them as competent instructors, as well as competent counselors. School counseling students, it seems, will benefit from opportunities to become competent at pedagogics during their training in order to provide balanced school counseling services.

Training experiences for school counselors might include opportunities to learn about structured, developmentally appropriate proactive group prevention and intervention programs for students, teachers, and parents; and opportunities to learn skills for presenting and delivering such programs effectively to students representing the students' own as well as other worldviews. Counselors planning and presenting structured programs to groups of students will be more successful if they are competent technically—at developing lesson plans and supplementing instruction with activities that are interesting and that complement the instructional goals—as well as competent multiculturally—able to make programs meaningful to individuals representing all worldviews in their schools.

All three of the initiatives for enhancing school counseling introduced in chapter 1 advocate the importance of proactive prevention programming competencies. Speaking for the ASCA National Model, Bowers and Hatch (2001) state that the components should include a guidance curriculum. Further, Gysbers and Henderson (2001) indicate that the curriculum should cover kindergarten through 12th grade and translate the ASCA National Standards (see Appendix A) into classroom activities delivered via structured groups. Indeed, the competencies in the ASCA National Standards offer a foundation for proactively designing strategies and producing activities to enhance student achievement and success in academic, career, and personal-social development.

Representing the National School Counselor Training Initiative, House and Hayes (2002) use the words *planner* and *program developer* among the desired competencies for school counselors. The Education Trust hopes to produce school counselors who can promote student achievement through well-articulated developmental school counseling programs. Through these programs, school counselors will teach students how to help themselves via improved organizational, study, and test-taking skills. House and Hayes also promote school counselor involvement in staff development for school personnel focused on learning how to promote high expectations and standards.

In the School-Community Collaboration Model, part of an interconnected system for meeting the needs of all students is having systems for promoting healthy development and preventing problems (i.e., primary prevention). Examples given are drug and alcohol education, parent involvement, and conflict resolution (Adelman & Taylor, 2002).

Excerpts from the professional literature illustrate the scope of counselor-initiated proactive prevention programming in the schools. Several recent and historical examples are provided as background.

Prevention Programming Focused on Enhancing Skills

Lapan, Gysbers, Hughey, and Arni (1993) experienced some success with a program that had school counselors and English teachers working together to have high-school juniors explore career issues and develop academic skills. Perceived changes occurred in mastery of career guidance competencies such as planning and developing careers, making decisions about college, and selecting vocations and training that "predicted positive change in vocational identity and attainment of higher English grades for girls" (p. 444).

Social problem-solving skills have been targeted as important for helping children and adolescents reduce trial-and-error behaviors, preventing them from resorting to maladaptive responses, enhancing their social interactions, encouraging more positive peer relationships, and providing a means of gaining social acceptance (Mehaffey & Sandberg, 1992). Galvin (1983) designed a systematic problem-solving training program for elementary-school children in which they learned to brainstorm solutions, make choices from an inventory of solutions, work on strategies for implementing the solutions, and evaluate the effects of their choices.

In their study of the program, "Succeeding in School," Gerler and Anderson (1986) report positive changes in attitudes toward school, classroom deportment, and language arts grades among fourth and fifth graders across North Carolina, and Gerler and

Herndon (1993) found that the program could enhance awareness of how to achieve success in school among sixth to eighth graders, also in North Carolina. A follow-up study by Lee (1993) indicates that academic achievement can also be influenced in a positive direction. In Lee's study, successes occurred in mathematics achievement. The participants were fourth through sixth graders in California from a variety of cultural and economic backgrounds. At the core of this program is a 10-session group guidance program led by school counselors. The "Succeeding in School" program is now online and can be seen at the following Internet site: www.scan21st.com.

Prevention Programming Focused on Enhancing Academic Performance

Delivering their program directly to 12- to-15-year-old students who had been certified as learning disabled, Omizo and Omizo (1987) viewed self-esteem enhancement as the key to improving academic performance. They believe that improved self-esteem will reduce self-defeating behaviors, which, in turn, will improve academic performance.

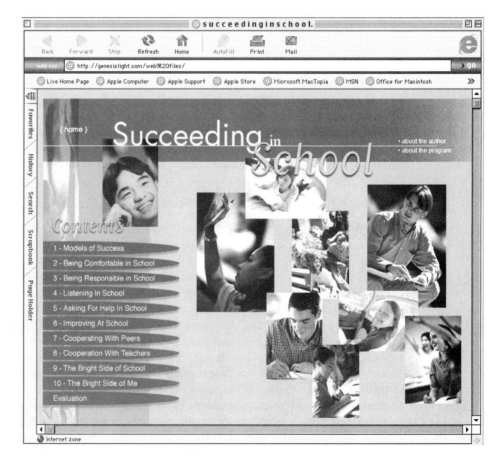

Academic achievement can be influenced in a positive direction.

Schlossberg, Morris, and Lieberman (2001) reported on effects of an intervention program designed to have a positive impact on the behavior, attitudes, and informational awareness of ninth graders attending a large, comprehensive, multiethnic high school in southeast Florida. The program consisted of six 45-minute sessions in a counselor-led developmental guidance unit. Program content was based on findings from a schoolwide needs assessment and focused on goal setting, problem solving, career exploration, and recognition of available resources within the school setting. The findings indicated significant differences between treatment and control conditions in student ratings for behavior, attitude, and information. The researchers concluded that programs such as this one have potential for helping students cope with the potentially overwhelming aspects of the transition to high school.

Prevention Programming Designed to Counter Cultural Oppression

Accepting Sue's (1992) contention that multiculturalism—recognizing and valuing diversity and cultural pluralism—"is the road less traveled" (p. 6), some have proposed curricular programs to counter monocultural and ethnocentric influences that have been dominant in the United States. The Getting on the Right Track Project, designed to encourage college-bound ninth-grade African American students, includes a component in which a counselor can meet with the participants to develop thinking and research skills through African-centered exploration (Locke & Faubert, 1993). Examples of projects the exploration activity generates are: learning why African American students do less well than others on standardized tests and studying about strategies for preventing students from dropping out of school early.

In response to low levels of academic achievement among Hispanics in the Los Angeles school district, a parent leadership program was initiated (Casas & Furlong, 1994). Counselors conducted twelve 2-hour, weekly classes in Spanish. To achieve a general goal of parental empowerment leading to greater participation in the school community, information about how the school operates is combined with developing such skills as getting the most out of parent-teacher conferences and communicating successfully with school officials.

Salzman and D'Andrea (2001) believe that "counselors can make a difference in the construction of a more harmonious and enriching multicultural environment if they intentionally choose to do so" (p. 346). This position is based in part on the findings from a study of the effects of a prejudice prevention program. The prejudice prevention intervention developed by Omizo and D'Andrea (1995) was presented to 28 ethnically diverse fourth graders attending a public school in Hawaii in 10 weekly 40-minute group guidance sessions by a school counseling intern under the supervision of the researchers. The program content included activities designed to foster positive social skills and self-esteem. Teachers observed significant improvement in the cooperative social skills of the students in the program in comparison to those in a control condition. This was viewed as evidence of the potential for this intentional prevention program, and similar ones, to help participants acquire social skills that lead to more harmonious, less prejudiced environments in school settings.

Prevention Programming Within the School Curriculum

One of the tenets of the comprehensive guidance and counseling model espoused by Gysbers and Henderson (2000) that influences the ASCA National Model initiative is that guidance (a.k.a. school counseling) should have its own curriculum in the schools just as English, science, and the others have. Lapan, Gysbers, and Petroski (2001) reported findings from a study of a statewide implementation of this curriculum-based model. The Missouri Comprehensive Guidance Program (MCGP) has been in place since 1984 and "has been adopted, in whole or in part, by many states and school districts across the country" (Lapan et al. 2001, p. 322). One of the components of the MCGP is a guidance curriculum.

Lapan et al. (2001) examined the impact on perceptions of safety in school, satisfaction with one's education, grades, perceptions of relationships with teachers, and perceptions of the importance and relevance of education to students' future. The participants were 22,601 seventh graders and 4,858 teachers from 184 schools. The findings were quite striking. According to Lapan et al. (2001), "the present study provided additional evidence that the implementation of comprehensive school counseling programs was consistently associated with important indicators of student safety and success" (p. 327) and "students . . . reported (a) feeling safer attending their schools, (b) having better relationships with their teachers, (c) believing that their education was more relevant and important to their futures, (d) being more satisfied with the quality of education available in their schools, (e) having fewer problems related to the physical and interpersonal milieu in their schools, and (f) earning higher grades" (p. 320).

BASIC INGREDIENTS OF PREVENTION PROGRAMMING

Point of View

Because prevention programming is analogous to teaching, it might be argued that the basic ingredients are drawn from the field of education. Education is an applied field, just as counseling is, and, like counseling, education has drawn from various disciplines for its foundations. For instance, psychology contributes ideas about human learning, philosophy is the source of ideas about the human condition, and sociology helps educators understand the role of the schools in the greater society. Basic education is also influenced by local, state, and national politics and by applied economics because the schools are primarily supported by taxes. Therefore, when counselors act like teachers and engage in prevention programming, they are not necessarily mimicking a field that is foreign to them.

The traditional training that counselor education programs impart includes knowledge and competencies that prepare counselors for prevention programming. However, the preparation is often not formalized or specified in traditional counselor education programs. Therefore, the field of education is the source of ideas for formalizing and specifying the ingredients of the prevention programming in counseling. What results is a marriage of ingredients from traditional counseling programs and from education that provides an organizing structure for prevention programming training in counselor education training programs.

This combination may not seem necessary for school counseling students who are experienced teachers with formal training in education. On the other hand, it is important to remember that teachers are trained to focus on the enhancement of cognitive abilities; in some cases, they learn to divorce thinking about the affective domain from their professional mind-set. Experienced teachers and counselor education students from other disciplines who are being trained as school counselors are challenged to focus on both the cognitive and affective domains in their prevention programming. Therefore, there is a place for formalized instruction in prevention programming within counselor education programs.

The competencies to be introduced are valid for all forms of prevention programming. Prevention programming can take different forms depending on the circumstances. For instance, the programming can be direct or indirect. The term *direct programming* indicates that programs are delivered directly to audiences (e.g., the school counselor leads groups designed to help students become better problem solvers). Indirect programming, on the other hand, indicates that audiences receive programs from third parties (e.g., the school counselor helps classroom teachers prepare for and deliver programs designed to help their students become better problem solvers).

The competencies are also valid for prevention programming that falls within a guidance curriculum or is independent of a curriculum. Some schools and school districts have guidance curriculums. That is, school counselors have their own set of courses (i.e., curriculum) in schools just as the academic disciplines do, and they have their own recognized area of specialization. They have prevention programs based on enhancing specific developmental goals that are sequenced by grade levels. Time for delivering the programs is scheduled by school administrators and recognized by classroom teachers. Essentially, school guidance counseling is accepted as an equally important curriculum and treated accordingly.

Many school counselors work in environments where they do not have guidance curriculums. They arrange to deliver prevention programs independently of the curriculum by working around the schedule. This requires cooperation from school administrators and teachers and leads to less comprehensive prevention programming than is the case with guidance curriculums. For example, during the fall semester of an academic year, a hypothetical elementary-school counselor might present a unit to enhance self-esteem in the classes of kindergarten teachers who want to cooperate and also might provide a study skills program for students who are interested and whose teachers will let them leave the classroom to participate.

Whether prevention programs are delivered via guidance curriculums or by working around the academic curriculums, the programs can be either direct or indirect. Prevention programs can be delivered directly and indirectly in guidance curriculums and in programs that are adapted to the academic curriculum. Whichever of these circumstances may occur, the competencies to be presented remain valid.

Formalizing and Specifying Prevention Programming

Foundations. According to the American School Counselor Association (1979), the fruits of prevention programming should be available to all students and should be focused on promoting maximum personal development. Dagley (1987) recommends

Counselors may coach students while helping them acquire desired skills.

that these general principles focus school counselor activities devoted to enhancing individual development on distinct goals related to lifelong learning, personal effectiveness, and life roles. Figure 4.1 presents a summary of Dagley's proposal. The goals and outcomes in Figure 4.1 offer an inventory of the foundations on which school counselors' prevention programming is based.

Like the counseling function, prevention programming is immersed in a developmental context. The importance of a developmental perspective was discussed in chapter 2. Erikson's theory was presented in chapter 2 to advocate presenting counseling interventions to meet the differing developmental needs of children and adolescents. A summary of Erikson's Eight Stages of Man is presented in Figure 2.2. Ivey's (1986) adaptation of Piaget's developmental theory, which is presented in chapter 5, can be used to match prevention programming efforts with the cognitive stages of individuals, groups of individuals, or individuals within groups. Table 5.2 provides a graphic representation of Ivey's position. Erikson's work focuses on psychological needs, and Ivey's material highlights the importance of cognitive development. Both remind us that human development is complex and varied and that individuals develop at different rates although common themes are found within age-groups. Knowledge of human development appears to be an imperative foundation for prevention programming by school counselors.

Ingredients.   Prevention programming seems to require careful planning. Adherence to specific steps is as important to prevention programming as it is to counseling and consulting interventions. The major steps in prevention programming are planning,

Personal Effectiveness Competencies	Self-Understanding (identity, autonomy, acceptance, validation)
	Human Relations (respect, empathy, social interest, conflict resolution)
	Health Development (intimacy, leisure, growth stages)
Lifelong Learning Competencies	Communication (reading and writing, listening, expressiveness, assertiveness)
	Information Processing (study and analysis, evaluation, problem solving)
	Personal Enrichment (time management, renewal, change)
Life Roles Competencies	Daily Living (child rearing, consumerism, community involvement)
	Career Planning (values clarification, decision making, planning, goal setting)
	Employability (self-placement, work habits, educational and occupational preparation)

Figure 4.1

Foundations on which prevention programming is based.

Source: "A New Look at Developmental Guidance: The Hearthstone of School Counseling," by J. C. Dagley, 1987, *School Counselor, 35,* p. 103. Copyright 1987 by American Counseling Association.

delivering, transferring, and evaluating. *Planning* includes assessing the needs of prospective recipients, setting goals and objectives, researching, and recruiting and selecting participants. *Delivering* includes lesson planning, instructing, demonstrating, and directing. *Transferring* involves providing opportunities for clients to transfer their learning to the real world. The ingredients of the delivering component are also important in transferring. *Evaluating* includes assessing, analyzing, and reporting. Together, these ingredients are the basic competencies of proactive prevention programming.

BASIC COMPETENCIES IN PREVENTION PROGRAMMING

Planning

Assessing Needs. Counselors are encouraged to engage in the measurement and assessment activities that will help them identify the perceived, expressed, and assumed needs of their public. Fall (1994) refers to this first step as asking questions. Direct measurement and assessment of perceived and expressed needs involve counselors in sampling and surveying activities with accompanying skills. Assumed needs can be learned from the professional and popular literature. Results of needs assessments may be reported to interested individuals and entities; thus, reporting is an important skill. Needs assessment, whatever the method, sets the stage for setting goals and objectives.

Setting Goals and Objectives.   The terms *goal* and *objective* have been used both interchangeably and separately—*goal* meaning a more general purpose, and *objective* meaning the more specific purposes assigned to general goal achievement. Whichever meanings counselors assign to these terms, the requisite skills are constant. Counselors are challenged to translate needs into goals. For instance, if a local needs assessment survey results in a public demand for the school system to do something about the drug abuse problem among teenagers, one goal will be to reduce drug abuse in that group. One objective related to that goal will be to teach adolescents at risk of abusing drugs to respond to peer pressure more assertively. Notice that the example goal and objective are stated in measurable terms. This allows the individuals delivering such programs to assess their ability to achieve the goals and objectives; that is, instances of increased or decreased drug use and acquisition of assertiveness skills can be measured. The results can be offered as evidence of achieving or not achieving the program goals and objectives. Counselors and their publics will be better served if they state their goals and objectives in measurable terms.

Researching.   Having established goals and objectives, counselors may use them to determine the content of their prevention programming. Necessary content may be material with which they are familiar or unfamiliar. When necessary, counselors may have to locate, read, and abstract material from various resources. Therefore, they will benefit from being familiar with available libraries; catalogs of publications, media, and assessment instruments; consultants; relevant professional organizations; and various governmental, service, private, fraternal, and special interest organizations that may have useful information. The Internet has expanded the potential for school counselors to engage in this researching function in the twenty-first century. There is a limit to the knowledge base that counselors should be expected to have at the outset. In other words, counselors will not be able to deliver all programs for all people on demand. What kinds of prevention programming should counselors be able to deliver initially?

One possibility is that counselors are able to use the competencies they acquired during graduate school. Much of what was learned in counselor education programs can be translated into prevention programming. Some examples are basic interpersonal communication and challenging skills training, decision-making and problem-solving training, peer helper training, teaching individuals to cope with and change irrational thinking, a variety of applications of behavioral rehearsal (e.g., applying for jobs, meeting new people, coping with stressful relationships), self-management training, assertiveness training, relaxation training, career information-seeking and information-processing, career planning, gaming, cartooning, playing, clarifying and sharing values, support groups, process groups, and parent and teacher groups that focus on any of this content. This is a relatively comprehensive list that can be expanded through research and experience, leaving the impression that counselors can offer much through their prevention programming.

Recruiting and Selecting Participants. On occasion, prevention programming might be offered on a voluntary basis, and counselors will need to recruit volunteers successfully. This involves using information-sharing skills and being able to motivate children and adolescents, as well as being truthful. Circumstances may lead counselors to select possible participants from a pool of volunteers, or counselors may have to determine group membership for individuals in the pool. When engaging in selection activities, counselors again may use their information-sharing skills. For example, they may be challenged to explain their selection decisions to inquiring individuals. In addition, they may use diagnostic and assessment skills to match the right opportunities with the appropriate individuals.

Delivering

Lesson Planning. Lesson planning involves several important components. The ideas culled from researching can be organized around the goals and objectives to form a coherent plan for delivering a program. Lesson plans are organized on a global and unit basis. A global lesson plan covers the entire program, detailing the proposed goals and events sequentially. The events are daily or single-unit lesson plans. Basic ingredients of lesson plans are objectives, materials/resources, identification of the audience, an outline of the planned action steps for presenting the program, identification of information individuals need to participate in the lessons, homework assignments, and evaluation strategies. A sample lesson plan follows:

Lesson Plan for an Anxiety Management Program

Objectives (stated so that each objective identifies specific desired outcomes behaviorally that can be measured)

1. Participants will be able to generate at least one self-defeating and one self-improving thought without assistance or coaching.
2. Participants will contribute to a discussion about applying self-statements to stressful situations in their lives.

Materials/Resources

1. Chalkboard and chalk to record information generated during the discussion.
2. Assertiveness handouts to be distributed as homework for the next lesson.

Audience

1. Male and female ninth-grade students who have volunteered to participate in the program.

Action Steps

1. Have participants generate a list of anxiety-provoking situations.
2. Review the notion of self-improving thoughts.
3. Have participants generate and share one self-defeating and one corresponding self-improving thought for the anxiety-provoking situations they previously listed.

4. Discuss how the self-statements may be applied in a stressful situation.
5. Distribute assertiveness handouts.
6. Introduce assertiveness training and review the important components of appropriate assertive responses by reading the handout aloud.
7. Ask participants to read the assertiveness handout and to practice applying coping self-statements in real-life stressful situations as homework.

Evaluation Strategies (parallel to the stated behavioral objectives)
1. Participants keep a record of the self-defeating and self-improving thoughts as they occur in their daily experiences.
2. Observe participation during the discussion.

Fall (1994) provides an example of a situation that might require a global plan. A fifth-grade teacher asks an elementary-school counselor for assistance with initiating a classroom guidance unit. Goals for the teacher include learning about group membership and developing skills for leading a group. Related objectives might be that the teacher will learn how to include all students in the group activities and how to get the students to work cooperatively in the group activities. Action steps might include providing printed information and helping the teacher understand and process that information. The counselor might follow this by demonstrating the targeted skills and by providing opportunities for the teacher to practice those behaviors via simulations. The counselor offers constructive feedback until the teacher is ready to engage in classroom guidance with the students.

Counselors are also challenged to create environments that ensure their lesson plans will be successful. In a school setting where there is no guidance curriculum, this involves arranging for rooms, adapting or developing the master schedule so that targeted individuals can participate, informing administrators and teachers of the program goals and obtaining their cooperation, and securing the cooperation of resource persons such as librarians, speakers and presenters, media coordinators, and custodians—all of whom are vital to the success of the program. Pursuing the example just presented, the counselor might ask the teacher to have the students engage in reading and writing assignments related to the guidance unit. For example, they might be encouraged to write in journals about preassigned topics that coincide with objectives for the guidance unit (Fall, 1994).

Instructing. The term *instructing* as used here refers to behaviors through which people who assume the instructor's role in prevention programming engage in the direct or indirect imparting of information to members of the group. Different forms of direct instructing occur in prevention-programming situations. Lecturing, explaining, and reading are prominent examples. Video, audio, film, and graphic media are indirect methods to impart information, as are printed and computer-generated materials. Providing information is an important component of prevention programming, and counselors will be challenged to do this in ways that are interesting and motivating. It seems as if it is as important to prevention programming for counselors to lecture, explain, and read to audiences interestingly as it is for them to listen empathically and to respond facilitatively during counseling interventions. It seems as if it is equally important for counselors to select and prepare media aids and handout materials that are interesting and motivating. Experience indicates that successful instructing leads to a mutually facilitative relationship between the leader and the members of a group, just as successful basic communicating leads to a facilitative counseling relationship. In both instances, acquisition of a facilitative relationship is the foundation for achieving goals successfully.

Demonstrating.   Guidance curriculum programs often focus on teaching such skills as communicating with other people more proficiently, making rational decisions, and asserting oneself. In these instances, counselors are challenged to demonstrate the skills adequately. The process is social modeling (Bandura & Jeffery, 1973). Models can be living people, or they can be symbolic—people in films or videos. Counselors may serve as models themselves, select and train others to serve as models, or develop or locate appropriate symbolic models to provide adequate demonstrations. In addition, counselors will benefit from being familiar with research on modeling to enhance the effectiveness of their demonstrations.

For example, effects are enhanced when there is a similarity between the model and the participants—a model who is coping well, though not perfectly, may be more effective than one who has mastered the skills. Repeated demonstrations are often necessary (Cormier & Cormier, 1998). For example, a counselor might help a teacher by demonstrating how to interact with students when trying to get them to work cooperatively in a group. If the counselor is viewed as a competent, coping model, the probability of helping the teacher is enhanced. Achieving the goal occurs through communicating to the teacher that the counselor is not perfect and does not expect the teacher to be perfect but is performing to the best of his or her ability and appears to the teacher to be providing useful suggestions. Successful demonstrating sets the stage for participants to rehearse the skills. As participants rehearse or practice, counselors direct.

Directing.   Several important behaviors are associated with directing. While helping participants acquire the desired skills, counselors may coach them through the steps and repetitions, provide encouragement, give accurate and useful feedback, determine helpful homework assignments, and discern when the participants have achieved a desirable level of skill or have gone as far as they can to achieve the targeted objectives. Coaching involves instructing and providing cues that help participants determine how they are doing or what to do next. Coaching may be manifested through recommending repeated practices, altering the time devoted to practicing, arranging and rearranging the sequence of practice activities, or offering verbal or physical support (Cormier & Cormier, 1998).

Encouraging is best done via applications of learning principles such as positive reinforcement, withdrawal of reinforcement, and time-outs. Feedback provides participants information about the quality of their rehearsing efforts. Counselors contribute by providing feedback that helps participants recognize what is desirable and undesirable about their efforts. When offering prevention programs, it is important to dispense feedback judiciously and with as much care and empathy as is provided when engaging in counseling interventions. Keeping up to date on research about feedback is as important as it is for modeling. For example, participants may have opportunities to assess their own performances, verbal assessment may be supplemented with objective assessment, and verbal feedback may contain encouragement and suggestions for improvement (Cormier & Cormier, 1998).

Appropriate homework assignments can help participants acquire the desired skills and knowledge and lay the foundation for developing desirable ideas. Helpful homework also lays the foundation for transfer-of-training. Counselors can give assignments to teachers (indirect delivery), and teachers or counselors can give assignments to the student participants (direct delivery). Counselors might ask teachers to practice in front of a mirror at home, reading information about leading small, structured groups, and instructing and encouraging students to work cooperatively. Teachers and counselors can ask students who are to be working cooperatively on an activity to distribute components of the activity among themselves voluntarily and set a date for each to have the assigned component ready for sharing and for integrating the components into one joint endeavor. The assignments help the participants engage in constructive, goal-directed activities that, if accomplished successfully, provide evidence that the participants have achieved skills commensurate with the goals of the project.

To be effective at giving homework assignments, counselors may need to explain the purpose and to inform participants about what they are to do, where it is to occur, how often it is to occur, and how it is to be recorded (Cormier & Cormier, 1998). At some time during the rehearsal and homework cycle, counselors will probably need to decide whether participants are achieving targeted levels of accomplishment. If the decision is affirmative, counselors can focus on transfer of training, closure, and evaluation. If the decision is negative, they can determine whether the best alternative is to recycle the participant(s) or to end the training. To make these decisions, counselors will be challenged to assess, to diagnose, and to make rational decisions. In so doing, counselors may find it necessary to apply all the basic and challenging counseling skills as carefully as they do when engaging in counseling interventions.

Transferring

The ultimate goal of prevention programming is transfer or generalization of training to one's natural environment. Goals, training activities, and homework assignments serve us best when they reflect a plan to help participants apply what is being taught to the real world. Procedures for achieving this transfer of training have been identified and discussed previously.

Evaluating

Assessing the effects of all counseling functions is important, and a full chapter in this text is devoted to evaluation and accountability. Here, suffice it to say that evaluating is among the requisite prevention programming skills. In chapter 13, philosophy and method are discussed, along with the importance of determining (a) whether prevention programming objectives have been met, (b) the opinions of influential people concerning prevention programs, and (c) the cost-effectiveness of those programs.

EXAMPLES OF PREVENTION PROGRAMMING

In this section we present information about prevention programs that have or could be developed. The first group is presented in an abbreviated fashion to add more breadth to this presentation while responding to the contingencies associated with having limited space with which to work. Additional details about the program content and effects are available in the reports cited in the presentation and listed in the references for this chapter.

A second group of programs is presented more comprehensively, each with its own heading. We did this because the problems to be prevented and the areas of human development to be enhanced seem very important in these times.

Overview of Sample Programs

Recognized nationally as an exemplary model, the *Primary Mental Health Project (PMHP)* has spawned related programs in New York and California (Deutsch, 1996). The Los Angeles (California) version, known as the *Primary Prevention Intervention Program (PIP)*, focuses on early identification and prevention of school adjustment difficulties. PIP is a school-based program that engages in systematic screening in kindergarten through third grade, employs trained paraprofessionals supervised by counselors and other mental health professionals, and emphasizes cooperation with local mental health entities. Counselors serve as trainers, consultants, and coordinators. A multimodal individual curriculum programming approach is used to achieve the program's goals.

The *Parent-Teen Empathy Enhancement Process (P-TEEP)* focuses on stimulating healthy communications among teenagers and their parents (Hawes, 1996). A format of ice breaking, group cohesion formation, interpersonal communication skills enhancement, and learning to discuss important issues with one's parent or teenager is used with groups of volunteers who are either parents or teenagers.

The *School Families Project* is a program designed to help middle-school students develop problem-solving skills, decision-making skills, and other life skills without distracting teachers and students from daily school activities (Lawson, McClain, Matlock-Hetzel, Duffy, & Urbanovski, 1997). *School Families* consists of one teacher, 20 to 25 students, and four to six community volunteers who meet for 45 minutes, 1 day per week during the school's activity period to engage in group mentoring via a primary prevention perspective.

Berube and Berube (1997) present a plan for offering a menu of small-group activities in an elementary school served by only one counselor. Following a needs assessment and recruitment of assistance from community resources, the counselor provided a menu that contained leadership training, peer mediation, My Future (career education goals), Special Study Hall (enhanced study environment), Lunch With the Principal (experience her as approachable), Lunch Bunch (forum for discussions with the counselor), a friendship group, Peer Buddies (help special education students interact with peers), Children of Alcoholics (coping focus), and Rainbow Groups (coping with loss).

Two high-school counselors met with 9th- through-12th-grade girls once per week for 8 weeks to help participants avoid abusive relationships and understand the effect of such relationships on self-esteem and decision making (Becky & Farren, 1997). Specific sessions focused on providing information about the context of abuse, offering warning signs and risk factors, helping participants understand and prevent date rape, managing conflict, and building interpersonal communication skills.

The *Kwanzaa Group* was established for male African American sixth graders who were underachieving academically and having difficulty controlling their classroom behavior. Participants are taught the seven Kwanzaa principles to instill a positive sense of self and achievement in a Eurocentric education system (Bass & Coleman, 1997). The program is conducted in two phases over a school year. In the first phase, participants are exposed to positive images of the African American culture to facilitate trust in Afrocentric principles. In the second phase, the rites of passage from learning about Kwanzaa principles to applying them are emphasized.

According to Green and Keys (2001), the American Psychological Association offers a database of reviews of preventive interventions. It is called Prevention Connection: Promoting Strength, Resilience, and Health in Children, Adults and Families (http://www.oslc.org/spr/apa/home.html).

Helping Students to Become Self-Regulated Learners

A schematic for helping students to become self-regulated, successful learners is offered by Lapan, Kardash, and Turner (2002). Self-regulated learning is "an active, constructive process whereby learners set goals for their learning and then attempt to monitor, regulate, and control their cognition, motivation, and behavior" (Pintrich, 2000). Self-regulated learners can control planning, performing, and completing stages of the learning process and focus on mastering tasks, improving skills, and understanding information. They also use a variety of strategies and tend to attribute poor performance to ineffective strategies rather than inability.

Lapan et al. (2002) elaborate on the value of helping students to become more engaged in academics, especially in consideration of national initiatives to help all students to be successful learners. Their presentation covers the importance of many of the competencies in a balanced program. In this chapter, we focus on their suggestions that can be translated into prevention programming.

The information presented by Lapan et al. (2002) suggests that school counselors could develop and initiate proactive prevention programs designed to help any student become a self-regulated learner. They offer the following categories of learning strategies that are known to enhance academic performance. The goals of a prevention program would be to teach students these effective learning strategies and to motivate them to use the strategies. The strategies are the ability to: (a) separate important from nonessential information, (b) identify main ideas, (c) relate new information to prior knowledge, (d) take effective notes, (e) organize information into useful subsets, (e) monitor whether information is truly understood, and (f) construct internal images that represent the meaning of information studied.

The following tactics for teaching effective learning strategies, recommended by Lapan et al. (2002), could be melded into a prevention program: (a) explain the effective learning strategy to the participants, (b) model/demonstrate the strategy while sharing thoughts aloud, (c) have participants practice the strategy continuously on several important learning tasks, (d) use both covert (e.g., mental imagery) and overt (e.g., physical performance) rehearsals, (e) have students practice with their peers, (f) help participants learn ways to monitor and evaluate their own performance,(g) help students realize concrete benefits of using the strategies, and (h) involve participants in the process of modifying and constructing new strategies.

Teaching Coping Skills

Teaching children and adolescents how to cope successfully with life's various stressors may prepare them for such events in advance of occurrences (primary prevention) or help them manage challenges that are already influencing their lives (secondary prevention). For example, Hains (1992, 1994) reports on the effectiveness of teaching youths to recognize, monitor, and alter stress-arousing or anxiety-provoking thoughts. Romano, Miller, and Nordness (1996) describe a stress management and student well-being curriculum for elementary-school students that consists of six 45-minute lessons integrated into the fifth- and sixth-grade curriculums, including the importance of physical exercise, good nutrition, focusing and identifying feelings and expressing them positively, communicating well with one's parents, and learning problem-solving skills. Some components of the program engage their parents as well. Deffenbacher, Lynch, Oetting, and Kemper (1996) found that teaching sixth-through-eighth-grade students with high anger thresholds to identify anger-provoking situations, acquire specific relaxation skills, and learn how their thoughts influence anger led to increased control of their expressions of anger. The sequential training includes learning how to calm down while visualizing anger-provoking situations and replacing the anger-producing thoughts with controlling thoughts that are more calming. Shechtman (2001) demonstrated that prevention goals may be achieved in small groups as well as in large-group interventions. She reported being able to reduce aggressive behaviors and enhance social skills of young children via a small counseling group intervention.

An example of a coping skills training program is found in Kiselica, Baker, Thomas, and Reedy (1994). Participants in the program were ninth graders enrolled in a guidance class in a rural high school. They met once per week during 60-minute sessions for 8 weeks. The program combines elements of Meichenbaum and Deffenbacher's (1988) stress inoculation training, assertiveness training (Galassi & Galassi, 1977), and progressive muscle relaxation (Bernstein & Borkovec, 1973).

After receiving instruction about stress, stressors, anxiety, and anxiety-related symptoms, participants generate examples of their own anxiety-provoking experiences. Next, participants are taught progressive muscle relaxation through a series of exercises, learning how to transfer the skills to in vivo situations. Then, participants are taught to elicit the relaxation response by repeating a cue word during anxiety-provoking situations. The following step is to teach participants how to identify negative thoughts that lead to self-defeating behaviors and replace them with self-improving thoughts, learning how the process (cognitive-restructuring) works. This process is combined with progressive muscle relaxation in practice sessions and in vivo homework. Following discussion of the importance of appropriate assertiveness, participants engage in simulations designed to enhance their assertiveness skills.

Combining cognitive restructuring with progressive muscle relaxation and assertiveness training approaches coping with anxiety arousal from a multimodal perspective. Because the school environment is a source of many anxiety-arousing experiences for children and adolescents, stress-inoculation training holds promise for providing coping skills that can be learned and generalized to the real world via proactive primary and secondary prevention programming (Baker, 2001).

Prejudice Prevention

Ponterotto and Pedersen (1993) believe that adolescents, because they are learning to depend on their cognitive skills and are becoming more comfortable with abstract thinking, are at a stage when prejudice prevention may be developmentally appropriate. Concluding that prejudice is caused by stereotypical beliefs that become more important than real people, Ponterotto and Pedersen recommend several exercises designed to increase awareness of ethnic, racial, and cultural identity. An example is the Label Game, the objective of which is to discover what others believe about each individual participant.

The steps in this exercise are (a) prepare a set of labels containing positive adjectives (e.g., friendly, generous, helpful) and attach one to the forehead or back of each participant so that the label cannot be seen by its wearer; (b) have participants mingle while discussing a topic of interest without any additional structure; (c) instruct participants to treat each individual in a manner that reflects the label he or she is wearing; (d) instruct participants not to inform each other about the content of the labels; and (e) instruct each participant to attempt to guess his or her own label before it is removed.

Debriefing includes asking the participants to share with each other how they used feedback from interacting with others to figure out the content of their own labels. They also discuss how it feels to be labeled and treated as if the label were accurate. Components of the exercise are used to introduce such concepts as stereotyping, prejudice, and communication barriers. It is hoped that participants become aware that we do label each other, that there are differences important to each person's identity, and that the differences are not always bad: Diversity is an important reality.

The remaining components of the program are designed to help participants engage in meaningful and enjoyable activities that lead to processing important information related to prejudice prevention.

Conflict Resolution

An important response to widespread concern about violence in the schools has been the development and implementation of conflict resolution programming. Attempts to implement conflict resolution programming vary from individual programs to those integrated into the core curriculum of a school system.

Carruthers, Carruthers, Day-Vines, Bostick, and Watson (1996) describe the core conflict resolution curriculum in the Wake County, North Carolina, public schools. The goals are to (a) help make the schools orderly and peaceful, (b) use conflict as an instructional tool, (c) teach participants to generalize what they have learned to future interpersonal interactions, and (d) reinforce the core curriculum goals and objectives.

This curriculum has a developmental overlay in which the focus shifts across grade levels to make units relevant to students at different grade levels (e.g., greater emphasis on interpersonal relations in the early grades, conflict resolution in the upper elementary grades, conflict at the middle-school level, violence in the high school). Examples of four objectives recommended for specific subjects in the curriculum are as follows:

- *Kindergarten:* The student will dramatize the appropriate behavior when confronted with various warning signs, sounds, and symbols (subject: health living).
- *Second grade:* The student will demonstrate the ability to infer (subject: science).
- *Fourth grade:* The student will propose alternatives to impulsive behavior (subject: healthful living).
- *Seventh grade:* The student will exercise social and interpersonal persuasion (subject: healthful living).

Carruthers et al. provide an inventory of instructional units, goals, and objectives in the appendix to their article.

One popular form of conflict resolution is *peer mediation,* which can be provided as a total school program, as an elective course, or by training selected mediators (Lupton-Smith, Carruthers, Flythe, Goettee, & Modest, 1996). Lupton-Smith et al. describe three peer mediation programs, one of which is in a middle school with the in-school suspension coordinator serving as the program coordinator. In the preliminary stage, a core group of school staff members are trained, and the entire staff agrees to refer conflicts between students to mediation before treating them as discipline problems. All sixth graders receive 10 days of conflict resolution instruction in their health classes and are informed about the function of peer mediation in their schools via mini-assemblies. Parents are informed at an open house. Selected student mediators receive 20 hours of training that focuses on (a) engaging in self-introspection, (b) considering how to deal with conflict, (c) learning how to use active listening skills in the mediation process, and (d) practicing in simulated sessions. Time is set aside for peer mediation sessions each day in a 30-minute period after lunch known as *teen development time.* Mediation sessions take place in a room adjacent to the coordinator's office with the door between the two rooms left open. Further details and a summary of the mediation steps are found in Lupton-Smith et al. (1996).

The importance of recruiting and selecting a diverse set of peer mediators is highlighted by Day-Vines, Day-Hariston, Carruthers, Wall, and Lupton-Smith (1996). They propose that, rather than be represented proportionally, all segments of the school's population should be represented equally.

Comprehensive Developmental Guidance

Considerably broader in perspective than the programs just covered, comprehensive developmental guidance programs, as perceived by Gysbers and Henderson (2000), are integrated into the school's curriculum. Primary characteristics of these programs are as follows: They (a) are similar to other programs in education (focused on student outcomes, have activities designed to help students achieve the outcomes, are facilitated by professionally recognized personnel, use curriculum-enhancing resources, and employ student evaluation), (b) are based on developmental principles, (c) represent a full range of guidance services (e.g., assessment, referral, placement, consultation), and (d) involve all school staff members.

The underlying theme or theoretical perspective of the guidance curriculum is *life career development.* "Life career development is defined as self-development over the life span through the integration of the roles, settings, and events in a person's life" (Gysbers & Henderson, 2000, p. 62). Four domains of human growth and development are emphasized in life career development: (a) self-knowledge and interpersonal skills; (b) life roles, settings, and events; (c) life career planning; and (d) basic studies and occupational preparation. The major delivery systems are the school counseling and instructional programs.

Prevention programming is an essential ingredient in comprehensive developmental guidance whether in the school counseling or the instructional program of a school, school district, or state school system. A concrete example, taken from Gysbers and Henderson (2000), is the following curriculum goals for a school district: Students will (a) understand and respect themselves and others; (b) behave responsibly in the school, family, and community; (c) develop decision-making skills; (d) use their educational opportunities well; (e) communicate effectively; and (f) plan and prepare for personally satisfying and socially useful lives. These goals will generate competencies that, in turn, generate educational strategies and materials to support them. For the goal "develop decision-making skills," the recommended competencies are (a) making wise choices, (b) managing change successfully, and (c) solving problems. Subcompetencies for "making wise choices" are (a) awareness of how decisions are made, (b) exploration of use of the process, and (c) implementation of the decision-making process.

More than as a method of implementing the prevention programming concept, Gysbers and Henderson (2000) view their idea as a way to reconceptualize school guidance and reform education. Sink and MacDonald (1999) report that, by 1997, 24 states had plans and 17 others had them in a developmental stage. Not all of them are replicas of the Gysbers and Henderson model. They do, however, represent the basic ideas just presented.

A Model Substance Abuse Prevention Program

Swisher, Bechtel, Henry, Vicary, and Smith (2001) describe a substance abuse prevention program that may be integrated into school curriculums under the leadership of school counselors. Adoption of Drug Abuse Training (Project ADAPT) is an initiative funded by the National Institute for Drug Abuse that was instituted and evaluated over a 5-year period prior to publication by Swisher et al. (2001). Project ADAPT employs Botvin's (1998) Life Skills Training concept by helping teachers to integrate targeted skills, concepts, and content into their subject matter curriculums. Because teachers are to be involved actively in the design and delivery of this programming, school counselors are viewed as excellent sources of consultation, modeling, and coaching. For example, Botvin's program includes such activities as group discussions, role-plays, and hands-on activities. School counselors may also contribute by helping teachers find and use developmentally appropriate teaching aids, recruiting capable teachers, and assessing the effects of program implementation. Project ADAPT staff members reported that participating teachers displayed a considerable amount of creativity and initiative.

The goals of Botvin's program are that student participants will: (a) learn to resist social pressure to use alcohol, tobacco, and other drugs; (b) develop an enhanced sense of self-direction; (c) be better able to cope with anxiety; (d) acquire improved decision-making skills; (e) improve their basic communication and social skills; (f) acquire increased knowledge about the risks associated with using alcohol, tobacco, and other drugs; and (g) develop healthy beliefs and attitudes consistent with avoiding substance abuse. Swisher et al. (2001) present a sample lesson plan matrix from a rural middle school that implemented the program. It indicates how specific life skills training components such as decision making, coping with anxiety, and assertiveness are infused/integrated into various curriculums. For example, decision making was approached in geography via a travel exercise in which routes had to be chosen on a map. In earth science, the students considered the pros and cons of space travel. They were taught the steps in personal decision making in a personal development course.

PREVENTION PROGRAMMING IN THE WAKE COUNTY ESSENTIAL GUIDANCE PROGRAM

In the balanced Wake County Essential Guidance Program, a component is designed to serve all students through prevention programming. Identified as "Topics to Be Developed in Classroom Guidance," the component is presented as follows:

Kindergarten
- How to Be Successful in School (two sessions)

First Grade
- How to Be Successful in School (two sessions)
- Cooperation: Working in Groups (two to four sessions)

Second Grade
- How to Be Successful in School (two sessions)
- Feelings and Emotions (two to four sessions)

Third Grade
- How to Be Successful in School (two sessions)
- What Is a Friend? (two to four sessions)

Fourth Grade
- How to Be Successful in School (two sessions)
- Safety and Preventing Abuse; Substance Abuse Prevention (two to four sessions)

Fifth Grade
- How to Be Successful in School (two sessions)
- Human Growth and Development (two to four sessions)
- Transition to Sixth Grade (two to four sessions)

Sixth Grade
- How to Be Successful in Middle School (two to four sessions)
- Getting Along With Peers and Adults; Getting Connected to Middle School

Seventh Grade
- How to Be Successful in Middle School (two to five sessions)
- Personal Success: Looking at My Interests; Talents; Attitudes; Family Changes; Stress; Assertiveness

Eighth Grade
- How to Be Successful in Middle School (two to four sessions)
- Four-Year Plan; Career/Interest Inventory; Decision Making; College Admissions Requirements

Ninth Grade
- How to Be Successful in High School (two or three sessions)
- Understanding High-School Climate; Relating to Teachers; Study Skills

Tenth Grade
- How to Be Successful in High School (two or three sessions)
- Emphasis on Preliminary Scholastic Aptitude Test; Postsecondary Career Information; Managing Academic and Social Stress

Eleventh Grade
- How to Be Successful in High School (two to four sessions)
- Emphasis on Decision Making; College and Career Planning; Résumé Writing; Interviewing

Twelfth Grade
- How to Be Successful (one session)
- Orientation to Postsecondary/Career Planning

PREVENTION PROGRAMMING IN THE WAYNESBORO *COMPREHENSIVE GUIDANCE PLAN*

The Waynesboro plan is modeled after the comprehensive guidance idea generated by Gysbers and Henderson (2000) cited earlier. A broad range of student activities, assignments of professionals responsible for implementation, and evaluation strategies are listed across goals for students ranging from kindergarten to 12th grade. For example, the goals for kindergarten are: Students will (a) make a positive transition from home to school, (b) demonstrate appreciation of self, (c) make friends, and (d) learn how to interact appropriately with other children.

PREVENTION PROGRAMMING TO ACHIEVE PREVENTION AND DEVELOPMENTAL GOALS: THE CHALLENGE

In a survey of elementary-, middle-, and high-school counselors selected randomly from the membership of the American School Counselor Association, Bowman (1987) posed several important questions about the state of "small group guidance and counseling" in basic education. He found that counselors at all levels agree that these are important functions, although high-school counselors find them less practical. A variety of topics such as decision making, communication skills and peer helping, self-concept, study skills, career, behavior, and family were identified as having been presented across grade levels with different emphases because of developmental needs. Finding time to engage in prevention programming, coping with resistance from others, and feeling competent in a pedagogical domain were the three categories in which the majority of respondents' professed problems occurred.

It seems clear that counselor education programs face a challenge: helping graduates learn about prevention programming and how to implement prevention programs. School counselors are challenged to know how to plan, deliver, and evaluate such programs; they also will benefit from ideas for coping with the practical challenges of competition for time and space, resistance, and ignorance that are associated with working in school systems. For instance, creative counselors, when attempting to resolve the time challenge, use lunch break groups, form groups of students attending the same study halls, make their groups an option during general activity periods, alternate class periods on a weekly basis to prevent participants from missing the same class every week, and cooperate with teachers to make their prevention programming ideas units in the teachers' classes. Just as it is important to incorporate evidence of students' acquisition of counseling competence as a goal of practicum and internship experiences, it is also important to incorporate evidence of prevention programming competence.

SUGGESTED ACTIVITIES

1. Take an inventory of prevention programming experiences and competencies you already possess. What additional competencies do you need to be more proficient at prevention programming? Why?
2. Debate one theme of this chapter—for example, prevention programming competence is equally as important in school counseling as is counseling competence.
3. Analyze, discuss, and/or debate the following statement: School counselors need not have been classroom teachers to offer prevention programming successfully.
4. Develop a set of lesson plans for a real or imaginary prevention program.
5. Prepare a document explaining how a counselor might convince parents or administrators that prevention programming is a valid school counseling function.
6. Make an inventory of ideas from the section "Examples of Prevention Programming" that are most appealing to you. What are your reasons for selecting these ideas?
7. Go to the following Internet site: www.scan21st.com. Identify and discuss the challenges of prevention programming on the Internet.

REFERENCES

Adelman, H. S., & Taylor, L. (2002). School counselors and school reform: New directions. *Professional School Counseling, 5,* 235–248.

American School Counselor Association. (1979, April 1). A new look at developmental guidance. *ASCA Counselor, 16,* 2–3, 11–12.

American School Counselor Association. (n.d.). *Guide to membership resources.* Alexandria, VA: Author.

Baker, S. B. (2001). Coping skills training for adolescents: Applying cognitive behavioral principles to psychoeducational groups. *Journal for Specialists in Group Work, 26,* 219–227.

Bandura, A., & Jeffery, R. W. (1973). Roles of symbolic coding and rehearsal processes in observational learning. *Journal of Personality and Social Psychology, 26,* 122–130.

Bass, C. K., & Coleman, H. L. K. (1997). Enhancing the cultural identity of early adolescent male African Americans. *Professional School Counseling, 1*(2), 48–51.

Becky, D., & Farren, P. M. (1997). Teaching students how to understand and avoid abusive relationships. *School Counselor, 44,* 303–308.

Bernstein, D. A., & Borkovec, T. D. (1973). *Progressive relaxation training.* Champaign, IL: Research Press.

Berube, E., & Berube, L. (1997). Offering a menu of small-group opportunities in response to students' expressed needs by drawing on school and community resources. *School Counselor, 44,* 294–302.

Botvin, G. J. (1998). *Life Skills Training: Promoting health and personal development.* Princeton, NJ: Princeton Health Press.

Bowers, J., Hatch, T., & Schwallie-Giddis, P. (2001, September–October). The brain storm. *ASCA Counselor,* 17–18.

Bowman, R. P. (1987). Small-group guidance and counseling in schools: A national survey of counselors. *School Counselor, 34,* 250–262.

Carruthers, W. L., Carruthers, B. J. B., Day-Vines, N. L., Bostick, D., & Watson, D. C. (1996). Conflict resolution as a curriculum: A definition, description, and process for integration in core curricula. *School Counselor, 43,* 345–373.

Casas, J. M., & Furlong, M. J. (1994). School counselors as advocates for increased Hispanic participation in schools. In P. Pedersen & J. C. Carey (Eds.), *Multicultural counseling in schools* (pp. 121–156). Boston: Allyn & Bacon.

Cormier, S., & Cormier, B. (1998). *Interviewing strategies for helpers: Fundamental skills and cognitive-behavioral interventions* (4th ed.). Pacific Grove, CA: Brooks/Cole.

Dagley, J. C. (1987). A new look at developmental guidance: The hearthstone of school counseling. *School Counselor, 35,* 102–109.

Day-Vines, N. L., Day-Hariston, B. O., Carruthers, W. L., Wall, J. A., & Lupton-Smith, H. (1996). Conflict resolution: The value of diversity in the recruitment, selection, and training of peer mediators. *School Counselor, 43,* 392–410.

Deffenbacher, J. L., Lynch, R. S., Oetting, E. R., & Kemper, C. C. (1996). Anger reduction in early adolescents. *Journal of Counseling Psychology, 43,* 149–157.

Deutsch, J. (1996). Primary intervention program makes a big difference for the ordinary kid. *ASCA Counselor, 34*(2), 15–16.

Fall, M. (1994). Developing curriculum expertise: A helpful tool for school counselors. *School Counselor, 42,* 92–99.

Galassi, M. D., & Galassi, J. P. (1977). *Assert yourself! How to be your own person.* New York: Human Sciences Press.

Galvin, M. (1983). Making systematic problem solving work with children. *School Counselor, 31,* 130–136.

Gerler, E. R., Jr., & Anderson, R. F. (1986). The effects of classroom guidance on success in school. *Journal of Counseling & Development, 65,* 78–81.

Gerler, E. R., Jr., & Herndon, E. Y. (2001). Expanding the developmental school counseling paradigm. *Professional School Counseling,* 84–95.

Green, A., & Keys, S. (2001). Learning how to succeed academically in middle school. *Elementary School Guidance and Counseling, 27,* 186–197.

Gysbers, N. C., & Henderson, P. (2000). *Developing and managing your school guidance program* (3rd ed.). Alexandria, VA: American Counseling Association.

Gysbers, N. C., & Henderson, P. (2001). Comprehensive guidance and counseling programs: A rich history and a bright future. *Professional School Counseling, 4,* 246–256.

Hains, A. A. (1992). Comparison of cognitive-behavioral stress management techniques with adolescent boys. *Journal of Counseling & Development, 70,* 600–605.

Hains, A. A. (1994). The effectiveness of a school-based, cognitive-behavioral stress management program with adolescents reporting high and low levels of emotional arousal. *School Counselor, 42,* 114–125.

Hawes, D. J. (1996). Who knows who best? A program to stimulate parent-teen interaction. *School Counselor, 44,* 115–121.

House, R. M., & Hayes, R. L. (2002). School counselors: Becoming key players in school reform. *Professional School Counseling, 5,* 249–256.

Ivey, A. E. (1986). *Intentional interviewing and counseling: Facilitating client development* (2nd ed.). Belmont, CA: Wadsworth.

Kiselica, M. S., Baker, S. B., Thomas, R. N., & Reedy, S. (1994). Effects of stress inoculation training on anxiety, stress, and academic performance among adolescents. *Journal of Counseling Psychology, 41,* 335–342.

Lapan, R. T., Gysbers, N. C., Hughey, K. F., & Arni, T. J. (1993). Evaluating a guidance and language arts unit for high school juniors. *Journal of Counseling & Development, 71,* 444–451.

Lapan, R. T., Gysbers, N. C., & Petroski, G. F. (2001). Helping seventh graders be safe and successful: A statewide study of the impact of comprehensive guidance and counseling programs. *Journal of Counseling & Development, 79,* 320–330.

Lapan, R. T., Kardash, C. M., & Turner, S. (2002). Empowering students to become self-regulated learners. *Professional School Counseling, 5,* 257–265.

Lawson, D. M., McClain, A. L., Matlock-Hetzel, S., Duffy, M., & Urbanovski, R. (1997). School families: Implementation and evaluation of a middle school prevention program. *Journal of Counseling & Development, 76,* 82–89.

Lee, R. S. (1993). Effects of classroom guidance on student achievement. *Elementary School Guidance and Counseling, 27,* 163–171.

Locke, D. C., & Faubert, M. (1993). Getting on the right track: A program for African American high school students. *School Counselor, 41,* 129–133.

Lupton-Smith, H., Carruthers, W. L., Flythe, R., Goettee, E., & Modest, K. H. (1996). Conflict resolution as peer mediation: Programs for elementary, middle, and high school students. *School Counselor, 43,* 149–157.

Mehaffey J. I., & Sandberg, S. K. (1992). Conducting social skills training groups with elementary schoolchildren. *School Counselor, 40,* 61–67.

Meichenbaum, D. H., & Deffenbacher, J. L. (1988). Stress inoculation training. *Counseling Psychologist, 16,* 69–89.

Merriam-Webster's collegiate dictionary (10th ed.). (1998). Springfield, MA: Merriam-Webster.

Morgan, C., & Jackson, W. (1980). Guidance as a curriculum. *Elementary School Guidance and Counseling, 15,* 99–103.

Omizo, M. M., & D'Andrea, M. (1995). Multicultural classroom guidance. In C. C. Lee (Ed.), *Counseling for diversity: A guide for school counselors and related professionals* (pp. 143–158). Boston: Allyn & Bacon.

Omizo, M. M., & Omizo, S. A. (1987). The effects of eliminating self-defeating behavior of learning-disabled children through group counseling. *School Counselor, 34,* 282–288.

Ponterotto, J. G., & Pedersen, P. B. (1993). *Preventing prejudice: A guide for counselors and educators.* Newbury Park, CA: Sage.

Romano, J. L., Miller, J. P., & Nordness, A. (1996). Stress and well-being in the elementary school: A classroom curriculum. *School Counselor, 43,* 268–276.

Salzman, M., & D'Andrea, M. (2001). Assessing the impact of a prejudice prevention project. *Journal of Counseling & Development, 79,* 341–346.

Schlossberg, S. M., Morris, J. D., & Lieberman, M. G. (2001). The effects of a counselor-led guidance intervention on students' behaviors and attitudes. *Professional School Counseling, 4,* 156–164.

Shechtman, Z. (2001). Prevention groups for angry and aggressive children. *Journal for Specialists in Group Work, 26,* 228–226.

Sink, C. A., & MacDonald, G. (1999). The status of comprehensive guidance and counseling in the United States. *Professional School Counseling, 2,* 88–94.

Sue, D. W. (1992). The challenge of multiculturalism: The road less traveled. *American Counselor, 1,* 6–14.

Swisher, J. D., Bechtel, L., Henry, K. L., Vicary, J. R., & Smith, E. (2001). A model substance abuse prevention program. In D. C. Locke, J. E. Myers, & E. L. Herr (Eds.), *The handbook of counseling.* Thousand Oaks, CA: Sage.

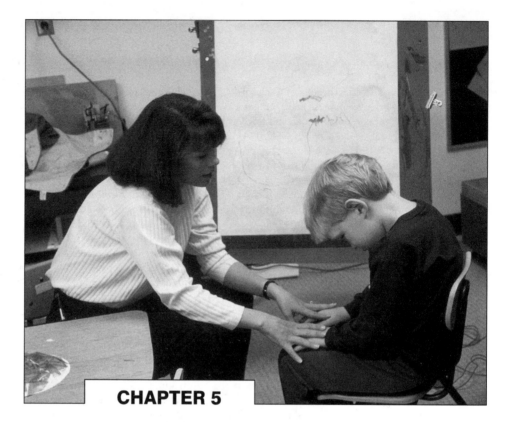

CHAPTER 5

Counseling in Schools

Goals: To provide evidence of the demand for counseling interventions from school counselors; to propose a set of basic competencies for a balanced school counseling program.

The many and varied service demands placed on school counselors is best character-ized in counselors' own words:

> *With so many broken homes and single parent families now, I spend most of my time giving support to kids—support they don't get at home.*

> *When I don't feel like going to work in the morning, I am heartened by remembering the times I've helped a teacher and child get along better, or I've listened to a child talk out some problem at home. These kinds of situations will keep the school counselor's work valuable.*

I think children turn to drugs and alcohol because of peer pressure. We counselors need to channel this pressure in more positive directions.

You'd be surprised at how much time I spend in classroom programs and activities that try to help children learn to cope with human relations problems at home—fighting between parents and arguments between brothers and sisters. I think these problems are timeless.

I've got many parents who are concerned about their children being overweight. I've tried to help these kids without much success. I'd like to see what would happen if I teamed up with some nutrition experts or some physical education specialists in doing some counseling groups for overweight children.

This variety of demands requires skills that are learned through preservice preparation and through on the job experience. This chapter explores some of the demands and the skills required to meet the demands.

DEMAND FOR SCHOOL COUNSELING INTERVENTIONS

The schools are a microcosm of society. Many problems that occur in the greater society also exist in the schools, affecting children and adolescents alike. Current circumstances seem to place more and more responsibility on educators for responding to childhood and adolescent manifestations of society's problems. In some instances, such responsibilities are actually imposed, as was the case with PL 94-142, which mandated that all children with disabilities be accommodated in the mainstream of basic education. Other problems have become the responsibility of the schools simply because they cannot be ignored and, for a variety of reasons, are not successfully treated elsewhere. One way to view this phenomenon is as an imposition, because the primary function of the schools is to impart knowledge. Another way to view the phenomenon, however, is as an inevitability, because the schools as a microcosm of the greater society share responsibility for responding to the problems. Beyond that, it seems illogical to expect the acquisition and use of knowledge to occur for many individuals whose personal and social problems are not treated.

Like the greater society, the schools have experienced varied success in treating personal and social problems. There are many reasons for this, some of which are related to the expertise of the professional staff. Most teachers and principals are not trained to intervene in students' personal and social problems. Specialists in social work, psychology, reading, speech, hearing, and the like are available only part-time. Among the full-time professional staff of the schools, the individuals most likely trained to provide interventions for personal and social problems are school counselors. Support for this position is found in the ethical standards of the American School Counselor Association (ASCA, 1992) under the heading "Responsibilities to Students": "The school counselor is concerned with the total needs of the student (educational, vocational, *personal*, and *social*) [italics added]." Therefore, without debating whether this system is fair, it seems obvious that school counselors will be challenged to prepare to provide counseling interventions.

All three of the initiatives presented in chapter 1 state that counseling is an important function for school counselors. In ASCA's National Model for Comprehensive

School Counseling Programs, counseling is considered a responsive service (Bowers, Hatch, & Schwallie-Giddis, 2001). As a responsive service, counseling is viewed from two perspectives (Gysbers & Henderson, 2001). Individual counseling is part of an individual planning process for which the goals are to help students monitor their career, academic, and personal development. Personal counseling is for students who experience problems with relationships, personal concerns, or normal developmental tasks.

The National School Counselor Training Initiative states that counseling remains an important role for school counselors, especially academic counseling for learning and achievement and supporting student success (House & Hayes, 2002). The School-Community Collaboration Model alludes to counseling as a function in systems for care (i.e., treatment of severe and chronic problems such as emergencies and crises) and systems of early intervention (i.e., responding early after the onset of problems)(Adelman & Taylor, 2002).

The competencies for counseling in schools, as presented in this textbook, lend themselves to preparing school counselors to function successfully in each of the initiatives just cited. School counselors who possess these competencies will be able to provide individual and personal counseling as defined in the ASCA model, academic counseling, crisis counseling, early interventions, and a host of other categories of important counseling services that are not highlighted in the initiatives.

A review of excerpts from recent school counseling literature offers a sample of challenging personal and social problems that manifest themselves in today's schools. They are all potentially within the realm of a school counselor's competence as a counselor.

Personal Problems

The terms *early identification and treatment* and *remedial intervention* were introduced in chapter 2 as classifications of the intervention function in school counseling. The personal problems cited here can require either type of intervention, depending on the degree of maladaptation.

Acting-Out Behaviors.   Children who act out announce by doing so that they have problems. Classrooms are disrupted, and the acting-out children often suffer academically (Hovland, Smaby, & Maddux, 1996; Patton, 1995). Counselors may be able to help discover how the behavior started, determine its purpose, and initiate ideas for managing it (Coffman & Roark, 1992; Hovland et al., 1996; Kann & Hanna, 2000). Group counseling shows promise as a method for helping students manifesting acting-out behaviors (Brantley, Brantley, & Baer-Barkley, 1996; Nelson, Dykeman, Powell, & Petty, 1996).

Underachievement.   Instead of accepting the challenge to perform up to expectations, underachieving students respond to academic challenges with apathy, depression, absenteeism, tardiness, and irresponsibility (Thompson, 1987). Underachievement seems to have many causes. Counselors are in a position to identify underachieving students early and may also be able to find ways to respond to the symptoms and causes of individual cases (Fall & McLeod, 2001; Schnedeker, 1991; Wirth-Bond, Coyne, & Adams, 1991).

Disabilities. The mainstreaming legislation mentioned previously ushered the schools into an era in which the attendance of exceptional students is common. Students trying to cope with physical, social, and emotional disabilities may also present exceptional challenges to the schools in that their personal needs may be more extreme and time-consuming than those of mainstreamed/included students. Counselors may be able to provide a variety of interventions, including person-centered counseling (Williams & Lair, 1991), self-management (Gumaer & Hudspeth, 1985), and career counseling (Humes & Hohenshil, 1985).

Grief. Because they lack experience and their cognitive development is incomplete, children and adolescents often respond to the death of loved ones and contemporaries maladaptively and may manifest inappropriate responses in school. Counselors can apply their knowledge of the grieving process by offering direct coping interventions (Lenhardt, 1997; Moore & Herlihy, 1993; Thompson, 1993) and indirect supportive interventions (Gray, 1988).

Suicide Ideation and Depression. Data indicate that suicide is the third leading cause of death among 11-to-24-year-olds (Malley, Kush, & Bogo, 1994). Therefore, counselors are challenged to be informed well enough to recognize the symptoms of at-risk individuals, determine the degree of severity, keep them alive with immediate interventions, provide needed support, and teach others how to recognize the symptoms (ASCA, 1990; King, Price, Telljohann, & Wahl, 2000; Malley & Kush, 1994; Malley et al., 1994).

Substance Abuse. An increasingly pervasive problem in American society, drug and alcohol abuse is also part of the school culture. In addition to a prevention program such as that highlighted in chapter 4, school counselors are challenged to provide responsive counseling services for those students who have personal problems related to substance abuse. To have any chance of making effective interventions with these at-risk individuals, counselors should know about drugs and the drug culture and be able to provide at least initial counseling services and support for those returning from inpatient treatment (Beauvais & Oetting, 1988; Chandler & Page, 1991). Children of alcoholic parents need support and help; school counselors can offer such assistance through both group and individual counseling interventions (Brake, 1988; Buwick, Martin, & Martin, 1988).

Social Isolation. Some children experience abnormally low frequencies of interaction with peers and low levels of peer acceptance (Nickolai-Mays, 1987). Helping these individuals become more sociable and accepted often requires subtle, well-planned interventions. Counselors can help identify such children, offer a supportive counseling relationship, and identify strategies to help bring about desired changes. Strategies well within the repertoire of any school counselor include providing useful and therapeutic books for the children to read (Nickolai-Mays, 1987) and helping the children express and discuss feelings by creating cartoons cooperatively with their counselors (Sonntag, 1985). Counselors are also able to assist with what is perhaps the most extreme form of social isolation—school phobia—through home and school collaboration (Jenni, 1997).

Help clients explore their problem situations and identify their resources.

Floundering Career Planning.   Most students expect to be employed after completing their schooling. What happens to individuals while in school significantly affects how they view the world of work and prepare themselves for it. Noeth, Engen, and Noeth (1984) reported that many of the 1,200 high-school students in their survey viewed school counselors as not being very helpful in their career planning. The researchers recommend that school counselors provide more direct career counseling. Approaching the same issue from a different perspective, Vondracek and Schulenberg (1986) suggest that counselors invest more time with school-age clients to assess factors that affect career development and provide helpful interventions. Individuals often need special assistance, however, because their needs are not served by group interventions. This may be particularly important at the time the individuals need to make their own educational and vocational decisions (Salamone, 1988).

Social Problems

Dysfunctional Families.   Our society is experiencing an increasing breakdown of the traditional family. In many instances, this results in families being dysfunctional.

Children in dysfunctional families must try to function in school successfully despite the lack of support at home. In fact, the home environment may be the source of problems that manifest themselves in school (Fontes, 2000). Dysfunction in a family may have one or more causes (e.g., divorce, addiction, mental illness, dual working parents, single parent). The symptoms also vary (e.g., running away, abuse, underachievement, social isolation). Counselors are challenged to recognize the symptoms early and to help children and adolescents from dysfunctional homes cope. Traditional strategies include individual counseling interventions, support groups, and peer helping. Beyond these approaches, some suggest that school counselors may need to offer family counseling interventions (Kammer & Schmidt, 1987; Robison, Smaby, & Williams, 1988).

Unwed Pregnant Students and Teenage Fathers. In earlier times, pregnant students were ostracized by the schools. Today, adolescent pregnancy, though certainly not advocated by school personnel, is often accepted, and mothers, prospective mothers, and adolescent fathers are viewed as individuals needing help. Counselors are among the schools' professional staff most likely to learn about individual pregnancies. Pregnant unwed young women and the fathers of their children value support and assistance with coping and planning. Also valued are individualized and group support and coping assistance during pregnancies and on returning to school after the babies are born (Kiselica, 1995; Kiselica & Pfaller, 1993; Thompson, 1984).

Homelessness. School counselors have witnessed increasing numbers of homeless children attending school (Daniels, 1992; Walsh & Buckley, 1994). School counselors occupy a unique position from which they can help these children by providing advocacy services to meet their basic needs and by offering counseling interventions to help them process their circumstances to enhance self-esteem (Daniels, 1992; Walsh & Buckley, 1994).

BASIC INGREDIENTS OF COUNSELING INTERVENTIONS

Point of View

Counseling is essentially a direct service that may be devoted primarily to intervention goals. It is an important function that requires considerable training to learn and develop the requisite skills. It also requires time to acquire the experience necessary for making appropriate decisions during counseling interviews and in case planning. Counseling is at the heart of the intervention function.

The more popular personality and counseling theories on which school counseling is founded were derived from the experiences of psychoanalysts and clinical psychologists (e.g., Sigmund Freud, Alfred Adler, Erik Erikson, Carl Rogers, Albert Ellis) and the research of experimental and social psychologists (e.g., B. F. Skinner, Albert Bandura). These foundations are useful, but counselor educators and school counselors find themselves translating the information, which is devoted to enhancing long-term psychoanalysis and psychotherapy, into appropriate models for short-term counseling of children and adolescents, most of whom are coping with normal developmental issues.

Historically, the fields of psychoanalysis, psychotherapy, and counseling have endured conflict among disciples of various theoretical camps over which approach is superior. Although differences of opinion still exist, time seems to have diffused some of them. The most common response by less invested persons to such disputes has been to advocate an eclectic approach. Supporters of eclecticism are quick to define what it is and is not. *Eclecticism* is a counselor's systematic, studied, and intelligent assimilation of ideas from differing theoretical perspectives into a personal hybrid that is defensible and identifiable. This individual eclectic theory is then adapted to the specific clientele and setting. Eclecticism is not a random set of acts and thoughts drawn from previous life experiences in response to immediate events.

Eclecticism appears to be the appropriate approach for school counseling. Sue (1992) points out that an eclectic approach may also be the path to achieving multicultural competence in one's counseling interventions by becoming culturally flexible:

> In counseling, equal treatment may be discriminatory treatment. And differential treatment is not necessarily preferential. Minority groups want and need equal access and opportunities, which may dictate differential treatment. . . . Counselors must be able to shift their counseling styles to meet not just developmental needs of their clients but also the cultural dimensions. There has to be recognition that no one style of counseling is appropriate for all populations and situations. (p. 14)

In the spirit of Herring's (1997) synergistic model, rather than use counseling interventions universally for all clients, school counselors will make the most appropriate use of the interventions selectively, having taken into account the attributes of individual client characteristics such as ethnicity, environment, culture, and gender. Sue, Ivey, and Pedersen (1996) refer to this as being aware of a *third presence* in counseling relationships: counselor, client, and culture. Readers are encouraged to think about the following hypothetical clients when reading the remainder of this chapter or when identifying their own alternative clients. How would the individual attributes of the following clients influence you in choosing from the menu of basic counseling competencies and strategies and in responding to client resistance or reluctance?

- John is a third-generation Italian American teenager whose close-knit family has recently moved to a metropolitan area of the southeastern United States. The family consists of two parents and six older siblings (three males and three females), all devout Roman Catholics. They own a restaurant, and all the family members work in some way in that business.
- Jennifer is a biracial middle-school student; she has two younger sisters. Her father is African American, and her mother is Asian American (Thai). The family is currently homeless because of a series of misfortunes that caused both parents to lose good jobs. The family is receiving welfare assistance.
- Brianna is a second grader whose mother is an employed single parent. Brianna just transferred to a new school and is having difficulty making friends because she is considered an outsider. Her younger sister has a hearing disability.

- Tomas dropped out of school a year ago because of substance abuse problems. Tomas has returned to school in an effort to graduate and get a diploma. He belongs to a gang whose negative attitudes about his decisions have caused him to be conflicted.

Because this book is intended to be used for training school counselors, the basic ingredients of eclectic school counseling are presented here. It is assumed that school counselors receive training to acquire basic competencies before accepting their first paid counseling positions. What follows, then, are recommended ingredients of the counseling intervention function competencies. It is also assumed that counselors will become lifelong learners after basic training. As lifelong learners, they will surely enhance that basic training through thoughtful analyses of their own counseling experiences, and intelligent applications of information from readings, workshops, conferences, and collegial discussions will enhance the basic competencies.

Foundations

School counselors are challenged to understand several important sets of knowledge to apply basic skills successfully. Such knowledge provides the necessary environment for successful counseling. Therefore, these foundation ingredients are addressed first. The list is presented here in no particular order; other writers may identify additional or different foundations:

- Knowledge about human ego defenses, such as rationalization, denial, and intellectualization
- Awareness that this nation is becoming increasingly pluralistic culturally
- Knowledge of the developmental tasks associated with childhood and adolescence
- Knowledge of changing social attitudes and conditions and economic opportunities
- Awareness that the vast majority of student clients need counselors who will help them overcome deficits and learn ways to cope better
- Self-awareness, leading to self-acceptance and a genuine interest in the welfare of all members of one's clientele

Developmental Perspective

Counseling is a dynamic, continuous process, and counselors are aided by road maps to help them find their way. On the assumption that all counseling has beginnings and endings—sometimes prematurely—a road map serves as a means of deciding what to do next (e.g., when the client's goals have been identified) and analyzing the situation when problems occur (e.g., when engaged in helping the client achieve previously established goals and the client suddenly resists). Several such road maps can be found in the professional literature. They often take the form of a stage-wise paradigm, appearing developmental, which counseling often is, and linear, which counseling often is not. The comment about the nonlinearity of counseling is important and usually is a disclaimer from authors of stage-wise models. One well-known stage-wise model applicable to school counseling was developed by Egan (1998).

Table 5.1

Egan's paradigm.

Stage	Goal
I.	Client's problem situations and unused opportunities are identified and clarified.
II.	Hopes for the future become realistic goals to which the client is committed.
III.	Strategies for reaching goals are devised and implemented.

Source: Data from *The Skilled Helper: A Problem-Management Approach to Helping* (6th ed.), by G. Egan, 1998, Pacific Grove, CA: Brooks/Cole.

Egan's paradigm consists of three stages, which he has subdivided for discussion and increased understanding. Each stage is characterized by goals and related counseling skills. Once familiar with this model or one like it, counselors can use it in making decisions about their own behaviors, analyzing client needs, and assessing progress in counseling relationships. A summary of Egan's paradigm is presented in Table 5.1.

Ivey (1988) presents a developmental idea for assessing client readiness that may be a useful adjunct to stepped counseling process models like Egan's, especially when clients are children and adolescents. Counseling process paradigms such as Egan's are designed to help counselors decide what to do with hypothetical average clients. They are not designed to help counselors respond to different levels of client readiness. Ivey's system, drawn from the work of Jean Piaget, challenges counselors to match their counseling behaviors with client levels of intellectual development. Thus, counselors match their responses to the client's intellectual capacity, knowing full well that capacity may change during development and will differ among clients. For example, an adolescent client may be self-directed when the issues are related to career decision making but preoperational when dealing with parental expectations. Table 5.2 presents a summary of Ivey's system.

Egan's system gives a road map for the counseling process; Ivey's provides one for client development. Together, they present developmental bases on which counselors can make educated decisions during the counseling process and when planning case management strategies. Egan's and Ivey's systems are consistent foundations on which to make decisions. The following hypothetical counseling example illustrates how the Egan and Ivey systems might be merged:

A middle-school counselor is working with a 12-year-old girl whose parents are separated and contemplating a divorce. During Egan's identification and clarification stage of the counseling relationship, the counselor establishes an empathic relationship and learns that the child is very upset about the prospect of her parents getting a divorce and her family breaking up. The counselor assesses the client's response to the problem as being preoperational according to the Ivey paradigm. The client is thinking irrationally and is without any viable alternative ideas for responding to the problem. Eventually realizing that she has little control over her parents' emotions and actions, the child joins the counselor in deciding that she wants to control her fear and depression over the problem—Egan's

Table 5.2
Ivey's levels of client development.

Level	Description
1. Preoperational	Client lacks intentionality; is stuck without alternatives or with limited ones; lacks skills; is unaware of discrepancies; may be irrational. All clients may experience some preoperational thought. (Influencing skills and environmental structuring are recommended.)
2. Concrete Operations	Client possesses some degree of intentionality; understands some incongruities; is often stuck on issues; has skills but is not always able to use them; may understand problem but be unable to operate on it concretely. (Suggests a balance of attending and influencing skills.)
3. Self-Directed Formal Operations	Client has intentionality that is not fully developed; needs a limited amount of assistance; is able to separate self from actions and thoughts. (Recommends attending skills and a limited amount of influencing skills.)
4. Mutual or Dialectic	Client is intentional; able to generate and choose from among alternatives; able to analyze self, own thinking processes, and environmental factors. (Needs support and assistance on specific issues.)

Source: Data from *Intentional Interviewing and Counseling: Facilitating Client Development* (2nd ed.), by A. E. Ivey, 1988, Belmont, CA: Wadsworth.

second stage of setting goals. Thinking that the client has possibly reached the self-directed formal operations stage of the Ivey model, the counselor introduces a strategy designed to teach her to recognize irrational and self-defeating thoughts and to cope with them by herself—Egan's third stage. When the client's response is not successful, the counselor realizes that the girl is more likely at the concrete operations stage than the self-directed formal operations stage of Ivey's paradigm, so the counselor decides to explore and clarify the client's responses to the treatment and her corresponding feelings—returning to Egan's first stage. Renewed exploration leads to validating the original goals—Egan's second stage—and initiating a treatment plan that includes support counseling with coping skills introduced gradually. This seems necessary because the child sometimes misunderstands the purpose of the coping skills; her anxieties sometimes interfere with her ability to do anything constructive. These incongruities require a balance of attending and influencing skills from the counselor because the client seems to be at the concrete operations stage of the Ivey paradigm.

THE NATURE OF SCHOOL COUNSELING INTERVENTIONS

Unlike the classic therapeutic hour that psychotherapists in private practice or counselors in college and university counseling centers set aside for appointments with clients, school counselors engage in a greater variety of counseling interventions, many of which are very brief. In addition, school counselors, because of the press of time or competence limits, are less likely to see student clients for more than one or a few consecutive appointments. Most school counseling interventions are short-term rather than long-term. Some interventions are short-term because the nature of the clients' needs demands nothing else. Others are shortened because a referral is better. More comprehensive information on referrals is provided in chapter 7.

Other factors that impinge on the length of school counseling sessions are (a) the large number of students that each counselor is to serve, (b) little time available for students to see a counselor because of tight academic scheduling, (c) concern about taking students away from their classroom studies for too long, (d) in secondary schools, scheduling periods that are about 40 to 45 minutes in length, and (e) school systems that do not provide activity periods or study halls for students. Faced with having to conduct brief or limited counseling interventions, school counselors are challenged to be efficient. Important to efficiency in brief/limited counseling is being able to establish a working alliance and to determine client goals expeditiously. Equally important is being able to provide the client something of value immediately. Some things of value can be as diverse as feeling understood and receiving something concrete such as valuable information or relief from negative affect (e.g., anxiety). Fortunately, Egan's (1998) helping model and the basic intervention competencies presented in this chapter lend themselves to conducting brief/limited counseling interventions. Being organized from the outset is also important.

BASIC COMPETENCIES FOR COUNSELING INTERVENTIONS

Counselors who have adequate developmental road maps will be able to respond to student clients intentionally. As defined by Ivey (1994),

> Intentionality is acting with a sense of capability and deciding from among a range of alternative actions. The intentional individual has more than one action, thought, or behavior to choose from in responding to changing life situations. The intentional individual can generate alternatives in a given situation and approach a problem from different vantage points, using a variety of skills and personal qualities, *adapting styles to suit different individuals and cultures.* . . . One of the critical issues in interviewing is the fact that the same skills may have different effects on people with different individual and cultural backgrounds. Intentional interviewing requires an awareness that cultural groups each have different patterns of communication. (p. 11)

Intentionality is enhanced when counselors possess a repertoire of appropriate behaviors or responses to changing situations and can choose freely from among these options—the epitome of eclecticism.

The information presented in this section about basic competencies for counseling in schools is offered as an overview for readers who may not yet have taken courses in counseling theories and methods, career counseling and development, assessment, pre-practicum, and practicum—with the caveat that the information is not intended to be a substitute for, or a primer in, the content of these courses. Indeed, the aforementioned courses will cover these topics more substantively with accompanying opportunities to observe counseling demonstrations and to engage in supervised practice with corresponding constructive feedback. Consider the following information as suggestions for good practice with examples inserted for clarification. Readers are encouraged to revisit this information during or after taking the courses in their training program similar to those generic courses just listed.

Identifying and Clarifying Problem Situations and Unused Opportunities

Whether engaged in individual or group counseling, school counselors are challenged to help clients explore their problem situations and identify their resources. Virtually all counselor training programs emphasize the core facilitative conditions of accurate empathy, genuineness, respect, and concreteness (Egan, 1998). Also emphasized is attending to clients physically via facing them squarely, adopting an open posture, leaning forward slightly, maintaining good eye contact, and trying to be relatively relaxed (Egan, 1998). Being able to attend to clients psychologically is equally important. Psychological attending manifests itself through listening carefully and focusing on the core or theme of what is being said and felt and then conveying having done so via verbal responses and physical behaviors. Several basic counseling or interviewing skills have been recommended for accomplishing the goals associated with successfully initiating counseling relationships. These basic skills remain important throughout all stages of counseling relationships. The basic verbal skills are: paraphrasing information, reflecting feelings, clarifying unclear material, summarizing information and feelings, inviting clients to talk, and questioning appropriately. The following example from a simulated counseling session provides examples of the respective basic verbal counseling skills.

An elementary-school student is seated in the office of a school counselor. The counselor smiles at the student client and asks, "How can I help you today?" (open-ended question/invitation to talk)

Client:	I don't like school. No one will play with me, and it's not fun. I hate all of them and wish they would move away. Sometimes I don't want to come to school.
Counselor:	No one will play with you, and school is not fun, (paraphrase) and the way the other children treat you hurts your feelings and makes you unhappy. (reflecting feeling)
Client:	Yes, they hurt my feelings. I wish I could just stay at home. They make me so unhappy that I want to go away.
Counselor:	Please tell me what you mean when you say "I want to go away." (clarifying unclear material)
Client:	Sometimes I feel like running away or moving away or going to my grandmother's house and living there. Then those kids will be sorry for what they did and I can play with someone who is nice.
Counselor:	So, you have thought about running or moving away. (paraphrase) Have you ever run away? (closed question)

Client:	No, I can't do that because I'd miss my mom and dad and it would be scary.

Client continues to identify and clarify her concerns and the counselor must close the interview.

Counselor:	I think we have gotten off to a good start today. You have shared some important information with me about how bad you feel when being rejected by other children, how much you would like to make friends, and how hopeful you are that we can work together to try to help you be happier. (summarizing information and feelings)

During his presentation on March 25, 2002, at the American Counseling Association (ACA) convention, William Glasser referred to the preceding competencies as "making nice" and stated his belief that anyone who cannot make nice does not belong in the counseling profession. He appeared to allude to a belief that the basic counseling skills are necessary for all counselors in every counseling situation.

Hopes for the Future Become Realistic Goals

Through problem clarification and self-exploration, individual clients and counseling group members learn how to present issues. They may also need help in setting goals. Setting goals is challenging and often requires stronger responses from counselors—responses that are more directive and influential than the ones listed previously. Whereas the previous responses focus on helping clients understand their own material better, challenging responses evolve from counselor perceptions and are therefore more direct in their influence. Cormier and Cormier (1998) describe these as *action responses* because they exert such direct influence on clients. For all these reasons, clients may respond in a negative fashion.

Unproductive client responses such as anger, denial, and attacks on the counselor may set the relationship back, cause a stalemate, or lead to client withdrawal from the counseling relationship. Challenging responses, in contrast, may cause clients to acquire insights impossible for clients to achieve by themselves, accept responsibility for their behavior, and change their thoughts or behavior or both constructively. Because challenging responses are so powerful, they are best used sparingly—only when needed—and skillfully. Rather than single behaviors, as are the previously cited skills (e.g., paraphrasing, reflecting, summarizing), the challenging skills are sets of behaviors that are logically combined to achieve specific goals. Important basic challenging skills are interpretation, self-sharing, confrontation, immediacy, information sharing, and goal setting. A common aspect of the challenging skills is to present them tentatively to allow clients to negotiate their responses, rather than be forced to defend themselves. Examples of each follow.

Interpretation.   Also known as *advanced accurate empathy*, interpretation occurs when a counselor challenges a client to think about what is implied rather than stated by the client's words and behaviors. Usually preceded by a paraphrase, reflection, and/or summary of what the client did say, an interpretation is the counselor's

Many children and adolescents are confronted with choices.

hypothesis of what was implied or stated tentatively (e.g., "You decided not to apply at Ivy University. I wonder whether your decision is related to doubts about your ability to succeed in that college."). Successful interpretations evolve from insights acquired by counselors from their clinical experiences and from closely following material presented by the client. When successful, interpretations provide clients either a new view of their material or another explanation for their thoughts and behaviors (Cormier & Cormier, 1998).

Self-Sharing. Also known as *self-disclosure*, self-sharing takes place when counselors share something about themselves with their clients. Usually prompted by a paraphrase, reflection, and/or summary of something about the client, the counselor presents related information and feelings with an attempt to be brief and an invitation for the client to use the information therapeutically (e.g., "You're afraid of flunking out of State University during the first semester and being too embarrassed to face your family. I remember having similar thoughts when trying to decide whether to take this job at Comprehensive High School. I wasn't sure whether the students would accept me, and I had to understand that I might not achieve my goal of working in a high-school counseling center if I wasn't willing to take that risk. There seem to be some similarities between your situation and that one of mine."). Successful self-sharing helps clients learn how to share and discover perspectives they had not considered previously (Egan, 1998). Effectiveness at self-sharing seems to require being selective and not overdoing the sharing by offering material that adds to the client's burden, is too verbose, or causes the roles to shift (i.e., client becomes attentive responder to counselor who is engaging in excessive self-talk).

Confrontation.   Confrontation occurs when counselors point out discrepancies, distortions, and conflicts in clients' messages. Best preceded by a summary of the detected discrepancies or distortion, confrontations contain a tentative description of what the counselor has observed as being discrepant, distorted, or conflicting, along with an invitation to think about the counselor's observations (e.g., "You say that not attending college has something to do with your fear of failure, yet you have been able to complete high school when there were trying times for you here."). Confrontations like this can help clients consider alternative ways to perceive their issues and become more aware of their discrepancies, distortions, and conflicts (Cormier & Cormier, 1998).

Immediacy.   Sometimes referred as *you-and-me talk*, immediacy achieves direct, mutual interactions between counselor and client when the counseling relationship itself is at issue. A counselor's summary of what is interfering with the counseling relationship is followed by a statement of the counselor's feelings about what is happening and the counselor's goals in bringing attention to the situation. The immediacy response concludes with an invitation to the client to participate in negotiating an amicable resolution. For example, a client accuses a middle-class European American counselor of overemphasizing concerns about possible academic difficulties as a college student because the client is African American and from a lower socioeconomic background. The client wonders whether the counselor is discouraging college attendance because of racist intentions. The counselor responds, "You think I believe college will be difficult for you because I am White and you are Black and I am a racist, and that both surprises and hurts me. We seem to be in danger of being at odds with each other because you interpreted my comments in a way I did not intend. I apologize for my part in that, and I want to get us back on the right track. Do you think we can resolve this, and if so, do you have any recommendations?"

Immediacy serves as a means of engaging clients in mutual assessments of problems in the counselor–client relationship that interfere with progress.

Information Sharing.   Information sharing, or giving instances, occurs when clients need information that may challenge them to view circumstances differently. Cormier and Cormier (1998) suggest that information giving can include the sharing of facts about experiences, events, alternatives, or people. Following a summary of the client's understanding of the information in question, the counselor asks whether the client is aware of, and interested in, additional information the counselor possesses. The counselor then shares the information, checking the client's reaction. For example, "You heard that all freshmen at Ivy University must take calculus and an advanced year of foreign language in the first semester. Are you aware that there is an alternative? . . . No? Would you like to know what it is? . . . Incoming freshmen at Ivy University who do not have the background to take calculus or an advanced year of foreign language are allowed to take other courses appropriate to their high-school preparation. How does that affect your thinking?"

Information sharing helps clients identify and evaluate alternatives they were not aware of previously, helps dispel myths they may harbor, and motivates them to examine issues they may have been avoiding (Cormier & Cormier, 1998).

Goal Setting. Understanding that most school counseling clients need help in adjusting or coping, learning new and better ways of behaving and thinking, and overcoming deficits in their environment, counselors may view themselves as participants in the counseling process, helping clients identify and achieve their goals. Goal setting is at the heart of this participatory relationship between counselors and clients, and counselors are challenged to help clients find a sense of direction, as well as share the responsibility for clients achieving their goals (Egan, 1998). Several basic counseling intervention skills are involved in the goal-setting process.

Initially, counselors explain the purpose of goal setting; this involves information-sharing skills. The basic verbal responses (paraphrasing and summarizing) will help clients identify and evaluate their options (What are the possible goals?). All the basic verbal and challenging skills may be needed to help clients select goals, clarify them, determine whose goals they really are, decide how to achieve them, and then proceed to achieve them. Helping clients set goals focuses their attention on acting constructively, gets them involved in the helping process, makes them aware of what needs to be accomplished, encourages them to act on their own behalf, and informs them that the counselor is a capable partner in the helping process. A hypothetical interaction between that elementary-school counselor and the unhappy student introduced earlier provides an example of one of the many approaches counselors might pursue when trying to help clients set goals:

Counselor:	So, we have talked about how bad you feel and how angry you are at the others. Tell me what you want right now.
Client:	I wish they would all disappear in a cloud of smoke!
Counselor:	I can see how that might make you feel better right now. Are you sure that is all you want?
Client:	Well, I wish someone would be nice to me.
Counselor:	Do you think that is something for us to work on—figuring out how to get someone to be nice to you?

The counselor has discovered a possible goal in the client's comments and offered it as a possible goal. At this point, the counselor and client may engage in negotiating whether or not this would be a viable goal.

Action Strategies for Reaching Goals

In the logic of Egan's (1998) three-stage counseling model, problem identification, successful clarification, and goal setting usher in constructive action designed to achieve client goals. The options available to counselors when helping clients act on their goals are far-ranging, and many counselors spend their careers trying to learn more about ideas in the counseling literature and to become more accomplished at applying those skills. This book focuses on selected basic action strategies, not all possible action strategies. The strategies presented here are suggested because they are appropriate for helping most school counseling clients achieve their goals. Therefore, the suggestions that follow are presented as basic action strategies for the school counselor's repertoire. Some strategies may be more appropriate for counseling children, some more appropriate for counseling adolescents, and others useful for both children and adolescents.

Readers are again reminded that the purpose of the following information is to provide an overview, rather than to be a substitute for other courses in one's training program. In this section, an overview of action strategies that appear to be useful is presented. Competence in these strategies will come from comprehensive training associated with course work in one's counselor education training program. After his comments about the necessity of the basic counseling skills (i.e., "making nice") during the 2002 ACA convention, William Glasser stated that the "hard work" follows, that is, helping clients achieve their goals.

Supportive Counseling.   Children and adolescents benefit from knowing that someone cares and is trying to understand their circumstances. They respond best to counselors who provide support and understanding by creative facilitative mutual relationships. These clients may be experiencing grief, confusion, pain, or apathy, and their goal may be to adjust, to understand, or to feel accepted. The skills popularly associated with client- or person-centered counseling (Rogers, 1951) are commonly used in supportive counseling. Interestingly, they are the same skills cited previously as the basic verbal counseling responses (e.g., paraphrasing content, reflecting feelings, clarifying unclear material). Thus, in this instance the action strategy takes the form of continuing counseling responses designed to elicit identification and clarification of client thoughts and feelings in advance of goal setting. What differs is the use of these responses to help clients achieve their goals.

For example, a high-school counselor is meeting with a student who is traumatized by the sudden death of a classmate killed in a car accident. Realizing that the client needs to identify and clarify feelings, the counselor uses paraphrases, reflections, clarifications, and summaries to provide an empathic atmosphere. Eventually, the counselor learns that the client "just needs someone to talk to." Deciding that needing someone to talk to is the client's immediate goal, the counselor continues to respond in much the same manner as was done initially to provide a supportive environment for the client to work through and process the thoughts and feelings that led to seeking help from the counselor.

Decision-Making Counseling.   Many children and adolescents are confronted with choices, and making the best decisions is critically important to them. This is another arena in which counselors can be of service. Counselors are faced with a broad range of client problems that require decision-making assistance. For instance, choices are to be made when seeking a job, selecting a college, or determining whether to pursue a vocational-technical curriculum. Choices are also to be made in the personal-social domain, such as whether to forgive a transgressing peer or to pursue dangerous activities.

When engaging in decision-making counseling as an action strategy, counselors have at their disposal several rational, stepped, decision-making counseling paradigms.

As Horan (1979) points out, they all have four major components in common; therefore, counselors will be able to follow these paradigms and assist many of their clients successfully by helping them do the following:

1. Define the problem as involving a decision.
2. Identify the alternative response options (by using basic clarifying and exploring skills).
3. Determine the advantages and disadvantages of each option.
4. Make a tentative choice (by using basic clarifying, exploring, and challenging skills).

Decision-making counseling involves a unique combination of the aforementioned basic responding and challenging skills in a strategy founded on the counselor leading the client through a set of predetermined helping steps. For example, the high-school client who was traumatized by the death of a classmate, having processed thoughts and feelings with the help of a supportive counselor, reaches a point of having to decide whether to tell someone about witnessing alcohol abuse by the driver of the car before the accident occurred (the problem is defined as involving a decision). Using the decision-making steps, the counselor helps the client decide what the alternatives are (e.g., tell someone, tell no one, or have someone else tell). Following identification of the alternatives, the counselor helps the client consider the advantages and disadvantages of each one. For instance, the counselor might say (using an open-ended question): "What are the advantages of telling someone?" Having discussed the advantages, the counselor will then ask, "What are the disadvantages?" After seemingly having together exhaustively discussed the various advantages and disadvantages, the counselor then asks the client which alternative seems to be the best choice. The response may be to make a choice, to not make a choice (which is actually a choice—to do nothing), or to think about the choices further—perhaps acquiring more information or opinions in the process. If more time is needed, the counselor invites the client to return and continue if desired. If a choice is made, the counselor helps the client make plans for implementing it and returning to meet with the counselor and process the effects. Notice the similarity between this process and that suggested for making ethical decisions in chapter 3.

Counseling for Rational Thinking. Although humans have the capacity to engage in thinking processes, that capacity is not always used rationally. Some irrational thoughts common among school-age individuals are "People don't like me because my nose is big," "Men who choose careers in nursing are sissies," "The principal is mean because she doesn't smile at me," and "I've got to do what the others are doing or else they won't like me." It is safe to conclude that much irrational thinking occurs during childhood and adolescence and that it often leads to maladaptive responses. Many clients whom school counselors encounter need help in identifying and coping with their irrational thoughts, and school counselors can use proven strategies to help them.

Rational emotive therapy (RET; Ellis & Dryden, 1997; Ellis, Gordon, Neeman, & Palmer, 1997) provides a system for seeking out irrational beliefs in what clients present and for pointing out the unfortunate consequences of those beliefs. For instance, the counselor working with the African American client discussed earlier in this chapter in the material on immediacy and believing that the accusation of racism was emotionally rather than factually based might borrow from RET as follows to introduce to the client the counselor's view of how the situation occurred and to induce mutual discussion.

> Counselor: So, when I mentioned challenges I thought you would face as a college student, you thought my motives were racist, and that led to your being angry, losing confidence in me, and telling me off.

Basic verbal counseling and challenging responses can be used to help the client become aware of irrational thinking. Counselor–client interactions can be quite challenging, and clients may either recognize their irrational cognitions or leave counseling.

Ellis and others offer systems for teaching clients to think more rationally. *Cognitive self-instruction* is a system for identifying self-defeating thoughts and teaching clients to replace them with coping thoughts (Meichenbaum, 1993, 1994). *Reframing* helps clients learn more rational ways of perceiving situations (Gendlin, 1996). These and other strategies for teaching clients to think more rationally follow the establishment of clients' goals as the acquisition of more rational coping responses. The common ingredients of these strategies are (a) explaining the procedure to the client (information sharing), (b) demonstrating the strategy (serving as a model), (c) helping the client rehearse the new behavior and cognitions (practicing), and (d) encouraging the client to use the skills in the real world (by using basic counseling and challenging skills when encouraging them).

The most challenging aspect of irrational ideation counseling occurs at the beginning: Counselors try to identify the irrational components of the client's cognitions and the behavioral consequences. Then they may find themselves disputing the client's irrational thinking patterns, which sometimes is very difficult to do. It follows that counselors who are rational thinkers themselves are more likely to help clients think more rationally.

Competence Enhancement Counseling.   It is not uncommon for school-age clients to set goals successfully and then feel stymied because they do not feel competent to achieve their goals. When these feelings of incompetence are products of inexperience, lack of information, or mild performance anxiety, counselors can help clients enhance or learn the requisite skills. As a result, clients will be better prepared to cope with the targeted situations and others like them, and they may feel better about themselves for having coped and acquired new or enhanced skills.

Participant modeling, also called *behavioral rehearsal,* is a competence-enhancing counseling strategy for the school counselor's basic action strategies repertoire (Bandura, 1986). The ingredients are modeling, rehearsal with feedback, and transfer of training. The strategy is explained to the client (information sharing), the targeted behavior is demonstrated by a model (observational learning), the client engages in repeated practice sessions—as many as needed—with possible repetitions of the modeling if necessary (basic counseling and challenging skills), and an effort is made to transfer the acquired or enhanced skills to the real world when the client is ready. Among the sample cases that have been presented in this chapter, the elementary-school student experiencing difficulty making friends might be helped through friendship training provided by the counselor's employing participant modeling as just described.

Another case that lends itself to behavioral rehearsal is the high-school client who, after receiving supportive and decision-making counseling assistance from a counselor following the death of a classmate in a car accident, decides to tell someone about having witnessed alcohol abuse by the driver of the car but is concerned about not being clear and convincing in the presentation. The counselor offers to help the client feel more confident by employing the participant modeling strategy. After exploring the client's concerns about telling someone, the counselor helps the client decide who it will be. Counselor and client then determine together how that person might act and how the client should act. Next, counselor and client engage in a series of practice sessions in which the two exchange playing the roles of the client and the person to whom the client is relating the information. When the counselor plays the client's role, modeling occurs; when the client plays the client's role, the counselor provides encouragement and helpful feedback after each rehearsal. Successive approximations are employed until the client either feels ready to carry out the decision or decides to delay action, to not act, or to rethink the alternatives.

Competence enhancement counseling is similar to teaching when counselors engage in participant modeling or behavior rehearsals with clients. Therefore, counselors are better prepared to be effective if they are familiar with such strategies as induction aids, reinforcing statements, coaching, and arranging the subskills of the targeted behavior into a hierarchy (Cormier & Cormier, 1998).

Assertiveness Counseling.   Children and adolescents who are unable to respond to others with appropriate levels of assertiveness are at risk of undesirable consequences that range from feeling unfulfilled (e.g., unable to approach others socially) to being endangered (e.g., unable to resist peer pressure to engage in life-threatening behaviors such as substance abuse or unprotected sexual intercourse). Realizing that there is a fine line between assertiveness and aggressiveness, counselors can help clients who are not assertive enough by enabling them to receive compliments, make normal requests of others, express affective feelings such as fondness and displeasure, initiate and maintain conversations, express their legitimate rights, and refuse illegitimate requests—recognize their deficits, establish appropriate goals, and be appropriately assertive (Galassi & Galassi, 1977; Lange & Jakubowski, 1976).

When clients engage in maladaptive, nonassertive behaviors, counselors may help them replace those behaviors with adaptive responses. When clients have deficits, new behaviors can be taught. As with other instructional counseling intervention strategies, the first step is to explain the purposes and procedures for the training. Second, the counselor teaches clients how to appraise situations and decide how to behave (information-sharing skills). Third, demonstration and practice with feedback are used to teach the actual assertion skills (observational learning and reinforcement menus). Finally, the skills are implemented in the real world. One of the easiest ways to encourage appropriate assertiveness is to reinforce such behaviors when clients exhibit them.

In the example of the client being helped to tell someone about the alcohol abuse of the driver in the car accident through participant modeling, one might conclude that the client was lacking in assertiveness and may have been helped to be more assertive through competence enhancement counseling. Therefore, it seems appropriate to conclude that although not all participant modeling involves enhancing assertiveness, it is a very useful strategy for helping individuals learn to be more assertive.

Self-Management Counseling. Counselors have direct influence over their clients only during periods of direct contact during counseling interviews or group sessions. Interviews and sessions seldom occur more than once per week and often less than that. It is fortunate if counselors spend as much as 45 minutes per week with clients individually or in groups. Consequently, clients are on their own most of the time. The influence of counselors may increase a bit when they arrange with third parties to assist in intervention programs. In those cases, however, their influence is indirect.

Because clients involved in various counseling programs are on their own most of the time, it behooves counselors to introduce a system of self-management to help clients be successful with their interventions. In essence, clients assume control of their own intervention programs. Counselors remain important partners in the arrangement, however, because they introduce the self-management system and because they receive dependable information about client progress. Therefore, counselors assume indirect control over the intervention program, with the self-management system serving as the third party. More work by the client may occur between counseling sessions than during them. This is good because much more time is devoted to the intervention program than if client action is restricted to the counseling sessions.

Self-management programs require workable systems that are taught to clients. Appropriate homework assignments provide clear explanations (information sharing), teach clients how to carry them out (pedagogical skills), and assess client success with self-management activities (e.g., self-evaluation, standard setting, self-reinforcement, self-monitoring, stimulus control; Cormier & Cormier, 1998).

An interesting secondary effect of self-management activities is that clients often experience more success than they might have otherwise simply because they pay more attention to the targeted behaviors.

In an example of self-management programming (self-monitoring) for a middle-school student, a counselor and the student have agreed that academic performance in school may improve if the student becomes involved in a self-managed schoolwork program. To initiate the program, the counselor explains to the student how it works:

Counselor:	I think the best way to do this is for you to set aside 2 hours for homework each evening and to write down on the chart I am giving you what you need to accomplish (goals), what you accomplish (outcomes), and how you feel about it (opinions) without spending too much time doing the record keeping. The chart is like a weekly and monthly calendar, and you can see how things are progressing. What do you think?
Client:	Sounds good to me.

Counselor: OK! Now let's decide when you will start, and set up a series of meetings between the two of us to analyze how you are doing and determine what to do next. OK?

Nonverbal Counseling.   Verbal interactions between counselors and their clients are not the only way to achieve counseling goals; in fact, nonverbal strategies may be better in some cases. Although the following strategies all include some verbal material and interactions, they are classified here as nonverbal because of the special importance of nonverbal material and activities.

Play therapy offers counselors an avenue into the world of young children that is less successfully traveled through verbalizations. Through play therapy, counselors are able to learn what children are thinking. Here, counselors can communicate with children indirectly by using basic counseling skills to inquire about the play activities. Understanding the play therapy process and having at one's disposal the necessary space or, at least, equipment is imperative (e.g., toys, games, materials; Keat, 1990b). Barlow, Strother, and Landreth (1985) recommend that teachers and principals be aware of the goals and benefits of play therapy to make them more understanding partners in the helping process.

O'Connor (1991) believes that play therapy can be adapted for children at all levels of functioning. Children at higher levels will find the treatment more cognitive than experiential. Therefore, it is important to have a sense of a child's level of cognitive development before initiating play therapy activities. When done well, play therapy provides an opportunity for children to have a new understanding with corresponding response options. Further information is available in the following sources: O'Connor and Schaefer (1994) provide a menu of theoretical approaches to play therapy (e.g., Adlerian, time-limited, and cognitive-behavioral); ideas for adapting play therapy to adolescent clients; and descriptions of several play therapy techniques. Schaefer and Cangelosi (1993) offer recommendations for a wide variety of play therapy techniques (e.g., using puppets, sand play, water play, using food, finger painting, checkers or chess, and Nintendo® games). Ideas for using play therapy in concert with specific presenting problems are suggested by Landreth, Homeyer, Glover, and Sweeney (1996; e.g., abuse and neglect, aggression and acting out, attachment difficulties, grief, reading difficulties, and social adjustment).

Kahn (1999) believes that art therapy is an effective medium for counseling adolescents in several important ways by helping them with developmental tasks such as individuation and separation from their families. This is accomplished by aiding them to achieve control over their expressions, stimulate their creativity, have pleasurable experiences, and employ media options that reflect personal and age-group symbols and metaphors. She also believes that school counselors can establish art stations in their offices, using a variety of materials, each selected for specific reasons (e.g., felt-tip markers can be used quickly and are relatively easy to control). Stressing that counselors do not need to be artistically talented themselves, Kahn points out that the process should be planful, normalized, and explained to parents, teachers, and administrators. She also stresses the importance of informing students that they are engaged in a communication process rather than a talent show and of maintaining the confidentiality of the artwork done by students—it is not for exhibition. Kahn closes with the presentation of a stage-wise art therapy case with a high-school junior who returned to school following alcohol abuse rehabilitation. In the last seven sessions, the client was able to summarize insights acquired about the role of alcohol in his schooling and interpersonal relationships coupled with a record free of alcohol-related or disciplinary actions.

Other physical activities in which clients can engage therapeutically are drawing and writing. Whereas drawing is useful for children and adolescents, writing is probably more useful with adolescents and possibly older children. These activities provide alternative avenues for clients to express themselves and may also be therapeutic action stage strategies. The process will be enhanced by counselors who can explain the strategies, help clients carry them out, and help them find meaning in their drawings and writings.

Film, video, audio, and printed media are also nonverbal resources that counselors can employ as action strategies for children and adolescents. Again, counselors are challenged to be able to explain the purposes and procedures involved in these strategies, help their clients carry them out, and help them find meaning in the messages. Knowing where to find media sources that are appropriate for specific client needs (e.g., grief, substance abuse, divorce) is a challenge. It behooves counselors to use media sources to enhance their intervention repertoires, and they may learn about media resources through catalogs, advertisements, annotated bibliographies, and journals. The April 1987 issue of *Elementary School Guidance and Counseling* has several articles on counseling with expressive arts ("Special Issue on Counseling With Expressive Arts," 1987). Included are articles on using play therapy, computer art, writing, drama, music, puppets, sand play, and poetry. See also Cochran (1996) and Fall (1994, 1997).

Group Counseling.   Sometimes a group mode is the most effective vehicle for achieving intervention goals. Group counseling has advantages over individual counseling. Krieg (1988) points out that group members may keep fellow members honest, preventing them from manipulating counselors as easily as they might during individual sessions. Dinkmeyer (1969) suggests that group relationships are more realistic than individual relationships between adult counselors and children or adolescents. In group settings, counselors can observe social interactions among the members, peers may serve as role models, peer feedback is available, clients have opportunities to help their peers, and they may become aware that they are not alone in their circumstances.

Group counseling differs from group guidance (prevention programming, group therapy, and sensitivity training; the distinctions are important considerations for school counselors). Two basic differences between group guidance and group counseling are the roles of the leaders and the goals of the groups. In group guidance, the goals are determined by the leaders and are usually instructive and preventive in nature. The role of the leader is pedagogical, instructing, informing, directing, and leading. In group counseling, the goals are determined by the needs of the members, and the role of the leader is therapeutic, using counseling skills to help members of the group achieve individual and common goals. Group counseling is appropriate for the schools and is within the scope of the school counselor's training. The members are usually volunteers who are functioning normally and possibly are at risk. Topics are personal, often related to normal developmental concerns, and are shared by the members. Desired outcomes include greater self-understanding, self-acceptance, and resolution of targeted concerns.

The basic individual counseling and challenging skills are important in group counseling. Counselors also use skills more specific to group counseling, such as forming groups, teaching members about group processes, understanding the finer points of the small-group process contrasted with individual counseling, and mediating between and among members. Group counseling is not without challenges. Scheduling time for counseling groups in the schools is more difficult than scheduling individual counseling sessions. The difficulty of bringing groups of students together for counseling is compounded by the need to find student volunteers who share the same goals and can be scheduled together. When working in groups, many counselors find that maintaining a leadership role is more difficult than working with individuals. Maintaining confidentiality is more challenging in group counseling because several individuals might breach it, rather than only two.

Group counseling appears to be more cost-effective than individual counseling, and sometimes that may be true. More important, group counseling may be the most successful strategy for school counselors to use to help some clients. Therefore, it appears to be an important part of the basic action strategies repertoire. An example of a group counseling intervention for elementary-school children points out that successful group counseling has many features that often do not come to the attention of casual observers (M. S. Corey & Corey, 1997):

> Students ranging in age from 6 to 11 years were referred to group counseling by a principal, their teachers, and the school nurse. The students were experiencing a host of problems that, in turn, influenced their academic performance. The counselor's goal was to alleviate school problems and prevent arrested development by helping the students cope with underlying problems. She hoped to identify maladaptive behaviors, teach the students to express their emotions constructively, and provide an atmosphere where they could express their emotions freely while understanding that problems are caused by the way they act on feelings, rather than by the feelings themselves. Important ingredients of the counseling process were as follows:
>
> - The counselor worked with the students individually and in small groups.
> - The students received tutoring from empathic tutors concurrently with the counseling.
> - The students and their parents agreed to participate only after informed consent sessions.
> - The counselor had continuous meetings with parents, teachers, the school nurse, school psychologists, and the principal during the helping process.
> - The counselor engaged in social action activities as needed to help the students and their families receive clothing, food, money, and special services.

Several groups were formed. Those deemed most successful consisted of three to five students of the same age and gender. In forming the groups, which were open to new members at any time, the counselor attempted to combine withdrawn and outgoing students and to keep together students experiencing similar problems. The typical group met twice per week for 30 to 60 minutes. Students could leave a session before it ended, although they were encouraged to stay. A termination date was set in advance, and the students were prepared for termination as it approached.

Activities designed to help the students express their emotions safely included role playing, play therapy, acting out special situations, painting, finishing stories started by the leader, puppet shows, playing music, and dancing. Most students manifested observable behavior changes. The leader commented that although the group provided an excellent setting for the students to learn and practice relational skills, the individual counseling provided opportunities to pay each student more attention and to develop a trusting relationship.

Crisis Counseling.

Although not labeled as such, school counseling offices are often viewed as drop-in counseling centers. Some students never drop in and have to be invited. Others make appointments. Some drop in to see whether a counselor is available. Emergencies or crises occur in the schools, as well as in the greater society. Some emergencies are handled in the main office, by nurses, or by other staff members. Students in crisis also find their way to the counseling office, and it behooves counselors to have crisis counseling skills in their intervention repertoire. For example, students grieving over the suicide of a classmate may be overwhelmed. Others who have just had a traumatic experience (e.g., a physical beating, taunts and insults from peers, a suddenly broken relationship, a rejection letter from a prospective college or employer, receipt of disappointingly low scores on a college entrance exam) may panic. In these cases and others like them, counselors do not have the advantage of making appointments or opening the interviews in a relatively calm working atmosphere.

Crisis counseling is an immediate, time-limited treatment process. Clients are clearly unable to employ the usual coping mechanisms, and counselors do not have time to move patiently through the usual counseling steps. Because clients in crisis are extremely amenable to being assisted, counselors who act quickly and appropriately can be very helpful. Even in crisis situations, counselors can follow potential helping stages (Caplan, 1961). First, the counselor can assess how effectively the client is functioning and whether an immediate referral is necessary (determine whether the client needs medical attention). Second, if an immediate referral is not needed, the counselor can help the client cope with powerful affect, accept that affect, and find out the causes of the affect (use basic counseling skills). Third, some sort of immediate resolution or plan to resolve the problem is negotiated with the client (use basic counseling and challenging skills). Next, after determining whether it is appropriate for the client to be allowed to leave (e.g., determine whether the client is expressing suicide ideation) or whether the client wishes to end the interview, the counselor will determine whether termination, referral, or an appointment is in order.

All that has been suggested about crisis counseling thus far is clearly within the basic intervention repertoire of school counselors. Interestingly, school counselors cannot choose whether to include crisis counseling in their intervention repertoires. Crises will seek them out, and they will be expected to respond successfully. Therefore, it is important for their clients' welfare and their own reputations that school counselors be prepared to respond to crises. A strategy that counselors may employ to be prepared for crises is to conduct controlled simulations of possible crisis interventions, following them with analyses of their performances to rectify problems encountered during the simulations.

Roberts (1995) provides an example of how a small, rural school system that was prepared in advance responded to a crisis. A 14-year-old student with a long, troubled history took his life 3 weeks after classes had dismissed for summer vacation. Although the school had a crisis prevention–intervention team, it was not prepared to respond during the summer vacation. Under the circumstances, the school counselor collected accurate information about the event, contacted those members of the team who could be located to ensure that they knew the facts and could dispel rumors, and got commitments from some of them to volunteer to hold conferences with students they had contact with in the community. Most of the immediate postvention responsibilities were handled by the counselor, the principal, and the school secretary.

The school served as the center for communications about everything, including the facts about the suicide and information about the funeral. Care was taken to protect the family's privacy and to prevent speculation and rumors. Telephone calls were answered and messages returned. The counselor scheduled supportive interviews with students and others in need (e.g., nurses in the hospital emergency room) on request. Members of the deceased student's peer group and their parents were contacted to provide support and to encourage the parents to provide support as well. Home visits were made to these students to provide immediate assistance, inform them about sources of help in the future, and assess their emotional stability. Local media outlets were requested to handle the matter tactfully. The school was kept open to assist students and adults from early morning until late at night for 5 days following the suicide.

Long-range postvention continued through the summer and into the next school year. For example, all faculty members were briefed at the first teachers' meeting, faculty members feeling guilt were seen by the counselor, and the student's peer group members were monitored for 18 months.

Brief Family Systems Counseling.

Intact traditional families have declined in number, and counselors find themselves working more and more with children and adolescents whose issues seem to require working with other members of the family in some way to adjust behaviors and attitudes of members of the client's family. Gerler (1993) notes that "many counselors are simply reacting to changing families and are helping children, parents, and other family members to cope.... [School counselors and others can benefit from] some new ways to improve the relationship between home and school" (p. 243). According to Peeks (1993), this goal can be achieved by counselors who are able to "implement problem-solving models based on the principles of family therapy and ... advocate for and organize extended parental involvement programs" (p. 249). Competencies that appear to be important in this process are (a) being able to recognize that causes of clients' presenting problems are connected to the extended social unit or family after having eliminated intraschool causes, (b) having the capability to gather information about the family that may help in the formulation of intervention plans, (c) being able to establish rapport with families, (d) consulting with families about child and adolescent behavior, and (e) carrying out interventions that involve one or more members of a client's family system (Hinkle, 1993; Peeks, 1993).

Brief Counseling. Models for brief counseling have appeared in the school counseling literature recently (Bruce, 1995; Littrell, 1998; Murphy, 1997). Bruce (1995) describes a brief counseling approach that is time limited by design, rather than by default. Essential components of this approach are (a) a strong working alliance between counselors and clients, (b) affirmation and use of client strengths and resources, (c) high levels of counselor and client affective and behavioral involvement, and (d) establishment of clear, concrete goals. Murphy (1994, 1997), referring to the approach as solution-focused counseling, believes that counselors should focus on increasing their clients' existing success, rather than on trying to eliminate problems. In this approach, counselors help clients identify exceptions and encourage clients to engage in the exceptions more often. An example follows:

> A middle-school counselor is seeing a female student whose presenting problem is stated vaguely as wanting to be more successful academically. The counselor quickly helps the client assess the problem in concrete terms. In this hypothetical case, the client and the counselor agree that academic success involves her doing her homework more consistently and correctly and then getting higher grades. Next, the counselor helps the client identify solutions to the problem that the client attempted previously, looking for exceptions (specific circumstances in which the presenting problem does not occur or occurs with less intensity; Murphy, 1994). The client indicates that when she takes her schoolwork home and completes it in a quiet environment and in a timely manner, she seems to be more successful. The counselor then helps the client determine short-term goals that are concrete, achievable, and measurable, establishing a deadline for achieving the goals. With the counselor's assistance, the hypothetical client decides that she wants to feel that she is getting her homework done successfully for the next month with the hope of improving her grades. They agree that the client will set aside a specific amount of time each evening to complete her homework in a quiet place at home.

The client now has control of her own solution, and measurable, achievable goals have been established. The plan just described could conceivably have been accomplished in one counseling session. Follow-up sessions are in order to determine how well the client is doing and whether the goals need to be revisited. Murphy (1997) refers to these as "booster sessions." Counselors use their social influence to help clients own and maintain their accomplishments. Another feature of the approach is the possibility that the effects of the intervention strategy will generalize to other aspects of the client's life. Bruce and Hopper (1997), LaFountain, Garner, and Eliason (1996), and Murphy (1997) report research that provides some empirical support for the claims of proponents of this approach, indicating that it has promise for school counseling both in individual and group counseling relationships.

Facilitating Naturally Occurring Environmental Resources. All clients have resources in their environments that may be helpful in the counseling process. Some clients may already be employing these resources; others may need help realizing that they may be more successful in achieving their goals if they draw on them. For example, in a case presented earlier in this chapter, John from the close-knit Italian American family may be able to draw on support from his family or his religious beliefs for assistance. All individuals have environmental resources that help sustain them. General categories in which help for specific clients may be found are family ties; religious and philosophical beliefs; health practices; education and training; and networks of interpersonal, professional, fraternal, and work associations. Egan (1998) points out the importance of naturally occurring resources when he writes about helping clients discover unused resources and opportunities and employ them in goal attainment. Lee (1996) stresses the importance of being open-minded about client resources that may be of value to clients even though they may be contrary or unfamiliar to the counselor's beliefs and experiences (e.g., nontraditional religious beliefs, participation in indigenous support and healing systems).

The challenge to employ naturally occurring environmental resources successfully begins with Herring's (1997) synergistic approach—using the basic counseling competencies to find out what individual environmental resources exist and helping clients use them to their benefit. For example, the counselor introduced earlier who was working with the client traumatized by the death of a classmate in a car accident learns during the supportive counseling process that the client has religious beliefs about death and life after death. In turn, the counselor is able to help the client apply those beliefs to a resolution of how to respond successfully to the other student's untimely death (e.g., the client believes that death visits everyone and has faith in a better existence after death for her- or himself and the other student).

Combining Basic Action Strategies. Counselors may find that a single action strategy is sufficient in some cases, whereas a combination of strategies is more successful in others. The case of the student experiencing difficulty in coping with the accidental death of a classmate provides an example of the multimodal strategy approach. Supportive counseling, decision-making counseling, competence enhancement counseling, relaxation counseling, crisis counseling, and employing naturally occurring resources were offered when deemed appropriate by the counselor. Therefore, it appears that school counselors should be competent in a repertoire of action strategies to be able to serve diverse clients with a variety of presenting problems and to be able to select from a menu of action stage responses to each client as the cases evolve and the needs present themselves. The next section introduces ideas for organizing the counseling process.

ORGANIZING THE COUNSELING PROCESS

Counselors often hear a variety of subplots when clients offer information and express feelings about problems and related issues. Organizing the material and choosing constructive action strategies can be very challenging. Systems for gathering and organizing information and for planning treatment strategies have been suggested here.

One system that has received considerable attention in the school counseling literature is the *multimodal approach.* In this approach, several categories for client assessment and intervention planning are offered. The original multimodal model was developed by Lazarus (1973). He uses the acronym BASIC ID to represent the seven identified categories. Additional explanation and an application of the BASIC ID strategy are presented in chapter 11 via the work of Seligman (1981).

Keat's (1990b) modification of Lazarus's multimodal model is represented by the acronym HELPING: H represents health issues such as diet, substance abuse, and physical health; E represents emotions and feelings, the affective domain; L represents learning and school-related concerns; P means personal relationships; I stands for imagery and interests; N is the cognitive or thoughts category, which is designated as "need to know"; and G stands for guidance of acts, behaviors, and consequences.

Counselors may use the multimodal categories as guides for organizing material their clients present and for determining counseling leads directed at acquiring information not volunteered. The categories can also be used to determine clients' needs following assessment interviews and then to plan action strategies. The term *multimodal* suggests that assessment activities and action planning cover all modes to ensure the most comprehensive response to client needs. It also suggests an eclectic approach because client needs may require a variety of action strategies over a period of time. Therefore, the multimodal approach also has potential for counselors wishing to be multiculturally competent. Much has been written about adaptations of the multimodal idea. The April 1990 issue of *Elementary School Guidance and Counseling* contains a useful integration of multimodal theory, research, and practice ("Special Issue on Multimodal Theory, Research, and Practice," 1990).

BASICS OF RESPONDING TO CLIENT AVERSION TO COUNSELING

Client aversion takes two forms: reluctance and resistance (Doyle, 1992; Ritchie, 1986). Reluctant clients do not want to be involved in a counseling relationship initially; resistant clients behave in counterproductive ways while involved in the counseling process. Resistance can be a trait or a state in that clients may be resistant throughout the counseling process (trait) or may resist engaging in goal-directed behaviors periodically (state). Reluctance and resistance are natural challenges—part of the counseling process.

Reluctance

School counselors work in a setting in which they do not always control referrals made to them, and their functions are viewed differently by teachers, administrators, and parents. For example, teachers may refer students to counselors because they are puzzled, baffled, or frustrated by the students' behaviors and want someone to change the students so that they will behave as desired in the classroom. Viewing counselors as behavior management specialists or wishing the counselors were such specialists, some teachers refer their troublesome students to counselors. Often, the referred students have not been appropriately prepared for the referral and are reluctant to participate. Administrators sometimes do the same thing; for instance, principals may send misbehaving students to the counselor's office after having administered disciplinary action, expecting the counselor to modify student behavior, validate the principal's disciplinary decisions, or initiate additional discipline. In all these cases, students are very likely to be reluctant to visit the counseling office.

Parents sometimes view counselors as their agents in the school, persons who will gather information about their children or who will support the parents' wishes. Viewing counselors as their agents, parents may expect them to initiate interviews with students at the parents' request. In such interviews, students are often reluctant to participate or cooperate. They may be reluctant because they are unfamiliar with counseling or the counselor or because they do not know why they have been summoned to the counseling office. In some of these instances, counselors are faced with clients who enter the relationship negatively. When individuals make inappropriate referrals or have unrealistic expectations of counselors, perhaps the best way to cope with the predictably reluctant clients is to find acceptable ways to avoid engaging in such interviews. More is presented on this matter in chapter 7, "Referring and Coordinating in School Counseling."

Suggestions for coping with reluctance recommend that counselors draw on their basic counseling skills to earn the client's trust and on their challenging skills to explain the counseling relationship and determine client-based goals (information sharing, goal setting). Trust and structure are important in counteracting client reluctance (Ritchie, 1986). The goal is to restructure the relationship to one in which counselors and clients work together in mutual understanding toward achieving client goals. If, during the process of trying to accomplish this, counselors can replace client reticence, suspiciousness, and defensiveness with trust, they will appear trustworthy and competent to their clients. Janis (1983) calls this "motivating power." Having become what Janis calls "referent persons," counselors are able to use their motivating power to challenge clients to achieve their goals successfully.

Keat (1990a) points out that children may often be reluctant parties at the beginning of counseling relationships because adults initiate the counseling and establish the outcome goals. He recommends that counselors try to convince reluctant children that counselors are special adults, different from other adults in their lives. Suggestions for employing this idea include (a) demonstrating that counselors have influence over other adults in the children's lives and can effect changes; (b) presenting themselves as adults who can help children by engaging them in activities they find useful, such as learning to relax and cope better with stress, or by giving them therapeutic gifts, such as tape-recorded information or readings; and (c) showing a genuine interest in the children's interests.

Resistance

Ritchie (1986) believes that the instances of resistance in counseling far outnumber those of reluctance, making it a more pervasive challenge. This seems true because a limited number of reluctant clients enter a counselor's life, but all clients exhibit resistance at some time. The reasons for resistance vary. Some clients do not understand what they are to do. Others lack the skills to carry on as expected. Fear of failure and other immobilizing emotions may prevent clients from responding. Sometimes clients receive more reinforcement for engaging in unproductive behaviors than in productive ones. Sometimes clients do not want to admit to needing to change or, if admitting it, do not want to change.

Suggestions for coping with resistance vary because the reasons for resistance vary. G. Corey, Corey, Callanan, and Russell (1992) and Ritchie (1986) advocate an eclectic approach that can be summed up as using what works best from among available strategies. Cormier and Cormier (1998) offer what might be called a systematic eclecticism (they recommend finding the cause of the resistance and responding accordingly). Causes of resistance may be categorized as being attributable to client variables (e.g., pessimism, anxiety), environmental variables (e.g., unable to change environment), or counselor or counseling process variables. Inventories of suggestions for coping with resistance present a variety of strategies crossing different theoretical underpinnings and having no absolute guarantees (G. Corey et al., 1992; Cormier & Cormier, 1998; Cowan & Presbury, 2000; Ritchie, 1986). Consequently, counselors may have to draw on many of their basic skills and creativity when faced with client resistance. What can be stated positively is that counselors are challenged to be prepared because resistance will occur during their careers, manifesting itself in forms ranging from the very subtle to the outrageous.

BASIC TERMINATION SKILLS

Individual and group counseling relationships are analogous to lives in that they have beginnings and endings. The endings may be good because the clients are ready, they may be difficult because the clients are resistant, or they may be bad because they occur prematurely. Ward (1984) recommends that termination be viewed as one of several stages in the counseling process. Indirectly supporting the termination-as-a-stage concept, Krieg (1988) advocates devoting 10% of the life of a group to termination.

Cummings (1986) suggests that therapy and counseling can be thought of as analogous to medicine without adopting the medical treatment model. He thinks that the ending of a counseling relationship is considered an interruption rather than a termination. Physicians treat patients for problems (e.g., the flu), and when the treatments are completed, the physician–patient relationship is interrupted. The relationship may be reactivated to treat different or recurring problems (e.g., headaches). The relationship is therefore continuous, with intermittent contacts when needed. If school counseling services are viewed similarly, then termination will not be treated as a permanent event. School counselors are encouraged to view termination as an interruption in counseling services and as a stage in the counseling process.

The basic counseling and challenging skills are important as counselors engage in terminating or interrupting individual and group counseling relationships. These skills provide an appropriate climate for carrying out the activities required to accomplish the following goals:

- Evaluating client readiness
- Resolving affective issues between clients and counselors or among group members
- Maximizing transfer of training to the real world
- Enhancing client self-reliance and confidence
- Coping with and responding to premature terminations
- Enhancing the prospects of clients being able to cope successfully after the terminations
- Making successful referrals when needed
- Ensuring that clients are aware of their counselors' availability after the terminations (G. Corey et al., 1992; Ward, 1984)

Achieving these goals is challenging because the issues are varied and because clients respond differently to the circumstances associated with termination/interruption. School counselors can achieve the goals eclectically, using what works from their repertoire of skills.

Although counseling interventions are conceivably available to all students, and counselors are employed to serve all clients to the best of their ability, as Yalom (1975) points out, the matching of interventions, counselors, and clients is less than perfect. Freedom to terminate or interrupt is an important option because it is a source of protection for the client. Although counseling interventions in the schools are imperfect, counselors can do much to increase the probability that the interventions are good by having a desire to serve and help their clients and by being knowledgeable about counseling and skillful at it. School counselors have the freedom to choose whether to do everything in their power to provide effective counseling interventions.

COUNSELING INTERVENTIONS IN THE WAKE COUNTY ESSENTIAL GUIDANCE PROGRAM

The Wake County, North Carolina, Essential Guidance Program was introduced in chapter 2 as an example of a balanced school counseling program. In that program, students with special needs are served through individual and small-group counseling interventions. An outline of that component of the balanced program follows:

Individual Counseling
- Individual counseling as needed with students identified from referrals in kindergarten through 12th grade
- Identification and monitoring of at-risk students accompanied by appropriate interventions in 6th through 12th grades

Small-Group Counseling
- Provided as needed in kindergarten through 12th grade (e.g., divorce and separation, newcomers, grief and loss)

COUNSELING INTERVENTIONS IN THE WAYNESBORO *COMPREHENSIVE GUIDANCE PLAN*

Also introduced in chapter 2, the Waynesboro, Pennsylvania, *Comprehensive Guidance Plan* serves as a model of a balanced program as well. Counseling interventions are provided through *Responsive Services*.

Personal Counseling
- On a small-group basis for students having difficulties with relationships, personal concerns, or normal developmental tasks

Crisis Counseling
- For students and families facing emergency situations

SUGGESTED ACTIVITIES

1. Analyze a counseling model in terms of the following:
   a. basic steps
   b. basic competencies
   c. multicultural potential
2. Make an inventory of competencies that are new to you and learn more about them.
3. From the counseling competencies suggested in this chapter, select those that you think are debatable and debate their merits.
4. Analyze, discuss, and/or debate the intent of the following statement: "School counselors have neither the credentials nor the training required to provide therapy, but they can offer therapeutic counseling services."
5. Discuss or debate the merits of eclecticism and multicultural competence in school counseling.
6. Among the various competencies cited in the chapter, identify those that are important or mostly important for counselors working in the elementary, middle, and secondary schools; identify those that are universal across all three levels. Which list is the largest? Why do you think it is the largest?
7. Compare the suggested basic competencies in this chapter with those taught in the curriculum in your own training program. Analyze your findings.
8. Evaluate the concept that the freedom to terminate counseling is an important protection for clients.
9. Watch a film or a televised talk show and analyze the differences among conversing, interviewing, and counseling.
10. Discuss the merits of brief, solution-focused counseling.
11. Go to the following Internet site: www.scan21st.com. Submit a recommendation for how the Internet might be used to enhance school counseling interventions.

REFERENCES

Adelman, H. S., & Taylor, L. (2002). School counselors and school reform: New directions. *Professional School Counseling, 5,* 235–248.

American School Counselor Association (ASCA). (1990). Special theme section: Suicide and the school counselor. *School Counselor, 37,* 328–390.

American School Counselor Association (ASCA). (1992). Ethical standards for school counselors. *School Counselor, 40,* 84–88.

Bandura, A. (1986). *Social foundations of thought and action: A social cognitive theory.* Upper Saddle River, NJ: Prentice Hall.

Barlow, K., Strother, J., & Landreth, G. (1985). Child-centered play therapy: Nancy from baldness to curls. *School Counselor, 32,* 347–356.

Beauvais, F., & Oetting, E. R. (1988). Adolescent drug use and the counselor. *School Counselor, 36,* 11–17.

Bowers, J., Hatch, T., & Schwallie-Giddis, P. (2001, September–October). The brain storm. *ASCA Counselor,* 17–18.

Brake, K. J. (1988). Counseling young children of alcoholics. *Elementary School Guidance and Counseling, 23,* 106–111.

Brantley, P. L., Brantley, P. S., & Baer-Barkley, K. (1996). Transforming acting-out behavior: A group counseling program for inner-city elementary school pupils. *Elementary School Guidance and Counseling, 31,* 96–105.

Bruce, M. A. (1995). Brief counseling: An effective model for change. *School Counselor, 42,* 353–363.

Bruce, M. A., & Hopper, G. C. (1997). Brief counseling versus traditional counseling: A comparison of effectiveness. *School Counselor, 44,* 171–184.

Buwick, A., Martin, D., & Martin, M. (1988). Helping children deal with alcoholism in their families.

Elementary School Guidance and Counseling, 23, 112–117.

Caplan, G. (1961). *An approach to community mental health.* New York: Grune & Stratton.

Chandler, C., & Page, R. (1991). Adolescent drug use in a southern, middle-class metropolitan high school. *School Counselor, 38,* 229–235.

Cochran, J. L. (1996). Using play and art therapy to help culturally diverse students overcome barriers to school success. *School Counselor, 43,* 287–298.

Coffman, S. G., & Roark, A. E. (1992). A profile of adolescent anger in diverse family configurations and recommendations for intervention. *School Counselor, 39,* 211–216.

Corey, G., Corey, M. S., Callanan, P., & Russell, J. M. (1992). *Group techniques* (2nd ed.). Pacific Grove, CA: Brooks/Cole.

Corey, M. S., & Corey, G. (1997). *Groups: Process and practice* (5th ed.). Pacific Grove, CA: Brooks/Cole.

Cormier, S., & Cormier, B. (1998). *Interviewing strategies for helpers: Fundamental skills and cognitive behavioral interventions* (4th ed.). Pacific Grove, CA: Brooks/Cole.

Cowan, E. W., & Presbury, J. H. (2000). Meeting client resistance and reactance with reverence. *Journal of Counseling & Development, 78,* 411–419.

Cummings, N. A. (1986). The dismantling of our health system. *American Psychologist, 41,* 426–431.

Daniels, J. (1992). Empowering homeless children through school counseling. *Elementary School Guidance and Counseling, 27,* 104–112.

Dinkmeyer, D. (1969). Group counseling theory and techniques. *School Counselor, 17,* 148–152.

Doyle, R. E. (1992). *Essential skills and strategies in the helping process.* Pacific Grove, CA: Brooks/Cole.

Egan, G. (1998). *The skilled helper: A problem-management approach to helping* (6th ed.). Pacific Grove, CA: Brooks/Cole.

Ellis, A., & Dryden, W. (1997). *The practice of rational emotive behavior therapy* (2nd ed.). New York: Springer.

Ellis, A., Gordon, J., Neeman, M., & Palmer, S. (1997). *Stress counseling: A rational emotive behavior approach.* Herndon, VA: Cassell.

Fall, M. (1994). Self-efficacy: An additional dimension in play therapy. *International Journal of Play Therapy, 3,* 21–32.

Fall, M. (1997). From stages to categories: A study of children's play. *International Journal of Play Therapy, 6,* 1–21.

Fall, M., & McLeod, E. H. (2001). Identifying and assisting children with low self-efficacy. *Professional School Counseling, 4,* 334–341.

Fontes, L. A. (2000). Children exposed to marital violence: How school counselors can help. *Professional School Counseling, 3,* 231–237.

Galassi, M. D., & Galassi, J. P. (1977). *Assert yourself! How to be your own person.* New York: Human Sciences Press.

Gendlin, E. T. (1996). *Focusing oriented psychotherapy: A manual of experiential methods.* New York: Guilford.

Gerler, E. R., Jr. (1993). Parents, families, and the schools. *Elementary School Guidance and Counseling, 27,* 243.

Gray, R. E. (1988). The role of school counselors with bereaved teenagers: With and without peer support groups. *School Counselor, 35,* 185–193.

Gumaer, J., & Hudspeth, T. (1985). Self-instructional training with an adolescent schizophrenic. *School Counselor, 32,* 371–380.

Gysbers, N. C., & Henderson, P. (2001). Comprehensive guidance and counseling programs: A rich history and a bright future. *Professional School Counseling, 4,* 246–256.

Herring, R. D. (1997). *Multicultural counseling in schools: A synergistic approach.* Alexandria, VA: American Counseling Association.

Hinkle, J. S. (1993). Training school counselors to do family counseling. *Elementary School Guidance and Counseling, 27,* 252–257.

Horan, J. J. (1979). *Counseling for effective decision making.* North Scituate, MA: Duxbury.

House, R. M., & Hayes, R. L. (2002). School counselors: Becoming key players in school reform. *Professional School Counseling, 5,* 249–256.

Hovland, J., Smaby, M. H., & Maddux, C. D. (1996). At-risk children: Empirical findings and counseling implications. *Elementary School Guidance and Counseling, 31,* 43–51.

Humes, C. W., & Hohenshil, T. A. (1985). Career development and career education for handicapped students: A reexamination. *Vocational Guidance Quarterly, 34,* 31–40.

Ivey, A. E. (1988). *Intentional interviewing and counseling: Facilitating client development* (2nd ed.). Belmont, CA: Wadsworth.

Ivey, A. E. (1994). *Intentional interviewing and counseling: Facilitating client development in a multicultural society* (3rd ed.). Pacific Grove, CA: Brooks/Cole.

Janis, I. L. (1983). The role of social support in adher-ence to stressful decisions. *American Psychologist, 38,* 143–160.

Jenni, C. B. (1997). School phobia: How home-school collaboration can tame this frightful dragon. *School Counselor, 44,* 206–216.

Kahn, B. B. (1999). Art therapy with adolescents: Making it work for school counselors. *Professional School Counseling, 2,* 291–298.

Kammer, P. P., & Schmidt, D. (1987). Counseling run-away adolescents. *School Counselor, 35,* 149–154.

Kann, R. T., & Hanna, F. J. (2000). Disruptive behav-ior disorders in children and adolescents: How do girls differ from boys? *Journal of Counseling & Development, 78,* 267–274.

Keat, D. B. (1990a). Change in child multimodal coun-seling. *Elementary School Guidance and Counseling, 24,* 248–262.

Keat, D. B. (1990b). *Child multimodal therapy.* Norwood, NJ: Ablex.

King, K. A., Price, J. H., Telljohann, S. K., & Wahl, J. (2000). Preventing adolescent suicide: Do high school counselors know the risk factors? *Professional School Counseling, 3,* 255–263.

Kiselica, M. S. (1995). *Multicultural counseling with teenage fathers.* Thousand Oaks, CA: Sage Publications.

Kiselica, M. S., & Pfaller, J. (1993). Helping teenage parents: The independent and collaborative roles of counselor educators and school counselors. *Journal of Counseling & Development, 72,* 42–48.

Krieg, E. J. (1988). *Group leadership training and supervision manual for adolescent group counseling in schools* (3rd ed.). Muncie, IN: Accelerated Development.

LaFountain, R. M., Garner, N. E., & Eliason, G. T. (1996). Solution-focused counseling groups: A key for school counselors. *School Counselor, 43,* 256–266.

Landreth, G. L., Homeyer, L. E., Glover, G., & Sweeney, D. S. (1996). *Play therapy interventions with children's problems.* Northvale, NJ: Jason Aronson.

Lange, A., & Jakubowski, P. (1976). *Responsible assertive behavior.* Champaign, IL: Research Press.

Lapan, R. T., Kardash, C. M., & Turner, S. (2002). Empowering students to become self-regulated learners. *Professional School Counseling, 5,* 257–265.

Lazarus, A. A. (1973). Multimodal behavior therapy: Treating the BASIC ID. *Journal of Nervous and Mental Disease, 156,* 404–411.

Lee, C. C. (1996). MCT theory and implications for indigenous healing. In D. W. Sue, A. E. Ivey, & P. B. Pedersen (Eds.), *A theory of multicultural counseling and therapy* (pp. 86–98). Pacific Grove, CA: Brooks/Cole.

Lenhardt, A. M. (1997). Disenfranchised grief/hidden sorrow: Implications for the school counselor. *School Counselor, 44,* 264–271.

Littrell, J. M. (1998). *Brief counseling in action.* New York: Norton.

Malley, P. B., & Kush, F. (1994). Comprehensive and systematic school-based suicide prevention pro-gram: A checklist for counselors. *School Counselor, 41,* 191–194.

Malley, P. B., Kush, F., & Bogo, R. J. (1994). School-based adolescent suicide prevention and intervention programs: A survey. *School Counselor, 42,* 130–136.

Meichenbaum, D. H. (1993). Stress inoculation training: A 20-year update. In P. M. Lehrer & R. L. Woolfolk (Eds.), *Principles and practices of stress management* (2nd ed., pp. 373–406). New York: Guilford.

Meichenbaum, D. H. (1994). *A clinical handbook: Practical therapist manual for assessing and treating adults with post-traumatic stress disorders.* Waterloo, Ontario: Institute Press.

Moore, J., & Herlihy, B. (1993). Grief groups for stu-dents who have had a parent die. *School Counselor, 41,* 54–59.

Murphy, J. J. (1994). Working with what works: A solution-focused approach to school behavior prob-lems. *School Counselor, 42,* 59–72.

Murphy, J. J. (1997). *Solution-focused counseling in middle and high schools.* Alexandria, VA: American Counseling Association.

Nelson, J. R., Dykeman, C., Powell, S., & Petty, D. (1996). The effects of a group counseling interven-tion on students with behavioral adjustment prob-lems. *Elementary School Guidance and Counseling, 31,* 21–33.

Nickolai-Mays, S. (1987). Bibliotherapy and the so-cially isolated adolescent. *School Counselor, 35,* 17–21.

O'Connor, K. J. (1991). *The play therapy primer: An integration of theories and techniques.* New York: John Wiley.

O'Connor, K. J., & Schaefer, C. E. (Eds.). (1994). *Handbook of play therapy: Vol. 2. Advances and innovations.* New York: John Wiley.

Patton, P. L. (1995). Rational behavior skills: A teach-ing sequence for students with emotional disabili-ties. *School Counselor, 43,* 133–140.

Peeks, B. (1993). Revolutions in counseling and education: A systems perspective in the schools. *Elementary School Guidance and Counseling, 27,* 245–251.

Ritchie, M. H. (1986). Counseling the involuntary client. *Journal of Counseling & Development, 64,* 516–518.

Roberts, W. B., Jr. (1995). Postvention and psychological autopsy in the suicide of a 14-year-old public school student. *School Counselor, 42,* 322, 330.

Robison, F. F., Smaby, M. H., & Williams, G. T. (1988). School counselors using group counseling with family-school problems. *School Counselor, 35,* 169–178.

Rogers, C. (1951). *Client-centered therapy.* Boston: Houghton Mifflin.

Salamone, P. R. (1988). Career counseling: Steps and stages beyond Parsons. *Career Development Quarterly, 36,* 218–221.

Schaefer, C. E., & Cangelosi, D. M. (Eds.). (1993). *Play therapy techniques.* Northvale, NJ: Jason Aronson.

Schnedeker, J. A. (1991). Multistage group guidance and counseling for low-achieving students. *School Counselor, 39,* 47–51.

Seligman, L. (1981). Multimodal behavior therapy: A case study of a high school student. *School Counselor, 28,* 249–256.

Sonntag, N. (1985). Cartooning as a counseling approach to a socially isolated child. *School Counselor, 32,* 307–312.

Special issue on counseling with expressive arts. (1987). *Elementary School Guidance and Counseling, 21.*

Special issue on multimodal theory, research, and practice. (1990). *Elementary School Guidance and Counseling, 24.*

Sue, D. W. (1992). The challenge of multiculturalism: The road less traveled. *American Counselor, 1,* 6–14.

Sue, D. W., Ivey, A. E., & Pedersen, P. B. (1996). *A theory of multicultural counseling and therapy.* Pacific Grove, CA: Brooks/Cole.

Thompson, R. A. (1984). The critical needs of the adolescent unwed mother. *School Counselor, 31,* 460–466.

Thompson, R. A. (1987). Creating instructional and counseling partnerships to improve the academic performance of underachievers. *School Counselor, 34,* 289–296.

Thompson, R. A. (1993). Post-traumatic stress and post-traumatic loss debriefing: Brief strategic intervention for survivors of sudden loss. *School Counselor, 41,* 16–22.

Vondracek, F. W., & Schulenberg, J. E. (1986). Career development in adolescence: Some conceptual and intervention issues. *Vocational Guidance Quarterly, 34,* 247–254.

Walsh, M. C., & Buckley, M. A. (1994). Rational behavior skills: A teaching sequence for students with emotional disabilities. *School Counselor, 43,* 133–140.

Ward, D. E. (1984). Termination of individual counseling: Concepts and strategies. *Journal of Counseling & Development, 63,* 21–25.

Williams, W. C., & Lair, G. S. (1991). Using a person-centered approach with children who have a disability. *Elementary School Guidance and Counseling, 25,* 194–203.

Wirth-Bond, S., Coyne, A., & Adams, M. (1991). A school counseling program that reduces dropout rate. *School Counselor, 39,* 131–138.

Yalom, I. D. (1975). *The theory and practice of group psychotherapy* (2nd ed.). New York: Basic Books.

CHAPTER 6

Consulting in School Counseling

Goals: To introduce a specific consultation role for school counselors and to cite the similarities and differences between consultation and other school counseling functions while proposing basic competencies and training recommendations.

Here is how a school counselor described how he began consulting with a parent:

Sondra, a 14-year-old, was experiencing difficulties at school and elsewhere. She was disruptive in class and disturbed other students while they worked. She often returned to class late following lunch breaks. She also used profanity and vulgar language to intimidate teachers and students. Outside school, Sondra was caught vandalizing vending machines and defacing public property.

Sondra's mother—a single parent, divorced for about 2 years—requested help to resolve Sondra's difficulties. She was concerned about raising Sondra without a father. The mother planned to remarry within a few months. Sondra disliked the prospect of having a stepfather.

Students often exhibit behaviors and describe feelings that require the school counselor to consult with parents and teachers as a way of alleviating the presenting problems and of preventing the occurrence of future problems. This chapter describes the school counselor as a consultant.

DEMAND FOR CONSULTING IN SCHOOL COUNSELING

Definitions of *consultation* abound in the professional literature; a perusal of them leads to the conclusion that the differences are largely varying degrees of comprehensiveness. When consultation is treated as a topic or process, the definitions are quite comprehensive. When consultation is treated as a competency, the definition is more narrow and compact (cf. Brack, Jones, Smith, White, & Brack, 1993; Dougherty, 1990; Kurpius, Fuqua, & Rozecki, 1993; Mendoza, 1993; Rockwood, 1993; Ross, 1993). Dougherty (1990) offers a useful, comprehensive definition:

Consultation is a process in which a human services professional assists a consultee with a work-related (or caretaking-related) problem with a client system, with the goal of helping both the consultee and the client system in some specified way. (p. 8)

Dougherty's (1990) definition introduces three terms that are important to a discussion of consulting: *human services professional, consultee,* and *client system.* In this chapter, the human services professional is referred to as a consultant, and the client system is referred to as a client. Consultation involves three parties, two of whom are working together to serve a third. The two working together are a consultant and a consultee; the recipient of their efforts is the client. At times, multiple consultants, consultees, or clients may be involved in the consultation process. For example, a school counselor (consultant) is approached by two parents (consultees) for consultation about helping their child (client) be more successful in school. When the school counselor and the parents agree to work together, a consulting relationship takes place in which the school counselor (consultant) works with the parents (consultees) to find ways to help their child (client). The school counselor's interactions with the child are most likely to be indirect. That is, the school counselor directly assists and interacts with others (e.g., parents and teachers) who are working directly with the child. Therefore, the school counselor might be depicted as working behind the scenes. The circumstances just depicted describe school-based consulting.

In most consulting relationships, consultants will help consultees by sharing their expertise in some way. Consultees, in turn, will use that help in their work with clients who receive the help. Therefore, a prime feature of school counselor consulting is that the school counselor participates in the helping process as a helper whose influence on the client is indirect, and the consultee's influence is direct.

Counselors have probably provided consultation as long as there have been counselors; however, a formalized consulting function has been an important part of the school counselor's repertoire only since the late 1970s. Earlier, the proposal that professionals branch out from one-to-one relationships to work with caretakers who, in turn, work with clients was popularized in the mental health field (Caplan, 1959). School counseling was one helping profession that incorporated the idea because the large student-to-counselor ratios in virtually every school district made more effective use of counselor time appealing. Consultation is one way counselors can use their skills to influence as many people as possible (Gerler, 1992). That consultation is considered an important function in counseling today and for the future is borne out in the appearance of special issues of counseling journals devoted to consultation (Dougherty, 1992; Kurpius & Fuqua, 1993a, 1993b) and in the specific attention devoted to it as one "basic intervention" emphasized in the role statement for school counselors advocated by the American School Counselor Association (n.d.):

> The counselor as a consultant helps people to be more effective in working with others. Consultation helps individuals think through problems and concerns, acquire more knowledge and skill, and become more objective and self-confident. This intervention can take place in individual or group conferences, or through self-development activities. (p. 23)

Although the idea has gained momentum and acceptance, the meaning of consultation has been less clear. There is no universal definition of consultation (Kurpius & Fuqua, 1993a). Various helping fields have differing versions of what the ingredients of consulting are, and consulting behaviors are based more on trial-and-error activities than on theory (Bardon, 1985; Gallessich, 1985). The lack of theory need not be as unsettling for school counselors as it is for counselor educators because the peculiar environment in which school counselors work creates a relatively specific consultation role for school counselor consulting.

School counselors work in the schools, where the natural recipients of consulting services are students, teachers, administrators, parents, and occasionally others in the school district. For example, school counselors might consult with civic leaders who want to establish a scholarship program for local students or with members of a local service club who want to establish a system for recruiting American Field Service (AFS) volunteers. Natural circumstances related to daily activities in school systems create situations in which individuals need consultation, and counselors often can provide the needed assistance. Counselors respond to teachers working with challenging students and/or planning units about which counselors have topical knowledge or implementation ideas. The first example involves a counseling intervention response and the second a prevention programming response, indicating that consultation services are important to both the counseling intervention and prevention programming domains. School counselors do not need to create a consulting service—one exists. Counselors who understand what exists can improve on it.

Excerpts from the professional literature indicate that school counselors are, in fact, engaging in consulting activities; the activities most often reported involve consulting with teachers as consultees and students as the indirect recipients of the counselors' consulting services.

The most common reports of school counselors consulting with teachers involve teachers receiving assistance with students who exhibit challenging behaviors. Through excerpts of a consultation dialogue between an elementary-school counselor and a teacher, Keat (1974) demonstrates that assistance provided by the counselor includes empathy, additional ideas, support, confirmation, and recommendations. Dowd and Moerings (1975) report a case in which an eighth grader's underachievement and social isolation were alleviated when a counselor consulted with three of the student's teachers and developed a treatment strategy. Off-task behaviors having a detrimental effect on the academic performance of six male and female sixth graders were reduced by modifications in the encouraging behaviors of teachers in consulting relationships (Rathvon, 1990). In a case in which the extent of the teacher's presented problem was unclear, Osterweil (1987) offers suggestions for achieving clarity and eventually suggests a treatment plan. Viewing teachers as information gatherers and hypothesis formers, Bauer and Sapona (1988) recommend that counselors have the expertise to help with students who exhibit challenging behaviors. Offering support for school counselor consultation, Bundy and Poppen (1986) report that significant improvements in student behavior, adjustment, or achievement were found in 77% of consultation studies they reviewed.

Strein and French (1984) point out that counselors are also an important consultation source for teachers in helping them foster affective growth in students. Therefore, counselors as consultants are seen as people who not only can help solve or treat existing problems but also can offer assistance with proactive preventive planning. Taking the prevention concept a step farther, Robinson and Wilson (1987) believe that counselor involvement in human relations training groups can be conceived as a form of consultation. Teachers of second and fifth graders in 13 elementary schools received 25 hours of human relations training that led to overall improvements in their skills. Robinson and Wilson also report evidence suggesting that teachers who learn to be more effective communicators may, in turn, enhance the academic achievements and self-concepts of their students.

Parents may also find value in the consultation services of school counselors. Purkey and Schmidt (1982) suggest that school counselors can help parents enhance their children's growth by adopting an invitational approach to family living. Purkey and Schmidt's ideas are practical and easily adopted and can be conveyed to parents in several relatively easy ways. Myrick (1977) also states that parent consultation is a potentially important function for school counselors, especially elementary-school counselors, because of the important role of parents in child development. He also notes, however, debate among various writers about the cost-effectiveness of taking time away from other functions to engage in consultations with parents. Mullis and Edwards (2001) suggest that, if school counselors view concerns expressed by parents through a family systems lens, they can help parents to plan interventions that may be successful in a time-efficient manner. We present more about this consulting approach later in the chapter.

Smaby, Peterson, Bergmann, Bacig, and Swearingen (1990) may have identified an approach to parental consultation that is cost-effective. They describe school-based, comprehensive, community suicide prevention and intervention programs in northeastern Minnesota in which school counselors serve as members of community intervention teams. Including teachers, social workers, community mental health workers, law enforcement officials, members of the clergy, and students, the teams develop and present workshops and train personnel from participating schools who, in turn, train others in their respective schools, agencies, and communities. Most of the consultation offered to parents by these school counselors is indirect, allowing them to help more people than direct service consultation could accomplish in this instance.

Mathias (1992) believes that "there is a myriad of interventions available to the [school counselor] consultant" (p. 191). She provides several examples, including listening to parent and teacher concerns about children and adolescents and helping them explore alternative ways to address those concerns, developing and locating helpful printed materials that can be distributed to parents and teachers, working with school librarians to develop bibliotherapy sections in the school library, participating in child study teams with other school professionals, and serving on committees designed to improve the school as a system.

The importance of consulting is highlighted in all three of the initiatives for enhancing school counseling that were introduced in chapter 1. In the ASCA's National Model for Comprehensive School Counseling Programs, consulting is considered as an important responsive service just as counseling is. Gysbers and Henderson (2001) depict consulting as dedicated to helping students manage and resolve personal/social, educational, and career concerns. Representing the National School Counselor Training Initiative, House and Hayes (2002) view consulting as an important function for helping parents enroll their children in academic courses that will lead to attending college and teaching them how to make formal requests to school officials successfully. They also believe school counselors can help all educators in the schools to resolve issues that involve the schools and their communities through consultation. Adelman and Taylor (2002) view consultation as part of an interconnected system for meeting the needs of all students via the School-Community Collaboration Model. More specifically, conflict resolution (a.k.a. mediation) is presented as a primary prevention strategy, and dropout and family support are seen as early intervention components.

BASIC INGREDIENTS OF CONSULTING IN SCHOOL COUNSELING

Although less voluminous, the consultation literature, like the counseling literature, offers several recommendations about how consulting may be conducted. As is the case with the basic counseling skills, the competencies of consulting are atheoretical; they can be learned, developed, and incorporated into the behavioral repertoire, and they can be applied according to one's own theoretical persuasion. Two major themes stand out in these positions: modes and steps or stages. *Consulting modes* are the methods individuals use or the ways they behave when engaging in consulting services.

Consulting steps or stages are the sequential behaviors in which individuals engage when carrying out any of the consulting modes. Because steps and stages depend on modes, modes are discussed first here.

School Counselor Consulting Modes

Kurpius (1978) suggests four modes that school counselors might use, each of which leads to different attitudes and behaviors and therefore requires different competencies. The following material extends Kurpius's ideas and also reflects thoughts expressed by Gallessich (1985).

We have added a fifth mode (mediation) to the four modes identified by Kurpius (1978). All five consulting modes are available to school counselors, and they are not mutually exclusive. It is very likely that some modes are more prevalent among practicing counselors and in counselor education training programs. It is also likely that some are preferred by counselors or are recommended by counselor educators more than others.

Prescription Mode.   Consultants provide intervention plans or aid in the selection of intervention strategies for predetermined problems. When doing so, consultants investigate and diagnose the circumstances, negotiating strategies and people to implement them. This is an indirect service. An example of the prescription mode is a case in which an elementary-school counselor (consultant) helps a frustrated teacher (consultee) establish a plan for a token economy program designed to enhance students'(clients) on-task behaviors and to reduce their acting-out behaviors. One-to-one consultation sessions with the teacher are accompanied by classroom observations by the counselor, who then analyzes students' behaviors prior to suggesting an intervention plan that the teacher may implement in the classroom.

Provision Mode.   Consultants provide direct services to clients because consultees lack time, interest, or competence. When doing so, counselors draw on competencies used in counseling and prevention programming. This differs from basic counseling or prevention programming because the assistance is initiated by a consulting relationship. An example of the provision mode might occur from the same concerns that led to the prescription consultation example in the preceding paragraph. In an alternate scenario, the teacher may feel unable to initiate the plan or may have tried unsuccessfully to do so. As a provision-mode consultant, the counselor could enter the classroom as a substitute or collaborator and implement the proposed token economy program to the students (clients). In this example, the counselor (consultant) serves as a model for the teacher (consultee), who will still have to become involved eventually because the program will take time to complete. If the program necessitates only one class session and the counselor replaces the teacher, the provided consultation services completely eliminate active participation by the teacher.

Initiation Mode.   Consultants contact prospective consultees proactively after having recognized and studied a problem, offering their consulting services. Depending on the nature of the problem, the consulting services may be either direct or indirect. An example of the initiation mode is a case in which a high-school counselor responds to a first-year teacher who makes many disciplinary referrals to the assistant principal's office, appears unhappy when with colleagues, and is heard making comments about leaving the school district or the profession. The counselor (consultant) responds by inviting the teacher (consultee) to meet and talk, taking the opportunity to mention the events and offering to help the teacher resolve the problem. In this example, the consultation mode can then become prescriptive, provisional, collaborative, or a combination. A happier, more confident teacher may make fewer disciplinary referrals and serve the students (clients) better.

Collaboration Mode.   Consultants respond to requests from consultees by engaging in mutual efforts to understand the problem, devise an action plan, and implement it. The services are usually indirect. A case of collaborative consulting will occur if the high-school teacher (consultee) who has classroom management problems agrees that help is needed and engages in a joint problem-solving relationship with the counselor (consultant). They might engage in such collaborative activities as defining the problem clearly, identifying alternative solutions, selecting mutually agreeable strategies, and figuring out ways to implement them. Their ultimate goal is to discover ideas that, when implemented, will help the teacher be more effective with the students (clients).

Mediation Mode.   Consultants respond to requests from two or more consultees to help them accomplish an agreement or a reconciliation by serving as facilitators. The services are direct. Mediation consulting may occur whenever two people or groups become locked in mutual disagreements and seemingly unresolvable differences of opinion. Antagonists may be teacher versus student, student versus parent, student versus student, or administrator versus student. If all sides agree, counselors can mediate by serving as intermediaries. An example is for a counselor (consultant) to help a teacher (consultee) having discipline problems work out differences with a student (client) angered by being sent to the principal's office. The mediating counselor can meet with both parties to help them share their explanations and try to achieve a mutual understanding and an improved relationship leading to a settlement of their differences. In so doing, the counselor might make suggestions but will never dictate resolutions to the disputing parties. It is also important that both the teacher and student believe that the counselor is a fair, impartial mediator. That mediation has become an important consulting mode is seen in the attention paid to conflict resolution in the counseling literature (Messing, 1993).

School Counselor Consulting Steps or Stages

Several writers deserve credit for helping counselors by spelling out important steps or stages to be considered when delivering consulting services (Bauer & Sapona, 1988; Brown, Wyne, Blackburn, & Powell, 1979; Dustin & Ehly, 1984; Kurpius, 1978; Myrick, 1977; Stum, 1982; Umansky & Holloway, 1984). They have more commonalities than differences. Essentially, their ideas fit into the three stages of Egan's (1998) helping paradigm presented in Table 5.1 (see chap. 5). Briefly, those stages are identifying and clarifying the problem, setting realistic goals, and devising and implementing strategies for achieving the goals. The same three stages were previously presented for organizing and implementing counseling interventions and are also advocated in conjunction with organizing and implementing consulting interventions. Therefore, the task of implementing the systems for both counseling and consulting interventions is easier because the systems are alike. An example follows:

> Reflect on the two parents (consultees) who approached a counselor (consultant) for consultation about ways to help their child (the client) become more successful in school (as described in the opening section of this chapter). The mode for this consulting relationship is collaboration. Implementing the first of Egan's stages (identify and clarify the client's [consultees'] problem situations and/or opportunities), the counselor/consultant uses basic interviewing skills to help the parents (consultees) tell their story, identify related affect, and discover resources available to them. Next, the counselor helps the consultees set goals based on a mutual understanding of the problem (Egan's second stage). Having agreed on what seemingly needs to be done, the consultant works with the consultees to identify strategies that can be employed to try to reach the goals that were established and to devise plans for implementing the strategies (Egan's third stage).

BASIC COMPETENCIES FOR CONSULTING IN SCHOOL COUNSELING

The nature of school counseling itself positions counselors as prospective consultants. Because opportunities for consulting may present themselves from at least five modes, the school counselor is challenged to be a versatile consultant, able to be the provider, the mediator, or the initiator. The five modes can be further categorized as representing either direct or indirect services. The basic skills of a comprehensive consulting model are presented here in the context of the three of stages of identification/clarification, goal setting/commitment, and implementation. Fortunately, consulting does not require a completely independent set of competencies. Instead, many of the counseling and some of the prevention programming competencies are simply applied in a different context. Research by Lin, Kelly, and Nelson (1996) indicates that many verbal behaviors are common to counseling and consulting interactions. The importance of being multiculturally competent—sensitive to the worldviews of consultees and their clients—remains as important as it is in counseling interventions and prevention programming.

Identifying and Clarifying the Problem Situations

Opening Consulting Interviews. Most often, consulting relationships are initiated by the individuals seeking consulting assistance. In such cases, counselors draw on the same skills used when opening counseling relationships initiated by clients—open invitations that encourage consultee sharing, identifying, and clarifying. When counselors initiate consulting relationships, clear explanations of the invitation and proposal are necessary, just as they are in counseling interviews initiated by counselors. For example, a counselor will respond with an open invitation to talk with a consultee as the elementary-school teacher did who approached a counselor for help out of frustration with students' acting-out behaviors. Horton and

Brown's (1990) review of research on the importance of interpersonal skills led them to conclude that successful clinical consultants establish facilitative relationships with their consultees. Therefore, the counselor's initial consulting goal is to find out what the teacher wants. The counselor who approached the high-school teacher having disciplinary difficulties in the "Initiation Mode" section of this chapter is an example of a prospective consulting relationship that needs to begin with an explanation. Having initiated the meeting, the counselor provides the teacher with an explanation of what appears to be happening and how the counselor as a consultant might help the teacher.

Identifying the Presenting Problem and Preparing Consultees for Consultation.
After opening the consulting interview successfully, counselors will invite prospective consultees to share their presenting or targeted (initiation mode) problems and establish a facilitative working alliance in the process. In this process, consultees can be encouraged to share pertinent information about themselves (e.g., experiences, feelings, perceived level of competence to resolve the current problem, motives, initial goals), clients (e.g., culture, age, gender, maturity, behaviors), interactions between clients and consultees (e.g., communications, behaviors, affect, attitudes, antecedents, reactions), and the context in which the interactions occurred (e.g., physical setting, contemporaries, peers, relationships, expectations, distractions, challenges). This process is similar to opening counseling interviews. Therefore, providing the core facilitative conditions, attending physically, and using the basic verbal counseling responses are as important to consulting as they are to counseling interventions.

While prospective consultees respond to invitations to share pertinent information about presenting problems, consulting counselors determine which mode is suggested by the circumstances and whether the consultees are ready, willing to proceed, and able to provide professional assistance. Then counselors are in a position to negotiate their roles and explain their own understanding of the presenting problems and the consultees' motives. Being clear with consultees about one's role as a consultant is important at the outset and remains important throughout the consultation process. Consequently, when providing consulting services, counselors make sure they and their consultees agree about expectations. More emphatically, it is recommended that, early in the consulting process, counselors periodically assess whether the expectations of all parties match and that counselors renegotiate and reiterate those expectations as necessary. One of the many reasons for doing this is that consultees sometimes have hidden agendas. For example, the teacher who expressed a desire for help in coping with a misbehaving student may also harbor a desire to punish that student. Another reason for assessing the consulting relationship periodically is that consultees sometimes misunderstand or misinterpret initial explanations. For example, in cases where consultants perceive their roles as mediators and the consultees expect arbitration, the consultees may be disappointed that the consultants do not dictate a solution.

Agreeing to Consult, Defining the Problem, and Exploring Possible Solutions.
At some point in the identifying and clarifying process, a decision to consult must be made. Assuming the decision is affirmative, the parties engage in further definition of the problem and exploration of possible solutions. Basic challenging skills (e.g., information sharing, immediacy, confrontation) and the basic

counseling competencies will be as useful at this time as they are in counseling relationships. This step in the consulting relationship is similar to identifying alternative response options in the decision-making counseling strategy presented in chapter 5. Consultants and consultees can brainstorm hypotheses about the problem and possible solutions. This is especially appropriate when counselors are using the initiation and collaboration consulting modes. In brainstorming, the idea is to identify as many solutions or hypotheses as possible without engaging in analyses of the ideas—a follow-up task. In the prescription mode, consultants explain the details of their treatment plans and brainstorm or negotiate who will implement them. In the provision and mediation modes, consultants may either brainstorm ideas about possible strategies or inform consultees about what they will do as they carry out their consulting services.

Exploring solutions leads to evaluating alternatives once they have been identified. Osterweil (1987) recommends using reasonability, workability, and motivation as criteria for evaluating potential solutions. Additional information about problem antecedents, consequences, and participant responses may be required before conclusions can be made and may require research by consultants and consultees (Umansky & Holloway, 1984). One important skill in this instance is to observe clients in natural settings unobtrusively and concurrently collect relevant data. After that has been done, the stage is set for establishing goals.

Recall again the case of the parents who desire more success for their child in school. After finding out the parents' goals, the counselor suggests that the goals be

The consultant works with consultees to identify strategies that can be employed.

considered tentative until there is an opportunity to collect baseline data about how well the child is currently doing in school. One means of collecting data will be for the counselor (consultant) to observe the child in classroom settings and/or ask the child's teacher to provide information based on observations. Observations are supplemented by data from standardized tests and performance on tasks and assignments in the classroom. After data are collected, the parents and counselor meet to continue solidifying goals and determining constructive action strategies.

Understanding the Situation and Setting Goals

As it is in counseling, goal setting is the heart of consulting, for consulting, like counseling, is a participatory helping relationship. Counselors as consultants help consultees find a sense of direction and share the responsibility of achieving their own goals. The same counseling skills that are important for goal setting in counseling relationships remain important in consulting relationships. Helping consultees set goals focuses their attention on acting constructively, involves them in the helping process either directly or indirectly, makes them aware of what needs to be accomplished, encourages them to act on their own behalf or on behalf of their clients, and informs them that counselors are capable partners in the consulting process.

For example, the counselor and the parents in the continuing hypothetical case, after having perused the data from observations and records, decide that two goals will suffice for the time being. They will remain open to reviewing the goals, revising them, and possibly changing them. The two goals are to ask the child's teacher to help by employing some strategies designed to keep the child on task when attention deficits occur and to have the parents set aside time each evening to discuss schoolwork with the child and to provide encouragement and, if necessary, appropriate assistance. The counselor agrees to approach the teacher, seek cooperation, and provide instruction. The counselor also helps the parents carefully define and, if necessary, rehearse their interactions with their child. Systems for monitoring the child's progress are determined, and a plan for meeting again to discuss the case is established.

Basic Action Strategies for Consulting in School Counseling

As discussed in chapter 5, counselors can choose among numerous strategies to achieve consulting goals. Therefore, the strategies presented here are those that seem most appropriate for school counselors in the majority of their consulting cases. Additions may occur with experience and in response to the peculiarities of one's professional setting.

Basic Strategies for Reaching Consulting Goals.   Most action strategies important for achieving counseling goals, presented in chapter 5, are also important in achieving consulting goals. Settings and applications may differ, but the importance of the skills remains constant. The supportive counseling strategy will prove useful in all consulting modes because of the importance of the basic counseling skills throughout the consulting process.

Table 6.1
Applicability of counseling strategies to consultation modes.

Counseling Strategies	Consultation Modes				
	Prescription	Provision	Initiation	Collaboration	Mediation
Support	Yes	Yes	Yes	Yes	Yes
Decision Making	Yes	Yes	Yes	Yes	Yes
Competence Enhancement	Yes	Yes	Yes	Yes	
Self-Management	Yes	Yes	Yes	Yes	
Nonverbal	Yes	Yes	Yes	Yes	
Rational Thinking		Yes			Yes
Assertion		Yes			
Group		Yes			
Crisis		Yes			

In all five consulting modes, consultees may need help making decisions. Consequently, decision-making counseling is another action stage strategy applicable to both counseling and consulting services. Other basic counseling service action strategies vary in their applicability to the five consulting modes. All the strategies seem applicable in the provision mode. Table 6.1 provides a summary of this discussion.

Assertiveness, group, and crisis counseling seem applicable only in the provision mode, whereas counseling for rational thinking seems applicable in the provision and mediation modes. Competence enhancement counseling seems applicable in the prescription, provision, initiation, and collaboration modes. Self-management and nonverbal counseling seem appropriate for the prescription, provision, initiation, and collaboration modes. The foregoing categorizations are logical but arbitrary, and it may be that the applications are broader or more limited than indicated here. Much depends on the individual counselor providing the consulting services. The most important theme is that the basic action strategies are applicable to both counseling and consulting services.

Consulting to Enhance Child and Adolescent Development. In the prescription, initiation, and collaboration modes, school counselors may find themselves trying to help consultees understand and use knowledge about human development to intervene appropriately. Parents, teachers, and administrators are sometimes at a loss to match expectations with maturational differences. Counselors who are knowledgeable about developmental expectations at various age levels and about individual differences within all age levels are in a position to help colleagues and parents understand the behaviors of their students and children more intelligently and make decisions about whether to respond accordingly. When the decision to respond is made in consultation with counselors, helpful interventions can be developed. The key assumption here is that school counselors who offer consultation to enhance child and adolescent development are indeed knowledgeable about the topic. The hypothetical case running through this chapter of the parents who want to help their child become more successful in school is an example of child development consulting.

Consulting With Teachers to Enhance Classroom Management. It is not unusual for counselors working in the prescription, initiation, or collaboration consulting mode to be assisting with management of student classroom behaviors, especially at the elementary- and perhaps middle-school levels. In these cases, specific undesirable behaviors such as acting out, aggressiveness, and withdrawal can be targeted through teacher/consultee reports and consultant observations. Counselors can introduce teacher/consultees to the importance of recognizing and collecting baseline data to have benchmarks about the presenting behaviors against which efforts to induce changes can be compared.

In general, classroom management consulting involves implementing behavior modification principles. Therefore, counselors responding to requests for such consultation are challenged to be versed in these basic principles. The principles are summarized in the following list and can be shared with teacher/consultees:

1. Behavior is learned when it is reinforced consistently.
2. Specific behaviors that require acceleration or deceleration can be identified and the child's strengths emphasized.
3. When engaging in behavior modification activities, small gains are to be anticipated initially.
4. Consequences of behavior must be meaningful to the student.
5. Consequences, rewards, or punishments are more meaningful if they follow the behavior immediately.
6. Reinforcement may be physical or social.
7. Purposes and goals should be clear.
8. The target behavior should be the best one for the particular student.
9. The aim of behavior control should be self-control. (Center for Studies of Child and Family Mental Health Principles, cited in Keat, 1974, p. 165)

These principles are applied to changing targeted behaviors. To help teacher/consultees achieve desired behavior changes, counselors may select from among several available behavior modification strategies. The most applicable strategies are response differentiation, fading, shaping, chaining, token systems, contingency management, and time-out procedures. Finally, counselors help teacher/consultees keep sufficient records for evaluating progress toward achieving desired objectives. (Evaluation involves assessment skills, a topic covered more comprehensively in chapter 10.) That part of the hypothetical case in this chapter in which the teacher is being asked to enhance the client's on-task behavior in class is an example of classroom management consultation. For instance, one strategy the teacher may use is shaping (e.g., gently reminding the student to pay attention to the desired task when off task, reinforcing on-task behavior with praise when noticed, and generally paying attention to on-task and off-task behavior).

Consulting With Individuals to Enhance Their Understanding of Schools as Organizations. Schools operate according to organizational principles. Sometimes this is manifested pathologically, or individual applications of and responses to these principles are pathological. Similar circumstances occur in organizations outside the school, and the effects may be manifested in the school. Organizational pathologies and pathological responses to organizations may lead to situations in which counselors engage in prescription, initiation, or collaboration consulting services. For example, students, parents, or teachers need assistance determining how to respond to school regulations they perceive as being repressive or unreasonable, such as dress codes and tardiness criteria. As with classroom management consulting, this form of consultation often takes the form of sharing knowledge with consultees that will empower them to behave more effectively.

To be effective at helping individuals in this way, it behooves counselors to understand the schools as organizations. Examples of information that may help counselors in this role are knowing how well educated staff members are and how liberal or conservative they are regarding new ideas and innovations. Better educated and secure professionals are more open to innovations (Brown et al., 1979). It is also useful to know whether the school's decision-making structure is centralized or decentralized, because centralized power tends to retard innovation, whereas distribution of decision making among groups seems to encourage it. It follows that counselors who are familiar with the balance of power in the school system are more likely to know how to influence it positively. Identifying the most influential people inside and outside the organization helps a counselor understand the sources of authority and influence. All others have little or no authority or influence unless they find ways to influence the decision makers (Haettenschwiller, 1970). Under these circumstances, most counselors, teachers, and students find that diplomacy and subtlety are the best avenues to effect influence.

In summary, counselors engaging in organizational consultation help consultees translate noble dreams into achievable goals that will increase the probability of success and decrease the probability of failure and abandonment (Ponzo, 1974). Acting as consultants, counselors can help consultees understand how the system works and establish action plans that seem to have the best chances of succeeding. At times, consulting counselors are proactive and serve as advocates for their consultees (e.g., representing student consultees or joining them in meetings with administrators). At other times, the assistance will be indirect (e.g., preparing student consultees for meetings with administrators through structured behavior rehearsals). Of course, the prospect of redesigning the strategy for additional follow-up efforts is necessary because no plan can be a guaranteed success. An understanding of the organization also helps counselors when offering consultation through in-service programs and when helping colleagues plan curriculum programs. A hypothetical example of organizational consultation follows:

> In a high-school setting, the administration (principal and assistants) arbitrarily dictated a student dress code to which some have strong objections. Several students ask to meet with a counselor to air their complaints about the new code and to ask for help. The counselor believes that the administrators have the right to determine policies; she also thinks that the students seem to have some legitimate complaints about the code. These beliefs lead to the counselor offering to serve as a consultant (collaborative mode) to the students to help them try to achieve their goals. Initially, the counselor helps the students identify and clarify their position and the affect associated with it. Next, using knowledge of the school as a system, the counselor helps the students devise a strategy that demonstrates respect for the

office of the principal, awareness of the lines of authority in the school system, and conformity with their goals. Having agreed on a strategy, the counselor helps the students prepare to implement it and develops a follow-up strategy for dealing with the range of possible responses from the school's administrators. For example, the counselor may help the students prepare to deliver to the principal an inventory of their objections to the dress code in a manner that is respectful yet appropriately assertive, after advising them on behaviors that seem to have the best potential for success. Follow-up activities will depend on the administration's response. Whether the administrators are conciliatory and willing to negotiate or steadfast in defending their position, the counselor remains available to consult with the students about the process, the outcomes, and the appropriate next step.

Consulting to Achieve Successful Mediation. In the mediation mode, counselors respond directly to requests from two or more consultees to facilitate a mutual agreement or reconciliation. For example, two students who have been feuding and fighting over issues they are unable to resolve agree to meet with a counselor to work out an amicable settlement. Initially, the consultees must understand the assumptions on which mediation is founded: The mediator is not expected to dictate a resolution, the consultees agree to declare a truce during mediation, the mediator facilitates communications between the disputing parties, the disputing parties listen to each other's views, the disputing parties agree that their goal is to achieve a mutually agreeable resolution, and mediation is completed successfully when the disputing parties achieve a mutually agreeable solution.

The mediator facilitates communications between disputing parties.

Counselors who understand and accept the assumptions on which mediation is founded will be quite capable of serving as mediation consultants. The basic counseling and challenging skills coupled with knowledge about interpersonal communications are the requisite skills for mediation consultation. Beyond that, counselors can draw on experience, previous formal knowledge, and familiarity with the schools to help mediation consultees. The following example introduces the use of mediation as a consulting strategy in conflict resolution. In a hypothetical case of conflict resolution, the counselor acts as a mediator in a student-teacher dispute with cultural diversity overtones:

> The participants in the simulation are an African American male counselor (the consultant), a European American female teacher (the consultee), and a 13-year-old African American female student (the client). Their middle school is located in a middle-class area of a predominantly European American community. The student is a client of the counselor's whom he has counseled previously regarding school adjustment and academic performance. One class (English) that has been discussed in their counseling sessions is taught by the consultee, and the student has mentioned disliking the teacher as a reason for not performing well in the class, without specifically elaborating on reasons. After about 40% of the school year passes, the teacher approaches the counselor for consultation about getting the student, who appears to be stubbornly refusing to complete assignments, to complete her schoolwork. The consultation relationship opens in the collaboration mode.
>
> Counselor (consultant)–teacher (consultee) discussions lead to defining the problem as student stubbornness, and they agree that the first step is that the counselor meet with the student to share the teacher's concern and position and try to determine whether the student can be persuaded to do her schoolwork. Before proceeding, the counselor makes sure that both the student and the teacher know of his previous relationships with each of them to avoid complications associated with having dual professional relationships (Dougherty, 1992). During the interview with the counselor, the student refuses to do any more homework than she is doing because she is passing the course; she also accuses the teacher of being racist, without providing specific examples of racist behaviors.
>
> The counselor suggests a meeting between the student and the teacher, with him present to serve as a mediator. They agree, although the student is not very hopeful in her comments when doing so. The counselor, as a consultant, has introduced the mediation mode. During the meeting, both the student and the teacher, despite the counselor's best efforts to explain how mediation works, behave as if the purpose of the meeting is to have the counselor take their side against the adversary. The student openly accuses the teacher of being racist and refuses to change her study behaviors, again citing her impression that she is passing. The teacher, while recognizing that the student is passing, tries to point out the folly of the student's actions and encourages her to try harder. Surprised by the accusation of racism, she denies it and defends herself as anything but a racist while also saying things that indicate her potential cultural insensitivity. The counselor, acting as a mediator, lets the interactions occur while trying to help

both parties clarify their positions and understand each other's. In addition, the counselor attempts to keep the parties focused on trying to resolve the conflict.

Within a week, the counselor, who believes that the mediation session went quite badly, checks with the teacher and the student to find out how things are progressing. To his surprise, he learns from the teacher that the student is turning in assignments and is not behaving belligerently in class. He learns from the student that the teacher's attitude has changed and is more acceptable. There are several possible explanations for why the conflict seems to be resolved. Perhaps the most important observation is that the counselor, using his mediation skills, provided an atmosphere in which the adversaries could find ways to communicate that worked best for them.

Responding to Consultee Reluctance and Resistance.   When attempting to initiate consulting, counselors may encounter reluctance from prospective consultees. The same competencies used for coping with reluctance when initiating counseling relationships are important when initiating consulting relationships. Because prescription, provision, collaboration, mediation, and arbitration consulting relationships are usually initiated by consultees, resistance is more common than reluctance in consulting relationships.

Resistance to consulting is similar to resistance to counseling. Therefore, the requisite competencies are similar. As with counseling, consulting relationships have such variables as individual personalities, different settings, and previous experiences that influence the counselor's responses to resistance and whether those responses work. In summary, when consulting, counselors may encounter reluctance and resistance just as they do when counseling, and the repertoire of possible responses is the same.

Closing Consulting Relationships.   The similarity between counseling and consulting relationships includes the closing phase. The same competencies are important in both. Evaluating consulting relationships is as important as evaluating counseling interventions and prevention programming. Chapter 13 is devoted to evaluation and accountability; suffice it to say here that if consulting goals have been established, they provide criteria for determining whether the goals were met. Also, because consultees are individuals with opinions about the services rendered to them, they can provide feedback about the consulting they received. Finally, cost-effectiveness can be determined from information readily available to counselors—the amount of time devoted to a consulting relationship and the counselor's approximate hourly pay.

Examples of Consulting in School Counseling

Planned Periodic Consulting in an Elementary-School Setting.   This example and those that follow are paraphrased from reports about consultation activities of school counselors that appeared in the professional literature or are derived from the professional experience of the authors. In the first example, Fall (1995) describes a *periodic planned consultation* idea between school counselors and teachers. With the knowledge and support of the principal, the counselor schedules 1-hour meetings with each teacher to whom the counselor is responsible to take place every 10 weeks (three times a year). Each consultation meeting may have its own topics. For example, determining the accuracy of student placement, assessing whether students' needs are being met, and asking how well the entire classroom is functioning may be topics for the first meeting.

Fall recommends a set of five steps that may be followed in each of the planned consultations. In the first step, the counselor observes the classroom for 30 minutes prior to the consultation meeting. Goals of the observation are acquiring background for understanding concerns the teacher may have; identifying classroom and teacher strengths; and noticing student behavior, particularly potential problem behaviors (e.g., appear withdrawn and unfocused). The second step consists of beginning the consultation session with positive comments from the observation step (e.g., "Your class worked well in groups. I was impressed by the way you let the students express themselves."). The goal of this interaction is to pave the way for accurate, nondefensive communication by being nonjudgmental and respectful.

During the third step, the counselor (consultant) employs reflective listening skills while the teacher is invited to share information about the entire classroom and specific students, including problems. This is followed by the counselor helping the teacher explore possible solutions. An excerpt from a hypothetical interaction follows:

Counselor:	It sounds like Ivey's behaviors are distracting the class and keeping him from being successful academically.
Teacher:	Some days are better than others. Mondays seem to be the worst.
Counselor:	That may be important. How does he do in subject areas?
Teacher:	He's OK when he pays attention. I've tried many things, and nothing seems to work unless I keep on him. I don't have time to do that.
Counselor:	Unquestionably, this has exasperated you. It appears as if attention from you works.
Teacher:	I hadn't thought of that, but I think you're right. (Fall, 1995)

The fourth step consists of exploring possible interventions for identified problems. Fall recommends doing this jointly, similar to the mutual counselor–consultee interaction presented in the collaboration mode described earlier in this chapter. This approach increases potential for identifying a host of possible solutions and for creating a good working alliance between the counselor (consultant) and teacher (consultee). The fifth step finds the counselor summing up what has been accomplished and making plans, jointly with the teacher, to follow up on plans for action that have been generated.

Gang Mediation in a Middle School. Tabish and Orell (1996) describe a middle-school gang intervention program for which the goal is to allow gang-involved youths to confront issues with rivals in a safe area where respect is maintained. To achieve this goal, Washington Middle School in Albuquerque, New Mexico, initiated peer and formal mediation in 1990. Peer mediation is for two rival gang members; formal mediation is for two or more rival gangs. Trained student mediators provide the peer mediation. The school's gang interventionist or selected outside mediators perform the formal mediations between rival gangs. An overview of the formal mediation process is provided here.

Initially, the interventionist meets with the rival gangs in a small assembly to explain the purpose, roles, and process. Participation is voluntary; however, it should be noted that the school's administration has made it known that negative gang behaviors will not be tolerated in the school. Each gang selects two representatives and an alternate to negotiate on their behalf. One to 3 hours per day for 3 to 5 days are devoted to the process. They meet in a room selected to provide a formal, serious atmosphere. The following rules are posted in the room: All parties must (a) try to solve the problem, (b) refrain from name calling and putting others down, (c) show respect by not interrupting each other, (d) be honest, (e) avoid using weapons, threats, and intimidating behaviors, and (f) maintain confidentiality. There is an agenda, and a list of gang members is distributed. The formalities are seen as indicating to the participants that the atmosphere is mature and serious. The mediation process itself is a form of social modeling that will help the participants generalize the process to other problems.

The process consists of four meetings. The introductory events just described occur during the first meeting. Establishing an atmosphere of mutual trust and understanding while allowing all parties to share their feelings and views is the focus of the second meeting. Witnesses may be called in to clarify the problem. Solutions to the problem are identified during the third meeting, using a brainstorming approach. Adjournment occurs only after an agreement is reached by all parties. The fourth meeting is devoted to reviewing and confirming the agreement. Follow-up meetings with representatives of both gangs in attendance or with each gang separately are held to evaluate the agreement and acquire signatures missed earlier.

The preceding information describes mediation provided by a trained professional consultant who could be a school counselor using the collaborative mode. An atmosphere of respect for each student was promoted.

Supervising Peer Counselors in a Secondary-School Setting.

A high-school counselor trained student volunteers to help their peers meet with the peer counselors on a regular basis to provide them with support and supervision. The following scenario represents a hypothetical supervisory relationship. The counselor supervisor is the consultant, the student peer counselor is the consultee, and the students whom she is helping are the clients:

The counselor-supervisor opens a supervision meeting with an open-ended question or open invitation to the peer counselor to share whatever concerns her most. The peer counselor describes the circumstances of a case that is particularly challenging for her. The client is a student who sought out the peer counselor for help because she is failing her mathematics course, having relationship problems with a boyfriend, and experiencing pressure from her parents about her schoolwork and the relationship. She believes that her parents have unrealistic academic expectations and should not try to influence her choice of boyfriends.

After helping the peer counselor tell her story and clarify the facts, the counselor consultant invites her to share her feelings about the case. The peer counselor wonders aloud whether she is competent enough to deal with the issues the client has presented. The consultant agrees that this may be a genuine concern and asks the peer helper what options she has considered, offering to help brainstorm them (collaboration mode). The brainstorming session leads the supervisor (consultant) to conclude that the peer helper (consultee) may be able to help the client in some ways but is not the appropriate person to respond to all the issues that were presented. The supervisor-consultant then offers suggestions for the peer helper to consider (initiation mode).

The consultant offers the following recommendations for the consultee to consider (prescription mode): (a) Meet with the client again and ask whether she is interested in receiving tutoring for her mathematics difficulties. If she is, the peer helper can then make the necessary arrangements for her to receive that help. (b) Inform the client that she (the peer counselor) discussed the case with the consultant supervisor, who, in turn, recommends that the client see one of the school's professional counselors about the relationship and parental issues, indicating that the supervisor is willing to receive the referral. Following discussion of the merits of the recommendations, the peer counselor agrees to the plan. After attempting to carry out the agreed-on strategy, the consultee will report what transpired with the client to the consultant, and together they will determine what to do next.

The hypothetical consulting relationship transpired across the three stages described earlier in the chapter, and the consultant used several consulting modes in the process. Switching modes is not uncommon. As presented herein, the modes are primarily means of classifying, studying, and understanding different ways to engage in consultation.

Solution-Focused School Consultation.

Kahn (2000) uses a middle-school setting to provide an example of solution-focused school consultation. Kahn emphasizes that school counselor (consultants) should help consultees (e.g., teachers or parents) to set goals that they can control rather than assessing their success in terms of client change. Kahn's (2000) approach is for the school counselor as consultant to begin with an orientation to solution-focused consulting and help the consultee to identify strengths and resources and set initial goals. In a case illustration, the school counselor (consultant) begins with an invitation to the teacher (consultee) to share what she hoped to accomplish in the first consulting session. The teacher reveals her frustration with a literature/language class. The counselor's response focuses on the teacher's recent accomplishments (e.g., started an after-school study hall and tailored her curriculum to students). After the teacher remembers that she has experienced success, the counselor restates the problem positively ("Let's see what we can do to help you feel like you are staying afloat"; p. 252). The counselor follows with a request for a survey of what's been happening in the teacher's class.

The teacher then describes a class out of her control and a specific student who takes over the class, sabotaging her lesson plans. The (counselor) consultant's brief response is to ask how the teacher will know when things are better for the most troublesome student in her classroom. When the teacher responds, the counselor attempts to help her be specific and use concrete terms (i.e., "When he's tuned in" becomes "He wouldn't disrupt my class"; p. 252). Next, the counselor asks the teacher how she will feel when the student is "tuned in." The teacher lists several positive outcomes. At this point, the goals have been established.

Having established goals early in the consultation process, the counselor proceeds to seek solutions that will be acceptable to the consultee. The process begins with the counselor helping the teacher to remember occasions when the troublesome student was not troublesome. This is followed by an analysis of the circumstances that led to his not being troublesome (e.g., "shorten his task . . . ask him what he needs during breaks between tasks"; p. 252). The counselor then asks: "What do you need to do to make it happen again?" (p. 253). When the teacher states that she should initiate again the procedures that once worked, the counselor gives her immediate positive verbal reinforcement. The counselor follows this with a recommendation to the teacher for evaluating the effects of her efforts ("So, if Jon is a four this week, what will have to happen for him to be a five by our next meeting?"; p. 253 [principle: incremental changes will cause a rippling effect]). The counselor closes the session by recommending that the teacher think about how she can react differently to the troublesome student and perhaps change their relationship before the next consultation session.

Kahn stresses that the solution-focused approach can be conducted in one or a few sessions, focuses on the future, uses the consultee's strengths as resources, and is collaborative in nature. The primary steps in the process, as just demonstrated, are: (a) perform initial structuring, (b) establish goals for consultation, (c) examine previously attempted solutions and exceptions, (d) help the consultee find a solution, and (e) summarize goals and praise the consultant for past successes. As presented, the model seems user-friendly for school counselors as consultants and their consultees.

SCHOOL COUNSELOR CONSULTATION IN THE WAKE COUNTY ESSENTIAL GUIDANCE PROGRAM

Consultation activities among counselors and teachers, administrators, and students exist on an informal, as-needed basis. Consulting opportunities for parents, in contrast, are planned as follows:

- *Kindergarten Through 12th Grade:* Individual consultation with parents is based on referrals by teachers, principals, and counselors on an as-needed basis.
- *Third Grade:* Consultation is initiated with parents whose children have been identified as being potentially at risk of being unsuccessful in school.
- *Sixth Through 12th Grades:* Individual consultation for parents of at-risk students is conducted.

SCHOOL COUNSELOR CONSULTATION IN THE WAYNESBORO *COMPREHENSIVE GUIDANCE PLAN*

Consultation is planned for within components of the guidance plan as follows:

- *Responsive Services:* Counselors consult with parents, teachers, other educators, and community agencies regarding strategies to help students.

• *System Support:* Counselors need to consult with teachers and other staff members regularly to provide information, support staff, and receive feedback on emerging needs of students.

CONSULTATION: A NATURAL FUNCTION FOR SCHOOL COUNSELORS

Consulting is a widely accepted counseling function. It is not as clearly understood as counseling interventions or prevention programming and varies across settings. Natural circumstances in the schools provide school counselors with a relatively specific consultation role that can manifest itself in several modes. Many students, teachers, administrators, and parents view counselors as being in a relatively neutral position in the schools and as possessing competencies that can be shared in consulting relationships. Therefore, being available for, and sought out by, others for consultation assistance is a natural function for school counselors. They are strategically located in the schools as people who might be trusted to serve as consultants via the various consulting modes introduced in this chapter. School counselors who recognize the interrelationships between consulting and other important school counseling functions can appreciate the unique qualities of consultation activities and recognize opportunities to consult in an organized fashion.

SUGGESTED ACTIVITIES

1. Debate the position taken in this chapter that school settings naturally determine the parameters of consulting for school counselors.
2. Take an inventory of the competencies taught in your core counseling methods course that are applicable to consulting.
3. Review the five consulting modes presented in this chapter; determine which ones you would be comfortable providing and which do not appeal to you.
4. Analyze, discuss, and/or debate the following statement: "Courses in school counselor training programs devoted only to consultation are unnecessary because there is so much in common between counseling and consulting."
5. List ways that consulting assignments can be incorporated into your field internship or practicum.
6. Debate the merits of the basic consulting action strategies mentioned in this chapter. Which ones seem appropriate to you and which do not? What are the reasons for your decisions?
7. Analyze the conflict resolution mediation consulting simulation (the simulation in which a female student thought her teacher was a racist) in this chapter from the perspective of critiquing the (counselor) consultant's actions and trying to hypothesize possible explanations for the outcomes.
8. After having read the section "Examples of Consulting in School Counseling," what new thoughts about consultation occurred to you?
9. Discuss or debate how the modes and stages of consultation presented in this chapter fit into a multicultural perspective of helping diverse consultees and clients with varied worldviews. Are they sufficient, or do they need to be altered in some way?
10. Go to www.scan21st.com and explain how this Internet site might assist school counselors in their consulting roles.

174 Chapter 6

REFERENCES

Adelman, H. S., & Taylor, L. (2002). School counselors and school reform: New directions. *Professional School Counseling, 5,* 235–248.

American School Counselor Association. (n.d.). *Guide to membership resources.* Alexandria, VA: Author.

Bardon, J. I. (1985). On the verge of a breakthrough. *Counseling Psychologist, 13*(3), 355–362.

Bauer, A. M., & Sapona, R. H. (1988). Facilitation and problem solving: A framework for collaboration between counselors and teachers. *Elementary School Guidance and Counseling, 23,* 5–9.

Brack, G., Jones, E. S., Smith, R. M., White, J., & Brack, C. J. (1993). A primer on consultation theory: Building a flexible worldview. *Journal of Counseling & Development, 71,* 619–628.

Brown, D., Wyne, M. D., Blackburn, J. E., & Powell, W. C. (1979). *Consultation: Strategy for improving education.* Boston: Allyn & Bacon.

Bundy, M. L., & Poppen, W. A. (1986). School counselors' effectiveness as consultants: A research review. *Elementary School Guidance and Counseling, 29,* 215–222.

Caplan, G. (1959). *Concepts of mental health and consultation.* Washington, DC: U.S. Department of Health, Education and Welfare, Children's Bureau.

Dougherty, A. M. (1990). *Consultation: Practice and perspectives.* Pacific Grove, CA: Brooks/Cole.

Dougherty, A. M. (1992). School consultation in the 1990s. *Elementary School Guidance and Counseling, 26,* 163–164.

Dowd, E. T., & Moerings, B. J. (1975). The underachiever and teacher consultation: A case study. *School Counselor, 22,* 263–266.

Dustin, R., & Ehly, S. (1984). Skills for effective consultation. *School Counselor, 32,* 23–29.

Egan, G. (1998). *The skilled helper: A problem-management approach to helping* (6th ed.). Pacific Grove, CA: Brooks/Cole.

Fall, M. (1995). Planning for consultation: An aid for the elementary school counselor. *School Counselor, 43,* 151–156.

Gallessich, J. (1985). Toward a meta-theory of consultation. *Counseling Psychologist, 13*(3), 336–354.

Gerler, E. R., Jr. (1992). Consultation and school counseling. *Elementary School Guidance and Counseling, 26,* 162.

Gysbers, N. C., & Henderson, P. (2001). Comprehensive guidance and counseling programs: A rich history and a bright future. *Professional School Counseling, 4,* 246–256.

Haettenschwiller, D. L. (1970). Control of the counselor's role. *Journal of Counseling Psychology, 17,* 437–442.

Horton, G. E., & Brown, D. (1990). The importance of interpersonal skills in consultee-centered consultation. *Journal of Counseling & Development, 68,* 423–426.

House, R. M., & Hayes, R. L. (2002). School counselors: Becoming key players in school reform. *Professional School Counseling, 5,* 249–256.

Kahn, B. B. (2000). A model of solution-focused consultation for school counselors. *Professional School Counseling, 3,* 248–254.

Keat, D. B. (1974). *Fundamentals of child counseling.* Boston: Houghton Mifflin.

Kurpius, D. J. (1978). Consultation theory and process: An integrated model. *Personnel and Guidance Journal, 56,* 335–338.

Kurpius, D. J., & Fuqua, D. R. (1993a). Consultation I: Conceptual, structural, and operational dimensions. *Journal of Counseling & Development, 71,* 596–708.

Kurpius, D. J., & Fuqua, D. R. (1993b). Consultation II: Prevention, preparation, and key issues. *Journal of Counseling & Development, 72,* 115–198.

Kurpius, D. J., Fuqua, D. R., & Rozecki, T. (1993). The consulting process: A multidimensional approach. *Journal of Counseling & Development, 71,* 601–606.

Lin, M., Kelly, K. R., & Nelson, R. C. (1996). A comparative analysis of the interpersonal process in school-based counseling and consultation. *Journal of Counseling Psychology, 43,* 389–393.

Mathias, C. E. (1992). Touching the lives of children: Consultative interventions that work. *Elementary School Guidance and Counseling, 26,* 190–201.

Mendoza, D. W. (1993). A review of Gerald Caplan's *Theory and Practice of Mental Health Consultation. Journal of Counseling & Development, 71,* 629–635.

Messing, J. K. (1993). Mediation: An intervention strategy for counselors. *Journal of Counseling & Development, 72,* 67–72.

Mullis, F., & Edwards, D. (2001). Consulting with parents: Applying family systems concepts and techniques. *Professional School Counseling, 5,* 116–123.

Myrick, R. D. (1977). *Consultation as a counselor intervention.* Washington, DC: American School Counselor Association.

Osterweil, Z. O. (1987). A structured process of problem definition in school consultation. *School Counselor, 34,* 245–252.

Ponzo, Z. (1974). A counselor and change: Reminiscence and resolutions. *Personnel and Guidance Journal, 53,* 27–32.

Purkey, W. W., & Schmidt, J. J. (1982). Ways to be an inviting parent: Suggestions for the counselor-consultant. *Elementary School Guidance and Counseling, 17,* 94–99.

Rathvon, N. W. (1990). The effects of encouragement on off-task behavior and academic productivity. *Elementary School Guidance and Counseling, 24,* 189–199.

Robinson, E. H., & Wilson, E. S. (1987). Counselor-led human relations training as a consultation strategy. *Elementary School Guidance and Counseling, 22,* 124–131.

Rockwood, G. G. (1993). Edgar Schein's process versus content consultation models. *Journal of Counseling & Development, 71,* 636–638.

Ross, G. J. (1993). Peter Block's flawless consulting and homunculus theory: Within each person is a perfect consultant. *Journal of Counseling & Development, 71,* 639–641.

Smaby, M. H., Peterson, T. L., Bergmann, P. E., Bacig, K. L. Z., & Swearingen, S. (1990). School-based community intervention: The school counselor as lead consultant for suicide prevention and intervention programs. *Elementary School Guidance and Counseling, 37,* 370–377.

Strein, W., & French, J. L. (1984). Teacher consultation in the affective domain: A survey of expert opinion. *School Counselor, 31,* 339–344.

Stum, D. L. (1982). DIRECT: A consultation skills training model. *Personnel and Guidance Journal, 60,* 296–301.

Tabish, K. R., & Orell, L. H. (1996). RESPECT: Gang mediation at Albuquerque, New Mexico's Washington Middle School. *School Counselor, 44,* 65–70.

Umansky, D. L., & Holloway, E. L. (1984). The counselor as consultant: From model to practice. *School Counselor, 31,* 329–338.

CHAPTER 7

Referring and Coordinating in School Counseling

Goals: To explain the unique circumstances of the referral and coordination

functions in school counseling. To propose competencies for counselor-

initiated referrals and a system for managing referrals to school counselors.

To highlight the place of coordination in the referral process.

Lakisha, an 8-year-old living in North Florida with her grandmother and grandfa-
ther, came to school almost every day wearing long-sleeved sweaters and heavy wool
pants. When teachers questioned her about wearing such heavy clothing in a warm
climate, Lakisha responded simply that she liked the way the clothes looked. She would
then lower her eyes and walk away quickly. One teacher, suspicious that something

was wrong, asked the school counselor to speak with Lakisha. Noticing that Lakisha moved with great care and with a grimace on her face, the counselor immediately referred Lakisha to the school nurse, who examined Lakisha and discovered burns and bruises on her arms and legs. The counselor and school nurse immediately contacted social services and began the difficult process of investigating and repairing the tragedy of Lakisha's existence. The process required the coordination of many professionals and involved diligence to avoid having Lakisha's case lost in a sea of bureaucracy.

School counselors are frequently called upon to refer and coordinate difficult cases like that of Lakisha. This chapter examines the skills and processes involved in these efforts.

DEMAND FOR REFERRAL AND COORDINATION IN SCHOOL COUNSELING

In previous chapters, a case was made for balanced school counseling programs consisting of equally important intervention and prevention emphases. Counseling, prevention programming, and consulting were presented as important competencies in a balanced program. All professionals are limited in expertise and time; they refer clients to others whose services are more appropriate. In addition, school counselors receive referrals from other professionals who also are limited in expertise and time. Consequently, school counselors are challenged to have the skills to make referrals, manage the referrals they receive, and coordinate the process once referrals have been made or accepted. Referring and coordinating are functions that fit within a broader school counselor role concept that appears to be increasingly important. Atkinson and Juntunen (1994) use the label *school-home-community liaison* for this role. As liaisons, school counselors work with students, parents, and members of the community to identify and use valuable human services inside and outside the school system that meet both remedial and enhancement goals for students, and they coordinate the acquisition and use of the services, acting at times like brokers.

Collaboration between the schools and their communities seems to be increasingly important. Students are faced with problems that require comprehensive services, many of which are beyond the capacities of the services the schools can provide. Hobbs and Collison (1995) found evidence that collaboration between the schools and local agencies (in their study, youth services teams in four communities in Oregon) is increasing. They believe that school counselors will need to reassess their role in the context of the community rather than the school and to develop or enhance collaboration skills. J. Downing, Pierce, and Woodruff (1993) picture this collaboration in the context of developing networks among the community's professional helpers inside and outside the schools, a challenging yet potentially fruitful undertaking.

The focus of this chapter is on two types of referrals. They are treated separately and referred to as either counselor-initiated referrals or referrals to counselors. Because counseling is a human services profession, it is important that counselors help clients receive needed services. At times, the needed services are beyond the scope and setting of school counseling. In such cases, school counselors help clients through a referral process. The direction of these referrals is away from school counselors toward other professionals or sources of help. These are counselor-initiated referrals. Prospective referees are encouraged to use the school's counseling services voluntarily and, in so doing, to understand the goals and limitations of those services. At other times, school professionals (e.g., teachers, administrators) and individuals outside the schools who are interested in students' welfare (e.g., parents) look to counselors as a source of help for their students/children and make referrals to counselors. This process works best when the prospective referees clearly understand the counselors' range of competencies. All parties are served best when school counselors inform others about their services and manage efficiently the referrals they receive.

Spokespersons for the three school counseling initiatives introduced in chapter 1 cite the importance of appropriate referrals and helpful coordination of the referral process. In the ASCA's National Model for Comprehensive School Counseling Programs, referral is depicted as a responsive service through which school counselors seek help for students from professional resources in and out of the school when necessary (Gysbers & Henderson, 2001). The National School Counselor Training Initiative places importance on the role of school counselors as brokers of services for parents and students from community and school system resources. To accomplish this goal, school counselors are challenged to understand and appreciate the contributions that these significant others can make (House & Hayes, 2002). Referring and coordinating seem to be subsumed under a somewhat broader context referred to as collaboration in the School-Community Collaboration Model (Adelman & Taylor, 2002). The citations attributed to Hobbs and Collison (1995) and Downing et al. (1993) offer a hint of what this broader context means. We elaborate more on collaboration competencies in chapter 12.

SCHOOL COUNSELOR-INITIATED REFERRALS

Point of View

In the *Code of Ethics and Standards of Practice* of the American Counseling Association (ACA) and in the American School Counselor Association's (ASCA) "Ethical Standards for School Counselors," referrals are presented as a mandate to do what is in the client's best interests:

> If counselors determine an inability to be of professional assistance to clients, they avoid entering or immediately terminate a counseling relationship. Counselors are knowledgeable about referral resources and suggest appropriate alternatives. If clients decline the suggested referral, counselors should discontinue the relationship. (ACA, 1995, Section A.11, paragraph b)
>
> The professional school counselor makes referrals when necessary or appropriate to outside resources. Appropriate referral necessitates knowledge of available resources and making proper plans for transitions with minimal interruption of services. (ASCA, 1998, p. 18)

Two delicate issues that counselors face in the referral process are the related possibilities of referring clients prematurely and of treating them too long. On the one hand, busy counselors may wrongly view referral as a way to divest themselves of part of their counseling burden. Then referral sources become repositories for excess work-loads. The motives behind such referrals are primarily selfish. Premature referrals may also result from counselors' feelings of inadequacy, low risk-taking thresholds, or fail-ure to appreciate their own ability. Although counselors' intentions may be honorable, the outcomes are still premature referrals.

On the other hand, counselors may continue working with clients too long for selfish reasons, such as a need to feel responsible for curing their clients. This mistaken motivation serves the needs of the counselors, rather than those of the clients. Counselors may also work with clients too long for altruistic reasons, as when clients convince them that no one else can help or refuse to be referred. Kimmerling (1993) refers to deciding when to refer a client as "When Saying No Is the Right Thing to Do" (p. 5).

Shertzer and Stone (1981) offer suggestions for resolving these referral fallacies. First, counselors realize that referral is not merely a technique they use when operat-ing a clearinghouse. Second, they understand that referrals are not limited to emer-gencies. Many emergencies can be averted by timely referrals. Third, referrals are not admissions of failure. Instead, they are intelligent decisions to provide the best possi-ble assistance to clients.

When approaching the referral decision, counselors are forced to look within themselves and beyond their work settings to ask several important questions. These questions draw on evaluations of their competencies, the competencies of their refer-ral sources, and their own motives. Assessing one's competencies realistically can be difficult and painful. Although counselors are the main sources of information about their own competencies, respected colleagues can provide wise counsel.

Knowing the competencies of potential referral sources requires careful intelli-gence gathering. Sources of information are numerous, and using them requires con-siderable effort. Information can be acquired through cooperative research with colleagues. Categories of important information that counselors might acquire about referees are offered by Weinrach (1984), who suggests that referees can make the refer-ral process more mutual by demystifying it. Important information that Weinrach rec-ommends counselors and clients should know about referees includes their qualifica-tions, expertise, and orientation; intake procedures, fee structures, and scheduling methods; whether the services are publicly or privately provided; follow-up proce-dures; and general attitudes toward clients.

Motives can be controlled if counselors hold their clients' welfare above their own needs. This is continuous because client cases change and counselors grow in experi-ence and competence. In all, the decision process requires honest introspection and a willingness to spend time and energy gathering information.

A unique aspect of the referral function in school counseling is that most clients are minors. Therefore, the referral process is complicated by the need for parental knowledge and cooperation. At times, all seems well until the clients' parents or guardians become involved. Parents may be the source of clients' attitudes that lead to ignoring or rejecting referral suggestions, and usually parents cannot be forced to respond as desired. On other occasions, clients who are minors may themselves make the referral process extremely difficult. They may not want their parents or guardians

Knowing the competencies of potential referral sources requires careful intelligence gathering.

to know about the issues leading to referral suggestions, or they may ignore or reject referral suggestions. Children and adolescents are less likely than adults to understand the referral process and to be objective about it.

School counselors face the additional challenge of working with parents or guardians through their children, often without authority to require desired responses. Because of this two-tiered decision-making situation, school counselors are challenged to be more adept at making referrals than many other helping professionals. They also face the dilemma of deciding whether to continue counseling clients who fail to accept referral suggestions, or to discontinue the relationships. Discontinuing counseling services under these circumstances is ethically acceptable. Yet, failing to respond to referral suggestions may be caused by parental attitudes, leaving clients caught in the middle and counselors struggling to determine whether their own services are better for the clients than none.

A recent challenge for school counselors is managed care. Many families may be insured by health maintenance organizations (HMOs) or preferred provider organizations (PPOs), which place restrictions on one's freedom to choose service providers. Therefore, even though student clients and their parents are cooperative, their insurance may not cover the services being recommended or the services can only be provided by a restricted group of preferred or contracted providers. Counselors will then be challenged to become aware of a larger cohort of approved providers across various organizations serving their clients' families.

Foundations

Counselor-initiated referring and coordinating beg for a systematic approach. A system helps counselors know in advance what to do and makes the process more efficient for everyone. The process is more likely to progress effectively, and clients are more likely to be treated appropriately. The three-stage helping model adapted from Egan (1998) for counseling and consulting is applicable to referring and coordinating, too. The three stages can be expressed as identifying and clarifying, setting goals based on an understanding of the problem, and implementing constructive action strategies. The following suggested competencies are woven into the fabric of these stages. They are culled from several sources in the professional literature (cf. Amatea & Fabrick, 1984; Baker, 1973; Bobele & Conran, 1988; C. J. Downing, 1985; Weinrach, 1984).

BASIC COMPETENCIES FOR SCHOOL COUNSELOR-INITIATED REFERRALS

Identifying and Clarifying the Problem

Counselors are challenged to know themselves and their referral sources—to evaluate realistically their own competencies as well as those of other referral sources. Beyond that, counselors who have sufficient knowledge about their clients make educated decisions about referral sources. The basic counseling competencies are again paramount because most referrals begin as counseling or consulting relationships. An example follows:

> A high-school teacher refers a student to a high-school counselor after witnessing a noticeable change in the student's affect indicating that the student seems depressed. The student responds to the counselor's invitation to have an interview. The counselor explains that the teacher is concerned about the student's welfare and has asked for help to be provided if needed. The student agrees that things are not good and agrees to talk with the counselor. Beginning the relationship as if it were a potential counseling intervention, the counselor asks the client to talk about the presenting problem and the feelings associated with it. Using the basic counseling intervention skills, the counselor helps the client try to identify and clarify the problem and concludes that the client seems quite depressed and is also at a loss to offer specific reasons for the depressed affect.

Setting Goals Based on Understanding the Problem

Bringing a counseling or consulting relationship to the point where goals are established helps counselors determine whether a referral needs to be suggested. Thus, the basic challenging skills are also part of the referral service. Under these circumstances, it might be appropriate to mention that Ivey (1994) uses the label *influencing skills* when classifying these counseling competencies, and in some instances *influencing* may be the more appropriate term to use. Because many clients and their parents do not necessarily think they need specialized help outside the school system, counselors may have to use influencing skills to challenge them to consider and accept a referral suggestion (e.g., advanced accurate empathy, confrontation, information sharing, immediacy). An example follows:

The case of the depressed high-school student moves to the goal-setting stage when the counselor, after having met with the client for two sessions to identify and clarify the situation, concludes that the client is deeply depressed, seemingly unable to identify causes, and apparently in need of help that is beyond the scope of the counselor's expertise. The counselor indicates to the client that the best source of help may be a referral to a clinician in private practice (e.g., psychologist, psychiatrist).

Counselor:	We have talked extensively about how miserable you seem to feel, and you have indicated a desire to get some relief. I agree that you need and should get some relief, and I also think that the best way to get relief is to see a professional who is a specialist and can devote the proper amount of time that is needed to help you, doing so in a setting that is more private than being seen here at school.
Client:	I don't know. That sounds expensive, and I don't know if my folks will agree to it. Besides, I don't want people to think I am crazy and have to see a "shrink."
Counselor:	So, you are concerned about the cost and what people will think, perhaps what you think about yourself as well [advanced accurate empathy]. Are you familiar with the services of Wellsprings?
Client:	No! What do they do?
Counselor:	They may be able to help you without it being too expensive and without your thinking of yourself as needing to see a "shrink." Do you wish to know more?
Client:	Yes!

The counselor then proceeds to provide accurate information about Wellsprings [information sharing]. After sharing the information, the counselor asks, "Well, what do you think?"

Client:	I don't know, it sounds pretty involved to me. I don't think I will have enough time, and my parents probably will object to my going there.
Counselor:	It sounds involved, and you worry about what your parents will say. On the other hand, you have indicated to me that things are really bad and you have to get some help, and I have pointed out that the kind of help you seem to need is not really available here in school, leading me to suggest Wellsprings. We can explore other alternatives, but before we do, I'm wondering if you need to think first about how badly you want help and whether or not you and your

parents are willing to make the commitment needed to take that first step. I want to help you, but I also think you need to take a good look at what you have just been saying. What do you think? [confrontation]

In the foregoing interaction, the counselor employed three influencing responses: advanced accurate empathy, information sharing, and confrontation. All are presented caringly and tentatively in the hope that the client will accept a referral suggestion to achieve expressed goals.

Implementing Constructive Action Strategies

Sometimes, counseling and consulting relationships move into the action stage before a referral suggestion is considered, or the act of referring becomes the constructive action stage of the helping relationship. In either case, where and how to refer become the basic referring objectives, and how to coordinate a successful referral becomes the third basic action strategy objective. Referring and coordinating competencies are devoted to responding to those questions.

Where to Refer Clients. Deciding where to refer clients requires knowing a variety of referral sources. Acquisition of such information demands investigative skills, using time and energy to locate and evaluate telephone books and the Internet, attending meetings of professional organizations, conferring with colleagues, interviewing potential service providers, and evaluating advertisements. School counselors may also have opportunities to acquire useful information from service organizations. Hollis and Hollis (1965) suggest that awareness includes identification of sources, a working knowledge of their services, knowledge of ways to use the services, and development of reciprocal services. Figure 7.1 lists various referral sources with which school counselors in any community might develop referral agreements.

Multiculturally aware counselors will develop resource lists of "educational and community support services to meet the socioeconomic and cultural needs of culturally diverse students and their families" (American School Counselor Association, 1989, p. 322). Recognizing the importance of cultural sensitivity in the referral process, Atkinson and Juntunen (1994) recommend that counselors be familiar with services offered both in ethnic communities and in the larger community. They also suggest that referrals can be traditional—that is, to remediate problems—and can be made to enhance the development of ethnic students. In the latter instance, the coordinating function comes into play as counselors refer students to such programs as Big Brothers and Big Sisters and children's workshops and to such organized, sponsored athletic programs as Little League baseball that may enhance their development. Although those recommendations are from writers whose focus is on serving ethnic minority students, the ideas are useful for, and applicable to, serving all students. Examples of referrals made to enhance development are as follows:

A middle-school counselor pursuing the school-home-community liaison role engages in the following related activities as a part of his or her overall functioning as a school counselor during 1 week.

Local Volunteer Organizations

Churches—Clergy	Job Placement Services	Rape Crisis Centers
Counseling Services	Medical Societies	Referral Services
Emergency Financial Assistance	Nursing Services	Runaway Hotlines
Health Councils	Parents Without Partners	Sheltered Workshops
Hospitals	Planned Parenthood Association	Thrift Shops
Information Services	Private Schools	

Government Agencies and Services

Bureau of Employment Security	County Board of Assistance	Home Health Services
Bureau of Special Health Services	County Health Services	Human Relations Commission
Bureau of Vocational Rehabilitation	Department of Agriculture	Mental Health/Mental Retardation
Child Welfare League of America	Department of Consumer Services	State Department of Health
Child Welfare Services	Department of Human Services	State Hospitals
Civil Service Commission	Department of Public Welfare	State Schools
Community Action	Family Planning Centers	Upward Bound
	Foster Home Care	Youth Service Bureau

National Nonprofit Organizations

Alanon	Easter Seal Society	National Association of Business and Professional Women
Alateen	Economic Opportunity Commission	National Federation of the Blind
Alcoholics Anonymous	Goodwill	National Runaway Hotline
Altrusa International	Junior Chamber of Commerce	Optimist International
American Association of University Women	Lions Club International	Rotary International
American Bar Association	Lutheran Social Services	Salvation Army
American Cancer Society	March of Dimes Foundation	Society for Crippled Children
American Heart Association	Narcotics Anonymous	Young Men's Christian Association (YMCA)
American Red Cross	National Association for the Advancement of Colored People	Young Women's Christian Association (YWCA)
Catholic Social Services		
Chamber of Commerce		

School District Services

Administrators	School Nurses	Teachers
Adult Education	School Psychologists	Other Pupil Personnel Specialists
Counseling Colleagues	School Social Workers	
Intermediate Service Units	Speech and Hearing Specialists	

Proprietary Services

Attorneys	Employment Agencies	Physical Therapists
Boarding Houses	Nurses	Physicians
Chiropractors	Occupational Therapists	Preparatory Schools
Clinical Psychologists	Opticians	Professional Resume Services
Counseling Psychologists	Optometrists	Psychiatrists
Counselors	Osteopaths	

Figure 7.1

Potential referral resources available to school counselors.

- The counselor coordinates arrangements for a group of students to visit nearby colleges and technical schools.
- The counselor, in conjunction with cooperating local employers, arranges for part-time work for several students who are borderline delinquents.
- The counselor recommends a Big Brother to an 11-year-old male student and coordinates a meeting between the student and a volunteer recommended by the Big Brother organization.
- A female student who has been attending an after-school drama workshop because the counselor recommended and arranged it stops by the office and reports that she is enjoying the activity.

After adequate information has been gathered, a system for storing and retrieving it is necessary. Options include personal memory and filing systems. In this age of microcomputers, the information can be stored relatively easily. Simplicity of organization and efficient retrieval are mandatory, so new information can be added, old information updated, and existing information accessed easily.

Counselors are challenged to be willing to serve as reciprocal referral sources. It seems logical that counselors do for others that which others request them to do. To implement a reciprocal arrangement, formal or semiformal agreements can make both parties aware of the services each is prepared to deliver to the other on request.

Carrying the idea of organization a step farther, a follow-up system can be considered. Among the benefits is the acquisition of helpful information about the clients and about the referral service. The follow-up can contain information from both parties covered in the referral service agreement. One example of a reciprocal feedback proposal follows:

> A school counselor successfully arranges for a referral of a client to Dr. X. Per their agreement, Dr. X supplies the counselor with appropriate information about the client after acquiring signed permissions from the client or the client's parents. The counselor expects this feedback from Dr. X and will seek it out if necessary. (paraphrased from Baker, 1973)

Because clients are the most important parties in the referral process, follow-up data from them are a valuable source of information about the adequacy of referral services. Some sort of client survey is suggested. Important questions can be incorporated into these surveys by using any one of several available formats. Here are some areas to cover by questions in client surveys:

- The client's level of satisfaction with the counselor's manner when making the referral suggestion
- The accuracy of the counselor's description of these referral services to the client
- The client's level of satisfaction with the helper's services
- The client's perception of the competence of the new helper
- The client's level of satisfaction with the new helper or the combination of original and referred helpers (Baker, 1973)

Such surveys measure client satisfaction with referral services. A more comprehensive evaluation of the referral services also includes procedures for acquiring outcome data based on referral objectives and enumerative data that determine cost-effectiveness of the referral services. More information about outcome data and cost-effectiveness is presented in chapter 13.

The follow-up procedures just described, including the survey, fall into the coordinating domain. As such, counselors are attempting to ensure success for referrals and to assess how successful the referring and coordinating efforts were.

How to Refer Clients.

Perhaps the most important facet of the referral process is the referral suggestion. Brammer, Abrego, and Shostrom (1993) think that the way the referral suggestion is introduced and explained has considerable influence on the chance for success. Two challenges confront counselors when suggesting referrals:

1. Clients may feel abandoned or rejected by the suggestion.
2. Clients may reject the suggestion.

Responding to the first challenge requires sensitivity and good communication skills. The second challenge requires resilience and persistence; if rejected, counselors are challenged to keep seeking answers to the challenges.

To avoid confusion when referrals are made, counselors determine whether referrals are partial or complete. A *partial referral* results in the continuation of the counseling relationship, with supplementary services being provided by the referral source. For instance, after arranging for a referral physical examination and pregnancy test, the counselor meets with the young woman again to discuss her possible alternatives once the medical results are known. A *complete referral* is just what the term implies: The client is referred to another helper, and the counselor who made the referral completely disassociates from the case.

Carey, Black, and Neider (1978) propose a plan for increasing the success of referral suggestions. They believe that client expectations about complete referrals are seldom fulfilled. Thus, partial referrals are likely to be the best choice in many cases. They suggest looking at the problem from the client's point of view, which is often a troubled one. They conclude that two variables, client motivation and confidence, have a strong effect on the success of any referral. Both variables can be influenced strongly by counselors. Carey et al. offer the following suggestions for increasing client motivation and confidence:

- Eliminate some client dilemmas by recommending partial referrals. This should increase client motivation.
- Know your referral sources well. Counselors who do are less likely to project ambiguity to clients.
- Communicate appropriate and important information about clients to the referral sources. Telling clients that you've done this provides an additional safeguard and increases client motivation and confidence in the referral.
- Give specific information about cost, time, location, and the like to clients to help make their decision easier.

- When necessary, help clients by becoming active in the referral process. This may require making direct contact with referral sources to arrange for appointments or accompanying or transporting clients to appointments.

All these suggestions can be implemented by school counselors. Becoming active in the referral process to the point of arranging appointments and providing transportation, however, gets counselors into the arena of legal and ethical decisions. It also raises the issue of whether such acts are within the school policies where one is employed. Deciding to accompany or transport minor clients is predicated on thorough consideration of ethical standards, legal precedents, insurance liability, and school district policies. A more thorough presentation of legal and ethical issues is offered in chapter 3.

It is virtually impossible to develop a foolproof, cookbook-type method for making referral suggestions. The following suggestions may increase the chances of success. When reading and processing the suggestions, reflect on the hypothetical case about a depressed high-school student presented earlier in this chapter, and think about how well the counselor followed the suggestions made here. Those suggestions that offer ideas that will be incorporated during the implementation of the constructive action strategies stage are accompanied by extensions of the counselor–client interactions introduced earlier in the chapter.

1. *Assess a client's readiness carefully before making the suggestion.* In so doing, attempt to determine the psychological and emotional climate. It is important to know the client's ability to cope not only with making the decision but also with the implications of making such a suggestion. In the hypothetical case of the depressed high-school student, the counselor first explored the client's presenting problem and the client's assets and assessed his or her own capabilities before introducing the referral suggestion.

2. *Treat the client as you would like to be treated.* Consider the following questions and their implications (paraphrased from Baker, 1973):

Would [the client] want the counselor to be attentive and nonthreatening? objective and factual? completely honest? partially honest? Should the counselor "sell" the referral service, or does the client want an objective evaluation with a choice of optional resources? Does the client want the counselor to assist with the arrangements, or would he or she rather do it alone?

3. *Whenever possible, discuss the potential referral with prospective referees before making the referral suggestion* (Weinrach, 1984). This can be accomplished without divulging confidential information. Counselors can describe the specifics without mentioning identifying information, or they can present case information hypothetically. After selecting potential referees, informing them about the case, and deciding to make the referral suggestion, communicate confidence in the client (Bobele & Conran, 1988). The way the counselor introduced the idea of making a referral to Wellsprings indicates a familiarity with its services that predates the interview with the client.

4. *Be able to explain that the referral suggestion is congruent with the client's goals and why the referee will be better able to meet those goals* (C. J. Downing, 1985). Avoid implying that problem severity is the main reason for the referral. Doing so may lead clients to think negatively about themselves. Allow ample time for presenting and discussing the referral suggestion with the client. Offer specific information about names, orientations of referees, fees, and procedures. Communicate an interest in knowing how the referral fared for the client—to the point of arranging follow-up meetings and providing support (C. J. Downing, 1985). The hypothetical case is continued below:

Client:	(in response to the counselor's confrontation) I guess you are right. I do need to do something about this situation because it seems to be getting worse instead of better. But it's so hard. I don't have any energy, and it seems overwhelming to go to that place and start telling my story all over again.
Counselor:	You realize something needs to be done, yet there seems to be no energy, making it appear almost impossible. Perhaps knowing that I can be of some help in the process and will be here for you even though you are seeing someone outside the school may help. What do you think?
Client:	You'll help me and will see me, too. How?
Counselor:	Before you do anything, I'll see to it that you and your mother receive all the information needed to better know the people at Wellsprings, what they do, how they operate their services, and how much it may cost. I'll also help your mother make an appointment if she wishes. Also, I'll work with you here at the school in cooperation with whomever you are working with at Wellsprings. That is usually the way it is done. It makes the whole process run more smoothly when someone here at the school coordinates these arrangements. So, what do you think about that?
Client:	It sounds good, but I haven't really told my mother about how bad I feel or about seeing you. Will you help me tell her?
Counselor:	Yes! Let's explore how we can do that.

5. *When client and parental permissions are granted, cooperate with referees by providing helpful information when it is requested* (Amatea & Fabrick, 1984).

6. Parental resistance to a referral suggestion may be natural because problems involving their children threaten family systems and may seem to reflect badly on the core of the parents' being. They wish to protect their family systems. Counselors may have to *use challenging/influencing skills to persuade resistant parents of the seriousness of the problem*. Amatea and Fabrick (1984) recommend, as one approach, that the counselor hold back on tentativeness and assume the stance of an authoritative expert. The hypothetical case continues after the counselor has helped the client tell the parents about the referral and the counselor and client have explained what has transpired thus far:

Parent:	As you know, I am a single parent, and this all sounds to me like it could be very expensive. I don't know if my insurance will cover this, and I'm also not sure it is as serious as you say. Can't my child just shake it off and straighten things out with your help and mine?
Counselor:	You have doubts, and that is a reasonable response. I agree that your child has the capacity to get better and that both of us can be helpful. However, I also believe that additional help is needed, both in terms of time and expertise, and that help is available at Wellsprings. Before thinking about the cost, let's think about the effect this situation is having on your child and what the human costs will be if sufficient help is not provided. What are your thoughts about that?
Parent:	Well, I like the idea of your helping us get information before making a decision. What do we do now?
Counselor:	I think we should ask your child to explain just how serious it is and then look carefully at the options, and if seeing someone at Wellsprings turns out to be part of the plan, we need to gather information that will answer your questions. Then, I hope you'll be ready for a decision. I'll try to help you as much as I can, whatever the decision.

7.   *Give very careful consideration to the arrangements for the first meeting and for follow-up procedures.* A successfully accomplished referral suggestion can be damaged severely by expecting the client to make the next move (Baker, 1973). Experts are divided on this issue. Some think that clients should initiate contacting referees (Amatea & Fabrick, 1984); others think that referees should initiate contacts (in this case, family therapists: Bobele & Conran, 1988); and others suggest that counselors should be willing to help clients and parents initiate contacts (Baker, 1973; C. J. Downing, 1985). The natural compromise is for counselors to be prepared to use all three approaches because circumstances will dictate which is best. Some clients are very independent; others need help with making arrangements. Be sure to deal with this part of the referring/coordinating process carefully and conscientiously. What do the circumstances dictate our hypothetical case?

8.   *Engage in this process with an awareness of the implications involved when entering into the referral process with clients and referees who represent different worldviews* (e.g., gender differences, different cultural backgrounds). This concern leads to being able to take cultural differences and levels of tolerance into consideration when trying to select referees for clients.

9.   *Understand that referrals are only one step in the counseling or consulting process.* They are not the end of the helping relationship. For example, the counselor in the hypothetical case running through this chapter may make arrangements for a partial referral in which the client continues to see the counselor while seeing a helper at Wellsprings, and the counselor serves as a coordinator of services the client is receiving in and out of school.

How to Coordinate a Successful Referral.   Where referring ends and coordinating begins is somewhat unclear. In our hypothetical case, it may be argued that the coordinating process begins when the school counselor volunteers to participate in the process of bringing the clients and referees together. It makes no difference whether referrals are partial or complete. Coordinating remains important in either approach. Important coordinating competencies include being able to (a) keep track of whether or not clients and referees met, (b) submit all information and materials that are needed by the referee, (c) help the client while not interfering with the work of the referee if the referral is partial, (d) serve as a consultant to the referee when necessary, and (e) evaluate the effects of the referral. What follows is an application of these recommendations to the hypothetical case running through this section of the chapter.

> Soon after the referral was made, the school counselor checks with the student and finds out that a relationship with a therapist at Wellsprings has been successfully initiated. Upon the request of the referee at Wellsprings, and with the approval of the parent, the counselor provides pertinent information about the student from the cumulative records. Next, the counselor meets with the client periodically to address issues that are appropriate and have been recommended by the referee at Wellsprings. As the helping process continues, the referee contacts the school counselor for consultation about the case, and the counselor responds cooperatively. Finally, when appropriate, the counselor gathers information from the client, parent, and referee that will help determine how effective the referral seemed to be. As well, the data are used to find ways to improve the process.

Clearly, making a good referral and coordinating it successfully require considerable thinking and conscientious organizing. To ignore the importance of devoting the necessary thought and effort to this task is to flirt with the danger of reducing the effectiveness of the school counseling program.

The information presented here recommends preferred practices. Data collected from a sample of 149 Ohio school counselors and analyzed by Ritchie and Partin (1994) provide evidence of differences between the recommendations and the realities of professional practice, leaving room for improvement. Included in their summary are the following comments:

> Our findings indicate that school counselors are faced with a host of concerns.... Emotional concerns, family concerns, alcoholism, drug abuse, and suspected child abuse were the concerns most frequently referred.... Although counselors claimed to be familiar with referral resources in their school, ... they were less familiar with referral resources outside of school.... Many counselors expressed a need for more formal training in ethical referral practices. (p. 270)

MANIFESTATIONS OF SCHOOL COUNSELOR-INITIATED REFERRING AND COORDINATING

The School Counselor as a Referral Service Coordinator

Referral service coordinating encompasses a blend of counseling, consulting, and referral services. Taken from DeVoe and McClam (1982), the following is a summary of proposed phases of referral service coordinating with examples of their implementation in the case of Brenda, a student with many overwhelming problems.

After establishing counseling relationships leading to awareness of goals and priorities, counselors may determine what information about a case is needed, collect critical information, organize it, and assess it to identify problems and goals. DeVoe and McClam call this the *information-retrieval phase*. Brenda is a young woman experiencing failure in school, abuse of drugs, possible child abuse, and possible pregnancy. Information about her perception of her problems is acquired via an accepting, participatory counseling relationship. In addition, physicians, teachers, school psychologists, social workers, and neighbors are asked for information that can help identify Brenda's needs. In some instances, those questioned are referees in partial referrals.

After receiving the information, counselors may determine how their own expertise can meet client needs and where referrals are needed. Evaluating one's professional capability, making appropriate referrals, establishing a timeline, and determining follow-up procedures make up the *information assessment phase*. With Brenda, the counselor realizes that some problems are beyond her own expertise and/or require more time and attention than she can offer. She then pursues a plan of joint, cooperative actions, setting up the information assessment phase.

While continuing to offer legitimate counseling services, the counselor acts as a coordinator of referral services. As coordinator, the counselor orchestrates the referral process and mobilizes the referral services by making referrals and devising plans for communications among referral services. In so doing, the counselor acts as an advocate for Brenda, ensuring that she does not get lost in the system. As the professional who is providing direct, caregiving services to Brenda in school, the counselor occupies the

Being a referee for other professionals and parents can be a source of professional satisfaction.

most strategic position for coordinating the helping services, including following up on referral services and incorporating them with the direct services when appropriate.

DeVoe and McClam view referral service coordination as a way for school counselors to alleviate concerns about not being able to meet all their clients' needs while also providing a more comprehensive set of services. Effective referral service coordination results in more effective counseling interventions. In the referral service coordination scenario described, the counselor used referrals as one means of helping the client while serving as a liaison between the various persons and agencies involved in providing services for Brenda.

School Counselors and Student Assistance Programs

Student assistance programs (SAPs) are approaches that the schools use to reach out to and help a variety of at-risk students. SAPs are helpful to school counselors because they bring into play sources of help, in responding to the challenges at-risk students present, that are more systematic and comprehensive than individual counselors are usually able to be when working independently with at-risk students and trying to make referrals.

Modeled on the concept of the employee assistance programs (EAPs) established in business and industry, SAPs are designed to identify high-risk students experiencing decreased productivity (declining academic performance) because of chemical abuse and other suspected mental health problems. Identification is followed by intervention and referral to appropriate community services. An aftercare component is provided to support those returning to school after having received counseling intervention services. One important distinction between EAPs and SAPs is that EAPs provide adult employees with voluntary participation and an option to resign; SAPs, in contrast, often demand that adolescent students participate or face expulsion (Roman, 1989). This circumstance occurs because the school differs from the workplace.

The school atmosphere favors acceptance of referral suggestions, although it is also more subject to abuse and exploitation unless great care is exercised. Because of legitimate national concern about chemical abuse and prevention of mental health problems, SAPs became increasingly popular in the late 1980s. As Roman points out, the rapid transfer of the core technology from the workplace (EAPs) to the school (SAPs) poses both advantages and disadvantages. High-risk adolescents and the school personnel trying to help them gain the advantages because SAPs offer additional systematic opportunities for help. Inconsistency of services is one disadvantage, however, because there is no national consensus on the definition of SAPs.

Three approaches to organizing SAPs have emerged (Borris, 1988). Some SAPs follow an externally based model, in which a specialized staff is available for services outside the school. Others have employed an internally based model, in which a specialized staff is available for services inside the school. Because it is the most common and cost-effective model, a third approach, the core team idea, is described in detail here.

Core team members are trained to screen, refer, intervene with, and support dysfunctional students. Diversity in team membership is recommended to represent all kinds of school personnel and to provide a variety of pathways to discovering potential clients. Therefore, central office and building administrators, teachers, counselors, nurses, school psychologists, and other specialists are members of core teams. Certified providers outside the school district can give specialized training, usually short term and intense, to core team members. The training often includes a knowledge base about SAPs, group process, chemical dependency and the disease concept, suicide prevention/intervention, symptoms of mental illness, theories of adolescent development, treatment recovery, continuity of care, and action planning. Some of these topics are similar to the basic training programs of school counselors. Simulations and rehearsals of confrontations with targeted adolescents and their parents/guardians are often included in the training. Having been trained themselves, core team members, in turn, provide training to other school personnel through in-service programs. Such faculty in-service training creates an informed and helpful professional staff supportive of the core team.

Core teams network with referral sources just as counselors do as part of their liaison function. In this instance, the networking involves a team of professionals that includes counselors, rather than counselors acting independently. Identification of at-risk students can therefore involve all professional school personnel because of the pyramid-like nature of core teams and the in-service training of others. Self-referrals and referrals from peers, parents, and others are welcomed. When at-risk students are identified, the core teams are responsible for investigating the referrals and meeting with the students and their parents/guardians if further action is deemed appropriate.

Informing and involving parents/guardians varies from school to school; the nature of such contacts seems to be independent rather than universal policy. Meetings with parents are informational in that the core teams share their findings and recommendations. The meetings may also be confrontational because of the possibility of denial and resistance from the students and/or their families. In these situations, school systems are often empowered to threaten suspension as a form of caring coercion if cooperation is not achieved. This occasional resorting to coercion may cause school counselors to be concerned about students' perceptions of them. This issue has not yet been resolved beyond the individual decision-making level.

Recommended intervention plans vary because of differing circumstances where SAPs exist. When appropriate services are provided outside the schools, core teams are responsible for assessing the readiness of returning students and for providing after-care services. When necessary services are not readily available, which is the case in many communities, or targeted families cannot afford the services, or both, core teams may have to devise alternative intervention programs. Sometimes such alternative services are provided by school personnel and are offered in the schools during or after the school day.

The nature of the problem also affects where students receive help. Students with discipline and attendance problems might receive help in the school, whereas students with substance abuse problems require more specialized help off-site. In some instances, counselors are among the staff professionals with competencies that enable them to serve as referees as well as referral recommenders. For example, Zubrod (1992) describes a situation where a school counselor provides ongoing counseling groups for students referred to the school's SAP. In this case, the counselor was able to help many participants achieve improved mental health, and all who indicated substance abuse problems reported change in a positive direction. Confidence in the viability of the group-counseling program, which was high at the outset, continued throughout.

Aftercare is another challenge facing core teams. A system must be established and monitored for accepting the referred student back in school or for determining whether problem behaviors have been changed successfully. Beyond that, support is needed to prevent or detect relapses or both. Aftercare seems to be natural for counselors as part of their intervention function. One way school counselors provide aftercare for these students is through ongoing counseling groups that returning students can join to process things in a safe environment while trying to adapt to having returned to the school after a substantial absence.

SAPs offer counselors an exceptionally useful adjunct to their referral services, whether they are members of core teams or are making referrals to core teams or to external and internal experts. Advantages include the team concept, the targeting of dysfunctional behaviors by informed staff members, and the comprehensive and systematic nature of the program.

SAPs are designed to identify, inform, and refer many more students than counselors can independently under their less-formalized referral services. To ensure appropriate counselor involvement in SAPs, Zimman and Cox (1989) make several recommendations:

- The program should be mandated by the school's administration to avoid turf battles between counselors and teachers.
- Services within the SAPs should be spelled out clearly to avoid confusion over what is to be referred internally (e.g., to counselors) and what is to be referred externally.
- Coordinators should be designated in a manner that conveys the broadest possible ownership of the program.
- The headquarters of the SAP program should be located in an office near but not within the counseling or administrative offices to give the program separate status.
- Responsibilities of all professionals should be clarified in advance.
- Allowances should be made for individual differences among counselors and grade-level differences among students when implementing the program.

A relatively recent idea, SAPs have already had a significant influence on the basic education scene. Designed originally to serve high-school adolescents, SAPs are gradually being implemented in junior high, middle, and elementary schools.

REFERRALS TO SCHOOL COUNSELORS

Referrals From Other Professionals and Parents

Being a referee for other professionals and parents can be a source of professional satisfaction, as well as frustration. Satisfaction is achieved from knowing that coworkers and parents know and appreciate one's services. Frustration occurs when services are misunderstood, expectations are unrealistic, and referrals are made inappropriately. Consider, for example, the following hypothetical and real cases:

- Tina's mother, Mrs. Jones, calls the counselor and requests an interview. In the interview, the counselor learns that Mrs. Jones is terribly worried about Tina's behavior in and out of school. She requests help from the counselor to find out what is wrong and perhaps bring about a cure.
- Gene has just arrived in the counselor's office. He has been brought by Ms. Smith, the principal, who finds Gene's behavior reprehensible. The principal requests that the counselor straighten Gene out and hints at more drastic methods if this does not work.
- Taking a survey of teacher-initiated referrals during 1 week of school, a counselor creates the following list: six cases of students fighting, four cases of classroom acting out, two cases of smoking, and one case of inappropriately affectionate behavior in the hallways.
- A analysis of 313 referral documents and findings from focus group interviews with 10 elementary-school teachers led Jackson and White (2000) to conclude that many teachers tend to view referrals from the perspective of a medical model. That is, many teachers assume that children are not responsible for their problems. Therefore, they attribute responsibility to the referees (i.e., school counselors), expecting them to solve the problem for the child (and possibly for the teacher as well).

These four frustrating scenarios demonstrate some pitfalls awaiting counselors who respond to referrals indiscriminately. Indeed, these cases dictate the challenge to organize the system by which referrals are made to counselors. The examples offer several ideas about how this aspect of the referral service can be organized. The ideas are organized around three basic questions: Who is my client? What is the proper referral procedure? and What is a legitimate referral?

Who Is My Client?   Mrs. Jones's request places the counselor in a dilemma from which there is no escape if the counselor attempts to serve her and her daughter at the same time. Initially, Mrs. Jones requests to be the client, but it is her daughter who is to receive the direct intervention. If the counselor initiates a counseling relationship with Tina, Tina will become a client. Then, from an ethical perspective (and legally in some states), Mrs. Jones can no longer be a client because whatever Tina shares with the counselor becomes confidential and the counselor cannot share it with Tina's mother. If the counselor decides to accept Mrs. Jones as a client, then consultation is in order. Then, Tina is the client and Mrs. Jones the consultee. With Mrs. Jones as the client, the counselor's services to Tina are indirect; that is, the counselor helps Tina by consulting with Mrs. Jones, who works directly with Tina. When Mrs. Jones's goals become clear to the counselor, it is time to clarify the issues and negotiate which client to serve directly. A third option is to work out a system for serving both clients if an understanding of mutually acceptable goals can be achieved. Mrs. Jones's request indicates a misunderstanding of the counseling services and naïveté about counseling ethics, problems counselors handle systematically or individually on a case-by-case basis.

What Is the Proper Referral Procedure?   Ms. Smith, the principal, expects the counselor to cure student Gene quickly and dramatically. The counselor is challenged to clarify for Ms. Smith what are and what are not legitimate expectations (referrals). Among other things, clarification involves requesting information from Ms. Smith about what transpired before the referral, what behavioral goals Ms. Smith has for Gene, and what outcomes he expects. In fairness to the counselor, this information will be the content of negotiations with Ms. Smith. This is also a "Who is my client?" situation because it is not Gene who initiated the request for counseling services. Ms. Smith wants an intervention to change Gene's behaviors. As is the case with Mrs. Jones and Tina, the "Who is my client?" question needs to be resolved quickly.

Ms. Smith essentially commands the counselor to perform a service. In this case, the counselor is not forewarned, availability of the counselor's services is assumed, and outcome expectations are vague. Such a situation underscores the need for communication with superiors and colleagues to establish a clearly defined referral system. Diplomacy is in order, leading to a systematic plan wherein the needs of all parties are being served.

What Is a Legitimate Referral?   The two hypothetical cases and the findings by Jackson and White (2000) require thought about whether counselor involvement in the interventions is appropriate. Neither Tina nor Gene asks the counselor for help. The list of reasons for the referrals demands that one ask whether demonstrations of affection or smoking in school are counseling problems or matters of rules and mores that should be regulated by either administrators or community consensus. The findings from the Jackson and White study indicate that expectations of teachers and others may be inappropriate when making referrals, placing school counselors in no-win situations. This raises two questions: How do the counselors help teachers and other referees understand that all involved parties, including students and teachers, are potentially involved in achieving solutions to problems that cause referrals? and Do school counselors view themselves as miracle workers or super-counselors who can fix all problems referred to them, or do they understand that all players, including teachers, students, and parents, are involved helping students realize their potential?

Another issue is the fact that all the referrals involved some form of acting out. No referral involved a student who exhibited symptoms of being overly passive or withdrawn. This narrowness of focus in recognizing problems indicates that members of the school staff seem not to be aware of a broader range of potential problems. The situation offers an opportunity to design an in-service presentation for other members of the faculty and staff.

A report by Wagner (1976) offers food for thought about referral patterns of elementary-school teachers. Teachers were invited to make referrals to groups helping students enhance personal problem-solving skills. Data from the teachers' responses showed they consistently recommended more boys than girls for this kind of help. This finding led Wagner to hypothesize that girls' problems in adjusting to home and school are more difficult to observe from their school-related attitudes and behaviors than boys' are and that perhaps expectations of boys in elementary school need further investigation. The latter hypothesis was based on Wagner's observation that, in general, boys are encouraged to be independent, active, and mobile but that exhibiting these behaviors in classrooms often leads to teacher distress and disciplinary referrals.

Are Referrals Being Made When Making Them Would Be Appropriate?

Another serious problem is the absence of referrals to the school counselor. Some colleagues and parents are apathetic or poorly informed. This suggests that counselors need to establish systems for receiving referrals and to make those systems known. Ingredients of any system are bound to differ among communities, schools, and counseling goals. Despite such differences, some basic suggestions are relevant to most school districts:

1. Distribute information about the services that school counselors provide (e.g., counseling, consulting, information).
2. Include examples of how those services are carried out (what kind of counseling is offered and the outcomes to expect).
3. Make public a referral system, explaining the process for making referrals to counselors and providing necessary forms. Make the system simple, efficient, and multiculturally appropriate.
4. Include procedures for providing feedback to referral sources.
5. Explain the policy regarding confidentiality.
6. Look for opportunities to explain the system. Do so proactively (e.g., faculty meetings, in-service programs, distributive materials).

Referrals From Students

Much of the preceding discussion of referrals from professionals and parents also holds true for students. They, too, have misperceptions and unrealistic expectations, and sometimes they are apathetic. They seldom refer a peer, although occasionally they do. Among those students who refer peers are those trained to be peer helpers. Ingredients of the counselor-initiated referrals described at the beginning of this chapter can be part of the training programs for peer helpers. More on training peer helpers is found in chapter 6 (Consulting in School Counseling).

In most instances, referrals from students are self-referrals, and counselors are challenged to present themselves to students clearly while also living up to realistic expectations. In their efforts to enhance the probability of student self-referrals, counselors face several difficult challenges. Park and Williams (1986) list the following negative expectations that make reaching some students more difficult:

- Adults are persons who give information to students, talking *to* them rather than *with* them.
- Adults give advice, and students view their own role as captive listeners who are forced to accept adult solutions.
- Adults respond critically and tell students how they should feel when students try to express feelings, leading to the conclusion that disclosing feelings is a risky business.
- Adults can be punitive; they have the power to make students feel shame or guilt over mistakes.

- Adults do not treat information about students confidentially. Often, they share it with other people, which sometimes leads to punitive responses.

Obviously, faced with these unflattering perspectives, counselors are truly challenged to prove that they are special adults who are dedicated to helping students and who are different from other adults.

Revisiting Wagner's (1976) study provides further food for thought about student self-referrals. It is less likely that boys who hypothetically might have been referred by teachers will refer themselves. It is also more likely that girls who hypothetically might have been referred by teachers will refer themselves for help. This indicates that boys who need help may be the least likely students to refer themselves. Elementary-school boys and girls, however, refer themselves at about an equal ratio, evidence that not all boys are reticent about referring themselves.

What to do? Realize that not all students need to refer themselves for counseling services. They wish to be able to avail themselves of these services if needed. When school counseling is not perceived positively and accurately by students, there are insufficient self-referrals. Insufficient student self-referrals diminish the impact of a counseling program or at least result in an unbalanced program. A proactive stance leads to counselors providing information about their services to students in a manner that is simple, truthful, and in the students' vernacular. Park and Williams (1986) offer an interesting suggestion for implementing this idea. Applying the principles of social modeling, they exposed elementary-school students to live or filmed performances of children modeling behaviors they wanted the students to learn. The targeted behaviors included social skills needed to initiate contacts with adults. Demonstrated were situations in which initiating contacts would be appropriate, showing how the models coped with the anxiety and reluctance associated with approaching adults.

Another idea is offered by LaFountain (1983), who asked elementary-school children to complete information-gathering graphic checklists during her weekly classroom visits. One of the checklists is the Smiley-Frowney Face Sheet, on which children in kindergarten and first and second grades are asked to make an X on the face that best depicts their feelings about school, friends, and family. Six faces, ranging from teary-eyed to openly smiling, are presented for each of the three categories. The reverse side of the paper is used for writing news to the counselor. A second graphic checklist is the Feelometer, which LaFountain used in third through sixth grades. Thermometers with scales ranging from *Very Unhappy* to *Very Happy* are located beside each of three questions asking how students are feeling about school, friends, and family. The Feelometer also contains boxes that can be checked by children who wish to see the counselor. In a space on the reverse side, children can write messages to the counselor. The information is used for reaching out to children proactively and as a resource when referrals are made to the counselor.

Student self-referrals occur more often if they are easy to make. Students desire to know that their counselors maintain confidentiality. Counselors who are visible and appear to students as adults who talk with them, participate in the decision-making process as equals, empathize with feelings, and accept individual differences are more likely to receive student self-referrals. To repeat the admonition made earlier in this chapter: Ignoring the importance of devoting the necessary thought and effort to this task is flirting with the danger of reducing the effectiveness of the counseling program.

SUGGESTED ACTIVITIES

1. Using the criteria suggested in this chapter, evaluate the referral services in the institution where you are employed and/or where you attended school for counselor-initiated referrals and for referrals to counselors.
2. Using the results of the previous activity, develop a proposal for improving the referral services.
3. List the referral sources you use. Check those with which you have reciprocal relationships. Make a different mark by those about which you have adequate knowledge. What do the results tell you? Are these sources appropriate for serving a multiculturally diverse population?
4. Add possible referral sources to your list.
5. Brainstorm ideas for enhancing the image of counseling among children and adolescents, and suggest ways to implement them. What are the underlying principles for your ideas?
6. Cooperatively generate a list of referral sources that can be used to enhance client development.
7. Go to www.scan21st.com and propose some ways that this Internet site might assist school counselors in developing referral sources.

REFERENCES

Adelman, H. S., & Taylor, L. (2002). School counselors and school reform: New directions. *Professional School Counseling, 5,* 235–248.

Amatea, E. S., & Fabrick, F. (1984). Moving a family into therapy: Critical referral issues for the school counselor. *School Counselor, 31,* 285–294.

American Counseling Association. (1995). *Code of ethics and standards of practice.* Alexandria, VA: Author.

American School Counselor Association. (1989). American School Counselor Association statement: Cross/multicultural counseling. *Elementary School Guidance and Counseling, 23,* 322–323.

American School Counselor Association. (ASCA) (1992). Ethical standards for school counselors. *School Counselor, 40,* 84–88.

Atkinson, D. R., & Juntunen, C. L. (1994). School counselors and school psychologists as school–home–community liaisons in ethnically diverse schools. In P. Pedersen & J. C. Carey (Eds.), *Multicultural counseling in schools* (pp. 103–120). Boston: Allyn & Bacon.

Baker, S. B. (1973). Referrals: Who? When? Where? How? *Pennsylvania Personnel and Guidance Journal, 1,* 19–23.

Bobele, M., & Conran, T. J. (1988). Referrals for family therapy: Pitfalls and guidelines. *Elementary School Guidance and Counseling, 22,* 192–198.

Borris, A. F. (1988). Organizational models. *Student Assistance Journal, 1,* 31–33.

Brammer, L. M., Abrego, P. J., & Shostrom, E. L. (1993). *Therapeutic counseling and psychotherapy* (6th ed.). Upper Saddle River, NJ: Prentice Hall.

Carey, A. R., Black, K. J., & Neider, G. G. (1978). Upping the odds on the referral gamble. *School Counselor, 25,* 186–190.

DeVoe, M. W., & McClam, T. (1982). Service coordination: The school counselor. *School Counselor, 35,* 95–101.

Downing, C. J. (1985). Referrals that work. *School Counselor, 32,* 242–246.

Downing, J., Pierce, K. A., & Woodruff, P. (1993). A community network for helping families. *School Counselor, 41,* 102–108.

Egan, G. (1998). *The skilled helper: A problem-management approach to helping* (6th ed.). Pacific Grove, CA: Brooks/Cole.

Gysbers, N. C, & Henderson, P. (2001). Comprehensive guidance and counseling programs: A rich history and a bright future. *Professional School Counseling,* *4,* 246–256.

Hobbs, B. B., & Collison, B. B. (1995). School-community agency collaboration: Implications for school counselors. *School Counselor, 43,* 58–65.

Hollis, J. W., & Hollis, L. U. (1965). *Organizing for effective guidance.* Chicago: Science Research Associates.

House, R. M., & Hayes, R. L. (2002). School counselors: Becoming key players in school reform. *Professional School Counseling, 5,* 249–256.

Ivey, A. E. (1994). *Intentional interviewing and counseling: Facilitating client development in a multicultural society* (3rd ed.). Pacific Grove, CA: Brooks/Cole.

Jackson, S. A., & White, J. (2000). Referrals to the school counselor: A qualitative study. *Professional School Counseling, 3,* 277–286.

Kimmerling, G. F. (1993). When saying no is the right thing to do. *American Counselor, 2,* 5–6.

LaFountain, R. (1983). Referrals. *Elementary School Guidance and Counseling, 17,* 226–230.

Park, W. D., & Williams, G. T. (1986). Encouraging elementary children to refer themselves for counseling. *Elementary School Guidance and Counseling, 21,* 8–14.

Ritchie, M. H., & Partin, R. L. (1994). Referral practices of school counselors. *School Counselor, 41,* 263–272.

Roman, P. M. (1989). Perils, payoffs of technology transfer. *Employee Assistance, 1,* 16–17.

Shertzer, B., & Stone, S. C. (1981). *Fundamentals of guidance* (4th ed.). Boston: Houghton Mifflin.

Wagner, C. A. (1976). Referral patterns of children and teachers for group counseling. *Personnel and Guidance Journal, 55,* 90–93.

Weinrach, S. G. (1984). Toward improved referral making: Mutuality between the counselor and the psychologist. *School Counselor, 32,* 89–96.

Zimman, R. N., & Cox, V. (1989). The role of guidance counselors. *Student Assistance Journal, 1,* 22–24.

Zubrod, A. R. (1992). The influence of group social skills development on attitudes and behaviors of at-risk adolescents. *Dissertation Abstracts International, 53–11A,* p. 3856. (University Microfilms No. AA19236928)

CHAPTER 8

Helping Students Acquire and Process Information

Goals: To point out the importance of helping children and adolescents acquire and process accurate, developmentally appropriate information. To identify the requisite counselor competencies for providing that assistance.

The following is a sample request showing how school counselors seek innovative ways to use online information tools such as the career key (Jones, 2000). This sample merges the kind of creative ideas that come from school counselors across the world.

I would like permission to make approximately 30 copies of your online instrument, the Career Key, for use with a group of academically at-risk seventh-grade students, who have indicated an intent to drop out of school or who have simply given up on the idea of ever escaping their difficult circumstances. I intend to use your instrument along with a hard copy of the *Occupational Outlook Handbook* to generate ideas of what these students may wish to consider for career and life goals. Once the students have an idea of some possibilities and what some of the educational requirements are for those occupations, I will have counselors from a local community college and from several state colleges present workshops on postsecondary admissions. I also intend to ask a financial aid representative to present a seminar for these students about available funding and qualification requirements.

I already have commitments from the at-risk students to attend the workshops. I am also working with several departments at a nearby state university to recruit college students to serve as tutors/mentors for my group of students. I hope these volunteers are from economically challenged communities and families, or are first-generation college students, and are maintaining high academic standards. These characteristics will provide the volunteers with credibility among my students. We are asking for a long-term commitment from these volunteers, so that once my students leave our school, they have a role model and mentor to keep them inspired.

I have also invited parents to attend the workshops, especially the financial aid workshop. Many of the parents are telling their children that they will never be able to afford college. I also have been speaking with parents about selecting high schools that offer some type of pre-college program such as Upward Bound that can help keep their children on a college track.

I am working with my school district to obtain one or more computers for the counseling office so that students in the future can come to my office and utilize your online Career Key program. My administration responded more favorably to this request than when I requested a recurring cost budget for career exploration items.

Some students who have access to a computer and the Internet have already used your online version of the Career Key. They are in the process of interviewing people in the occupations that are of interest to them. They express a little skepticism about achieving the outcome but have put their trust in me that if they work hard and follow the directions all of these professionals give to them, we will show them how to overcome the obstacles. But when they talk to the rest of the group, they now have a grin on their face, a twinkle in their eye, and—this is something new—a spark of hope.

I am of the opinion that if we wait until these students are sophomores, if they stay enrolled that long, they will feel overwhelmed with all of the classes and skills they will need to acquire in a short period of time, and will fail to make the commitment to strive for something more.

We finally have a homework center and all of the students who entered into the career exploration/career development contract with me have attended daily. I also offer study skills and test-taking strategy sessions. Teachers have not been very supportive of allowing me class time, so the students and I brown bag these sessions during their lunch breaks. I am pleased with these sessions because many of my students are gang members from opposing factions, but when they are with me at the homework center or at other sessions, they put it aside and work with me and slowly but surely work together.

DEMAND FOR INFORMATION

Useful information is the foundation for intelligent choices. Individuals are faced with choices constantly. Children and adolescents, lacking experience in the decision-making process, often need useful information and assistance in processing it. Knowledge is power, and useful information is a foundation of knowledge. Providing information and helping students process it are important components of the prevention programming, counseling, and consulting functions. Therefore, counselors serve student clients by providing them with opportunities to acquire useful information and to process it adequately.

Information most likely to be disseminated by school counselors can be classified into two general categories: *educational/vocational* (e.g., college entrance requirements, educational and work environments, job descriptions) and *personal/social* (e.g., substance abuse awareness, sex, marriage and family, mental health). Helping student clients process such information requires that counselors have expertise and resources to help students use the information productively (e.g., decision-making counseling skills, computer-assisted career exploration resources).

Information services have always been important in guidance and counseling. Initially, information was simply dispensed or made available to clients. Later, the counselor's role expanded to include the processing of the information. Current counselor training programs include courses that help make sense of information services and that teach how to help clients process information in several ways. For example, counselor education students are taught decision-making skills and procedures for teaching children and adolescents how to process acquired information. Through prevention programming, counseling, and consulting, counselors are in a unique and important position to help student clients gain the power associated with making informed decisions.

From the educational/vocational information perspective, the acquisition of useful information plays an important role in the major career development and choice theories. The developmentalists/constructivists (e.g., Savickas, 2002; Super, 1953, 1990) view career development as synonymous with personal development, complete with stages and tasks. Useful information helps individuals cope with the tasks associated with these stages. For instance, in Savickas's expanded version of Super's theory, the Exploration stage occurs during adolescence in most individuals. Savickas (2002) points out that "the first task of the explorations stage—*crystallizing vocational preference*—requires that an individual explore broadly to form tentative ideas about where they fit into society" (p. 172). Successful accomplishment of crystallization hinges on acquiring and processing useful information. According to Paa and McWhirter (2000), "Opportunities for self-exploration and access to information about the world-of-work are critical for fostering career expectations that are realistic and likely to lead to satisfaction"(p. 41).

Career-choice theorists emphasize the importance of personality characteristics over a developmental process (e.g., Holland, 1997). Individual development is considered important to the extent that it leads to acquiring individual personality predispositions. Useful information is important to help individuals form accurate impressions about various occupations, leading to choosing jobs or careers that match their own personality predispositions. For example, according to Holland's theory, individuals with a personality predisposition that might be labeled as *realistic* (aggressive behavior; interest in activities requiring motor coordination, skill, and physical strength) need accurate information about occupational roles that use these attributes, such as military officers, police officers, or skilled artisans. Individuals need to identify careers that appeal to them so that they can make intelligent decisions.

The theoretical positions summarized here, though useful, are based on what seems to be most true for individuals from the majority culture. Herr and Niles (1994, p. 182) point out that "many of the career development issues that confront students from culturally diverse backgrounds are the same as those confronting students from the majority culture." They continue: "Additional issues also emerge for members of cultures with world views and perspectives that are different. . . . Such factors require the culturally skilled counselor to be able to use varied approaches with different clients." Among the "varied" approaches Herr and Niles suggest are exploring cultural identity, acculturation, and racial consciousness and providing accurate information about areas of potential occupational growth and sets of skills needed to be competitive for jobs in the future.

Viewing the demand for information from a personal/social development perspective, having useful information and assistance with processing it enhances developmental guidance, the goals of which are acquisition of enhanced life skills, bolstered self-esteem, and more effective learning competencies (Myrick, 1987). W. Johnson and Kottman (1992) point out the importance, to the development of middle-school students, of self-knowledge, information, reading, and hearing and telling stories, and Holcomb (1990) highlights the potential impact that relevant information can have on the perceptions of elementary-school children. This is supported by Schrank's (1982) finding that bibliotherapy—that is, enhancing self-understanding through literature or media (Bodart, 1980)—changes attitudes, promotes mental health, enhances self-concepts, and reduces anxiety.

Useful information fulfills a theoretical purpose. If the theories have merit, then the information-providing and -processing function is important when used constructively. An investigation by Miller (1982), using a sample of community-college students, suggests that information seeking is a coping skill that helps individuals deal with developmental problems. This finding adds empirical support to the theoretical suggestions. Results of two surveys, however, indicate that student use of information services in their schools is infrequent and inadequate (Carroll, 1982; Chapman & Katz, 1983). Recommendations about improving these circumstances focus on improving information delivery and processing in the schools. This is a healthy approach; it is fruitless to blame students for behaving like the children and adolescents they are.

Theoretically and empirically, arguments support the importance of having information delivery and processing in elementary-, middle-, and secondary-school counseling. The necessary information and how it is processed differ across grade levels. Empirical data suggest that counselors face a challenge in trying to provide helpful information services because the information available may be inadequate and infrequently used (Carroll, 1982; Chapman & Katz, 1983). This chapter is devoted to identifying basic ingredients and competencies needed to meet the challenge.

The three school counseling initiatives introduced in chapter 1 attribute importance to information as well. In the ASCA's National Model for Comprehensive School Counseling Programs, it is viewed as a responsive service. That is, school counselors need to respond to the information-seeking needs of students, parents, and teachers (Gysbers & Henderson, 2001). In the National School Counselor Training Initiative, school counselors are challenged to teach students and their families how to access support systems for academic success by informing them about tutoring and academic enrichment programs (House & Hayes, 2002). In the School-Community Collaboration Model, information is viewed as part of an interconnected system for meeting the needs of all students (Adelman & Taylor, 2002). Examples are providing information to enhance general health, prevent drug and alcohol abuse, prevent child abuse, and help families learn how to support students with their homework.

BASIC INGREDIENTS OF INFORMATION DISSEMINATING AND PROCESSING

Understanding the Information Needs of Student Clients

The world is complex and promises to become more so in the twenty-first century. This complexity can appear overwhelming to anyone. Children and adolescents, lacking the experience of adults, find it even more challenging. Information is a source of power to overcome the complexities and to manage life more successfully. If all students understood this and simply sought out the necessary information and processed it successfully, none would need professional help. However, most children and adolescents are not aware of the importance of information. Their attention spans are brief and attuned to their own interests. Consequently, they need help acquiring and processing useful information. They were not born with the requisite motivation and skills.

The expectations of students serve as filters, and only part of what they receive is processed. Therefore, children and adolescents need information that is accurate, recent, and available, and they need time to acquire and process it. Given these characteristics, counselors are challenged to plan information services carefully and acquire client feedback to determine what was learned and how it was assimilated. All of this points to the importance of considering the information function as a process, rather than as an event or a series of unrelated events, viewing it developmentally with a K–12 concept in mind. If information dissemination and processing are planned according to developmental needs and delivered accordingly, each operation will build on those that preceded it and set up those that follow.

Information-seeking and exploration activities are more likely to occur if reinforced. Students benefit from understanding alternatives in order to learn about relationships. In a classic, yet timely, book about occupational information, Hoppock (1957) suggested that useful information serves several important needs:

- Increasing feelings of security
- Encouraging natural curiosity
- Extending horizons

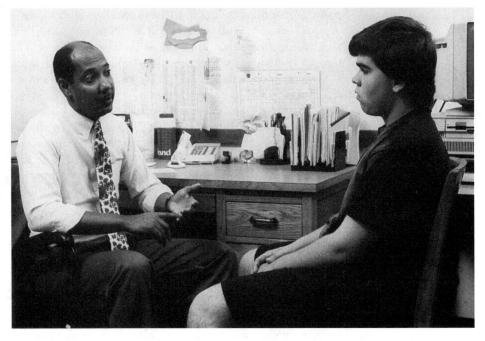

Culturally flexible counselors will also take the client's worldview into consideration.

• Encouraging wholesome attitudes
• Developing desirable approaches to decision making
• Being helpful when pragmatic decisions, such as selecting school programs or courses, deciding which college to attend, and determining whether to drop out of school, have to be made

Understanding the information needs of clients also leads to power for counselors—power to use the information constructively and well. It follows that a second basic ingredient of the information service is that it should be versatile. Versatility in the provision and processing of information allows counselors to respond to the many needs of children and adolescents and opens the way to treating the service as a process.

Versatility

When attempting to achieve versatility, counselors are encouraged to realize the limits to the amount of information they themselves can know. One of the harsh realities that beginning counselors face is discovering they cannot have all the information suitable for their clients and consultees readily in mind. If counselors cannot know it all, what can they do? More information is acquired with experience. Using information also leads to adding it to one's memory bank. Beyond that, counselors may become familiar with resources to which they can refer or refer others. Also, students can be expected to participate fully in information finding and processing. Therefore, counselors are challenged to encourage children and adolescents to engage in as much of the work as possible. Attempting to do too much for them places counselors in a cost-inefficient time-use bind and prevents clients from getting full value from the information-seeking process.

In another timeless publication, Morrill and Forrest (1970) elaborated on what they described as different dimensions of counseling for career development. Their dimensions provide suggestions about how versatile counselors can be when helping individuals process information. In the first dimension, counselors use information to help clients make specific decisions. These authors suggest that most counseling is like this. A second dimension involves helping clients understand the factors involved in making a decision, teaching them to make decisions and use information appropriately. Focusing on the idea that all decisions are part of a process, the third dimension attends to using information in a process of serial or continual choice making. The fourth dimension finds counselors helping individuals use information to influence future choices and to achieve self-determination.

Restating the information-is-power theme, Morrill and Forrest's (1970) dimensions suggest that counselors assist clients with specific decisions, teach them to make decisions, help them think serially, and help them achieve self-determination. Doing so successfully may help clients achieve this lofty and important goal. This demands versatility of counselors.

BASIC COMPETENCIES IN INFORMATION DISSEMINATING AND PROCESSING

Finding and Acquiring Useful Information

Information is available everywhere. Finding it is not a problem. Finding *useful* information, however, may be a problem. Knowing what to look for and where to find it are skills one acquires over time. Because beginners have not acquired these skills, the most efficient procedure and perhaps the one most likely to produce higher quality information is to let others locate it. As used here, *others* refers to professionals trained to compile useful information. The training of school counselors includes learning how to recognize useful information. Courses in the counseling curriculum are devoted partly to this topic, so it is not covered in great detail in this chapter. The advent of the Internet and the World Wide Web has opened a mammoth new source of information to those who have access. Although many student clients will have access to the Internet, many as yet do not. Therefore, other sources as well are addressed in this chapter.

Information acquisition will probably involve a combination of counselors and associates seeking and finding sources, as well as receiving unsolicited information from various providers. The school library and its personnel may be helpful. State or regional clearinghouses can be useful, too, when and where available. Clearinghouses can provide such services as explanatory information about resources, listings, samples, and evaluations. Inquire about the existence of clearinghouses.

Organizing and Storing Information

Sheer volume makes the task of organizing, storing, and keeping information up-to-date monumental. A systematic approach is necessary to achieve an orderly information service. Consequently, Baer and Roeber's (1964) advice is still appropriate. These authors of another classic publication about occupational information recommended that one's information service be kept current with changing technology. The best conceptual technology for systematizing the organization and storage of information is the information resource center idea.

Information resource centers—also known as career resource centers, career information centers, and career development resource centers—are founded on the principle of maintaining a centrally located area for organizing, storing, and disseminating useful information. A centralized location provides opportunities to organize materials systematically; to monitor, maintain, and enhance their use; and to make the center a focal point for programming activities (Zunker, 1998). The central location can serve a single school or a cluster of schools (McDaniels & Puryear, 1991).

Practical considerations associated with establishing an information resource center include the following, taken, in part, from McDaniels and Puryear (1991) and Zunker (1998):

- Create and form an advisory committee.
- With the committee's assistance, determine the resource center's objectives, the parameters of information to be kept there, and a plan for evaluation and accountability.
- Use this information to initiate a budget-setting process. Resource allocation depends on administrative and school board support.
- Assess the existing services to determine the base from which to begin, identifying information currently held that is to be gathered for the resource center.
- Begin the process of finding space, acquiring furniture and equipment, and collecting and storing information. The two most common locations for information resource centers are counseling office suites and school libraries. Neither has a clear advantage over the other, and deciding which to use will depend on local variables such as space, politics, and funds.
- Set up a system for disseminating, monitoring, and maintaining the information. McDaniels and Puryear recommend stations through which students can work at their own pace over several days or weeks. The four stations are (a) educational-occupational information; (b) self-awareness tools such as inventories, checklists, pamphlets, and books; (c) taking-action strategies such as writing resumes; and (d) life management issues such as time management and self-esteem. It may be useful to establish working alliances with school librarians to use their expertise and link the major instructional information centers in the schools. Even though state-of-the-art methods for disseminating information may not be within the budget, it still behooves planners and implementers to know what those methods are, to aspire to move toward using them, and gradually to improve local methods as much as possible.
- Initiate programming efforts that involve the center. One example is to develop a career exploration unit in cooperation with the English Department that uses resources in the center. As an added touch, Zunker suggests having a grand opening of the center.

These recommendations focus primarily on disseminating educational-vocational information to secondary-school students, leaving questions about disseminating personal-social information to all students and educational-vocational information to elementary- and middle-school students. It is feasible to work with librarians to disseminate personal-social information systematically in secondary, middle, and elementary schools. Gladding and Gladding (1991) remind us that, since the 1930s, librarians have compiled lists of books with therapeutic potential and worked with counselors to make those materials available for achieving bibliotherapy goals. At the elementary-school level, counselors usually work with teachers who have access to the same students most of the day, calling perhaps for a centralized system in the counselors' offices and satellites of the center in the classrooms. Many recommendations from McDaniels and Puryear and from Zunker can be applied to this setting as well.

Disseminating Information

Information dissemination can take many forms. Given that individuals mature differently and have diverse worldviews, their readiness to seek and use information will vary. Matching information dissemination strategies with developmental stages and worldviews is a challenge that demands versatility. Therefore, strategies need to be varied. The following sections are devoted to reviewing comments about strategies for disseminating information to children and adolescents. None is superior or inferior to the others; each may be helpful when used appropriately. In the spirit of versatility, counselors are encouraged to know various ways to disseminate information and to be able to apply them according to circumstances.

Printed Materials. Printed information was the most common method of acquiring occupational-educational information in the first half of the twentieth century. Bibliotherapy dates back to the 1930s (Gladding & Gladding, 1991). Printed materials are the traditional vehicle for information acquisition and bibliotherapy. Although print is currently not the only approach, it remains an important one. These materials have improved with the expansion of dissemination ideas and associated technology. Counselors are challenged to help clients acquire useful information from printed materials.

The reading levels of print materials pose a challenge for counselors. Over a half-century ago, Brayfield and Reed (1950) found that the information they sampled was difficult to read. More than a decade later, Sharp (1966) found the situation had changed very little. Assuming that some publishers may be trying to correct this situation whereas others are not even aware of it, the problem probably still exists to some degree. How do counselors ensure that clients use materials they can read? Research by Billups and Peterson (1994) indicates a relationship between reading level and levels of cognitive development. Higher levels of both tend to lead to greater appreciation of thought-provoking content. These researchers also found that adolescents prefer to read factual information consistent with their own interests. A general recommendation that Billups and Peterson offer is to consider the importance of individual differences when acquiring and making printed materials available for dissemination.

A second challenge for counselors is content bias. Unfortunately, much information is biased in various ways. Counselors are challenged to combat the biases because monitoring all materials is virtually impossible. How pervasive is bias? No one knows. That it exists is borne out by a report on the 1982–1983 edition of the *Occupational Outlook Handbook* (*OOH*), a respected publication of the U.S. Department of Labor. Salamone and Seniecle (1985) found that ethnic minorities were overrepresented, women were underrepresented, workers under age 30 and over age 49 were underrepresented, and disabled workers were not illustrated in a random sampling of pictures in the *OOH*.

Bachelder and Cole (1980) believe that printed materials cannot be equally suitable across all age levels. They found themselves adapting materials designed for older and younger audiences. In presenting suggestions, they highlight the importance of being specific, the need to embellish facts with materials that enhance individual self-exploration of values, and the use of nonprint materials for unenthusiastic or poor readers. Books are an important vehicle for helping children acquire information. Informational books provide useful facts, and fictional books offer symbolic role models.

Counselors can recommend to teachers books that can be incorporated into curricular activities and that can be used in group counseling and guidance activities for bibliocounseling and biblioguidance (Gladding & Gladding, 1991). In support of this thesis, Christenbury, Beale, and Patch (1996) published an annotated bibliography of 60 fiction and nonfiction selections deemed useful for interactive bibliocounseling. The authors present their recommendations under several categories (e.g., illness and death, self-destructive behaviors, family relationships, identity, violence and abuse). Pursuing this admonition, Borders and Paisley (1992), while warning against simply collecting and labeling books and then categorizing children by problems, recommend that counselors help children make connections between books and their lives and help them select books that have potential for enhancing their developmental growth. Realizing the challenge their recommendation represents, Borders and Paisley suggest working with librarians, media specialists, and parents while also referring counselors to such journals as *Hornbook* and *School Library Journal*, both of which contain reviews and supply lists.

Examples of counselors involved in bibliocounseling are offered by Gladding and Gladding (1991). One approach is to have individuals read targeted literature before meeting with a counselor or with a counseling or guidance group. Gladding and Gladding depict what might happen as a follow-up to the pre-session reading assignment: "Each participant might talk about their reaction to what they read . . . about how personal perceptions differ according to experience" (p. 10). This process, in turn, might be followed by discussing the book's central theme and sharing pieces of literature that have personal meaning to the client(s). In another example, children are presented with dilemmas, such as prejudice or dealing with disappointments, following their reading of a series of short stories, after which they discuss ways characters in the stories, serving as symbolic models, respond to the dilemmas.

Person-to-Person Approaches.   Observational learning, formal presentations, and simulations are examples of person-to-person approaches. Such approaches provide interpersonal interactions in the information dissemination process. In classic studies of the influence of observational learning, Krumboltz and Schroeder (1965) and Krumboltz and Thoresen (1965) found that social modeling and positive reinforcement generated self-initiated, information-seeking behaviors by high-school students. This research led to a series of related studies on the influence of symbolic models (tape-recorded or filmed), live models, gender differences, and group versus individual settings. Later, Thoresen and Hamilton (1972) found that social modeling also helped students process information. These studies established the importance of observational learning—learning skills and acquiring attitudes by watching others perform targeted behaviors successfully and receive positive reinforcement for doing so.

A recent application of the observational learning concept is an activity called *work shadowing.* In work shadowing, children and adolescents accompany cooperating workers as they go about their business—observing behaviors, responsibilities, and a myriad of details involved in the models' work (Herr & Watts, 1988). Attractive models, whether real or symbolic, are potent influencers of targeted behaviors such as seeking information independently and processing it. Access to live models on the intimate scale that work shadowing provides offers opportunities for individuals to acquire and process large amounts of comprehensive information.

Effective models are especially important for children, to mitigate their tendency to eliminate viable occupations that seem incompatible with their gender or with their social status at the time. Of particular importance is the presentation of models engaged in atypical occupations. According to Gottfredson (2002), children tend to reduce the number of personally acceptable occupations, rather than to expand their horizons. Attractive models may cause children to keep their options more open. Research by Bailey and Nihlen (1989) supports this reduction-and-elimination-of-options thesis. They suggest interventions by elementary-school counselors, including interactions with various workers (modeling) coupled with useful information. An example of this occurs when a counselor arranges for children to shadow workers in various targeted occupations, such as teachers, secretaries, and carpenters. The work shadowing experience is accompanied by printed and media information about each career and related discussions of the children's reactions.

An important ingredient of the modeling process, as highlighted by Bailey and Nihlen, is providing children with opportunities to interact with live models so that they can ask questions and test their own hypotheses. During follow-up activities, children's questions can be initially generated from classroom simulations and brainstorming sessions.

Formal presentations may include, but are not restricted to, observational learning strategies. Oral presentations by qualified individuals place those individuals in the position of being models at the same time they are using additional teaching strategies to inform their audiences successfully. Formal presentations can also be instructive. Instructors serve as potential social models while engaging audiences in other learning activities. They may use oral presentations and a variety of other pedagogical strategies. Formal presentations employ group formats and offer counselors opportunities to disseminate information more efficiently. Group work has the potential for identifying those who need subsequent individualized attention. The formalized group approach provides members with opportunities to learn from peer activities. It also has the potential for bringing together those who are not cohorts, such as parents and their children.

Simulated activities allow students to try their skills on relevant subject material in a safe environment. Such activities can help students develop decision-making skills, learn about unfamiliar options otherwise unavailable, have opportunities for creative thinking, and learn important group interaction skills. Krumboltz and Rude (1981) found that simulated work experiences increase the number of career options that participants explore. In the typical simulation, a gamelike environment prevails. A mock real-life situation is created, and the players act out roles that take them beyond the present in a make-believe fashion. Decisions are evaluated according to predetermined probabilities of success based on history and programmed into the simulation materials. Gamelike simulations such as S. S. Boocock's Life Career Game (produced by Western Publishing Co.) and J. D. Krumboltz's Job Experience Kits (by Science Research Associates) have enjoyed some popularity.

More recently, a set of simulations referred to as the Real Game Series has become available. Seven simulations in the series are either ready for use or are in production. The Real Game (1996), designed for Grades 7 and 8, consists of 17 sessions that take approximately 30 hours to complete. Byrd (1997, p. 2) describes it as "an innovative career exploration program." It can be used in prevention programming conducted by counselors, or it can be integrated into the school's curriculum. Other simulations in the set are Jouer Pour Vrai (1997, Grades 7 and 8, in French), the Be Real Game (1998, Grades 9 and 10), the Real Small Business Game (1999, Grades 4 through 6), the Get Real Game (1999, Grades 11 and 12), and the Real Spin Game (2000, Grades 1 through 3). Further information about the stated goals and the procedures used can be acquired from the publisher's World Wide Web page: http://realgame.ca.

Critics point out that no game can duplicate all the complexities and nuances of the real world, making what is learned through simulations distorted. It is also claimed that even motivated and involved students are not necessarily learning anything new. When players get competitive, some respond conservatively to enhance their chances to win. Others play impetuously, knowing it's only a game, and hence taking risks that would be ruinous and foolhardy in real life. Despite such limitations, simulations offer interesting tools when linked effectively to other person-to-person techniques (e.g., formal instruction).

Computerized Approaches: Interactive Guidance Systems. Although computers are not the only information-disseminating approach that involves person-to-machine relationships (others include microfiche and microfilm readers), they have been the most influential. McDaniels (1982) surmised that the expanded role of technology is the most visible change in occupational-information dissemination since 1950, and computerized systems are the most notable contributors to that change. From the early developmental stages through the 1970s, computerized guidance systems progressed through three or four generations. They evolved from storehouses of information that could be kept up-to-date and retrieved quickly, to comprehensive interactive systems. Rayman and Harris-Bowlsbey (1977) reported that the third-generation systems provided users with direct communication with the computers; access to stored information about themselves; the ability to search and redo files; the capacity to perform computer-assisted instruction and simulation exercises on values clarification, decision making, and clarification of occupations; the ability to assess levels of career development; and the option to have tests administered and interpreted.

The 1980s brought sophistication to comprehensive interactive systems. Dependence on mainframes was eliminated with the proliferation of microcomputers, which might be referred to as the fourth generation. The amount of time required by individuals when interacting with computers was reduced. Both developments reduced the cost per pupil of using computerized guidance systems. Currently, providers are achieving greater speed in reaction time, increased comprehensiveness of services, and improved cost-effectiveness in their systems.

Depending on such factors as local demand, financial resources, sophistication levels, and readiness of local personnel, school systems incorporate computerized guidance systems at different rates. The school districts with which the authors are familiar and that use interactive computerized systems use DISCOVER II (by the American College Testing Service) exclusively. Adaptable to microcomputers and pro-grammed by high-school students, DISCOVER II has four primary units, each of which can be used independently:

- *Self-Information* measures the user's interests, aptitudes, and values. The en-tered data and online responses to computer-generated questions lead to a computer-generated list of occupations to explore, as well as to interpretations and summaries.
- *Strategies for Identifying Occupations* allows users to enter scores from other interest inventories and aptitude tests. These data are added to those generated from assessments done online by the system. They are used by the system to provide printouts of occupational options related to values, interests, abilities, and educational levels.
- *Occupational Information* provides users with two options for acquiring lists of occupations that include brief descriptions of job families. One option involves browsing the World of Work Map. The other offers a more detailed operation that generates increased information.
- *Searches for Educational Institutions and Jobs* offers lists of post–high-school ed-ucational institutions that meet user-entered criteria such as cost, enrollment, and major field preferences (Heppner, 1985).

Chronicle Guidance Publications has an interactive program entitled ComputerLinked Exploration of Careers and Training (C-LECT). It is also designed for high-school students. Self-administered temperament and interest survey data or the occupational composite from the Armed Services Vocational Aptitude Battery (ASVAB) are processed by users as they explore occupational, educational, and financial aid infor-mation. The C-LECT modules are these:

- *Educational Investigation,* through which users enter their preferences for types of schools, geographic regions, and college or vocational-school majors in con-junction with the self-report information.
- *Educational Information,* which allows users to investigate selected schools more thoroughly.

• *Financial Aid and Apprenticeship Information,* which offers specific information and a system for seeking additional facts about financial aid.

Burnett, Magel, Harrington, and Taylor (1989) developed a prototype that provides computer-generated health feedback information for high-school students. Referred to as *computer-assisted behavioral health counseling* by its authors, the program consists of individualized feedback based on factors of weight, smoking, and diet in the form of risk information, practical suggestions, and encouragement for self-reported improvement. Information is disseminated, and an interactional component is involved as well. Early research efforts indicate that self-reported student health behavior was influenced positively by interacting with the computerized program. Previously, all known computerized information dissemination systems seemed to focus on educational-occupational information. Although access to this information is crucial to making intelligent career-related decisions, the equally important area of personal-social decision making has been ignored in the drive to improve the information dissemination process. The work of Burnett et al. is important, in part, because it opened the way to more research and development in this area.

Another advancement in programming designed to help students gain access to personal-social information is a computer-assisted drug curriculum for middle-school students entitled "The Dilemma in Drug Education" (Gerler, 1994). An important element in the curriculum is the inclusion of computer-generated simulations designed to stimulate thinking about drug use. The simulations present students with dilemmas, an example of which follows:

> Jim had just moved and was enrolled in his new high school. He hated the thought of having to make all new friends. . . . Today, a guy named Bill from math class asked Jim to eat with him. . . . When they left the cafeteria, Bill said, "I've noticed that nobody talks to you. . . . I've got something here in my back pack that will make you forget about the unfriendly kids here." . . . Jim wanted a friend, but he wasn't sure if he wanted to get involved in drugs. What should Jim do? (Gerler, 1994, p. 1)

The increasing popularity of computerized guidance systems raises some issues, including whether computer-assisted guidance is effective. In a study designed to answer that question, Myers, Lindeman, Thompson, and Patrick (1975) found that 10th-grade boys and girls increase their degree of efficiency as well as their knowledge and use of resources for career exploration as they increase the time spent on a computer-based educational and occupational exploration system. Luzzo and Pierce (1996) found that rural middle-school students who worked with the DISCOVER program 1 hour per day over 2 weeks experienced significant gains in career maturity.

Clinical experiences of school counseling interns whom the authors have supervised lead to the conclusion that many adolescents need person-to-person assistance when interacting with computerized guidance systems. One problem the interns encountered was that many students were impatient and expected the decision-making process to take place quickly. For example, students use the computer as a video game when assessments get too long and tedious. In addition, they respect the information generated by computers too highly because of the aura of accuracy and invincibility that computer information enjoys among students and other individuals who may believe that whatever comes from computers is infallible. More specifically, with the DISCOVER II program, students lacking the sophistication to determine accurately the size of their community or the enrollment of their high school enter inaccurate information into the program. "Garbage in, garbage out" is a common phrase in this computer age. Further, lacking adult maturity, adolescents espouse immature values when responding to information requests from the program. For example, they indicate the highest levels of education and income as their goals. This leads to receiving discrete categories of information of no use without understanding how to investigate other options.

Clearly, it is important for counselors to help their clients use computerized information systems successfully. Help may include proactive instructions and monitoring systems, prevention programming, and follow-up of individual users to determine how they are processing the information. When the processing seems deficient, remedial or treatment-focused responses are in order. Unless counselors are involved closely with students using computerized guidance systems, either directly or indirectly through surrogates such as trained paraprofessionals or peers, all the advantages of the systems will be only a mirage, good for public relations but a sham with regard to individual outcomes.

Practical issues have always existed with computerized guidance systems. One is cost-effectiveness. Issues like start-up costs, maintenance of the systems, and amount of student time online wait to be resolved.

Johnston, Buescher, and Heppner (1988) call attention to an issue that had previously received little or none. Viewing computerized guidance systems as comparable to standardized tests, they question why the computerized guidance systems have not been put to the same rigorous challenges that tests have received. They also ask why providers of the systems have not been expected to offer evidence of validity, reliability, flexibility, accuracy, readability, and the like. Perhaps, as they suggest, it is time that computerized guidance programs be put on the same plane as standardized tests and the same qualitative demands be placed on them. Until that time arrives, a *caveat emptor* (let the buyer beware) environment prevails. In that atmosphere, it seems appropriate to close this section with a summary of suggested criteria for selecting computerized guidance systems. The following suggestions are taken from Brown and Srebalus (1988) and Snipes and McDaniels (1981):

• Determine the characteristics of prospective users, ascertaining their developmental needs and limitations.
• Determine the counseling staff's goals for how the system is to fit into the existing counseling services and how the staff members expect to interact with the system.
• Learn about the systems. On what theories were they designed? Are the theories manifested consistently throughout the systems? Are the assessment instruments used in the systems valid and reliable? What analytic skills are assumed of users? What skills are taught by the systems? Are the actual outcomes consistent with the advertised objectives?
• Ask some practical questions. What are the start-up and long-term costs? How quickly do the systems respond to individual users, and how much time do users spend online on average? Will the systems hold the attention of individual users and motivate them to complete modules successfully? Is customer service good when problems occur?

In a thought-provoking article that remains timely today, Harris-Bowlsbey (1984) suggested that counselors view computers as partners in helping clients achieve their goals. She treats the relationship as one analogous to a marriage, with challenges that require planning, hard work, and mutual learning. Harris-Bowlsbey recommends that counselors be computer literate, aware that computer programs are imperfect, aware of their own counseling theory preferences, and able to understand possible uses of computerized guidance in various theoretical positions. Her point of view is based on the premise that all counseling, like computer programming, is systematic and that all counseling theories also have a system.

Computerized Approaches: The World Wide Web. The most important new source of information at the beginning of the twenty-first century is the World Wide Web. This textbook is unique, for example, in that it is the foundation for an evolving online network, the School Counseling Activities Network (www.scan21st.com), whereby graduate students, their professors, and practicing school counselors can work together to bring the graduate classroom and the practice of school counseling into closer harmony.

Individuals able to gain access through a variety of servers may reach thousands of websites throughout the world on the Internet and have at their disposal the most comprehensive amount of information yet known to be available by merely "surfing the Net" on their computers any time of the day or night. Much of this information is developmentally appropriate and useful for children and adolescents, and much of it is free. Helping individuals surf the Net has become a cottage industry. For example, Riley, Roehm, and Oserman (1998) have published a guide to Internet job searching that purports to assume no prior knowledge of online resources. Information about websites and how to use them abounds.

The questions of how school counselors go about using computer and networking technology in counseling far outnumber the current applications in the field. How can computer technology be applied to counseling beyond data analysis, record keeping, and simple information dissemination? How can counseling make the best use of international computer networks? Given the limited budgets that have traditionally been allocated for school counseling and related social programs, where can counselors find the needed technological expertise to help in the discovery of computer applications? Since counselor education programs have been increasing the number of hours required to complete master's degrees in the field, how can graduate students preparing for careers in school counseling be given the time and opportunity for exploring and inventing computer applications in counseling? Because most students who apply to school counseling graduate programs derive much of their work satisfaction from areas other than computer technology, how are we going to find individuals to take the lead in doing the creative work needed for applying computer technology to counseling in the schools?

A creative application of Internet technology to counseling is the development by Lawrence K. Jones of a website that provides free career counseling. At this site, users have free access to a career interest inventory Jones published in 1987 known as the Career Key. Both Internet and paper-and-pencil versions are available to youths and adults. The paper-and-pencil version may be printed from the website at no charge.

The Career Key employs six career/personality typologies and the *Guide for Occupational Exploration.* Those who use the Internet version of the Career Key also have access to the *Occupational Outlook Handbook,* from which they can acquire information about occupations highlighted from responding to the Career Key. The address is http://www.careerkey.org/english/.

Van Horn and Myrick (2001) reported that the use of Internet technology is increasing at a rapid rate in the nation's schools. They identified several ways through which information can be retrieved and disseminated via this medium. These opportunities include electronic mail, electronic newsletters, online journals, and websites. Websites offer a variety of information seeking and processing opportunities such as virtual tours of college campuses, information about financial aid, and numerous databases.

School counselors can benefit particularly from newly emerging professional publications that have significant online offerings. The *Journal of Technology in Counseling* offers many opportunities for school counselors to explore inventive ways for applying computer and networking technology. The Internet address for the journal is http://jtc.colstate.edu/

Journals with significant online presence are emerging on other topics of interest to school counselors. The *Journal of School Violence,* for instance, offers school counselors theory, research, and practice related to preventing and dealing with violence in schools. The journal's Internet address is http://genesislight.com/JSV.html. This site offers links to international sources of help on violence in schools. Here are some examples:

Center for the Prevention of School Violence

http://www.ncsu.edu/cpsv/

Established in 1993, the center serves as a primary resource for dealing with the problem of school violence. The center, a public agency not motivated by profit, focuses on ensuring that schools are safe and secure so that every student is able to attend a school that is free of fear and conducive to learning.

Connect

http://www.gold.ac.uk/connect/

This initiative brings together practitioners and researchers throughout Europe to provide substantial and authoritative reports on school violence and to examine intervention strategies that appear most promising in terms of prior work and wide European applicability.

Hamilton Fish Institute

http://www.hamfish.org/

The institute, with assistance from the U.S. Congress, was founded in 1997 to serve as a national resource to test the effectiveness of school violence prevention methods and to develop more effective strategies. The institute's goal is to determine what works and what can be replicated to reduce violence in America's schools and their communities.

Institute on Violence and Destructive Behavior

http://darkwing.uoregon.edu/~ivdb/

The institute helps schools and social service agencies understand violence and destructive behavior to ensure the safety of young people and to facilitate the academic achievement and healthy social development of children and youth.

National Association of Students Against Violence Everywhere

http://nationalsave.org/

The mission of S.A.V.E. is to decrease the potential for violence in our schools and communities by involving students in meaningful crime prevention, conflict management, and community service activities.

In summary, the challenge of applying computer and networking technology, especially in human service areas such as school counseling, is actually greater than the engineering problems involved in designing and creating the technology. There is, in fact, the very real possibility that we may become so enamored with the marvels of computers that we lose sight of how the technology can be realistically applied to meeting human needs. To those of us involved in school counseling who are excited by the potential of computer technology, it is stimulating to imagine and invent applications to serve students, parents, teachers, and school administrators. Our special challenge is to make possibilities seem reasonable and workable to colleagues who are less inclined toward technology and to school counseling professionals who have had little opportunity to explore the available technology.

Helping Children and Adolescents Process Information

Most ideas in the professional literature for helping individuals process educational-vocational information seem to be labeled *career education, career guidance,* or *career counseling.* Ideas about helping students process personal information seem to come most often from the literature about bibliotherapy and alcohol and drug education. In the career education domain, Peterson, Sampson, Lenz, and Reardon (2002) recommend approaching matters when working with adolescents and adults from a cognitive information-processing conceptual perspective. Peterson et al. developed a system based on helping clients acquire self-knowledge, occupational knowledge, and decision-making skills. Efforts to achieve these goals are based on assessing client readiness to engage in career problem solving and decision making and then responding accordingly. Initial assessments during the career counseling process focus on learning about such areas as information needed, typical decision making methods, and existing faulty metacognitions. For example, the findings may lead to those assessed to have high readiness and support, being encouraged to use Internet sources, such as the Career Key, independently. Those deemed to have low readiness and support may be helped best via individual and small group counseling and career courses that have small group interactions.

A report of research by some of the authors just mentioned provides evidence in support of a contention that computer-assisted guidance systems are best used when accompanied by counseling (Sampson, Peterson, Reardon, et al., 1992). Therefore, it appears as if computerized guidance programs will best serve student clients if accompanied by a systematic program such as the one just presented, which is designed to help individuals process the information successfully. An abbreviated example of how their ideas might be incorporated follows:

> During the first interview with an adolescent student, a counselor asks questions that help determine the client's goals, decision-making methods, and possible faulty metacognitions. The information is used to recommend activities and strategies designed to help the client acquire information and process the information usefully, a step that may include the client interacting with a computerized career guidance system such as the Career Key. This step is followed by appointments designed to help clients think clearly about the information, ask and seek answers to related questions, and possibly engage in systematic decision making, all of which may be facilitated by a counselor. Culturally flexible counselors will also take into consideration the client's worldview and those cultural circumstances that may affect the processing of career information, such as culturally biased assessment instruments, self-defeating cognitions, and restricted environmental conditions.

Hansen (1997) views the process of helping clients make decisions metaphorically as piecing together a life quilt. All panels are necessary to complete a quilt, and all areas of one's life should be considered when making career decisions. Hansen cites six tasks that are crucial components of the decision-making process: (a) Find work in an ever-changing global context that needs to be done; (b) think of work as a meaningful part of one's life; (c) look for harmony between work and one's family; (d) accept, value, and celebrate diversity; (e) include exploration of one's spiritual beliefs and life purpose in the process; and (f) prepare for transitions and changes in one's life and career.

Working with children poses challenges that differ from those one encounters when working with adolescents. Bailey and Nihlen (1989, pp. 143–144) recommend the integration of career-awareness programs into elementary-school curricula. They believe that children need time to personalize the world of work and to become inoculated against sex role stereotyping and gender circumscription. Five specific suggestions for helping children process career information are offered:

- Provide "information that focuses on the responsibilities and structure of occupations."
- Present a "curriculum that provides time and opportunities for young children to share their present knowledge of the world of work and experiences they have had with workers in various occupations."
- Offer "opportunities for young children to interact with various workers on a personal level."
- Develop a "curriculum that provides the students with the opportunity to discover how people in various occupations feel about their chosen professions."
- Provide "a curriculum that exposes and counteracts the sex-role stereotyping inherent in the labor force."

Individuals mature differently and have diverse worldviews; their readiness to seek and use information will vary.

Stein (1991) offers examples of how these ideas might be implemented creatively for children. She elaborates on "book talk," in which books about occupational information are used to generate information processing; "athletic talk," through which sports equipment is used; "picture-zine scrapbook," by which children learn about careers when making scrapbooks from used magazines; "barber shop talk," in which children are assigned homework to talk with friends and relatives about their work; and "career-ween day," an activity in which children create objects that represent specific careers, play a role in costume, and discuss characteristics of that role.

Gladding and Gladding (1991) point out that bibliotherapy, like counseling, lends itself to a variety of ways to help individuals process information. For example, counselors may read excerpts after explaining the topic or have participants read excerpts in advance of individual or group bibliocounseling or group biblioguidance sessions. Participants can be asked to share their thoughts and impressions and, if in a group, discuss individual and collective thoughts, questions, and reactions. Gladding and Gladding believe that it is important for participants to close the sessions with some sort of personal commentary about how much or little was gained personally from the bibliotherapeutic experience. If the participants are in third grade or above, Gladding and Gladding recommend having them each write a sentence or paragraph of personal commentary. Follow-up sessions are noted as important in helping participants process bibliotherapy experiences, with recommendations to follow up differentially (e.g., sooner with younger children).

In her presentation on alcohol and drug education in elementary schools, Bradley (1988) stresses the importance of recognizing and responding to the characteristics of the developmental stage of the participants and establishing an atmosphere of mutual respect and positive interpersonal communications. Bradley goes on to suggest using stories, puppets, simulations, and films with children in the beginning years; exciting information, simulations, communications skills activities, and class discussions that stimulate reasoning skills in the middle elementary grades; and research activities based on formulated questions supplemented by films and models in the upper elementary grades.

In concluding this section on helping children and adolescents process information, it is important to stress taking into account additional considerations when working with student clients having differing worldviews. All counselors need to examine their own biases and stereotypes and how those might influence the way they help multicultural clients process information (Bowman, 1993). Other considerations may be determining whether group or individual interactions are most effective, whether family members should be included, whether race- and gender-appropriate role models should be used, and whether languages other than English should be employed (Borodovsky & Ponterotto, 1994; Bradley, 1988; Herr & Niles, 1994).

Concluding Comments About School Counselors as Information Disseminators

Thinking about what it takes to provide an adequate information service can be mind-boggling! With the enormous amount of available information and the large variety of choices to make, counselors can easily be overwhelmed by their responsibility to help clients acquire and process adequate and useful information. The central themes of the task are achieving a systematic organization; providing useful information via user-compatible systems; integrating information services with counseling, consulting, and prevention programming; and providing opportunities to process the information successfully.

SUGGESTED ACTIVITIES

1. Figure out the role of useful information in your approach to counseling. Be as specific as you can.
2. Select three occasions in your life when useful information provided by others was obviously an important factor—that is, the information significantly empowered you. Elaborate on the reasons for your conclusions.
3. Using criteria gleaned from this chapter, evaluate the information services at the high school, junior high school, middle school, or elementary school you attended; one where you are interning; or one where you are employed. Offer recommendations for changes if you think changes are necessary. Justify your recommendations.

4. If you have access to a computerized guidance system, use and evaluate it according to criteria presented in this chapter. Have you discovered anything new? Explain your answer.

5. Find the Career Key on the World Wide Web and go through all its phases. What, in your opinion, are the advantages and disadvantages?

6. Take an inventory and discuss ways that the information function can be integrated with the counseling, consulting, and prevention programming functions.

7. Develop a comprehensive plan for helping student clients process information. How will you start? What are the important elements? How will you know whether the plan is successful?

8. Go to www.scan21st.com and propose how some of the tools on this Internet site might assist school counselors to help students acquire and process information.

REFERENCES

Adelman, H. S., & Taylor, L. (2002). School counselors and school reform: New directions. *Professional School Counseling, 5*, 235–248.

Bachelder, L., & Cole, C. G. (1980). Career education materials for the middle school. *Vocational Guidance Quarterly, 29*, 159–163.

Baer, M. F., & Roeber, E. C. (1964). *Occupational information: The dynamics of its nature and use* (3rd ed.). Chicago: Science Research Associates.

Bailey, B. A., & Nihlen, A. S. (1989). Elementary school children's perceptions of the world of work. *Elementary School Guidance and Counseling, 24*, 135–145.

Billups, A., & Peterson, G. W. (1994). The appreciation of career literature in adolescents. *Career Development Quarterly, 42*, 229–237.

Bodart, J. (1980). Bibliotherapy: The right book for the right person at the right time and more. *Top of the News, 36*, 183–188.

Borders, S., & Paisley, P. O. (1992). Children's literature as a resource for classroom guidance. *Elementary School Guidance and Counseling, 27*, 131–139.

Borodovsky, L. G., & Ponterotto, J. G. (1994). A family-based approach to multicultural career development. In P. Pedersen & J. C. Carey (Eds.), *Multicultural counseling in schools* (pp. 195–206). Boston: Allyn & Bacon.

Bowman, S. L. (1993). Career intervention strategies for ethnic minorities. *Career Development Quarterly, 42*, 14–26.

Bradley, D. F. (1988). Alcohol and drug education in the elementary school. *Elementary School Guidance and Counseling, 23*, 99–105.

Brayfield, A. H., & Reed, P. A. (1950). How readable are occupational information booklets? *Journal of Applied Psychology, 34*, 325–328.

Brown, D., & Srebalus, D. J. (1988). *An introduction to the counseling profession.* Upper Saddle River, NJ: Prentice Hall.

Burnett, K. K., Magel, P. E., Harrington, S., & Taylor, C. B. (1989). Computer-assisted behavioral health counseling for high school students. *Journal of Counseling Psychology, 36*, 63–67.

Byrd, D. (1997). The Real Game. *Guidance and Social Work Lead.* Raleigh, NC: Wake County Public Schools.

Carroll, M. R. (1982). Student use of career information resources. *NVGA Newsletter, 21*, 6–7.

Chapman, W., & Katz, M. R. (1983). Career information systems in secondary schools: A survey and assessment. *Vocational Guidance Quarterly, 31*, 65–177.

Christenbury, L., Beale, A. V., & Patch, S. S. (1996). Interactive bibliocounseling: Recent fiction and non-fiction for adolescents and their counselors. *School Counselor, 44*, 133–145.

Gerler, E. R., Jr. (1994). *The dilemma in drug education.* Unpublished manuscript, North Carolina State University, Raleigh.

Gladding, S. T., & Gladding, C. (1991). The ABCs of bibliotherapy for school counselors. *School Counselor, 39*, 7–14.

Gottfredson, L. S. (2002). Gottfredson's theory of circumscription, compromise, and self-creation. In D. Brown and Associates (Ed.) *Career choice and development* (4th ed. pp. 85–148). San Francisco: Jossey-Bass.

Gysbers, N. C., & Henderson, P. (2001). Comprehensive guidance and counseling programs: A rich history and a bright future. *Professional School Counseling, 4,* 246–256.

Hansen, L. S. (1997). *Integrative life planning: Critical tasks for career development and changing life patterns.* San Francisco: Jossey-Bass.

Harris-Bowlsbey, J. (1984). High touch and high technology: The marriage that must succeed. *Counselor Education and Supervision, 24,* 6–16.

Heppner, M. J. (1985). DISCOVER II, SIGI, and Micro SKILLS: A descriptive review. *Journal of Counseling & Development, 63,* 323–325.

Herr, E. L., & Niles, S. G. (1994). Multicultural career guidance in schools. In P. Pedersen & J. C. Carey (Eds.), *Multicultural counseling in schools* (pp. 177–194). Boston: Allyn & Bacon.

Herr, E. L., & Watts, A. G. (1988). Work shadowing and work-related learning. *Career Development Quarterly, 37,* 78–86.

Holcomb, T. F. (1990). Fourth graders' attitudes toward AIDS issues: A concern for the elementary school counselor. *Elementary School Guidance and Counseling, 25,* 83–90.

Holland, J. L. (1997). *Making vocational choices: A theory of vocational personalities and work environments* (5th ed.). Odessa, FL: Psychological Assessment Resources.

Hoppock, R. E. (1957). *Occupational information.* New York: McGraw-Hill.

House, R. M., & Hayes, R. L. (2002). School counselors: Becoming key players in school reform. *Professional School Counseling, 5,* 249–256.

Johnson, W., & Kottman, T. (1992). Developmental needs of middle school students: Implications for counselors. *Elementary School Guidance and Counseling, 27,* 3–14.

Johnston, J. A., Buescher, K. L., & Heppner, M. J. (1988). Computerized career information and guidance systems: Caveat emptor. *Journal of Counseling & Development, 67,* 39–41.

Jones, L. K. (2000). *The career key.* http://www.careerkey.org/english/

Krumboltz, J. D., & Rude, S. (1981). Behavioral approaches to career guidance. *Behavioral Counseling Quarterly, 1*(2), 108–120.

Krumboltz, J. D., & Schroeder, W. W. (1965). Promoting career planning through reinforcement and models. *Personnel and Guidance Journal, 44,* 19–26.

Krumboltz, J. D., & Thoresen, C. E. (1965). The effect of behavioral counseling in group and individual settings on information-seeking behavior. *Journal of Counseling Psychology, 11,* 324–333.

Luzzo, D. A., & Pierce, G. (1996). The effects of DISCOVER on career maturity of middle school students. *Career Development Quarterly, 45,* 170–172.

McDaniels, C. (1982). Comprehensive career information systems for the 1980s. *Vocational Guidance Quarterly, 30,* 344–350.

McDaniels, C., & Puryear, A. (1991). The face of career development centers for the 1990s and beyond. *School Counselor, 38,* 324–331.

Miller, M. F. (1982). Interest pattern structure and personality characteristics of clients who seek career information. *Vocational Guidance Quarterly, 31,* 28–35.

Morrill, W. H., & Forrest, D. J. (1970). Dimensions of counseling for career development. *Personnel and Guidance Journal, 49,* 299–305.

Myers, R. A., Lindeman, R. H., Thompson, A. S., & Patrick, T. A. (1975). Effects of an educational and career exploration system on vocational maturity. *Journal of Vocational Behavior, 6,* 245–254.

Myrick, R. D. (1987). *Developmental guidance and counseling: A practical approach.* Minneapolis, MN: Educational Media Corporation.

Paa, H. K., & McWhirter, E. H. (2000). Perceived influences on high school students' current career expectations. *Career Development Quarterly, 49,* 29–44.

Peterson, G. W., Sampson, J. P., Jr., Lenz, J. G., & Reardon, R. C. (2002). A cognitive information processing approach to career problem solving and decision making. In D. Brown and Associates (Ed.), *Career choice and development* (pp. 312–372). San Francisco: Jossey-Bass.

Rayman, J. R., & Harris-Bowlsbey, J. (1977). DISCOVER: A model for a systematic career guidance program. *Vocational Guidance Quarterly, 26,* 3–12.

Riley, M., Roehm, F., & Oserman, S. (1998). *The guide to Internet job searching.* Lincolnwood, IL: VGM Career Books.

Salamone, P. R., & Seniecle, J. C. (1985). Bias in *Occupational Outlook Handbook* illustrations: A new look. *Vocational Guidance Quarterly, 34,* 41–46.

Sampson, J. P., Jr., Peterson, G. W., Reardon, R. C., Lenz, J. G., Shahnasarian, M., & Ryan-Jones, R. E. (1992). The social influence of two computer-assisted career guidance systems: DISCOVER and SIGI. *Career Development Quarterly, 41,* 75–83.

Savickas, M. L. (2002). Career construction: A developmental theory of vocational behavior. In D. Brown and Associates (Ed.), *Career choice and development* (pp. 149–205). San Francisco: Jossey-Bass.

Schrank, F. A. (1982). Bibliotherapy as an elementary guidance tool. *Elementary School Guidance and Counseling, 16,* 218–227.

Sharp, B. L. (1966). Readability of school guidance materials. *School Counselor, 14,* 106–109.

Snipes, J. K., & McDaniels, C. (1981). Theoretical foundations for career information delivery systems. *Vocational Guidance Quarterly, 29,* 307–314.

Stein, T. S. (1991). Career exploration strategies for the elementary school counselor. *Elementary School Counseling and Guidance, 26,* 153–157.

Super, D. E. (1953). A theory of vocational development. *American Psychologist, 9,* 185-190.

Super, D. E. (1990). A life span, life space approach to career development. In D. Brown & L. Brooks (Eds.), *Career choice and development: Applying contemporary theories to practice* (2nd. ed., pp. 197–261). San Francisco: Jossey-Bass.

Thoresen, C. E., & Hamilton, J. A. (1972). Peer social modeling in promoting career behaviors. *Vocational Guidance Quarterly, 20,* 210–216.

Van Horn, S. M., & Myrick, R. D. (2001). Computer technology and the 21st century school counselor. *Professional School Counseling, 5,* 124–130.

Zunker, V. G. (1998). *Career counseling: Applied concepts of life planning* (5th ed.). Monterey, CA: Brooks/Cole.

CHAPTER 9

Providing Transition Assistance in School Counseling

Goals: To highlight the importance of helping students make transitions from home to school, from school to school, and from school to work, and in so doing to approach each transition as a process rather than as a series of isolated events.

Melissa knew that her schoolwork had suffered after moving to a large high school in Detroit. She had to move to Detroit because of her mother's new job at an automobile plant in the city. Melissa had spent all her life in South Carolina; she liked growing up near the ocean. She missed all the friends she had grown so close to at her junior high school. She feared that kids would make fun of her in Detroit because she didn't know how to act in a big city high school. Melissa's mother tried to make the move exciting, but Melissa was angry and thought her mother was being selfish—looking out for her own career plans without thinking about how it would affect Melissa's high school years. Melissa's anger boiled over one day at her high school in Detroit; her history teacher suggested that she visit with one of the school counselors.

Melissa's story is not unusual. School counselors are constantly asked to help students make transitions from one school to another, from school to work, and from home to school. This chapter focuses on how school counselors carry out this responsibility.

DEMAND FOR HELPING STUDENTS MAKE TRANSITIONS

Why are people required to attend school until they reach an arbitrary age? One reason is that school is considered to be preparation for life as a responsible adult. Responsible adults are productive workers able to support themselves and their dependents, as well as contribute to the general welfare. What becomes of adolescents who reach the minimum age to leave and/or graduate from high school? Those who seem to be making normal progress toward responsible adulthood continue their education or acquire gainful employment. Others struggle to find themselves during this time, but eventually they become gainfully employed or acquire further education or both. Some never make the transition from adolescence successfully. All these individuals at some time need a sense of direction during their transition from childhood to adolescence to adulthood. The sense of direction that individuals achieve is influenced by their transitions from home to school, from school to school, and from school to work, in which success provides a feeling of belonging, of achievement, and of progress toward future goals.

Sometimes individuals achieve this independently; at other times individuals need help. Helping people make transitions successfully is part of the schools' and the school counselor's role. Schooling contributes to preparation for the transition into adulthood. An awareness of the importance of the transitions and of the influence of a systematic, proactive response is an important ingredient of enlightened educational planning.

Although enhancing transitions is a concern for all educators, it has been a specific part of school counseling since the earliest days of formalized practice. Over the years, the transition enhancement philosophy of school counseling programs has changed. The changes have been influenced, in part, by different preoccupations of the U.S. Department of Labor's Bureau of Employment Security, the widespread acceptance of career development and developmental guidance theory, the increasing mobility of Americans, greater diversity in the nation's population, and the increasing complexity of the array of choices confronting individuals in U.S. society.

Helping students make transitions can be defined as a means by which the schools assist students in making eventual transition to their post-high-school endeavors. Usually,

Help students explore a wide range of postsecondary options.

that next endeavor involves further education, training, or employment. As Isaacson (1977) points out, most students do not consider transitions important until they approach the school-leaving age. Consequently, they and their parents view the process narrowly—as an event or series of events culminating in the transition from school to job or to another school. Some school counselors also view transitions as events or a sequence of events and define their responses as lists of functions: holding assemblies for incoming students; scheduling mass, brief visits by incoming students; completing transcripts; posting job openings; maintaining a file of college catalogs; meeting college and military representatives; and offering information about college entrance examinations.

A more enlightened approach is to view transitions as a process (Baker, 1981; Herr & Cramer, 1996; Isaacson, 1977; Kosmo, 1977). Elaborating on the transitions-as-a-process idea, Isaacson (1977) notes that school counseling services are increasingly being organized around the concepts of developmental theory. He concludes that those same concepts should be the foundation of effective transition enhancements. Developing the theme further, Kosmo (1977) stresses the need to extend the definition of *transition* to include intervention in instructional and school counseling programs. An instructional program is proactive and provides opportunities for students to gain the skills and knowledge necessary to qualify for entry into a variety of endeavors. A school counseling program, in turn, allows students access to the information and counseling necessary to select from among the available alternatives. Thus, school counselors are challenged to look both back at the experiences that students have had and ahead to the skills they will need. Herr and Cramer (1996) concur with these views, pointing out that career guidance, counseling, and school-to-work transitions are neither synonymous nor mutually exclusive—nor should they be viewed as events. Effective transitions, then, are one phase of a developmental process.

Viewed as a process, enhancing transitions complements the information, counseling, prevention programming, and consulting functions. The schools support this idea by acknowledging that successful transitions are a goal of school counseling. Although specific, identifiable behaviors are involved for counselors, more important is their attitude. School counselors must believe that helping students achieve successful transitions is important and allow that belief to influence their behaviors.

The three initiatives to enhance and advance school counseling recognize the importance of helping students make transitions successfully. For the ASCA National Model for Comprehensive School Counseling Programs, Dahir (2001) states that school counselors should help students make transitions from grade to grade, from school to postsecondary education, and from school to the world of work. Further, Gysbers and Henderson (2001) view placement and follow-up for transitions from school to work or additional educational training as important parts of the individual planning component in comprehensive school counseling.

In the National School Counselor Training Initiative, the importance of preparing students for the transition from school to higher education is a resounding theme (House & Hayes, 2002). Within the School-Community Collaboration Model, the interconnected system for meeting the needs of all students includes work and job programs and support for transitions such as changing schools, changing grades, being included in the mainstream from special education, making transitions before and after school, and making the transition from school to work or postsecondary education (Adelman & Taylor, 2002).

BASIC INGREDIENTS OF HELPING STUDENTS MAKE TRANSITIONS

Understanding the Transition Needs of Students

Support. Many children and adolescents are challenged by the transition from home to school and from school to school. Making these transitions successfully is truly a developmental task that, if not mastered successfully, may lead to arrested development. Some problems that individuals experience are common manifestations of anxiety about the uncertainty of new settings and discomfort over leaving familiar and comfortable surroundings. Others are more severe and likely to lead to maladaptive responses if not addressed successfully.

Awareness. Because it is not in their nature to think about and plan for the future, children and adolescents benefit from reminders and activities to help them realize that they must eventually make a transition from high school to work or further training. Early twenty-first-century America is a complex place with increasingly complicated technologies and rapid change. Today's children and adolescents need help in preparing for those challenges.

School-to-work transition is a process of guidance and instruction that can begin at the elementary-school level (Kosmo, 1977). At this level, attention can be paid to developing attitudes and habits, expanding horizons, and offering relevant general information. Once established, these emphases can be continued and expanded through the middle- and high-school years. As students mature, additional emphasis can be placed on learning how to gain access to information, making rational decisions, and acquiring relevant skills.

Implementation of the school-to-work concept requires both prevention programming and counseling interventions. Developing attitudes and habits, expanding horizons, offering relevant information, teaching students how to gain access to information and make rational decisions, and helping them acquire relevant skills are all proactive goals that can be achieved via prevention programming. Doing this requires a state of mind that includes transition goals with prevention-programming goals. This process is often categorized as career education, and there is a considerable body of literature on this topic. We address the idea later in this chapter. When individuals demonstrate attitudinal and skill deficiencies in these important placement-related categories, counselors are challenged to work with them to establish relevant intervention goals. For example, when working with a senior who is undecided about what to do after high school, a counselor uses a stepped decision-making counseling process to help the client make a tentative decision. In the process, the client also learns how the rational decision-making process works and how to employ it in the future. This process is often referred to as career counseling. Again, a significant body of literature has evolved about career counseling. We also address this topic later in the chapter.

Skills. All skills acquired during basic K–12 education are important in the transition process, including reading, writing, and arithmetic. Some specific transition skills are more in the domain of counseling than of classroom instruction: job hunting, employment interviewing, résumé writing, and college selection. Primarily the basis of the vocational guidance movement, these skills are as important to the school-to-work transition process as are the basic skills. In fact, basic skills are components of these transition skills. For example, job hunting requires reading skills, and résumé writing requires writing skills. Helping students acquire adequate school-to-work transition skills requires proactive prevention programming (i.e., career education) and reactive counseling interventions (i.e., career counseling) from school counselors. The teaching of skills follows students' acquisition of understandings and attitudes that make skill acquisition relevant. School counselors are challenged to be aware of the important transition skills and to be able to teach them in developmentally relevant ways.

Coordinating Transition-Enhancing Activities

The relevant professional literature that addresses transition issues tends to be separated into information about home-to-school and school-to-school transitions. Terms such as *articulation* and *orientation* are applied to home-to-school and school-to-school issues, and school-to-work information is sometimes categorized as *placement activities*.

Several articulation points are found in any educational system—home-to-school, elementary-to-middle- (or junior-high) school, middle- (or junior-high) to-high-school (or vocational-technical school). Most school districts believe in orientation programs to help students make these transitions, and school counselors are typically involved. However, different philosophies are applied in school systems throughout the country. Some treat orientation as an event, a short-time occurrence in which several activities take place in a massive but brief attempt to orient people to a new setting. Others treat it as a process—a longer series of less massive events. Examples of the two approaches follow, the first being an event, the second a process:

All eighth or ninth graders are excused from their classes and transported to the high school they will be attending the following year. On arriving, they are greeted by selected high-school faculty during a general meeting or assembly. They then form small groups that are guided around the school by older students who provide verbal highlights and explanations, answer questions, and distribute prepared printed materials such as maps of the building. The visitors are then treated to a typical lunch in the cafeteria. In the afternoon, they attend another assembly where they are greeted by the principal and then provided with verbal and audiovisual information about important aspects of the high-school program. The assistant principal, head counselor, athletic director, music coordinator, student council president, and representatives of academic units and clubs and organizations participate in the presentation. Printed handouts are distributed, and time is allowed for questions and answers. The visitors are bused back to their schools prior to dismissal time. As a follow-up to the visit, junior-high/middle-school counselors and teachers begin aiding the students with high-school course selection during the week after the visit. The work is completed within 2 to 3 weeks, and counselors often are involved in the planning and implementation of the programs.

During the fifth-grade year, a series of planned, coordinated orientation activities are provided for students prior to their articulation to the middle school as sixth graders. These activities are spread over that school year and are planned to supplement each other. Examples of the activities are audiovisual presentations about the middle school, visitations from middle-school personnel, visits to the middle school for students and parents, periodic mailings of orientation materials to the home, inclusion of preparatory material and activities into fifth-grade teaching units, and a systematic series of pre-articulation group and individual counseling sessions planned to reach all students. The process is continued through the summer and into the fall. During the first year of attendance at the middle school, a systematic series of group and individual counseling sessions serving all students continues. The counseling staff working with the students in these sessions, however, is now the middle-school staff. In addition to this, a "thematic interconnection" is made between one or more academic courses and the orientation program (Ducat & Lieberman, 1978). Counselors and teachers cooperatively blend academic curriculum content and guidance orientation ideas into an academic course. In this way, the orientation process is systematically carried through the sixth-grade year in a directed effort to help students gradually assimilate into their new school with minimal trauma.

The American School Counselor Association (ASCA, n.d.) is on record in support of the school-to-work transition function for school counselors in a position statement adopted in 1984. Referring to school counselors as "career guidance professionals" who "assume leadership in the implementation of career development outcomes," the ASCA position continues:

> Career Guidance is a delivery system that systematically helps students reach the career development outcomes of self-awareness and assessment, career awareness and exploration, career decision-making, career planning and placement. It has consistently been seen as a high priority needed by youth, their parents, school boards, the private sector, and the general public. . . . The certain rapidity of occupational change, coupled with the uncertain nature of the emerging service/information oriented high technology society, have combined to change guidance practices in significant ways. The school counselor's role covers many areas within the school setting and career guidance is one of the most important contributions to a student's lifelong development. (p. 31)

Various federal and state agencies provide placement services for high-school graduates and dropouts. Colleges, universities, community colleges, trade and technical schools, and proprietary schools also have placement services. In addition, some high-school departments such as business education, cooperative education, vocational–technical education, and agricultural education have placement services. All may be important to some of a school counselor's clients. These services tend to be specialized, however, and dependent on clients referring themselves for assistance.

A basic ingredient of an effective school-to-work transition is the coordination of various resources both in and out of the school system. Counselors are in a position to coordinate these services somewhat like a broker. Counselors are strategically located in the schools, where they have access to students, know their placement needs, and have access to the useful services of other agencies. Counselors are able to bring students and agencies together when appropriate. An example is when a school counselor refers students to the state bureau of employment security to be given the General Aptitude Test Battery as a first step toward employment by a local industry.

School counselors also know about the placement services of differing departments in the school system. They can help students avail themselves of such services. Counselors can work cooperatively with department faculties toward achieving mutual placement goals. For instance, counselors may cooperate with business education faculty members by training business education majors to be skillful job interviewers, and the business education faculty, in turn, provides business graduates with entry-level job openings.

School-to-work transition is best coordinated across grade levels. Proactive prevention programming designed to influence attitudes and teach skills related to transition goals will be most effective if started early, with subsequent efforts building on previous ones. Without coordination of these programs, important content may be repeated unnecessarily or overlooked. If this occurs, transition programming will be haphazard and inconsistent.

School counselors are challenged to realize that their transition activities need to be relevant for children and adolescents having varied worldviews. Therefore, planning ways to enhance transitions from home to school, from school to school, and from school to work must be done from a multicultural perspective.

BASIC COMPETENCIES FOR THE HOME-TO-SCHOOL AND SCHOOL-TO-SCHOOL TRANSITIONS

Understanding the Advantages and Disadvantages of Optional Transition Enhancement Approaches

As described earlier in this chapter, the home-to-school or school-to-school transition can be treated as an event or a process. The advantages of treating it as an event are its being structured, subject to organizational efficiency, and economical in the use of everybody's time and energy. All necessary information is imparted. In the example, the middle- or junior-high school students are given an opportunity to become familiar with the physical plant and with the various program offerings. They get a schedule for their high-school courses, and provisions are made for their assimilation into high school.

This type of transition program also has disadvantages. One disadvantage is the possibility of overkill: Too much information may have to be processed by students in too short a period of time; as a result, selective perception may leave different students with different conclusions. A second disadvantage is that so many students are involved in the event that it is virtually impossible to determine their individual needs or to respond to even a small portion of them in that short period of time. This problem is exacerbated in settings where participants vary culturally and are treated as if they were a homogeneous group. Another disadvantage is insufficient follow-up. After a massive transition event is held, students are expected to proceed on their own. Most, if not all, follow-up is dependent on student-initiated requests for help.

Among the advantages of transition as a process is the opportunity to supply necessary information gradually, over a longer period of time and in small doses. This increases the chances of retention and correct interpretation. Students have more time to give thought to the situation, to formulate and ask questions, and to analyze the answers to their questions. Also, a series of well-planned activities extending over a period of time is less likely to cause students to feel the anxiety that may result from abrupt change. Because of the challenges of working with students having diverse worldviews, approaching transitions as a process may make it easier to attend to their individual differences successfully.

This approach also has several disadvantages. The total amount of time and energy that must be devoted to such a transition process may be prohibitive. When balanced against other demands and needs, the costs, time, and energy demanded by an orientation process may be too heavy to be considered worthwhile. Decision makers may think that an orientation event is more practical and just as effective. Certainly it is more visible. Another disadvantage of transition as a process is that it may be more difficult to orchestrate because of its longer duration. Thus, it may be prone to more systemic breakdowns. Also, those in control of an orientation process may overapply the plan, making it more elaborate than is necessary, again resulting in breakdowns of the system and concurrent disenchantment with it.

Advantages of the event approach are primarily administrative and practical, whereas advantages of the process approach are more person-centered. The fact that the process approach is less administratively feasible makes implementing it a greater challenge for school personnel. This may explain why many schools seem to adhere to the event approach.

Being Aware of the Developmental Tasks Faced by Children and Adolescents

There is not enough space here to discuss specifically the many developmental tasks that children and adolescents face and how they interact with the transitions that occur during their in-school years. Holland-Jacobsen, Holland, and Cook (1984) sum them up efficiently as needing to find an acceptable place among new peers, being able to meet academic and behavioral standards for grade level, and being accepted by their teachers. School counselors are challenged to be aware of these tasks and to participate in designing and delivering transition events or processes or both with potential for helping children and adolescents achieve them successfully.

Akos (2002) provides several insights that are based on a study of students making the transition from fifth to sixth grade. Questions these students raised were dominated by a need for information about rules and procedures in the new setting. The students also exhibited a variety of worries (e.g., getting lost, bullying by older students, and succeeding academically). On the other hand, their worries were countered by an equal amount of enthusiasm and confidence. This led Akos to recommend highlighting those aspects of the new setting that students may look forward to (e.g., increased freedom and choices) during the orientation process. The findings also indicated the benefits of including a variety of participants in the orientation process (e.g., friends, parents, teachers, and trained peer helpers). Finally, based on the findings, Akos stated: "Transition programs should evolve throughout the transition year as student perceptions and needs change" (2002, p. 345).

A review of the literature on educational aspirations of children and adolescents led Wahl and Blackhurst (2000) to make several conclusions that led to recommendations for school counselors. Their conclusions included: (a) students from lower socioeconomic backgrounds often lack access to important informational resources and lack the skills to take advantage of what is available; (b) Native Americans and Hispanics have the lowest and least stable aspirations; (c) if students of color are to have college aspirations, parental support is needed; and (d) students of color who do have high academic aspirations often lack realistic information about colleges. Their recommendations include: (a) begin career exploration through prevention programming in the early elementary-school grades; (b) use prevention programming to help middle-school students acquire realistic ideation about postsecondary options, need for training, and how to prepare for success in various fields; and (c) help high-school students explore a wide range of postsecondary options. Space limitations allow us to present only part of the findings and recommendations, and readers are encouraged to read this article for a number of excellent ideas for helping all students become better prepared for postsecondary transitions.

Knowing Specific Transition Strategies and Being Able to Implement Them

The professional literature does not contain many entries about this topic, yet those that have been published seem practical and helpful. The sample of recommendations we offer was discovered by searching the professional journals. This is a skill that individual counselors are encouraged to develop.

Holland-Jacobsen et al. (1984) recommend parent meetings, get-to-know-the-school nights, special tutoring programs, buddy systems, and periodic meetings with new students. In their description of a program specifically designed for transition to junior high school, Allan and McKean (1984) recommend visitations to feeder elementary schools by junior-high-school counselors, a welcoming event at the junior high school (when prospective new students meet professional school personnel and are guided around the school by students who had attended their elementary schools), visits with the prospective students by students from the junior high school to answer questions about life at the junior high school, a parent night followed by a staff meeting with teachers to discuss students, visits to classrooms by counselors and school nurses during the first month in attendance at the junior high school, and a buddy program that pairs new students with older students who help them adjust to the new school setting. N. S. Wilson (1983) describes an innovative idea in the form of a play entitled *What Can the School Do for Me?* and Childress (1982) describes implementation of the play idea. Johnson (1995) offers specific recommendations for transition strategies that may enhance multicultural relations. Among the ideas not already mentioned are evaluating the English and native-language proficiency of new immigrant students, providing special educational screening, forming newcomer clubs in the elementary schools through which new students are invited to join in activities with established students, and conflict-resolution and peer-mediation programs designed to teach students alternative ways to deal with interpersonal differences.

Focusing on providing support for students making transitions from one school district to another—that is, transfer students—C. Wilson (1993) stresses the importance of recognizing signs of stress, helping transfer students ease into the new environment, and providing as much stability in their lives as possible. Among the specific strategies she implemented in a suburban Washington, D.C., secondary school that was experiencing a high student mobility rate were these:

- Paying comprehensive attention to basic needs when students enroll (e.g., selecting courses, receiving needed information, inventorying students' interests and goals)
- Providing each student with a peer helper
- Entering each student in a new-student support group co-led by school counselors and meeting weekly

Interestingly, Matter and Matter (1988), in presenting ideas for helping elementary-school children cope with relocation stress, cite the same goals as Wilson: recognizing signs of stress, providing stability, and easing children into the new environment. Matter and Matter mention the usefulness of helping children prepare for relocation via discussions about the move, what might be enjoyable about it, and the opportunities that might occur. They also highlight the importance of working with parents and of reminding parents of the role of maintaining links with the former environment. Counselors can provide direct assistance by being available when children need stability, using bibliotherapy to help the children ease into their new environment, and remaining alert for signs of maladaptive behaviors.

Wood and Beale (1991) call attention to the additional challenge of assisting special students (e.g., students with disabilities) with the transition process (i.e., inclusion to the mainstream). In general, the challenge for counselors with these students is greater than with other students. Beyond the ideas that have already been discussed that are also applicable to this group of students, according to Wood and Beale, counselors are in a good position to develop teamwork among themselves and other professionals, and these students may need special considerations to make successful home-to-school and school-to-school transitions. Examples of possible special considerations are curriculum modifications, parent conferences, and individual counseling interventions.

BASIC COMPETENCIES FOR THE SCHOOL-TO-WORK TRANSITION

Helping Students Understand the Contingencies of the Process

Helping students understand the contingencies of the school-to-work process is, in part, a matter of providing useful information and helping recipients process it. Counselors are challenged to be aware of what students need to know, when they are best able to learn it, how to get their attention when presenting it, and how to help them process the information usefully. Counselors are also challenged to be able to address the placement needs of their clientele. Educational and vocational placements deserve to be given equal status. If specialization is introduced, specialists should be available to serve the needs of all students (e.g., entry-level job counselors, as well as college counselors). The ratio of one specialization to the others may be determined by the corresponding ratio of student needs; that is, if 90% of students attend college after high school, then 90% of placement service efforts should be educational placement.

Although not including all the school-to-work information that students need, the following sample may be helpful. To make informed decisions, it is important for students to separate facts from myths about the job market (e.g., "If one can't find a job, it proves that few of them are out there"; "employers are in the driver's seat"; Bolles, 1981). Dispelling myths about the job market is a service that counselors can provide through both prevention and treatment programming.

Beyond being freed from mythical thinking, students can be prepared to assert themselves appropriately. Appropriate assertiveness includes setting goals and developing confidence in one's ability to achieve them, identifying the skills one possesses that can be used in the workplace, learning how to join networks that share useful information, and learning how to promote oneself to prospective employers (Worzbyt, Stacy, & Rieseman, n.d.). Being able to assert oneself appropriately when approaching the job market results in being empowered, which is healthier than being reactive.

Achieving empowerment requires planning, which counselors can advocate. In that vein, DeMont and DeMont (1983) created an interesting application of situational leadership theory and generated four approaches to career planning. If DeMont and DeMont's application is followed, counselors can benefit from viewing individual career planning as being differential, situational, and developmental. This is especially important in the light of already stated differences in worldviews that school counselors encounter. Career planning is *differential* in that individuals vary in their planning approaches. Some need mentoring, others are independent, and others exhibit various combinations of dependence and independence. Career planning is *situational* because individual circumstances generate behaviors anywhere along the dependence-independence continuum. For example, an individual who has undertaken the college selection process independently may need mentoring to be ready for on-campus selection interviews. Career planning can be *developmental* when the dominant initial approach of individuals is dependent but progresses toward independence over time.

This application of situational leadership theory offers suggestions for strategies for helping students plan the future. The strategy offers a diagnostic and planning vehicle; it can be used to diagnose the approaches of clients, to plan how to respond to their current needs, and to plan efforts to help them progress toward a desired approach. Although careful planning is admittedly important, developing students also need to be aware of the role of luck or happenstance. Defined by M. J. Miller (1983) as unexpected events that may alter one's behaviors and plans, *happenstance* cannot be forecast. Students should be aware of the possibility and potential impact of happenstance events.

Counselors can help developing students become aware of their values. Many youngsters are not overtly aware of the influence of their values and the values of others on decisions they make. Consequently, covert influences may affect their eventual placements in ways that are unknown and undesired. In the domain of work values, research indicates that there may be differences between parents and children (Vodanovich & Kramer, 1989). Such generational differences, though signaling the possibility of parent-child conflicts, also indicate that counselors and their student clients may have differing work values. A counselor's ability to help clients clarify their values is dependent on the counselor's self-awareness and openness to individual differences. Having achieved these characteristics, counselors may help students identify and clarify their values in the context of their potential influence on current and future decisions. Awareness of the values of their constituents provides counselors with information useful in developing individualized helping strategies. For instance, adolescents pursuing nontraditional careers may need supportive counseling as they proceed toward implementing decisions manifested by their nontraditional values (S. Wilson, 1982).

Children, too, can be helped to understand the contingencies of the transition process. Catlett (1992) offers an idea for kindergartners, the goals of which are to foster respect for all jobs, increase understanding of the importance of work, and develop an appreciation of school as work. Designed to give the children an overview of work that causes an examination of what it is and means, Catlett describes a program, presented over 2 weeks, consisting of three activities: people at work, children at work, and a work-setting simulation.

Helping Students Acquire the Requisite Skills

In addition to being aware of what developing students need to know, counselors are challenged to be aware of what students need to do and how to help them do it successfully. Helping students acquire requisite skills is another way to help them achieve empowerment in the transition process. Skill acquisition requires training, either as prevention programming designed to develop skills that will eventually be needed or as counseling interventions for individuals deficient in skills currently important. It is not possible to address all transition skills in this chapter. Instead, an inventory of basic transition skills is discussed briefly. Some skills are exclusive to educational placement, others to job placement, and others are universal. In the spirit of giving equal status to both educational and job placements, no categorizing of skills along those lines is provided. All are presented as important basic transition skills that school counselors can help their clients acquire.

Evaluating Recruitment Materials.   It stands to reason that adult counselors can help inexperienced youths read recruitment materials carefully and intelligently. Faculty members, such as English teachers and librarians, and knowledgeable adults outside the schools can also be helpful. Inexperienced youths will be better prepared to evaluate recruitment materials objectively when they know how to make rational decisions. Some evidence suggests that training in rational decision making leads to improved action planning and superior choice making for some individuals (Krumboltz, Sherba, Hamel, & Mitchell, 1982). In a stepped decision-making process, individuals are encouraged to identify their options, investigate the advantages and disadvantages of the options, and make choices based on the information they acquire from the process. The importance of the stepped approach to rational decision making has been stressed in previous chapters. Transition skills are another area in which the ideas can be applied usefully in either a specialized or general fashion. Decision-making skills can be taught in a unit on evaluating recruiting materials or in a general prevention program.

Children and adolescents are helped if made aware of the importance of staying power.

Completing Applications. Junge, Daniels, and Karmos (1984) found that personnel managers of companies they surveyed ranked highly the ability to follow verbal instructions and to write Standard English. Skill in this area comes partly from being informed about the nuances of application forms and of the expectations and goals of those who read the applications. Counselors can help by giving instructions and by providing important information. Simulations in which students complete mock applications and get feedback are also helpful. Repetitions of the simulations should enhance student sophistication.

Taking Selection Tests.   Helping students be prepared to perform successfully on selection tests introduces counselors to three challenging topics: test-wiseness, coaching, and test anxiety. *Test-wiseness* involves knowledge of the characteristics and formats of tests that allows individuals to achieve scores reflecting their true capacities not influenced by the structure of the test (Millman, Bishop, & Ebel, 1965). Performance tests have right and wrong answers and are the kind of standardized selection examinations most commonly used. Test-wiseness can be taught; such training includes instruction in developing strategies for time use, error avoidance, guessing, deductive reasoning, test constructor intent consideration, and cue using (Sarnacki, 1979). Brown (1982) offers a test-wiseness program for children that appears to be a modification of the principles published in Sarnacki's review. Brown's suggestions reflect an awareness of developmental differences and focus on enhancing familiarity with tests, learning how to answer test items, and using time efficiently.

Coaching, both similar to and different from general test-wiseness training, is the preparation of individuals to take specific tests. Among the tests most often targeted for coaching efforts are college and professional-school entrance tests, such as the Scholastic Aptitude Test (SAT) and the American College Test (ACT). In earlier times, counselors and students accepted claims by the publishers of these tests that coaching produced minimal gains and was unethical. Eventually, however, commercial coaching programs flourished, partly because of their advertised claims of dramatic test score gains. The claims attracted customers and caused counselors to wonder which position was accurate. Empirical investigations of the discrepant claims led to the current belief that, on average, coaching gains are greater than the test publishers once claimed but less than the commercial coaching schools advertise. Some individuals, however, especially those residing in disadvantaged environments, are capable of making dramatic gains.

As stated previously, school counselors can help by providing test-wiseness training (Powers, Alderman, & Noeth, 1983). Beyond that, counselors can inform students about commercial coaching programs and warn them of the cost-effectiveness risks. This may represent an opportunity for decision-making counseling services. In schools where many students need coaching and are unable to afford commercial programs, counselors may consider establishing in-school coaching as well as test-wiseness programs, inasmuch as many school counselors are capable of doing what commercial coaches do.

A resource that counselors who endeavor to coach students might use is ACTive Prep, a test-preparation software program developed by the ACT Educational Services Division. Designed to help students prepare for the ACT college admissions assessments,

ACTive Prep employs graphics, videos, and music to provide comprehensive reviews in English, mathematics, reading, and science reasoning. The software will create a customized plan for each student and provides advice for taking the ACT assessments. For more information see the www.act.org website.

Test anxiety is the tendency of individuals to respond to the stress associated with testing situations with worried, negative, self-centered ideation (Spielberger, Anton, & Bedell, 1976). This results in lowered performances. A considerable body of research on test anxiety has been generated, and no single or simple cure has been found. Some individuals can be helped by enhancing their test-wiseness. For others, test anxiety is a complicated phobic response. School counselors are challenged to be able to prevent some test anxiety by making students more skillful and knowledgeable test takers. Others, for whom more help is needed, can be identified and referred to clinical or counseling specialists. Some cases of test anxiety can be treated by school counselors familiar with strategies that are sometimes successful (e.g., cognitive self-instruction, stress inoculation, systematic desensitization). Some individuals can be helped through direct intervention, and others through referrals: School counselors can identify all individuals who require help in order to begin the process of getting it for them.

Test anxiety prevention can be approached via prevention programming. Cognitive self-instruction and stress inoculation are coping skills that can be used to prevent test anxiety and a host of other thinking-related anxieties. Test anxiety can be treated as the sole focus of such groups or as one of several foci. Group interventions designed to teach coping skills can be offered from upper-elementary through high-school levels. One example, cited in the professional school counseling literature, is summarized here: Wilkinson (1990) recommends that elementary-school counselors offer mini-lectures and classroom guidance programs to help children overcome test anxiety. Wilkinson suggests that students be helped to realize when they engage in negative self-talk. Examples of negative self-talk are "I can't ever finish on time" and "My parents will hate me if I fail." Students can be taught to replace such negative self-talk with positive thoughts. This strategy is known as *cognitive self-instruction*, and it is based on the principle that one cannot have two competing thoughts concurrently. The positive thoughts are used to interrupt and replace the negative thoughts. Wilkinson also recommends helping children improve time management and study techniques to reduce the probability that the reasons for having test anxiety are legitimate.

Engaging in Selection Interviews.

Engaging in formal interviews with adults who are strangers and who are looking for their weaknesses is a new experience for most adolescents. Preparing adolescents for selection interviews by demystifying the process is a crucial component of school-to-work transition. Preparation for engaging in selection interviews successfully can be given through instructions and simulations. Galassi and Galassi (1978) refer to the process of helping interviewees increase their chances of success as *image management.* Instruction directed toward competence at image management can provide students with information about important considerations, such as the kinds of questions to expect, different interviewing strategies, dress codes, and questions to ask interviewers. Simulations provide opportunities for rehearsals and for receiving constructive performance feedback.

Kerr, Claiborn, and Dixon's (1982) suggestions for teaching persuasion skills, though originally targeted for training counselors, provide food for thought. The basic idea is to help adolescents learn to project expertness, trustworthiness, and attractiveness. The skills that Kerr et al. associate with these qualities are behavioral. Thus, the skills are identifiable and associated with such actions as smiling, establishing direct eye contact, and dressing appropriately. The instructional and simulation components of programs designed to demystify selection interviewing for adolescents are well within the realm of the basic competencies of school counselors. Wild and Kerr (1984) found that persuasion skills training enhanced the ability of adolescents to convince employers that they were the right people for the jobs. The same procedures can prepare younger students to acquire part-time employment. Learning about image management at an early age may be an important foundation for success in the future.

Producing Résumés and Other Transition-Related Compositions.

Using instructions and simulations is advocated for teaching developing students the skills needed to produce documents such as résumés or autobiographies. In addition to informing students of the purposes of each document, instruction will teach them the methods used to gather information and the skills needed to produce the documents (e.g., outlining, choosing appropriate words, making the document persuasive). Simulations allow students to practice producing documents with supervision that provides opportunities for constructive feedback. Repetitions of the simulations, coupled with constructive feedback, allow students to perfect their skills gradually while enhancing their self-esteem. A transition-related composition of increasing importance to high-school students is writing admission essays. Cook (2001) presents information about the importance of these essays and offers some helpful recommendations. For more information, see EssayEdge.com.

Understanding the Difference Between Getting Accepted and Achieving Success.

Counselors are challenged to help their clients realize the importance of staying power, which is arguably a combination of attitudes and skills. *Staying power* refers to following through after being accepted for a job or by a higher education institution, by holding the job or finishing the educational program. Transition-to-work and -school goals include helping students make a transition and succeed after the transition has been made.

Children and adolescents are helped if made aware of the importance of staying power so that it becomes one of their goals. They also benefit from assistance in acquiring the skills that will help them achieve staying power. Those skills are difficult to define clearly. Mastery of the basic skills such as reading, writing, and arithmetic is important and points to the need for getting the most out of one's lessons and classes in school. The importance of mastering the requisite skills for performing an entry-level job or for succeeding in an institution of higher education has been highlighted through survey research (Junge et al., 1984). In holding down a job, being able to get along with supervisors and coworkers may be more important than the ability to perform job-related duties. Failure to establish successful peer and faculty relationships may lead to greater likelihood of leaving school. Getting along well with others draws on the entire range of human relations skills.

Basic communication skills are teachable when students are motivated to learn them. Other human relations skills, such as learning to accept individual differences, are more complex and difficult to teach. Preparing students to get along with others is an important staying-power goal that challenges school counselors to inventory their entire range of competencies in order to offer constructive assistance. It is best to begin training for enhanced human relations in elementary school and to continue that training thereafter. Enhancing staying power is only one of many potentially positive outcomes of programs designed to improve human relations throughout the basic K–12 education years.

Developing Attitudes, Expanding Horizons, and Offering Relevant Information. Kosmo (1977) was cited previously as having advocated starting the placement process in the elementary schools. She suggests that the goals of placement programming at the elementary- and middle-school levels should be developing attitudes, expanding horizons, and offering relevant information.

Making children more aware of the world of work and the place of work in their lives is one important way to operationalize the goals suggested by Kosmo. Edington (1976) reports on two approaches for helping primary-age children expand their horizons. One approach is to take the children on field trips to work sites. A second, though less effective, method is to develop classroom interest centers. In Edington's study, the interest center is in a house-shaped enclosure and contains mannequins dressed for specific occupations, tools for different trades, and recorded interviews with workers. The children in Edington's study were kindergartners. In a series of studies assessing the effects of integrating materials on nontraditional role concepts into kindergarten and preschool curricula, Weeks and Porter (1983) and Weeks, Thornburg, and Little (1977) found that they were able to modify some occupational stereotypes, especially in girls.

The importance of presenting children with live models is emphasized in the work of Bailey and Nihlen (1989) and R. R. Miller (1986). Providing opportunities to interact with live models while asking questions and testing hypotheses is an important way to help children keep their options open. Bailey and Nihlen also point out the importance of providing useful information for children in conjunction with their interactions with workers.

Tinsley, Benton, and Rollins (1984) studied the effect of values clarification techniques on enhancing the career decision-making competencies of seventh and eighth graders. They found the eighth graders better able to respond to the program successfully, becoming aware of the need to cope with their values but not necessarily able to crystallize them. In an attempt to expand the career horizons of eighth-grade girls while not denigrating traditional careers, Cramer, Wise, and Colburn (1977) developed an 11-hour unit containing definitions and discussions of stereotypes, information about differing work roles, and data about the workforce. They also had the participants investigate sex stereotyping in the media. Also working with seventh- and eighth-grade students, J. Wilson and Daniel (1981) developed a role clarification workshop to modify sex role stereotypes and to expand career choices. The workshop is a blend of role clarification and vocational role appraisal exercises. Modest effects in both the J. Wilson and Daniel and the Cramer et al. studies indicate promise for such programs.

Hoyt's (2001) data point out the importance of helping students and parents make "reasoned" decisions about attending college. He believes that, although baccalaureate degrees are valuable for many individuals, many others can benefit more from other postsecondary training options that can lead to happiness and success. According to Hoyt (2001, 2002), students and their parents will be better prepared to make "reasoned" decisions if, in addition to receiving information about baccalaureate-degree colleges and universities, they also receive and are helped to process information about community colleges, technical institutes, publicly supported career institutions, proprietary career-oriented institutions, federally sponsored career training programs, and career-oriented programs in the Armed Services. Hoyt (2002) believes that acquiring and accurately processing information about this wider range of choices will better prepare high-school students to avoid the pain and frustration associated with dead-end jobs and postsecondary training programs.

Making Students Aware of Useful Self-Help Resources

School-to-work transition is analogous to counseling interventions in that clients are on their own more often than they are in the presence of teachers, counselors, and other helpers. This time-ratio discrepancy points to the importance of self-management in achieving transition goals, just as it does in achieving counseling goals. To enhance the probability that students will make adequate progress toward achieving transition goals when on their own, counselors can make them aware of self-help resources and can make useful resources available. To do so requires counselors to be familiar with such resources. This circumstance highlights the interrelatedness of the information and transition enhancement functions. Self-help resources are informational and may be used to achieve transition-to-work goals. One example is that students have access to and independently use informational materials that prepare them for the transition from high school directly to work or to postsecondary education in preparation for work. The self-help resources discussed in this section are not exhaustive; they are examples of the types of topics that may be addressed in self-help resources.

Government agencies are quite productive. On the federal level, for example, the U.S. Department of Labor produces such documents as the *Occupational Outlook Quarterly*. State bureaus of employment security also have useful materials. Commercial publishers are good sources because of an appreciable demand for self-help materials. Perhaps the most well-known writer of commercial self-help materials is R. N. Bolles, author of *What Color Is Your Parachute: A Practical Manual for Job Hunters and Career Changes* (1999), published by Ten Speed Press. Other offerings from Ten Speed Press focus on such topics as helping readers hunt for jobs, prepare résumés, prepare for interviewing, move up the career ladder, negotiate for salaries, and earn degrees in nontraditional ways. Bolles published *Job Hunting on the Internet* (1997), which discusses the advantages and disadvantages of the Internet and the World Wide Web. A list of web addresses for job hunting and evaluations of their usefulness are available as well. On the one hand, numerous self-help offerings are in the marketplace, and the right combination of materials and individual sources can be very productive. On the other hand, leading students to self-help resources is similar to providing them with helpful computerized career guidance programs: Not all resources are equally helpful, nor are all developing students equally ready to process the contents successfully. Consequently, if self-help resources are to be used and promoted in the transition-to-work process, counselors need to be involved constructively. Constructive involvement includes, but is not limited to, knowing the content and usefulness of materials recommended to students and encouraging students to seek professional assistance with the processing of the resources.

Communicating Successfully With Placement Personnel

It stands to reason that, in high schools having transition-to-work services, counselors will have contacts with individuals representing the employers of their graduates and the schools to which their graduates matriculate after high school. At issue is how much contact should take place and what communications are necessary to make these relationships successful. Logic indicates that extremes should be avoided. One extreme scenario is counselors who have few, if any, such direct contacts, taking a laissez-faire attitude toward establishing productive relationships. The other extreme is a scenario in which counselors are so involved in the transition process that they are advocating and influencing the employment or selection of specific students. One manifestation of this extreme is that the competence of such counselors may be determined by their ability to get a sufficient number of students accepted to the right schools or employed by the right employers.

The first extreme leads to underserving one's clients; the latter leads to excessive attention to the school-to-work transition and the use of shallow, inappropriate accountability criteria such as "hit rates" for college acceptances and employment. A reasonable assessment of the situation leads to advocacy of a middle-of-the-road position—sufficient attention to communicating with placement personnel but not overattention. At the least, counselors can make placement personnel welcome on occasions when they visit their schools, provide access to interested students within the regulations of the school district and according to the ethical codes of the profession, visit schools and businesses of interest to their students if possible, prepare and distribute transcripts and letters of recommendation in an informative and timely manner, send personal communications with requests for informational materials, and inform both placement personnel and students of the school's transition-to-work goals. Counselors who behave accordingly will be student advocates who themselves are highly regarded by representatives of prospective employers and higher education institutions. Students will be served well by counselors who create a positive impression about the school, its employees, and its students without going overboard in their efforts.

Providing Comprehensive Direct Transitions From School to Work

Characteristics of Traditional Programs.   Although every generalization has exceptions, most school transition-to-work programs can probably be characterized fairly accurately by the following observations: Although there is some organization, the program is not organized systematically to serve all students; as a result, some students are served better than others. Minimal educational transition programs usually include writing recommendations, completing applications and transcripts, holding college nights, arranging college visitations, providing hospitality for post-high-school educational recruiters, assisting with arrangements to take entrance examinations, assisting in the interpretation of results of entrance examinations, assisting with locating and acquiring financial aid, providing decision-making counseling, and providing access to useful printed materials.

Minimal direct-to-work transition programs usually consist of notifying students about job opportunities brought to the school's attention by prospective employers, writing recommendations, releasing transcripts or other information when requested appropriately, excusing students for job interviews, making referrals to employment agencies, offering decision-making counseling, and providing access to useful printed materials. Although the overall transition-to-work programs in many schools often leave something to be desired, the general opinion is that the schools are more deficient in job placement than in educational placement (Bottoms, Gysbers, & Pritchard, 1972).

This deficiency has been decried for at least 30 years (Hoyt, Hughey, & Hughey, 1995). Recent attention to the situation has focused on the perceived national need to have individuals who do not pursue post-high-school training in 4-year colleges and universities acquire postsecondary vocational-technical training to acquire the requisite skills for surviving in the nation's and the world's emerging high-tech/high-skills marketplace. Commentaries by individuals such as Hoyt et al. (1995) and Parnell (1986) and reports such as those of the William T. Grant Foundation Commission on Work, Family, and Citizenship (1988) and the U.S. Department of Labor (1989) highlight the perceived importance of this matter. Hoyt et al. report the implementation of a project entitled "Counseling for High Skills: Vo-tech Career Options" that is designed to disseminate information to help school districts deal with this challenge better, primarily through enhanced school counseling responses in this area. The support of this effort by the DeWitt Wallace Reader's Digest Fund and the attention given to the challenge in the professional and popular press seem to indicate that school counselors may need to pay more attention to these students, referred to as the "forgotten half" in the W. T. Grant Foundation report, in the coming decade.

Findings from a study by Barker and Satcher (2000) indicate that efforts to arouse more interest in the so-called forgotten half may have been effective. The findings indicated that high-school counselors in a southeastern state perceived that it was just as important for work-bound students to acquire workplace skills and career development competencies as it was for college-bound students.

Parnell is credited with introducing the Tech Prep idea as an alternative to the so-called general education track for students not planning to attend 4-year baccalaureate degree programs (Chew, 1993). Funded by the Carl D. Perkins Vocational and Applied Technology Act, the Tech Prep initiative has spawned programs in several states. In general, Tech Prep is to bring about new and creative partnerships among secondary schools, the business community, and postsecondary vocational-technical institutions, leading to technical preparation in associate degree or 2-year certificate programs for non-college-bound students. School counselors are to be involved in several ways, including knowing about the new curriculum initiatives, coordinating the requisite partnership efforts, and implementing needed developmental guidance and counseling interventions (Chew, 1993).

Developing a Comprehensive Direct Transition-to-Work Program. All the functions attributed to traditional transition-to-work programs are useful. Taken as a whole, however, they are not comprehensive enough. They probably cannot be offered to all students by the typical school-counseling program because the counseling staff is too small and because of the many other demands on staff time. Therefore, it is unrealistic to expect the typical school counseling staff to provide comprehensive direct transition-to-work programs. The best solution to the dilemma of high expectations versus staff resources is to engage in cooperative transition programs that include using human resources from outside the school system. There is no universally accepted plan for implementing this idea. Suggestions have been offered earlier. For example, collaborations can be established with the state bureau of employment security. The ability to do this is affected by changing federal and state emphases on funding and on periodically changing program emphases. Currently, it may be easier to work out arrangements with these agencies for students representing special populations than for all students. At one time, the U.S. Department of Labor considered out-stationing employment service counselors and occupational information specialists in the schools (Odell, Pritchard, & Sinick, 1974). Although that plan was not implemented universally, it remains a good idea. It may be possible to bring specialists into the schools through the out-stationing of employees of agencies or organizations that are prepared to do so. It is more likely that additional human resources stationed outside the schools will need to be recruited.

Because students and counselors are located in the schools, school counselors are the logical candidates for serving as coordinators. When counselors do not coordinate services, each outside agency will work independently, and services will be delivered haphazardly. Among the resources that might be drawn into cooperative arrangements are military representatives, admissions officers of nearby institutions of higher and vocational-technical education, bureau of employment security personnel, and bureau of vocational rehabilitation personnel. Members of the school faculty can help, such as agriculture education, business education, cooperative education, and vocational-technical education departments responsible for placement of students majoring in their programs. Whatever the mixture of people in the cooperative enterprise, school counselors can coordinate and check the quality and appropriateness of the services contributed by cooperating agencies and individuals. Following is a listing of suggested direct placement services that can be included in such a school-to-work transition cooperative:

- Keeping placement records up-to-date. This includes the following:
  a. Job opportunities
  b. Training opportunities
  c. Potential employers
  d. Listings of full- or part-time jobs
  e. Up-to-date retrieval systems
  f. Placement credentials service

g. Records of placements made

h. Follow-up and follow-through services for graduates and dropouts

- Providing office facilities for prospective employers and representatives of educational institutions.
- Conducting surveys on job and educational needs and opportunities and posting or publishing the findings.
- Promoting and organizing field trips to schools, personnel offices, job sites, and the like.
- Having a system for making referrals to employers.
- Providing a comprehensive skills training component.
- Making students aware of their rights. For example, Title VII of the Civil Rights Act of 1964 prohibits discrimination in employment on the basis of race, sex, color, religion, or national origin.
- Making appropriate referrals to intermediary employment services, such as the bureau of employment security.
- Holding periodic management meetings with members of the placement cooperative.
- Providing counseling for current and former students engaged in the placement process.

CONCLUDING COMMENTS ABOUT ENHANCING TRANSITIONS

Every student has transition needs. Everyone eventually leaves the school system to make the transition to work, to further education, or to a less identifiable stage. Counselors can do much toward making the transition successful. To do so, they need help, and they need to approach the implementing of their transition programming carefully. Success requires a unique combination of being an organizer and a practitioner.

SUGGESTED ACTIVITIES

1. Analyze the strengths and weaknesses of the transition functions in a school you attended or where you are or were employed, using the criteria in this chapter.
2. Outline changes that would be necessary to improve those transition services. How expensive in time and funds would those changes be? List any workable compromises that might improve matters.
3. Read one or two of the self-help placement resources on the market and evaluate their effectiveness. What criteria will you use?
4. Debate the merits of each of the following position statements:
   a. Transition should be viewed as a process.
   b. Implementation of the transition process will require prevention programming and counseling interventions.
   c. Educational and vocational transitions must be given equal status.
5. Debate the merits of providing follow-up and follow-through transition services to individuals after they have left school.
6. Go to www.scan21st.com and propose some ways that this Internet site might help school counselors provide transition assistance to students.

REFERENCES

Adelman, H. S., & Taylor, L. (2002). School counselors and school reform: New directions. *Professional School Counseling, 5,* 235–248.

Akos, P. (2002). Student perceptions of the transition from elementary to middle school. *Professional School Counseling, 5,* 339–345.

Allan, J., & McKean, J. (1984). Transition to junior high school: Strategies for change. *School Counselor, 32,* 43–48.

American School Counselor Association (ASCA). (n.d.). *Guide to membership resources.* Alexandria, VA: Author.

Bailey, B. A., & Nihlen, A. S. (1989). Elementary school children's perceptions of the world of work. *Elementary School Guidance and Counseling, 24,* 135–145.

Baker, S. B. (1981). *School counselor's handbook: A guide for professional growth and development.* Boston: Allyn & Bacon.

Barker, J., & Satcher, J. (2000). School counselors' perceptions of required workplace skills and career development competencies. *Professional School Counseling, 4,* 134–139.

Bolles, R. N. (1981). *The three boxes of life and how to get out of them.* Berkeley, CA: Ten Speed Press.

Bolles, R. N. (1997). *Job hunting on the Internet.* Berkeley, CA: Ten Speed Press.

Bolles, R. N. (1999). *What color is your parachute? A practical manual for job hunters and career changes.* Berkeley, CA: Ten Speed Press.

Bottoms, J. E., Gysbers, N. C., & Pritchard, D. H. (1972). Career guidance, counseling, and placement. In J. R. Cochran & H. J. Peters (Eds.), *Guidance and introduction.* Upper Saddle River, NJ: Merrill/Prentice Hall.

Brown, D. (1982). Increasing test-wiseness in children. *Elementary School Guidance and Counseling, 16,* 180–186.

Catlett, J. C. (1992). The dignity of work: Schoolchildren look at employment. *Elementary School Guidance and Counseling, 27,* 150–154.

Chew, C. (1993). *Tech prep and counseling.* Madison, WI: Center for Education and Work.

Childress, N. W. (1982). Orientation to middle school: A guidance play. *Elementary School Guidance and Counseling, 17,* 89–93.

Cook, G. (2001, January/February). Admissions essays: The best-kept secret for getting into college. *ASCA Counselor,* 14–15.

Cramer, S. H., Wise, P. S., & Colburn, E. D. (1977). An evaluation of a treatment to expand the career perceptions of junior high school girls. *School Counselor, 25,* 124–129.

Dahir, C. (2001). The National Standards for School Counseling Programs: Development and implementation. *Professional School Counseling, 4,* 320–327.

DeMont, B., & DeMont, R. (1983). Personal approaches to career planning. *Vocational Guidance Quarterly, 32,* 6–15.

Ducat, D., & Lieberman, R. K. (1978). Articulating a freshman orientation program with a social science course. *Personnel and Guidance Journal, 57,* 61–62.

Edington, E. D. (1976). Evaluation of methods of using resource people in helping kindergarten students become aware of the world of work. *Journal of Vocational Behavior, 8,* 125–131.

Galassi, J. P., & Galassi, M. D. (1978). Preparing individuals for job interviews: Suggestions from more than 60 years of research. *Personnel and Guidance Journal, 57,* 188–192.

Gysbers, N. C., & Henderson, P. (2001). Comprehensive guidance and counseling programs: A rich history and a bright future. *Professional School Counseling, 4,* 246–256.

Herr, E. L., & Cramer, S. H. (1996). *Career guidance and counseling through the lifespan: Systematic approaches* (5th ed.). New York: HarperCollins.

Holland-Jacobsen, S., Holland, R. P., & Cook, A. S. (1984). Mobility: Easing the transition for students. *School Counselor, 32,* 49–53.

House, R. M., & Hayes, R. L. (2002). School counselors: Becoming key players in school reform. *Professional School Counseling, 5,* 249–256.

Hoyt, K. B. (2001). Helping high school students broaden their knowledge of postsecondary education options. *Professional School Counseling, 5,* 6–12.

Hoyt, K. B. (2002, March/April). The right tools. *ASCA Counselor,* 19–20, 22–23.

Hoyt, K. B., Hughey, J. K., & Hughey, K. F. (1995). An introduction to the "Counseling for High Skills: Vo-tech Career Options" project. *School Counselor, 43,* 10–18.

Isaacson, L. E. (1977). *Career information in counseling and teaching.* Boston: Allyn & Bacon.

Johnson, L. S. (1995). Enhancing multicultural relations: Intervention strategies for the school counselor. *School Counselor, 43,* 103–113.

Junge, D. A., Daniels, M. H., & Karmos, J. S. (1984). Personnel managers' perceptions of requisite basic skills. *Vocational Guidance Quarterly, 33,* 138–146.

Kerr, B. A., Claiborn, C. D., & Dixon, D. D. (1982). Training counselors in persuasion. *Counselor Education and Supervision, 21,* 138–148.

Kosmo, S. J. (1977). *Career education, career guidance, and occupational competence.* Madison: Wisconsin Vocational Studies Center.

Krumboltz, J. D., Sherba, D. S., Hamel, D. A., & Mitchell, L. K. (1982). Effect of training in rational decision making on quality of simulated career decisions. *Journal of Counseling Psychology, 29,* 618–625.

Matter, D. E., & Matter, R. M. (1988). Helping young children cope with the stress of relocation: Action steps for the counselor. *Elementary School Guidance and Counseling, 23,* 23–29.

Miller, M. J. (1983). The role of happenstance in career choice. *Vocational Guidance Quarterly, 32,* 16–20.

Miller, R. R. (1986). Reducing occupational circumscription. *Elementary School Guidance and Counseling, 20,* 250–254.

Millman, J., Bishop, C. H., & Ebel, R. (1965). An analysis of test-wiseness. *Educational and Psychological Measurement, 25,* 707–726.

Odell, C. E., Pritchard, D. H., & Sinick, D. (1974). Whose job is placement? *Vocational Guidance Quarterly, 23,* 138–145.

Parnell, D. (1986). *The neglected majority.* Washington, DC: Community College Press.

Powers, D. E., Alderman, D. L., & Noeth, K. J. (1983). Helping students prepare for the SAT: Alternative strategies for counselors. *School Counselor, 30,* 350–357.

Sarnacki, R. (1979). An examination of test-wiseness in the cognitive test domain. *Review of Educational Research, 49,* 252–279.

Spielberger, C. D., Anton, W. D., & Bedell, J. (1976). The nature and treatment of test anxiety. In M. Zuckerman & C. D. Spielberger (Eds.), *Emotions and anxiety* (pp. 317–341). Mahwah, NJ: Lawrence Erlbaum.

Tinsley, H. E. A., Benton, G. L., & Rollins, J. A. (1984). The effects of values clarification exercises on the value structure of junior high school students. *Vocational Guidance Quarterly, 32,* 160–167.

U.S. Department of Labor. (1989). *Work-based learning: Training America's workers.* Washington, DC: U.S. Department of Labor, Employment and Training Administration.

Vodanovich, S. J., & Kramer, T. J. (1989). The examination of the work values of parents and their children. *Career Development Quarterly, 37,* 365–374.

Wahl, K. H., & Blackhurst, A. (2000). Factors affecting the occupational and educational aspirations of children and adolescents. *Professional School Counseling, 3,* 367–374.

Weeks, M. D., & Porter, E. P. (1983). A second look at the impact of nontraditional role models and curriculum on the vocational role preferences of kindergarten children. *Journal of Vocational Behavior, 23,* 64–71.

Weeks, M. D., Thornburg, K. R., & Little, L. (1977). The impact of exposure to nontraditional role models on the vocational role preferences of 5-year-old children. *Journal of Vocational Behavior, 10,* 139–145.

Wild, B. K., & Kerr, B. A. (1984). Training adolescent job seekers in persuasion skills. *Vocational Guidance Quarterly, 33,* 63–69.

Wilkinson, C. M. (1990). Techniques for overcoming test anxiety. *Elementary School Guidance and Counseling, 24,* 234–237.

William T. Grant Foundation Commission on Work, Family, and Citizenship. (1988). *The forgotten half: Pathways to success for America's youth and young families.* Washington, DC: Author.

Wilson, C. (1993). Providing support for high school transfer students. *School Counselor, 40,* 223–227.

Wilson, J., & Daniel, R. (1981). The effects of a career-options workshop on social and vocational stereotypes. *Vocational Guidance Quarterly, 29,* 341–349.

Wilson, N. S. (1983). "What can the school do for me?": A guidance play. *School Counselor, 30,* 374–380.

Wilson, S. (1982). A new decade: The gifted and career choice. *Vocational Guidance Quarterly, 31,* 53–59.

Wood, J. W., & Beale, A. V. (1991). Facilitating special students' transition within the school. *Elementary School Guidance and Counseling, 25,* 261–268.

Worzbyt, J. C., Stacy, R., & Rieseman, R. (n.d.). *The job connection: Advocacy and employment.* Washington, DC: Association for Counselor Education and Supervision.

CHAPTER 10

Assessment in School Counseling

Goals: To describe the strategic role of counselors in the total assessment services of the schools. To identify basic competencies for fulfilling associated responsibilities.

We recently had an opportunity to hear a North Carolina school counselor voice a complaint not uncommon among counselors who work in schools:

> *I spend too much of my time worrying about tests, especially end-of-grade tests. Since North Carolina decided to emphasize testing of students, I've become the testing coordinator for my school. I have little time to do what I really need to do to help students with all the other things going on in their lives. The emphasis on testing has also*

created new problems for kids. I spend many hours visiting with parents who are concerned about whether or not their children will pass the required tests at the end of the year. The children also worry. I can hardly believe how many cases of test anxiety I handle involving fourth graders. They feel as if their lives will be total failures if they don't make a passing mark on end-of-grade tests. I am at a loss to know how to handle all of this. What can I do?

School counselors have always been concerned about their role in testing. The profession has seen a lively debate over the years about this very matter. This chapter addresses some of the many issues school counselors face as they consider their roles in testing and assessment.

DEMAND FOR ASSESSMENT IN SCHOOL COUNSELING

The term *assessment* is used here instead of the more traditional term *testing* because the scope of these activities has now expanded from the exclusive use of standardized tests to the inclusion of nonstandardized methods. Therefore, *assessment* more accurately represents the comprehensive nature of the activities. Assessment activities are a wide range of strategies, including standardized testing, used to gather information about students that is useful in individual and institutional decision making.

The demand for assessment in school counseling is wrapped up in the history of standardized testing and the demand for testing in society and in education. Scholarly activities by psychologists in Western Europe and later in the United States during the late nineteenth and early twentieth centuries led to the development of efforts to assess individual differences and, in so doing, to employ methods that were scientifically rigorous (orderly, accurate, and reproducible). The work was conducted in laboratories and universities by such individuals as Wilhelm Wundt, Sir Francis Galton, James T. Cattell, Edward L. Thorndike, and Charles Spearman, all of whom eventually became recognized as pioneers of the testing and assessment movement (Linden & Linden, 1968).

Primarily a scholarly enterprise conducted without much fanfare and with only limited applications, standardized assessment received a major boost in popularity during World War I when a committee of scholars developed group tests of intelligence, known as Army Alpha and Beta, to help the military determine which recruits were fit for service. In the period following World War I, scholarly assessment ideas were applied on a much larger scale, and testing became a business. Several factors were at work: Massive immigration to the United States at the turn of the century, industrialization and urbanization of what had been primarily a rural society, and legislation to protect children from industrial usury and to enhance their educational opportunities, which led to a changing educational philosophy—away from exclusivity and toward mass education.

The growth in the number of children attending school and the need to assimilate immigrants into American society created an environment where standardized assessment flourished. The availability of tests that could be administered to groups of schoolchildren and that could provide information about individual differences as well as individual and group achievement helped make standardized testing a big business.

Test results were used primarily for institutional decision making, such as for classifying students into instructional tracks and for comparing the academic achievement of a particular school's students with achievements from national samples. These purposes for using standardized tests in the schools became traditional uses that are as important now as they were 90 years ago, helping make such testing a multimillion dollar business.

Concurrently, vocational guidance professionals, influenced by the publication of Parsons's book *Choosing a Vocation* (1909), were able to use standardized tests as one source of dependable information for individuals attempting to make occupational choices. As noted in chapter 1, the influence of vocational guidance on the schools was minimal at that time. The psychological testing movement eventually led to tests being used as important school guidance tools, primarily for trying to predict academic and occupational success. By the end of the 1930s, test scores, particularly from aptitude tests and interest inventories, had become a major component of vocational guidance in the schools, and prediction was the primary purpose for using them.

The demand for standardized tests was further enhanced by the National Defense Education Act (NDEA) of 1958. The NDEA influenced the growth of school counseling significantly by drawing attention to the need for effective guidance of gifted and talented students and by infusing large sums of money into the schools in an effort to improve guidance and instruction. One outcome was an increase in the purchase and use of standardized tests in the schools. School districts received federal funds to buy tests to identify gifted students. Another outcome was to highlight the importance of assessment as a school counseling function. Traditional uses of standardized tests to make institutional placement and curriculum decisions continued, and school counselors found that they had become associated with *all* the schools' testing programs. Consequently, it was common for school counselors to use tests in guidance and counseling, as well as to participate in and direct programs designed to gather information for placing, tracking, and monitoring the performance of local students on achievement tests. This happened particularly often in elementary schools, where counselors often were assigned responsibility for coordinating testing services. Additionally, counselors had become responsible for arranging students' access to entrance testing for postsecondary education and to placement testing for transitions from school to work. In the minds of many administrators and classroom teachers, school counseling and testing became synonymous.

In the years after the popularization of standardized assessment, widespread use led to abuses and to concerns about inherent biases. Warnings and criticisms in scholarly writings and in popular publications led to technical improvements in tests and their accompanying explanatory materials, to the publication of standards for tests and testing applications, and to improvements in the training of users. Yet, the continued growth of applications and the increase in users were so great that further abuses were inevitable.

In the early 1970s, Goldman (1972) attracted the attention of counseling professionals and test publishers to this issue. Describing the relationship between tests and counseling as analogous to a failed marriage, Goldman suggested that most tests were developed for selection purposes and that, though useful for such institutional decisions in the military services, business and industry, and colleges and universities, they were of little use in one-to-one or small-group counseling because the predictive valid-ity of the tests was too low. He went on to point out that the same tests were even less useful for disadvantaged populations, noting that most counselors lacked the skills needed to derive whatever limited value the tests do have to offer. He concluded with a recommendation for reducing the use of tests in counseling and for limiting test interpretations to highly qualified specialists.

Goldman's statements came amid criticisms that were leveled at standardized test-ing and test corporations and that called for moratoriums on testing. These criticisms included allegations of racial and gender bias in the tests, invasion of privacy by the testing procedures, and declining performances on college entrance examinations. Spurred, in part, by these criticisms, as well as by improvements naturally generated by corporate competition and scholarly research, changes occurred. In the early 1980s, a group of scholars examining the years since Goldman's failed marriage analogy made the following observations:

- Counselors are increasingly privy to nonstandardized assessment instruments that emphasize process over outcomes (Zytowski, 1982).
- Publishers are producing standardized instruments accompanied by computer-generated counseling information, which changes the emphasis from using tests for predicting to using them as tools in a self-discovery/future-potential exploratory process.
- Major problems are still associated with using standardized assessment instru-ments with disadvantaged populations (Goldman, 1982).

Survey data indicated a trend away from using maximum performance tests mea-suring achievement, intelligence, and aptitude and toward using typical performance instruments measuring interests, attitudes, and personality attributes. This trend indi-cated a need for even greater counselor sophistication than was the case when Goldman leveled his criticism in the early 1970s (Zytowski & Warman, 1982). A con-current survey indicated that testing was important in most schools and that career guidance was the primary purpose for using tests in counseling (Engen, Lamb, & Prediger, 1982).

In 1994, *Measurement and Evaluation in Counseling and Development* published another scholarly discussion of Goldman's (1972) marriage metaphor. Bradley (1994), Goldman (1994), Prediger (1994), and Zytowski (1994) agreed that the reductionistic scientific view of using a regression model to make predictions from test scores, espe-cially ability measures such as the Scholastic Assessment Test (SAT) and the American College Test (ACT), is outdated. Both Prediger and Zytowski believe that a discrimi-nant model in which membership in, or similarity to people in, groups when blended or applied to estimates of one's potential is more useful and is the wave of the future for using tests in counseling. An example of this model is to use data from interest inventories like the Strong Interest Inventory (SII) to indicate to clients how similar or dissimilar their expressed interests are when compared with those of successful, employed women and men representing several work categories or groups (e.g., teach-ers, psychologists, physicists). In the model, counselors will help individuals process the discriminant data in combination with self-assessments and other data about their abilities when making decisions about how to use the assessment data to understand themselves and to make plans for their lives. Goldman continued to believe that standardized tests have limited usefulness for counselors and that perhaps 10% possess the requisite skills and attitudes to use them properly. He thought the remaining 90% should use qualitative assessment techniques such as card sorts, simulations, and observations that require no statistical or psychometric sophistication.

Additional comments were expressed by individuals who were concerned about culturally sensitive assessment. For example, Facundo, Nuttal, and Walton (1994) pointed out that, in many cases, the people conducting cognitive, academic, personality, and social functioning assessments are of different national, ethnic, racial, or social class backgrounds from the children being assessed. Referring to this phenomenon as "cross-cultural assessment," Facundo et al., focusing primarily on the challenges of assessing Latino children, believe in what appears to be an eclectic, culturally sensitive approach that includes the following:

1. Establishing rapport with the families and making them feel comfortable in the school environment
2. Using assessment instruments that are appropriate for the populations being served
3. Writing culturally sensitive assessment reports

Reporting on the RACE 2002 conference at Arizona State University, Arredondo and D'Andrea (2002) addressed the issue of whether current assessments are culturally informed. One presenter stated that, since the standardized testing industry will not self-destruct, cultural experts must voice their collective perspectives. Ideas presented at the RACE 2002 conference included (a) increasing the representation of minority groups in standardization studies, (b) developing and applying ethnic-specific assessment processes, (c) using qualitative approaches and methods to learn more about the influence of cultural background and socialization processes on gaining access to educational and vocational opportunities and being successful, and (d) approaching assessment from a culturally informed perspective. The tone and nature of the presentations indicate that cultural experts believe much improvement is needed in order to overcome the disadvantages such groups as African Americans and Latinos experience when taking many standardized tests. The cultural experts appear to know much more about what is wrong than what to do to correct it. This then seems to be their greatest challenge in the twenty-first century.

Giordano, Schwiebert, and Brotherton (1997) surveyed approximately 120 school counselors in Illinois and found that even though counselors reported believing in the usefulness of a wide range of assessment instruments (intelligence tests, personality inventories, substance abuse instruments, eating disorder inventories, depression assessments, achievement tests, and interest inventories), they tended to actually use a narrower range. The assessment instruments used most often were primarily achievement tests and interest inventories. The five highest ranked instruments according to use were the Wechsler Intelligence Scale for Children (WISC-R), Career Orientation Placement and Evaluation Survey/Career Abilities Placement Survey/Career Occupational Preference Survey (COPES/CAPS/COPS), Scholastic Assessment Test

(SAT), Myers-Briggs Type Indicator (MBTI), and Career Assessment Inventory (CAI). The WISC-R is usually administered for diagnostic purposes, such as placement in special education programs and identification of gifted students. Clinical, counseling, and school psychologists usually administer the tests. The SAT is administered at designated testing centers under the auspices of the College Board, and postsecondary education institutions use the scores for admissions decisions. The remaining three instruments are typical performance measures of personality types and interests used to help middle- and secondary-school students learn more about themselves in the career guidance and counseling process.

President Bush's No Child Left Behind initiative includes yearly achievement testing, a feature that places increased emphasis on the use of standardized tests for educational accountability purposes. Hayes (2001) reported that the instruments will be selected by states and local school districts, and standards will be flexible enough for current state standards to be acceptable. The apparent popularity of the initiative indicates that general public confidence in standardized test data is as strong as or stronger than it previously was. Some have referred to this as a "high stakes" testing era (Hayes, 2001).

School counseling leaders and school counselors predict that the brunt of the additional work required in order to implement the testing mandate in the schools will fall upon school counselors. These school counseling representatives, as well as leaders in the Association for Assessment in Counseling (AAC) and the testing industry also point out how important it is for school counselors, teachers, and administrators

School counselors are in a strategic position to promote responsible use of tests.

to have appropriate levels of sophistication and skills in order to ensure that tests and test-generated data are used appropriately (Hayes, 2001).

Assessment remains an important school counseling function, and providing useful assessment services has become even more difficult. Whether school counselors are up to the challenge is unknown. Complicating matters further for counselors, the mid-1980s ushered in an era of general educational criticism and demands for reform, leading to recommendations for minimum competency tests not only for students graduating from high school but also for adults receiving teaching certificates or holding their teaching positions. Such recommendations imply a widespread belief that standardized tests can precisely identify competence and incompetence, indicating that the general public, politicians, and some educators were as naive as their predecessors in the 1920s.

Surrounded by a charged environment in which students, teachers, administrators, parents, and the general public expect much of but know little about formal and informal assessment tools, counselors walk a tightrope between understanding the limited data those instruments provide and helping individuals use those data successfully. Refusing to participate in the assessment services does not seem to be an option for most school counselors. In fact, many counselors are routinely drawn into performing noncounseling assessment services such as giving group achievement and intelligence tests across all grade levels, interpreting the results, preparing reports about the results, and keeping the results in the counseling offices. If refusing to participate is not an option, helpful participation demands competence. Much is expected, less can probably be delivered, and school counselors are challenged to understand what they are doing to educate consumers about realistic expectations and to deliver services that meet reformulated expectations.

Spokespersons for the three initiatives for enhancing school counseling presented in chapter 1 promote the importance of assessment. In the ASCA National Model for Comprehensive School Counseling Programs, appraisal (also known as assessment) is a process for which the goal is helping students carry out the individual planning process. Through data from a variety of assessment activities, students receive help in interpreting their abilities, interests, skills, and achievements (Gysbers & Henderson, 2001). In addition, Dahir (2001) stresses the importance of using measurable indicators to determine whether or not students experience achievement in academic, career, and personal-social development. In the first context, assessment is viewed as a process tool for helping students make informed decisions about their futures. In the second context, assessment is viewed as an accountability tool. A more detailed coverage of accountability is presented in chapter 13.

In the National School Counselor Training Initiative, school counselors are viewed as having a unique, strategic, schoolwide perspective that can be used to help students become successful academically. This perspective includes quantitative and qualitative data (e.g., students' cumulative files, reports about whole school and individual student academic successes and failures, student course placement information, course-taking patterns, teacher characteristics, parental contacts with the school, and the status of community resources). House and Hayes (2002) believe school counselors can use these data to promote and effect systematic change and teach students to help themselves (e.g., improved test-taking, organizational, and study skills). House and Hayes appear to present assessment as a process for collecting data to be used by school counselors in a leadership role. We cover leadership more thoroughly in chapter 12.

The role of assessment in the School-Community Collaboration Model was not specifically mentioned in the material we read. On the other hand, we assumed that it was important in this model because the interconnected system for meeting the needs of all students presented in Adelman and Taylor (2002) includes an early identification and treatment component. Logic indicates that early identification and treatment require diagnostic data that would be derived from assessment processes. Thus, assessment is presented in a diagnostic light in this model—more about diagnostic assessment later in this chapter. We believe that Adelman and Taylor would expand the assessment function beyond diagnosis if presented with a direct question to that effect.

BASIC INGREDIENTS OF ASSESSMENT IN SCHOOL COUNSELING

The authors believe that the only legitimate assessment functions for school counselors are those used to achieve counseling goals. *Counseling* is defined globally here and includes all the counseling functions—prevention programming, consulting, referring and coordinating, providing information, enhancing transitions, advocating, leading and collaborating, and counseling students. Unfortunately, this is an unrealistic stance in light of the long-standing tradition of having counselors involved in virtually all group assessments that occur in the schools. A strong coalition of students, teachers, administrators, and taxpayers believe that school counseling and assessment are synonymous.

Some counselor educators and counselors may believe that involvement in assessment for classifying and tracking students and in determination of levels of student academic achievement is not legitimate for school counselors because those functions are designed to achieve instructional and administrative goals. Counselors' ability to change these circumstances in most school systems in the near future, however, is very limited. Changes usually have to be achieved through subtle educational strategies and negotiations because teaching colleagues and administrators may have to assume additional responsibilities when the desired changes are made. For example, many elementary-school counselors are assigned responsibility for administering the achievement testing programs in their schools. Results from this testing are most commonly used to evaluate instructional goals and to compare the performance of the schools' students with performances in a national sample. These are instructional and administrative goals, indicating that teachers and administrators are the more legitimate coordinators of such programs. What the authors consider nonlegitimate assessment services for school counseling programs are included in this discussion as basic ingredients of the assessment services because in reality they do exist in most school counseling programs.

The following information is meant to be an overview of, and not a substitute for, a comprehensive tests and measurement course. Readers are encouraged to seek general understanding and not be taken aback by technical terms with which they are not familiar. Readers are also encouraged to review this material while enrolled in, or after having completed, their tests and measurement, assessment, or appraisal course.

Assessment for Enhancing Student Development

Helping individuals with personal decision making is one legitimate use of assessment services in school counseling. Many standardized and nonstandardized assessment tools are designed to help individuals acquire information about themselves that can be combined with information from other sources when making educational and vocational decisions. In many instances, the decision-making process will be enhanced by individuals who can help the decision makers travel the road more successfully. School counselors are qualified by their specialized training to provide this assistance. A useful term for the process is *individual self-exploration.* School counselors can use standardized and nonstandardized assessment tools in conjunction with their own counseling and prevention programming skills to enhance the self-exploration of individual clients.

Standardized measures of interests and aptitudes can be used in the self-exploration process. Examples of standardized interest measures useful with high-school students are the Jackson Vocational Interest Survey (published by Research Psychologists' Press), the Self-Directed Search (Psychological Assessment Resources), and the Strong Interest Inventory (Consulting Psychologists' Press). At the junior-high-, middle-, and upper-elementary-school levels, the Harrington-O'Shea Career Decision-Making System (American Guidance Services), the Kuder General Interest Survey (Science Research Associates), and the Interest Determination, Exploration and Assessment System (NCS Professional Assessment Services) may be useful. All can be used for the same general purpose—helping individuals acquire information that may be used in making informed decisions. These measurement tools are designed to serve adolescents and children at different developmental stages.

Examples of standardized, group aptitude test batteries for high-school students are the General Aptitude Test Battery (U.S. Employment Service), the Armed Services Vocational Aptitude Battery (U.S. Department of Defense), and the Differential Aptitudes Test (DAT; The Psychological Corporation). The DAT may also be useful with junior-high- and middle-school students. Aptitude testing below these levels is not recommended because the attributes being measured have not developed sufficiently in children, and the norms are not useful.

Profiles, computerized printouts, and graphic report forms that can be helpful in the exploratory process are generated for many of these instruments. Card sorts are examples of nonstandardized tools for assessing interests that deformalize the process, and work samples may be used to assess important attitudes and abilities in ways that are not applicable with standardized instruments.

Some publishers have designed programs for converting data from standardized sources (e.g., interest inventories, aptitude tests) and nonstandardized sources (e.g., grades, self-reported experiences) into comprehensive counseling tools to be used to achieve self-exploration goals. One such conversion is the Career Planning Program (American College Testing Service), which is designed to help adolescents organize their thoughts about decisions related to professional and technical careers. Others have included assessment components in computerized guidance programs, allowing users to generate data from assessment instruments built into the programs or to enter relevant data from assessments taken independently of the computer programs. The trend in the direction of developing and publishing assessment tools designed to enhance individual self-exploration is definitely a turn in the right direction. As these instruments and ideas become more sophisticated and are designed to serve increasingly younger consumers, the challenge to get meaning out of them increases. Most children and adolescents need help making sense of the information generated by these instruments. Therefore, school counselors are challenged to make themselves capable of helping their clients. To do this, they are challenged to make sense of the output generated by these advanced assessment tools and to transmit that understanding to their clients. An example follows.

> Middle-school counselors conducting a career exploration program (prevention programming) include having students complete an age-appropriate interest inventory as a part of the program. They also acquire the students' latest general aptitude test scores from their files. In a segment of the program, the counselors explain the meaning of the scores and the purpose of the measures to the students collectively. The students then work on assignments designed to have them incorporate the test data with other information about themselves and to try to integrate all the information into a meaningful set of information about themselves. This activity is followed by another group presentation on future planning, which is then followed up by individual counseling sessions by a counselor with each student in order to help the students process what they have learned and to find out whether they understand the meaning of the test scores correctly. During the counseling sessions, students are encouraged to share how the data affect their self-perceptions and future plans.

Assessment for Diagnosing Student Status

Using assessment tools for diagnostic purposes seems to be a common role in elementary-school counseling. It is also a legitimate assessment role in secondary-school counseling. Elementary-school counselors often work with children too young for the kind of self-exploration previously described. They more commonly use assessment tools to appraise individual children for diagnostic purposes. Specific purposes include diagnosis as a prelude to counseling, as a part of consultation, and as a part of referral and coordination services. Whatever the diagnostic assessment goals, Keat (1974) recommends that the questions to be answered be relevant and that constructive action follow the assessments.

Counseling services offered to elementary-school children often are therapeutic in nature. Therefore, diagnostic assessment is an important precursor to implementing intervention strategies. Elementary school counselors who apply a counseling model similar to the multimodal approach advocated by Keat (1990) and others use assessment tools and strategies as part of the identification and clarification stage of the counseling relationship, mixing data collecting with relationship establishing.

Because children are less able to engage in semi-independent reconstruction of irrational cognitions and in self-management of their treatment programs, more collaboration among adults significant in their lives is required than is usually the case with adolescent and adult clients. The need for collaboration when helping children leads to consulting relationships. Elementary-school counselors often consult with teachers and parents in joint efforts to help individual children. Assessment data commonly serve as the foundation for therapeutic plans devised by counselors in cooperation with parents and teachers.

Recommendations that children be referred for specialized services are often based on assessment information acquired by counselors. The assessment data are usually collected to respond to referrals by colleagues or parents to counselors. Consequently, school counselors, acting as professionals who are both providers and recipients of referrals, need to assess situations and targeted individuals to respond usefully.

Diagnostic assessment expectations of school counselors should be within their range of expertise. Unless they have received specialized training, school counselors do not have the same expertise as school psychologists; clinical and counseling psychologists; or reading, speech, and hearing specialists. In many instances, these specialists can be called on for assessment assistance, although delays may occur before referral requests can be honored.

What is the range of diagnostic assessment expertise of school counselors? The following assessment strategies seem important enough to be part of the basic training of school counselors, particularly elementary-school counselors:

- *Taking case histories:* being able to collect accurate descriptive data from records, reports, and interviews of significant others about a variety of important topics as diverse as statistical information and relationships
- *Observing and diagnosing behavior:* being able to observe targeted individuals unobtrusively, organize one's observations, and report them diagnostically
- *Performing individual assessment:* being able to select and administer standardized and nonstandardized instruments usable within the confines of one's training and to report the results accurately (e.g., using intelligence and achievement screening tests as preliminary estimates of academic potential and achievement)
- *Acquiring sociometric data:* being able to survey classrooms of students and compile the results meaningfully (e.g., in sociograms)

It seems as if secondary-school counselors should also be able to take case histories, give individual tests, and, to a lesser extent, observe and diagnose behavior and acquire sociometric data. As do elementary-school counselors, secondary-school counselors use diagnostic assessment services in support of counseling and consulting relationships and as part of the referral and coordination, advocacy, leadership, and collaboration functions.

External Assessment Expectations

As part of the transition function, secondary-school counselors help students acquire information about, and make arrangements for, various tests required for entrance into institutions of higher education, the military service, and some job placements. Examples are the Scholastic Assessment Test, the Armed Services Vocational Aptitude Battery, and the General Aptitude Test Battery. Additionally, individual students need help understanding the results of these tests, deciding what to do, and knowing what kinds of decisions institutional personnel and prospective employers make on the basis of the test results. These tests are referred to as external because entities outside the school system create the demand for students to take them. School personnel assume the responsibility for helping students gain access to higher education, military, and employment opportunities by creating clearinghouses for information and by serving as support personnel for the testing corporations and prospective educators and employers. Support takes the form of distributing information, giving tests, submitting completed test results, interpreting the results, and helping students process the information. This is another legitimate assessment component. For example, counselors in many high schools take the responsibility for making the Preliminary Scholastic Assessment Test (PSAT) available to students. This requires those counselors to announce the availability of the testing program and its purpose, identify students who wish to take the test, be responsible for the test-taking logistics, send the completed answer sheets to the Educational Testing Service, distribute the results on their return, and help students process their results.

Assessment for Classification, Placement, and Curriculum Evaluation

The acquisition of accurate information about individual students in order to make placement decisions was once an accepted and important purpose for assessment in the schools. Currently, that practice is under attack. Originally, the idea of grouping or tracking students held merit because of the potential for modifying instruction to fit the needs of students whose intellectual abilities and rates of cognitive development differed. Over the years, flaws in the implementation of the idea led to criticisms. For example, on the one hand, some students who are placed in accelerated groups receive average grades, causing them to experience self-esteem problems. They do not realize that their accomplishments are well above those of students who receive top grades in lower academic tracks. On the other hand, those in the lower tracks have no models of academic competence to imitate or by which to be tutored. They are usually encouraged by peer pressure to perform only to the group's already low expectations. Their self-esteem is seriously damaged by the knowledge that they are identified by the system as dummies. Unfortunately, tracking such as this often occurs in comprehensive schools.

The first author has observed that once students are assigned to a track, they are seldom reevaluated and considered for revised placements. The common practice is to use the assessment data to make initial placement decisions but seldom to follow up on the progress or to diagnose the accuracy of individual placements. The negative side of the tracking concept achieved national attention in the case of *Larry P. v. Riles* (1980). A federal district judge in San Francisco, California, ruled that intelligence tests administered individually to assign students to classes for the educationally mentally retarded are biased against minority children. Although not consistent with decisions handed down elsewhere, the California case publicized accusations that some educational classifications lead to biased placement decisions. In the decision, the California judge used the term *dead end* to describe his opinion of the quality of the educational program the students in question were receiving (Aiken, 1988).

Tracking remains an instructional management method in many schools, as does assessment for classification and placement, because the system has not been completely negated. It is under scrutiny, however, and sparks of criticism abound. Because it is clearly a system intended to enhance instruction, should counselors be involved in the implementation process? In the authors' opinion, counselor involvement leads to inappropriate and negative attitudes about the counselor's role in the assessment process. For instance, how does a student experiencing confusion and lowered self-esteem because of low grades in an accelerated academic track receive help and understanding from a counselor who is administering the system? Will that student seek help from a counselor who is a party to the system? Also, how can parents who think their children have been placed incorrectly have confidence in the objectivity of a consultation from counselors who are gatekeepers for the system?

The goals of assessment for tracking placements are instructional in nature, some students are inadvertently abused because of tracking placements, and counselors are generally viewed as student advocates rather than as instructional associates. Because of these elements, it seems that counselors will better fulfill their student advocacy goals by being constructive critics of the system than by being part of it. Ideally, instructional and administrative personnel should administer the assessment services for classification and placement.

Curriculum evaluation is also an instructional function. Yet, many school counselors engage in the administration of group achievement tests and in compiling, reporting, disseminating, and storing the resultant data. This phenomenon seems especially prevalent among elementary-school counselors. Although involvement in curricular assessment does not have the potential for endangering one's student advocacy role that assessment for placement purposes does, it clearly robs counselors of time that could be devoted to legitimate counseling functions. It also places counselors in the uncomfortable position of participating in evaluations of their teaching colleagues. Curriculum assessment functions are best conducted by administrative and instructional personnel, leaving school counselors to use the data diagnostically in their counseling, consulting, and referral activities.

Leadership in Promoting Responsible Use of Standardized Tests in Assessment

Although assessment has been an important function of basic education for some time, many administrators, teachers, and counselors are not very well informed about tests and measurement and related ethical positions. As the professionals on the school staff probably most knowledgeable in these areas—as well as those usually responsible for most assessment functions—school counselors are in a strategic position to promote responsible use of tests among their colleagues.

Test users face many challenges. Traditional challenges include determining whether the decision to test is correct, selecting the appropriate tests, administering the tests, scoring the tests accurately, and interpreting or communicating the results. Additional challenges have evolved from the knowledge that test content and norms reflect existing inequalities in U.S. society (Castenell & Castenell, 1988; Miller-Jones,

1989) and from the fact that testing can now be computerized efficiently, which raises concerns about confidentiality (Sampson, 1983; Wood, 1984).

As advocates for the responsible use of standardized tests, school counselors can strive to promote positive assessment environments. Assuming that individuals who abuse tests do so out of ignorance rather than guile, counselors can use an educational strategy. Many abuses can be corrected if all users become better informed. This is certainly something school counselors are capable of achieving.

Talbutt (1983) suggests resources that counselors can employ to help colleagues become responsible users of tests. He recommends that school counselors become knowledgeable about regulations and guidelines of local and state boards of education. They should also be aware of the ethical standards of the counseling profession (see chapter 3). Other resources are relevant publications by professional organizations (e.g., *The Responsibilities of Test Users*, American Association for Counseling and Development, 1989) and important publications of other organizations (e.g., *Guidelines for Computer-Based Tests and Interpretation*, American Psychological Association, 1986). Counselors are challenged to keep up-to-date by perusing journals for relevant information and by attending appropriate sessions at professional meetings.

Talbutt's recommendations call for informed counselors to transmit useful information to colleagues. The appropriate application of one's acquired knowledge is action. Therefore, school counselors can be models of responsible test use. Counselors who are viewed by their colleagues as competent and responsible may serve as models of appropriate behavior. They are more likely to influence the attitudes and behaviors of their colleagues positively than are counselors who are not desirable models.

COMPETENCIES FOR BASIC SCHOOL COUNSELING ASSESSMENT

Knowledge About Principles of Measurement

Without basic knowledge of measurement principles, test users are navigating without compasses. They know they are going somewhere, but they don't know where or how to get there. Test users who lack basic knowledge about measurement will harm the individuals they are trying to serve. Those individuals would have been better served by no service at all. Unfortunately, most people whose use of tests is coupled with misinformation about measurement are not aware of that shortcoming or do not realize how crucial their behavior can be.

What should school counselors know about measurement? This is a difficult domain to master, yet it ranks low in the minds of many counseling students. In addition, measurement can appear complex if taught in a manner that befuddles counseling students and/or if taught by instructors who cannot apply it to using tests in counseling. Beginning school counselors cannot be expected to know all the intricacies of measurement at the outset of their careers. They are encouraged to increase their knowledge after their graduate-level training. Following is an attempt to identify a set of important assessment competencies. This information cannot replace the knowledge acquired from courses in descriptive statistics, measurement, and assessment. A goal of these subsections is to give relevance to the large body of information presented in such courses.

Scales and Scoring Systems.

All standardized and some nonstandardized assessment instruments have scales and scoring systems that report individual and group results. School counselors are challenged to be familiar with these systems in order to understand the results correctly and to help others understand and use the results appropriately. The following simulation supports the contention that counselors serve students better if they understand the scales and scoring systems of various assessment instruments:

> *Simulation:* All students in the elementary schools of a school district participate in an annual achievement-testing program. Standardized achievement tests are given in each grade to compare the average scores of the school district with national norms, to evaluate teachers, to locate content areas that need to be improved, and to identify students who need remedial or advanced work. One of the scales used by the test publisher is known as *grade equivalents.* Individual scores on specific content area subtests are reported as grade levels with corresponding months above and below the first month in that grade level. For instance, Jafar, a fourth-grade student, receives scores of Second Grade–Third Month, Second Grade–Fifth Month, Second Grade–Tenth Month, and Third Grade–First Month on the language, reading, arithmetic, and social studies subtests, respectively. Jamilah, also a fourth-grade student, receives scores of Sixth Grade–Seventh Month, Sixth Grade–Eighth Month, Sixth Grade–Tenth Month, and Seventh Grade–First Month on the same subtests. In addition, approximately half of the fourth-grade class had average scores below Fourth Grade–First Month.

> The following false conclusions were made about this information by otherwise intelligent and well-meaning persons. Jafar's teacher entertained thoughts of recommending that he be given second-grade materials to study as part of a remedial program. Jamilah's parents considered requesting that she be advanced to sixth grade. The principal was upset to learn that half of the fourth grade was below grade level on the tests. Why were these false conclusions made, and what were the reasons for making them?

> Jafar's teacher, Jamilah's parents, and the school principal, not knowing the scoring system on which grade equivalent scales are based, interpreted the words literally and came to apparently logical conclusions. Counselors are challenged not to make such conclusions. Their job is to understand the scales and scoring systems used in various assessment programs and therefore to be able to help others avoid such errors. Detailed information about grade equivalents can be presented as part of well-designed and comprehensive courses on assessment, including information about measurement systems.

> Briefly, Jafar's teacher and Jamilah's parents made conclusions without knowing that Jafar's and Jamilah's test results had only been compared with those of other fourth graders. They had not been compared with second, third, sixth, or seventh graders. The grade equivalents in Jafar's case indicated that he is

well below average fourth graders. Jamilah is well above average. On grade-equivalent scales, test publishers use grade levels higher and lower than the one of interest—in this case, fourth grade—for scores outside the 10 months of the school year. Therefore, Fifth Grade–First Month follows Fourth Grade–Tenth Month, and Third Grade–Tenth Month precedes Fourth Grade–First Month even though the scale is used exclusively for fourth graders.

The school principal did not realize that the average score for fourth graders should identify them as being where they were when they took the test—which was the Fourth Grade–First Month. If they achieve average performance on the tests, they will be at that point. Those who score below the middle will have third-grade or lower grade equivalents. If the class has a normally distributed group of fourth-grade students, about half of them will have scores below the average or middle of the distribution of scores. Therefore, it is to be expected that a substantial number of students have grade equivalents below Fourth Grade–First Month. The fact that half of the students are below grade level merely means that half of them are below the middle or average score.

This example shows only a few of the many problems that can occur when assessment data are misunderstood. Scales and scoring systems represent an important technology about which school counselors are challenged to be sophisticated. It appears as if minimum competence should include knowledge about the following:

- The different kinds of scales (nominal, ordinal, interval, and ratio) and their properties
- The scoring systems derived from the basic scales used in psychological and educational assessment (e.g., standard scores, percentile ranks)
- The standard normal distribution and its properties—leading to an understanding of the role of norms in assessment
- Sampling theory for selecting test items and establishing norms or reference groups
- Basic descriptive statistics (e.g., measures of central tendency, such as means, medians, and modes; measures of dispersion from the center of a distribution, such as standard deviations and ranges)

Reliability and Validity.   Simply stated, *validity* means that assessment tools should achieve the goals they are designed to achieve. Validity also means that tests should be used appropriately. *Reliability* means that the assessment tools perform consistently. The following simulation highlights the importance of counselors being knowledgeable about these measurement principles:

Simulation: Middle- and junior-high-school students are given a vocational interest inventory as part of a career exploration unit. One purpose of the inventory is to provide food for thought—to suggest careers about which participants might acquire further information because they demonstrated higher interest in them than most other individuals of their age and gender. Jana brought her results home and announced that they indicated she should be an artist. Jarek filed his results and discovered them 3 years later when planning for life after high school. He used the results to begin a search for information about careers appropriate for him to pursue.

Both Jana and Jarek used the results of their interest inventories inappropriately because they knew nothing about validity and reliability. That is to be expected in most instances. Therefore, school counselors are challenged to prevent these situations as often as possible. Jana misinterpreted the purpose of the inventory and ascribed a degree of certainty to the results that was not intended by the test publisher or by the individuals who designed the career exploration program. She invalidated the results by assuming that they identified a specific career for her when, in fact, the inventory was designed to compare her interests with those of others of her age and gender.

Jarek created a reliability problem when he assumed that the results were useful 3 years later. Because of the dramatic changes that occur in individuals as they mature from childhood through adolescence, it was likely that Jarek's interests had changed in 3 years and that his later responses would be quite different from the earlier ones. The reliability of interest inventories over a period of 3 years is limited—not in every case, but certainly in many cases. Jarek would have been served better by the results of an inventory taken concurrently with his career search activities, and a school counselor who understood reliability principles would have been able to provide Jarek with helpful information in that regard.

Reliability and validity are important concepts; minimally, a school counselor should know the following:

- Classic reliability theory, including the concepts of true scores and observed scores
- Methods for estimating reliability used by test publishers, such as the test-retest, parallel forms, split halves, and internal consistencies strategies
- Basic statistical procedures used when reporting most reliability and some validity estimates (correlation analyses and correlation coefficients)
- Methods used by test publishers for estimating validity (content validity, construct validity, predictive validity, and concurrent validity)
- Procedures used to translate reliability and validity data into counseling information (e.g., the standard error of measurement, the standard error of estimate, expectancy tables)

Knowledge About Standardized Tests

Standardized tests vary in their designs and purposes. It is important to understand their differences, limitations, and purposes. One way to make sense of the information is to categorize it. One system for categorizing standardized tests is according to the purpose. Standardized tests used by school counselors usually fall into one of the following five purpose categories: intelligence, aptitude, achievement, interests, and personality.

Intelligence Tests.   Intelligence tests are designed to provide a general or global measure of academic potential. That academic potential is usually expressed by a single score. The score is expressed as an intelligence quotient (IQ) with a scale score attached to it. For example, Emily's IQ of 115 indicates that her intelligence ranks 15 points higher than the average of 100. Among the most common uses of intelligence tests are determining which individuals should be placed in special education or gifted programs and classifying students for grouped or tracked academic programs in the schools.

Aptitude Tests.   Also designed to provide information about individual potential, aptitude tests are more specific than intelligence tests. They are designed to identify specific attributes or aptitudes, such as verbal, mechanical, artistic, musical, numerical, and spatial. Some aptitude tests address only one aptitude; others cover several, providing a profile of aptitude scores. An example of the latter approach is the General Aptitude Test Battery (published by the U.S. Employment Service). This test provides scores for 12 subtests or aptitudes. Some aptitude tests are used in predicting future performance and therefore support the decisions of personnel and admissions workers in business and industry, the military services, or colleges and universities. Other aptitude tests help individuals acquire information about their capabilities to use in a process of educational and career decision-making.

Achievement Tests.   Designed to find out what individuals have learned up to the time they are tested, achievement tests are used to evaluate curriculum efforts in the schools. Individual students, their teachers, the schools, and communities may be evaluated by achievement testing results. Performances by local students are compared collectively to national standards. The national standards usually are the results of a sampling of schools and students from across the country at each grade level. Achievement tests cover important academic areas such as language arts, reading, arithmetic, social studies, and science. In addition to being compared to national norms, individual scores may also be used diagnostically to identify academic deficiencies and initiate remedial instructional programming. For instance, in the simulation presented earlier, Jafar had relatively low grade-equivalent scores on the language, reading, arithmetic, and social studies subtests of an achievement test battery. That information could be used in designing a remedial instructional program.

Interest Inventories.   These instruments are most often used to initiate career exploration activities. Therefore, they are primarily counseling tools. Individuals are usually asked to rate the attractiveness of activities in some manner. Examples of such activities are persuading others of the merits of one's point of view, meeting new people, and working out solutions to arithmetic problems. Two approaches are used in designing interest inventories. One compares the respondents' answers with answers of other individuals of their own age and gender, providing information about the strength of their interests in comparison with their peers. The second approach compares the respondents' answers with those of individuals successful in specific occupations. The basis of this approach is that people of similar interests are more likely to find success in similar careers. This is the discriminant information advocated by Prediger (1994) and Zytowski (1994) in comments about the state of the marriage between tests and counseling earlier in this chapter. Interest inventory results are often very comprehensive and require careful interpretations to avoid misunderstandings.

Counselors can incorporate test interpretations into the counseling process.

Personality Measures.   These instruments provide information about individual emotional, motivational, interpersonal, and attitudinal characteristics (Anastasi, 1997). In psychiatry, clinical psychology, and counseling psychology, they may help develop or determine clinical diagnoses, as well as help individuals better understand themselves and their thoughts and actions—a common use in education. In business, industry, and the military, personality measures are sometimes used to make selection decisions.

A variety of such instruments are published, representing several different methods of test development. Some have questions and scoring systems based on particular personality theories. Some are developed through statistical procedures that provide useful scoring systems. An example of the statistical approach, instruments developed from factor analyses provide information about individual placement along bipolar scales. Such scales include trust versus defensiveness, activity versus lack of energy, and masculinity versus femininity. A second example is criterion-referenced keying, which provides the kind of information referred to previously in the section on interest inventories—comparing the answers of respondents with those of specific categories of other people. As with interest inventories, results of personality measures are often very comprehensive and demand care in interpretation.

A second system for categorizing standardized tests is according to the type of motivation respondents are expected to have when taking the tests. Two motivational categories can be determined: maximum performance and typical performance.

Motivation for Maximum Performance.   On intelligence, aptitude, and achievement tests, the questions have right or wrong answers, and those who use the test results require accurate estimates of the respondents' capabilities. Therefore, respondents need to be motivated to do their best when answering items on these assessment instruments.

Motivation for Typical Performance.   Interest inventories and personality measures do not have questions for which there are right or wrong answers. All answers have meaning according to the scales or keys developed for the instruments. Therefore, it is important that respondents be truthful when answering the questions. This requires the individuals to take the test in a frame of mind that is usual or typical of them at times when they are not responding to the test.

A third system for categorizing standardized tests is according to the kind of counseling information they provide. Goldman (1971) names three categories, or bridges, into which test results may be classified: norms, discriminant, and regression. Goldman uses the bridge analogy to depict the role of test interpretations in counseling. The interpretations bridge the gap between the test results and client understanding of the results. It is important that counselors understand what bridge the test results represent, what kind of information is available, and the limitations of that information to avoid overstating or misinterpreting the information or allowing clients to do so.

Norms Bridges.   Normative test results allow for comparisons between the scores of respondents and some reference or norms group. They answer the question "How do I compare with the norms group?" An example is informing a high-school student that her Scholastic Assessment Test (SAT) scores were at a percentile rank of 90, meaning that 90% of the norms group had scores equal to or below hers. All intelligence, aptitude, and achievement tests—and some interest inventories and personality measures—provide normative data. It is the most common form of reporting standardized test results.

Discriminant Bridges.   Less commonly, discriminant data are found in some interest inventories and personality measures. Discriminant data are derived from the empirical criterion keying technique mentioned in the previous section on personality measures. The technique is used to identify questions that distinguish people who have been successful in specific careers, such as teaching mathematics, being a YMCA administrator, or plumbing, from people in general. Answers are compared to those of specific reference groups (e.g., mathematics teachers) and to those of people in general. Discriminant scoring scales allow respondents to learn how similar or dissimilar their answers are to those of specific groups and to those of people in general. One whose answers are more similar to those of mathematics teachers, for example, than to those of people in general can be encouraged to find out more about that profession because of having something in common with mathematics teachers.

Regression Bridges.   Data for regression bridges are generated from test results and formulated into tables or formulas that are used in estimating or predicting future events. Aptitude tests are most often used to acquire regression data, and intelligence and achievement tests may be used in the same manner. An example of a future event of interest to school counselors and their clients is whether a student will get into and succeed in a college. College entrance examination scores and the grade point averages of freshmen are often analyzed statistically by the colleges to generate expectancy tables and prediction formulas. These can be used in estimating the grade point averages of high-school students for whom college entrance examination scores are available. The entrance examination scores are used as predictors of the future event: grade point averages. The predicted grade point averages provide an estimate of how successful students are likely to be. This is the reductionistic approach to using assessment data that Bradley (1994), Goldman (1994), Prediger (1994), and Zytowski (1994) refer to as outdated.

Expectancy tables generate such information as: The probability of your achieving a 2.00 grade point average is 75% on the basis of individuals with entrance examination scores similar to yours at State University last year. In this case, the data are used to answer the question "What is my relative chance of being successful?" Formulas are used to estimate the grade point average. For example, given your scores of 400 and 550 on the Scholastic Assessment Verbal and Math Tests and your high-school grade point average, the formula estimates your first college semester grade point average to be 2.26. There is a 68% chance that it will be above 3.00 or below 2.22. In this case, the data estimate an answer to the question "How well am I likely to do in college?"

Because of all the work involved in generating regression bridge data, such data are relatively rare but can be found in college admissions. In addition, tests are imperfect predictors. That imprecision is clearly seen in the disclaimer about the accuracy of the prediction from the formula in the previous paragraph and the positions taken by Bradley (1994), Goldman (1994), Prediger (1994), and Zytowski (1994).

Knowledge About Nonstandardized Assessment Strategies

Goldman (1972) declared that standardized tests, representing a quantitative approach, failed to live up to their promise as counseling tools. He suggested that qualitative strategies may contribute more to counseling than standardized tests (Goldman, 1982, 1994). Qualitative strategies are not standardized; they are devoid of cumbersome and confusing statistical data; the instruments are readily adapted to different age-groups, reading levels, and settings; and their administration involves counseling—or at least has implications for decision making, problem solving, and planning—a more active role for clients, Goldman (1982, 1990, 1994) claims. He continued by suggesting several nonstandardized strategies for acquiring qualitative assessment data in counseling, three of which—card sorts, work samples, and observation—are elaborated on here.

Card Sorts. Used to assess interests and values, card sorts are done during one-to-one sessions between counselors and clients. Clients are presented with a stack of cards, each with a printed stimulus. For example, the cards may contain names of various occupations. Usually, counselors ask clients to sort the cards according to categories such as Might Choose, Would Not Choose, and Uncertain. Follow-up strategies can include asking clients to reclassify the cards in the Uncertain category and to rank order the cards in the Might Choose pile. Possible counseling strategies include exploring the reasons for the choices, inquiring about the training required for specific choices, asking about opportunities, recommending information-seeking activities beyond the counseling session (e.g., reading, interviewing), and helping clients process the information they acquired between counseling sessions.

Work Samples.   Work samples provide an alternative to aptitude testing. They are most useful for individuals who have a disability of some kind or who are very gifted. Standardized tests are either too difficult for such individuals or too simple. In either case, work samples provide more comprehensive information. In general, work sampling involves analyzing important components of a task that occurs in specific jobs or activities. The analysis is used to develop a simulation of the task. For example, it is possible to simulate the basic tasks of repairing watches. Clients can be carefully observed as they attempt to follow the steps in the instructions. They can be timed, their behaviors noted, and their ability to perform the skills assessed. The information may be used diagnostically, educationally, or for selection purposes. Most schools cannot afford to develop or purchase work samples. However, they are available at many vocational rehabilitation services. Counselors may be able to use the referrals to make them available to some clients. Kapes and Whitfield's *A Counselor's Guide to Career Assessment Instruments* (2002) is a good source of information about specific commercial card sorts and sets of work samples.

Observation.   Goldman (1990) defined *qualitative observation* as collecting comments and impressions. Quantitative observation entails translating observations into standardized scoring systems or counting the number of times specific behaviors occur. Collecting comments can take the form of asking elementary-school teachers to share comments about students in their classrooms. This might be done to verify observations of others or to acquire narrative information about student behaviors. The information may be used diagnostically to plan counseling interventions or to determine the effects of interventions already under way. Collecting impressions through observations might occur through work shadowing. For example, children and adolescents can accompany working adults as they proceed through all or part of their days at work and can formulate impressions of the jobs while they do so.

The multimodal approach to counseling and therapy offers a system for using observation in the process of assessing a client's current level of functioning (diagnosis) and proceeding to develop intervention plans. The multimodal approach is founded on the principles of comprehensiveness and eclecticism. The diagnoses are to be broad-based according to a predetermined plan and the interventions selected from a wide spectrum of strategies that work. Two plans for organizing diagnostic information have been popularized in the counseling and therapy literature. Each suggests several categories of information to acquire when making diagnostic assessments through interviews, observations, and instrumental data gathering. The categories help counselors organize their findings and suggest information that should be collected. Assessments are not restricted to presenting problems. All categories should be investigated even though no suggestions of problems in those areas have been reported. This procedure implements the comprehensiveness principle.

Lazarus's (1976) plan is identified by the acronym BASIC ID, and Keat's (1990) plan has a HELPING acronym. The categories in the BASIC ID plan are these:

B = Behavior

A = Affect

S = Sensation

I = Imagery

C = Cognition

I = Interpersonal relationships

D = Drugs/Diet

The HELPING plan categories are these:

H = Health

E = Emotions/feelings

L = Learning/school

P = Personal relationships

I = Imagination/interests

N = Need to know/think

G = Guidance of acts, behaviors, and consequences

Table 10.1 contains a summary of the findings of a multimodal assessment and plans for the subsequent treatment. The BASIC ID was used, and the client was a 16-year-old female high-school sophomore. The case study by Seligman (1981), too long to present here, provides an interesting example of applying the multimodal idea. Case studies involving child clients may be found in Keat (1990). Not all treatment plans are initiated at once, but several can be under way concurrently, as the categories of information about clients are interdependent.

Nonstandardized assessment strategies lend themselves to the goals of culturally sensitive assessment because counselors are better able to accommodate linguistic challenges and to determine stages of acculturation when engaged in nonstandardized assessment activities (Facundo et al., 1994). Despite these advantages, the challenges of engaging in cross-cultural assessments exist, with the need for being fair and sensitive remaining.

Knowledge About Managing School Testing Programs

When school counselors are given full or partial responsibility for school testing programs, they are faced with a challenge to be good managers. How to meet that challenge is an administrative question, and the contingencies that influence the system used will be affected by the views and practices of school and district administrators, as well as by a host of other factors that make setting up a system situation-specific. Setting up a system is, however, imperative. What follows is an inventory of important factors to be considered when establishing a system for managing a school-testing program:

1. A budget for purchasing tests and supplies is needed in addition to a system for making purchases and accounting for expenditures.

Table 10.1

Findings from a multimodel assessment.

Modality	Problem	Treatment
Behavior	Excessive eating, weight gain	Participation in weight control program
	Circumscribed range of activities	Behavioral rehearsal; defining and planning pleasurable activities
	Negative self-statements	Nonreinforcement; positive self-talk assignments
Affect	Depression, suicidal feelings	Increasing experiences providing positive reinforcement
	Expression of anger	Role-playing
	Loneliness, emptiness	Relationship building; communication skills
Sensation	Lack of positive sensory experiences	Sensate focusing; planned pleasurable experiences
	Feelings of being bloated, obese	Diet, exercise
	Headaches, stomachaches	Relaxation, improved eating habits
	Tension	Relaxation
Imagery	Image of self as grossly overweight	Thought-stopping
	Suicidal fantasies	Thought-stopping; rational self-talk
Cognition	Poor study habits	Study skills training; assertiveness training
	Lack of educational and occupational information	Career counseling; including assessment and information giving
	Irrational beliefs; irrational self-talk	Corrective self-talk; rational disputation
	Sexual misinformation	Sex education; bibliotherapy
Interpersonal relations	Fears of social situations	Behavioral rehearsal
	Competitiveness with female peers	Group counseling
	Inconsistent relationships with parents	Family conferences; role playing; attending weight control sessions with mother
Drugs/Diet	Poor dietary habits	Involvement in weight reduction program
	Excessive smoking, some solitary drinking	Self-administered behavior modification program; jogging

Source: From "Multimodel Behavior Therapy: A Case Study of a High School Student" by L. Seligman, 1981, *School Counselor, 28,* pp. 255–256. Copyright 1981 by American Counseling Association. No further reproduction authorized without written permission of the American Counseling Association.

2. The program is founded on goals. The goals can define the reasons why all tests are used, what information is desired from the test results, and how that information is to be used effectively.
3. The specific responsibilities of school counselors in the testing program are explicated. In addition, the roles and responsibilities of administrators, teachers, and support personnel are clearly defined.
4. Testing practices conform to professional ethical standards and other established principles for using tests. Counselors can serve as monitors of testing practices in their schools and can educate their colleagues proactively.
5. Advisory committees can be established to help determine testing policies, monitor test uses, and educate various publics about testing and assessment.

Knowledge About Assessment Issues

School counselors knowledgeable about basic measurement principles understand the different sides in issues involving assessment services. Basic knowledge about measurement will be more useful if counselors also are familiar with the viewpoints of the protagonists. A combination of knowing what the protagonists believe and the basics about measurement will allow counselors to explain the issues and to help their clientele draw objective conclusions. For example, knowledge about the principles associated with normal distributions will help counselors lead others away from stereotyping members of different racial groups.

To elaborate on the example, it has not been uncommon for people to assume that the mean or average difference between European Americans and African Americans on standardized intelligence tests indicates that European Americans are more intelligent than African Americans because the average for European Americans is higher. Accurate knowledge of normal distributions, however, makes one realize that greater differences are found within each group than between groups. Figure 10.1 demonstrates that many African Americans have higher intelligence test scores than many European Americans even though the average score for European Americans is higher. This indicates that individual members of a group should not be stereotyped or labeled according to the statistically average group member. Rather, all members of a group are individuals with their own combinations of attributes. Intelligence test data about individuals can be used to determine where one ranks in a group, and different groupings can be established (e.g., gender groups, racial groups, age-groups).

Following is an inventory of several issues that are important because they are about assessment uses and abuses that touch the lives of children and adolescents. They rank high among the assessment issues important for school counselors to understand.

Using Standardized Tests Leads to Invasion of Privacy. Those who feel this way about tests generally object to item content or to required assessments. More specifically, critics have raised the following objections:

- Selected items on personality tests, when taken out of context, seem outrageous.
- Attitude surveys may present questions to individuals that are upsetting or request information about behaviors that some parents do not want their children even to consider.

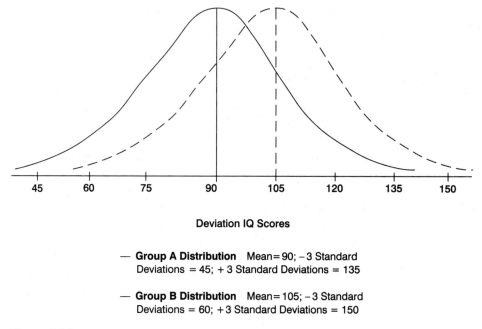

Deviation IQ Scores

— **Group A Distribution**   Mean = 90; –3 Standard
Deviations = 45; +3 Standard Deviations = 135

— **Group B Distribution**   Mean = 105; –3 Standard
Deviations = 60; +3 Standard Deviations = 150

Figure 10.1
Differences within and between groups when attributes are distributed normally.

- Results of some tests may be kept in computer banks by institutions or agencies whose motives are questionable.
- Some schools require all students to take targeted tests.

Counselors are in a strategic position to provide information, offer support, or serve as consultants, depending on the demands of the situation. For instance, concerns about the meanings of individual test items may be alleviated if people understand the purpose of the questions in the context of the entire test. Concerns about test content and required participation may be alleviated by recommending that participation be voluntary and that the decision whether to participate be preceded by an opportunity to learn the purposes of the testing program and the tests in question.

An example of how test content can lead to the problems just cited occurred in Pennsylvania during the 1970s when the schools were required to administer a battery of tests called the Educational Quality Assessment Program (EQA). The EQA was designed to provide information about achievement and attitudes across all the school districts. This, in turn, was used to make comparisons to a set of state standards. Reports were issued to school districts, indicating the areas in which they were deficient and those in which they were doing well. The tests were given at specified points from elementary through the high-school grades. Some parents objected to having their children answer specific attitudinal questions and filed civil suits. One objectionable question was "Have you ever used marijuana?" Those who objected did not want the idea of using marijuana even suggested to their children. Eventually, participation in the program was made voluntary.

Standardized Tests Are Biased, and Their Use Furthers Discrimination Against Some People.

These objections surround the use of tests for classification and selection and for helping individuals choose careers. Specifically, it is believed that African Americans, Hispanics, members of other minority racial and ethnic groups, women, people with disabilities, and individuals from economically disadvantaged backgrounds are, on average, less likely than others to appear desirable on standardized tests used to select who goes where to college, who is placed in special education and accelerated K–12 basic education trackings, who gets jobs, and who gets scholarships. Additionally, some believe that women are encouraged to consider a more limited range of career possibilities than are men when aptitude tests with separate gender scores and interest inventories that present limited choices are used in career counseling.

School counselors who are well informed about this issue are in a position to provide assistance in several ways. They can inform students, parents, and colleagues that some test scores reflect educational and social shortcomings that need to be identified and corrected. They can act as advocates for students' rights when they have evidence that results of tests used by the school system are leading to decisions that unfairly place some students at a disadvantage. They can be careful and discriminating when selecting tests to be used in career counseling. When the alleged bias is attributable to the use of external tests, counselors can try to help students find alternative ways to enhance their desirability or to achieve their goals (e.g., through test-wiseness training; see chapter 9 for more information). Counselors can act as advocates for individuals with disabilities by establishing opportunities for alternative testing arrangements (e.g., arranging special environments for dyslexic students so that they have more time to complete the tests and opportunities to ask questions to clarify material that confuses them).

Some Assessment Issues Create a Stressful Environment in Schools While Not Necessarily Influencing Clients Directly.

Concern over declining entrance exam scores and pressure for minimum competency tests for teachers are examples of issues that may influence students indirectly. Since the 1960s, concern over declining performance on college entrance exams has created puzzlement over the causes of the declines, as well as criticisms of teachers. The declining averages and other negative impressions of the nation's schools have led to an erosion of confidence in the competence of teaching professionals, which has manifested in some states by the institution of minimum competency tests for teachers.

School counselors can help students, parents, and colleagues put the highly publicized declining entrance exam scores issue in perspective by informing them about the history of the issue and the fact that it is a phenomenon that also leaves the experts puzzled. That is, explanations are as diverse as outdated norms, birth order, and family sizes. Additionally, concerned individuals can be informed that other measures of student performance should be considered, such as standardized achievement tests. If the entrance exam scores indicate problems, there are constructive ways to respond. Examples are enhancing and altering the curriculum, teaching students to be more proficient test takers, and changing the anxious atmosphere sometimes associated with the college selection process to make it more rational.

Minimum competency examinations for teachers have created a highly charged atmosphere in states where they have been used and recommended. School counselors can serve as consultants to their colleagues and to their professional organizations about the flaws in the current applications of the minimum competency examination idea. The tendency is to set the cutoffs so low that only a few individuals are unable to pass. The cost of implementing the examination may be so high that, in combination with low discrimination rates, the exams may be very cost-ineffective, leading to a lowering of public opinion and demoralization among teachers (Shepard & Kreitzer, 1987). Colleagues can be helped, just as students can, by learning to be better test takers and by having their anxieties about the examination reduced. Test-wiseness training and programs designed to help colleagues cope with test anxiety, which were suggested for students as part of the transition from school to work in chapter 9, can also be given to colleagues.

Knowledge About Selecting and Administering Assessment Instruments

The reasons for counselors to become involved in the selection of assessment tools and strategies are varied. One reason is to select instruments to be used for institutional decision making, such as group intelligence and achievement tests. A second reason is to select diagnostic instruments and strategies, such as quick intelligence tests, case study outlines, and observation-recording strategies, to support one's counseling activities. A third reason is to select tests that individual student clients can take when trying to make educational and career decisions.

When school counselors are involved in the process of selecting tests for institutional decision-making purposes, they can draw on their knowledge about basic measurement principles and testing issues to make significant contributions to the selection process. The basic ingredient of this selection process is a systematic approach, including specifications of goals and inquiries about the technical and practical attributes of the various tests being considered. Counselors will also contribute by suggesting that those involved in the selection process read certain appropriate test reviews that have been published. Useful sources of test reviews are the *Mental Measurement Yearbooks* (I through IX) and *Tests in Print* (I through IV), and *A Counselor's Guide to Career Assessment Instruments* (Kapes & Whitfield, 2002, published by the National Career Development Association). The same approach can be used by individual counselors when selecting instruments and techniques to be used diagnostically. In addition, they can consult with colleagues and mentors for their ideas.

Sampson (2000) identified several Internet websites that provide information about tests by title and category. Brief descriptions can be downloaded, and there are links to published test reviews. Sampson's (2000, p. 356) appendix of testing-related Internet websites includes the following:

Assessment & Evaluation on the Internet
    (http://ericae.net/intass.htm)

Association of Test Publishers
   (http://www.testpublishers.org/)

Buros Institute of Mental Measurements
   (http://www.unl.edu/buros/)

Buros/ERIC Test Publisher Directory—Search
   (http://ericae.net/testcol.htm#Testpub)

ERIC Clearinghouse on Assessment and Evaluation
   (http://ericae.net/)

Mental Health: Assessment Search and Evaluation on the Internet
   (http://ericae.net/sintbod.htm)

Test Review Locator—Search
   (http://ericae.net/testcol.htm#trev)

When school counselors engage in selecting tests for individual decision making, degree of client involvement becomes an issue. School counselors know about tests and have more life experience than their clients. Yet, clients, being involved in a decision-making method, seem to need to share the responsibility for selecting the tests. Counselors can provide information about tests that they can interpret competently and use their decision-making counseling skills to help clients choose the tests in the clients' best interests. With this process, test selection becomes part of the counseling process, rather than an adjunct activity.

Good test administration is essentially having concern for accuracy and caring for the test takers. Test publishers provide explicit instructions that must be followed by those who administer the tests to enhance the validity of the outcomes. Testing environments are best when test takers are comfortable and are allowed to do their best. A good principle for test administrators to follow is to create a testing environment similar to one in which they would be willing to participate.

The challenges of test administration are expanded when students take tests on the Internet (Sampson, 2000). On the one hand, distance barriers are broken down when individuals can take tests via the Internet rather than traveling to test sites. On the other hand, there is increased potential for circumstances that detract from the standardized conditions that should be found at any test site. Although Sampson alludes to test-publisher-protected and fee-charging self-assessment websites, there are also self-assessment sites that are free (see The Career Key: http://www.careerkey.org/english/).

Knowledge About Communicating Assessment Information Accurately

Test interpretations in counseling might be described as efforts by counselors to help test takers make sense out of the results and process the information to use it constructively. Test interpretation, like the test selection process, is best accomplished by making it a part of the counseling process, rather than an adjunct activity. Therefore, counselors can incorporate test interpretations into the counseling process. To accomplish this, counselors blend their knowledge of basic measurement principles with their counseling competencies. The following presentation suggests how the blending might occur.

If one is viewing test interpretation as part of the decision-making counseling process, the first step or goal is to establish a mutually acceptable working relationship between the counselor and the client. These attitudes and competencies are described in chapter 5. Beyond that, the reasons for taking the test are made clear to all involved, and the counselors know what their clients' expectations are. Unrealistic or misinformed expectations may need to be challenged immediately, and unmet expectations will need to be addressed eventually. Judicial use of basic communication skills will help counselors learn about expectations.

Relationship development and expectation assessment set the stage for disseminating the information if the client is ready and interested. The information is often technical and sometimes comprehensive, leaving counselors with the challenge of keeping it from overwhelming and confusing the client. In meeting this challenge, counselors will share their technical knowledge about tests and measurement while remembering their communication skills. They will translate technical terms into words and phrases understandable to the client and not use those terms directly with the client unless necessary. For example, clients seldom need to know what methods were used to estimate the reliability or validity of a test. They can be helped to understand the concept of the standard error of measurement without being introduced to the term *standard error of measurement* or to the formula for estimating it. The developmental stage of clients will also serve as a guide to what technical information they can process. Certainly, children need to be treated differently than high-school adolescents.

Graphic aids such as publisher-generated profiles provide visual assistance to counselors and clients. The counselor can help clients by making sure they are able to see the aids clearly and understand them. Computerized printouts from test publishers or from the Internet can also be very helpful, providing printed and graphic interpretive information. Many clients will need help with the computer-generated printouts because such reports often provide more information than clients can process successfully and may include information clients do not understand.

Because the information dissemination segment of the test interpretation process contains so much that needs to be shared and explained, there is a danger of too much counselor and too little client involvement in the process. Counselor overactivity and client passivity can be avoided through the use of counseling skills. The counselor can draw clients into the information dissemination process by asking clients to summarize at strategic points, to answer questions that will inform the counselor how well they understand the information, and to explain in their own words after having observed counselor demonstrations. It may also help to incorporate segments of client data processing into the dissemination process. Getting clients involved in the information dissemination process should be primary in counselors' minds and within their range of basic skills.

Client processing of the information leads to a continuation of the decision-making process, completing the test-interpreting component. Basic counseling skills can be used to invite clients to begin processing the information. For example, a counselor might ask, "What are your thoughts about these test results?" after sharing the appropriate information. Client processing can lead the counseling relationship in several directions, such as decision-making counseling and support counseling. Accurate communication of assessment information requires attitudes and skills that are commensurate with good counseling. The ingredient that differentiates these interpretations from other counseling endeavors is the technical information generated by the assessments that begs to be translated clearly in order to be useful. As Goldman (1971) implies, competent counselors can bridge the gap between the assessment data and constructive client use of those data.

The following simulation is an abbreviated example of a test interpretation interview. The student, Ned, is an eighth grader who took the Differential Aptitudes Test as an assignment in a career-planning unit led by the counselor, Ms. Bigelow (prevention programming with an assessment component). The purpose of the testing is to use data from the test to help Ned and his classmates think about future plans and, more immediately, make course selections for ninth grade. Ned is having difficulty understanding the information on the profile of scores provided by the test publisher and seeks out Ms. Bigelow for assistance:

Ms. Bigelow (B):	Hello, Ned, what can I do for you?
Ned (N):	Hi! Ms. Bigelow, I'm having trouble understanding these test scores. Can you help me?
B:	I certainly will try. Tell me what you think you know about the scores and what you hope to learn from them.
N:	Well, I hope to find out what I want to do when I grow up and what courses I should take next year—and I'm not sure what I know about the scores.
B:	Okay! You would like to use the information to make plans for the future, and it appears as if you are really confused about the scores. Should we begin with them?
N:	Yes! I'm really confused about all the numbers and graphs.
B:	They can be confusing for many people. In fact, it took me a while as an adult student in graduate school to feel that I understood the information well enough to explain it to others. Let's look at the profile sheet you have together. Okay?
N:	Yes.
B:	Some of the information can be read. For example, the name of the test, Differential Aptitudes Test, the names of the subtests, and descriptions of each of the subtests and what they are supposed to measure. Are you experiencing any difficulty understanding that part of the profile?
N:	No. I don't think so. It seems clear right now.
B:	Okay! Let's look at the graphic and numerical parts. There seem to be two kinds of numerical scores—percentile ranks and standard scores—and there are shaded areas on each

	graph, about an inch in length, above and below where your scores fall on the scale. Do you see all that?
N:	Yes. I see them but am not sure how to use them.
B:	Let's choose a place to start because several subtests and different kinds of scores are reported. Do you have a preference?
N:	Not especially. Let's start with the numerical section. That seems to be my worst score, and I don't like math very much. Yet, my dad says that I'll need to take a lot of math to get along well in the world.
B:	Okay! Let's look at your math score on the profile. Do you understand percentile ranks?
N:	I don't know. Does that mean the percentage of questions I got right?
B:	Not exactly, but that is a conclusion many people make when first experiencing percentile ranks because the word *percentile* is used. Actually, your performance on the test is being compared to the performances of a large group of people your age who already took the test, and the percentile rank informs us how you compared to that group. Does that make sense?
N:	I think so.
B:	So, on the numerical section the number of questions you answered correctly was equal to or higher than 40% of the people in that comparison group, which is labeled as a norms group. On the other hand, 60% of the norms group had higher scores on the test than you did. Does that help?
N:	I think so.
B:	Well, let's check you out by looking at the verbal section next. Why don't you explain to me what it means so that I can check out how well you understand that information.
N:	My score on the verbal section is at the 80th percentile, which means my score is higher than 80% of the norms group.
B:	That's pretty good! What percentage of the norms group scored higher than you did?
N:	Twenty percent.
B:	Correct. You seem to understand it quite well now.

Note: At this time, the counselor may decide to explain the nuance about Ned's score actually being equal to or higher than those in the norms group and may also choose to explain the concept of standard error of measurement and how it is applied via the darkened areas of the graphic materials above and below each specific score. Having taken care of these matters, the counselor may also then make sure the client is able to engage in the same process without prompting on the remaining sub-test scores on the test. The simulation resumes after these procedures have been completed:

B: Well, you seem to have a better understanding now. At least, that is the way it appears to me because you are now able to explain to me what the scores mean. Do you have any more questions about the scores?

N: No. I think I understand them better now. Thanks!

B: Good! Now, earlier in our interview you mentioned some things that I believe it would be important to discuss further. One is that you hope the scores will help you decide what to do when you grow up. Another is that you hope they will tell you what courses to take next year. Yet another comment was that you believe math is your weak academic area and that your father believes you should continue taking math courses because they are important for getting along in the world. Finally, I think we should talk about your reaction to your performance on the test; that is, how do you feel about your scores? Those seem to be some important issues we probably should discuss further. Would you like to do that?

N: Okay. That's something I wanted to talk about too, and I was hoping the test scores would be helpful.

B: Fine. If it is OK with you, tell me what you think the test scores should be able to do for you. . . .

Ms. Bigelow has helped Ned understand the scoring system of the test further by involving him in the process and providing him with information he can understand. She also has identified issues that need to be addressed further as a part of the counseling process. Several tracks are possible at this point, all of which may be interwoven: (a) clarifying Ned's too narrow perception about the usefulness of the test scores, (b) processing his thoughts about his father's beliefs and their influence on him, (c) thinking more about career planning, (d) helping Ned plan his course of studies for ninth grade, and (e) processing negative affect derived from his performance on the test.

The simulation presents one of many possible scenarios involving the application of assessment to counseling. In this case, the assessment was part of a prevention programming effort. The counselor provided a direct service in response to a request for assistance from the client. Basic counseling and assessment skills were combined to help the client, and the test interpretation opened the door to further counseling with the client. It appeared as if the counselor was sufficiently competent to explain the technical information associated with standardized testing in a manner that the client could comprehend, and she involved him in the process while doing so.

Competent counselors can bridge the gap between assessment data and constructive client use of those data.

Knowledge About Ethical Responsibilities in the Assessment Process

Both the ACA and ASCA codes offer ethical guidance for using tests in counseling. Section E of the ACA Code of Ethics provides considerable guidance for counselors. Examples are: (a) counselors are to recognize the limits of their competence (E.2.a.) and are responsible for the appropriate application, scoring, interpretation, and use of assessment instruments (E.2.b.); (b) counselors are cautious when selecting tests for culturally diverse populations (E.6.b.); (c) counselors administer tests under the same conditions that were established in their standardization (E.7.a.); (d) counselors indicate any reservations they have about test validity or reliability when reporting results (E.9.a.); and (e) counselors do not use data or test results that are obsolete or outdated (E.11.). For greater detail, see Appendix C.

The ASCA ethical standards include a section devoted to evaluation, assessment, and interpretation (A.9.). See Appendix D.

SUGGESTED ACTIVITIES

1. Take an inventory of testing and assessment abuses of which you are aware. Suggest possible solutions for each abuse. Share your observations with colleagues, and discuss the similarities and differences.
2. Make an inventory of tests you feel competent to interpret at this time. Add to the list those tests you plan to become competent to interpret in the near future.
3. Make an inventory of nonstandardized assessment techniques you feel competent to use, and add to the list those you plan to become competent with in the near future.
4. Debate the merits of the following statement: "The only legitimate assessment services are those used to achieve counseling goals."
5. In the light of what you know about the use of tests in school counseling today, what is your response to Goldman's claim that the marriage between tests and counseling has failed?
6. Discuss the merits of computerized and Internet testing and what the role of counselors should be.
7. Compare your thoughts with the authors' ideas about the basics in measurement that all school counselors should possess. Which expectations are the greatest? Why do you think this is so?
8. Which, if any, assessment issues presented in this chapter have influenced your life? Have they been resolved? If so, how? If not, did you acquire any information that might lead to a resolution?

9. Make an inventory of the tests that are mandated in the state where you currently reside or work. What is your impression of this condition?
10. Analyze the performance of the counselor in the test interpretation simulation from a counseling skills perspective. What were her strengths? What are your recommendations for improving her performance?
11. Go to www.scan21st.com and propose some ways that this Internet site might assist school counselors in their various assessment functions.

REFERENCES

Adelman, H. S., & Taylor, L. (2002). School counselors and school reform: New directions. *Professional School Counseling, 5*, 235–248.

Aiken, L. R. (1988). *Psychological testing and assessment* (6th ed.). Boston: Allyn & Bacon.

American Association for Counseling and Development. (1989). The responsibilities of test users. *Guidepost 31*(6), 11, 16, 18, 27–28.

American Psychological Association. (1986). *Guidelines for computer-based tests and interpretation.* Washington, DC: Author.

Anastasi, A. (1997). *Psychological testing* (7th ed.). Upper Saddle River, NJ: Prentice Hall.

Arredondo, P., & D'Andrea, M. (2002, March). Are assessments culturally informed? *Counseling Today, 28,* 32.

Bradley, R. (1994). Tests and counseling: Did we ever become partners? *Measurement and Evaluation in Counseling and Development, 26,* 224–226.

Castenell, L. A., Jr., & Castenell, M. E. (1988). Norm-referenced testing and low-income Blacks. *Journal of Counseling & Development, 67,* 205–206.

Dahir, C. (2001). The National Standards for School Counseling Programs: Development and implementation. *Professional School Counseling, 4,* 320–327.

Engen, H. B., Lamb, R. R., & Prediger, D. H. (1982). Are secondary schools still using standardized tests? *Personnel and Guidance Journal, 60,* 287–290.

Facundo, A., Nuttal, E. V., & Walton, J. (1994). Culturally sensitive assessment in schools. In P. Pedersen & J. C. Carey (Eds.), *Multicultural counseling in schools: A practical handbook* (pp. 225–238). Boston: Allyn & Bacon.

Giordano, F. G., Schwiebert, V. L., & Brotherton, D. L. (1997). School counselors' perceptions of the usefulness of standardized tests, frequency of their use, and assessment training needs. *School Counselor, 44,* 198–205.

Goldman, L. (1971). *Using tests in counseling* (2nd ed.). New York: Appleton-Century-Crofts.

Goldman, L. (1972). Tests and counseling: The marriage that failed. *Measurement and Evaluation in Guidance, 4,* 213–220.

Goldman, L. (1982). Assessment in counseling: A better way. *Measurement and Evaluation in Guidance, 15,* 70–73.

Goldman, L. (1990). Qualitative assessment. *Counseling Psychologist, 18*(2), 205–213.

Goldman, L. (1994). The marriage is over . . . for most of us. *Measurement and Evaluation in Counseling and Development, 26,* 217–218.

Gysbers, N. C., & Henderson, P. (2001). Comprehensive guidance and counseling programs: A rich history and a bright future. *Professional School Counseling, 4,* 246–256.

Hayes, L. (2001, September). Testing, 1-2-3. *Counseling Today,* 8–9.

House, R. M., & Hayes, R. L. (2002). School counselors: Becoming key players in school reform. *Professional School Counseling, 5,* 249–256.

Kapes, J. T., & Whitfield, E. A. (Eds.). (2002). *A counselor's guide to career assessment instruments* (4th ed.). Alexandria, VA: National Career Development Association.

Keat, D. B. (1974). *Fundamentals of child counseling.* Boston: Houghton Mifflin.

Keat, D. B. (1990). *Child multimodal therapy.* Norwood, NJ: Ablex.

Larry P. v. Riles, 495 F. Supp. 926 (N.D. Cal. 1979) appeal docketed, No. 80–4027 (9th Cir., Jan. 17, 1980).

Lazarus, A. A. (1976). Multimodal assessment. In A. A. Lazarus (Ed.), *Multimodal behavior therapy* (pp. 25–47). New York: Springer.

Linden, K. W., & Linden, J. D. (1968). *Modern mental measurement: A historical perspective.* Boston: Houghton Mifflin.

Miller-Jones, D. (1989). Culture and testing. *American Psychologist, 40,* 360–366.

Parsons, F. (1909). *Choosing a vocation.* Boston: Houghton Mifflin.

Prediger, D. J. (1994). Tests and counseling: The marriage that prevailed. *Measurement and Evaluation in Counseling and Development, 26,* 227–234.

Sampson, J. P., Jr. (1983). Computer-assisted testing and assessment: Current status and implications for the future. *Measurement and Evaluation in Guidance, 15,* 293–299.

Sampson, J. P., Jr. (2000). Using the Internet to enhance testing in counseling. *Journal of Counseling & Development, 78,* 348–356.

Seligman, L. (1981). Multimodal behavior therapy: A case study of a high school student. *School Counselor, 28,* 249–256.

Shepard, L. A., & Kreitzer, A. E. (1987). The Texas teacher test. *Educational Researcher, 16*(6), 22–31.

Talbutt, L. C. (1983). The counselor and testing: Some legal concerns. *School Counselor, 30,* 245–250.

Wood, S. (1984). Computer use in testing and assessment. *Journal of Counseling & Development, 63,* 177–179.

Zytowski, D. G. (1982). Assessment in the counseling process for the 1980s. *Measurement and Evaluation in Guidance, 15,* 15–21.

Zytowski, D. G. (1994). Tests and counseling: We are still married and living in discriminant analysis. *Measurement and Evaluation in Counseling and Development, 26,* 219–223.

Zytowski, D. G., & Warman, R. E. (1982). The changing use of tests in counseling. *Measurement and Evaluation in Guidance, 15,* 147–152.

CHAPTER 11

Advocacy in School Counseling

Goal: To recommend a place for advocacy in school counseling and suggest

implementation strategies for a balanced program.

Children and adolescents are among the most powerless people in twenty-first-century society. They can be moved from home to home and from school to school with little or no recognition of their needs or rights. The following is an example:

> *Sanchez was a 6-year-old boy. He lived in one of the wealthiest suburbs of Denver. He was adopted when he was 5 years old, not long after he appeared on a local television news program that featured children who needed a home. Sanchez appeared to be a handsome, strong, healthy youngster during his television appearance, and several callers to the television station requested opportunities to meet Sanchez and to consider*

adopting him. An affluent couple in Denver, who had tried unsuccessfully for years to give birth to a child, adopted Sanchez and set out to provide a wonderful home for him. Shortly after the adoption, the couple learned that Sanchez had a serious disease that would consume much of their time and wealth to manage. The couple, fearing the loss of their wealth and freedom, neglected Sanchez and rejected him emotionally. Sanchez came to the attention of his school counselor because of the neglect and rejection he faced at home.

What should a school counselor do in a case like this one? How can the counselor advocate for kids like Sanchez? What advocacy skills does the counselor need? What dilemmas will school counselors face as they advocate for students? Advocacy is an important role for school counselors; this chapter discusses that role.

THE LEGACY OF ADVOCACY

As stated in chapter 1, "guidance first appeared in the schools like any other subject. Guidance had a curriculum, the goals of which evolved from the social reform movements of the late nineteenth and early twentieth centuries. Guidance teachers also sought to have a positive impact on the moral development of their charges." At that time, the need for reform was primarily linked to the negative effects of the Industrial Revolution. The rapid transition from an agrarian to an industrial society in the United States caused some people to find their vocations obsolete, others to be uprooted from familiar surroundings, and still others to be unskilled and powerless employees of powerful and relatively unregulated industrialists.

Aubrey (1977) suggested the process by which social reformers made an impact on the problems when he described the relationship between the social reform movement and vocational guidance:

> The linkage between this movement and vocational guidance was largely built on the issue of the growing exploitation and misuse of human beings. This linkage centering on the two conditions of economic waste and human suffering was to be used time and again as a means of pricking the conscience of the public, especially legislators. Lawmakers, visibly absent among the ranks of social reformers, were forced to be responsive to the persistent and ceaseless cries of social reformers. As a consequence, Congress in 1917 passed the landmark Smith-Hughes Act for secondary vocational education and teacher training. This beginning of enabling legislation was to be strengthened during the next twenty years. (p. 290)

Cremin (cited in Aubrey, 1977) is credited for noting that some reformers viewed the schools as vehicles for improving individuals' lives. Referred to as humanitarians and progressives, these reformers included Horace Mann and John Dewey, who founded the Progressive Education Association. Cremin (1965) was among those who viewed school counselors as the professionals in the schools whose role and functions most epitomized the goals of the progressive movement. In pointing out that Cremin's thought was more of a compliment than a reality, Aubrey observed that the tendency to elevate school counseling idealistically beyond reality reached its zenith with the publication of John Brewer's *Education as*

Guidance in 1932. Brewer's point of view and that of the progressives faded during World War II and the postwar years.

In the years immediately following World War II, the United States found itself among the wealthiest and most powerful of nations. Many social problems of the late nineteenth and early twentieth centuries had abated, and some goals of the reformers had been achieved. School counseling entered a period of rapid expansion following the passage of the National Defense Education Act of 1958 (NDEA). Much attention was devoted to training new counselors, retraining employed counselors, and developing counselor education programs. The support provided by the NDEA for these efforts was predicated on the assumption that the needs of the nation will be served if its youth are guided into careers that will strengthen the nation in its struggle against Communism and keep it strong and prosperous.

The need for social reform still existed. It did not have the high priority in school counseling and in education it had once enjoyed, however, and those who insisted on telling others the right answers, as some early reformers did, were not very popular. An indication of some social problems in the middle of the twentieth century was provided by Wrenn (1962) in *The Counselor in a Changing World.* He cited racial discrimination, occupational restrictions on women, the influence of automation on employment opportunities, increasing divorce rates, and inner-city income and cultural deprivation among the challenges for which new directions in school counseling were needed.

The 1960s and early 1970s were a period of great social unrest in the United States. Exacerbated by a growing confusion over the country's military involvement in Vietnam, many young Americans clashed with their elders over national priorities, social mores, and personal rights and responsibilities. The Vietnam War and the civil rights and women's rights movements were leading factors in the polarization of attitudes. A return to militancy toward social problems developed concurrently with the appearance of individuals whose voices sounded a demanding, uncompromising, and accusing tone.

Contributors to the professional counseling literature during this era encouraged counselors to respond to the conditions proactively. Terms like *activist, advocacy, social action,* and *change agent* became prominent in the literature (cf. Hansen, 1968; Harris, 1967; Rousseve, 1968; Shaw, 1968; Stewart & Warnath, 1965; Stone & Shertzer, 1963). Clearly, school counselors were being challenged to try to change the circumstances causing various social problems and alleviating the effects. Focusing on the problems of urban America in particular, though also alluding to related problems in rural and suburban areas, Menacker (1974) advocated an interventionist role for school counselors. He argued as follows:

> The most fundamental guidance issue, finally, is the response that guidance ought to take to the concept that the student's out-of-school psychological, social, and physiological environment (food, housing, parents, peers, and so on) are more important determinants of school achievement than anything that occurs inside the school building. (p. 23)

Menacker insisted that school counselors should respond to "the forces outside the school as those within it and, in so doing, actively support the student" (1974, p. 22). His recommendation places school counselors idealistically in the role of advocates.

Herr (1979) sees this as "a source of both vulnerability and promise—vulnerability in the sense that many of the problems encountered by school counselors are of long duration of resolution, promise in the sense that the school counselor is a symbol of hopefulness that the school is a caring, humane place that has regard for individual purpose among all students" (p. 11).

Advocacy was not on the front burner in school counseling during the 1980s. Attention to the advocacy concept came primarily from champions for multiculturalism and multicultural counseling competencies in the 1990s. In 1999, the American School Counselor Association (ASCA) issued a position statement on multicultural counseling that calls for facilitation of student development through an understanding of and appreciation for multiculturalism and diversity. Currently, one can find articles written by advocates for numerous disenfranchised populations in the professional counseling literature, several of which will be cited later in this chapter.

All three of the initiatives for enhancing school counseling promote advocacy. In the ASCA National Model for Comprehensive School Counseling Programs, advocacy is a responsive service through which school counselors reach out to administrators and the community to help students achieve their goals (Gysbers & Henderson, 2001). Representing the National School Counseling Training Initiative, House and Hayes (2002) highlight the importance of being advocates for all students. Access to school-wide and community data places counselors in a unique position to achieve this goal. School counselors are viewed as advocates for school-community collaboration in the School Community–Collaboration Model (Adelman & Taylor, 2002). They are encouraged to take the lead in planning and advocating for less costly interventions for students and their families.

Kiselica and Robinson (2001) remind us that advocacy has several synonyms that may be found in the professional literature and that essentially mean the same thing. *Advocacy counseling, social action,* and *social justice* are among the most recent synonyms. Bradley and Lewis (2000) define advocacy as the act of speaking up or taking action to make environmental changes on behalf of clients. Dinsmore, Chapman, and McCollum (2002) supplement the definition by pointing out that advocacy can focus on responding on behalf of clients or empowering clients to work on their own behalf. Furthermore, Lee (1998) reminds us that the goal of advocacy in school counseling is to help clients challenge institutional and social barriers that are impediments to academic, career, or personal-social development. Comparing advocacy to the more traditional responsive counseling competencies such as counseling and consulting, Kiselica and Robinson (2001) point out that advocating for clients expands the counselor's focus. That is, the focus is expanded from intrapsychic concerns to include responding to extrapsychic forces that may be detrimental to clients. Their analysis implies that different competencies may be needed as well.

CHALLENGES OF THE NEW MILLENNIUM

Two centuries after the Industrial Revolution's beginnings, this nation still faces social problems, and the schools and school counselors are in the midst of those problems. Changing circumstances have caused some traditional problems to decline in importance and new ones to occur, whereas other traditional problems remain pervasive. In the first decade of the twenty-first century, American society is faced with social issues as challenging as ever. The struggle for equality continues for individuals with disabilities, racial and ethnic minority groups, women, senior citizens, homeless individuals and families, immigrants, migrants, drug-addicted babies, AIDS victims, and gays and lesbians. Substance abuse has reached proportions of great magnitude. Drug lords openly vie with public officials for power in some countries, and the staggering value of drugs shipped to and sold in the United States compares favorably with major segments of the federal budget. Alcohol, cigarette, and fast-food manufacturers argue with critics in an effort to protect their investment domains. The environment is threatened by by-products of industrialization, the immense need for energy-producing fuels, and people's disinterest in recycling waste products. Vulnerable pregnant teenagers are caught between forces advocating and seeking to legislate right-to-life and pro-choice viewpoints on abortion. Suicide is a national problem among adolescents, especially sexual minority students. The traditional family has declined as the norm, with the children of many single-parent, dual-working-parent, and disintegrated families left to fend for themselves. AIDS has demanded new views on interpersonal relationships while also creating a new source of stress and uncertainty for young people. Because of rapid changes in the economy, the workplace, and employment opportunities, many Americans have found themselves unemployed after years of employment or underemployed, with a corresponding decline in their standard of living. The same conditions threaten to engulf those young people who, for one reason or another, fail to cope with the expectations of the workplace and condemn themselves to unfulfilling futures living below the economic subsistence level. Statistics on child abuse indicate a problem whose dimensions are more pervasive than once known.

The litany of problems cited in the previous paragraph can make one feel depressed and overwhelmed. They represent current and future challenges with which society must continue to struggle. The schools and school counselors are in the midst of this struggle; they cannot ignore the problems because individuals affected by the problems attend and will attend the schools. And, these problems will prevent those children from being successful academically. Like it or not, the schools have become more than a place to impart knowledge. They have become, seemingly more than before, one institution that must help victims or potential victims of debilitating social problems, using both reactive and proactive responses. School counselors have a place in this scene as collaborators with other professional colleagues. School counseling was born in the social reform movement of another era, the legacy lives on, and it will continue to flourish.

In a call for social action in counseling, Lee and Sirch (1994) point out that the new millennium will usher in "a more global view of human need and potential" (p. 91). While striving to present their vision of an enlightened world society, Lee and Sirch also recommend two ways the counseling profession may promote their vision through social action, which they refer to as *counseling for an enlightened world society.*

First, counselors must believe in the vision of an enlightened world society and, in so doing, adopt *a sense of social responsibility.* Lee and Sirch view this commitment as manifesting itself in philosophical commitment to the need for global social change and a willingness to become *social change agents* in the spirit of the models promoted by the activist contributors to the counseling literature of the 1960s and 1970s. Second, counselors are challenged to work with clients from diverse cultural backgrounds, to be able to facilitate client development via traditional intervention and prevention strategies, and to help clients "assess the meaning of life and significant relationships within it" (1994, p. 95).

More recently, Lee (2001) issued a challenge for school counselors as follows: "[Demographic trends indicate that] as never before, U.S. schools are becoming a social arena where children who represent truly diverse behavioral styles, attitudinal orientations, and value systems have been brought together with one goal—to prepare them for academic, career, and social success in the twenty-first century" (p. 257). Lee continued by challenging counselors to be able to respond to students representing an expanded set of worldviews in order to ensure them access to services that promote optimal academic, career, and psychosocial development. Finally, he challenges us to "move beyond the myth of a monolithic society to the reality of cultural diversity" (p. 261).

In the authors' opinion, the pervasiveness of these social problems and the call for advocacy require school counselors to respond with patience and care. Setting goals and working with others to achieve them is a better strategy than working independently and impulsively to resolve issues. Demanding change may be less palatable to decision makers than leading the way with information and reasoned debate. When singular efforts fail, planning and renewed efforts are needed. These social problems may not be eradicated for a generation or more. Yet, some individuals can be helped. Many counselors attempting to help many individuals can be very influential. The remainder of this chapter elaborates on advocacy competencies and provides vignettes in which the competencies are demonstrated.

A CLOSER LOOK AT ADVOCACY

The popularity of Carl Rogers's nondirective or person-centered approach to counseling in the mid-twentieth century led to an atmosphere in which most school counselors viewed their role as somewhat clinical in nature. Much emphasis was placed on individual counseling, one-to-one relationships, and counseling interventions. In developmental counseling—the counseling of individuals who were dealing with developmental issues such as selecting courses of study, planning for the future, coping with schoolwork, and getting along with others—many counselors also used client-centered response modes. That client-centered counseling dominated the repertoires of many counselors indicated that they found it effective. Numerous clients were helped by school counselors who were using a predominantly client-centered model or other models that allowed them to work mainly in their offices, responding to referrals from colleagues and self-referrals by students.

Although effective for some student clients, this counseling model is also a passive, reactive one in which clients are expected to take responsibility for helping themselves. Therefore, the solutions to problems, choices, and challenges confronting these clients are often viewed as being within the grasp of the clients themselves if they can figure out how to solve the problems, make the choices, and meet the challenges successfully. In this approach, school counselors use listening and responding skills to create an accepting and empathic environment for their clients. Clients are helped because they can use that environment to feel understood, to clarify their thoughts and feelings, and to move freely toward decisions or feel better about themselves and their circumstances. As an alternative method, counselors can share the wisdom of their experience to offer student clients advice based on the expectation that the clients will be responsible for carrying out that advice. To sum up, in the mid-twentieth century, most school counselors used helping models drawn primarily from psychological theories that stressed passive verbal interaction and self-directed client activity (Menacker, 1976). It is not a helping model that encourages advocacy, nor is it a training model that produces counselors who are active interventionists. Into this setting came the unrest of the 1960s. With that unrest came dissatisfaction with the accepted counseling models because school counselors seemed too passive and uninvolved and because some clients could not achieve their goals through their own self-directed efforts. Several descriptive terms were used to label different approaches being advocated; yet, advocates of these approaches seemed to recommend that school counselors become more active, more directive and challenging, and more helpful to individuals confronted by issues whose resolutions were beyond their own self-directed efforts. A sample follows.

Menacker (1974) highlights the importance of a nontraditional, more active role for school counselors in the urban schools. His position is based on his conclusions that the out-of-school environment of urban students is more important than anything that occurs inside the school building and that urban school bureaucracies have inertia and resistance to change, which challenges counselors to adopt an activist, interventionist role to prevent themselves from becoming part of a stifling bureaucracy. Recommended manifestations of this role include the following:

- Adopting a multiple guidance control model in which central guidance officials, principals, local guidance workers, teachers, students, and parent-community representatives are all involved in planning, monitoring, implementing, and evaluating the counseling program
- Resisting bureaucratic pressures to achieve maintenance goals and instead advocating goals that serve students and promise to improve their circumstances
- Engaging in environmental alteration when such changes seem appropriate, both in the school and in the community as a community resource specialist

In his theory of activist guidance, Menacker (1976) advocates a shift away from philosophical underpinnings deeply rooted in psychology and toward a greater emphasis on sociology, anthropology, and political science. He believes this will bring about increased understanding of the importance of social class and race in schooling, the impact of social change on communities and the schools, the importance of socioeconomic status, the importance of reference groups, and the effect on learning of the environment outside school. Menacker believes that a pervasive amount of activist philosophy in the approach of school counselors will change their traditional work patterns and their relations with other professionals. New work patterns will include spending more time away from the office and the school interacting with employers, parents, and community leaders and will lead to different work patterns (e.g., evening and weekend hours). New relations will occur when clients find counselors advocating more assertively for students, sometimes appearing more like attorneys or ombuds-men than mediators.

Implementation of Menacker's activist guidance theory is founded on the follow-ing principles:

1. Direct counselor activity is focused on concrete action that objectively helps students. Activist counselors can achieve empathy through direct, concrete helping activities.
2. There should be mutual client-counselor identification of environmental con-ditions that may facilitate or retard goals and self-development. Counselors should attempt to capitalize on the positive and to eliminate the negative client elements.
3. Activist guidance recognizes the distinction between client goals and values and those of educational institutions. Thus, rather than always adjusting the student, it may be necessary to acknowledge that the institution is sometimes the patho-logical element that needs time to adjust or to be adjusted.

Standing out among Menacker's principles are the ideas that direct helping activities can achieve empathy and that the institution may need to be adjusted. Traditional empa-thy takes the form of verbal and nonverbal responses by counselors that lead clients to feel understood. One might hypothesize that acts of direct help when help is needed also make clients feel understood. Therefore, empathy might be achieved in ways other than listening and responding passively. Few will claim that the schools are perfect institu-tions. Yet, the tendency for bureaucratic thinking among school personnel often leads to the expectation that students and parents, even teachers and counselors, must adjust to the system. The traditional goal of verbal counseling often has been to help individuals adjust to the system. Menacker would have counselors attempt to alter the system in those instances when it is the system, and not the student, that seems wrong or patho-logical and to help students adjust only when it is they who are wrong.

Beyond the importance of activist counseling for all students lies the potential for helping disadvantaged students. Sue (1992) summarizes the position succinctly:

> Evidence continues to accumulate, for instance, that economically and educationally disadvantaged clients may not be oriented toward "talk therapies," that self-disclosure in counseling may be incompatible with cultural values of Asian Americans, Latinos and American Indians, that the sociopolitical atmosphere may dictate against working openly with the counselor, and that some minority clients may benefit from the coun-selor's active intervention in the system. (p. 14)

In an approach he labels *synergistic counseling,* Herring (1997a, 1997b) believes that if school counselors are to serve as advocates for culturally different students, they will be challenged to employ a *cultural- and ethnic-specific model*. Herring describes synergistic counseling as going beyond eclecticism and the communication skills approaches. The basic themes are that traditional counseling models are incom-plete and that school counselors will be more helpful if able to employ counseling strategies that are responsive to students' goals, cultures, and environments. Cultural and environmental factors, as well as psychodynamics, are important in the helping process.

The School Counselor as an Advocate: A Case Study

When interviewing a 17-year-old male student who was having academic difficulties, a rural high-school counselor learned that the client had moved away from home and was living in his own apartment. The student was working as many hours as possible after school in a local food market in an effort to earn enough money to support himself. He had too little time for his studies and was often so tired that he overslept or fell asleep in school. The counselor's response was to contact county social services agencies whose services were available to the student. These were services about which the student was uninformed. By contacting the targeted agencies on the student's behalf, the counselor was able to help the client receive assistance that made it possible for him to afford to live alone and finish his high-school education. In this case, the counselor recognized the client's needs, knew or found out how they could be met, took the initiative to intercede for a client who was too naive to help himself, and changed the circumstances that were impeding the student's successful academic performance.

Challenges Associated With Advocacy

Activism has a traditional place in school counseling, along with the more passive, traditional models. Passive and active counseling strategies are different, however, and the special challenges that face counselors who attempt to achieve activist goals are addressed in closing this section. Among these challenges are the possibility of appearing to be an adversary to those one is trying to influence and the real possibility of becoming burned out.

In a classic example of a school counselor who demanded that the system do things the way he truly believed it should, Ponzo (1974) reflects on what he learned from his Pyrrhic victory—one in which he achieved his immediate goals but destroyed his relationships with some fellow professionals and part of the community:

> For a host of reasons, systems—human, animal, and social—tend to resist change. The strength of this resistance is dependent on the system's awareness of its need to change, its confidence in its ability to change, and its perception of the entity that proposes to bring the change about. It is prudent as well as necessary for a change agent to consider these factors as part of the change process. In Lincoln I attempted to bring about change without considering those factors. I barged in as if I were asked, wanted, and trusted. I failed to recognize that my "client" was very security conscious and had its borders well guarded. I failed to recognize that I was an outsider looking in. I failed to recognize that much of my behavior created additional barriers to change rather than removing existing ones. (p. 29)

Were he to do it over again, Ponzo would change his strategies, adopting a more diplomatic approach:

1. One must understand himself or herself. Your own personality is a strong tool, but it can be administered in dosages that are too heavy.
2. One must understand the system. This corresponds to developing a facilitative relationship with a client. Empathy, warmth, concreteness, and understanding serve to prevent the system (client) from fearing you.

3. Learn how the system works. The chances for success increase if one is a consultant who facilitates change rather than a foreign intruder who demands it.
4. Noble dreams must be translated into achievable program goals. This will increase the probability of success and decrease the probability of failure and abandonment.

One of Ponzo's recurring themes is the recommendation to learn the system and then use that knowledge to negotiate differences and initiate new proposals. Counselors will be successful more often if others in the system view them as competent. Counselors are then in a better position to promote competing goals in an appropriately assertive manner and to take positions that are not necessarily popular. The ultimate negotiating goal is to have all sides gain something in the end, with everyone believing that they won something and that the counselor's goals were accomplished.

An overly literal interpretation of the information about advocacy can lead a counselor to work night and day every day of the week. Few individuals can keep up that pace without burning out. Therefore, the advocacy model, to be effective, must provide for prevention against burnout. Individuals who engage in advocacy need rest and recreation. Gunnings (1978) offers two useful suggestions for preventing burnout and enhancing the effectiveness of advocates. One suggestion is to give school counselors 12-month contracts so that they will have time to develop community contacts. A second suggestion is to provide additional funding to reduce the ratio of counselors to students, especially in districts requiring high levels of advocacy. Additional strategies are released time during weekdays for counselors who work evening and weekend hours, periodic sabbatical leaves, and supportive counseling and supervision services for counselors.

If the legacy of advocacy is to be kept alive, school counselors who accept the challenge need to be skillful change agents, not martyrs, so that advocacy goals can be achieved and clients served. Such counselors need to protect themselves from burnout and to be protected by enlightened supervisors and administrators. Otherwise, they will be used up by the same systems they are trying to help their clients understand and manage; the losses will be great because some will leave the profession, and many will continue to function at a level much less proficient and helpful than they should, cheating both themselves and their clients.

COMPETENCIES FOR ADVOCACY IN SCHOOL COUNSELING

Advocating on Behalf of Clients

There are situations when it seems clear to counselors that clients face challenges that lie beyond their coping capacity. These are opportunities to be advocates for our clients. These are also situations that present significant challenges. What do I do? How do I do it? What are the consequences? Will I place myself, or my job, at risk? These questions represent a myriad of challenges school counselors who would be advocates on behalf of their clients will face. In this section, we address the "How do I do it?" question with a set of recommendations taken from recent contributions to the professional literature.

Lee (2001) believes that counselors need to possess cultural awareness, that is, an understanding of the diverse cultural realities of all students. This includes an awareness of one's own cultural blind spots. Also required are an awareness of the systemic barriers to quality education that clients face and knowledge of, and competence in, how to challenge the barriers effectively.

Marinoble (1998) suggests that a strategy for challenging systemic barriers successfully is trying to influence school policies, curriculum, and staff development when appropriate. For example, school counselors might lobby for including sexual orientation in the language of nondiscrimination clauses of teacher contracts and school policies about treatment of students and parents, for establishing and enforcing school policies forbidding homosexual slurs and jokes, and for permitting mention of gay and lesbian topics in school publications.

Kiselica and Robinson (2001) highlight the importance of a capacity for appreciating human suffering as well as a capacity for being able to commit to advocating for those in need. To influence groups that might help clients, or may be affecting them negatively, counselors are challenged to understand group change processes. As emphasized earlier by Menacker (1974), organizations or systems (e.g., schools and school systems) sometimes engage in practices or policies that are harmful to students. In advocacy challenges of this nature, Dinsmore, Chapman, and McCollum (2000) recommend being able to: (a) ensure that clients and their families receive accurate information, (b) serve as a mediator for clients and organizations, (c) negotiate with organizations on behalf of clients, (d) engage in lobbying efforts on behalf of clients, and (e) submit articulate complaints.

New work patterns will include spending more time away from the office and school.

Another approach is to try to influence significant others such as colleagues and members of the community by raising the level of discussion (D'Andrea & Daniels, 1997). One such potential discussion topic is racism and how it impedes opportunities for many students to be successful academically.

In closing this section we share strong words about advocating on behalf of clients from Kiselica and Robinson (2001): "We are convinced that it is not possible for us as counselors to engage in genuine social action unless we discover a personal moral imperative to serve as a drawing force behind our work" (p. 396).

Advocating for Clients to Work in Their Own Behalf

Helping clients work in their own behalf begins with the basic listening and responding skills presented in chapter 5. Kiselica and Robinson (2001) stress the importance of being able to listen and respond to clients who need advocates and to help them communicate effectively for themselves. An example would be to help a gay youth who wants to do so to be able to "come out." Arredondo and D'Andrea (2001, 2002) agree that all communication skills are appropriate in counseling relationships. They stress that the importance of realizing which skills to use and how to use them may vary across cultural groups. Ethnic and cultural differences across clients highlight the importance of multicultural competence.

This focus on multicultural competence introduces the Multicultural Counseling Standards (Sue, Arredondo, & McDavis, 1992) that are found in Appendix E. Designed as guides to interpersonal counseling interactions, the standards define multicultural counseling as "preparation and practices that integrate culture-specific awareness, knowledge and skills into counseling interactions" (Arredondo & D'Andrea, 1995, p. 28) and identify the context as application to "African/Black, Asian, Caucasian/European, Hispanic/Latino, and Native American or indigenous groups which have historically resided in the continental United States and its territories" (p. 28). Note when viewing the standards in Appendix E that the major section headings refer to awareness of one's own values and biases, awareness of the client's worldview, and use of culturally appropriate interventions.

These headings allude to the importance of competence based on knowledge and awareness. According to Arredondo and D'Andrea (2002), one cannot apply culturally competent skills without awareness and knowledge, and the process requires life-long learning; it begins with classes and textbooks and continues with experience and learning from others.

EXAMPLES OF ADVOCACY IN SCHOOL COUNSELING

The following examples are a mixture of cases found in the professional literature and others that are hypothetical. We attempted to present a variety of clients needing advocacy and of approaches to advocacy; yet, we realize that there are numerous other possible examples. The narrative will reveal both specific and implied advocacy competencies. Our format is to first provide background about the advocacy challenge. The overview will be followed by a narrative summary of the advocate's response and an analysis of the advocacy process involved.

Empowering Her to Be All That She Can Be

Background. That women have not achieved a status equal to men is a widely accepted and documented proposition. One domain in which these differences have clearly manifested themselves is occupational opportunities (Bartholomew & Schnorr, 1994; Pedersen, 1988). Bartholomew and Schnorr highlight the need to enhance the confidence of many young women to enable them to take advantage of career opportunities opening up to them, especially in mathematics and science. The several recommendations Bartholomew and Schnorr offer for responses by counselors add up to a challenge to conceive and implement a broad range of efforts aimed at enhancing the self-esteem of female students so that they will view themselves as capable of pursuing expanding career opportunities.

Summary. When meeting with an 11th-grade female client to discuss her plans for the future, a male counselor asked her what she wanted to be when she graduated from high school. The client, who was a better than average student, stated that she was planning to go to college and try to find a major or career field that would not prevent her from being a successful homemaker and having children and a family. When the counselor asked her to elaborate on the criteria for careers that did not prevent her from being a successful homemaker, she responded in a manner that indicated she had considerably restricted her college field and career opportunities.

When the counselor asked her if there were college fields and careers that she might consider pursuing that were not being considered because of her previously stated beliefs, she listed several. Then, the counselor asked the client what had prevented her from considering them too and learned that she had been influenced not to do so by her parents and her junior-high-school counselor. Those parties had informed her she should restrict her options to courses and majors that did not require math and science because girls were not as strong in those disciplines as boys and that she should not waste her time in a major or career that was too challenging or required too much of a commitment because she would probably be getting married and raising a family in the not too distant future.

The counselor's advocacy responses were as follows. He provided her with accurate information about all the careers of interest to her, about her math and science aptitudes, and about related college majors. He also provided age-appropriate gender equity information for her to read. The information dissemination was accompanied by counseling sessions to help her process the information thoroughly while trying to empower her to make her own decisions. In addition, the counselor volunteered to visit with the student's parents about this concern if she wished and made a note to himself to try to find a way to raise the gender equity consciousness of his junior-high-school counseling colleague.

Analysis. Much of the activity in this advocacy response occurred in the counselor's office. He recognized the client's need for someone to empower her to be all that she can be, apparently because he believed in gender equity. He then helped her find and process useful information. Realizing that the student may not be able to deal with her parents alone, the counselor volunteered to help her beyond the confines of his office. Finally, the counselor seemed ready to try to influence the system by approaching the counselor colleague who seemed to be in need of gender equity consciousness-raising in an effort to induce change.

An Advocate in the School for the Family

Background. Exceptional children have a physical, emotional, or intellectual status that places them outside the normal range and therefore causes them to be categorized as having a *disability*. The welfare of this constituency historically concerned counselors, but they had little direct contact with such children until November 1975. Any question about whether school counselors believed in equity for exceptional children became academic with the passage of PL 94-142, the Education for All Handicapped Children Act, in 1975. This piece of federal legislation made equity for exceptional children mandatory across the country and challenged school counselors to implement their social activism tradition.

Humes (1978) points out that PL 94-142 is very specific about what is to be done. One specific ingredient of the law is that all individuals between the ages of 3 and 21 have to be given a free, appropriate public education in some form and setting. That education is to be provided, to some degree, in the same environment with able individuals. This concept is known as *mainstreaming*. Implementation of the mainstreaming concept is specified through annual individualized educational plans (IEPs) that are developed for every child. IEPs must include information about the child's current level of functioning, annual goals, measurable short-term objectives, and an inventory of specific educational services the child requires. IEPs are drawn up by multidisciplinary teams of teachers, administrators, and pupil service specialists (including counselors) in cooperation with parents. Parents of exceptional children are granted specific due process rights that include the right to independent educational evaluations, the option of requesting hearings by impartial officials, and the inspection of all evaluative records. Chief among the categories of people whose education is governed by PL 94-142 are those children evaluated as being deaf, deaf-blind, hard of hearing, mentally retarded, multihandicapped, orthopedically impaired, other health impaired, seriously emotionally disturbed, specific learning disabled, speech impaired, and visually impaired (Fagan & Wallace, 1979).

Passage of the Education for Handicapped Amendments (PL 99-457) in 1986 expanded the mainstreaming concept to working with both the child and the family through individualized family service plans (IFSPs). This legislation calls for school personnel to work closely with the family and the child to identify early intervention services. Greer, Greer, and Woody (1995) believe that PL 99-457 expands the role of counselors in the mainstreaming process.

Concern about programming in schools that seemed to be defeating the principles in PL 94-142 led to enactment of the Education of All Handicapped Act Amendments of 1990 (PL 101-476). PL 101-476 calls for *inclusion*, which means that all students, no matter the severity of their disability, must be included in all aspects of school life. The present vignette is drawn loosely from Hourcade and Parette (1986).

Summary. A school counselor received a telephone call from the parents of a child with epilepsy who revealed that the child needed an anticonvulsant medicine administered while in school. Unfortunately, unenlightened school personnel resisted responding to the parents' request, and their family physician referred them to the school counselor. The counselor recognized that the family needed an advocate to act as a liaison between them and the school—a champion for their position.

First, the counselor informed the parents that he would try to act as a liaison if they wished. With their approval, the counselor diplomatically informed the unenlightened school personnel about the student's rights under the applicable federal legislation, the parents' due process rights, and the responsibilities of the school personnel. Upon achieving cooperation from the targeted school personnel, the counselor informed the parents and proceeded to coordinate the process of ensuring that the student received the requisite anticonvulsant medicine. Coordinating the process involved informing/educating all school personnel who were to participate in the process about their responsibilities and roles, arranging the medicine administrations (e.g., times and places, excuses from classes for the student), ensuring the client was cognizant of the system that had been set up, informing the parents about what to expect and their due process rights, keeping notes about important events and agreements in the process, monitoring the process as it took place, and evaluating the success of the advocacy intervention.

Analysis. In this vignette, the counselor was appropriately informed about the related legislation while also understanding the client's rights and the school's responsibilities. The counselor also viewed the student's family as part of the client system and realized they needed help from someone familiar with the school system and personnel. Beyond that, the counselor was willing to take the risk of advocating for them and upsetting the previously uncooperative school personnel. It also appears as if the counselor knew how to approach the school personnel in a manner that got their attention and cooperation. Finally, the counselor was willing and able to coordinate the process once it was initiated.

A Proactive Effort to Expand the Range of Possibilities

Background. This example is based on a project reported by Vontress (1966). Advocacy is a theme that runs through the multicultural literature (cf. Casas & Furlong, 1994; Gibbs, 1973; Haettenschwiller, 1971; Kopala, Esquivel, & Baptiste, 1994; Luftig, 1983; Rogler, Malgady, Constantino, & Blumenthal, 1987; Ruiz & Padilla, 1977). Pallas, Natriello, and McDill (1989) advocate a role for counselors outside the schools that might be conceived of as a community resource specialist, working with families and communities, helping them learn to use their power and reintegrating them with the schools. Acting in this manner causes a counselor to become known in the community as someone who cares. LaFromboise and Jackson (1996) suggest that doing whatever is possible to help clients control their own lives leads to empowerment—that is, clients exerting interpersonal influence, improving performance, and maintaining effective support systems. Vontress (1966) described an all-out attempt to widen the range of possibilities for African American children in a large inner-city school.

Summary.   Viewing themselves as advocates for all the children in their school, the counselors developed and initiated a plan for a school-community collaboration program. They conducted an analysis of the needs of the students and their families, particularly those needs they were unable to meet through the services their staff could provide. Then, by concentrating on what needed to be done, they initiated a number of intervention strategies such as evening parent conferences, home visits, driving parents to visit colleges, talking to newspaper reporters, making television appearances, meeting with civic leaders, and finding part-time jobs for students. This multifaceted set of interventions consisted of working with students individually and reaching out to several targeted constituencies (e.g., families, the school board, and business/community groups).

Analysis.   Realizing that they were unable to meet all the important needs of their clients, these counselors were willing to extend their services by engaging in advocacy activities. To accomplish their goals, the counselors were willing and able to engage in activities that might be depicted as public relations and social work. They understood that enriching the current environment and opportunities for their students might have positive long-term benefits for their lives. Their efforts also resulted in the formation of school-community partnerships that had potential for being continuous.

Advocacy for Sexual Minority Youths

Background.   Marinoble (1998) writes:

> A favorite self-esteem activity among elementary school children involves listening to a story about a "very special person" who can be seen by opening a colorful box. One-by-one the children lift the lid, peer inside, and see their own reflection in a mirror. . . . Most children giggle with glee, pride, or self-consciousness. It is fun, and it encourages children to feel good about the person they see. . . . For some children though, the mirror begins to develop a blind spot—a part of themselves they cannot see or, at best, cannot bring into focus. As these children progress through childhood and adolescence, their schools, families, and communities often collaborate to reinforce the blind spot. The results of this collaboration may range from mild to tragic. The blind spot is homosexuality—a sexual orientation that appears to be natural for approximately 10% of the population. (p. 4)

"Gay adolescents face the same developmental challenges as their heterosexual counterparts, with the added burden of attempting to incorporate a stigmatized sexual identity" (Fontaine, 1998, p. 13). For some sexual minority youths, the burden may be too much to bear. Suicide is the number one cause of death among these youths, two to three times more than among heterosexual youths (Cooley, 1998; Logan & Williams, 2001; McFarland, 1998). Higher rates of substance abuse, psychiatric treatment, school problems, and running away from home have been documented as well (Remafedi, 1987; Remafedi, Farrow, & Deisher, 1991). For others, the burden may be sufficiently challenging to require counseling interventions. Collectively, Black and Underwood (1998), Cooley (1998), Fontaine (1998), Marinoble (1998), and Omizo, Omizo, and Okamoto (1998) provide an inventory of burdens that is both impressive and saddening: identity confusion and conflict, depression, family disruptions, fear of exposure, internalized hostility, peer relationship problems, self-doubt and low self-esteem, social isolation, unfriendly environments (e.g., institutional homophobia), and concerns and doubts about the future. Although heterosexual youths face many of these challenges as well, some are clearly more applicable to homosexual youths (fear of exposure, unfriendly environments) or have the potential for being more severe if one has a homosexual orientation (identity confusion and conflict, family disruptions, peer relationship problems, social isolation, concerns and doubts about the future).

Many sexual minority youths attend schools in which institutionalized homophobia ranges from outright intolerance to benign neglect. McFarland and Dupuis (2001) report about the decisions in three court cases that collectively indicate schools must ensure safe educational environments for gay and lesbian students. Two examples of advocacy interventions found in the professional literature are presented here.

Summaries. Bauman and Sachs-Kapp (1998) provide an example of counselors helping an alternative high school in Fort Collins, Colorado, manifest its goal to achieve tolerance toward diversity. The focus of the counselors' efforts was to create schoolwide workshops on a variety of diversity issues, the most controversial of which was sexual orientation, that were well organized and facilitated by students. The counselors recruited and trained those students who would lead the workshops. An overview of the workshops follows.

Student leaders were trained in a for-credit minicourse. Team building, self-awareness enhancement, demonstrations of effective teaching and facilitating skills, and practice with constructive feedback were features of the training program. Students were not required to attend the workshops. An alternative workshop covering fear and intolerance in more general terms was offered by a popular teacher. A daylong format involving the entire school was followed. A guest speaker keynoted the workshops with a presentation that focused on individual humanity being more important than sexual orientation when dealing with people. Three panels followed, all of which the students experienced via a rotation format. Guest panel members, chosen by students, included gay, lesbian, and bisexual individuals (one panel); individuals whose family members were gays, lesbians, and bisexuals (a second panel); and professional psychologists considered experts in human behavior (a third panel). All three panels were requested by students to focus on the theme *How Hate Hurts*. Following the panel rotations, small discussion groups, consisting of no more than 10 students and one or two staff members, were facilitated by the trained students. These groups focused on processing the experience and talking about feelings. The leaders followed a structured format they learned during their training. The closing event was an exercise for all in attendance scripted by the counselors and led by a popular teacher. Students who were willing to identify themselves as being gay, lesbian, or bisexual or as having friends and family members who are (*the targets*) were invited to move silently to the opposite side of the room from the remainder of those present (*the nontargets*).

Ninety-five percent of students opted to participate in the primary program. Follow-up evaluation survey data indicated that, on a 5-point scale, the average rating of the educational value of the workshop was 3.8.

Muller and Hartman (1998) provide suggestions for group counseling, including issues that may be the focus of the group intervention (homophobia, loneliness and isolation, identity issues, alienation from families, suicide, substance abuse). They describe a counseling support group that was conducted in a suburban Maryland public high school. The general goal for this group was to provide an atmosphere for universality, hope, and interpersonal learning. Overt methods for identifying prospective members included posters in hallways encouraging sexual minority youths to see a counselor if they wanted to talk about their concerns, posting rainbows and pink triangles around the school with invitations from the counselors, posting antihomophobic slogans in the school counseling area, and the counselors wearing buttons declaring support for sexual minority youths. Teachers known to be trusted by sexual minority youths were informed about the proposed group. Seven students eventually responded and participated. An overview of the group intervention follows.

Two heterosexual female counselors led the group. Both had extensive preparation. Goals for the group counseling process focused on identifying and discussing feelings, developing coping skills, and building a support system. Twenty-five weekly sessions of 45 minutes each were held; meeting times were rotated to prevent students from missing the same class more than once a month. A more detailed description of the content and methods is offered in Muller and Hartman (1998) who state: "Many sessions were devoted entirely to interpersonal issues which arose in the group. Anger and resentments among members and resulting feedback enriched sessions and became the focus of the group on many occasions" (p. 41).

Analysis. Both interventions involved groups organized by counselors in their schools. The first group required prevention programming competencies, and the second group counseling competencies. Probably speaking for the organizers of both group interventions, the author-counselors in the second intervention point out the importance of being aware of their own assumptions and beliefs and of having the support of their principal in advance of and during the program. As well, they state that school system policies on any kind of sexual harassment must be in effect (Muller & Hartman, 1998). Beyond competence, awareness, and acquiring support, the counselors were also risk-takers, willing to demonstrate their advocacy for sexual minority youths in a potentially hostile school and community environment. All the elements just cited required careful planning by the counselors. They also had to be able to organize and manage the programs efficiently and successfully.

Bully Busting Advocates for Violence Prevention/Intervention

Background. The following case is hypothetical and based on information presented in Roberts and Morotti (2000) and Hanish and Guerra (2000). School violence has received considerable national attention in recent years, especially in the context of horrific instances where students take the lives of other students and teachers (Sandhu, 2000). Bullying is one manifestation of violence in schools, and, in some recent instances reported recently in the press, those who took the lives of classmates were bullying victims who responded in a very drastic manner. In our vignette, the counselor views the bully and the bully's target as individuals in need of an advocate.

Summary. Reports from a couple of teachers indicate that a middle-school 8th-grade boy has been bullying a much smaller, shy, and introverted 6th-grade boy for two months since students returned from summer vacation. The counselor's first step was to call in the target, or victim, in order to get acquainted, establish rapport, and decide when it was appropriate to ask about the bullying. Feeling comfortable with the counselor, the target related a tale of physical and mental abuse that had him both frightened and angry. The counselor immediately indicated that the target student's tale had been believed, that an effort would be made to help him and immediately, and that the student was invited to come to the counselor's office immediately if either an act of bullying occurred or he felt like retaliating.

The counselor initiated a plan to work with the target and the bully concurrently. To help the target, the counselor: (a) met with the victim to help him process his feeling about the situation and determine proactive strategies for protecting and feeling better about himself; (b) worked with teachers and administrators to make necessary modifications in the school climate to help the victim and reduce the likelihood that the bully would have opportunities to act; and (c) met with the victim's parents to help them process their concerns, determine what they could do to help, and understand that something constructive was being done.

Concurrently, the counselor met with the bully. The first step was to make the contact nonthreatening and listen to what the bully had to say about himself and the situation. Eventually, specific unacceptable behaviors and their possible consequences were described to the bully. The counselor attempted to find opportunities to help the bully achieve increased self-awareness leading to change. Targets for the self-awareness effort were the bully's home environment and the sources of vicarious reinforcement for the bullying behaviors. This led to the counselor working with both the bully and his parents in an effort to induce change. Finally, once the effort was under way, the counselor provided attention, support, and long-term follow-up.

Analysis. The counselor recognized the need for advocacy—for the victim *and* the bully—immediately. In addition, the counselor responded quickly, and the response was multifaceted. Interventions involved both the victim and the bully, and they were undertaken concurrently. The multifaceted response involved clients, school personnel, school climate, and parents. The counselor as an advocate achieved collaboration with others and served as a coordinator of the intervention process.

Achieving Professional Identity: Advocating for the School Counseling Profession

Background. Confusion and debate about the role of school counselors seem to have accompanied the profession from its beginnings in the early part of the twentieth century. More than three decades ago, Shertzer and Stone (1963) referred to role confusion as an "old ghost." The professional literature was then, and is now, sprinkled

Enriching the current environment and opportunities for students might have positive long-term benefits for their lives.

with articles discussing, lamenting, and offering solutions for role confusion (cf. Carmichael & Calvin, 1970; Gibson & Mitchell, 1981; Hutchinson, Barrick, & Groves, 1986; Knapp & Denny, 1961; Smith, 1955). Although old and timeworn, it remains an important and unresolved issue. Sarbin (1954) likens the importance of being able to define one's role to adjustment of one's individual self-identity.

Haettenschwiller (1971) described counselors as being in a weak or boundary position within the power and status framework of the schools, receiving demands from parents, administrators, and teachers who are able to bestow both positive and negative sanctions. Willower, Hoy, and Eidell (1967) found that school administrators and teachers whose dominant attitudes toward the school environment tended to be custodial, favored maintenance of control or order, and caused humanistic teachers and counselors to remain silent or pay lip service to custodial concerns. School counselors may often find themselves in environments where some of their more influential colleagues and supervisors have beliefs that are contrary to the counselors' preferences and the ideals expressed in their training, possibly leading to role confusion. A spate of reports about surveys of the school counselor's role appeared in *Journal of Counseling & Development, School Counselor,* and *Elementary School Guidance and Counseling* between 1985 and 1991 (cf. Boser, Poppen, & Thompson, 1988; Gibson, 1990; Helms & Ibrahim, 1985; Hutchinson et al., 1986; Hutchinson & Bottorf, 1986; Hutchinson & Reagan, 1989; Miller, 1989; Moles, 1991; Morse & Russell, 1988; Peer, 1985; Remley & Albright, 1988; Tennyson, Miller, Skovholt, & Williams, 1989; Wilgus

& Shelley, 1988). Common themes from those surveys are presented here (Baker, Kessler, Bishop & Giles, 1993).

Clear, consistent themes emerged. The most common challenges are as follows: (a) The role of school counselors is not well defined; (b) student-to-counselor ratios are too high; (c) counselors are engaged in auxiliary work too often; and (d) different publics have conflicting expectations (e.g, students want counselors, parents want consultants, teachers want faculty advocates, and principals want administrative assistants). Some unfortunate influences of these challenges are that many students may view counselors as too busy with paperwork to see them, parents may perceive counselors as ineffective, teachers may distance themselves from counselors, and principals may under- or overvalue counselors for the wrong reasons. Some counselors may acquiesce to these conditions and become minimally effective professionals. Others may become frustrated and leave the profession. Yet others may adjust in a manner that makes them as effective as they can be but less effective than they might be. Johnson (2000) attests to the currency of this situation:

> After decades of struggling through a virtual role-identity crisis, it is time for school counselors to recognize their operational existence by revisiting their stated purpose, functions, and relationship within the system. The new millennium affords transformative opportunities for school counselors to refine their professional identity as highly trained practitioners, whose goal is to facilitate all students to become effective learners through the provision of a contemporary, integrated school counseling program that promotes the achievement of developmentally based competencies across academic, career, and personal-social domains. (p. 32)

The enduring nature of this role confusion indicates that school counselors and counselor educators were not very successful in meeting the challenge during the twentieth century. Perhaps professional self-advocacy, the road less traveled, is the approach that needs to be emphasized in the twenty-first century. Although advocacy directed toward achieving universal recognition of the desired identity for school counselors by individual counselors and counselors within school systems is necessary, it is probably also not sufficient (Baker et al., 1993). A profession that agrees on its mission, role, and functions may be more likely to achieve dramatic change collectively rather than individually. Advocacy for this purpose must occur in each locality *and* collectively, beginning at the grass roots (Baker, 2001).

The following vignette is based on recommendations found in Johnson (2000). Our case describes a group of school counselors who decide to become advocates for their own professional identity.

Summary.   The scenario that we present can conceivably happen anywhere, and we hope it will happen in numerous school systems. A group of school counselors within a school system decided to advocate for themselves as primary players in their educational system. Their first step was to conduct internal discussions among themselves and determine a shared, clear vision that consisted of goals and objectives for the program, functions required to achieve those goals, and the estimated time and resources required to achieve those goals.

This first step was carried out as follows. The counselors conducted a needs assessment—that is, of students, teachers, parents, administrators, and community members. A more detailed coverage of needs assessments is found in chapter 13. The needs assessment data were used to identify goals for their program (e.g., What outcomes do we want to achieve over the next five years?). This led to writing a mission statement that reflected their vision for the future, one that can be understood by their publics and used when promoting their cause. Next, they developed a school counseling program plan outlining objectives, activities, services, and expected outcomes across all grade levels. They established a calendar designating what services would be provided and when. The counselors included professional development for themselves within the plan. Going into more detail, the counselors created formal job descriptions for themselves at each level. They invited input from school administrators, union officials, professional organizations, and state legislative and education department representatives. Finally, the counselors selected a strong leader for their unit, someone who could be their advocate throughout the school system.

The second step was to determine a strategy for promoting the plan that had been developed. This led to an ongoing public relations campaign designed to inform students, parents, teachers, administrators, the community, and the school board. All components of the plan were systematically integrated. The strategy included: (a) presentations about the role of the school counseling program and accountability data about the effects of its services; (b) membership in school-community-based committees and publication of a newsletter for parents and the community that informed readers about program goals, roles, and accomplishments; (c) development of a booklet that informed readers about specific services to special populations; (d) visits to all classrooms in the fall to introduce the counseling program to teachers and students; (e) preparation of an annual accountability report that was distributed to building and central administrators, the school board, and appropriate parent and community groups; (f) invitations to teachers and administrators to visit classroom guidance sessions; (g) arrangements with local service clubs and organizations to offer counselors as speakers on topics related to the mission; (h) development of professional portfolios for each counselor to be made available to the public; and (i) a website that provided information about the mission, accountability data, a calendar of school counseling activities, and links for students and the community.

Analysis.   The counselors in this vignette appeared to believe in themselves and the value of their program. They were proactive in their efforts, united as a team, and clear about their goals. They worked their way through a plan to achieve their goals systematically and became advocates for themselves and their profession. Indirectly, they were also advocates for their students, schools, and community, all of whom would become beneficiaries of the accomplishments of the program. The plan was based on an awareness of good practice derived from professional standards. Their strategy for promoting the plan was multifaceted and reached out to all their publics. The public relations efforts exposed their important services to the various publics, were enhanced by accountability data, and brought attention to their mission. Since this is a hypothetical vignette, we cannot report on the actual outcomes. We believe that professional advocacy strategies of this nature have excellent potential for successful outcomes.

We believe that grassroots efforts such as were depicted in this vignette are necessary for the school counseling profession to enhance itself in the twenty-first century. In addition, counselor educators and national professional organizations, such as the ASCA and ACA and their affiliates, will benefit from working together. The next generation of school counselors will have to be more active than their predecessors if the counselor role challenge is to be resolved. That resolution will require being active rather than passive in responding to the challenges, being informed, being committed to providing the best possible counseling services, becoming skilled at being successful advocates, and supporting the efforts of national professional counseling associations that are directed toward achieving uniformity and clarity in the school counselor's role.

SUGGESTED ACTIVITIES

1. Browse through back issues of *ASCA Counselor* or *Counseling Today,* the newsletters of the American School Counselor Association and the American Counseling Association, respectively; make an inventory of advocacy issues related to its articles.
2. Read several articles in *ASCA Counselor* or *Counseling Today* back issues. Try to determine what, if any, philosophical trends run through the articles that might suggest whether the American School Counselor Association and the American Counseling Association are consistent in their philosophy.
3. Take an inventory of your personal stance on social problems on the following scale:
   reactionary . . . conservative . . . moderate . . . liberal . . . radical
   Discuss these views in class.
4. Use the same scale to rate yourself on specific issues.
5. Use the same scale to rate yourself as an advocate.
6. If you have activist leanings, take stock of your chance of being successful versus turning others off or being impatient and undiplomatic. Do you need to make changes, or do you believe that confrontation is the best first option? Support your answer.
7. Organize a debate among classmates on question 6.
8. Make an inventory of general strategies that counselors might use in the schools to initiate change diplomatically and without being perceived as a threat by the system.
9. Make an inventory of current and future issues in the schools that are most likely to require advocacy to resolve.
10. Debate the merits of Menacker's idea that "activist counselors may achieve empathy through direct, concrete helping activities."
11. Go to www.scan21st.com and propose some ways that this Internet site might help school counselors become more effective advocates.

REFERENCES

Adelman, H. S., & Taylor, L. (2002). School counselors and school reform: New directions. *Professional School Counseling, 5,* 235–248.

Arredondo, P., & D'Andrea, M. (1995, September). AMCD approves multicultural counseling competency standards. *Counseling Today,* pp. 28–29, 32.

Arredondo, P., & D'Andrea, M. (2001, April). Changing paradigms in organizations. *Counseling Today,* pp. 38, 44.

Arredondo, P., & D'Andrea, M. (2002, June). What do culturally competent practices look like? *Counseling Today,* pp. 28, 32.

Aubrey, R. E. (1977). Historical development of guidance and counseling and implications for the future. *Personnel and Guidance Journal, 55,* 288–295.

Baker, S. B. (2001). Reflections on forty years in the school counseling profession: Is the glass half full or half empty? *Professional School Counseling, 5,* 75–83.

Baker, S. B., Kessler, B. L., Bishop, R. M., & Giles, G. N. (1993). *School counselor role: A proposal for ridding the profession of an "old ghost."* Unpublished manuscript, Penn State University, University Park.

Bartholomew, C. G., & Schnorr, D. L. (1994). Gender equity: Suggestions for broadening career options of female students. *School Counselor, 41,* 245–256.

Bauman, S., & Sachs-Kapp, P. (1998). A school takes a stand: Promotion of sexual orientation workshops by counselors. *Professional School Counseling, 1*(3), 42–45.

Black, J., & Underwood, J. (1998). Young, female, and gay: Lesbian students and the school environment. *Professional School Counseling, 1*(3), 15–20.

Boser, J. A., Poppen, W. A., & Thompson, C. L. (1988). Elementary school guidance evaluation: A reflection of student–counselor ratio. *School Counselor, 36,* 125–135.

Bradley, L., & Lewis, J. (2000). Introduction. In J. Lewis & L. Bradley (Eds.), *Advocacy in counseling: Counselors, client & community* (pp. 3–4). Greensboro, NC: ERIC Clearinghouse on Counseling and Student Services.

Brewer, J. M. (1932). *Education as guidance.* New York: Macmillan.

Carmichael, L., & Calvin, L. (1970). Functions selected by school counselors. *School Counselor, 17,* 280–285.

Casas, J. M., & Furlong, M. J. (1994). School counselors as advocates for increased Hispanic parent participation in schools. In P. Pedersen & J. C. Carey (Eds.), *Multicultural counseling in schools: A practical handbook* (pp. 121–156). Boston: Allyn & Bacon.

Cooley, J. J. (1998). Gay and lesbian adolescents: Presenting problems and the counselor's role. *Professional School Counseling, 1*(3), 30–34.

Cremin, L. A. (1965). The progressive heritage of the guidance movement. In R. L. Mosher, R. E. Carle, & C. D. Kehas (Eds.), *Guidance: An examination* (pp. 3–12). New York: Harcourt, Brace & World.

D'Andrea, M., & Daniels, J. (1997). Continuing the discussion about racism: A reaction by D'Andrea and Daniels. *ACES Spectrum, 58*(2), 8–9.

Dinsmore, J. A., Chapman, A., & McCollum, V. J. C. (2000, March). *Client advocacy and social justice: Strategies for developing trainee competence.* Paper presented at the Annual Conference of the American Counseling Association, Washington, DC.

Dinsmore, J. A., Chapman, A., & McCollum, V. J. C. (2002, March). *Client advocacy and social justice: Strategies for developing trainee competence.* Paper presented at the Annual Conference of the American Counseling Association, New Orleans, LA.

Fagan, T., & Wallace, A. (1979). Who are the handicapped? *Personnel and Guidance Journal, 58,* 215–220.

Fontaine, J. H. (1998). Evidencing a need: School counselors' experiences with gay and lesbian students. *Professional School Counseling, 1*(3), 8–14.

Gibbs, J. T. (1973). Black students/White university: Different expectations. *Personnel and Guidance Journal, 51,* 463–470.

Gibson, R. L. (1990). Teachers' opinions of high school guidance and counseling programs: Then and now. *School Counselor, 37,* 248–255.

Gibson, R. L., & Mitchell, M. H. (1981). *Introduction to guidance.* New York: Macmillan.

Greer, B. B., Greer, J. G., & Woody, D. E. (1995). The inclusion movement and its impact on counselors. *School Counselor, 43,* 24–132.

Gunnings, T. S. (1978). Guidance and counseling in special settings. In *The status of guidance and counseling in the nation's schools* (pp. 147–156). Washington, DC: American Personnel and Guidance Association.

Gysbers, N. C., & Henderson, P. (2001). Comprehensive guidance and counseling programs: A rich history and a bright future. *Professional School Counseling, 4,* 246–256.

Haettenschwiller, D. L. (1971). Counseling Black college students in special programs. *Personnel and Guidance Journal, 50,* 29–36.

Hanish, L. D., & Guerra, N. G. (2000). Children who get victimized at school: What is known? What can be done? *Professional School Counseling, 4,* 113–119.

Hansen, L. S. (1968). Are we change agents? *School Counselor, 15,* 245–246.

Harris, P. R. (1967). Guidance and counseling: Where it's been—Where it's going. *School Counselor, 15,* 10–15.

Helms, B. J., & Ibrahim, F. A. (1985). A comparison of counselor and parent perceptions of the role and function of secondary school counselors. *School Counselor, 32,* 266–274.

Herr, E. L. (1979). *Guidance and counseling in the schools: Perspectives on the past, present, and future.* Falls Church, VA: American Personnel and Guidance Association.

Herring, R. D. (1997a). *Counseling diverse and ethnic youth: Synergistic strategies and interventions for school counselors.* Ft. Worth, TX: Harcourt Brace College Publishers.

Herring, R. D. (1997b). *Multicultural counseling in schools: A synergistic approach.* Alexandria, VA: American Counseling Association.

Hourcade, J. J., & Parette, H. P., Jr. (1986). Students with epilepsy: Counseling implications for the hidden handicapped. *School Counselor, 33,* 279–285.

House, R. M., & Hayes, R. L. (2002). School counselors: Becoming key players in school reform. *Professional School Counseling, 5,* 249–256.

Humes, C. W., II (1978). School counselors and PL 94–142. *School Counselor, 25,* 192–195.

Hutchinson, R. L., Barrick, A. L., & Groves, M. (1986). Functions of secondary school counselors in the schools: Ideal and real. *School Counselor, 34,* 87–91.

Hutchinson, R. L., & Bottorf, R. L. (1986). Selected high school counseling services: 1986 student assessment. *School Counselor, 53,* 350–354.

Hutchinson, R. L., & Reagan, C. A. (1989). Problems for which seniors would seek help from school counselors. *School Counselor, 36,* 271–279.

Johnson, L. S. (2000). Promoting professional identity in an era of educational reform. *Professional School Counseling, 4,* 31–40.

Kiselica, M. S., & Robinson, M. (2001). Bringing advocacy counseling to life: The history, issues, and human dramas of social justice. *Journal of Counseling & Development, 79,* 387–397.

Knapp, D. L., & Denny, E. W. (1961). The counselor's responsibility in role definition. *Personnel and Guidance Journal, 40,* 48–50.

Kopala, M., Esquivel, G., & Baptiste, L. (1994). Counseling approaches for immigrant children: Facilitating the acculturative process. *School Counselor, 41,* 352–359.

LaFromboise, T., & Jackson, M. (1996). MCT theory and Native American populations. In D. W. Sue, A. E. Ivey, & P. B. Pedersen (Eds.), *A theory of multicultural counseling and therapy* (pp. 192–203). Pacific Grove, CA: Brooks/Cole.

Lee, C. C. (1998). Counselors as agents for social change. In C. C. Lee & G. R. Walz (Eds.), *Social action: A mandate for counselors* (pp. 3–16). Alexandria, VA: American Counseling Association.

Lee, C. C. (2001). Culturally responsive school counselors and programs: Addressing the needs of all students. *Professional School Counseling, 4,* 257–262.

Lee, C. C., & Sirch, M. L. (1994). Counseling in an enlightened society: Values for a new millennium. *Counseling and Values, 38,* 90–97.

Logan, C., & Williams, C. B. (2001, April). Ethical issues in counseling gay youth. *Counseling Today,* pp. 41–42.

Luftig, R. L. (1983). Effects of schooling on the self-concept of Native American students. *School Counselor, 30,* 251–260.

Marinoble, R. M. (1998). A blind spot in the mirror. *Professional School Counseling, 1*(3), 4–7.

McFarland, W. P. (1998). Gay, lesbian, and bisexual student suicide. *Professional School Counseling, 1*(3), 26–29.

McFarland, W. P., & DuPuis, M. (2001). The legal duty to protect gay and lesbian students from violence in school. *Professional School Counseling, 4,* 171–179.

Menacker, J. (1974). *Vitalizing guidance in urban schools.* New York: Dodd, Mead.

Menacker, J. (1976). Toward a theory of activist guidance. *Personnel and Guidance Journal, 54,* 318–321.

Miller, G. D. (1989). What roles and functions do elementary school counselors have? *Elementary School Guidance and Counseling, 24,* 77–88.

Moles, O. C. (1991). Guidance programs in American high schools; A descriptive portrait. *School Counselor, 38,* 163–177.

Morse, C. L., & Russell, T. (1988). How elementary counselors see their role: An empirical study. *Elementary School Guidance and Counseling, 23,* 54–62.

Muller, L. E., & Hartman, J. (1998). Group counseling for sexual minority youth. *Professional School Counseling, 1*(3), 38–41.

Omizo, M. M., Omizo, S. A., & Okamoto, C. M. (1998). Gay and lesbian adolescents: A phenomenological study. *Professional School Counseling, 1*(3), 35–37.

Pallas, A. M., Natriello, G., & McDill, E. L. (1989). The changing nature of the disadvantaged population: Current dimensions and future trends. *Educational Researcher, 18*(5), 16–22.

Pedersen, J. S. (1988). Constraining influences on the vocational guidance of girls from 1910 to 1930. *Career Development Quarterly, 36,* 325–336.

Peer, G. G. (1985). The status of secondary school guidance: A national survey. *School Counselor, 32,* 181–189.

Ponzo, Z. (1974). A counselor and change: Reminiscence and resolutions. *Personnel and Guidance Journal, 53,* 27–32.

Remafedi, G. (1987). Adolescent homosexuality: Psychosocial and medical implications. *Pediatrics, 79,* 331–337.

Remafedi, G., Farrow, J. A., & Deisher, R. W. (1991). Risk factors in attempted suicide in gay and bisexual youth. *Pediatrics, 87,* 869–875.

Remley, T. P., Jr., & Albright, P. L. (1988). Expectations for middle school counselors: Views of students, teachers, principals, and parents. *School Counselor, 35,* 290–296.

Roberts, W. B., Jr., & Morotti, A. A. (2000). The bully as victim: Understanding bully behaviors to increase the effectiveness of interventions in the bully-victim dyad. *Professional School Counseling, 4,* 148–155.

Rogler, L. H., Malgady, R. G., Constantino, G., & Blumenthal, R. (1987). What do culturally sensitive mental health services mean? The case of Hispanics. *American Psychologist, 42,* 565–570.

Rousseve, R. J. (1968). The role of the counselor in a free society. *School Counselor, 16,* 6–10.

Ruiz, R. A., & Padilla, A. M. (1977). Counseling Latinos. *Personnel and Guidance Journal, 55,* 401–408.

Sandhu, D. S. (2000). Foreward. *Professional School Counseling, 4,* iv.

Sarbin, T. R. (1954). Role theory. In G. Lindzey (Ed.), *Handbook of social psychology.* London: Addison-Wesley.

Shaw, M. C. (1968). The function of theory in guidance programs. *Guidance Monograph Series I.* Boston: Houghton Mifflin.

Shertzer, B., & Stone, S. (1963). The school counselor and his publics: A problem in role definitions. *Personnel and Guidance Journal, 41,* 687–693.

Smith, G. E. (1955). *Counseling in the secondary school.* New York: Macmillan.

Stewart, L. H., & Warnath, C. F. (1965). *The counselor and society.* Boston: Houghton Mifflin.

Stone, S. C., & Shertzer, B. (1963). The militant counselor. *Personnel and Guidance Journal, 42,* 342–347.

Sue, D. W. (1992). The challenge of multiculturalism: The road less traveled. *American Counselor, 1,* 7–14.

Sue, D. W., Arredondo, P., & McDavis, R. J. (1992). Multicultural competencies/standards: A pressing need. *Journal of Counseling & Development, 70,* 477–486.

Tennyson, W. W., Miller, G. D., Skovholt, T. M., & Williams, R. C. (1989). How they view their role: A survey of counselors in different secondary schools. *Journal of Counseling & Development, 67,* 399–403.

Vontress, C. (1966). *Counseling the culturally different adolescent: A school community approach.* Moravia, NY: Chronicle Guidance Publications.

Wilgus, E., & Shelley, V. (1988). The role of the elementary school counselor: Teacher perceptions, expectations, and actual functions. *School Counselor, 35,* 259–266.

Willower, D. J., Hoy, W. K., & Eidell, T. L. (1967). The counselor and the school as a social organization. *Personnel and Guidance Journal, 46,* 228–234.

Wrenn, C. G. (1962). *The counselor in a changing world.* Washington, DC: American Personnel and Guidance Association.

CHAPTER 12

Leadership and Collaboration in School Counseling

Goal: To discuss and advocate the role of leadership and collaboration in school counseling and identify leadership and collaboration competencies.

Some years ago one of our prized graduate students was invited to do an internship at an inner-city school that had no school counselor. The school had a nurse and was served by a school psychologist but never had built a school counseling program of any kind. The new principal of the school had a counseling degree and was anxious to hire school counselors and to begin a counseling program at her school. She agreed to supervise our intern.

The intern eagerly accepted the challenge of this special situation. She quickly learned, however, that the parents at the school did not understand school counseling and were not eager to waste school resources on a program that was unfamiliar to them. Several parents complained to the principal that having an inexperienced intern work with their children was simply a ploy to begin a school counseling program.

Undaunted by the complaints from parents and supported by a courageous principal, the intern launched a public relations campaign for her school counseling efforts. She worked to receive speaking invitations at church meetings in the community, at social organizations, and at business groups. Her speeches reflected her sense of humor, her dedication to the counseling profession, and her commitment to serving students. At the end of 6 weeks, her skillful leadership had won over a school community to the importance of having a counseling program. The program has grown and matured over the years and is currently thriving.

Individuals often enter school counselor preparation programs because they want to work closely with students, parents, and teachers. Seldom do these aspiring counselors consider the leadership skills that are required to build and maintain successful school counseling programs. This chapter focuses on school counselors as leaders and collaborators.

DEMAND FOR LEADERSHIP AND COLLABORATION IN SCHOOL COUNSELING

The call for leadership and collaboration in school counseling is something of a twenty-first-century phenomenon. Leadership has not been a traditional function in the repertoire of school counselors. Spokespersons for each of the three initiatives presented in chapter 1 have indicated that leadership and collaboration are requisite functions for school counselors and school counseling programs because of the circumstances that exist in the world, in the nation, in communities, and in schools. We present here summaries of the three positions. Each has its own underlying reasons for promoting leadership and collaboration. Combined, the reasons generated by the three initiatives are, in our opinion, more compelling than any one is alone.

Representing the ASCA's National Model for Comprehensive School Counseling Programs (One Vision One Voice), Lapan, Kardash, and Turner (2002) state: "School counselors have a central leadership role to play in working with teachers and students to increase the use of effective learning strategies thus encouraging more self-regulated learning" (p. 264). Gysbers and Henderson (2000) call for school counselors to take the primary leadership role in organizing and managing comprehensive school counseling programs.

The primary emphasis of the leadership function in the ASCA initiative seems to be on taking charge of the planning, initiating, and managing of comprehensive school counseling programs and the associated guidance curriculums. By so doing, students will benefit. The leadership function begins around and within the school counseling programs themselves. This, in turn, requires collaboration with administrators, teachers, students, families, and the greater community to achieve the program goals.

In the National School Counselor Training Initiative, House and Hayes (2002) call for proactive leaders who advocate for the success of all students. As leaders, school counselors are to advocate for equal opportunity for all students to achieve high aspirations. Collaboration involves counselors with students, parents, education professionals, and community agencies to build a sense of community.

This initiative appears to focus on leadership in relation to the current educational reform movement. That is, school counselors are called to be leaders in efforts to ensure that all students have equal access to rigorous academic programs and, therefore, to success in life.

Adelman and Taylor (2002), presenting for the School–Community Collaboration Model, state that "school counselors and all other school personnel concerned must find their way to leadership tables so that system-wide changes are designed and implemented" (p. 240). The goal is to connect schools, families, and communities (Taylor & Adelman, 2000). As leaders, school counselors will establish collaborations that connect schools with home and community resources. In so doing, considerable effort will be required to link health and human services with the schools.

In this initiative, the leadership emphasis appears to be on linking schools with community services in order to achieve the school-community collaboration. This approach focuses on the perceived need to enhance the services available to students and their families in order to respond to social, emotional, and physical health barriers to student academic success by bringing outside services into the schools.

BASIC INGREDIENTS OF LEADERSHIP AND COLLABORATION IN SCHOOL COUNSELING

Are leaders born or made? This question has been studied for some time, and we do not intend to address it in this edition of the textbook. We are aware that leadership has not traditionally been treated as an important function in the training of school counselors. Indeed, we believe that many individuals who entered school counseling previously did not view themselves as leaders. Otherwise, they may have entered training programs for educational administrators.

There also are conditions in the schools that make leadership a challenge for school counselors. Haettenschwiller (1971) describes counselors as being in a weak or boundary position within the power and status framework of the schools, receiving demands from parents, administrators, and teachers who are able to bestow both positive and negative sanctions. Furthermore, school counselors may often find themselves in environments where some of their more influential colleagues and supervisors have beliefs that are contrary to the counselors' preferences and ideals (Willower, Hoy, & Eidell, 1967). This may cause them to be silent or pay lip service to the preferences of their more dominant colleagues.

It seems as if some individuals are by nature and nurture more likely to seek or respond to leadership opportunities successfully. Others may not want to be, or be capable of being, good leaders. With regard to school counselors already in the field, perhaps the best thing that can be done is to inform and attempt to motivate them about the importance of leadership and help them if they are so inclined. With regard to future students, counselor educators who believe in the importance of leadership can attempt to select individuals who are willing and able to be leaders as well as

Are leaders born or made?

become competent in all the other aspects of the profession. Having done so, they can then provide training opportunities that enhance the potential to be successful leaders. Perhaps practicum and internship experiences will help. On the other hand, it may not be until counseling students are on the job in the real world that they will have the opportunity to emerge as leaders. Then, they will have to be both willing and able.

COMPETENCIES IN BASIC LEADERSHIP AND COLLABORATION IN SCHOOL COUNSELING

It appears to us that the basic competencies are rather complex combinations of many specific behaviors. We have derived a set of behaviors that seem appropriate for leaders and collaborators. We also believe that these behaviors will be appropriate when used successfully. Using the behaviors successfully depends on a combination of one's genetic proclivities and one's socialization. It is not necessary to exhibit all the following behaviors in order to be a leader because there are numerous ways one can lead, depending on the circumstances. For example, one person may exhibit leadership qualities by taking charge during the process of developing and implementing a school counseling program. Another individual may demonstrate leadership in more subtle ways, such as being a mediator during a dispute, recruiting volunteers for collaborations, or helping community and school representatives build a sense of community. The following behaviors were taken from the work of Adelman and Taylor (2002), Bemak (2000), Bemak and Cornely (2002), Dahir (2001), Gysbers and Henderson (2000, 2001), Hatch and Bowers (2002), House and Hayes (2002), Keys (2000), and Rowley, Sink, and MacDonald (2002). The order in which they are presented does not reflect an opinion of their importance. We have tried to order them in a manner that makes sense to us. A leader in school counseling should be able to:

- Cause, lead, implement, and maintain a comprehensive school counseling program.
- Form and lead committees, including chairing committees, planning agendas, and establishing meeting schedules.
- Coordinate the objectives, strategies, and activities of a comprehensive school counseling program.
- Serve as a missionary for the program.
- Develop mechanisms for educating and involving others.
- Develop support systems for yourself and other school counseling personnel.
- Conduct meetings, make commitments for action, form and convene steering committees, form and convene school and community advisory committees, establish work groups, and meet with district administrators and school boards.
- Demonstrate leadership skills as an active member of programs and committees.
- Identify and use complementary skills.
- Mediate conflicts.
- Recognize differences such as race, gender, experience, preferred learning styles, and work roles and use that information to engage in creative problem solving even though it may involve conflict.
- Recognize opportunities for empowerment.
- Know how work groups operate, especially teams, and how to build effective teams.
- Recruit volunteers to assist in school programs.
- Build a sense of community in the schools.
- Know how to effectively manage school and community bureaucracies.
- Build a consensus and work collaboratively with a broad range of professionals and concerned citizens in order to achieve a sense of community.
- Keep your fingers on the pulse of the needs of students and on the mission and goals of the school.
- Adopt a systems perspective.
- Facilitate family-school partnerships.
- Break down bureaucratic turf boundaries.
- Work collaboratively with school administrators.
- Bring community services into the schools and coordinate them.
- Develop mutual prevention/intervention programs with community agencies.
- Work closely with other support personnel in the schools (e.g., school psychologists, school social workers, nurses, and special educators).

- Support, consult, and work with teachers.
- Collect and share data (e.g., document obstacles to student growth and development).
- Develop a crisis team that is educated in emergency response procedures.
- Inform administrators about the contributions you plan to make rather than asking them what to do.

EXAMPLES OF LEADERSHIP AND COLLABORATION BY SCHOOL COUNSELORS

Transforming the School Culture: An Example of Leadership

This vignette is based on a report by Littrell and Peterson (2001) about an elementary-school counselor in Oregon whose goal was to transform the school's culture from one of negativity and high stress to one of problem solving at all levels. The counselor had a vision of a school in which all children were problem solvers. Littrell and Peterson depicted the counselor as having a guiding vision, defined values and beliefs, a willingness to confront the school about her vision, and the ability to clarify how she functions in the system.

We do not know the exact sequence of steps in which the counselor engaged. The following specific acts of leadership were reported by Littrell and Peterson. The counselor adopted a four-step problem-solving model that helped her to think systematically. Through a combination of previous experience, meetings, and consultation, she learned about and understood the school climate. Having a vision and knowledge of the school climate, the counselor introduced "a new, but natural and familiar, 'language' that was easy for all to understand—the language of problem solving" (Littrell & Peterson, 2001, p. 314). For example, she would ask such questions as "What is the problem?" and "What have you tried so far?" Through teaching the language of problem solving, she bonded with students. Eventually, parents picked up the problem-solving language as well.

Eventually, the counselor designed and implemented a developmental curriculum that was based on problem solving. For example, second graders learned 10 ways to solve conflicts. Having established a problem-solving curriculum in classrooms, the counselor also found ways to implement the curriculum content elsewhere (e.g., a problem-solving wheel in the principal's office). In response to numerous referrals by teachers of students who were classroom behavior problems, the counselor created several counseling groups or clubs, beginning with six that were topic focused (e.g., students who get everything done and want to do more and students who need to develop their own unique strengths).

The counselor's systematic approach led to identifying four factors that influenced her individual counseling: (a) accenting client strengths, (b) providing a caring relationship, (c) knowing her counseling theories and techniques, and (d) providing hope. Viewing the entire school as a community, the counselor built partnerships at all levels (e.g., the lunchroom supervisor, the new junior-high-school counselor, teachers, and parents). As a leader, the counselor engaged in advocacy activities such as lobbying legislators in order to influence policy and mobilizing local merchants to acquire clothing for poor children. The report also highlighted the counselor's effectiveness at planning and organizing, her attempts to ensure self-renewal, and an incidence of her efforts being self-sustaining six years later.

Littrell and Peterson (2001) conclude their report as follows:

> [She] was not a perfect counselor; however, we chose to study her because her work as a school counselor was exemplary and inspiring. The uniqueness of our model is in the emphasis on the counselor as a person and on the counselor's ability to assess the context and align vision, identity, beliefs/values, capabilities, and behaviors in the interest of creatively conceiving and realizing a programmatic vision. Our hope is that this model helps counselors to be visionary educational leaders. (p. 318)

School-Based Clinicians: An Example of Collaboration

The following vignette was derived from a report by Porter, Epp, and Bryant (2000). The school-based clinicians in the vignette are part of a larger program sponsored by the Community Psychiatry Department of Johns Hopkins University in Baltimore, Maryland. The Johns Hopkins program partnership includes the departments of social services, juvenile justice, health, and police, and the mental health clinicians include professional counselors, psychologists, arts therapists, and social workers.

Our example took place in an urban high school in which the clinician was a welcome guest because of high incidences of challenging mental health problems. The clinician worked with the difficult mental health cases in order to allow the school counselors to provide developmental guidance and college counseling services to a broad range of students.

The school's director of guidance implemented a collaborative system that could be established in other schools. She created a school mental health team that consisted of all the school counselors, a vice principal, a school nurse, a faculty member, and the school-based clinician. The guidance director chaired the committee and served as coordinator.

The school was referring clients to a clinician from an outside agency that was being paid by Medicaid. Therefore, a system of oversight and referral was needed. According to Porter et al. (2000), the committee was egalitarian, multidisciplinary, and free of turf battles. On the other hand, there were a number of challenges from within the school and the community. For example, the magnitude of presenting problems challenged the committee to figure out how to respond within the confines of their resources and not become overwhelmed. Also, some members of the faculty were less than friendly and cooperative, and the committee had to engage in quiet diplomacy in that domain. Occasionally, the committee faced dilemmas about which they were divided (e.g., reporting child abuse) and had to recognize the value of their common mission.

Porter et al. teased out the following lessons about collaboration that can overcome the potential barriers: (a) use the multidisciplinary team meetings to solve problems and make decisions, (b) ensure cultural sensitivity of clinicians through training, (c) develop a common language across the represented disciplines, (d) develop open and flexible attitudes, and (e) standardize procedures. Porter et al. (2000) conclude:

> School counselors are in a unique position to facilitate the collaborative process needed to ensure the provision of comprehensive, accessible mental health services. Collaboration is a major challenge, but when professionals are able to use their varied skills and experiences in a complimentary, collaborative way, they can transcend any barriers. (p. 322)

SCHOOL COUNSELORS AS LEADERS AND COLLABORATORS

We find the potential for school counselors to be leaders and collaborators as just depicted exciting. School counseling is a human service career, and school counselors are exposed to numerous situations that challenge their ability to serve all clients who are in need. We believe that leadership and collaboration are avenues through which school counselors can be of greater service to a broad range of clients. Perhaps the most important ingredients are the desire and will to do so.

Work closely with other support personnel in the schools.

SUGGESTED ACTIVITIES

1. Debate the current assumption that school counselors should be leaders.
2. Interview one or more school counselors and ask their opinion about whether or not they should be leaders.
3. Follow up with the school counselors who believe that they should be leaders, and ask them to provide an inventory of circumstances in which they believe school counselor leadership is needed and appropriate.
4. Study the list of leadership characteristics in this chapter and make a checklist of those with which you agree. Also, check off those you believe you possess and those you believe you should try to acquire.
5. Discuss the interrelationships among leadership, collaboration, and advocacy.
6. Make an inventory of both your leadership strengths and challenges.
7. Working independently or collectively with colleagues, develop a profile of the characteristics of a school counselor who is a good leader.
8. Make an inventory of the risks associated with being a leader as a school counselor. Then, make an inventory of possible ways to prevent or minimize the risks while still being successful.
9. Make an inventory of the disadvantages associated with failing to provide leadership, collaboration, and advocacy as a school counselor. Then, make an inventory of the potential beneficiaries of good school counseling leadership. Finally, compare the two inventories and process your reactions to the comparisons.
10. Discuss the affect you feel when being called to be a leader in the school counseling profession.
11. Go to www.scan21st.com and propose some ways that this Internet site might assist school counselors in their roles as leaders and collaborators.

REFERENCES

Adelman, H. S., & Taylor, L. (2002). School counselors and school reform: New directions. *Professional School Counseling, 5,* 235–248.

Bemak, F. (2000). Transforming the role of the counselor to provide leadership in educational reform through collaboration. *Professional School Counseling, 3,* 323–331.

Bemak, F., & Cornely, L. (2002). The SAFI model as a critical link between marginalized families and schools: A literature review and strategies for school counselors. *Journal of Counseling & Development, 5,* 322–331.

Dahir, C. (2001). The National Standards for School Counseling Programs: Development and implementation. *Professional School Counseling, 4,* 320–327.

Gysbers, N. C., & Henderson, P. (2000). *Developing and managing your school guidance program* (3rd ed.). Alexandria, VA: American Counseling Association.

Gysbers, N. C., & Henderson, P. (2001). Comprehensive guidance and counseling programs: A rich history and a bright future. *Professional School Counseling, 4,* 246–256.

Haettenschwiller, D. L. (1971). Counseling Black college students in special programs. *Personnel and Guidance Journal, 50,* 29–36.

Hatch, T., & Bowers, J. (2002, May/June). The block to build on. *ASCA Counselor,* 13–17.

House, R. M., & Hayes, R. L. (2002). School counselors: Becoming key players in school reform. *Professional School Counseling, 5,* 249–256.

Keys, S. G. (2000). Living the collaborative role: Voices from the field. *Professional School Counseling, 3,* 332–338.

Lapan, R. T., Kardash, C. M., & Turner, S. (2002). Empowering students to become self-regulated learners. *Professional School Counseling, 5,* 257–265.

Littrell, J. M., & Peterson, J. S. (2001). Transforming the school culture: A model based on an exemplary counselor. *Professional School Counseling, 4,* 310–319.

Porter, G., Epp, L., & Bryant, S. (2000). Collaboration among school mental health professionals: A necessity, not a luxury. *Professional School Counseling, 3,* 315–322.

Rowley, W. J., Sink, C. A., & MacDonald, G. (2002). An experiential and systemic approach to encour-

age collaboration and community building. *Professional School Counseling, 5,* 360–365.

Taylor, L., & Adelman, H. S. (2000). Connecting schools, families, and communities. *Professional School Counseling, 3,* 298–307.

Willower, D. J., Hoy, W. K., & Eidell, T. L. (1967). The counselor and the school as a social organization. *Personnel and Guidance Journal, 46,* 228–234.

CHAPTER 13

Accountability in School Counseling

Goal: To promote comprehensive evaluation strategies and understandable, informative accountability information.

A group of school counselors in a local school system was asked to develop an Internet site that outlined the school counseling services offered across the school system. One requested feature for the site was a set of data documenting the successes attributed to school counseling programs. These data included school attendance, dropout figures, and other related documentation of school counseling's importance to the school system.

The initial concern of the school counselors was developing the Internet site. They had no experience creating web pages or transferring files to servers. This concern, however, was quickly resolved after a few consultation meetings with a graphic designer. The Internet site grew quickly and was widely praised across the school system. A persistent school superintendent, not swayed by the attractiveness of the site, continued to demand the display of data showing the benefits of school counseling. The counselors worked closely with the superintendent, were able to develop a suitable display, and were able to use the Internet site as a source for collecting additional data about their programs.

Professional educators across the United States are being asked to account for what they do. School counselors, in particular, must attend to documenting their value as partners in the community of educators.

DEMAND FOR ACCOUNTABILITY IN SCHOOL COUNSELING

As presented in this textbook, the words *evaluation* and *accountability* are neither interchangeable nor synonymous. Each represents an important ingredient of the accountability domain, and both functions are important. Each complements the other. "Collecting information about the effectiveness of services rendered represents evaluation. Using that information to demonstrate competence is accountability" (Baker, 1983, p. 52). *Evaluation* is the act of gathering information about one's services; *accountability* is the act of reporting the results of the evaluation. Evaluation precedes accountability. Translating evaluative data into accountability information completes the process and leads to accomplishing the goals of the accountability process.

Evaluation

Program evaluation has been a common theme in education in general, and school counseling in particular, for some time. Educators and counselor educators have espoused the idea when preparing students for careers in education and in counseling, and textbooks usually include chapters devoted to the topic. The failure of most counselors to engage in systematic evaluations of their programs has been one weakness of school counseling.

The American School Counselor Association (n.d.) recognized the importance of evaluation through a position statement that was adopted in 1978, reaffirmed in 1984, and revised in 1986. An excerpt from the statement follows:

> Since the primary purpose of the evaluation process is to assure the continued professional growth of school counselors, the ASCA is committed to the continued improvement of the process. It is recommended that each counselor be evaluated with regard to the implementation of the district's written counseling program and school counselor job description. The plan and the school counselor need to be evaluated and reviewed annually. The plan needs to contain specific goals along with objectives which emphasize student outcomes. (p. 41)

Notice the emphasis placed on having a written school district counseling program and job description and on reviewing it annually. This, of course, provides counselors with the opportunity to influence their roles and the evaluations of their work by being actively involved in the process of establishing job descriptions.

Why have school counselors, although apparently trained to evaluate their work, failed to do so effectively? When trying to answer this question, Shaw (1973) asserted that the reasons vary from situation to situation. He suggested, however, that common reasons include counselors being busy meeting daily demands, feeling confident that they are working hard and effectively, having attitudes that reject evaluation activities, failing to have appropriate role models, and working in settings where counseling programs operate without clearly stated goals. Another possible reason is related to this last idea. In many school systems, the counseling programs were established by administrative fiat; counselors performed services in response to the school administration. In that environment, many counselors wait for directives from above regarding evaluation activities.

More recently, Frith and Clark (1982) considered this problem and generated 10 common myths they thought prevent practitioners from evaluating their programs. Frith and Clark attribute these myths to irrational or self-defeating thoughts:

1. Evaluation requires sophisticated skills.
2. Extensive evaluations are too expensive for most school systems.
3. Students' opinions are not good sources of evaluation data.
4. Evaluations must be restricted to objective procedures.
5. Parents' opinions are not good sources of evaluation data.
6. Evaluation is too time-consuming.
7. Data-gathering requires large samples.
8. School administrators will not support extensive evaluations.
9. The primary purpose of evaluations is for research publications.
10. Extensive statistical analyses are required in order to interpret evaluation data.

Adding their viewpoint to this discussion, Bernard and Goodyear (1998) believe that counselors seem to have trouble with summative evaluation (evaluating the effects of their work). Two factors come to the forefront. One factor is that evaluation seems to be incompatible with the therapeutic models counselors use; that is, if counselor accountability is measured in terms of client progress toward goals, often the clients' goals are vague and changing and may be less ambitious than the counselors' goals for clients. The second factor is the ambiguity of the field about which methods represent good counseling practice and which criteria should be used to evaluate counselors. The field is still uncertain about which counseling methods are best for which clients under what conditions.

Accountability

The historical information in chapter 1 pointed out that the money from the National Defense Education Act of 1958, in combination with other factors, led to an expansion of school counseling programs. The 1970s brought changing times economically, and those changes influenced education. This highwater mark was signaled by Arbuckle (1970) in an article entitled "Does the School Really Need Counselors?" Presented as what seemed to be a challenge to the profession, Arbuckle's negative response to the title question included observations that a wide gap existed between the preparation and the actual practices of many school counselors; that the services rendered by school counselors are not unique and could be delivered by other professionals; that little or no research has been conducted on the effectiveness of school counselors; and that many working counselors demonstrate relatively little interest in their professional organizations, indicating little or no sense of professional identity or loyalty. Arbuckle's criticisms highlighted apparent shortcomings in a relatively young profession that needed time to right itself.

What followed was an era of accountability with a corresponding survival mentality. A spate of articles appeared in the school counseling literature thereafter, referring to the need for accountability. Some were thought-provoking articles on various aspects of evaluation and accountability (e.g., Baker, 1977; Bardo, Cody, & Bryson, 1979; Hays & Linn, 1977); others suggested procedures in the form of models or systems (e.g., Helliwell & Jones, 1975; Krumboltz, 1974; Miller & Grisdale, 1975).

Although some school counseling programs instituted improved evaluation systems and some individual counselors became more sophisticated than had previously been the case, evidence still indicated that many counselors resisted the idea when Lombana (1985) reported her findings. In the early 1980s, the accountability issue became embroiled in the national concern over excellence in education. One state, Mississippi, initiated an educational reform act that required a system for assessing the performances of all certified personnel working in the schools, including counselors. With permission from the Mississippi State Department of Education, the Mississippi Counseling Association (MCA) developed a set of 11 competencies and 42 indicators of performance of those competencies for elementary- and secondary-school counselors (Hously, McDaniel, & Underwood, 1990). A survey of 700 counselors indicated that, in general, the assessment process was a beneficial experience (Hously et al., 1990). The counselors were forced to participate by a legislative mandate, a professional organization representing the counselors took the initiative and developed an acceptable evaluation system, and the results—accountability data—were generally favorable rather than threatening.

Basic education receives its financial support from taxes paid by local, state, and national citizenries, all of whom want their money's worth. School boards are elected by the citizens of their school districts and have authority over budgetary and personnel matters. They seek to allocate limited financial resources in a businesslike manner. Therefore, it is imperative that they have accurate evidence of the effectiveness of the services in their educational enterprises so that they can make intelligent financial and personnel decisions. The demand for accountability, then, comes partially from school boards, and accountability is expected of all individuals employed by the school districts. This demand is imposed on counselors and their colleagues by their employers. The demand takes different forms across the nation's school districts. Because the demand for accountability varies with each school district, counselors have both the opportunity and the responsibility to influence the conduct of evaluations of their services. Not to do so will cause counselors to risk having others less knowledgeable about school counseling impose accountability systems that are inherently unfavorable and inaccurate.

The demand for accountability can also have personal and collegial origins. School counselors are professionals employed in a service occupation. They share responsibilities for providing high-quality services with other professionals such as teachers, administrators, and school psychologists. As professionals, they have a duty to abide by the standards of their profession and to uphold the traditions and maintain the reputation of that profession. To do so requires behaviors that include assessments of the needs of their clientele and of the quality and effectiveness of their own efforts, information to be used to discover ways to serve their clientele effectively. Therefore, claims to professionalism should be accompanied by efforts to assess client needs and to evaluate one's effectiveness in meeting those needs.

From the authors' perspective, it seems logical that all individuals gainfully employed, including school counselors, would want information providing evidence of their effectiveness with suggestions for positive changes. Receiving information about one's effectiveness is a challenging experience that ranges from the exhilaration of success to the depression of failed or misunderstood efforts. Responding to both extremes and all levels of evaluative information in between requires caution—not becoming too self-confident or self-deprecating—and objectivity—using the information constructively and knowing that the future will provide opportunities to improve or falter. Evaluative information offers counselors reinforcement for their appreciated and successful efforts and criticism, if documented sufficiently, that can be used constructively. Making the effort to initiate and control the evaluative methods that provide evidence of their accountability is a worthwhile endeavor for school counselors because then they will be able to dictate the range and depth of information they receive. Otherwise, those who know less about counseling will define the evaluations.

When school counselors are the decision-makers themselves, objectivity is of the utmost importance.

The demand for accountability is multifaceted. It comes from external and internal sources. Externally, the taxpaying public generally and parents/guardians specifically expect cost-effectiveness and desire high-quality services. More subtle external demands are associated with membership in, or implied association with, a profession that has published standards and achieved respectability. That recognition carries with it responsibilities, including being accountable to one's clientele. Internal demands for accountability are more personal. Assuming that all professional counselors are motivated, in part, by a desire to be of service, it stands to reason that they want feedback about those services. A desire for information about one's performance is a legitimate component of the accountability function for it is natural to want feedback. It is also natural to prefer positive over negative feedback. Therefore, using negative feedback constructively is an acquired skill. The overriding challenge for school counselors is to develop a response that meets all the demands for accountability. One goal of this chapter is to provide useful suggestions for meeting those demands.

Spokespersons for the three initiatives for enhancing school counseling that were introduced in chapter 1 all highlight the importance of evaluation and accountability in school counseling. For the ASCA's National Model for Comprehensive School Counseling Programs, Bowers, Hatch, and Schwallie-Giddis (2001) stress the importance of a data-driven evaluation/accountability system, and Dahir (2001) points out that the ASCA National Standards are measurable indicators of student achievement in academic, career, and personal-social development. Furthermore, Gysbers and Henderson (2001) state that program evaluation is a responsive service that may lead to continuing development and updating of the guidance curriculum.

House and Hayes (2002), representing the Education Trust's National School Counselor Training Initiative, point out that accountability for school success is everyone's responsibility. If school counselors are part of a comprehensive program in which the mission and vision focus on improving school success, then they may be able to document how they helped participate in the process of achieving improvement. That is, measurable evaluation data leading to evidence of accountability would be increasing numbers of students completing school who are academically prepared to choose from a wide range of substantive postsecondary options, including college.

For the School–Community Collaboration Model, Adelman and Taylor (2002) stress the importance of empirically supported, cost-effective interventions that will improve the state of the art in school counseling. Action research data from such interventions will provide evidence of accountability.

INGREDIENTS OF THE ACCOUNTABILITY FUNCTION

Given the busy environment in which school counselors find themselves, evaluation activities need to be convenient and efficient. Also, given the press of external demands for accountability, supporting data need to be comprehensive, informative, and understandable to noncounseling professionals and laypeople. Finally, accountability data are most helpful when used constructively.

Convenient and Efficient Evaluation

Accountability activities will be less burdensome and aversive if fitted in with all other counseling activities. One important factor to be controlled is the amount of time devoted to evaluation and accountability activities; it would be ridiculously cost-inefficient to spend an inordinate amount of time collecting and reporting information about one's own performance. It would also be cost-inefficient and demoralizing for counselors to have to engage in antiquated, burdensome, and time-consuming data-collecting behaviors. Time can be better managed and convenience enhanced if data collection and reporting are streamlined and systematic.

A second important factor to be controlled is the procedure for collecting data. To avoid demoralization and increase efficiency, the procedures can be made convenient by streamlining the process and using systems that are not overly sophisticated and confusing. The systems and procedures should be commensurate with the basic training that school counselors at the master's level have received. Specific suggestions for the basic training of school counselors are offered later in this chapter.

Comprehensive Accountability Data

Comprehensiveness is a desirable characteristic of the accountability function because the services provided by school counselors have many facets, and school counselors have a varied set of publics to serve. Therefore, no one approach to evaluation is broad enough to be all-encompassing. Indeed, to rely on a narrow repertoire of evaluation approaches is to risk missing important information, underserving one's publics, and being judged unfairly. Following is an inventory of recommended categories of evaluation data that together represent a comprehensive set of approaches.

Assess Consumer Needs. In a service occupation such as school counseling, it is important to find out what the expectations and needs of the consumers are. Theoretically, the consumers of school counseling are the children and adolescents served by the school district. Realistically, parents, guardians, school board members, and all the citizenry have expectations of the school counselor, too. Therefore, school counselors are challenged to find ways to learn what all these consumers need and expect. Whether the needs and expectations of the consumers are legitimate is a moot point. School counselors will be better decision makers and more able to serve their consumers if they are aware of the range of expectations and needs that exist among their consumers. It will then be possible to separate the legitimate from the unrealistic expectations and to develop plans to meet the legitimate needs. It is also important to respond with alternatives and thoughtful explanations to criticisms from those whose unrealistic expectations are not being met. Knowing how to assess consumer needs is an important accountability competency.

Assess the Final Effects of One's Efforts. In the conduct of assorted services to various consumers, school counselors engage in many functions repeatedly. Knowledge of the outcomes of one's efforts is an important ingredient in accountability. It is useful to learn how one succeeded in performing the requisite behaviors. *Outcome data* is a term used to describe summative evaluative information collected to assess the effects of one's efforts. Assessment of outcomes implies the existence of goals and objectives in advance of actions. Having goals and objectives and knowing how to assess whether they have been achieved are important ingredients of accountability.

Assess *Intermediate Effects of One's Services.*   The achievement of goals may be more likely if information about progress is acquired along the way. Data acquired while one is in the process of responding to consumer needs will allow school counselors to make adjustments and revisions if necessary or to gain confidence from the knowledge that sufficient progress is occurring. Knowing how to gather this formative process data is another important component of accountability.

Assess *Consumer Satisfaction.*   School counseling is a profession in which consumer goodwill is built on the perception that quality services accompany wholehearted efforts. Dissatisfied consumers can boycott the counseling services and influence their peers to do so as well. Perceptions of the school counselor's publics cannot be ignored in comprehensive accountability activities. Information about the opinions of various consumers of their services will give counselors a picture of existing specific and general attitudes. The information may be used in conjunction with outcome and process data to determine whether and where changes need to be made and to plan how to respond to unfair opinions in order to prevent them from undermining the counseling services. Knowing how to collect and use opinion data is yet another important ingredient of accountability.

Assess *Cost-Effectiveness.*   The importance of cost-effectiveness was emphasized previously. School boards are likely to run the schools like businesses. In doing so, they sometimes make decisions that have a business rather than an educational or a humanitarian orientation. Cost-effectiveness may be the key factor in those decisions. In economically hard times, school districts have historically tended to designate counselors among the first to be furloughed when personnel cutbacks are used as a cost-cutting procedure. Therefore, evidence of one's own cost-effectiveness may be important for job security and survival. Cost-effectiveness data serve other purposes as well. For instance, such data may persuade administrative decision makers that changes in responsibilities and duties are needed. Additionally, cost-effectiveness information may help individual counselors take a more informed view of their activities. In all, cost-effectiveness information is best used when it leads to improved services to child and adolescent consumers. Ability to enumerate one's activities and to report that information clearly is an important component of accountability.

Understandable and Informative Accountability Data

Collecting evaluative information, though important, is not an end in itself; the information is inert data unless understood by those who have collected it and presented it to others in an informative fashion. The word *understand* is used two-dimensionally here. One dimension is that school counselors have the necessary sophistication to conduct basic evaluation activities. Many requisite competencies, such as setting goals, developing surveys, and using descriptive statistics, are part of counselors' graduate training, and the remainder are part of their continuing education. The second dimension is the ability to make evaluation data understandable to laypeople, colleagues, and supervisors. Doing this requires an ability to translate one's understanding of the data into a form that is familiar to those receiving the information.

Data presented informatively can be used appropriately and constructively, which is a goal of being accountable. Therefore, being able to design and implement informative accountability presentations is crucial to the success of the total counseling program. Informative accountability presentations are a key to influencing impressions about individual school counselors and counseling programs.

Constructive Use of Accountability Data

Historically, guidance or counseling specialists are the most recent arrivals in the schools, arriving after teachers and administrators established their professional credibility (Shaw, 1973). Teachers' and administrators' roles and the importance of their functions are widely recognized and understood. The roles and functions of school counselors, in contrast, have not been fully understood by a large part of the public or by many of their teaching and administrative colleagues. This lack of clarity has been exacerbated by differences between practicing school counselors, who often define their work by what it is, and counselor educators, who define it as what it should be, a discrepancy that exists to a much lesser extent in the teaching and administrative professions.

To prevent lowered morale, superficial evaluations, and trivialization of the school counseling profession, accountability activities can be founded on constructive principles. School counselors are challenged to view accountability as something other than an imposition, and others must be interested in more than simply determining whether the school counseling program is justified. Employers and supervisors can help by recognizing good work and by becoming better informed about the roles and functions of their counselors.

Accountability activities offer school counselors more than information that helps them survive economically. First is the satisfaction of accomplishing goals that represent quality services and hard work. Second is the satisfaction of knowing that one's consumers appreciate one's efforts and accomplishments. Third is the satisfaction that one has mastered the competencies of the profession, including the knowledge and skills to evaluate one's own services effectively and to report the results informatively. Fourth is access to information that can improve one's services or influence one's image positively. Accountability data empower counselors to challenge themselves to grow professionally and to demonstrate their accomplishments to others. The key is to realize there are reasons for accountability activities of a higher purpose than survival.

COMPETENCIES FOR BASIC ACCOUNTABILITY IN SCHOOL COUNSELING

Assessing Consumer Needs

Needs Assessment.   *Needs assessment* is a common term referring to activities designed to acquire information about consumer needs. Cook (1989) sums up the needs assessment process as identifying those to be assessed, determining a method

for reaching them, devising a measuring plan, and interpreting the results to those who will make relevant decisions.

Whose Needs Should Be Assessed?   Needs assessments are best conducted with a broad brush. It is good to know the expectations and perceived needs of a wide range of potential consumers, including minority and special populations. Knowing the needs of all prospective consumers, however, is not synonymous with guaranteeing delivery to all of them or even with agreeing that their expectations are legitimate. Eventually, school counselors learn they cannot be all things to all people. Service delivery is best approached from a realistic perspective. Knowledge of the range of expectations and needs allows counselors to make informed decisions about using limited time and resources.

How Should Needs Be Assessed?   Needs may be assessed in several ways, some of which are more challenging and time-consuming than others. Comprehensiveness is an important guiding principle. Possibilities include the following:

- Publications about child and adolescent development offer suggestions about the common needs that individuals have in various stages of life.
- Key individuals in the school and the community can share what they know about the setting. One has to guard against views representing only a particular bias when gathering this kind of information or when receiving unsolicited offerings (Cook, 1989).
- Community forums provide access to groups that have garnered consensus about some needs and expectations. Care must be taken to achieve true representation or to recognize that it has not been achieved (Cook, 1989).
- Consumers can be surveyed to learn about their needs and expectations.

A survey is probably the most popular and common approach to assessing needs. It is also probably the most time-consuming, challenging, and expensive approach. The challenge, in addition to time and expense, is in having the requisite skills to design a survey, administer it, and evaluate the results. Fortunately, others have designed needs assessment surveys and published them, and consultants are able to assist in the design and conduct of needs assessments or have surveys to share.

Needs assessment surveys can take one of two approaches: (a) Ask respondents what their needs are, or (b) offer them a predetermined list of possibilities from which to choose (Cook, 1989). Each approach has advantages and disadvantages. Open-ended surveys may be easier to design. They also allow respondents to state their own minds, volunteering ideas that surveyors using a predetermined list might not think of asking. Results, however, may be more difficult to understand. Respondents are limited to immediate needs and often cannot forecast needs they will have eventually but whose importance they do not realize at the time. Surveys based on predetermined lists often include topics that counselors know are important but that might not have been thought of by naive respondents. These surveys are more difficult and time-consuming to develop. Fortunately, once developed, they are easier to interpret than open-ended surveys and can be used repeatedly. They are limited to the range of questions the designers think to ask, however, and the potential range of needs is enormous.

Which Needs Assessment Strategy Should Be Used? The information presented in the preceding section paints a picture of two incomplete approaches, which may leave the impression that the best approach is to use both the open-ended and predetermined listing methods to get comprehensive coverage of the consumers' needs. Development of surveys representing either approach or a combination begins with goals and objectives. The surveyors then develop survey questions that reflect those goals and objectives. Specifying objectives helps surveyors design questions, open-ended or specific, that address the issues. The basic competencies required are stating goals and objectives in measurable terms, designing survey items that measure those objectives appropriately, and conducting surveys scientifically. If these skills were not developed adequately in one's counselor training program, they can be learned through continued education efforts. An alternative is to acquire the consultant services of others who already possess the requisite competencies.

Additionally, those who would employ the needs assessment survey approach must keep in mind the differences in students. Plans for surveying children differ from those for surveying adolescents. Goals and objectives may remain similar, but methods are different. Younger respondents will be less able to answer in writing, for example, and oral responses may be necessary in some cases. Finding that the professional literature did not provide any needs assessment surveys that had useful formats for primary-age children, Kelly and Ferguson (1984) developed their own instrument. The survey was administered orally to a randomly selected sample of children from Grades 1 through 5 to determine whether the children understood the questions and could complete the survey in 30 to 40 minutes. Kelly and Ferguson reported engaging in the following steps:

1. Determine what you want to know.
2. Decide on the best approach for acquiring the desired information.
3. Develop survey items, paying attention to language levels.
4. Have the items reviewed by colleagues, change the items as necessary, and then pilot-test them with a sample of children to determine the adequacy.
5. When the items are given orally to young children, the authors recommend:
   • Opening with an overview of the survey and its purpose
   • Explaining each item in detail and encouraging discussion to uncover misunderstandings
   • Reviewing the items to allow children to mark the ones they wish to learn more about
   • Allowing children to review their answers if time permits to identify incorrect responses

Surveying teachers, parents, and the professional literature, which are indirect needs assessment approaches, may be more productive than direct assessments. An example of what might be learned from teachers is provided by G. Schmidt (1986). In a survey inviting teachers to rate an elementary-school counselor in different performance categories (opinion data), one item asked for additional comments and suggestions. Schmidt learned that some teachers want help understanding achievement test results and that others have concerns with school record keeping. These needs assessment data serve as reference points when the counselor engages in consulting with teachers who have responded to the survey.

How Will the Results Be Interpreted to Decision Makers?   Because the ultimate purpose of assessing consumer needs is to determine the best ways to serve those consumers, decision makers should be involved in the process at the outset. If this is done, they can become informed of the assessment's intentions and are better able to respond to the results intelligently. Working with decision makers in this manner helps school counselors know their expectations. Counselors can then plan for those expectations throughout the assessment process. When school counselors are the decision makers themselves, objectivity is of the utmost importance.

Advisory committees may be beneficial in the decision-making process (Fairchild & Seeley, 1995). Said committees, having representation from various publics (e.g., parents, community members, faculty members, students), can provide useful feedback and be helpful in the needs assessment process. Because of their commitment, advisory committee members are likely to become knowledgeable about the program and supportive of its efforts to respond to consumer needs. All this, in turn, has potential for enhancing public relations.

Assessing the Final Effects of One's Efforts: Summative Evaluation

School counselors engage in helping behaviors that have been identified and elaborated on in previous chapters. Those activities are predicated on stated or implied goals and objectives. Virtually all purposeful activities in which counselors engage professionally are designed to achieve these goals and objectives. Therefore, it follows that determining whether they have been achieved is an important component of accountability. Shaw (1973) used the term *outcome data* for the effects of school counseling activities, and that term is used here to categorize data about the final effects of the efforts of school counselors to achieve goals they and their consumers have set.

Determining Outcome Goals and Objectives.   For the sake of simplicity, the word *goals* is used in the remainder of this chapter as a global term representing goals and objectives because of the tendency for the terms to be used differently in the professional literature. Determining what outcome data to collect and how to collect them depends on the goals one is trying to achieve. Therefore, the collection and reporting of outcome data depend on the identification of outcome goals. Sometimes the goals and the means of assessing them are clear. On other occasions, the goals may be clear but the means of assessing them are difficult to identify. At still other times, both the goals and the means of assessing them are difficult to discern. Two important skills emerge. School counselors are challenged, first, to be able to identify goals for their professional endeavors that can be assessed objectively and, second, to identify outcomes that measure whether those goals were achieved.

Often, counselors engage in activities for which the goals are implied or determined by others. In responding to the demands for such activities, counselors find themselves proceeding without fully realizing what the underlying goals are. Instead, they simply do what they are expected to do. For example, many secondary-school counselors find themselves heavily involved in the gatekeeping and clerical chores associated with scheduling, such as determining whether students should be allowed to make schedule changes, recording the changes, and monitoring the master schedule. On the surface, the goals appear to have been imposed by the school's administration. Indeed, some implied administrative goals are measurable: Is the system running smoothly? Has everyone who desired services been served? Is the paperwork in order? Are the class sizes balanced? Additionally, each student who seeks scheduling-related counseling services has his or her own goals. In these individual cases, counselors and clients can determine goals cooperatively, giving counselors a foundation for determining the outcomes for which to strive.

On some occasions, counselors can set goals in advance of their activities. For example, an elementary-school counselor planned a primary prevention program that was to be delivered in selected classrooms by basing the activity on predetermined goals. On still other occasions, counselors set goals after engaging in activities. This is often the case when counselors engage in individual counseling. Goal setting usually follows time spent exploring and clarifying the presentation of issues and feelings.

The underlying principle here is that there are goals for all the programs and interventions that counselors render. Some are predetermined by clients, administrators, and teachers. Some are determined by counselors. Others are negotiated. Realizing that all their activities are goal directed is the first step counselors can take to understand how to assess the final effects of their efforts. The next step is actively interpreting those goals as desired outcomes of the services they rendered. For example, a middle-school student was miserable because her friends were shunning her. She did not know what to do. The goal was to help her determine a plan of action. The outcome was a workable plan. Once counselors make the identification of goals a conscious behavior, they are in a position to consider methods for assessing outcomes. Perhaps another way to state this belief in the importance of goals is to put it in terms of job satisfaction. A clear understanding of goals will lead to a clear job description, whereas a lack of goals or unclear goals will, in turn, lead to an unclear job description.

Assessing Outcomes.   Having mastered the art of identifying goals and translating them into outcomes, counselors then need outcome measures. Although not limitless, the universe of possible outcome measures is large and impossible to inventory in this textbook. Essentially, the desired outcomes dictate the measures to be used in assessing those outcomes. For example, in the cases cited previously in which counselors helped students make decisions about their schedules, whether a decision was made is an example of outcome data for one client. In the case of the middle-school student who was being shunned, whether a plan for responding was developed would be outcome data. Whether the plan worked successfully would be outcome data for another goal: to carry out the plan. In such cases, the outcome data are unique to one client and do not lend themselves to summarizing and categorizing.

In the situation of the elementary-school counselor planning a prevention program with goals determined in advance, means for measuring the outcomes can also be planned in advance, allowing the counselor to choose one or more measures to be given at strategic times during the program. For example, if the purpose of the program is to make children aware of nontraditional careers, the counselor might present an inventory of pictures or titles of careers to participants at the outset to determine how many of the nontraditional careers presented in the inventory are familiar to them. The same inventory can be given at the close of the program to determine how much was learned. The same inventory can also be presented to students not in the program at the same points in time to compare results and to rule out reasons other than the program for changes in participants' performances. If changes in the program participants are greater than changes in nonparticipants, then the outcome data are evidence of program effectiveness. Another measure the counselor can use in the same manner is to assess whether the attitudes of participants toward the nontraditional careers become more favorable after the program. The following cases are offered as examples of how outcome data are collected and used. The results were reported in professional counseling journals.

Cobb and Richards (1983) used selected questions from a published behavior problem checklist to acquire outcome data for assessing the effectiveness of a program designed to improve classroom climate and conduct of fourth and fifth graders. The questions were first used by independent observers of the children in the classrooms to measure the level of problem behaviors before the program was instituted. Observations were made after the program was completed to determine any positive changes, and also after a designated period of time to determine whether the changes had lasted. Half the students who were observed did not receive the program; they served as a control group to compare with those who received the program. The findings led to the conclusion that the program could achieve the goals of improving classroom climate and conduct.

Some data-collecting strategies require considerable time and effort, as was the case in the report by Cobb and Richards (1983). Outcome data can also be collected easily. An example is provided by Bollendorf, Howrey, and Stephenson (1990), who suggest using program attendance numbers as outcome data for structured invitational events, such as college nights and a career speaker series, that were part of a career development program offered to ninth graders.

Outcome data from counseling intervention cases can be useful, too, individually and collectively. An example is provided by Liu and Baker (1993), who reported the progress of efforts to help a 4-year-old Chinese girl who was experiencing culture shock when attending a day-care center at a large American university. The child's progress in response to a counselor's friendship training program was charted graphically. Figure 13.1 depicts the child's progress at achieving the targeted outcome behaviors—increased verbal contacts with peers—graphically. The evaluation design, known as ABA, is one of several single-case designs that can be used to plot the progress of individual clients (Barlow & Herson, 1984). In this case, A represents the time when no intervention occurs, and B represents the time when the intervention is in progress. Thus, the first A-phase allows a counselor to collect baseline data, the B-phase provides information about a client's progress during the intervention, and the second A-phase

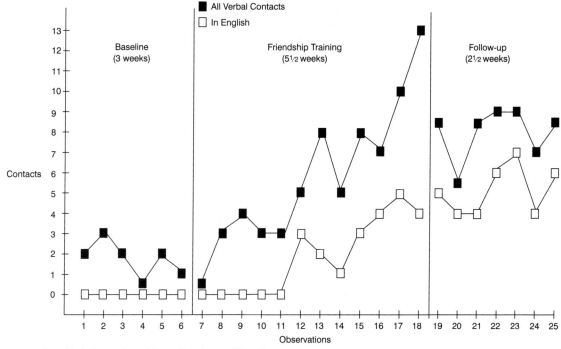

Figure 13.1
Number of self-initiated verbal contacts.

Source: From "Enhancing Cultural Adaptation Through Friendship Training," by Y. C. Liu and S. B. Baker, 1993, *Elementary School Guidance and Counseling, 28,* p. 97. Copyright 1993 by American Counseling Association.

offers data depicting the client's progress after the intervention is completed. In this case, client progress is visible and relatively easy to determine. The process itself is also relatively easy. A key factor in using this approach is being able to identify outcomes that lend themselves to observing and counting behaviors. When working with cases of this nature, the single-case design is useful for school counselors. From an account-ability perspective, counselors can present graphic representations from several cases, with clients' identity protected, as evidence of effectiveness. This provides promise for counselors who feel nagged by criticisms that no one knows what is being done that is worthwhile behind the closed doors to their counseling sessions.

Keeping case notes in an organized manner may help resolve the time and effort challenge. Fairchild and Seeley (1995) recommend keeping case notes in a systematic manner, even to the point of using a case notes form that may include sections for demographic data, details of referral concerns, and information about client present-ing problems and progress toward goals that does not include privileged information. The notes may be used in summarizing data and, if necessary, in responding to chal-lenges about time invested in cases and perceived outcomes of the cases. Following Fairchild and Seeley's recommendation is part of what Gillies (1993) refers to as *diagnostic action research:* identifying a problem, diagnosing the causes, considering responses, and making recommendations for resolutions. Keeping systematic case notes allows counselors to be accountable in their diagnostic action research efforts.

Gillies (1993) uses the term *action research* in a manner that is synonymous with evaluation. Her other three approaches to action research also fit into assessing outcomes. She writes about *participant action research*, through which data are collected, analyzed, and used to make recommendations; *empirical action research*, in which planning and evaluating the effects of programs and interventions are added to making recommendations; and *experimental action research*, which adds the element of comparison or control groups. An example of participant action research is found in the report by Elmore, Ekstrom, Diamond, and Whittaker (1993), who conducted a survey and used the results in making recommendations about test interpretation, administration, and selection practices of counselors. Hughey, Lapan, and Gysbers (1993) provide an example of empirical action research by reporting effectiveness data from surveys and interviews of students who participated in a high-school career guidance program. An example of experimental action research is provided by Zinck and Littrell (2000) who found that group counseling with at-risk adolescent girls decreased problem severity, led to moderate progress toward goal attainment, and influenced changes noticeable to the participants.

Assessing the Intermediate Effects of One's Efforts: Formative Evaluation

Process data are used to determine the intermediate effects of one's efforts and are collected while the phenomenon of interest is still in progress. The data are used to estimate one's progress toward achieving goals to determine whether changes need to be made. For example, if the elementary-school counselor delivering the primary prevention program on nontraditional careers wants to check the effectiveness of the program at the midway point, the outcome measures can be given at that time, too; the same comparisons described previously can be made.

School counselors do not need to collect process data for every activity in which they engage. Individual counseling and consulting cases that last a relatively long time and curriculum programs of an appreciable duration lend themselves to the collecting of process data to acquire intermediate feedback and to make changes if necessary. Ultimately, the decision is one that counselors have to make for themselves. Knowing the importance of process data for intermediate feedback is the key to making the decision. Data-collecting skills are the key to acquiring the desired information. The following case is an example of how process data were used by one school counselor:

> Haugaard (1986) reported adapting the Goal Attainment Scaling (GAS) system, initially developed for evaluating community mental health programs, to an elementary-school counseling program. With it, Haugaard was able to encourage students to set goals and monitor their progress toward those goals. The GAS system employs sheets of paper containing rectangular boxes in which students enter their goals, the strategies they expect to use to attain them, and five possible outcomes: Best Outcome, Better Than Acceptable Outcome,

Acceptable Outcome, Less Than Acceptable Outcome, and Worst Outcome. Each box is completed at the outset, and records are updated periodically under the heading Where I Stand. Under the GAS system, students whose achievements are below the Best Outcome level can be helped to assess their progress and to redesign strategies or goals.

Assessing Satisfaction

Knowledge of consumer satisfaction comes directly from consumers. Asking for their opinions is a relatively common practice in the business world, where corporations employ experts to find out what customers want and how much they value the services they have received, and in politics where the opinions of prospective voters are valued highly. When school districts evaluate their services, consumer opinions are also a popular source of information. Because formally assessing consumer satisfaction is not a routine counseling function, the process can be onerously time-consuming and frustrating, especially if the people involved have little experience and expertise with surveys. School counselors are challenged to know how to identify their consumers, what to ask them, and how to acquire the desired information.

Identifying Consumers.   Who are the consumers of the counselor's services? The authors prefer a broad definition, believing that individuals who are served both directly and indirectly should be included. Also, individuals with opinions about the services, even though they are not clients, should be surveyed. Categorically, then, this broad definition includes currently enrolled students, former students, members of the teaching faculty, members of the administration, members of the school board, parents and guardians, and citizens without direct ties with the schools.

Determining What Information Should Be Asked of Consumers.   A popular saying in the computer sciences is "Garbage in, garbage out." A poorly conceived opinion survey generates information that will haunt those who developed it and who depend on that information. The key principles are that surveys must contain questions that elicit relevant information and that the items are constructed and phrased so that the desired responses are achieved. Accomplishing these goals requires direct involvement of those who know what the relevant information is. They pay close attention to how the items are worded and constructed.

School counselors are most likely to know what the relevant information is. Therefore, it will be to their advantage to have direct involvement in the construction of opinion surveys. Committees can be established to work on developing surveys for specific consumers, and representatives of those consumer populations can be invited to participate in the survey construction. For example, school counselors working on surveys for teachers and parents may invite representatives of those groups to join their committee.

Item construction requires some sophistication about wording questions so that their intent is clear to the readers, they are easy to score objectively, and they generate information that is constructive while not being unwittingly deceptive. Clarity is enhanced by proper grammar, simple sentence structure, jargon-free terminology, and sequencing of items according to a logical system.

Open-ended questions are useful for finding out what is on the respondents' minds. Therefore, a place is included for a limited number of open-ended questions at the close of the survey. (Be sure to leave enough room on the paper for responses.) Used as the primary item strategy for opinion surveys, open-ended questions create problems that mitigate the initial advantage of generating them more quickly than closed-end questions. First, open-ended questions are difficult to score collectively and objectively, presenting surveyors with interpretation, tabulation, and presentation difficulties. Second, such questions limit the range of provided information to that which is in the front of the respondents' minds.

Closed-end questions, though more time-consuming to develop, have advantages that make them preferred for the bulk of opinion surveys. One advantage is that they can be scored objectively. There are several common types of objective scoring systems for opinion and attitude surveys, all of which are easy to tabulate and generate information easily understood by professionals and laypeople. For instance, questions that can be answered Yes or No can be tabulated so that the percentages of affirmative and negative responses can be reported. In an example, student responses to the survey item "Do you think that counselors are available to the students?" were Yes = 75%, No = 25%. Another common tactic is to employ some sort of rating system using numbers. One example is asking respondents to rate the career counseling services on a scale from 1 to 10, with 10 being the most positive. The average of the individual ratings can be reported. For instance, the average rating of the career counseling services was 6.76 on such a 10-point scale. A very simple scoring system is to have respondents check or leave blank items according to predetermined instructions. For example: "Check the services listed below that you knew existed before you received this survey." The total number of students who checked each service can be reported, as well as the percentage of all students who completed the questionnaire: Counseling Interventions = 750 students (75% of the student population); Curriculum Programming = 375 students (37.5% of the student population); and so forth. A set of opinion surveys developed by committees of professional school staff members is listed in Appendix F.

Another advantage to using closed questions is that survey constructors can ensure that they have developed items to represent all the topics they wish to have covered. This forces respondents to think about all the topics the designers deem important, some of which the respondents would not have known prior to the survey. Also, it is easier to report the results of surveys with closed questions. In the previous examples, percentages and totals were cited as tabulating methods that can be used to report the results. These methods and others like them allow opinion surveyors to report simply the collective results of surveys given to groups of respondents.

Acquiring Desired Information.   After developing the surveys, the next step is to use them in the field. Decision making focuses on whether to survey all the targeted population or to sample it; whether to have the respondents fill in their own answers or to have the questions presented by others who may also have to fill in the answers; whether to mail the surveys, use electronic mail, or use another delivery system; and whether to make responding a requirement or a voluntary act. If a survey program is comprehensive, all the above decisions are made. Possible decisions are these: when the

School counselors are challenged to be competent in translating evaluative data to meaningful accountability information.

number of administrators in a school system is small, all will be surveyed; because many adults are in the school district, an arbitrarily determined percentage of them will be surveyed randomly; older children, adolescents, and adults will complete their own survey, but primary-grade teachers will read the questions to their students and fill in the answers for them if necessary; and all administrators will be expected to complete a survey, whereas students and other adults will be allowed to do so voluntarily.

After such decisions have been made, opinion-surveying skills have to be employed. For instance, respondent anonymity must be protected, appropriate sample sizes determined, and strategies for getting adequate responses from mailed surveys developed. Some of these competencies are within the range of professional school counselors and their colleagues, and some may have to be acquired from professional literature or from consultants. *Surveys, Polls, and Samples: Practical Procedures* by Parten (1966) is one classic source of information. It includes planning strategies, sampling ideas, survey construction suggestions, procedures for mailing questionnaires, and techniques for tabulating data.

Getting started may seem like a monumental task. Indeed, it is a lot of work. Most of the work is at the beginning, however. Once surveys have been designed, they can be used with some necessary modifications at other times. In addition, not all consumer groups need to be surveyed all the time, nor do all members of a targeted group need to be surveyed at any one time. Samples can be selected and surveyed periodically according to a predetermined schedule. Therefore, getting started represents the major time commitment, one that must be made if there is a desire or a need to acquire meaningful opinion data. In the following cases, differing sources of, and uses for, opinion data are presented.

Bruckner and Thompson (1987) reported using surveys with sentence completion items to evaluate developmental group guidance meetings for fourth, fifth, and sixth graders. Student responses to the open-ended sentences were rated on a 5-point scale ranging from *outright accepting or positive attitude* to *outright rejecting or negative attitude* by independent judges. Two types of data were made available: (a) average numerical ratings from the judges using the scales and (b) the actual comments the students made when completing the sentences.

Teachers were asked to rate their high-school counseling programs in two surveys reported by Gibson (1990). The surveys were identical, given in 1965 and 1987 to different samples of teachers. Gibson used the information to discover the current opinions of a sample of teachers and to compare them with those collected 22 years earlier. Chief among Gibson's conclusions are that secondary-school teachers view the contributions of their counseling programs positively and that school counselors continue to need to do a better job of communicating clearly their roles and goals to teaching colleagues. An example of more specific information learned from opinion surveys is in the responses to one item on the survey that asked respondents to rank-order the school counseling services. In both the 1965 and 1987 surveys, the top three services, in order, were individual counseling, career information, and test administration.

Assessing Cost-Effectiveness

Counselors inventory their activities to acquire cost-effectiveness data. The term *enumerative data,* taken from Shaw (1973), is used to classify such information here. Enumerating data usually takes the form of keeping records of how individuals use their time; enumerative data consist of identifying targeted behaviors and tallying their frequency and duration.

Consider the following simulation. The evaluation stage has two parts:

1. Counselors in a school district make a list of the activities they engage in when carrying out their responsibilities and trying to achieve program goals. Some activities are general and some are specific to elementary-, middle-, and high-school levels.
2. Individual counselors keep records of how often the activities are performed and how much time is devoted to each of them. The enumerative data are recorded as hours per activity (e.g., for one counselor in 1 week: individual counseling = 5 hours, scheduling = 15 hours).

The accountability stage also has two parts:

1. The hours-per-activity data are then multiplied by the hourly pay rate of the respective counselors to acquire evidence of cost-effectiveness. If the hourly pay rate for the counselor is $20, for example, then the amount of money spent

on individual counseling services and scheduling is $100 for the 5 hours of counseling and $300 for the 15 hours of scheduling.
2. Decision makers will have enumerative data indicating how much time and money are devoted to each activity, and that information can be used in making cost-effectiveness decisions. The decisions will be based on the goals and priorities of the decision makers and those whom they represent.

In the example, the amount of money spent on scheduling is three times that devoted to individual counseling. Determining whether the expenditures of time and money are cost-effective is based on a variety of factors important to those making the cost-effectiveness decisions. Questions they must answer when establishing a foundation for making cost-effectiveness decisions include these:

- What is the relative importance of the individual counseling and scheduling functions? (If one is more important than the other, it seems that more time and money should be spent on it.)
- What is being accomplished during the time devoted to each function?
- Is the money spent on each function worth the outcomes being achieved?

Notice that enumerative data do not provide qualitative information. Data that answer such questions as "How much?" or "How many?" are quantitative and objective and are not qualitative unless outcome goals have been determined. Therefore, enumerative data cannot be used to provide qualitative information unless accompanied by outcome data. Using the enumerative data from this example, outcome data are added to provide an example of the previous point.

Outcome data were reported for each client who received individual counseling and scheduling assistance as follows: In the 5 hours devoted to individual counseling, two students made decisions with which they were satisfied, one received needed support for anxieties associated with enrolling in a new school, and two thought the counselor understood them well enough to make appointments for follow-up interviews. In the 15 hours devoted to scheduling, 10 schedules were changed as requested, 3 could not be changed as requested but alternatives were determined, and 2 remained unchanged.

The combination of enumerative and outcome data provides information about how much time is used and what goals are accomplished. The addition of opinion data may complete the picture when trying to determine the cost-effectiveness of the counselor's activities. Using the information from Gibson's (1990) report, teachers ranked individual counseling as the most important activity. Scheduling or administrative duties ranked 10th of 10 activities.

Given all this information, a decision maker's thoughts might be as follows:

1. The amount of time and money devoted to the lowest ranked activity is three times that devoted to the highest ranked activity.
2. The achievements associated with individual counseling seem clearer and more important than those associated with scheduling.
3. Therefore, it appears that the counselors' time is not being used in a cost-effective manner.

This is one of many possible responses to the data. Responses differ, depending on the goals and biases of individual decision makers.

Presenting Evaluation Data Successfully

The act of collecting evaluative information, though important, is not sufficient in itself. Evaluative information has to be shared with others in a manner that leads to understanding. Making their evaluative data understandable and informative is primarily the responsibility of school counselors. Therefore, school counselors are challenged to be competent in translating evaluative data into meaningful accountability information. This means that school counselors must be able to implement understandable and informative data-reporting systems.

Some data-reporting systems have been described in the professional counseling literature, and many other adequate systems remain to be developed by creative minds. Although reporting systems differ, they share some basic principles that make them understandable and informative:

- The information is summarized and organized systematically.
- The presentation is clear, concise, and understandable to laypeople.
- Reports are as brief as possible without omitting valuable information.

A classic accountability system that seems to meet these criteria was developed by Krumboltz (1974). Krumboltz's system emphasizes the importance of (a) using agreed-upon general counseling goals, (b) measuring outcomes in terms of observable behaviors, (c) stating counseling activities in terms of cost-effectiveness rather than activities accomplished, (d) focusing reports on the promotion of effectiveness and self-improvement, (e) recognizing that not every effort is successful but that something positive can be derived from failure, (f) including all users in the designing of accountability systems, and (g) being willing to evaluate and modify systems once they are in place.

When implementing a Krumboltz-style accountability system, users begin by determining general goals for their counseling services—for example, helping students develop more adaptive and constructive behavior patterns. Next, counselors estimate their hourly pay rate as concisely as possible (e.g., $14.00/hr in the Krumboltz example). As shown in Table 13.1, categories and subcategories organize and present data in the Krumboltz system.

Each general goal is a main category, and two subgoals are established under each main goal. The subgoals are Accomplishment (outcome data) and Cost (cost-effectiveness, enumerative data), which are further divided as shown. Information in the Accomplishment category can take various forms:

- Details about each problem, case, or cluster of like functions, such as specific treatment cases, similar treatment cases, specific prevention programs, and similar prevention programs; identifying names can be replaced with codes that make individuals anonymous.
- Brief descriptions of methods, tactics, or strategies used.
- Outcome data.

Table 13.1
A sample of Krumboltz's suggested accountability plan.

Accomplishment			Cost		
Problem Identification	Method	Outcome	Activity	Hours	Dollars
Olive's mother phones: Olive depressed, talking vaguely of suicide, no friends	Analysis of social reinforcers for Olive; social skill training; assigned Olive to help new transfer student	Olive increased frequency of initiating social contacts from 0/month to 4/month; reports having 1 good friend vs. 0; mother reports Olive's depression gone—suicide talk from 1/month before referral to 0/month for 3 consecutive months	Conferences with Olive	38	532
			Conferences with mother	3	42
			Conferences with teachers	2	28
					602
Student X came to me worried about his dependence on mood drugs; requested anonymity	Discussions to find other satisfactions, ways of getting his gang to change	Temporary progress in reducing frequency of drug use offset by relapse each time	Conferences with Student X	25	350
			Conferences with physician	0.5	7
					357

Source: From "An Accountability Model for Counselors" by J. D. Krumboltz, 1974, *Personnel and Guidance Journal, 52,* pp. 639–646. Copyright 1974 by American Counseling Association.

The Cost category includes information about specific activities, time devoted to each activity, and the dollar cost of accomplishing each activity, which can be summed up across problems within general goal categories, across goals, and for each counselor or group of counselors.

Keeping track of the amount of time devoted to each professional activity can be an oppressive undertaking. Traditionally, evaluation activities have been the least attractive tasks for school counselors; they have, therefore, been performed least often. The reasons are both practical and psychological. Among the practical reasons have been a lack of data-collecting skills and a lack of time to keep track of counselors' time use. Because of these challenges, school counselors need enumerative data-keeping systems that are easy and efficient. The best the authors have discovered is a coded data card system such as one developed in the Erie, Pennsylvania, school district. (Copies of the cards are shown in Appendix G.)

Predesigned data cards are developed for six major categories of counseling services:

Individual Student Counseling

Individual Student Information/Service

Individual Adult Conference In-School

Adult Group and Out-of-School Activity

Solitary In-School Activity

Student Group Activity

Each card has the name of a service category at the top, with space for the names of the counselor and the school, and is printed on identifying colored paper. Most of the space on the cards is devoted to time-use categories ranging from less than 10 minutes to 90 minutes or more. A list of different counseling behaviors is included under each counseling service. When the system is used, counselors have stacks of each of the six kinds of cards, which they pull out at a convenient time after individual activities. They circle the appropriate categories in a matter of seconds and place the card in a stack of completed cards. Completed cards are then collected, and the data are transferred to a computerized system for tabulation. Variations on this theme can be designed to fit different systems and technologies. For instance, counselors who have access to personal computers in their offices may find spreadsheet programs useful tools they can adapt to this endeavor. The primary principle is to develop a data-collecting scheme that is efficient and easy to use and from which data can be tabulated easily and accurately. Given these conditions, school counselors, like all busy professionals, are more likely to cooperate and to view the activities positively.

The Krumboltz (1974) proposal includes both outcome and enumerative data and is devoid of opinion data. Fortunately, the model is open to reporting opinion data. When collected, opinion data can be reported in the outcome column. For example, client/student opinion about the counseling interventions and curriculum programs can be collected via surveys. Opinion data can also be reported in the outcome column in instances when the general goal and specific problems are designed specifically to address opinion data collecting. For example, the general goal might be to learn the opinions of all consumers about the school counseling services, and the specific problems might include measuring the opinions of current students, teachers, administrators, former students, parents, and taxpayers.

The Krumboltz idea appears to be user-friendly while also being compatible to outcome, opinion, and enumerative data reporting. Therefore, it can be used to present comprehensive accountability data that are understandable and informative. It represents a good starting point from which school counselors can depart to additional ideas that seem useful and important.

Assembling Accountability Data: A Portfolio

Portfolios containing collections of a variety of products that display evidence of one's accomplishments over time can be used by counselors in assembling and storing their evaluation/accountability data (Rhyne-Winkler & Wooten, 1996). The professional literature contains suggestions about what might be included in a portfolio and how it might be constructed. Counselors are free to choose their own approaches should they decide that keeping portfolios is advantageous. Rhyne-Winkler and Wooten offer a comprehensive inventory of recommended components, which include (a) introductory information (e.g., title page, table of contents), (b) program planning materials (e.g., needs assessment findings, time management data), and (c) service/program delivery information (e.g., assessments of individuals; group counseling activities; consulting activities; and documentation of coordination, appraisal, and professional activities). Portfolios provide an advantage of being able to store samples of one's accomplishments for presentation when accountability data are requested or when one wishes to share the materials with interested parties.

A Plan for Implementing Accountability Activities

Following is an outline of how the foregoing information might be applied in a school system. It is divided into three categories or levels:

- School district accountability activities
- Accountability activities in specific schools
- Individual counselor's accountability activities

At all three levels, a sampling plan is used to keep the process from being overly formidable. With a sampling plan, data are collected periodically in a systematic fashion by using the plan for obtaining data that represent all seasons of the year and the total population of possible respondents.

School District Accountability Activities
1. Engage in districtwide needs assessments.
2. Establish districtwide goals.
3. Develop a districtwide evaluation system that includes collecting outcome, opinion, and enumerative data.
4. Develop a districtwide accountability plan for organizing and presenting the evaluation data.
5. Use the districtwide accountability data for organizing and presenting evaluation data to the school board.

Accountability Activities in Specific Schools
1. Implement the districtwide system.
2. Conduct needs assessments in the school.
3. Establish school goals.
4. Use the districtwide system for collecting outcome, opinion, and enumerative data in the school.
5. Use the districtwide accountability system for organizing and presenting evaluation data from programs at the school to administrators, teachers, and parents.

An Individual Counselor's Accountability Activities

1. Establish goals for individual prevention programs and consulting and counseling interventions.
2. Collect outcome, opinion, and enumerative data for individual services.
3. Use the districtwide accountability system for organizing and presenting evaluation data from individual counseling services.

Accountability as a Means of Enhancing Public Relations

The evaluation/accountability process provides school counselors with ample opportunities to influence public relations. Of the programs offered by the schools, counseling is usually less well understood by the public than teaching and administering. Consequently, misinformation and misperceptions about the counseling program are more likely to occur. This circumstance challenges school counselors to inform the various publics about their goals, programs, and accomplishments. Notice the assumption that programs with goals are in place before public relations activities are undertaken. Failure to do so entertains the risk of advertising one's shortcomings in advance of attempting to recognize and correct them if they exist.

Strategies for planfully influencing public opinion are numerous. For example, *advisory committees* consisting of cross sections of people from one's school and community provide important feedback for counseling programs and educate these influential members about the intricacies of the program (Fairchild & Seeley, 1995). Another strategy is to hold *accountability conferences* with one's administrators. Such conferences encourage administrators to be actively involved in the accountability process, keep them informed, encourage them to be allies, and enlist their support (Fairchild & Seeley, 1995). Another strategy with promise is to prepare a *formal written report* that brings together all the program's accountability data into one document that, in turn, can be shared with one's publics. Fairchild and Seeley recommend that, once the report has been prepared and disseminated, a school board presentation and presentations to the teaching faculty be requested. Both meetings provide opportunities to inform important publics and to correct misinformation that has occurred. Fairchild and Seeley cite other opportunities to enhance public relations that can be undertaken as well, including speaking to parent groups, civic organizations, and classrooms of students. Such meetings can focus on accountability data and can be used to share the expertise of the counseling staff through accurate, helpful information-sharing or town meeting formats. Clearly, systematic public-relations activities have an important place in the accountability function, and the evaluation data collected by counselors can be the centerpiece of public relations efforts.

ACCOUNTABILITY: A SPECIAL CHALLENGE FOR SCHOOL COUNSELORS

The authors' experience lends support to Myrick's (1984) contention that although most school counselors philosophically recognize the importance of being accountable, many detest the tasks related to accountability activities and resent having to be accountable. Part of this problem is attitudinal and may even be typological: The type of person attracted to the helping professions often prefers working with people and has antipathy for data collecting. Training may be another factor. Shaffer and Atkinson (1983) report that the counselor education programs they surveyed devote twice as much instruction time to scientific research as to program evaluation competence. Perhaps trainers of school counselors are not devoting enough attention to helping them learn the basics of evaluation (action research) and accountability. If true, the combination of having a low tolerance toward data and knowing little about program evaluation via action research makes the probability of school counselors engaging willingly in good accountability services seem very slim.

Results of a survey of a national but relatively small sample of school counselors ($N = 239$ respondents with usable returns) support those contentions. Fairchild and Zins (1986) reported only 55% of their respondents engaging in collecting some sort of evaluative data. Of that group, 91% reported collecting enumerative data; 70%, opinion data; 50%, intermediate outcome data; and 44%, final outcome data. Auspiciously, up to 75% of respondents who reported collecting evaluative data were using it to achieve a variety of accountability goals—some proactive and some reactive. In support of Shaffer and Atkinson's (1983) findings from a survey of counselor educators, only 41% of respondents indicated that they learned their accountability skills in basic counselor education training. Reasons for not engaging in evaluative activities vary, including a perceived lack of skills, the assumption that the process is too time-consuming and cumbersome, not thinking about doing it, and the fear of negative consequences. Several of these reasons support the contention that school counselors reject evaluation and accountability activities for attitudinal reasons.

These findings suggest both solutions and problems. The lack of good training in some counselor education programs can be corrected, but improved training will accomplish little if negative attitudes toward data collecting and analyzing persevere among individuals now in school counseling and those who will enter the field in the future. Changing selection strategies to attract different types of students to counseling will probably be counterproductive and create problems; individuals who appreciate data more may appreciate people less.

The rising tide of technological advances may usher in an era of user-friendly computerized systems. Although tempted to predict that the new wave of computer technologies will be the answer, the authors' sense is that, among people already working as school counselors, many of the same people who reject data collecting also resist learning to use computers. This may be less of a problem in the twenty-first century as more individuals who grow up using computers enter the counseling field.

With regard to accountability, school counseling has a problem that may persist well into the future; that is, many school counselors do not and will not proactively engage in accountability activities. As long as this situation exists, accountability activities will continue to be sporadic and ineffective. The profession may suffer for this both internally and externally. If accountability activities proliferate and improve in the future, the reason for the proliferation will probably be reactive. Many school counselors will engage in accountability activities because they have to do so. This will be unfortunate because then the accountability systems will be dictated by people other than counselors, and counselors' reactionary mentality will reinforce negative feelings about the accountability activities. Because they do not have a solution at this time, and perhaps not even agreeing that a problem exists, school counselors might continue to struggle with the issues related to accountability well into the twenty-first century. Fortunately, the keys to resolving the problem are within their grasp: Develop positive attitudes, learn the necessary skills, and approach accountability proactively.

AN ALTERNATIVE: EXTERNAL REVIEWS

J. J. Schmidt's (1995) recommendation, based on the belief that individual school counselors will seldom design and implement program evaluations despite efforts to assist them, is to employ external reviewers. Advantages of this approach include reduced time for counselors to devote to evaluation/accountability tasks and less demand for counselor expertise in this domain. Schmidt describes two evaluations conducted by external reviewers, one in a comprehensive school system and the other in a more rural school district. The reviewers' responsibilities included on-site visits by a team of consultants and preparation of opinion surveys for students, parents, and teachers. On-site visits consisted of structured interviews of principals, counselors, groups of teachers, the superintendent, and selected central staff personnel.

J. J. Schmidt's report of the evaluations indicates that the external reviews uncovered areas that needed to be improved in both school systems. Evidence that external reviews can be informative and helpful is provided in Schmidt's report.

A CASE STUDY: PROTECTING A SCHOOL COUNSELING PROGRAM

Hughes and James (2001) relate the case of an elementary-school counselor challenged by the decision of the school's site-based decision-making council to increase her classroom guidance time to more than the existing 50%. The reason for the council's decision was to provide more planning time for teachers. More planning time was needed because budget cuts in other areas had reduced collaborative planning time. The school counselor had 5 years of experience and was admittedly deficient in record-keeping, organizational, and accountability procedures. Her goal became explaining the school counselor's various roles and the total value of the school counseling program. She began with data for the previous year (evaluation) and considered ways to present it (accountability).

The counselor sought and received consulting assistance from a counselor educator and the professional literature on program accountability. The counselor decided to focus on enumerative data in order to help the site-based council members understand how she used her time and how her time use compared to a national study on counselor time usage. She presented the information graphically, and the council members realized how their decision would reduce the amount of time she would have for individual counseling, group counseling, consultation, and coordination.

The school counselor supported her enumerative presentation with a packet of information that included a mission statement, documentation of the grade levels served and topics covered in her prevention programming curriculum, her job description, and the state's professional standards for school counselors. The presentation generated constructive discussion leading to more informed decision making. The outcome was a victory for the status quo with the council agreeing to find alternative ways to provide teachers with more planning time. For the counselor, this was a preliminary step in a process for which the goal was to further improve her time use in order to serve students better.

In this case, the school counselor benefited from a helpful consultant, useful entries in the professional literature, an open-minded site-based decision-making council, support from her principal, and her own willingness to do the work needed to achieve her goals. Note that she was admittedly unprepared at the outset and had to respond reactively rather than proactively. Consequently, it is not surprising that she made the following recommendations to school counselors: (a) keep a collection of references from the professional school counseling literature handy, (b) adopt a personal school counseling model or set of standards, (c) record time spent on each school counseling activity (enumerative data), and (d) save documents that will inform others about the goals and services of one's school counseling program.

The heroine in this case study was able to accomplish her goals with enumerative data. Others may need more comprehensive data to accomplish their goals. It is useful to know that accountability goals can be achieved with relatively simple sets of data if they are on target and presented successfully. Also enlightening was her willingness to seek and use the help of consultants and the professional literature as well as her ability to respond to the challenge intellectually—figuring out what needed to be done and how it might be done. Finally, she was willing to admit competency deficits and do something constructive about it, especially learning how and preparing to present her accountability data in a manner that was convincing. Readers should view her as a coping model, learning from her vicariously. She is *any counselor,* an effective model for all school counselors!

SUGGESTED ACTIVITIES

1. Discuss the contention that many school counselors reject accountability activities because of the type of people they are.
2. Discuss the merits of proactive versus reactive accountability activities.
3. Discuss whether there are suitable alternative definitions of the terms *evaluation* and *accountability* to those used in this chapter.
4. Evaluate carefully and in detail the suggestions in this chapter for collecting evaluation data and reporting them for accountability purposes. Do you think the ideas are as good as the authors seem to think they are? Explain your position.
5. Debate the merits of the authors' prediction that accountability problems will persist for school counselors into the twenty-first century.
6. Develop samples of measurable outcome goals and useful opinion survey items.
7. Make an inventory of important enumerative data items across the various services that school counselors provide.
8. Investigate the feasibility of using commercial personal computer programs to record and store evaluation data and to organize them for accountability purposes successfully.

9. Debate the advantages and disadvantages of using accountability data for public relations purposes.
10. Debate the merits of employing external reviewers versus doing one's own evaluation and accountability activities.
11. Go to www.scan21st.com and propose some ways that this Internet site might help school counselors document and present their professional effectiveness.

REFERENCES

Adelman, H. S., & Taylor, L. (2002). School counselors and school reform: New directions. *Professional School Counseling, 5*, 235–248.

American School Counselor Association (n.d.). *Guide to membership resources.* Alexandria, VA: Author.

Arbuckle, D. (1970). Does the school really need counselors? *School Counselor, 17*, 325–330.

Baker, S. B. (1977). An argument for constructive accountability. *Personnel and Guidance Journal, 56*, 53–55.

Baker, S. B. (1983). Suggestions for guidance accountability. *Pennsylvania Journal of Counseling, 2*, 52–69.

Bardo, H. R., Cody, J. J., & Bryson, S. L. (1979). Evaluation of guidance programs: Call the question. *Personnel and Guidance Journal, 57*, 204–208.

Barlow, D. H., & Herson, M. (1984). *Single-case experimental designs: Strategies for studying behavior changes* (2nd ed.). New York: Pergamon Press.

Bernard, J. M., & Goodyear, R. K. (1998). *Fundamentals of clinical supervision* (2nd ed.). Boston: Allyn & Bacon.

Bollendorf, M., Howrey, M., & Stephenson, G. (1990). Project career REACH: Marketing strategies for effective guidance programs. *School Counselor, 37*, 273–280.

Bowers, J., Hatch, T., & Schwallie-Giddis, P. (2001, September/October). The brain storm. *ASCA Counselor,* 17–18.

Bruckner, S. T., & Thompson, C. L. (1987). Guidance program evaluation: An example. *Elementary School Guidance and Counseling, 21*, 196–198.

Cobb, H. C., & Richards, H. C. (1983). Efficacy of counseling services in decreasing behavior problems of elementary school children. *Elementary School Guidance and Counseling, 17*, 180–187.

Cook, D. W. (1989). Systematic needs assessment: A primer. *Journal of Counseling & Development, 67*, 462–464.

Dahir, C. (2001). National Standards for School Counseling Programs: Development and implementation. *Professional School Counseling, 4*, 320–327.

Elmore, P. B., Ekstrom, R. B., Diamond, E. E., & Whittaker, S. (1993). School counselors' test use patterns and practices. *School Counselor, 41*, 73–80.

Fairchild, T. N., & Seeley, T. J. (1995). Accountability strategies for school counselors: A baker's dozen. *School Counselor, 42*, 377–392.

Fairchild, T. N., & Zins, J. E. (1986). Accountability practices of school counselors: A national survey. *Journal of Counseling & Development, 65*, 196–199.

Frith, G. H., & Clark, R. (1982). Evaluating elementary counseling programs: 10 common myths of practitioners. *Elementary School Guidance and Counseling, 17*, 49–51.

Gibson, R. L. (1990). Teachers' opinions of high school counseling and guidance programs: Then and now. *School Counselor, 37*, 248–255.

Gillies, R. M. (1993). Action research for school counselors. *School Counselor, 41*, 69–72.

Gysbers, N. C., & Henderson, P. (2001). Comprehensive guidance and counseling programs: A rich history and a bright future. *Professional School Counseling, 4*, 246–256.

Haugaard, J. J. (1986). Idea exchange: Goal attainment. *Elementary School Guidance and Counseling, 20*, 227–229.

Hays, D. G., & Linn, J. K. (1977). *Needs assessment! Who needs it!* Washington, DC: American School Counselor Association.

Helliwell, C. B., & Jones, G. J. (1975). Reality considerations in guidance program evaluation. *Measurement and Evaluation in Guidance, 8*, 155–162.

House, R. M., & Hayes, R. L. (2002). School counselors: Becoming key players in school reform. *Professional School Counseling, 5*, 249–256.

Hously, W. F., McDaniel, L. C., & Underwood, J. R. (1990). Mandated assessment for counselors in Mississippi. *School Counselor, 37*, 294–303.

Hughes, D. K., & James, S. H. (2001). Using accountability data to protect a school counseling program: One counselor's experience. *Professional School Counseling, 4*, 306–309.

Hughey, K. F., Lapan, R. T., & Gysbers, N. C. (1993). Evaluating a high school guidance–language arts career unit: A qualitative approach. *School Counselor, 41,* 96–101.

Kelly, F. R., Jr., & Ferguson, D. G. (1984). Elementary school guidance needs assessment: A field-tested model. *Elementary School Guidance and Counseling, 18,* 176–180.

Krumboltz, J. D. (1974). An accountability model for counselors. *Personnel and Guidance Journal, 52,* 639–646.

Liu, Y. C., & Baker, S. B. (1993). Enhancing cultural adaptation through friendship training. *Elementary School Guidance and Counseling, 28,* 92–103.

Lombana, J. H. (1985). Guidance accountability: A new look at an old problem. *School Counselor, 32,* 340–346.

Miller, J. V., & Grisdale, G. A. (1975). Guidance program evaluations: What's out there? *Measurement and Evaluation in Guidance, 8,* 145–154.

Myrick, R. D. (1984). Measurement forum: Beyond the issues of school counselor accountability. *Measurement and Evaluation in Guidance, 16,* 218–222.

Parten, M. (1966). *Surveys, polls, and samples: Practical procedures.* New York: Cooper Square.

Rhyne-Winkler, M. C., & Wooten, H. R. (1996). The school counselor portfolio: Professional development and accountability. *School Counselor, 44,* 146–150.

Schmidt, G. (1986). Idea exchange: Guidance program evaluation. *Elementary School Guidance and Counseling, 20,* 225–227.

Schmidt, J. J. (1995). Assessing school counseling programs through external reviews. *School Counselor, 43,* 114–122.

Shaffer, J. L., & Atkinson, D. R. (1983). Counselor education courses in program evaluation and scientific research: Are counselors prepared for the accountability press? *Counselor Education and Supervision, 23,* 29–34.

Shaw, M. C. (1973). *School guidance systems: Objectives, functions, evaluation, and change.* Boston: Houghton Mifflin.

Zinck, K., & Littrell, J. M. (2000). Action research shows group counseling effective with at-risk adolescent girls. *Professional School Counseling, 4,* 50–59.

CHAPTER 14

Beyond the Training Program: A School Counseling Career

Goals: To offer suggestions for enhancing the professional identity and well-being of school counselors and discuss future prospects for school counselors.

Here is a testimonial we heard from a school counselor whose experience in the profession covered 35 years:

> *I have been a school counselor for 35 years. As I reflect on my years in counseling, I realize that I could not have chosen a better, more rewarding career for myself. Students I have counseled have attended fine universities and distinguished themselves in prominent careers. I have seen some of my favorite students graduate, join*

the military, go off to war, and then return to my office years later to reflect on the horrors they had seen or to grieve about the physical scars they suffered in battle. I have helped adolescent girls, raising children by themselves, struggle to complete the courses needed to graduate from high school. I have listened to African American youngsters—devalued by teachers—as they struggle to prove their worth in an unfriendly academic environment. I have been awakened on several nights by phone calls from parents who were trying to cope with the loss of a child in an automobile accident. I have sat with teachers, ready to leave their profession, because they no longer could tolerate the disrespect they experienced in the classroom. I have watched gifted young artists express themselves through painting and music. I have helped a fine athlete overcome his alcohol abuse and obtain a scholarship to a small college that valued his talent. I have found so many friends among teachers and parents who were willing to listen when I was confused and troubled in the work I had chosen for myself. I am retiring next year. I am glad to have found a profession that embraced me for who I am.

COUNSELORS IN SCHOOLS

According to Holland (1997), persons and environments interact, and both individuals and working environments may have personality types or structures. Of the six Holland types, school counselors tend to be primarily social. Social types value helping others, and tend to be friendly, enthusiastic, understanding, receptive, warm, and generous. They function best in predominantly social environments. In many schools, the predominant environment is not social. Unfortunately, the dominant environment in many schools is conventional, and conventional environments tend to be conservative and dogmatic. Preferred traits in conventional environments are conformity, conscientiousness, practical-mindedness, neatness, obedience, and docility.

The primary actors in creating and maintaining the school's environment are the administrators and teachers, in that order. Principals clearly influence the environment in their schools. What they value most will influence their own behavior and what they reinforce positively or negatively in the values and behaviors of their subordinates, in the school rules, and in the assignment of responsibilities within their purview. Teachers will influence the environment because they are the largest single group of professionals in a school. Depending on the circumstances, the teachers may or may not reflect the environmental preferences of the principal, especially if the principal was not involved in hiring them. Although teachers and counselors may differ from their principal(s) with respect to personality type, Holland (1997) believes that the most powerful individual in the environment will have the greatest influence. A principal can influence the environment as a model or by force of personality and will.

What does this mean for school counselors in training? Most prospective school counselors look forward enthusiastically to a career of applying the values, knowledge, and competencies acquired from their training in an environment that is conducive to achieving their goals. Unfortunately, many school administrators and teachers have other ideas about what counselors should do. Fitch, Newby, Ballestero, and Marshall (2001) found that, although many of the future school administrators they surveyed were aware of and appreciated roles and duties for school counselors that were commensurate with their training, some of them also rated noncounseling functions such as discipline, record keeping, and registration as important.

Two factors about school administrators and their training have been and will continue to be challenges for school counselors. First, many individuals who become school administrators are more conventional than social types of people. Second, programs that train school administrators rarely attempt to inform trainees about the roles and functions of school counselors according to either the content of the counselor education training programs or the content of the standards for training school counselors of the respective states. While counselor educators have attempted to address the second challenge both individually and collectively, their efforts have not been very successful; and we do not envision a breakthrough in that domain in the near future. Therefore, the brunt of trying to do something constructive about this challenge seems to fall upon the shoulders of individual school counselors at the grassroots level—each trying to make an impact on his or her own environment in order to make it more congruent.

Some beginning school counselors experience the challenge of incongruent environments as interns and others do so in their first jobs. Not all school counselors will experience this incongruence. Some will find themselves in a school environment that is congruent with their type and goals. Others will not, and we do not know the exact probabilities. Regarding this challenge, Fitch et al. (2001) highlight the importance of the job interview. They recommend using the first interview to present a summary of one's programmatic plans and goals to the chief school administrator. The administrator's response to this introduction is an important indicator of what the environment is and will be like for the prospective counselor. Thus, one way to deal with the possibility of environmental incongruence is to avoid it if possible. For those who cannot or did not, we next discuss some of the challenges that school counselors may have to face when working in incongruent environments.

CHALLENGES TO THE PROFESSIONAL IDENTITY OF SCHOOL COUNSELORS

You Never Told Us About . . .

Occasionally, interns and former students challenge us about not preparing them for the often onerous noncounseling functions they encounter on the job as school counselors. The implicit message is that, somehow, we should have included preparation for those functions in the training program. Should we write chapters about, and teach units on, how to build and monitor master schedules; coordinate testing programs; discipline misbehaving students; set up filing systems; and conduct lunchroom, hall, and bus duty? We think not! These are not functions that are included in role statements by the American School Counselor Association (ASCA), the Council for the Accreditation of Counseling and Related Educational Programs (CACREP), and state departments of education or public instruction. We view our role as ensuring that the training program meets the standards of the relevant professional and educational oversight organizations. We must prepare school counselors to be proficient at what they are supposed to do. On the other hand, we are very aware that many school counselors are assigned noncounseling tasks. Therefore, we do feel responsible for preparing school counseling students to cope with the noncounseling challenges. Our formula for meeting the challenges is as follows.

First, school counselors must know what they should be doing and be proficient at the requisite competencies. Proficiency leads to demonstrated competence that garners support from significant others, such as parents, students, teachers, and administrators. Second, school counselors will be challenged to advocate for themselves and their profession, as are counselor educators. Third, school counselors, as advocates, are challenged to provide leadership in helping colleagues and administrators discover better ways to get things done and use counselor time and talents wisely.

Our role as counselor educators then is to make students aware of the noncounseling challenges and prepare them to cope successfully—not train them to be proficient at noncounseling tasks. The remainder of this section of the chapter addresses some of the most prevalent noncounseling functions that school counselors may be requested to perform.

Dealing With Responsibility for Noncounseling Functions

Because of its diverse origins, school counseling has experienced greater identity problems than other professions in the field of education. On the one hand, most laypeople and professional educators have clear and relatively similar ideas about the roles of schoolteachers and administrators. On the other hand, those same people have widely differing opinions about the role of school counselors. Counselor education and training programs for school counselors have gradually reached the point where they have more similarities than differences; the differences often reflect the experiences and preferences of the counselor educators more than radical differences in the training programs. Professional organizations dedicated to promoting the counseling professions (the ACA, ACES, and ASCA) have developed and promoted role statements such as "Role Statement: The School Counselor" (ASCA, 1990) and developed training standards. In addition, CACREP is an accrediting agency whose attention is focused on counselor training programs. A relatively new accrediting agency, CACREP may have considerable influence in the twenty-first century.

Although counselor education has gradually developed a somewhat uniform identity for school counselors through its training programs and professional literature, the message has not reached the decision makers in the schools; many school counselors still find themselves engaging in functions that are unrelated or only remotely related to their training. These noncounseling functions, often highly regarded by individual principals and teachers, receive higher priority than counseling functions, leaving counselors to attend to noncounseling duties first and to engage in counseling functions in the remaining time. These conditions discourage some from entering the school counseling field; cause others to leave early, defeated and disappointed; cause some to adjust and become pseudo-counselors; confuse students, parents, and colleagues about the roles and functions of counselors; and leave many counselors disappointed in their training and trainers because they were not properly prepared for the noncounseling responsibilities and because their mentors cannot relieve them of the onerous responsibilities.

Because role senders are individuals in positions of authority or influence, they send messages both directly and implicitly to other individuals in institutional settings that influence the behaviors of those individuals (Haettenschwiller, 1970). Those who receive and react to the messages are boundary people who have little or no authority in the institutions. School counselors tend to be boundary people who have weak power status because they are a relatively small contingent of professionals and because they often differ from their teaching and administrating colleagues with regard to priorities. For example, Willower, Hoy, and Eidell (1967) found that administrators and teachers have high regard for custodial goals (or maintaining order), whereas counselors have high regard for humanistic goals (or those focused on promoting an environment for interaction and experience). As boundary people, school counselors traditionally receive messages from role senders that cause them to have responsibility for some custodial, noncounseling tasks. Cumulatively, these have considerable influence on determining an image of school counselors that is some distance from the ideal established by professional role statements and training standards. Until this situation is changed, school counselors will be unable to achieve either professional autonomy or the promise implied in the content and emphases of their training programs.

Scheduling.   School counselors have traditionally acquired some noncounseling functions. One of the most onerous and time-consuming is the gatekeeping and custodial tasks associated with scheduling. This administrative function has become the traditional responsibility of counselors in most secondary schools. Secondary-school counselors, responding to a survey from Tennyson, Miller, Skovholt, and Williams (1989), reported that as a group they are involved more frequently in scheduling than in any other activity. Although it is a lesser task in middle and elementary schools, scheduling may still be among the responsibilities of middle- and elementary-school counselors. Gatekeeping occurs when counselors must determine which students will be allowed to enroll in specific classes and which ones will be allowed to change classes. These responsibilities place counselors in potentially adversarial relationships with students and teachers, groups who should view counselors in more positive ways for counseling services to be received favorably. Students, and sometimes their parents, view counselors as adversaries whom they must cajole or entreat in order to receive limited resources (e.g., oversubscribed courses) or exceptions to the rules (e.g., making a course change after a course-drop deadline has passed). These encounters are hardly conducive to healthy helping relationships outside the scheduling domain. For some students, these are the only or initial encounters, and their impressions are colored unfavorably thereafter.

Teachers may view counselors as adversaries because, as gatekeepers, the counselors are directly responsible for fluctuating class enrollments. All teachers want class enrollments that are both consistent and sufficient. Receipt of additional students after the term has started creates stress for teachers, as does having students leave classes suddenly. Not having enough students in an elective course is threatening to teachers whose jobs are vulnerable. The number of students in their classes and the amount of student traffic into and out of their classes are annoyances that teachers attribute to the scheduling gatekeepers. When they are unhappy with the results of gatekeeping efforts, they blame the gatekeepers. These authors' experiences as school counselors, counselor educators, and consultants has led to the conclusion that the opinions of most secondary-school teachers about the value and competence of their counselors are heavily influenced by the way counselors are perceived to deal with scheduling gatekeeping chores. Not being able to please teachers as scheduling gatekeepers may condemn many school counselors to eternal disfavor, negating all their counseling accomplishments in the minds of these important colleagues.

Custodial tasks associated with scheduling include correcting mistakes on individual students' schedules and on master schedules; organizing, filing, and distributing student schedules; and screening individual student schedule requests for mistakes. These are tasks that can be performed by clerical personnel or mechanically (via computer) but are often done manually by school counselors. When the schools begin their academic years, they are captive to the activities and abilities of a handful of counselors who are trying to fit all students into the master schedule. Doing such work on a large scale is a demeaning and wasteful misuse of professionals trained to deliver much different services. Students and teaching colleagues, observing counselors performing these custodial functions, conclude that counselors are essentially professional clerks. Therefore, they, too, often dismiss counselors as having few worthy services to offer or as being too busy with clerical tasks to be bothered with higher order needs of students and colleagues.

Working school counselors form peer supervision groups similar to those they experienced as graduate students.

Scheduling is an administrative function, but principals, usually fewer in number than counselors, do not have the time or the inclination for most gatekeeping or custodial tasks. Interestingly, however, they usually control scheduling policies tightly. If scheduling is an administrative function and if the role of administrators is making policy, then they do need help with such gatekeeping and custodial responsibilities. The authors' position is that using counselors as gatekeepers and custodians is a mistake. If counselors are not the appropriate choice, who is? Even though scheduling is an administrative function, it serves teachers as well, providing them with a system that controls enrollments, assigns students to appropriate courses, and indicates where the participants are to meet. Therefore, because teachers benefit so greatly from the scheduling function, one can argue that they should be involved in the process. They should be involved in scheduling but not in the gatekeeping and custodial tasks any more than counselors should. Placing these responsibilities on teachers will have the same negative effects on them as it has on counselors.

Because the master schedule is an essential component of basic education and touches the lives of everyone in the schools, a team approach to making it work seems appropriate and fair. Baker (1982) offers an idea for implementing the team approach that provides basic responsibilities and leaves the details to those who might adapt the idea to specific settings. Specific task categories are identified. Adapted from that idea, five task categories are recommended here:

1. *Instruction* consists of administrators' informing counselors, teachers, students, parents and guardians, and other interested persons about the purposes, procedures, and content of the schedule and the scheduling process.

2. *Direction and control*, or gatekeeping, is an administrative function, so this can be the responsibility of administrators with the assistance of teachers, counselors, and clerical and paraprofessional personnel as consultants.

3. *Consultation* involves teachers, counselors, and students in the process of advising administrators about the strengths and weaknesses of the scheduling process and about the needs of individuals and of the system. For example, teachers can suggest that students be assigned to certain classes, counselors can provide information about student problems associated with scheduling, and students can make their own needs and opinions known. Administrators can serve as clearinghouses for this information with the assistance of clerical and paraprofessional personnel.

4. *Counseling* occurs when counselors, administrators, and teachers help students make decisions that affect their choices and schedules. In a system managed by administrators who make the policies, it stands to reason that they should also be the gatekeepers, setting rules about entering and leaving courses and making decisions when the rules are appealed or challenged. Teachers and counselors may provide counsel when asked.

5. *Custodial tasks* (e.g., processing and filing documents) are to be performed by clerical and paraprofessional personnel responsible to administrators.

This plan places the gatekeeping responsibilities in the administrative domain where they should be, recommends that clerical and paraprofessional personnel perform the custodial tasks they have been trained to do, and places teachers and counselors in the active and professional roles of fulfilling the consultation and counseling functions they have been trained to provide. If implemented, plans of this nature will free counselors from some undesirable noncounseling responsibilities and offer enhanced opportunities to provide professional services more attuned to their training.

Discipline.   Many counselors find that students they have requested to come to their office for service-oriented reasons often arrive displaying symptoms of tension and anxiety. The more assertive students want to know what they did wrong, and others behave reticently until put at ease by a quieting explanation or simply by an opportunity to experience a friendly, empathic atmosphere. Why do so many children and adolescents approach appointments with school counselors with tension and anxiety? Why do they think they must be in trouble if a counselor has asked to see them? To attribute these reactions to one cause would be an oversimplification of what is probably a complex set of reasons. Two very real and important reasons are that some counselors have disciplinary responsibilities and that others are assumed to have them. In either case, school counselors are viewed as disciplinarians by many students.

Discipline and guidance may have been linked through the concept of deans of men and women that was popular in student services before the influence of Rogers's client-centered counseling ideas and before the counseling professions developed clear statements of roles and functions. Early, simpler models of guidance viewed student services workers (e.g., deans) as wise, caring, and authoritarian individuals who were parent figures, providing support, advice, and discipline as needed. Currently, discipline is an administrative function in elementary, middle, and secondary schools. All disciplinary actions are subject to the scrutiny of school administrators. The schools that have assistant principals recognize them as having student discipline among their responsibilities. Discipline and counseling are antithetical when students are to be lectured, scolded, punished, interrogated, or accused. If counselors engage in such negative interactions with students, no matter how deserving, it will be very difficult to also establish empathic, unconditional helping relationships with them. Students will then view going to the counselor's office as an aversive experience—one to be avoided if at all possible.

If discipline is an administrative function, how did counselors get involved? One reason is history. Because of the way it was, some expect the situation to continue or assume it is continuing. Another reason is guilt by association. Because counselors work in offices often near the principal's, the activities of administrators, including discipline, are attributed to counselors, too. Another reason is the outright assignment of disciplinary responsibilities to counselors. This is more likely to happen in the schools where principals do not have assistants, and many of the more onerous disciplinary responsibilities are assigned to counselors. It can also happen in the schools where discipline has been assigned to school counselors by principals because those principals believe that counselors should be involved.

One of the best solutions to this dilemma will be recognition by the school administrators' profession, trainers of school administrators, and individual administrators that school counselors are professionals with their own definite and valuable programs to offer; they are not administrative assistants. Although individual counselors may contribute to this change, most are too isolated and powerless to do so; those who are successful may have only local or regional influence. A solution to this problem and to all the other noncounseling responsibilities that interfere with counseling services will probably have to come at a national level, through the efforts of professional organizations like the NEA, ACA, ACES, and ASCA. These organizations may influence members of other professional organizations such as the National Association of Secondary School Principals (NASSP) and perhaps legislators and the public. In the meantime, counselors are left with the challenge to devise solutions at the local and area levels.

School counselors who balk at the assignment of disciplinary responsibilities will probably have to determine ways to change the thinking of those who assign them such responsibilities. Successful attention-getting approaches may range from diplomacy to confrontation. Whatever approach is used, it will probably have to be accompanied by efforts to educate those who make the decisions. Professional counseling associations have helpful resources, primarily publications and media, and counselor educators may also be willing to offer consultation services.

Overcoming the image of being a disciplinarian requires more subtle efforts. Proactive strategies seem in order. The best way to change an undesirable image is to create a desired one. For example, elementary-school counselors can engage in preventive and counseling activities in the classroom that help them achieve counseling and developmental goals while introducing them to students as the kinds of professionals they want to be known as—caring, empathic, helpful, nonthreatening, and knowledgeable. Middle- and secondary-school counselors can engage in similar activities. All school counselors may also be able to use individual counseling contacts to introduce themselves appropriately. Get-acquainted interviews allow counselors to reach out to prospective student clients proactively and to establish a preferred agenda. Included in topics for get-acquainted interviews can be open-ended questions about interests and hobbies, future plans, progress in school, recreational activities, and perceptions of the counseling services. Responses to open-ended questions may lead to specific topics on which students wish to work once they accept the counselor as someone to trust who may be helpful (e.g., "What things interest you?" "What else would you like to talk about today?"). Personal topics (e.g., "Tell me about your family") and questions that focus the response on other individuals (e.g., "Who is your favorite teacher?") may be too threatening for students to handle in get-acquainted interviews.

The way invitations to students are made may prevent students from assuming the worst before learning the truth. Students who are invited with an advance explanation of the purpose of the interview, oral or printed, are less likely to think they have been summoned to the office for a threatening purpose. The purpose of get-acquainted interviews is to provide students with accurate perceptions of the kinds of people counselors are and the reasons why students might visit them again, either by appointment or self-referral. Additional proactive activities include newsletters for adults and older students, in-service programs for adults, and presentations for children—all designed to communicate accurate and understandable information about counselors and their services. A proactive approach to image management requires advance planning and assertiveness in gaining opportunities to meet with those whose favorable impressions are desired.

Secretarial and Clerical Tasks.

Secretaries and clerks perform noble and useful work. They choose to do so and prepare themselves accordingly before beginning their careers. School counselors, in contrast, receive specialized training at the graduate level to perform tasks other than secretarial and clerical work. School counselors need secretarial and clerical support because of the nature of their work. They must request or provide college transcripts, letters of recommendation to prospective employers, cumulative records, lesson plans and handouts for prevention programming activities, individualized educational plans (IEPs), newsletters, informational flyers and memos, drop-in requests for appointments, incoming telephone calls, media and materials for the information service, tests and testing reports, and various other items. These tasks are all reasons why school counselors need clerical and secretarial support to carry out their professional responsibilities successfully. Noncounseling responsibilities, such as scheduling, create additional needs for clerical and secretarial support.

Despite these legitimate reasons, many school counselors have either no secretarial and clerical support or too little. One result is that counselor time and energy that should be devoted to legitimate professional activities are spent on such support tasks. Another result is that the tasks are not done at all, or not done well, because there is too little time, interest, or talent for them. The first situation leads to making counselors into undertrained, part-time clerk-secretaries, and the second leads to diminished effectiveness and negative impressions by students, colleagues, and administrators. All these people are influenced by their first impressions of the obvious components of a professional's services—neatness, punctuality, availability, responsiveness, dependability, and organization.

The advent of microcomputers with useful word-processing, record-keeping, and printing capabilities has provided technological assistance to counselors for both counseling and noncounseling tasks. Although these technological advances may make better secretaries and clerks out of counselors, counselors are still doing secretarial and clerical work. Advanced technology is not the solution. An appropriate level of secretarial and clerical support is the solution. Freeing school counselors from secretarial and clerical tasks is another challenge for national professional organizations such as the NEA, ACA, ACES, and ASCA. School counselors, like other professionals, must have sufficient secretarial and clerical support for them to achieve their professional potential.

Paraprofessional Tasks.

For some counselors, responsibilities include selling lunch tickets, monitoring bus schedules, determining whether students have met graduation requirements, organizing and monitoring student fund-raising activities, monitoring prom and banquet planning, planning and conducting award ceremonies, and monitoring the distribution of diplomas at graduation ceremonies. All these are time-consuming noncounseling functions, administrative in nature, that have been assigned to counselors by their administrators. The implication is that these tasks are as important as the counseling functions for which the counselors were trained. Few can argue that these tasks are unimportant in the life of the school, but the counseling profession argues that they are not appropriate assignments for school counselors (ASCA, 1990). Based on a survey of school counselors, Astramovich and Holden (2002) reported that the participants supported the employment of paraprofessionals. They also found that secondary-school counselors were more likely to make this recommendation than elementary-school counselors, probably because they were more inundated with paraprofessional tasks.

Assigning such tasks to counselors places them in a role best identified as an administrative assistant—not only conducting paraprofessional tasks but also having their competence judged largely on the performance of these tasks. A widely held assumption in educational administration is that school counselors are supposed to serve primarily

Counselors are challenged to keep current and to achieve continuous self-renewal.

as administrative assistants to principals. How else can one explain the widespread assignment of so many noncounseling duties to school counselors? This mistaken assumption must be altered if school counseling is to achieve its necessary professional identity. In the authors' opinion, the only way this assumption and the actions it inspires will be changed is through a concerted effort by all national professional organizations that represent school counselors. School counselors, in turn, can unite and work through their professional organizations and take leadership responsibilities for this undertaking, something that has not happened on a large enough scale thus far.

Changes may require assertive and provocative actions by school counselors and their colleagues to get the attention of consumers, who may offer sympathetic support, and in educating administrators, who may respond in an adversarial fashion to proposals that threaten their assumptions about the role of school counselors. To do little or nothing about this will support the status quo; counselors in the twenty-first century, though possibly better prepared than their predecessors, will still be administrative assistants performing many noncounseling tasks.

Substitute Teaching.

Administrators sometimes find it convenient and cost-effective to call on school counselors to substitute for missing teachers and school nurses. The false assumptions and negative outcomes stated earlier apply in these instances as well. In addition, students are likely to receive lower quality instruction than from a qualified substitute teacher, and counselors engaging in substitute teaching or nursing are more vulnerable to accusations of negligence or malpractice than are qualified substitutes or than the counselors would be if they were engaging in responsibilities for which they have been trained and certified/licensed. Perhaps counselors will serve themselves and the profession better by being more the devil's advocate than the good guy or gal when asked to help out in this manner.

Challenges From Individuals and Groups Outside the School System.

In the 1990s, school counseling experienced challenges to elements of and entire school counseling programs. For example, a disagreement over materials and methods led to the cancellation of an entire school counseling program in Clackamas, Oregon, and self-esteem programs in the Capistrano, California, school district were challenged as unlawful (McCullough, 1994). Although it is difficult to predict exactly what might be challenged in the future, previous challenges seem to have focused on materials, programs, and practices that are viewed by some individuals and groups as invasions of privacy, religious in nature; as unlawful psychotherapeutic interventions, sacrilegious in nature; and as in opposition to the values of the dissenting groups or individuals. The issues become emotional and tend to polarize communities, leading to nastiness, attempts at censorship, political pressuring, and bad publicity for professionals and communities.

McCullough (1994) cites prevention advice from Greg Brigman, a counselor educator who recommends the following responses:

- Contact the ASCA for information on resources and procedures.
- Have district policies for reviewing curriculum materials and follow them.

- Keep the educational community informed about programs and materials.
- Have a clear idea of what the national and local communities want children to learn in schools.

McCullough's article provides additional specific advice to counselors. Although it is tempting to view the challengers as reactionaries, these events contain an important message for all school counselors. A careful examination of the teaching/instruction domain of the schools will usually lead one to discover that the content of courses taught in English, social studies, mathematics, science, kindergarten, third grade, and the like is the result of a curriculum development process and that the content is based on foundational principles and guidelines, studied, and approved by committees, administrators, and school boards before it is implemented. Sometimes prevention programming by school counselors has gone through much less rigorous planning and scrutiny, leaving the programs and the counselors more vulnerable when challenged. Therefore, an important message the challenges seem to provide for school counselors is that their prevention programming should be developed with as much care and scrutiny as are the academic curricula in their schools. Doing so will help make school counselors less vulnerable to outside challenges.

Keeping Motivated

Burnout is a widely used label for a broad range of symptoms leading to losing the interest or competence to perform one's job effectively. It is something to be avoided. No one wishes to be burned out. Yet, many professionals receive the label. Without getting overly diagnostic, several challenges cause school counselors to experience burnout. One may be the stress associated with trying to be all things to all people while having too little control over their professional identity. Principals who treat counselors like administrative assistants, teachers who are unhappy with class enrollments, parents who blame counselors because their children fail to get accepted to a preferred college, students who cannot be successfully helped, student-to-counselor ratios that are too large to manage, and insufficient secretarial and clerical support are but a few additional examples. Low status in the professional hierarchy, insufficient budgetary support and resources, low pay, professional isolation, loss of competence and confidence, and personal problems are also examples of stressors school counselors face that may take their toll and lead to burnout. Using the Counselor Occupational Stress Inventory (COSI), Moracco, Butcke, and McEwen (1984) documented the causes of stress among a sample of 361 ASCA members. Their analysis led to an observation that occupational stress seems to be a multidimensional concept. The dimensions they identify in their factor analysis are lack of decision-making authority, financial stress (small rewards), nonprofessional duties, job overload, and dissatisfying professional relationships with teachers and principals. Behannon (1996) assembled comments from several counseling professionals that, in summary, pointed out that the nature of their work makes school counselors at high risk of burning out.

The purpose of this discourse is not to lament these problems, for school counselors are not the only individuals who experience such stressors and suffer from burnout. Rather, they are presented as challenges. Individually and collectively, school counselors are challenged to accept stressors as a fact of life and do everything within their power to prevent themselves from burning out, treating the symptoms quickly and appropriately when they occur. As can be determined from the sampling of causes listed earlier, school counselors have many stressors with which to cope. Some can be managed individually or in cooperation with colleagues, and support from larger bodies, such as professional organizations and legislatures, and from enlightened individuals with sufficient influence to cause change is also needed. What can individual counselors do to prevent burnout? The authors' belief is that keeping motivated and current are strategies within the control of each counselor that have promise for self-enhancement and burnout prevention.

The theme of this presentation on keeping motivated is "Be proactive." We are challenged to take the responsibility for motivating ourselves. Many strategies for implementing this idea exist. Following is a presentation of goals, not to be considered a listing of strategies. Strategies are varied and numerous and do not work universally. Readers can more easily respond to suggested goals, determining whether they are personally appropriate and deciding on their own strategies for implementing them. In a book aptly entitled *A Survival Guide for the Secondary School Counselor*, Hitchner and Tifft-Hitchner (1987) suggest establishing consulting alliances with colleagues to find sanity in numbers and leaving the emotions associated with problems at work so that they do not interfere with one's home life. Both are commendable goals that may be accomplished differently by individual counselors.

Cognitive Health. One arena over which individuals have potential control is their own thoughts. Self-acceptance is an important goal. Self-acceptance is founded on the belief that one is doing her or his best and making decisions in good faith. A belief in having acted in good faith allows individuals to accept constructive criticism as challenging rather than as damning. Recognizing irrational and self-defeating thoughts may prevent corresponding irrational ideation and self-defeating behaviors. The same tactics that counselors use to recognize and treat irrational ideation experienced by student clients can be applied to themselves.

Physical Health. A second arena over which individuals have potential control is their physical health. Some symptoms of stress can be treated and prevented physically. Relaxed individuals with healthful diets are less likely to experience burnout. The health sciences offer numerous suggestions for achieving and maintaining good physical health. Physical health will make individuals better able to cope with stress while also causing them to think about themselves more positively. Some symptoms of stress can be treated successfully by such physical responses as deep diaphragmatic breathing and progressive muscle relaxation. These treatments may be even more effective if used in conjunction with cognitive strategies for coping with irrational and self-defeating ideation (Cormier & Cormier, 1998).

Healthy Interactions. A third arena over which control can be achieved is interactions with others. The environment includes other people. Achieving appropriate assertiveness is an important goal for coping with others. Individuals are challenged to achieve direct or open, honest, and appropriate expressions of their affectionate or oppositional feelings, preferences, needs, and opinions (Fitch et al., 2001; Galassi & Galassi, 1977). Appropriate assertiveness means that one is able to give and receive compliments; make requests; express liking, love, and affection; initiate and maintain conversations; express one's legitimate rights; refuse requests; and express justified annoyance, displeasure, and anger. Performing all these behaviors successfully will improve the working environment of school counselors. A pleasant, sufficiently spacious, private, and appropriately heated and ventilated physical environment can also work wonders. Counselors can achieve some of these goals on their own, whereas other goals may require assertive action.

Counselors who understand the goals and expectations of other individuals in their environment are better able to develop ways to cope with them successfully. For example, teachers may expect counselors, as coprofessionals, to take their side in disputes with students, rather than approach disputes as student advocates; principals, who have broad definitions of their own jobs, may define counselors' jobs similarly; and parents may view counselors as individuals who will readily share information with them about their children regardless of whether the information is confidential. Some combination of creative thinking, appropriate assertiveness, and diplomacy is required to cope with these and other misperceived expectations and to keep from being worn down by them.

Reasonable Workload.   Student-to-counselor ratios are determined predominantly by the financial condition of the school district and secondarily by the perceived worth of the guidance program (Shaw, 1973). Universal ratios are very difficult to dictate because of individual differences associated with the severity of student problems, amount of available secretarial and clerical assistance, curriculum options, and referral support. In a time of a generally perceived need for good counseling, when it was thought that the United States was threatened by Soviet technological advances, Conant (1959) recommended 250 to 300 students to each counselor. This was probably a compromise between providing high-quality counseling services and what was economically feasible for school districts. As reported by Peters (1978), the Education Task Force of the 1971 White House Conference on Youth recommended a ratio of 50 to 1 throughout elementary and secondary schools. Peters himself recommended 200 to 1, again as a compromise.

In *A Nation at Risk: The Imperative for Educational Reform*, reported by the National Commission on Excellence in Education in 1983, no mention was made of school counseling (Hitchner & Tifft-Hitchner, 1987). That report and others like it emphasize the importance of improving the knowledge and work habits of Americans to cope with the economic challenges from political allies in the Far East and Western Europe. Consequently, attention was devoted to the cognitive domain. The theme is to produce better educated and disciplined citizens. Although the report is useful, with important goals, it falls short because it does not recognize the affective needs of students, too.

These affective needs are likely to grow. Figures from the 1980 census led to projections that one third of the population in the United States would be either African American or Hispanic by 2020. Historically, children of poverty have come primarily from minority groups. Women are increasingly entering the labor force; 50% of the labor force in 1985 was women. The number of single-parent homes and latchkey children is increasing dramatically, and drop-out rates, already significant in some areas of the country, promise to become even more problematic (Hitchner & Tifft-Hitchner, 1987). Poverty, minority status, having a working mother, and coming from a single-parent family are highly correlated with school failure (William T. Grant Foundation Commission on Work, Family and Citizenship, 1988). School failure leads to dropping out or to floundering within the system. The Grant Commission views these individuals, "the forgotten half," as being in danger of not finding places for themselves in the economic system. In addition, individuals from these highly vulnerable groups who are capable of benefiting from the opportunities associated with receiving a higher education are not likely to receive adequate precollege guidance (College Entrance Examination Board, 1986).

All the preceding findings lead one to conclude that an emphasis placed solely on improving the environment for cognitive development is insufficient for the United States to meet the economic challenges of the twenty-first century. This was highlighted in earlier chapters by referring to the work of Adelman and Taylor (2002). Counseling programs with better proactive and reactive counseling responses, in conjunction with improved instruction, are crucial, and they go hand in hand (Dahir, 2001; Gysbers & Henderson, 2001). Better counseling programs are linked to lower student-to-counselor ratios, especially where the most vulnerable students are attending the schools. Exactly what the ratios should be is a moot question. They must be decreased for counselors to be more effective and to perceive themselves as such. The challenge probably has to be met collectively through efforts of national professional organizations. Currently, "the ASCA recommends a ratio of 1/100 (ideal) to 1/300 (maximum) to implement a standards-based, comprehensive developmental school counseling program" (Campbell & Dahir, 1997, p. 13).

Efficiency Enhancement.   Being able to operate efficiently will enhance counselors' motivation, providing a sense of control over their time and work. Adapting computer technology seems key to achieving greater efficiency for school counselors. Hoskins and Rosenthal (1983) reported using a microcomputer to schedule 1,400 students into career exploration groups in 12 hours. This job had previously taken three to four people up to 100 hours, a testimony to the efficiency of using a microcomputer in that instance. Much has been published about microcomputers in the recent counseling literature. What do microcomputers have to offer?

Computer technology has been available to school counselors since at least the 1960s. Access to that technology was limited and expensive until the advent of microcomputers in the 1980s. In the twenty-first century, counselors and students have access to the World Wide Web on the Internet. Suggestions for using microcomputers to achieve efficiency goals include tutoring, filing, scheduling, calculating, computer-assisted counseling, simulating real-life situations, and providing accountability data. Tutoring efforts can be enhanced by programs that provide repetitive practice opportunities, simulations of real-life operations, competency testing, and performance analyses (Gaushell, 1984). Custodial administrative tasks are particularly suitable for microcomputer technology; a relatively broad range of ever-improving software is available for managing filing, scheduling, calculating, and document-producing functions (Gaushell, 1984; Kennedy, 1987). As can be discerned from the web activities associated with this textbook, the Internet abounds with opportunities to use computer technology in school counseling.

Challenges are associated with the introduction of computer technology to the counseling profession. Some counselors resist computers because they think that the machines will interfere with their ability to work with people directly, think that working with computers requires abstract abilities they do not have, and have negative stereotypes of people who use computers (Childers & Podemski, 1984). Others disdain computer technology because having to learn a very challenging technology causes them anxiety, or they assume that computer technology can replace counselors (Lindsay, 1988). Research by Sampson et al. (1992) indicates that career counseling clients perceive computerized career guidance systems as more effective if accompanied by opportunities to work with human counselors, a conclusion that has been discovered by other researchers as well. This information should be encouraging to counselors who worry about being replaced by, or perceived as less effective than, computers.

Learning how to use a microcomputer can be formidable, especially for people not raised on computers since childhood. Attitude seems to be the important ingredient. Griffin, Gillis, and Brown (1986) found that familiarity breeds acceptance while unfamiliarity breeds contempt. Further, those not threatened by computers accept them (Cairo & Kanner, 1984). One of the major sources of feeling threatened—thinking computers will replace counselors—seems to be a fallacy, at least for the foreseeable future. Computers are not competitive in this respect because programs are very limited in their ability to process natural human language (Lawrence, 1986). As Sampson (1987) recommends, counselors should view computers as tools useful to aid or assist humans in the counseling process. Therefore, computers can be accepted for use in subordinate roles in the counseling and behavior-changing process. If counselors view computers as tools that provide useful but limited subordinate services, they will be more likely to use computers wisely to enhance the efficiency of counseling services, perhaps even achieving a greater sense of control and motivation. Assuming that counselors are able to accept and use computers, such issues as the differential influence of various systems and programs on users becomes a concern for future research and development (Kivlighan, Johnston, Hogan, & Mauer, 1994); that is, counselors and researchers, putting aside lower order concerns, will be able to concentrate on ways to enhance and refine the use of computers in counseling.

Enhanced Competence. Becoming a Licensed Professional Counselor (LPC) is an opportunity available to counselors in most states. Being an LPC is not a requisite for certification/licensure as a school counselor. Therefore, many counselors have this option as a way of keeping current and motivated. Although LPC requirements may vary from state to state, becoming an LPC usually requires having one's credentials reviewed, passing an examination (e.g., the National Counseling Examination), and providing evidence of postgraduate course work and/or clinical supervision. These are activities that help one become and remain current. They may also lead to a sense of personal accomplishment, add to one's perceived professional stature, and provide an opportunity for economic enhancement (e.g., private counseling practice or consultation services).

In a survey of 267 members of the American School Counselor Association who were school counselors, Page, Pietrzak, and Sutton (2001) found that 29% were receiving peer clinical supervision, and 57% wanted to receive it. Those expressing a preference for peer clinical supervision expressed a desire that it be provided by school counselors who were trained to provide supervision.

Sutton and Page (1994) and Agnew, Vaught, Getz, and Fortune (2000) reported on the advantages of peer supervision activities as a way to keep motivated. Working school counselors form peer supervision groups similar in nature to those they experienced in counseling and internship practicums while graduate students. Agnew et al. found that counselors who participated in a peer group clinical supervision program experienced improved professional relationships, believed they had increased the opportunities to learn counseling skills and techniques, and experienced an increased sense of professionalism. The report also stressed the importance of administrative support, training in clinical supervision, adequate funding, and adequate time in making the activity successful.

Keeping Current

At mid-twentieth-century, one axiom stated in counselor training programs was that there will be jobs in the future that do not exist today. That turned out to be true, accurately depicting the rapid changes in the second half of the twentieth century and indicating a continuation of the same circumstances in the early twenty-first century. Rapidly changing times feature increasing educational and technological developments. Consequently, matriculating from the most up-to-date and comprehensive counselor training program may still leave a graduate's preparation dated within a decade unless an effort is made to keep current with new developments—an effort to seek self-renewal (Baker, 1981). Walz and Benjamin (1978) suggest that self-renewal be viewed from two perspectives. The first perspective defines self-renewal as updating and streamlining previously acquired skills and knowledge to ensure that one knows what has been learned and adds new ideas to old approaches. From the second perspective, counselors can use self-renewal to acquire techniques, ideas, and skills they never had before, making them even more versatile. Thus, whether keeping current involves refurbishing the old model or developing a new hybrid, the need for self-renewal is a real and constant issue confronting school counselors.

Counselors are challenged to keep current and to achieve continuous self-renewal. This can be done in many ways, some creative and some traditional. Among the traditional ways to keep current are attending workshops; enrolling in university and college courses; reading professional journals, books, and reports; listening to audio and observing visual media; attending professional conferences and conventions; and teaching—that is, sharing one's knowledge and skills with others. Creative responses are determined by the ideas each counselor generates individually. For instance, those who have access to the information highway provided by the Internet may find exploring the World Wide Web an opportunity to gain useful information and mastering the Internet an interesting challenge.

The National Board for Certified Counselors (NBCC) provides an opportunity for counselors to keep current while engaging in a certification process. The NBCC certifies counselors who pass NBCC examinations, referring to them as National Certified Counselors (NCCs). Among the certificates is that for National Certified School Counselor (NCSC). Preparation for the examinations and involvement in NBCC-approved workshops and continuing education programs are examples of ways to keep current that have been sponsored by professional counseling associations such as the ACA and ASCA. They are designed to meet the needs of practicing counselors.

Of all the challenges to the professional identity of school counselors, keeping current may be the one most within the power of individual counselors to achieve. No less important than the others, it is a goal that can be achieved at any time. Perhaps it should be the first goal set by graduates of counselor training programs. The trainers, having done their best to make students up-to-date when they complete training, pass to their students the responsibility for keeping the torch of knowledge lit. Students, in turn, by keeping the flame burning, make themselves valuable to their consumers throughout their years of service.

BEYOND THE PRESENT: WHAT DOES THE FUTURE HOLD FOR SCHOOL COUNSELORS?

As editors of *The Handbook of Counseling*, Locke, Myers, and Herr (2001) contributed their own chapter on "counseling in the future." Their thoughts were based in part on a review of the material in the 43 chapters from contributors to the handbook, including the authors of the present textbook (Baker & Gerler, 2001). Among their concluding comments were the following thoughts:

> Professional counselors will need a broad knowledge base to deliver comprehensive counseling services and also will need specialized knowledge to cope with changes in client conditions. . . . These changes are assumed to affect all areas of the counseling profession. . . . Counselors will be functioning on a more professional level as a result of changes in practice environments and will expect to be treated as colleagues rather than the subordinates of the past. . . . Commonly understood descriptions of what counselors do for clients are essential if counseling is to be recognized as a principal contributor to mental health care. Counselors need to work in collaboration, not competition, with other mental health care providers to increase the effectiveness of the mental health delivery system. (Locke, Myers, & Herr, 2001, p. 691)

The focus of the thinking of Locke et al. is on the broad field of professional counseling. More specific to school counseling, Schmidt (2003) states that:

> Traditional guidance and counseling services will no longer meet the needs of future students and families. School counselors at all levels—elementary, middle, and high school—can be expected to adjust their goals, create expanded services, develop new skills, and serve broader populations in the years to come. To meet these challenges, future counselors will 1. Develop a broader knowledge of human knowledge

throughout the life span. . . . 2. Adapt to new technology. . . . 3. Increase the use of group practices. . . . 4. Expand their professional development. . . . 5. Measure the outcome of their services. . . . 6. Become professionally and perhaps politically active through state and national counseling associations to ensure the integrity of the school counseling profession. (p. 308)

In a special issue of *Professional School Counseling* (*PSC*) on the past, present, and future of school counseling, one of us wrote:

> These are not the comments of a pessimist. I am by nature an optimist. My view of school counseling is probably most appropriately labeled as realistic optimism. . . . As a realistic optimist, I predict that improvements will occur slowly and inconsistently over the decades to come if circumstances remain as they are. . . . Is the glass half full or half empty? For this realistic optimist, it is half full. . . . How does the profession implement these wonderful ideas expeditiously and systematically? In my opinion, this is the question that raises the primary challenge to the school counseling profession at the present time. (Baker, 2001, p. 82)

Other writers contributed to the special issue of *PSC* devoted to the future of school counseling. Gysbers (2001) advocated "fully implemented comprehensive guidance and counseling programs in every school district in the United States, serving all students and their parents, staffed by active, involved school counselors" (p. 103). He continued by pointing out that fully implemented comprehensive guidance programs would place school counselors and their programs in the center of education rather than on the periphery. Paisley and McMahon (2001) described the ideal school counselor of the future who completed a CACREP accredited program, was familiar with the larger school community, and was committed to lifelong learning. The ideal counselor would "be equally grounded in the three domains of academic, career and personal/social development" (p. 113). Finally, the ideal counselor would be competent in the several areas of competence covered in the present textbook. Green and Keys (2001) pointed out that, although the comprehensive developmental model had aligned the profession more closely with the needs of students, there remained the need to address the contextual factors that hinder the promotion of healthy development for those students who have little access to the benefits of a good education.

Note that these presentations address some of the ideas advocated in the three initiatives presented initially in chapter 1 and highlighted throughout this textbook. Gysbers (2001) spoke directly about comprehensive school counseling programs, and Paisley and McMahon (2001) mentioned the importance of counselors being grounded in academic, career, and personal/social development. These ideas are crucial components of the ASCA's National Model for School Counseling Programs. In addition, Green and Keys's (2001) attention to those students who have little access to the benefits of a good education addressed a central theme for both the Education Trust's National School Counselor Training Initiative and the School–Community Collaboration Model. Further analysis of the Green and Keys (2001) article will indicate that they are strong proponents of the School–Community Collaboration Model.

A second issue of *Professional School Counseling* presented reactions to the four presentations just cited. From his position as a school counselor and former president of the ASCA, Kuranz (2002) agreed with the views that promoted comprehensive school counseling programs and stated that "real success requires change . . . to develop and move forward" (p. 178). In her presentation, Whiston (2002) wondered whether the existing comprehensive developmental programs were indeed truly comprehensive—a point similar to that made by Green and Keys (2001). She also pointed out that none of the writers in the first issue had addressed "a significant dearth of research on school counseling" (p. 154). She concluded this theme by suggesting that the future of school counseling may hinge on the profession's being able to document evidence of its effectiveness.

As spokespersons for the Education Trust's National School Counselor Training Initiative, Sears and Granello (2002) expressed concern about inconsistency in language and failure to espouse alternative views in the four articles. They believe school counselors will need additional skills that empower them to be advocates for change, and that this will best occur via significant changes in the preparation of school counselors. Those additional skills will allow school counselors to provide leadership, collaboration, coordination, and advocacy.

After digesting the four articles, Sink (2002) concluded that the school counseling profession had "made significant strides forward and its future is bright" (p. 161). He also discerned from the four articles a theme suggesting that "the profession cannot simply rest, so to speak, on its laurels; rather, school counselors must actively engage in dialogue with their advocates and detractors, learning what they can about pertinent and effective educational and counseling innovations, and disagreeing respectfully with those notions that depart substantially from the profession's core beliefs and goals" (p. 161).

Although clearly not in full agreement, all of the writers just cited have a passion for the school counseling profession—past, present, and future. While unable to predict and arbitrarily mold the future, they are trying to influence it in a positive way. In spite of their efforts, our concern about how effectively ideas from professional association leaders and counselor educators will influence school counseling programs remains. School counselors and other stakeholders such as administrators, teachers, parents, and communities will clearly influence what happens. Yet, we are very impressed with the efforts of the ASCA National Model for School Counseling Programs, the National School Counselor Training Initiative of the Education Trust, and the School–Community Collaboration Model.

We applaud what has been accomplished within each of these three initiatives thus far and have highlighted their positions throughout this textbook. Spokespersons for all three initiatives have specified the connections with current educational reform initiatives, and that seems to be a strategically wise decision. Yet, as Borders (2002) points out, many of the goals of these initiatives were important in school counseling before the current reform movement, and "riding the wave of educational reform, however (whatever the reform movement focus of a particular time may be), does subject school counseling to the tides of public opinion and legislative decision making" (p. 183).

Remembering the influence of the National Defense Education Act of 1958 30 to 40 years ago, we understand the importance of riding the wave of the current educational reform movement. We also agree with Borders's (2002) point, viewing it as a recommendation to accept the current initiatives as something more than responses to the current educational reform movement. We believe the value of the three initiatives extends well beyond the focus of the current educational reforms and holds promise for strengthening the school counseling profession well into the twenty-first century. We also believe that the initiatives have promise for achieving grassroots support from school counselors across the land and from their administrators, teachers, students and families, and communities.

Having offered our support for the initiatives individually, we also wish to state our belief that together they offer much more than any of them offers alone. The ASCA National Model for Comprehensive School Counseling Programs provides the performance-based ASCA National Standards and advocacy for comprehensive school counseling programs. The emphasis upon performance-based comprehensive programs is important because it focuses on school counseling as a program with a curriculum. In addition, the ASCA linkage with Norman Gysbers and colleagues offers the strength of building on their work of over a decade across the country. These counselor educators and professional counselors know how to build consensus among grassroots school counselor groups and negotiate successfully with state departments of education and local school boards and have already caused several states to adopt the comprehensive guidance model. They have mastered important networking competencies.

The Education Trust's National School Counselor Training Initiative provides strength through its focus on upgrading the training of school counselors, especially in the leadership, collaboration, and advocacy domains. The Trust has established training prototypes in several counselor education programs. In addition, the initiative has captured the attention of decision makers at the federal level, especially for its focus on school counselors as leaders within the current No Child Left Behind reform activities and on making rigorous, high-quality educational opportunities available to all students.

In our opinion, the School–Community Collaboration Model provides the missing piece in this design for the future of school counseling. While access to all the benefits of a good education for all students is a noble cause, some students will not benefit from merely being placed in more rigorous courses of study. We draw on Maslow's (1954) hierarchy of needs to make this point. If the basic needs of students are not met, then they will be unable to respond to enhanced educational opportunities. In recognition of the mental health, physical health, and social service needs of students from impoverished and dysfunctional circumstances, proponents of the School–Community Collaboration Model promote collaborations between school systems and community services systems within and outside the schools. These collaborations will improve the potential for students and their families to receive needed services that will allow the students to attend to the higher order needs that rigorous academic offerings present, and school counselors are viewed as key players in coordinating the collaborations.

Our position on the future of school counseling thus stated, we close with a comment about competencies, a subject highlighted throughout this textbook. As stated earlier, we believe the competencies presented here are generic to any model for school counseling. We also believe these competencies will remain important in the future. Therefore, we encourage all school counseling students and school counselors to be skillful across all of these competency domains. Whatever the circumstances may be, competent, flexible school counselors are better positioned to provide high-quality services to their publics and make their programs relevant than are those who are inadequately competent and inflexible. This appears to be one important way that each school counselor can have an impact on his or her own future.

SUGGESTED ACTIVITIES

1. Survey a sample of school counselors about their attitudes toward scheduling.
2. Discuss the merits, limits, and cautions associated with computer-assisted counseling and using the Internet in school counseling.
3. Independently establish a plan for keeping current, and then share your ideas with others.
4. Discuss the merits of the various attempts in this chapter to predict or influence the future of school counseling.
5. Go to www.scan21st.com and propose some ways that this Internet site might help communicate the appeal of a career in school counseling.

REFERENCES

Adelman, H. S., & Taylor, L. (2002). School counselors and school reform: New directions. *Professional School Counseling, 5*, 235–248.

Agnew, T., Vaught, C. C., Getz, H. G., & Fortune, J. (2000). Peer group clinical supervision program fosters confidence and professionalism. *Professional School Counseling, 4*, 6–12.

American School Counselor Association (ASCA). (1990). Role statement: The school counselor. *ASCA guide to membership resources.* Alexandria, VA: Author.

Astramovich, R. L., & Holden, J. M. (2002). Attitudes of American School Counselor Association members toward utilizing paraprofessionals in school counseling. *Professional School Counseling, 5*, 203–210.

Baker, S. B. (1981). *School counselor's handbook: A guide for professional growth and development.* Boston: Allyn & Bacon.

Baker, S. B. (1982). Free school counselors from gatekeeping and custodial tasks. *National Association of Secondary School Principals Bulletin, 66*, 110–112.

Baker, S. B. (2001). Reflections on forty years in the school counseling profession: Is the glass half full or half empty? *Professional School Counseling, 5*, 75–83.

Baker, S. B., & Gerler, E. R., Jr. (2001). Counseling in schools. In D. Locke, J. E. Myers, & E. L. Herr

(Eds.), *The handbook of counseling* (pp. 289–318). Thousand Oaks, CA: Sage.

Behannon, M. (1996). Overworked and under stress. *Counseling Today, 39*(2), 17.

Borders, L. D. (2002). School counseling in the twenty-first century: Personal and professional reflections. *Professional School Counseling, 5*, 180–185.

Cairo, P. C., & Kanner, M. S. (1984). Investigating the effects of computerized approaches to counselor training. *Counselor Education and Supervision, 24*, 212–221.

Campbell, C. A., & Dahir, C. A. (1997). *Sharing the vision: The national standards for school counseling programs.* Alexandria, VA: American School Counselor Association.

Childers, J. H., Jr., & Podemski, R. S. (1984). Removing barriers to the adoption of microcomputer technology by school counselors. *School Counselor, 31*, 223–228.

College Entrance Examination Board. (1986). *Keeping the options open: An overview.* New York: Author.

Conant, J. B. (1959). *The American high school today.* New York: McGraw-Hill.

Cormier, S., & Cormier, B. (1998). *Interviewing strategies for helpers: Fundamental skills and cognitive behavioral interventions* (4th ed.). Pacific Grove, CA: Brooks/Cole.

Dahir, C. (2001). The National Standards for School Counseling Programs: Development and implementation. *Professional School Counseling, 4,* 320–327.

Fitch, T., Newby, E., Ballestero, V., & Marshall, J. L. (2001). Future school administrators' perceptions of the school counselors' role. *Counselor Education and Supervision, 41,* 89–99.

Galassi, M. D., & Galassi, J. P. (1977). *Assert yourself! How to be your own person.* New York: Human Sciences Press.

Gaushell, W. H. (1984). Microcomputers: The school and the counselor. *School Counselor, 31,* 229–233.

Green, A., & Keys, S. (2001). Expanding the developmental school counseling paradigm: Meeting the needs of the 21st century student. *Professional School Counseling, 5,* 84–95.

Griffin, B. L., Gillis, M. K., & Brown, M. (1986). The counselor as a computer consultant: Understanding children's attitudes toward computers. *Elementary School Counseling and Guidance, 20,* 246–249.

Gysbers, N. C. (2001). School guidance and counseling in the 21st century: Remember the past into the future. *Professional School Counseling, 5,* 96–105.

Gysbers, N. C., & Henderson, P. (2000). Developing and managing your guidance program (3rd ed.). Alexandria, VA: American Counseling Association.

Haettenschwiller, D. L. (1970). Control of the counselor's role. *Journal of Counseling Psychology, 17,* 437–442.

Hitchner, K. W., & Tifft-Hitchner, A. (1987). *A survival guide for the secondary school counselor.* West Nyack, NY: Center for Applied Research in Education.

Holland, J. L. (1997). *Making vocational choices: A theory of vocational personalities and work environments* (3rd ed.). Odessa, FL: Psychological Assessment Resources.

Hoskins, R. G., & Rosenthal, N. R. (1983). Microcomputer-assisted guidance scheduling for career information programs. *Vocational Guidance Quarterly, 32,* 122–124.

Kennedy, C. E., II. (1987). Techniques and technology. *School Counselor, 35,* 78–79.

Kivlighan, D. M., Jr., Johnston, J. A., Hogan, S., & Mauer, E. (1994). Who benefits from computerized career counseling? *Journal of Counseling & Development, 72,* 289–294.

Kuranz, M. (2002). Cultivating student potential. *Professional School Counseling, 5,* 172–179.

Lawrence, G. H. (1986). Using computers for the treatment of psychological problems. *Computers in Human Behavior, 2,* 43–62.

Lindsay, G. (1988). Strengthening the counseling profession via computer use: Responding to the issues. *School Counselor, 35,* 325–330.

Locke, D. C., Myers, J. E., & Herr, E. L. (2001). Counseling and the future. In D. C. Locke, J. E. Myers, & E. L. Herr (Eds.), *The handbook of counseling* (pp. 683–691). Thousand Oaks, CA: Sage.

Maslow, A. H. (1954). *Motivation and personality.* New York: Harper.

McCullough, L. (1994). Challenges to guidance programs: How to prevent and handle them. *Guidepost, 36*(8), 1, 12.

Moracco, J. C., Butcke, P. G., & McEwen, M. K. (1984). Measuring stress in school counselors: Some research findings and implications. *School Counselor, 32,* 110–118.

Page, B. J., Pietrzak, D. R., & Sutton, J. W., Jr. (2001). National survey of school counselor supervision. *Counselor Education and Supervision, 41,* 142–150.

Paisley, P. O., & McMahon, H. G. (2001). School counseling for the 21st century: Challenges and opportunities. *Professional School Counseling, 5,* 106–115.

Peters, D. (1978). The practice of counseling in the secondary school. In *The status of guidance and counseling in the nation's schools* (pp. 81–100). Washington, DC: American Personnel and Guidance Association.

Sampson, J. P., Jr. (1987). Computer-assisted or computerized: What's in a name? *Journal of Counseling & Development, 66,* 116–117.

Sampson, J. P., Jr., Peterson, G. W., Reardon, R. C., Lenz, J. G., Shahnasarian, M., & Ryan-Jones, R. E. (1992). The social influence of two computer-assisted career guidance systems: DISCOVER and SIGI. *Career Development Quarterly, 41,* 75–83.

Schmidt, J. J. (2003). Counseling in schools: Essential services and comprehensive programs (4th ed.). Boston: Allyn & Bacon.

Sears, S. J., & Granello, D. H. (2002). School counseling now and in the future: A reaction. *Professional School Counseling, 5,* 164–171.

Shaw, M. C. (1973). *School guidance systems: Objectives, functions, evaluation, and change.* Boston: Houghton Mifflin.

Sink, C. A. (2002). In search of the profession's finest hour: A critique of four views of 21st century school counseling. *Professional School Counseling,* *5,* 156–164.

Sutton, J. M., Jr., & Page, B. J. (1994). Post-degree clinical supervision of counselors. *School Counselor,* *42,* 32–39.

Tennyson, W. W., Miller, G. D., Skovholt, T. G., & Williams, R. G. (1989). Secondary school counselors: What do they do? What is important? *School Counselor, 36,* 253–259.

Walz, G. R., & Benjamin, L. (1978). Professional development and competency. In *The status of guidance and counseling in the nation's schools*

(pp. 127–136). Washington, DC: American Personnel and Guidance Association.

Whiston, S. C. (2002). Response to the past, present, and future of school counseling: Raising some issues. *Professional School Counseling, 5,* 148–155.

William T. Grant Foundation Commission on Work, Family and Citizenship. (1988). *The forgotten half: Non-college youth in America: An interim report on the school-to-work transition.* Washington, DC: Author.

Willower, D. J., Hoy, W. K., & Eidell, T. L. (1967). The counselor and the school as a social organization. *Personnel and Guidance Journal, 46,* 228–234.

Key Components of the National Standards for School Counseling Programs

American School Counselor Association

INTRODUCTION

All students growing up in America face the usual challenges of coping with everyday problems. In addition, societal challenges in expectations, values, and behavioral norms create confusion for students and the adults who guide them. Added to this are children who have been abused or neglected, who are frustrated with the cycle of personal and academic failure, who have a disability that requires special support or attention, who are substance abusers, who engage in sexual activity, who feel worthless, and who are homeless. One in five children lives in poverty, and almost one third of the children in the country under age 18 do not live with both parents (U.S. Bureau of the Census, 1993, 1995).

Coupled with these societal challenges is the national standards movement, the current educational reform agenda that focuses on raising expectations for teaching and learning. Many students face emotional, physical, social, and economic barriers that inhibit successful learning. What mechanisms exist to ensure that these barriers to academic success will be eliminated? School counselors are actively committed to helping students understand that the choices they make will affect their future educational and career options. Students are constantly reminded that academic success is the key to opening the door of opportunity. The school counseling program is the foundation of school success.

How do we, the school counselor community, reach all these students, touch their lives, and help them find ways to achieve the skills and knowledge needed for success in the twenty-first century? We begin by guaranteeing that all children receive the services of a credentialed or certified school counselor who delivers a school counseling program that is comprehensive in scope and developmental in nature. The purpose of the school counseling program is to affect specific skills and learning opportunities through academic, career, and personal/social development experiences in a proactive and preventive manner for all students.

How will the National Standards for School Counseling Programs help? Standards are a public statement of what students should know and be able to do as a result of participating in a school counseling program. Standards represent what a school counseling program should contain, serve as an organizational tool to identify and prioritize the elements of a quality school counseling program, and ensure equitable access to school counseling programs for all students. Adopting and implementing national standards will change the way school counseling programs are designed and delivered across the country.

Accountability is the key to determining the success of school counseling programs. Decisions at the building and system level will be needed to determine the degree to which students have acquired the skills and knowledge defined by the standards. Aligning school counseling programs with national standards requires a rethinking of priorities, time, resources, and outcomes. A school counseling program based on national standards necessitates the involvement of the entire school community to integrate academic, career, and personal/social development of students into the mission of each school. Measurable success resulting from this effort can be documented by an increased number of students completing school with the academic preparation, career awareness, and personal/social growth essential to choose from a wide range of substantial postsecondary options, including college.

For years, school reform initiatives have been enacted in the name of achieving excellence in education. Since the late 1980s, leaders in the counseling profession have called for a revitalization and transformation in school counseling programs. Organizations that have an interest in the work of school counselors, such as the

ACT, College Board, and National Association of College Admissions Counselors (NACAC), have advocated the reorganization of school counseling programs to meet the needs of all students. Historically, the professional association, the American School Counselor Association (ASCA), has established positions and goals for the profession in statements that guide the practitioner in implementation. More specifically, the ASCA has published role definitions, a program philosophy, and monographs that speak to the role of guidance and counseling in the educational system. Until now, however, this effort had not been supported by a national focus on a design or framework for program development and delivery.

The current movement to design national standards and world-class benchmarks in the academic disciplines ensures that all graduates of our high schools and postsecondary institutions can compete in a global economy. The challenge lies in providing all students with conditions for learning to help them achieve the expectations of rigorous academic standards. Effective school counseling programs ensure that all students have equal access to quality academic programs and the needed support in academic, career, and personal/social development to meet the demands of these challenges.

The ASCA's decision to participate in this educational reform agenda through the development of national standards for school counseling programs offers an opportunity for the school counseling profession to implement the goals deemed important by the profession, to promote its mission in educational reform, and to ensure that all students have an opportunity to participate in a school counseling program as part of the learning experience.

DOCUMENT OVERVIEW

The National Standards for School Counseling Programs is organized in the following manner:

The first chapter of this document defines standards and provides the ASCA's rationale for the development of the National Standards for School Counseling Programs. It also outlines the process the ASCA used to develop standards for school counseling programs.

The second chapter provides a brief overview of the history of the school counseling profession and defines the school counseling program. The goals of the school counseling program are outlined, and the major components of the program are described, along with the benefits that may be derived by its constituencies.

The third chapter outlines the standards for each student development area: academic, career, and personal/social. The standards are followed by a list of student competencies that define the specific knowledge, attitudes, and skills students should obtain or demonstrate as a result of participating in a school counseling program.

The fourth chapter focuses on the initial stages of implementation and evaluation for a standards-based school counseling program. Sample activities of standards into practice are presented.

DEFINITION OF A SCHOOL COUNSELING PROGRAM

A comprehensive school counseling program is developmental and systematic in nature, sequential, clearly defined, and accountable. It is jointly founded on developmental psychology, educational philosophy, and counseling methodology (ASCA, 1994). The school counseling program is integral to the educational enterprise, is proactive and preventive in its focus, and assists students in acquiring and using lifelong learning skills. More specifically, school counseling programs employ strategies to enhance academics, provide career awareness, develop employment readiness, encourage self-awareness, foster interpersonal communication skills, and impart life success skills for all students.

The school counseling program has characteristics similar to other educational programs, including a scope and sequence, student outcomes or competencies, activities and processes to assist students in achieving these outcomes, professionally credentialed personnel, materials and resources, and accountability methods.

School counseling programs are developed by design, focusing on needs, interests, and issues related to the various stages of student growth. Included are objectives, activities, special services, and expected outcomes, with an emphasis on helping students learn more effectively and efficiently. The commitment is to individual uniqueness and the maximum development in three major areas: academic, career, and personal/social (ASCA, 1990).

Most school counselors agree that their skills, time, and energy should be focused on direct services to students. School counseling programs and the role of the school counselor should be determined by the educational, career, and personal developmental needs of students. The comprehensive school counseling program places the counselor in a key position to identify the issues that affect student learning and achievement. The school counselor is at the core of school planning, school programs, and school environment.

The school counselor is not the counseling program. The school counselor and the school counseling program use a collaborative model as their foundation. Counselors do not work alone; all educators play a role in creating an environment that promotes the achievement of identified student goals and outcomes. The counselor facilitates communication and establishes linkages for the benefit of students, with teaching staff, administration, families, student service personnel, agencies, business, and other members of the community. School success depends on the cooperation and support of the entire faculty, staff, and student services personnel.

As student advocates, school counselors are committed to participate as members of the educational team. They consult and collaborate with teachers, administrators, and parents to assist students in being successful academically, vocationally, and personally. School counselors are recognized as indispensable partners of the instructional staff in the development of good citizens and leaders. As schools and communities initiate and establish partnerships to address common concerns, it is important that these efforts are implemented in a manner that facilitates the educational process and the full use of school and other community resources on behalf of students and their families.

Our educational system is being challenged by the growing needs of today's students and the rising expectations of society. Some students attend school with emotional, physical, and interpersonal barriers to learning as a result of societal and other factors. All students, however, require systematic support for their development. Therefore, in a comprehensive school counseling program, less emphasis is placed on crisis-oriented services. The emphasis is on development for all students. An effective school counseling program begins when students enter the school system and continues as they progress through the educational process. School counseling is an integral part of the total educational enterprise.

Our nation is rich in multicultural diversity. Effective school counseling programs and trained staff reflect and are responsive to the diversity in our schools and communities. Effective school counseling programs serve all students and acknowledge that diversity and individual differences are valuable to all. Programs and staff ensure that communication is open and that the community is represented and involved as counseling programs are developed and implemented. Counseling programs help ensure equal opportunity for all students to participate fully in the educational process.

The school counseling model supports and is compatible with *GOALS 2000* (1994). The School to Work Opportunities Act (1994), the Elementary Counseling Demonstration Act (1995), the *Children's Defense Fund Report* (1990), the Secretary's Commission on Achieving Necessary Skills (U.S. Department of Labor, 1991) and the *National Career Development Guidelines* (NOICC, 1989) support the school counseling program and acknowledge the role of the school counselor as essential to student success.

THE GOAL OF SCHOOL COUNSELING PROGRAMS

The primary goal of the school counseling program is to promote and enhance *student learning* through the three broad and interrelated areas of *student development*. Each of these areas of student development encompasses a variety of desired student learning competencies, which, in turn, are composed of specific knowledge, attitudes, and skills that form the foundation of the developmental school counseling program. The three areas of student development are (a) academic development, (b) career development, and (c) personal/social development. Recognizing that all children do not develop in a linear fashion according to a certain timetable, the overlap among grade levels (elementary, middle school/junior high, and high school) is intentional. The school counseling program reflects the progression of student development throughout the pre-K through 12 experience. It is understood that mastery of basic skills facilitates the mastery of higher-order skills in each area of development. The school counselor uses a variety of strategies, activities, delivery methods, and resources to promote the desired student development. The school counselor's responsibilities include the design, organization, implementation, and coordination of the program.

NATIONAL STANDARDS FOR SCHOOL COUNSELING PROGRAMS

Overview

The purpose of a counseling program in a school setting is to promote and enhance the training process. To that end, the school counseling program facilitates student development in three broad areas: academic development, career development, and personal/social development.

The standards for each content area are intended to provide guidance and direction for states, school systems, and individual schools to develop quality and effective school counseling programs. The emphasis is on success for all students, not only those students who are motivated, supported, and ready to learn. The school counseling program based on national standards enables all students to achieve success in school and to develop into contributing members of society.

School success requires that students make successful transitions from elementary school to middle/junior high school to high school. Graduates from high school have acquired the attitudes, skills, and knowledge essential to the competitive workplace of the twenty-first century.

A school counseling program based on national standards provides the elements for all students to achieve success in school. School counselors continuously assess their students' needs to identify barriers and obstacles that may be hindering success, and they also advocate for programmatic efforts to eliminate these barriers.

Each standard is followed by a list of student competencies that articulate desired student learning outcomes. Student competencies define the specific knowledge, attitudes, and skills that students should obtain or demonstrate as a result of participating in a school counseling program. These listings are not meant to be all-inclusive, nor is any individual program expected to include all the competencies in the school counseling program. The competencies offer a foundation for what a standards-based program should address and deliver. These can be used as a basis to develop measurable indicators of student performance.

The program standards for academic development guide the school counseling program to implement strategies and activities to support and maximize each student's ability to learn.

Academic development includes acquiring skills, attitudes, and knowledge that contribute to effective learning in school and across the life span; employing strategies to achieve success in school; and understanding the relationship of academics to the world of work and to life at home and in the community. Academic development standards and competencies support the premise that all students meet or exceed the local, state, and national academic standards.

The purpose of a counseling program in a school setting is to promote and enhance the learning process.

The program standards for career development guide the school counseling program to provide the foundation for the acquisition of skills, attitudes, and knowledge that enable students to make a successful transition from school to the world of work and from job to job across the life span.

Career development includes employing strategies to achieve future career success and job satisfaction, as well as fostering the understanding of the relationship among personal qualities, education and training, and the world of work. Career development standards and competencies ensure that students develop career goals as a result of participation in a comprehensive plan of career awareness, exploration, and preparation activities.

The program standards for personal/social development guide the school counseling program to provide the foundation for personal and social growth as students progress through school and into adulthood.

Personal/social development contributes to academic and career success. Personal/social development includes the acquisition of skills, attitudes, and knowledge that help students understand and respect self and others, acquire effective interpersonal skills, understand safety and survival skills, and develop into contributing members of society. Personal/social development standards and competencies ensure that students have learned to negotiate their way successfully and safely in the increasingly complex and diverse world of the twenty-first century.

National Standards for School Counseling Programs

I. Academic Development

Standards in this area guide the school counseling program to implement strategies and activities to support and enable the student to experience academic success, maximize learning through commitment, produce high-quality work, and be prepared for a full range of options and opportunities after high school.

The academic development area includes the acquisition of skills in decision making, problem solving and goal setting, critical thinking, logical reasoning, and interpersonal communication and the application of these skills to academic achievement.

The school counseling program enables all students to achieve success in school and to develop into contributing members of our society.

Standard A: Students will acquire the attitudes, knowledge, and skills that contribute to effective learning in school and across the life span.

Student Competencies: Improve academic self-concept, acquire skills for improving learning, and achieve school success.

Standard B: Students will complete school with the academic preparation essential to choose from a wide range of substantial post-secondary options, including college.

Student Competencies: Improve learning and plan to achieve goals.

Standard C: Students will understand the relationship of academics to the world of work and to life at home and in the community.

Student Competencies: Relate school to life experiences.

II. Career Development

Standards in this area guide the school counseling program to implement strategies and activities to support and enable the student to develop a positive attitude toward work and to develop the necessary skills to make a successful transition from school to the world of work and from job to job across the life career span. Also, standards in this area help students understand the relationship between success in school and future success in the world of work. Career development standards reflect the recommendations of the Secretary's Commission of Achieving Necessary Skills (SCANS, 1991) and the content of the *National Career Development Guidelines* (NOICC, 1989).

The school counseling program enables all students to achieve success in school and to develop into contributing members of our society.

Standard A: Students will acquire the skills to investigate the world of work in relation to knowledge of self and to make informed career decisions.

Student Competencies: Develop career awareness and develop employment readiness.

Standard B: Students will employ strategies to achieve future career goals with success and satisfaction.

Student Competencies: Acquire career information and identify career goals.

Standard C: Students will understand the relationship among personal qualities, education, training, and the world of work.

Student Competencies: Acquire knowledge to achieve career goals and apply skills to achieve career goals.

III. Personal/Social Development

Standards in the personal/social area guide the school counseling program to implement strategies and activities to support and maximize each student's personal growth and enhance the educational and career development of the student.

The school counseling program enables all students to achieve success in school and to develop into contributing members of our society.

Standard A: Students will acquire the knowledge, attitudes, and interpersonal skills to help them understand and respect self and others.

Student Competencies: Acquire self-knowledge and acquire interpersonal skills.

Standard B: Students will make decisions, set goals, and take necessary action to achieve goals.

Student Competencies: Self-knowledge applications.

Standard C: Students will understand safety and survival skills.

Student Competencies: Acquire personal safety skills.

Note: In the complete document containing the ASCA National Standards, each of the student competencies is followed by a listing of desired student outcomes. There is not enough space herein to list all of them.

Source: This appendix was written by Chari A. Campbell, Ph.D., University of South Florida; and Carol A. Dahir, Ed.D., Nassau BOCES, Westbury, New York.

Source: Standards from "The National Standards for School Counseling Programs" (pp. coversheet, 1, 2, 9–11, 17–31), by American School Counselor Association, 1998, Alexandria, VA: American School Counselor Association. Copyright 1998 by American School Counselor Association.

Lesson Outlines for "Succeeding in School Online"

http://genesislight.com/web%20files/index.htm

Section 1, Models of Success, helps make students aware of successful people and how they achieved their success. The section helps students be aware that they will experience failures in school and elsewhere and that failure often aids learning. Here are some of the topics covered in Section 1:

A. The need for children to be aware of successful people.

B. Examples of successful people (Sally Ride, astronaut; Michael Jordan, athlete; John Hope Franklin, historian; Bill Gates, computer expert) and what they have in common.

C. What it takes to be successful.

D. Why success in school is not always possible.

E. How occasional failures aid learning.

F. How success and failure in school will affect students' lives in the future.

G. How to achieve success in school.

Section 2, Being Comfortable in School, helps students view the classroom as an enjoyable and comfortable place to be. Although effective learning climates involve some tension and anxiety, students should feel comfortable at school and not regularly experience feelings that lead to avoiding school. Students need to learn how to cope with feelings of anxiety about school and should occasionally participate in games and other activities that are intended to be relaxing and to create a calm classroom environment. Although physical exercise, proper diet, and adequate sleep contribute to children's feeling comfortable at school, teachers and children sometimes need to discuss how to relax and feel comfortable. Here are some of the topics covered in Section 2:

A. Stress and relaxation.

B. Why and how different people relax.

C. What might cause students to feel nervous or anxious at school.

D. What it means to be relaxed at school.

E. Methods of relaxation that students can practice in the classroom and elsewhere.

F. How teachers can help students feel comfortable at school.

Section 3, Being Responsible in School, helps students see the importance of putting work ahead of play and the value of acting responsibly in their relations with peers, teachers, and family. Since students are easily distracted from behaving responsibly, they need to receive instruction and to participate in discussions about responsibility. Students may learn much about responsibility from observing respected adults and peers behaving responsibly. Students need to consider the good feelings and beneficial outcomes associated with acting responsibly. Here are some of the topics covered in Section 3:

A. A definition of responsibility in terms of self and others.

B. How children can learn the meaning of responsibility through observing responsible people at home and elsewhere.

C. The importance of taking roles that require responsible behavior.

D. What it means to behave responsibly at school.

E. The effects of being responsible at school.

F. Responsibility and students' future lives.

G. How students can encourage each other to be responsible.

Section 4, Listening in School, helps students understand that academic responsibility requires attentive listening in the classroom. Teachers often model effective listening skills and encourage students to practice these skills. Here are some of the topics covered in Section 4:

A. Why responsible behavior at school requires listening.

B. How listening pays off at school and elsewhere.

C. Skills needed for effective listening.

D. How listening among students can be improved in the classroom.

E. How teachers improve listening among students.

Section 5, Asking for Help in School, associates listening with the need for students to ask for help when they do not understand what they hear. Many students do not ask questions due to their fears of being put down by adults or being made fun of by peers. These students need to understand that learners are not passive; they are instead quick to ask questions and to seek out information. Here are some of the topics covered in Section 5:

A. How listening and asking for help are complementary.

B. Why students may be afraid to ask for help.

C. Ways for students to overcome their fears about asking for help.

D. Positive results from asking for help.

E. How students may improve their abilities to ask for help.

Section 6, Improving at School, helps students become aware of their academic strengths and weaknesses. Students need to ask themselves such questions as "What subjects am I good at?" and "What subjects do I need to improve in?" It is especially important for students to understand their academic strengths. Often students are deterred from academic progress by focusing solely on their failures. If students are aware of their academic strengths, they are more willing and able to work toward improving weak areas. Here are some of the topics covered in Section 6:

A. What students need to know about their strengths and weaknesses in order to improve at school.

B. Why it is important for students to focus on their academic strong points.

C. An overview of study skills needed for academic improvement.

D. How teachers can help students monitor improvement in schoolwork.

E. How students benefit by seeing themselves improve academically.

F. How students may help each other focus on academic improvement.

Section 7, Cooperating With Peers, considers the importance of peer relationships and examines the need for students to cooperate at school. Some educators and researchers have concluded that nearly all instruction should take place within a cooperative environment. Some, in fact, have specifically recommended peer tutoring and cross-age tutoring as avenues to promoting both cooperation and achievement. Although competition often motivates students and promotes their academic success, students need to recognize that cooperation often results in satisfying and important academic successes. Here are some of the topics covered in Section 7:

A. The importance of friendship in the lives of students.

B. How relations with peers may affect academic success.

C. The importance of cooperative learning in the classroom.

D. The value of peer and cross-age tutoring.

E. Helping students focus on ways to help each other at school.

Section 8, Cooperating With Teachers, discusses the importance of empathy between teachers and students. Teacher expectations of students, for example, is a major influence on achievement. Students perceived as low in ability and high in effort receive more positive feedback than high ability–high effort students. Similarly, pupils believed to be low in ability and low in effort receive more positive feedback than high ability–low effort students. It is essential, therefore, that teachers and students make every effort to understand each other and that students learn to show initiative in developing cooperative working relations with teachers. Here are some of the topics covered in Section 8:

A. The importance of empathy, genuineness, and positive regard between students and teachers.

B. The role of self-disclosure in creating a cooperative environment in the classroom.

C. How students can help teachers be more effective.

D. Specific avenues of cooperation between teachers and students.

Section 9, The Bright Side of School, helps students focus on pleasant aspects of school life. Since negative discussions about school are prevalent among students, this section provides an unusual opportunity for considering the positive side. Focusing on the positive aspects of school should be at least a start in fostering positive attitudes toward school and ultimately in reducing truancy and numbers of school dropouts. Students who do not like school, especially to the point of being truant, are unlikely to experience academic success. Here are some of the topics covered in Section 9:

A. The value of a positive attitude toward school.

B. What factors contribute to a student's attitude toward school.

C. An overview of positive aspects of school life.

D. How students can work to improve their view of school.

E. Helping students focus on the bright side of school.

Section 10, The Bright Side of Me, focuses on helping students feel good about themselves. Most educators acknowledge that children benefit academically from high self-esteem. Teachers need to concentrate on bolstering the self-image of children, recognizing the strong relationship between self-image and achievement. Here are some of the topics covered in Section 10:

A. An overview of the relationship between self-image and student achievement.

B. Factors that affect a student's self-image.

C. How school contributes to a student's self-image.

D. A classroom environment that promotes positive self-image.

American Counseling Association *Code of Ethics* and *Standards of Practice*

(Approved by the Governing Council, April 1995)

Preamble

The American Counseling Association is an educational, scientific and professional organization whose members are dedicated to the enhancement of human development throughout the life span. Association members recognize diversity in our society and embrace a cross-cultural approach in support of the worth, dignity, potential, and uniqueness of each individual.

The specification of a code of ethics enables the association to clarify to current and future members, and to those served by members, the nature of the ethical responsibilities held in common by its members. As the code of ethics of the association, this document establishes principles that define the ethical behavior of association members. All members of the American Counseling Association are required to adhere to the *Code of Ethics* and the *Standards of Practice*. The Code of Ethics will serve as the basis for processing ethical complaints initiated against members of the association.

CODE OF ETHICS

Section A: The Counseling Relationship

A.1. Client Welfare

A. *Primary Responsibility.* The primary responsibility of counselors is to respect the dignity and to promote the welfare of clients.

B. *Positive Growth and Development.* Counselors encourage client growth and development in ways that foster the clients' interest and welfare; counselors avoid fostering dependent counseling relationships.

C. *Counseling Plans.* Counselors and their clients work jointly in devising integrated, individual counseling plans that offer reasonable promise of success and are consistent with abilities and circumstances of clients. Counselors and clients regularly review counseling plans to ensure their continued viability and effectiveness, respecting clients' freedom of choice. (See A.3.b.)

D. *Family Involvement.* Counselors recognize that families are usually important in clients' lives and strive to enlist family understanding and involvement as a positive resource, when appropriate.

E. *Career and Employment Needs.* Counselors work with their clients in considering employment in jobs and circumstances that are consistent with the clients' overall abilities, vocational limitations, physical restrictions, general temperament, interest and aptitude patterns, social skills, education, general qualifications, and other relevant characteristics and needs. Counselors neither place nor participate in placing clients in positions that will result in damaging the interest and the welfare of clients, employers, or the public.

A.2. Respecting Diversity

A. *Nondiscrimination.* Counselors do not condone or engage in discrimination based on age, color, culture, disability, ethnic group, gender, race, religion, sexual orientation, marital status, or socioeconomic status. (See C.5.a., C.5.b., and D.1.i.)

B. *Respecting Differences.* Counselors will actively attempt to understand the diverse cultural backgrounds of the clients with whom they work. This includes, but is not limited to, learning how the counselor's own cultural/ethnic/racial identity impacts her/his values and beliefs about the counseling process. (See E.8. and F.2.i.)

A.3. Client Rights

A. *Disclosure to Clients.* When counseling is initiated, and throughout the counseling process as necessary, counselors inform clients of the purposes, goals, techniques, procedures, limitations, potential risks and benefits of services to be performed, and other pertinent information. Counselors take steps to ensure that clients understand the implications of diagnosis, the intended use of tests and reports, fees, and billing arrangements. Clients have the right to expect confidentiality and to be provided with an explanation of its limitations, including supervision and/or treatment by team professionals; to obtain clear information about their case records; to participate in the ongoing counseling plans; and to refuse any recommended services and be advised of the consequences of such refusal. (See E.5.a. and G.2.)

B. *Freedom of Choice.* Counselors offer clients the freedom to choose whether to enter into a counseling relationship and to determine which professional(s) will provide counseling. Restrictions that limit choices of clients are fully explained. (See A.1.c.)

C. *Inability to Give Consent.* When counseling minors or persons unable to give voluntary informed consent, counselors act in these clients' best interests. (See B.3.)

A.4. Clients Served by Others

If a client is receiving services from another mental health professional, counselors, with client consent, inform the professional persons already involved and develop clear agreements to avoid confusion and conflict for the client. (See C.6.c.)

A.5. Personal Needs and Values

A. *Personal Needs.* In the counseling relationship, counselors are aware of the intimacy and responsibilities inherent in the counseling relationship, maintain respect for clients, and avoid actions that seek to meet their personal needs at the expense of clients.

B. *Personal Values.* Counselors are aware of their own values, attitudes, beliefs, and behaviors and how these apply in a diverse society, and avoid imposing their values on clients. (See C.5.a.)

A.6. Dual Relationships

A. *Avoid When Possible.* Counselors are aware of their influential position with respect to clients, and they avoid exploiting the trust and dependency of clients. Counselors make every effort to avoid dual relationships with clients that could impair professional judgment or increase the risk of harm to clients. (Examples of such relationships include, but are not limited to, familial, social, financial, business, or close personal relationships with clients). When a dual relationship cannot be avoided, counselors take appropriate professional precautions such as informed consent, consultation, supervision, and documentation to ensure that judgment is not impaired and no exploitation occurs. (See F.1.b.)

B. *Superior/Subordinate Relationships.* Counselors do not accept as clients superiors or subordinates with whom they have administrative, supervisory, or evaluative relationships.

A.7. Sexual Intimacies With Clients

A. *Current Clients.* Counselors do not have any type of sexual intimacies with clients and do not counsel persons with whom they have had a sexual relationship.

B. *Former Clients.* Counselors do not engage in sexual intimacies with former clients within a minimum of two years after terminating the counseling relationship. Counselors who engage in such relationship after two years following termination have the responsibility to thoroughly examine and document that such relations did not have an exploitative nature, based on factors such as duration of counseling, amount of time since counseling, termination circumstances, client's personal history and mental status, adverse impact on the client, and actions by the counselor suggesting a plan to initiate a sexual relationship with the client after termination.

A.8. Multiple Clients

When counselors agree to provide counseling services to two or more persons who have a relationship (such as husband and wife, or parents and children), counselors clarify at the outset which person or persons are clients and the nature of the relationships they will have with each involved person. If it becomes apparent that counselors may be called upon to perform potentially conflicting roles, they clarify, adjust, or withdraw from roles appropriately. (See B.2. and B.4.d.)

A.9. Group Work

A. *Screening.* Counselors screen prospective group counseling/therapy participants. To the extent possible, counselors select members whose needs and goals are compatible with goals of the group, who will not impede the group process, and whose well-being will not be jeopardized by the group experience.

B. *Protecting Clients.* In a group setting, counselors take reasonable precautions to protect clients from physical or psychological trauma.

A.10. Fees and Bartering (See D.3.a. and D.3.b.)

A. *Advance Understanding.* Counselors clearly explain to clients, prior to entering the counseling relationship, all financial arrangements related to professional services including the use of collection agencies or legal measures for nonpayment. (See A.11.c.)

B. *Establishing Fees.* In establishing fees for professional counseling services, counselors consider the financial status of clients and locality. In the event that the established fee structure is inappropriate for a client, assistance is provided in attempting to find comparable services of acceptable cost. (See A.10.d., D.3.a., and D.3.b.)

C. *Bartering Discouraged.* Counselors ordinarily refrain from accepting goods or services from clients in return for counseling services because such arrangements create inherent potential for conflicts, exploitation, and distortion of the professional relationship. Counselors may participate in bartering only if the relationship is not exploitive, if the client requests it, if a clear written contract is established, and if such arrangements are an accepted practice among professionals in the community. (See A.6.a.)

D. *Pro Bono Service.* Counselors contribute to society by devoting a portion of their professional activity to services for which there is little or no financial return (pro bono).

A.11. Termination and Referral

A. *Abandonment Prohibited.* Counselors do not abandon or neglect clients in counseling. Counselors assist in making appropriate arrangements for the continuation of treatment, when necessary, during interruptions such as vacations, and following termination.

B. *Inability to Assist Clients.* If counselors determine an inability to be of professional assistance to clients, they avoid entering or immediately terminate a counseling relationship. Counselors are knowledgeable about referral resources and suggest appropriate alternatives. If clients decline the suggested referral, counselors should discontinue the relationship.

C. *Appropriate Termination.* Counselors terminate a counseling relationship, securing client agreement when possible, when it is reasonably clear that the client is no longer benefiting, when services are no longer required, when counseling no longer serves the client's needs or interests, when clients do not pay fees charged, or when agency or institution limits do not allow provision of further counseling services. (See A.10.b. and C.2.g.)

A.12. Computer Technology

A. *Use of Computers.* When computer applications are used in counseling services, counselors ensure that: (1) the client is intellectually, emotionally, and physically capable of using the computer application; (2) the computer application is appropriate for the needs of the client; (3) the client understands the purpose and operation of the computer applications; and (4) a follow-up of client use of a computer application is provided to correct possible misconceptions, discover inappropriate use, and assess subsequent needs.

B. *Explanation of Limitations.* Counselors ensure that clients are provided information as a part of the counseling relationship that adequately explains the limitations of computer technology.

C. *Access to Computer Applications.* Counselors provide for equal access to computer applications in counseling services. (See A.2.a.)

Section B: Confidentiality

B.1. Right to Privacy

A. *Respect for Privacy.* Counselors respect their clients' right to privacy and avoid illegal and unwarranted disclosures of confidential information. (See A.3.a. and B.6.a.)

B. *Client Waiver.* The right to privacy may be waived by the client or their legally recognized representative.

C. *Exceptions.* The general requirement that counselors keep information confidential does not apply when disclosure is required to prevent clear and imminent danger to the client or others or when legal requirements demand that confidential information be revealed. Counselors consult with other professionals when in doubt as to the validity of an exception.

D. *Contagious, Fatal Diseases.* A counselor who receives information confirming that a client has a disease commonly known to be both communicable and fatal is justified in disclosing information to an identifiable third party, who by his or her relationship with the client is at a high risk of contracting the disease. Prior to making a disclosure the counselor should ascertain that the client has not already informed the third party about his or her disease and that the client is not intending to inform the third party in the immediate future. (See B.1.c. and B.1.f.)

E. *Court Ordered Disclosure.* When court ordered to release confidential information without a client's permission, counselors request to the court that the disclosure not be required due to potential harm to the client or counseling relationship. (See B.1.c.)

F. *Minimal Disclosure.* When circumstances require the disclosure of confidential information, only essential information is revealed. To the extent possible, clients are informed before confidential information is disclosed.

G. *Explanation of Limitations.* When counseling is initiated and throughout the counseling process as necessary, counselors inform clients of the limitations of confidentiality and identify foreseeable situations in which confidentiality must be breached. (See G.2.a.)

H. *Subordinates.* Counselors make every effort to ensure that privacy and confidentiality of clients are maintained by subordinates including employees, supervisees, clerical assistants, and volunteers. (See B.1.a.)

I. *Treatment Teams.* If client treatment will involve a continued review by a treatment team, the client will be informed of the team's existence and composition.

B.2. Groups and Families

A. *Group Work.* In group work, counselors clearly define confidentiality and the parameters for the specific group being entered, explain its importance, and discuss the difficulties related to confidentiality involved in group work. The fact that confidentiality cannot be guaranteed is clearly communicated to group members.

B. *Family Counseling.* In family counseling, information about one family member cannot be disclosed to another member without permission. Counselors protect the privacy rights of each family member. (See A.8., B.3., and B.4.d.)

B.3. Minor or Incompetent Clients

When counseling clients who are minors or individuals who are unable to give voluntary, informed consent, parents or guardians may be included in the counseling process as appropriate. Counselors act in the best interests of clients and take measures to safeguard confidentiality. (See A.3.c.)

B.4. Records

A. *Requirement of Records.* Counselors maintain records necessary for rendering professional services to their clients and as required by laws, regulations, or agency or institution procedures.

B. *Confidentiality of Records.* Counselors are responsible for securing the safety and confidentiality of any counseling records they create, maintain, transfer, or destroy whether the records are written, taped, computerized, or stored in any other medium. (See B.1.a.)

C. *Permission to Record or Observe.* Counselors obtain permission from clients prior to electronically recording or observing sessions. (See A.3.a.)

D. *Client Access.* Counselors recognize that counseling records are kept for the benefit of clients and therefore provide access to records and copies of records when reasonably requested by competent clients, unless the records contain information that may be misleading and detrimental to the client. In situations involving multiple clients, access to records is limited to those parts of records that do not include confidential information related to another client. (See A.8., B.1.a., and B.2.b.)

E. *Disclosure or Transfer.* Counselors obtain written permission from clients to disclose or transfer records to legitimate third parties unless exceptions to confidentiality exist as listed in Section B.1. Steps are taken to ensure that receivers of counseling records are sensitive to their confidential nature.

B.5. Research and Training

A. *Data Disguise Required.* Use of data derived from counseling relationships for purposes of training, research, or publication is confined to content that is disguised to ensure the anonymity of the individuals involved. (See B.1.g. and G.3.d.)

B. *Agreement for Identification.* Identification of a client in a presentation or publication is permissible only when the client has reviewed the material and has agreed to its presentation or publication. (See G.3.d.)

B.6. Consultation

A. *Respect for Privacy.* Information obtained in a consulting relationship is discussed for professional purposes only with persons clearly concerned with the case. Written and oral reports present data germane to the purposes of the consultation, and every effort is made to protect client identity and avoid undue invasion of privacy.

B. *Cooperating Agencies.* Before sharing information, counselors make efforts to ensure that there are defined policies in other agencies serving the counselor's clients that effectively protect the confidentiality of information.

Section C: Professional Responsibility

C.1. Standards Knowledge

Counselors have a responsibility to read, understand, and follow the *Code of Ethics* and the *Standards of Practice*.

C.2. Professional Competence

A. *Boundaries of Competence.* Counselors practice only within the boundaries of their competence, based on their education, training, supervised experience, state and national professional credentials, and appropriate professional experience. Counselors will demonstrate a commitment to gain knowledge, personal awareness, sensitivity, and skills pertinent to working with a diverse client population.

B. *New Specialty Areas of Practice.* Counselors practice in specialty areas new to them only after appropriate education, training, and supervised experience. While developing skills in new specialty areas, counselors take steps to ensure the competence of their work and to protect others from possible harm.

C. *Qualified for Employment.* Counselors accept employment only for positions for which they are qualified by education, training, supervised experience, state and national professional credentials, and appropriate professional experience. Counselors hire for professional counseling positions only individuals who are qualified and competent.

D. *Monitor Effectiveness.* Counselors continually monitor their effectiveness as professionals and take steps to improve when necessary. Counselors in private practice take reasonable steps to seek out peer supervision to evaluate their efficacy as counselors.

E. *Ethical Issues Consultation.* Counselors take reasonable steps to consult with other counselors or related professionals when they have questions regarding their ethical obligations or professional practice. (See H.1.)

F. *Continuing Education.* Counselors recognize the need for continuing education to maintain a reasonable level of awareness of current scientific and professional information in their fields of activity. They take steps to maintain competence in the skills they use, are open to new procedures, and keep current with the diverse and/or special populations with whom they work.

G. *Impairment.* Counselors refrain from offering or accepting professional services when their physical, mental or emotional problems are likely to harm a client or others. They are alert to the signs of impairment, seek assistance for problems, and, if necessary, limit, suspend, or terminate their professional responsibilities. (See A.11.c.)

C.3. Advertising and Soliciting Clients

A. *Accurate Advertising.* There are no restrictions on advertising by counselors except those that can be specifically justified to protect the public from deceptive practices. Counselors advertise or represent their services to the public by identifying their credentials in an accurate manner that is not false, misleading, deceptive, or fraudulent. Counselors may only advertise the highest degree earned which is in counseling or a closely related field from a college or university that was accredited when the degree was awarded by one of the regional accrediting bodies recognized by the Council on Postsecondary Accreditation.

B. *Testimonials.* Counselors who use testimonials do not solicit them from clients or other persons who, because of their particular circumstances, may be vulnerable to undue influence.

C. *Statements by Others.* Counselors make reasonable efforts to ensure that statements made by others about them or the profession of counseling are accurate.

D. *Recruiting Through Employment.* Counselors do not use their places of employment or institutional affiliation to recruit or gain clients, supervisees, or consultees for their private practices. (See C.5.e.)

E. *Products and Training Advertisements.* Counselors who develop products related to their profession or conduct workshops or training events ensure that the advertisements concerning these products or events are accurate and disclose adequate information for consumers to make informed choices.

F. *Promoting to Those Served.* Counselors do not use counseling, teaching, training, or supervisory relationships to promote their products or training events in a manner that is deceptive or would exert undue influence on individuals who may be vulnerable. Counselors may adopt textbooks they have authored for instruction purposes.

G. *Professional Association Involvement.* Counselors actively participate in local, state, and national associations that foster the development and improvement of counseling.

C.4. Credentials

A. *Credentials Claimed.* Counselors claim or imply only professional credentials possessed and are responsible for correcting any known misrepresentations of their credentials by others. Professional credentials include graduate degrees in counseling or closely related mental health fields, accreditation of graduate programs, national voluntary certifications, government-issued certifications or licenses, ACA professional membership, or any other credential that might indicate to the public specialized knowledge or expertise in counseling.

B. *ACA Professional Membership.* ACA professional members may announce to the public their membership status. Regular members may not announce their ACA membership in a manner that might imply they are credentialed counselors.

C. *Credential Guidelines.* Counselors follow the guidelines for use of credentials that have been established by the entities that issue the credentials.

D. *Misrepresentation of Credentials.* Counselors do not attribute more to their credentials than the credentials represent, and do not imply that other counselors are not qualified because they do not possess certain credentials.

E. *Doctoral Degrees From Other Fields.* Counselors who hold a master's degree in counseling or a closely related mental health field, but hold a doctoral degree from other than counseling or a closely related field do not use the title, "Dr." in their practices and do not announce to the public in relation to their practice or status as a counselor that they hold a doctorate.

C.5. Public Responsibility

A. *Nondiscrimination.* Counselors do not discriminate against clients, students, or supervisees in a manner that has a negative impact based on their age, color, culture, disability, ethnic group, gender, race, religion, sexual orientation, or socioeconomic status, or for any other reason. (See A.2.a.)

B. *Sexual Harassment.* Counselors do not engage in sexual harassment. Sexual harassment is defined as sexual solicitation, physical advances, or verbal or nonverbal conduct that is sexual in nature, that occurs in connection with professional activities or roles, and that either: (1) is unwelcome, is offensive, or creates a hostile workplace environment, and counselors know or are told this; or (2) is sufficiently severe or intense to be perceived as harassment to a reasonable person in the context. Sexual harassment can consist of a single intense or severe act or multiple persistent or pervasive acts.

C. *Reports to Third Parties.* Counselors are accurate, honest, and unbiased in reporting their professional activities and judgments to appropriate third parties including courts, health insurance companies, those who are the recipients of evaluation reports, and others. (See B.1.g.)

D. *Media Presentations.* When counselors provide advice or comment by means of public lectures, demonstrations, radio or television programs, prerecorded tapes, printed articles, mailed material, or other media, they take reasonable precautions to ensure that (1) the statements are based on appropriate professional counseling literature and practice; (2) the statements are otherwise consistent with the *Code of Ethics* and the *Standards of Practice;* and (3) the recipients of the information are not encouraged to infer that a professional counseling relationship has been established. (See C.6.b.)

E. *Unjustified Gains.* Counselors do not use their professional positions to seek or receive unjustified personal gains, sexual favors, unfair advantage, or unearned goods or services. (See C.3.d.)

C.6. Responsibility to Other Professionals

A. *Different Approaches.* Counselors are respectful of approaches to professional counseling that differ from their own. Counselors know and take into account the traditions and practices of other professional groups with which they work.

B. *Personal Public Statements.* When making personal statements in a public context, counselors clarify that they are speaking from their personal perspectives and that they are not speaking on behalf of all counselors or the profession. (See C.5.d.)

C. *Clients Served by Others.* When counselors learn that clients are in a professional relationship with another mental health professional, they request release from clients to inform the other professionals and strive to establish positive and collaborative relationships. (See A.4.)

Section D: Relationships With Other Professionals

D.1. Relationships With Employers and Employees

A. *Role Definition.* Counselors define and describe for their employers and employees the parameters and levels of their professional roles.

B. *Agreements.* Counselors establish working agreements with supervisors, colleagues, and subordinates regarding counseling or clinical relationships, confidentiality, adherence to professional standards, distinction between public and private material, maintenance and dissemination of recorded information, workload, and accountability. Working agreements in each instance are specified and made known to those concerned.

C. *Negative Conditions.* Counselors alert their employers to conditions that may be potentially disruptive or damaging to the counselor's professional responsibilities or that may limit their effectiveness.

D. *Evaluation.* Counselors submit regularly to professional review and evaluation by their supervisor or the appropriate representative of the employer.

E. *In-Service.* Counselors are responsible for in-service development of self and staff.

F. *Goals.* Counselors inform their staff of goals and programs.

G. *Practices.* Counselors provide personnel and agency practices that respect and enhance the rights and welfare of each employee and recipient of agency services. Counselors strive to maintain the highest levels of professional services.

H. *Personnel Selection and Assignment.* Counselors select competent staff and assign responsibilities compatible with their skills and experiences.

I. *Discrimination.* Counselors, as either employers or employees, do not engage in or condone practices that are inhumane, illegal, or unjustifiable (such as considerations based on age, color, culture, disability, ethnic group, gender, race, religion, sexual orientation, or socioeconomic status) in hiring, promotion, or training. (See A.2.a. and C.5.b.)

J. *Professional Conduct.* Counselors have a responsibility both to clients and to the agency or institution within which services are performed to maintain high standards of professional conduct.

K. *Exploitive Relationships.* Counselors do not engage in exploitive relationships with individuals over whom they have supervisory, evaluative, or instructional control or authority.

L. *Employer Policies.* The acceptance of employment in an agency or institution implies that counselors are in agreement with its general policies and principles. Counselors strive to reach agreement with employers as to acceptable standards of conduct that allow for changes in institutional policy conducive to the positive growth and development of clients.

D.2. Consultation (See B.6.)

A. *Consultation as an Option.* Counselors may choose to consult with any other professionally competent person about their clients. In choosing consultants, counselors avoid placing the consultant in a conflict of interest situation that would preclude the consultant being a proper party to the counselor's efforts to help the client. Should counselors be engaged in a work setting that compromises this consultation standard, they consult with other professionals whenever possible to consider justifiable alternatives.

B. *Consultant Competency.* Counselors are reasonably certain that they have or the organization represented has the necessary competencies and resources for giving the kind of consulting services needed and that appropriate referral resources are available.

C. *Understanding With Clients.* When providing consultation, counselors attempt to develop with their clients a clear understanding of problem definition, goals for change, and predicted consequences of interventions selected.

D. *Consultant Goals.* The consulting relationship is one in which client adaptability and growth toward self-direction are consistently encouraged and cultivated. (See A.1.b.)

D.3. Fees for Referral

A. *Accepting Fees From Agency Clients.* Counselors refuse a private fee or other remuneration for rendering services to persons who are entitled to such services through the counselor's employing agency or institution. The policies of a particular agency may make explicit provisions for agency clients to receive counseling services from members of its staff in private practice. In such instances, the clients must be informed of other options open to them should they seek private counseling services. (See A.10.a., A.11.b., and C.3.d.)

B. *Referral Fees.* Counselors do not accept a referral fee from other professionals.

D.4. Subcontractor Arrangements

When counselors work as subcontractors for counseling services for a third party, they have a duty to inform clients of the limitations of confidentiality that the organization may place on counselors in providing counseling services to clients. The limits of such confidentiality ordinarily are discussed as part of the intake session. (See B.1.e. and B.1.f.)

Section E: Evaluation, Assessment, and Interpretation

E.1. General

A. *Appraisal Techniques.* The primary purpose of educational and psychological assessment is to provide measures that are objective and interpretable in either comparative or absolute terms. Counselors recognize the need to interpret the statements in this section as applying to the whole range of appraisal techniques, including test and nontest data.

B. *Client Welfare.* Counselors promote the welfare and best interests of the client in the development, publication, and utilization of educational and psychological assessment techniques. They do not misuse assessment results and interpretations and take reasonable steps to prevent others from misusing the information these techniques provide. They respect the client's right to know the results, the interpretations made, and the bases for their conclusions and recommendations.

E.2. Competence to Use and Interpret Tests

A. *Limits of Competence.* Counselors recognize the limits of their competence and perform only those testing and assessment services for which they have been trained. They are familiar with reliability, validity, related standardization, error of measurement, and proper application of any technique utilized. Counselors using computer-based test interpretations are trained in the construct being measured and the specific instrument being used prior to using this type of computer application. Counselors take reasonable measures to ensure the proper use of psychological assessment techniques by persons under their authority.

B. *Appropriate Use.* Counselors are responsible for the appropriate application, scoring, interpretation, and use of assessment instruments, whether they score and interpret such tests themselves or use computerized or other services.

C. *Decisions Based on Results.* Counselors responsible for decisions involving individuals or policies that are based on assessment results have a thorough understanding of educational and psychological measurement, including validation criteria, test research, and guidelines for test development and use.

D. *Accurate Information.* Counselors provide accurate information and avoid false claims or misconceptions when making statements about assessment

instruments or techniques. Special efforts are made to avoid unwarranted connotations of such terms as IQ and grade equivalent scores. (See C.5.c.)

E.3. Informed Consent

A. *Explanation to Clients.* Prior to assessment, counselors explain the nature and purposes of assessment and the specific use of results in language the client (or other legally authorized person on behalf of the client) can understand, unless an explicit exception to this right has been agreed upon in advance. Regardless of whether scoring and interpretation are completed by counselors, by assistants, or by computer or other outside services, counselors take reasonable steps to ensure that appropriate explanations are given to the client.

B. *Recipients of Results.* The examinee's welfare, explicit understanding, and prior agreement determine the recipients of test results. Counselors include accurate and appropriate interpretations with any release of individual or group test results. (See B.1.a. and C.5.c.)

E.4. Release of Information to Competent Professionals

A. *Misuse of Results.* Counselors do not misuse assessment results, including test results, and interpretations, and take reasonable steps to prevent the misuse of such by others. (See C.5.c.)

B. *Release of Raw Data.* Counselors ordinarily release data (e.g., protocols, counseling or interview notes, or questionnaires) in which the client is identified only with the consent of the client or the client's legal representative. Such data are usually released only to persons recognized by counselors as competent to interpret the data. (See B.1.a.)

E.5. Proper Diagnosis of Mental Disorders

A. *Proper Diagnosis.* Counselors take special care to provide proper diagnosis of mental disorders. Assessment techniques (including personal interview) used to determine client care (e.g., locus of treatment, type of treatment, or recommended follow-up) are carefully selected and appropriately used. (See A.3.a. and C.5.c.)

B. *Cultural Sensitivity.* Counselors recognize that culture affects the manner in which clients' problems are defined. Clients' socioeconomic and cultural experience is considered when diagnosing mental disorders.

E.6. Test Selection

A. *Appropriateness of Instruments.* Counselors carefully consider the validity, reliability, psychometric limitations, and appropriateness of instruments when selecting tests for use in a given situation or with a particular client.

B. *Culturally Diverse Populations.* Counselors are cautious when selecting tests for culturally diverse populations to avoid inappropriateness of testing that may be outside of socialized behavioral or cognitive patterns.

E.7. Conditions of Test Administration

A. *Administration Conditions.* Counselors administer tests under the same conditions that were established in their standardization. When tests are not administered under standard conditions or when unusual behavior or irregularities occur during the testing session, those conditions are noted in interpretation, and the results may be designated as invalid or of questionable validity.

B. *Computer Administration.* Counselors are responsible for ensuring that administration programs function properly to provide clients with accurate results when a computer or other electronic methods are used for test administration. (See A.13.b.)

C. *Unsupervised Test-Taking.* Counselors do not permit unsupervised or inadequately supervised use of tests or assessments unless the tests or assessments are designed, intended, and validated for self-administration and/or scoring.

D. *Disclosure of Favorable Conditions.* Prior to test administration, conditions that produce most favorable test results are made known to the examinee.

E.8. Diversity in Testing

Counselors are cautious in using assessment techniques, making evaluations, and interpreting the performance of populations not represented in the norm group on which an instrument was standardized. They recognize the effects of age, color, culture, disability, ethnic group, gender, race, religion, sexual orientation, and socioeconomic status on test administration and interpretation and place test results in proper perspective with other relevant factors. (See A.2.a.)

E.9. Test Scoring and Interpretation

A. *Reporting Reservations.* In reporting assessment results, counselors indicate any reservations that exist regarding validity or reliability because of the circumstances of the assessment or the inappropriateness of the norms for the person tested.

B. *Research Instruments.* Counselors exercise caution when interpreting the results of research instruments possessing insufficient technical data to support respondent results. The specific purposes for the use of such instruments are stated explicitly to the examinee.

C. *Testing Services.* Counselors who provide test scoring and test interpretation services to support the assessment process confirm the validity of such interpretations. They accurately describe the purpose, norms, validity, reliability, and applications of the procedures and any special qualifications applicable to their use. The public offering of an automated test interpretations service is considered a professional-to-professional consultation. The formal responsibility of the consultant is to the consultee, but the ultimate and overriding responsibility is to the client.

E.10. Test Security

Counselors maintain the integrity and security of tests and other assessment techniques consistent with legal and contractual obligations. Counselors do not appropriate, reproduce, or modify published tests or parts thereof without acknowledgment and permission from the publisher.

E.11. Obsolete Tests and Outdated Test Results

Counselors do not use data or test results that are obsolete or outdated for the current purpose. Counselors make every effort to prevent the misuse of obsolete measures and test data by others.

E.12. Test Construction

Counselors use established scientific procedures, relevant standards, and current professional knowledge for test design in the development, publication, and utilization of educational and psychological assessment techniques.

Section F: Teaching, Training, and Supervision

F.1. Counselor Educators and Trainers

A. *Educators as Teachers and Practitioners.* Counselors who are responsible for developing, implementing, and supervising educational programs are skilled as teachers and practitioners. They are knowledgeable regarding the ethical, legal, and regulatory aspects of the profession, are skilled in applying that knowledge, and make students and supervisees aware of their responsibilities. Counselors conduct counselor education and training programs in an ethical manner and serve as role models for professional behavior. Counselor educators should make an effort to infuse material related to human diversity into all courses and/or workshops that are designed to promote the development of professional counselors.

B. *Relationship Boundaries With Students and Supervisees.* Counselors clearly define and maintain ethical, professional, and social relationship boundaries with their students and supervisees. They are aware of the differential in power that exists and the student's or supervisee's possible incomprehension of that power differential. Counselors explain to students and supervisees the potential for the relationship to become exploitive.

C. *Sexual Relationships.* Counselors do not engage in sexual relationships with students or supervisees and do not subject them to sexual harassment. (See A.6. and C.5.b.)

D. *Contributions to Research.* Counselors give credit to students or supervisees for their contributions to research and scholarly projects. Credit is given through coauthorship, acknowledgment, footnote statement, or other appropriate means, in accordance with such contributions. (See G.4.b. and G.4.c.)

E. *Close Relatives.* Counselors do not accept close relatives as students or supervisees.

F. *Supervision Preparation.* Counselors who offer clinical supervision services are adequately prepared in supervision methods and techniques. Counselors who are doctoral students serving as practicum or internship supervisors to master's level students are adequately prepared and supervised by the training program.

G. *Responsibility for Services to Clients.* Counselors who supervise the counseling services of others take reasonable measures to ensure that counseling services provided to clients are professional.

H. *Endorsement.* Counselors do not endorse students or supervisees for certification, licensure, employment, or completion of an academic or training program if they believe students or supervisees are not qualified for the endorsement. Counselors take reasonable steps to assist students or supervisees who are not qualified for endorsement to become qualified.

F.2. Counselor Education and Training Programs

A. *Orientation.* Prior to admission, counselors orient prospective students to the counselor education or training program's expectations, including but not limited to the following: (1) the type and level of skill acquisition required for successful completion of the training; (2) subject matter to be covered; (3) basis for evaluation; (4) training components that encourage self-growth or self-disclosure as part of the training process; (5) the type of supervision settings and requirements of the sites for required clinical field experiences; (6) student and supervisee evaluation and dismissal policies and procedures; and (7) up-to-date employment prospects for graduates.

B. *Integration of Study and Practice.* Counselors establish counselor education and training programs that integrate academic study and supervised practice.

C. *Evaluation.* Counselors clearly state to students and supervisees, in advance of training, the levels of competency expected, appraisal methods, and timing of evaluations for both didactic and experiential components. Counselors provide students and supervisees with periodic performance appraisal and evaluation feedback throughout the training program.

D. *Teaching Ethics.* Counselors make students and supervisees aware of the ethical responsibilities and standards of the profession and the students' and supervisees' ethical responsibilities to the profession. (See C.1. and F.3.e.)

E. *Peer Relationships.* When students or supervisees are assigned to lead counseling groups or provide clinical supervision for their peers, counselors take steps to ensure that students and supervisees placed in these roles do not have personal or adverse relationships with peers and that they understand they have the same ethical obligations as counselor educators, trainers, and supervisors. Counselors make every effort to ensure that the rights of peers are not compromised when students or supervisees are assigned to lead counseling groups or provide clinical supervision.

F. *Varied Theoretical Positions.* Counselors present varied theoretical positions so that students and supervisees may make comparisons and have opportunities to develop their own positions. Counselors provide information concerning the scientific bases of professional practice. (See C.6.a.)

G. *Field Placements.* Counselors develop clear policies within their training program regarding field placement and other clinical experiences. Counselors provide clearly stated roles and responsibilities for the student or supervisee, the site supervisor, and the program supervisor. They confirm that site supervisors are qualified to provide supervision and are informed of their professional and ethical responsibilities in this role.

H. *Dual Relationships as Supervisors.* Counselors avoid dual relationships such as performing the role of site supervisor and training program supervisor in the student's or supervisee's training program. Counselors do not accept any form of professional services, fees, commissions, reimbursement, or remuneration from a site for student or supervisee placement.

I. *Diversity in Programs.* Counselors are responsive to their institution's and program's recruitment and retention needs for training program administrators, faculty, and students with diverse backgrounds and special needs. (See A.2.a.)

F.3. Students and Supervisees

A. *Limitations.* Counselors, through on-going evaluation and appraisal, are aware of the academic and personal limitations of students and supervisees that might impede performance. Counselors assist students and supervisees in securing remedial assistance when needed, and dismiss from the training program supervisees who are unable to provide competent service due to academic or personal limitations. Counselors seek professional consultation and document their decision to dismiss or refer students or supervisees for assistance. Counselors assure that students and supervisees have recourse to address decisions made, to require them to seek assistance, or to dismiss them.

B. *Self-Growth Experiences.* Counselors use professional judgment when designing training experiences conducted by the counselors themselves that require student and supervisee self-growth or self-disclosure. Safeguards are provided so that students and supervisees are aware of the ramifications their self-disclosure may have on counselors whose primary role as teacher, trainer, or supervisor requires acting upon ethical obligations to the profession. Evaluative components of experiential training experiences explicitly delineate predetermined academic standards that are separate and not dependent upon the student's level of self-disclosure. (See A.6.)

C. *Counseling for Students and Supervisees.* If students or supervisees request counseling, supervisors or counselor educators provide them with acceptable referrals. Supervisors or counselor educators do not serve as counselors to students or supervisees over whom they hold administrative, teaching, or evaluative roles unless this is a brief role associated with a training experience. (See A.6.b.)

D. *Clients of Students and Supervisees.* Counselors make every effort to ensure that the clients at field placements are aware of the services rendered and the qualifications of the students and supervisees rendering those services. Clients receive professional disclosure information and are informed of the limits of confidentiality. Client permission is obtained in order for the students and supervisees to use any information concerning the counseling relationship in the training process. (See B.1.e.)

E. *Standards for Students and Supervisees.* Students and supervisees preparing to become counselors adhere to the *Code of Ethics* and the *Standards of Practice.* Students and supervisees have the same obligations to clients as those required of counselors. (See H.1.)

Section G: Research and Publication

G.1. Research Responsibilities

A. *Use of Human Subjects.* Counselors plan, design, conduct, and report research in a manner consistent with pertinent ethical principles, federal and state laws, host institutional regulations, and scientific standards governing research with human subjects. Counselors design and conduct research that reflects cultural sensitivity appropriateness.

B. *Deviation From Standard Practices.* Counselors seek consultation and observe stringent safeguards to protect the rights of research participants when a research problem suggests a deviation from standard acceptable practices. (See B.6.)

C. *Precautions to Avoid Injury.* Counselors who conduct research with human subjects are responsible for the subjects' welfare throughout the experiment and take reasonable precautions to avoid causing injurious psychological, physical, or social effects to their subjects.

D. *Principal Researcher Responsibility.* The ultimate responsibility for ethical research practice lies with the principal researcher. All others involved in the research activities share ethical obligations and full responsibility for their own actions.

E. *Minimal Interference.* Counselors take reasonable precautions to avoid causing disruptions in subjects' lives due to participation in research.

F. *Diversity.* Counselors are sensitive to diversity and research issues with special populations. They seek consultation when appropriate. (See A.2.a. and B.6.)

G.2. Informed Consent

A. *Topics Disclosed.* In obtaining informed consent for research, counselors use language that is understandable to research participants and that: (1) accurately explains the purpose and procedures to be followed; (2) identifies any procedures that are experimental or relatively untried; (3) describes the attendant discomforts and risks; (4) describes the benefits or changes in individuals or organizations that might be reasonably expected; (5) discloses appropriate alternative procedures that would be advantageous for subjects; (6) offers to answer any inquiries concerning the procedures; (7) describes any limitations on confidentiality; and (8) instructs that subjects are free to withdraw their consent and to discontinue participation in the project at any time. (See B.1.f.)

B. *Deception.* Counselors do not conduct research involving deception unless alternative procedures are not feasible and the prospective value of the research justifies the deception. When the methodological requirements of a study necessitate concealment or deception, the investigator is required to explain clearly the reasons for this action as soon as possible.

C. *Voluntary Participation.* Participation in research is typically voluntary and without any penalty for refusal to participate. Involuntary participation is appropriate only when it can be demonstrated that participation will have no harmful effects on subjects and is essential to the investigation.

D. *Confidentiality of Information.* Information obtained about research participants during the course of an investigation is confidential. When the possibility exists that others may obtain access to such information, ethical research practice requires that the possibility, together with the plans for protecting confidentiality, be explained to participants as a part of the procedure for obtaining informed consent. (See B.1.e.)

E. *Persons Incapable of Giving Informed Consent.* When a person is incapable of giving informed consent, counselors provide an appropriate explanation, obtain agreement for participation and obtain appropriate consent from a legally authorized person.

F. *Commitments to Participants.* Counselors take reasonable measures to honor all commitments to research participants.

G. *Explanations After Data Collection.* After data are collected, counselors provide participants with full clarification of the nature of the study to remove any misconceptions. Where scientific or human values justify delaying or withholding information, counselors take reasonable measures to avoid causing harm.

H. *Agreements to Cooperate.* Counselors who agree to cooperate with another individual in research or publication incur an obligation to cooperate as promised in terms of punctuality of performance and with regard to the completeness and accuracy of the information required.

I. *Informed Consent for Sponsors.* In the pursuit of research, counselors give sponsors, institutions, and publication channels the same respect and opportunity for giving informed consent that they accord to individual research participants. Counselors are aware of their obligation to future research workers and ensure that host institutions are given feedback information and proper acknowledgement.

G.3. Reporting Results

A. *Information Affecting Outcome.* When reporting research results, counselors explicitly mention all variables and conditions known to the investigator that may have affected the outcome of a study or the interpretation of data.

B. *Accurate Results.* Counselors plan, conduct, and report research accurately and in a manner that minimizes the possibility that results will be misleading. They provide thorough discussions of the limitations of their data and alternative hypotheses. Counselors do not engage in fraudulent research, distort data, misrepresent data, or deliberately bias their results.

C. *Obligation to Report Unfavorable Results.* Counselors communicate to other counselors the results of any research judged to be of professional value. Results that reflect unfavorably on institutions, programs, services, prevailing opinions, or vested interests are not withheld.

D. *Identity of Subjects.* Counselors who supply data, aid in the research of another person, report research results, or make original data available take due care to disguise the identity of respective subjects in the absence of specific authorization from the subjects to do otherwise. (See B.1.g. and B.5.a.)

E. *Replication Studies.* Counselors are obligated to make available sufficient original research data to qualified professionals who may wish to replicate the study.

G.4. Publication

A. *Recognition of Others.* When conducting and reporting research, counselors are familiar with and give recognition to previous work on the topic, observe copyright laws, and give full credit to those to whom credit is due. (See F.1.d. and G.4.c.)

B. *Contributors.* Counselors give credit through joint authorship, acknowledgment, footnote statements, or other appropriate means to those who have contributed significantly to research or concept development in accordance with such contributions. The principal contributor is listed first and minor technical or professional contributions are acknowledged in notes or introductory statements.

C. *Student Research.* For an article that is substantially based on a student's dissertation or thesis, the student is listed as the principal author. (See F.1.d. and G.4.a.)

D. *Duplicate Submission.* Counselors submit manuscripts for consideration to only one journal at a time. Manuscripts that are published in whole or in substantial part in another journal or published work are not submitted for publication without acknowledgment and permission from the previous publication.

E. *Professional Review.* Counselors who review material submitted for publication, research, or other scholarly purposes respect the confidentiality and proprietary rights of those who submitted it.

Section H: Resolving Ethical Issues

H.1. Knowledge of Standards

Counselors are familiar with the *Code of Ethics* and the *Standards of Practice* and other applicable ethics codes from other professional organizations of which they are a member, or from certification and licensure bodies. Lack of knowledge or misunderstanding of an ethical responsibility is not a defense against a charge of unethical conduct. (See F.3.e.)

H.2. Suspected Violations

A. *Ethical Behavior Expected.* Counselors expect professional associates to adhere to Code of Ethics. When counselors possess reasonable cause that raises doubts as to whether a counselor is acting in an ethical manner, they take appropriate action. (See H.2.d. and H.2.e.)

B. *Consultation.* When uncertain as to whether a particular situation or course of action may be in violation of Code of Ethics, counselors consult with other counselors who are knowledgeable about ethics, with colleagues, or with appropriate authorities.

C. *Organization Conflicts.* If the demands of an organization with which counselors are affiliated pose a conflict with Code of Ethics, counselors specify the nature of such conflicts and express to their supervisors or other responsible officials their commitment to Code of Ethics. When possible, counselors work toward change within the organization to allow full adherence to Code of Ethics.

D. *Informal Resolution.* When counselors have reasonable cause to believe that another counselor is violating an ethical standard, they attempt to first resolve the issue informally with the other counselor if feasible, providing that such action does not violate confidentiality rights that may be involved.

E. *Reporting Suspected Violations.* When an informal resolution is not appropriate or feasible, counselors upon reasonable cause take action such as reporting the suspected ethical violation to state or national ethics committees unless this action conflicts with confidentiality rights that cannot be resolved.

F. *Unwarranted Complaints.* Counselors do not initiate, participate in, or encourage the filing of ethics complaints that are unwarranted or intend to harm a counselor rather than to protect clients or the public.

H.3. Cooperation With Ethics Committees

Counselors assist in the process of enforcing Code of Ethics. Counselors cooperate with investigations, proceedings, and requirements of the ACA Ethics Committee or ethics committees of other duly constituted associations or boards having jurisdiction over those charged with a violation. Counselors are familiar with the ACA Policies and Procedures and use it as a reference in assisting the enforcement of the Code of Ethics.

STANDARDS OF PRACTICE

All members of the American Counseling Association (ACA) are required to adhere to the *Standards of Practice* and the *Code of Ethics.* The *Standards of Practice* represent minimal behavioral statements of the *Code of Ethics.* Members should refer to the applicable section of the *Code of Ethics* for further interpretation and amplification of the applicable Standard of Practice.

Section A: The Counseling Relationship

Standard of Practice One (SP–1)

Nondiscrimination

Counselors respect diversity and must not discriminate against clients because of age, color, culture, disability, ethnic group, gender, race, religion, sexual orientation, marital status, or socioeconomic status. (See A.2.a.)

Standard of Practice Two (SP–2)

Disclosure to Clients

Counselors must adequately inform clients, preferably in writing, regarding the counseling process and counseling relationship at or before the time it begins and throughout the relationship. (See A.3.a.)

Standard of Practice Three (SP–3)

Dual Relationships

Counselors must make every effort to avoid dual relationships with clients that could impair their professional judgment or increase the risk of harm to clients. When a dual relationship cannot be avoided, counselors must take appropriate steps to ensure that judgment is not impaired and that no exploitation occurs. (See A.6.a. and A.6.b.)

Standard of Practice Four (SP–4)

Sexual Intimacies With Clients

Counselors must not engage in any type of sexual intimacies with current clients and must not engage in sexual intimacies with former clients within a minimum of two years after terminating the counseling relationship. Counselors who engage in such relationship after two years following termination have the responsibility to thoroughly examine and document that such relations did not have an exploitative nature.

Standard of Practice Five (SP–5)

Protecting Clients During Group Work

Counselors must take steps to protect clients from physical or psychological trauma resulting from interactions during group work. (See A.9.b.)

Standard of Practice Six (SP–6)

Advance Understanding of Fees

Counselors must explain to clients, prior to their entering the counseling relationship, financial arrangements related to professional services. (See A.10.a.–d. and A.11.c.)

Standard of Practice Seven (SP–7)

Termination

Counselors must assist in making appropriate arrangements for the continuation of treatment of clients, when necessary, following termination of counseling relationships. (See A.11.a.)

Standard of Practice Eight (SP–8)

Inability to Assist Clients

Counselors must avoid entering or immediately terminate a counseling relationship if it is determined that they are unable to be of professional assistance to a client. The counselor may assist in making an appropriate referral for the client. (See A.11.b.)

Section B: Confidentiality

Standard of Practice Nine (SP–9)

Confidentiality Requirement

Counselors must keep information related to counseling services confidential unless disclosure is in the best interest of clients, is required for the welfare of others, or is required by law. When disclosure is required, only information that is essential is revealed and the client is informed of such disclosure. (See B.1.a.–f.)

Standard of Practice Ten (SP–10)

Confidentiality Requirements for Subordinates

Counselors must take measures to ensure that privacy and confidentiality of clients are maintained by subordinates. (See B.1.h.)

Standard of Practice Eleven (SP–11)

Confidentiality in Group Work

Counselors must clearly communicate to group members that confidentiality cannot be guaranteed in group work. (See B.2.a.)

Standard of Practice Twelve (SP–12)

Confidentiality in Family Counseling

Counselors must not disclose information about one family member in counseling to another family member without prior consent. (See B.2.b.)

Standard of Practice Thirteen (SP–13)

Confidentiality of Records

Counselors must maintain appropriate confidentiality in creating, storing, accessing, transferring, and disposing of counseling records. (See B.4.b.)

Standard of Practice Fourteen (SP–14)

Permission to Record or Observe

Counselors must obtain prior consent from clients in order to electronically record or observe sessions. (See B.4.c.)

Standard of Practice Fifteen (SP–15)

Disclosure or Transfer of Records

Counselors must obtain client consent to disclose or transfer records to third parties, unless exceptions listed in SP–9 exist. (See B.4.e.)

Standard of Practice Sixteen (SP–16)

Data Disguise Required

Counselors must disguise the identity of the client when using data for training, research, or publication. (See B.5.a.)

Section C: Professional Responsibility

Standard of Practice Seventeen (SP–17)

Boundaries of Competence

Counselors must practice only within the boundaries of their competence. (See C.2.a.)

Standard of Practice Eighteen (SP–18)

Continuing Education

Counselors must engage in continuing education to maintain their professional competence. (See C.2.f.)

Standard of Practice Nineteen (SP–19)

Impairment of Professionals

Counselors must refrain from offering professional services when their personal problems or conflicts may cause harm to a client or others. (See C.2.g.)

Standard of Practice Twenty (SP–20)

Accurate Advertising

Counselors must accurately represent their credentials and services when advertising. (See C.3.a.)

Standard of Practice Twenty-one (SP–21)

Recruiting Through Employment

Counselors must not use their place of employment or institutional affiliation to recruit clients for their private practices. (See C.3.d.)

Standard of Practice Twenty-two (SP–22)

Credentials Claimed

Counselors must claim or imply only professional credentials possessed and must correct any known misrepresentations of their credentials by others. (See C.4.a.)

Standard of Practice Twenty-three (SP–23)

Sexual Harassment

Counselors must not engage in sexual harassment. (See C.5.b.)

Standard of Practice Twenty-four (SP–24)

Unjustified Gains

Counselors must not use their professional positions to seek or receive unjustified personal gains, sexual favors, unfair advantage, or unearned goods or services. (See C.5.e.)

Standard of Practice Twenty-five (SP–25)

Clients Served by Others

With the consent of the client, counselors must inform other mental health professionals serving the same client that a counseling relationship between the counselor and client exists. (See C.6.c.)

Standard of Practice Twenty-six (SP–26)

Negative Employment Conditions

Counselors must alert their employers to institutional policy or conditions that may be potentially disruptive or damaging to the counselor's professional responsibilities, or that may limit their effectiveness or deny clients' rights. (See D.1.c.)

Standard of Practice Twenty-seven (SP–27)

Personnel Selection and Assignment

Counselors must select competent staff and must assign responsibilities compatible with staff skills and experiences. (See D.1.h.)

Standard of Practice Twenty-eight (SP–28)

Exploitive Relationships With Subordinates

Counselors must not engage in exploitive relationships with individuals over whom they have supervisory, evaluative, or instructional control or authority. (See D.1.k.)

Section D: Relationships With Other Professionals

Standard of Practice Twenty-nine (SP–29)

Accepting Fees From Agency Clients

Counselors must not accept fees or other remuneration for consultation with persons entitled to such services through the counselor's employing agency or institution. (See D.3.a.)

Standard of Practice Thirty (SP–30)

Referral Fees

Counselors must not accept referral fees. (See D.3.b.)

Section E: Evaluation, Assessment, and Interpretation

Standard of Practice Thirty-one (SP–31)

Limits of Competence

Counselors must perform only testing and assessment services for which they are competent. Counselors must not allow the use of psychological assessment techniques by unqualified persons under their supervision. (See E.2.a.)

Standard of Practice Thirty-two (SP–32)

Appropriate Use of Assessment Instruments

Counselors must use assessment instruments in the manner for which they were intended. (See E.2.b.)

Standard of Practice Thirty-three (SP–33)

Assessment Explanations to Clients

Counselors must provide explanations to clients prior to assessment about the nature and purposes of assessment and the specific uses of results. (See E.3.a.)

Standard of Practice Thirty-four (SP–34)

Recipients of Test Results

Counselors must ensure that accurate and appropriate interpretations accompany any release of testing and assessment information. (See E.3.b.)

Standard of Practice Thirty-five (SP–35)

Obsolete Tests and Outdated Test Results

Counselors must not base their assessment or intervention decisions or recommendations on data or test results that are obsolete or outdated for the current purpose. (See E.11.)

Section F: Teaching, Training, and Supervision

Standard of Practice Thirty-six (SP–36)

Sexual Relationships With Students or Supervisees

Counselors must not engage in sexual relationships with their students and supervisees. (See F.1.c.)

Standard of Practice Thirty-seven (SP–37)

Credit for Contributions to Research

Counselors must give credit to students or supervisees for their contributions to research and scholarly projects. (See F.1.d.)

Standard of Practice Thirty-eight (SP–38)

Supervision Preparation

Counselors who offer clinical supervision services must be trained and prepared in supervision methods and techniques. (See F.1.f.)

Standard of Practice Thirty-nine (SP–39)

Evaluation Information

Counselors must clearly state to students and supervisees in advance of training, the levels of competency expected, appraisal methods, and timing of evaluations. Counselors must provide students and supervisees with periodic performances appraisal and evaluation feedback throughout the training program. (See F.2.c.)

Standard of Practice Forty (SP–40)

Peer Relationships in Training

Counselors must make every effort to ensure that the rights of peers are not violated when students and supervisees are assigned to lead counseling groups or provide clinical supervision. (See F.2.e.)

Standard of Practice Forty-one (SP–41)

Limitations of Students and Supervisees

Counselors must assist students and supervisees in securing remedial assistance, when needed, and must dismiss from the training program students and supervisees who are unable to provide competent service due to academic or personal limitations. (See F.3.a.)

Standard of Practice Forty-two (SP–42)

Self-Growth Experiences

Counselors who conduct experiences for students or supervisees that include self-growth or self-disclosure must inform participants of counselors' ethical obligations to the profession and must not grade participants on their nonacademic performance. (See F.3.b.)

Standard of Practice Forty-three (SP–43)

Standards for Students and Supervisees

Students and supervisees preparing to become counselors must adhere to the *Code of Ethics* and *Standards of Practice* of counselors. (See F.3.e.)

Section G: Research and Publication

Standard of Practice Forty-four (SP–44)

Precautions to Avoid Injury in Research

Counselors must avoid causing physical, social, or psychological harm or injury to subjects in research. (See G.1.c.)

Standard of Practice Forty-five (SP–45)

Confidentiality of Research Information

Counselors must keep confidential information obtained about research participants. (See G.2.d.)

Standard of Practice Forty-six (SP–46)

Information Affecting Research Outcome

Counselors must report all variables and conditions known to the investigator that may have affected research data or outcomes. (See G.3.a.)

Standard of Practice Forty-seven (SP–47)

Accurate Research Results

Counselors must not distort or misrepresent research data, nor fabricate or intentionally bias research results. (See G.3.b.)

Standard of Practice Forty-eight (SP–48)

Publication Contributors

Counselors must give appropriate credit to those who have contributed to research. (See G.4.a. and G.4.b.)

Section H: Resolving Ethical Issues

Standard of Practice Forty-nine (SP–49)

Ethical Behavior Expected

Counselors must take appropriate action when they possess reasonable cause as to whether counselors or other mental health professionals are acting in an ethical manner. (See H.2.a.)

Standard of Practice Fifty (SP–50)

Unwarranted Complaints

Counselors must not initiate, participate in, or encourage the filing of ethics complaints that are unwarranted or intended to harm a mental health professional rather than to protect clients or the public. (See H.2.f.)

Standard of Practice Fifty-one (SP–51)

Cooperation With Ethics Committees

Counselors must cooperate with investigations, proceedings, and requirements of the ACA Ethics Committee or ethics committees of other duly constituted associations or boards having jurisdiction over those charged with a violation. (See H.3.)

References

The following documents are available to counselors as resources to guide them in their practices. These resources are not a part of the *Code of Ethics* and the *Standards of Practice*.

American Association for Counseling and Development/Association for Measurement and Evaluation in Counseling and Development. (1989). *The responsibilities of users of standardized tests (revised)*. Washington, DC: Author.

American Counseling Association. (1988). *American Counseling Association code of ethics and standards of practice*. Alexandria, VA: Author.

American Psychological Association. (1985). *Standards for educational and psychological testing (revised)*. Washington, DC: Author.

American Rehabilitation Counseling Association, Commission on Rehabilitation Counselor Certification, and National Rehabilitation Counseling Association. (1995). *Code of professional ethics for rehabilitation counselors*. Chicago: Author.

American School Counselor Association. (1992). *Ethical standards for school counselors*. Alexandria, VA: Author.

Joint Committee on Testing Practices. (1988). *Code on fair testing practices in education*. Washington, DC: Author.

National Board for Certified Counselors. (1989). *National Board for Certified Counselors code of ethics*. Alexandria, VA: Author.

Prediger, D. J. (Ed.) (1993, March). *Multicultural assessment standards*. Alexandria, VA: Association for Assessment in Counseling.

Source: "The American Counseling Association Code of Ethics and Standards of Practice," by American Counseling Association, 1995, Alexandria, VA: American Counseling Association. Copyright 1995 by American Counseling Association. No further reproduction authorized without written permission of the American Counseling Association.

APPENDIX D

Ethical Standards for School Counselors
American School Counselor Association
(Revised June 25, 1998)

Preamble

The American School Counselor Association (ASCA) is a professional organization whose members have a unique and distinctive preparation, grounded in the behavioral sciences, with training in clinical skills adapted to the school setting. The school counselor assists in the growth and development of each individual and uses his/her specialized skills to protect the interests of the counselee within the structure of the school system. School counselors subscribe to the following basic tenets of the counseling process from which professional responsibilities are derived:

• Each person has the right to respect and dignity as a unique human being and to counseling services without prejudice as to person, character, belief, or practice regardless of age, color, disability, ethnic group, gender, race, religion, sexual orientation, marital status, or socioeconomic status.
• Each person has the right to self-direction and self-development.
• Each person has the right of choice and the responsibility for goals reached.
• Each person has the right to privacy and thereby the right to expect the counselor-client relationship to comply with all laws, policies, and ethical standards pertaining to confidentiality.

In this document, ASCA specifies the principles of ethical behavior necessary to maintain and regulate the high standards of integrity, leadership, and professionalism among its members. The Ethical Standards for Counselors were developed to clarify the nature of ethical responsibilities held in common by school counseling professionals. The purposes of this document are to:

• Serve as a guide for the ethical practices of all school counselors regardless of level, area, or population served, or membership in this professional Association.
• Provide benchmarks for both self-appraisal and peer evaluations regarding counselor responsibilities to counselees, parents, colleagues, and professional associates, schools and communities, self, as well as one's self and the counseling profession.
• Inform those served by the school counselor of acceptable counselor practices and expected professional behavior.

A.1. Responsibilities to Students

The professional school counselor:

A. Has a primary obligation to the counselee, who is to be treated with respect as a unique individual.
B. Is concerned with educational, career, emotional, and behavioral needs and encourages the maximum development of each counselee.
C. Refrains from consciously encouraging the counselee's acceptance of values, lifestyles, plans, decisions, and beliefs that represent the counselor's personal orientation.
D. Is responsible for keeping informed of laws, regulations, and policies relating to counselees and strives to ensure that the rights of counselees are adequately provided for and protected.

A.2. Confidentiality

The professional school counselor:

A. Informs the counselee of the purposes, goals, techniques, and rules of procedure under which she/he may receive counseling at or before the time when the counseling relationship is entered. Disclosure notice includes confidentiality issues such as the possible necessity for consulting with other professionals, privileged communication, and legal or authoritative restraints. The meaning and limits of confidentiality are clearly defined to counselees through a written and shared disclosure statement.

B. Keeps information confidential unless disclosure is required to prevent clear and imminent danger to the counselee or others or when legal requirements demand that confidential information be revealed. Counselees will consult with other professionals when in doubt as to the validity of an exception.

C. Discloses information to an identified third party who, by her or his relationship with the counselee, is at a high risk of contracting a disease that is commonly known to be communicable and fatal. Prior to disclosure, the counselor will ascertain that the counselee has not already informed the third party about her or his disease and he/she is not intending to inform the third party in the immediate future.

D. Requests the court that disclosure not be required when the release of confidential information without a counselee's permission may lead to potential harm to the counselee.

E. Protects the confidentiality of counselee's records and releases personal data only according to prescribed laws and school policies. Student information maintained in computers is treated with the same care as traditional student records.

F. Protects the confidentiality of information received in the counseling relationship as specified by federal and state law and applicable ethical standards. Such information is only to be revealed to others with the informed consent of the counselee, consistent with the counselor's ethical obligations. In a group setting, the counselor sets a norm of confidentiality and stresses its importance, yet clearly states that confidentiality in group counseling cannot be guaranteed.

A.3. Counseling Plans

The professional school counselor:
works jointly with the counselee in developing integrated and effective counseling plans, consistent with both the circumstances and abilities of the counselee and counselor. Such plans will be regularly reviewed to ensure continued viability and effectiveness, respecting the counselee's freedom of choice.

A.4. Dual Relationships

The professional school counselor:
avoids dual relationships which might impair her or his objectivity and increase the risk of harm to the client

(e.g., counseling one's family members, close friends, or associates). If a dual relationship is unavoidable, the counselor is responsible for taking action to eliminate or reduce the potential for harm. Such safeguards might include informed consent, consultation, supervision, and documentation.

A.5. Appropriate Referrals

The professional school counselor:
makes referrals when necessary or appropriate to outside resources. Appropriate referral necessitates knowledge of available resources and making proper plans for transitions with minimal interruption of services. Counselees retain the right to discontinue the counseling relationship at any time.

A.6. Group Work

The professional school counselor:
screens prospective group members and maintains an awareness of participants' needs and goals in relation to the goals of the group. The counselor takes reasonable precautions to protect members from physical and psychological harm resulting from interaction within the group.

A.7. Danger to Self and Others

The professional school counselor:
informs the appropriate authorities when the counselee's condition indicates a clear and imminent danger to the counselee or others. This is to be done after careful deliberation and, where possible, after consultation with other professionals. The counselor informs the counselee of actions to be taken so as to minimize his or her confusion and clarify expectations.

A.8. Student Records

The professional school counselor:
maintains and secures records necessary for rendering professional services to the counselee as required by laws, regulations, institutional procedures, and confidentiality guidelines.

A.9. Evaluation, Assessment, and Interpretation

The professional school counselor:

A. Adheres to all professional standards regarding selecting, administrating, and interpreting assessment measures. The counselor recognizes that computer-based testing programs require specific training in administration, scoring, and interpretation which may differ from that required in more traditional assessments.

B. Provides explanations of the nature, purposes, and results of assessment/evaluation measures in language counselee(s) can understand.

C. Does not misuse assessment results and interpretations and takes reasonable steps to prevent others from misusing information.

D. Uses caution when utilizing assessment techniques, making evaluations, and interpreting the performance of populations not represented in the norm group on which an instrument is standardized.

A.10. Computer Technology

The professional school counselor:

A. Promotes the benefits of appropriate computer applications and clarifies the limitations of computer technology. The counselor ensures that (1) computer applications are appropriate for the individual needs of the counselee, (2) the counselee understands how to use the applications, and (3) follow-up counseling assistance is provided. Members of underrepresented groups are assured of equal access to computer technologies and are assured the absence of discriminatory information and values within computer applications.

B. Counselors who communicate with counselees via Internet should follow the NBCC Standards for Web-Counseling.

A.11. Peer Helper Programs

The professional school counselor:
has unique ethical responsibilities in working with peer helper programs. The school counselor is responsible for the welfare of counselees participating in peer programs under her or his direction. School counselors who function in training and supervisory capacities are referred to the preparation and supervision standards of professional counselor associations.

B. Responsibilities to Parents

B.1. Parent Rights and Responsibilities

The professional school counselor:

A. Respects the inherent rights and responsibilities of parents for their children and endeavors to establish a cooperative relationship with parents to facilitate the counselee's maximum development.

B. Adheres to laws and local guidelines when assisting parents experiencing family difficulties that interfere with the counselee's effectiveness and welfare.

C. Is sensitive to cultural and social diversity among families and recognizes that all parents, custodial and noncustodial, are vested with certain rights and responsibilities for the welfare of their children by virtue of their role and according to law.

B.2. Parents and Confidentiality

The professional school counselor:

A. Informs parents of the counselor's role, with emphasis on the confidential nature of the counseling relationship between the counselor and counselee.

B. Provides parents with accurate, comprehensive, and relevant information in an objective and caring manner, as appropriate and consistent with ethical responsibilities to the counselee.

C. Makes reasonable efforts to honor the wishes of parents and guardians concerning information that he/she may share regarding the counselee.

C. Responsibilities to Colleagues and Professional Associates

C.1. Professional Relationships

The professional school counselor:

A. Establishes and maintains relationships with faculty, staff, and administration to facilitate the provision of optimal counseling services. The relationship is based on the counselor's definition and description of the parameter and levels of his or her personal roles.

B. Treats colleagues with professional respect, courtesy, and fairness. The qualifications, views, and findings of colleagues are represented to accurately reflect the image of competent professionals.

C. Is aware of and optimally utilizes related professions and organizations to whom the counselee may be referred.

C.2. Sharing Information With Other Professionals

The professional school counselor:

A. Promotes awareness of and adherence to appropriate guidelines regarding confidentiality; the distinction between public and private information; and staff consultation.

B. Provides professional personnel with accurate, objective, concise, and meaningful data necessary to adequately evaluate, counsel, and assist the counselee.

C. If a counselee is receiving services from another counselor or mental health professional, the counselor, with client consent, will inform the other professional and develop clear agreements to avoid confusion and conflict for the counselee.

D. Responsibilities to the School and Community

D.1. Responsibilities to the School

The professional school counselor:

A. Supports and protects the educational program against any infringement not in the best interest of counselees.

B. Informs appropriate officials of conditions that may be potentially disruptive or damaging to the school's mission, personnel, and property while honoring the confidentiality between the counselee and counselor.

C. Delineates and promotes the counselor's role and function in meeting the needs of those served. The counselor will notify appropriate school officials of conditions which may limit or curtail her or his effectiveness in providing programs and services.

D. Accepts employment only for positions for which he/she is qualified by education, training, supervised experience, state and national professional credentials, and appropriate professional experience. Counselors recommend that administrators hire only qualified and competent individuals for professional counseling positions.

E. Assists in the development of (1) curricular and environmental conditions appropriate for the school and community, (2) education procedures and programs to meet counselee's developmental needs, and (3) a systematic evaluation process for comprehensive school counseling programs, services, and personnel. The counselor is guided by findings of the evaluation data in planning programs and services.

D.2. Responsibility to the Community

The professional school counselor:
collaborates with agencies, organizations, and individuals in the school and community in the best interest of counselees and without regard to personal reward or remuneration.

E. Responsibilities to Self

E.1. Professional Competence

The professional school counselor:

A. Functions within the boundaries of individual professional competence and accepts responsibility for the consequences of his or her actions.

B. Monitors personal functioning and effectiveness and does not participate in any activity which may lead to inadequate professional services or harm to a client.

C. Strives through personal initiative to maintain professional competence and keep abreast of professional information. Professional and personal growth are ongoing throughout the counselor's career.

E.2. Multicultural Skills

The professional school counselor:
understands the diverse cultural backgrounds of the counselees with whom he/she works. This includes, but is not limited to, learning how the school counselor's own cultural/ethnic/racial identity impacts her or his values and beliefs about the counseling process.

F. Responsibility to the Profession

F.1. Professionalism

The professional school counselor:

A. Accepts the policies and processes for handling ethical violations as a result of maintaining membership in the American School Counselor Association.

B. Conducts herself/himself in such a manner as to advance individual ethical practice and the profession.

C. Conducts appropriate research and reports findings in a manner consistent with acceptable educational and psychological research practices. When using client data for research or for statistical or program planning purposes, the counselor ensures protection of the individual counselee's identity.

D. Adheres to ethical standards of the profession, other official policy statements pertaining to counseling, and relevant statutes established by federal, state, and local governments.

E. Clearly distinguishes between statements and actions made as a private individual and those made as a representative of the school counseling profession.

F. Does not use his or her professional position to recruit or gain clients, consultees for her or his private practice, seek and receive unjustified personal gains, unfair advantage, sexual favors, or unearned goods or services.

F.2. Contribution to the Profession

The professional school counselor:

A. Actively participates in local, state, and national associations which foster the development and improvement of school counseling.

B. Contributes to the development of the profession through sharing skills, ideas, and expertise with colleagues.

G. Maintenance of Standards

Ethical behavior among professional school counselors, Association members and nonmembers, is expected at all times. When there exists serious doubt as to the ethical behavior of colleagues, or if counselors are forced to work in situations or abide by policies which do not reflect the standards as outlined in these Ethical Standards for School Counselors, the counselor is obligated to take appropriate action to rectify the condition. The following procedure may serve as a guide:

1.   The counselor should consult confidentially with a professional colleague to discuss the nature of the complaint to see if she/he views the situation as an ethical violation.

2.   Whenever feasible, the counselor should directly approach the colleague whose behavior is in question to discuss the complaint and seek resolution.

3.   If resolution is not forthcoming at the personal level, the counselor shall utilize the channels established within the school, school district, the state SCA, and the ASCA Ethics Committee.

4.   If the matter still remains unresolved, referral for review and appropriate action should be made to the Ethics Committees in the following sequence.

- state counselor association
- American School Counselor Association

5.   The ASCA Ethics Committee is responsible for educating—and consulting with—the membership regarding ethical standards. The Committee periodically reviews and recommends changes in the code. The Committee will also receive and process questions to clarify the application of such standards. Questions must be submitted in writing to the ASCA Ethics Chair. Finally, the Committee will handle complaints of alleged violations of our ethical standards. Therefore, at the national level, complaints should be submitted in writing to the ASCA Ethics Committee, c/o the Executive Director, American School Counselor Association, 801 North Fairfax, Suite 310, Alexandria, VA 22314.

H. Resources

School counselors are responsible for being aware of, and acting in accord with, the standards and positions of the counseling profession as represented in such official documents as those listed below:

American Counseling Association. (1995). Code of ethics and standards of practice. Alexandria, VA. (5999 Stevenson Ave., Alexandria, VA 22034) 1-800-347-6647 www.counseling.org.

American School Counselor Association. (1997). The national standards for school counseling programs. Alexandria, VA. (801 North Fairfax Street, Suite 310, Alexandria, VA 22314) 1-800-306-4722 www.schoolcounselor.org.

American School Counselor Association. (1998). Position Statements. Alexandria, VA.

American School Counselor Association. (1998). Professional liability insurance program. (Brochure). Alexandria, VA.

Arredondo, Toperek, Brown, Jones, Locke, Sanchez, and Stadler. (1996). Multicultural counseling competencies and standards. *Journal of Multicultural Counseling and Development*, Vol. 24, No. 1. See American Counseling Association.

Arthur, G.L., and Swanson, C.D. (1993). Confidentiality and privileged communication. See American Counseling Association.

Association for Specialists in Group Work. (1989). Ethical guidelines for group counselors. Alexandria, VA. See American Counseling Association.

Corey, G., Corey, M.S., and Callanan. (1998). *Issues and ethics in the helping professions.* Pacific Grove, CA: Brooks/Cole (Brooks/Cole, 511 Forest Lodge Rd., Pacific Grove, CA 93950) www.thomson.com.

Crawford, R. (1994). Avoiding counselor malpractice. Alexandria, VA. See American Counseling Association.

Forrester-Miller, H. and Davis, T.E. (1996). A practitioner's guide to ethical decision-making. Alexandria, VA. See American Counseling Association.

Herlihy, B., and Corey, G. (1996). ACA ethical standards casebook. Fifth ed. Alexandria, VA. See American Counseling Association.

Herlihy, B., and Corey, G. (1992). Dual relationships in counseling. Alexandria, VA. See American Counseling Association.

Huey, W.C., and Remley, T.P. (1988). Ethical and legal issues in school counseling. Alexandria, VA. See American Counseling Association.

Joint Committee on Testing Practices. (1988). Code of fair testing practices in education. Washington, DC: American Psychological Association (1200 17th Street NW, Washington, DC 20036) 202-336-5500.

Mitchell, R.W. (1991). Documentation in counseling records. Alexandria, VA. See American Counseling Association.

National Board for Certified Counselors. (1998). National board for certified counselors: Code of ethics. Greensboro, NC (3 Terrace Way, Suite D, Greensboro, NC 277403-3660) 336-547-0607 www.nbcc.org.

National Board for Certified Counselors. (1997). Standards for ethical practice of webcounseling. Greensboro, NC.

National Peer Helpers Association. (1989). Code of ethics for peer helping professionals. Greenville, NC (P.O. Box 2684, Greenville, NC 27836) 919-522-3959 nphaorg@aol.com.

Salo, M., and Schumate, S. (1993). Counseling minor clients. Alexandria, VA. See American School Counselor Association.

Stevens-Smith, P., and Hughes, M. (1993). Legal issues in marriage and family counseling. Alexandria, VA. See American School Counselor Association.

Wheeler, N., and Bertram, B. (1994). Legal aspects of counseling: Avoiding lawsuits and legal problems (Videotape). Alexandria, VA. See American School Counselor Association.

Ethical Standards for School Counselors was adopted by the ASCA Delegate Assembly, March 19, 1984. The first revision was approved by the ASCA Delegate Assembly, March 27, 1992. The second revision was approved by the ASCA Governing Board on March 30, 1998, and adopted on June 25, 1998.

Multicultural Counseling Standards

I. Counselor Awareness of Own Cultural Values and Biases

A. Attitudes and Beliefs

1. Culturally skilled counselors have moved from being culturally unaware to being aware of and sensitive to their own cultural heritage and to valuing and respecting differences.

2. Culturally skilled counselors are aware of how their own cultural backgrounds and experiences and attitudes, values, and biases influence psychological processes.

3. Culturally skilled counselors are able to recognize the limits of their competencies and expertise.

4. Culturally skilled counselors are comfortable with differences that exist between themselves and clients in terms of race, ethnicity, culture, and beliefs.

B. Knowledge

1. Culturally skilled counselors have specific knowledge about their own racial and cultural heritage and how it personally and professionally affects their definitions of normality-abnormality and the process of counseling.

2. Culturally skilled counselors possess knowledge and understanding about how oppression, racism, discrimination, and stereotyping affect them personally and in their work. This allows them to acknowledge their own racist attitudes, beliefs, and feelings. Although this standard applies to all groups, for White counselors it may mean that they understand how they may have directly or indirectly benefited from individual, institutional, and cultural racism (White identity development models).

3. Culturally skilled counselors possess knowledge about their social impact on others. They are knowledgeable about communication style differences, how their style may clash or foster the counseling process with minority clients, and how to anticipate the impact it may have on others.

C. Skills

1. Culturally skilled counselors seek out educational, consultative, and training experience to improve their understanding and effectiveness in working with culturally different populations. Being able to recognize the limits of their competencies, they (a) seek consultation, (b) seek further training or education, (c) refer out to more qualified individuals or resources, or (d) engage in a combination of these.

2. Culturally skilled counselors are constantly seeking to understand themselves as racial and cultural beings and are actively seeking a nonracist identity.

II. Counselor Awareness of Client's Worldview

A. Attitudes and Beliefs

1. Culturally skilled counselors are aware of their negative emotional reactions toward other racial and ethnic groups that may prove detrimental to their clients in counseling. They are willing to contrast their own beliefs and attitudes with those of their culturally different clients in a nonjudgmental fashion.

2. Culturally skilled counselors are aware of their stereotypes and preconceived notions that they may hold toward other racial and ethnic minority groups.

B. Knowledge

1. Culturally skilled counselors possess specific knowledge and information about the particular group they are working with. They are aware of the life experiences, cultural heritage, and historical background of their culturally different clients. This particular competency is strongly linked to the "minority identity development models" available in the literature.

2. Culturally skilled counselors understand how race, culture, ethnicity, and so forth may affect personality formation, vocational choices, manifestation of

psychological disorders, help-seeking behavior, and the appropriateness or inappropriateness of counseling approaches.

3. Culturally skilled counselors understand and have knowledge about sociopolitical influences that impinge upon the life of racial and ethnic minorities. Immigration issues, poverty, racism, stereotyping, and powerlessness all leave major scars that may influence the counseling process.

C. Skills

1. Culturally skilled counselors should familiarize themselves with relevant research and the latest findings regarding mental disorders of various ethnic and racial groups. They should actively seek out educational experiences that foster their knowledge, understanding, and cross-cultural skills.

2. Culturally skilled counselors become actively involved with minority individuals outside of the counseling setting (community events, social and political functions, celebrations, friendships, neighborhood groups, and so forth) so that their perspective of minorities is more than an academic or helping exercise.

III. Culturally Appropriate Intervention Strategies

A. Attitudes and Beliefs

1. Culturally skilled counselors respect clients' religious and/or spiritual beliefs and values, including attributions and taboos, because they affect worldview, psychosocial functioning, and expressions of distress.

2. Culturally skilled counselors respect indigenous helping practices and respect minority community intrinsic help-giving networks.

3. Culturally skilled counselors value bilingualism and do not view another language as an impediment to counseling (monolingualism may be the culprit).

B. Knowledge

1. Culturally skilled counselors have a clear and explicit knowledge and understanding of the generic characteristics of counseling and therapy (culture bound, class bound, and monolingual) and how they may clash with the cultural values of various minority groups.

2. Culturally skilled counselors are aware of institutional barriers that prevent minorities from using mental health services.

3. Culturally skilled counselors have knowledge of the potential bias in assessment instruments and use procedures and interpret findings keeping in mind the cultural and linguistic characteristics of clients.

4. Culturally skilled counselors have knowledge of minority family structures, hierarchies, values, and beliefs. They are knowledgeable about the community characteristics and the resources in the community as well as the family.

5. Culturally skilled counselors should be aware of relevant discriminatory practices at the social and community level that may be affecting the psychological welfare of the population being served.

C. Skills

1. Culturally skilled counselors are able to engage in a variety of verbal and nonverbal helping responses. They are able to *send* and *receive* both *verbal* and *nonverbal* messages *accurately* and *appropriately*. They are not tied down to only one method or approach to helping but recognize that helping styles and approaches may be culture bound. When they sense that their helping style is limited and potentially inappropriate, they can anticipate and ameliorate its negative impact.

2. Culturally skilled counselors are able to exercise institutional intervention skills on behalf of their clients. They can help clients determine whether a "problem" stems from racism or bias in others (the concept of health paranoia) so that clients do not inappropriately personalize problems.

3. Culturally skilled counselors are not adverse to seeking consultation with traditional healers and religious and spiritual leaders and practitioners in the treatment of culturally different clients when appropriate.

4. Culturally skilled counselors take responsibility for interacting in the language requested by the client and, if not feasible, make appropriate referral. A serious problem arises when the linguistic skills of a counselor do not match the language of the client. This being the case, counselors should (a) seek a translator with cultural knowledge and appropriate professional background and (b) refer to a knowledgeable and competent bilingual counselor.

5. Culturally skilled counselors have training and expertise in the use of traditional assessment and testing instruments. They not only understand the technical aspects of the instruments but are also aware of the cultural limitations. This allows them to use test instruments for the welfare of the diverse clients.

6. Culturally skilled counselors should attend to as well as work to eliminate biases, prejudices, and discriminatory practices. They should be cognizant of sociopolitical contexts in conducting evaluation and providing interventions and should develop sensitivity to issues of oppression, sexism, elitism, and racism.

7. Culturally skilled counselors take responsibility in educating their clients to the processes of psychological intervention, such as goals, expectations, legal rights, and the counselor's orientation.

Source: From "Multicultural Competencies/Standards: A Pressing Need," by D. W. Sue, P. Arredondo, and R. J. McDavis, 1992, *Journal of Counseling & Development, 70,* pp. 485–486. Copyright 1992 by the American Counseling Association. Reprinted with permission.

Opinion Surveys Developed by Counselors in the State College, Pennsylvania, Area School District

State College Area School District
Counseling and Guidance Department

Teacher Survey

Dear Teacher: The guidance staff is in the process of a year-long self-study. Please help us by giving an honest response to each of the following survey items. A quick return is needed in order to analyze the information. Please return completed surveys to the mailbox of a counselor in your building as soon as possible.

Please circle the appropriate information relative to the grade level of the students you teach:

Elementary   Junior High   Senior High

In the following section use one of the three responses given below for each question.

Y = Yes   N = No   ? = Uncertain

1. Do you believe that you understand the purposes of the guidance program in your school? .... ____(01)
2. Do you believe that counselors and teachers are trying to accomplish similar purposes in your school? .... ____(02)
3. Do you think a good counseling service can be helpful to teachers? .... ____(03)
4. Do you believe that you are part of the guidance program? .... ____(04)
5. Is the counseling service in your school helpful to you? .... ____(05)
6. Do you have adequate time to see the counselor when the need arises? .... ____(06)
7. Do you think the counseling service in your school is helpful to students? .... ____(07)
8. Do you think that the guidance facilities are adequate? .... ____(08)
9. Do you think the counseling service should be limited to students with special problems? .... ____(09)
10. Do you think the counseling service should be concerned with the developmental needs of all students? .... ____(10)
11. Is the student able to see a counselor easily when a need arises? .... ____(11)
12. Do the counselors keep you informed of their work with your students? .... ____(12)
13. Have you ever requested a conference with the counselor to discuss ways you might work more effectively with an individual or group of students? .... ____(13)
14. Is the counselor usually available within a reasonable amount of time when you ask for a conference? .... ____(14)
15. Are your classes often disrupted unnecessarily by counselors? .... ____(15)
16. Are you able to include any developmental counseling topics in your classroom? (e.g. peer relationships, self-concept, career development, problem solving, decision making, etc.) .... ____(16)
17. Do you think parents are sufficiently involved with the counseling service? .... ____(17)
18. Do you think career development should be an integrated part of the K–12 curriculum? .... ____(18)
19. Do you ever refer students to the counselor? .... ____(19)

Source: From the school counseling staff of the State College Area School District, State College, Pennsylvania.

20. Are you aware of counselor referrals to outside agencies? .... ____(20)
21. Have you ever had any feedback from a referral agency? .... ____(21)
22. Do you think each student referred by you should be seen individually by the counselor? .... ____(22)
23. Are you aware of any group work being done by the counselors? .... ____(23)
24. Do you think group counseling is beneficial for some students? .... ____(24)
25. Do you think some students can be helped by an appropriate contingency management or behavior modification program? .... ____(25)
26. Do you think talking to a counselor is helpful to most students who see one? .... ____(26)
27. Do you think that the counselors are helpful when they participate in a conference involving the parents of one of your students? .... ____(27)
28. Do you think the counselor should facilitate communication between staff members? .... ____(28)
29. Do you think the counselor should facilitate communication between teaching staff and principal? .... ____(29)
30. Do you think it is helpful to have the counselor participate in staff planning meetings? .... ____(30)
31. Do you understand how to interpret standardized test results? .... ____(31)
32. Do you feel that the guidance testing program is helpful? .... ____(32)
33. Is the guidance orientation program in our school adequate? .... ____(33)

The statements below tell about some ways that teachers might feel about their school counselor. Please "score" each statement to show how you feel about your counselor(s).

Mark each statement on the following scale:
Mark 1—If the statement is very true (you feel strongly that it is true).
Mark 2—If the statement is probably true.
Mark 3—If you just cannot say about this (use as little as possible).
Mark 4—If the statement is probably not true.
Mark 5—If the statement is definitely not true.

34. He or she respects me (The rest of the items will all use "he," no matter if the counselor is a woman) .... ____(34)
35. He tries to see things the way I do and understands how I feel .... ____(35)
36. His interest in me depends on what I am talking about .... ____(36)
37. He tells me his opinions more than I want to know them .... ____(37)
38. It seems to bother him when I talk or ask about certain things .... ____(38)
39. His feeling toward me depends on how I feel toward him .... ____(39)
40. It is hard for me to know what he is really like as a person .... ____(40)
41. Sometimes he is warm and friendly; sometimes not so friendly .... ____(41)
42. He does not realize how strongly I feel about some of the things we discuss .... ____(42)
43. There are times when I think that what he says does not show what he really feels .... ____(43)
44. He hurries me through my business with him .... ____(44)
45. I often feel that he has more important things to do when I am talking to him .... ____(45)
46. He usually understands all of what I say to him .... ____(46)
47. Even when I can't say what I mean clearly, he still seems to understand me .... ____(47)
48. It seems that things (like the phone) often interrupt us when we're talking .... ____(48)

Listed below are elements of a counseling and guidance program. Will you please evaluate the counseling and guidance services as you see them operating in your school. There are two columns; one on each side of the page. The column to the left represents your feeling about the advisability of the service being offered by counselors, in general. The column on the right represents your feeling about whether or not the counselors at your school are actually performing this service up to expectations. Answer the questions in the left-hand column by checking either "Yes" or "No." Answer the questions in the right-hand column by using the following rating scale.

0 = Not being done   1 = Low level of performance
2 = Average level   3 = High level

Should counselors perform this service?

What is the quality of this service as it is now performed?

Yes	No		Rating (0, 1, 2, or 3)
___ (49)	___ (50)	a. Keep an up-dated system of pupil records	___ (51)
___ (52)	___ (53)	b. Interpretation of standardized testing results	___ (54)
___ (55)	___ (56)	c. Providing career information (e.g., occupational, educational, etc.)	___ (57)
___ (58)	___ (59)	d. Individual counseling (e.g., educational, social, vocational, personal, or some combination)	___ (60)
___ (61)	___ (62)	e. Group counseling (e.g., classroom groups, smaller groups, personal concerns, achievement, peer relationships, personal hygiene, etc.)	___ (63)
___ (64)	___ (65)	f. Maintain communication among the staff concerning pupil concerns	___ (66)
___ (67)	___ (68)	g. Provide counseling services to parents relative to their children in school	___ (69)
___ (70)	___ (71)	h. Serve as liaison with community agencies and referral sources	___ (72)
___ (73)	___ (74)	i. Function in a team approach with other pupil personnel specialists	___ (75)
___ (76)	___ (77)	j. Provide orientation activities for students entering post-secondary education	___ (78)
___ (79)	___ (80)	k. Provide placement counseling for students seeking the labor market	___ (81)
___ (82)	___ (83)	l. Provide placement counseling for students entering post-secondary education	___ (84)
___ (85)	___ (86)	m. Conduct research on student characteristics for various publics (e.g., teachers, administrators, parents)	___ (87)
___ (88)	___ (89)	n. Provide consultation for teachers (e.g., concerning student behavior, curriculum ideas, school policy ideas, approaches to interaction with and among students)	___ (90)
___ (91)	___ (92)	o. Help teachers to plan and conduct teaching units wherein the materials and concepts are related to guidance (e.g., career development, self-awareness, peer relationships, decision making)	___ (93)

1. What do you consider to be the major strengths of your guidance staff? (Please be as specific as possible.)
2. What do you consider to be the primary weaknesses of your guidance staff? If possible, include recommendations for improving these weaknesses.

State College Area School District
Counseling and Guidance Department
Parent Survey

The following brief survey has been designed to assess the extent and effectiveness of the guidance services you and your child have received through the school. How many children do you now have in grades:

1–6	____	01*
7–9	____	02
10–12	____	03

Part One

Directions: If you have children in more than one of the levels indicated above, please rate each counseling service for each child separately. Use column E to indicate an elementary rating, column J a junior high rating, and column H a senior high school rating.

　　Example: In response to Item 1 you might place a 1 in column H indicating one meeting at the senior high school and 2 in column J indicating two meetings at the junior high.

Type of Contact	Columns		
	E	J	H
1. Participated in a large group meeting conducted by the counselor or in which the counselor participated (P.T.A., special parent meeting)	____04	____05	____06
2. Individual conference with counselor	____07	____08	____09
3. Telephone conversation with counselor	____10	____11	____12
4. Received newsletter or bulletin prepared by the counselor	____13	____14	____15
5. Received special written reports prepared by the counselor about your child's progress in school	____16	____17	____18
6. Home-visitation by counselor	____19	____20	____21
A. Other contact. (Please specify.)			
....	____	____	____
....	____	____	____
....	____	____	____
....	____	____	____

* NOTE: Ignore numbering on the right-hand side of the page. It is for data processing.

Part Two

Directions: Using your knowledge of the contacts your child has had with his or her guidance counselor, please complete the following section by indicating the approximate number of times he has had each type of contact. As in Part One, use the appropriate column.

Type of Contact	Columns		
	E	J	H
7. My child participated with a small group of students in school, organized by the guidance counselor to discuss problems and concerns.	____22	____23	____24
8. My child participated with large and small groups for things other than problems and concerns (i.e., affective groups—college information, career nights, etc.).	____25	____26	____27
9. My child has had an individual interview or meeting with the guidance counselor.	____28	____29	____30
10. My child requested and received individual help from the guidance counselor.	____31	____32	____33
11. My child received special materials prepared by or secured by the guidance counselor (e.g., books, brochures, pamphlets).	____34	____35	____36

B. Other contact. (Please specify.)

....   ____   ____   ____

....   ____   ____   ____

....   ____   ____   ____

....   ____   ____   ____

Part Three

Directions: The following statements represent the intentions of the State College Area guidance program. In responding to these items, use the same columns as you did in Parts One and Two. However, use the following key when responding to these items:

>   1—very well
>   2—well
>   3—unsure
>   4—poor
>   5—much more needs to be done
>   6—no opinion

>   Example: If you think that the junior high school guidance personnel performed "well" in regard to item 15, place a 2 (2—well) in column J (J—junior high).

Please fill in all of the blanks although you may not have children attending school in each category.

Statements		Columns	
The guidance personnel . . .	E	J	H
12. Help parents to better understand their child's academic progress in school.	___37	___38	___39
13. Help parents to better understand their child's interests and abilities (i.e., test results).	___40	___41	___42
14. Help parents to better understand the school's total educational program.	___43	___44	___45
15. Make it easier for parents to relate to the school concerning their children.	___46	___47	___48
16. Help students to improve academically.	___49	___50	___51
17. Help students to better cope with school and developmental problems and concerns.	___52	___53	___54
18. Help to promote healthy attitudes and values in students.	___55	___56	___57
19. Assist students in decision-making skills relative to such concerns as career planning, course selection, post-high school training, etc.	___58	___59	___60
20. Assist students through the provision of materials, special programs, etc. relative to career planning, educational planning, and personal needs.	___61	___62	___63
21. Assist parents to better understand the behavior of school-age persons.	___64	___65	___66
22. Offer ideas which help parents to better understand and cope with students' behavior.	___67	___68	___69
23. Provide individual counseling upon reasonable demand by students	___70	___71	___72
24. Provide information on sources of help for the child that are available in the community.	___73	___74	___75
25. Assist parents in making decisions concerning the child's welfare.	___76	___77	___78
26. Assist children in assuming personal responsibility.	___79	___80	___81
27. Provide consultation services to parents concerning children and young people.	___82	___83	___84

Parent Reaction Space: (Please comment on the overall effectiveness of the guidance program—strong points, weaknesses, needed additions, etc.).

_____

_____

_____

_____

_____

_____

_____

_____

Your prompt return of this questionnaire will greatly enhance the effectiveness of the Self-Study of which this is one part. A self-addressed, stamped envelope has been provided for your convenience.

State College Area School District
Counseling and Guidance Department

Follow-up Study

Former State College Area High School Graduates

HELP! DID YOUR SCHOOL PROVIDE YOU WITH ADEQUATE COUNSELING AND GUIDANCE?
PLEASE HELP US TO FIND OUT BY COMPLETING THE FOLLOWING BRIEF SURVEY.

What year did you graduate from State College High? _____

a. Which of the following best describes the course of studies you pursued while in high school? (check one)	Business education	_____ (01)
	College preparatory	_____ (02)
	General studies	_____ (03)
	Vocational-technical	_____ (04)
	Work study	_____ (05)
b. Sex (check one)	Female	_____ (06)
	Male	_____ (07)
c. Which of the following best describes what you are doing with the majority of your time and energy? (check one)	Employed	_____ (08)
	Homemaker	_____ (09)
	Military	_____ (10)
	Student	_____ (11)
	Unemployed	_____ (12)
Other (please specify) _____		_____ (13)

For questions d through o, please use the following key:
   1 = little, 2 = uncertain, 3 = much, 4 = did not seek this service
        (Example: If your answer to question d is "much," place a "3" in blank number 14.)
How helpful were the school counselors to you in each of the following areas?

d. Selecting and scheduling your courses.   _____ (14)
e. Making your future plans.   _____ (15)
f. Solving a problem with a teacher.   _____ (16)
g. Understanding your grades.   _____ (17)
h. Solving a problem with your parents.   _____ (18)
i. Understanding your abilities.   _____ (19)
j. Seeking information on jobs or schools.   _____ (20)
k. Solving a problem with another student.   _____ (21)
l. Understanding achievement test scores.   _____ (22)
m. Improving yourself academically.   _____ (23)
n. Solving a personal problem.   _____ (24)
o. How free did you feel to contact a counselor when you had a problem?   _____ (25)

p. How many full-time jobs (30+ hours per week) have you had since leaving high school? (place answer in blank 26) If your answer to question "p" is zero or none, leave this section and move on to question "v." _____ (26)

q. List the full-time job titles you have had: _____

_____

r. After you seriously began looking, how long did it take for you to find your first job? (check one)	0 to 3 months	_____ (27)
	3 to 6 months	_____ (28)
	More than 6 months	_____ (29)
	Had job arranged before leaving school	_____ (30)
s. Which of the following best describes your degree of satisfaction with your present job? (check one)	very satisfied	_____ (31)
	satisfied	_____ (32)
	uncertain	_____ (33)
	dissatisfied	_____ (34)
	very dissatisfied	_____ (35)

t. What features of this job caused you to be satisfied: _____

_____

_____

_____

u. What features of this job caused you to be dissatisfied: _____

_____

_____

_____

v. Have you been a full-time student since leaving high school?	Yes	_____ (36)
If your answer is "Yes," continue with the following questions.	No	_____ (37)
If your answer is "No," see the note at bottom of page.		

w. Name of school(s) attended: _____

_____

x. Course(s) of study: _____

_____

For questions y through bb, please use the following key:
    1 = little, 2 = uncertain, 3 = much, 4 = did not seek this service
       (Example: If your answer to question "y" is "little," place a "1" in blank number 38.)

y. How much help in choosing a school did you receive from school counselors? _____ (38)

z. How much help in finding information relative to your choice of school did you receive from your school counselors? _____ (39)

aa. How much help related to the decision: "Should I go on to school?" did you receive from your school counselors? _____ (40)

bb. How satisfied are you with the school you attended or are presently attending since leaving high school? _____ (41)

| cc. Did you leave that school before completing the course of studies? If your answer is "Yes," why? _____ | Yes | _____ (42) |
| _____ | No | _____ (43) |

Thank you for taking the time to fill out this survey. Please mail it right back to us in the stamped envelope which is provided.

State College Area School District Counseling and Guidance Department
Senior High School Guidance Awareness Survey

The purpose of this survey is twofold: 1. to allow you to help evaluate your present counseling and guidance staff and 2. to learn more about your own future plans. You can help by being thoughtful, fair, and honest.

Grade level: _____   Sex (check one): Female _____ Male _____

Directions: When you answer questions a through bb, be sure to remember the general question, "Does your counselor do these things?" Choose only one answer for each statement (Yes, No, or Not their responsibility). Does your school counselor do these things?

	Yes	No	Not their responsibility
a. Help you learn how to study.	(01) _____	(02) _____	(03) _____
b. Help you become acquainted with the school (the building, the rules, courses, etc.).	(04) _____	(05) _____	(06) _____
c. Help you to plan school programs and courses.	(07) _____	(08) _____	(09) _____
d. Help you plan for education after high school.	(10) _____	(11) _____	(12) _____
e. Help you to learn of ways to finance your education.	(13) _____	(14) _____	(15) _____
f. Working mostly with college bound students.	(16) _____	(17) _____	(18) _____
g. Help you to plan for careers after high school.	(19) _____	(20) _____	(21) _____
h. Help you to find a job when you leave high school.	(22) _____	(23) _____	(24) _____
i. Help you to get part-time jobs while in high school, if you so wish.	(25) _____	(26) _____	(27) _____
j. Help you to find out how to qualify for jobs you would like to have.	(28) _____	(29) _____	(30) _____
k. Help you to learn about different jobs.	(31) _____	(32) _____	(33) _____
l. Help you to learn how to get along better with others.	(34) _____	(35) _____	(36) _____
m. Attempt to help you to solve personal problems.	(37) _____	(38) _____	(39) _____
n. Help you find out how to get along better with teachers.	(40) _____	(41) _____	(42) _____
o. Discuss interpersonal relations with you.	(43) _____	(44) _____	(45) _____
p. Discipline you when you are in trouble.	(46) _____	(47) _____	(48) _____
q. Try to help you if you are in trouble.	(49) _____	(50) _____	(51) _____
r. Give and explain to you tests which measure your ability to do school work.	(52) _____	(53) _____	(54) _____
s. Give and explain to you tests that tell your interests.	(55) _____	(56) _____	(57) _____
t. Give and explain to you tests that measure special skills and talents (e.g., mechanical, artistic, etc.).	(58) _____	(59) _____	(60) _____

Does your school counselor do these things?

	Yes	No	Not their responsibility
u. Give and explain to you tests that measure how much you know about school subjects.	(61) _____	(62) _____	(63) _____
v. Keep your records.	(64) _____	(65) _____	(66) _____
w. Help you and your parents understand each other better.	(67) _____	(68) _____	(69) _____
x. Refer you to places outside of school for special help, if necessary (e.g., medical, psychological, etc.).	(70) _____	(71) _____	(72) _____
y. Hold group meetings to discuss problems, school regulations, or other topics.	(73) _____	(74) _____	(75) _____
z. Is interested in and concerned about what you have to say.	(76) _____	(77) _____	(78) _____
aa. Is someone you can trust not to repeat what you told him/her.	(79) _____	(80) _____	(81) _____
bb. Is around when you need him/her.	(82) _____	(83) _____	(84) _____

The following is a list of things counselors do. Check the three you believe the counselors in your school spend most of their time doing.

a. Talking to students individually .... _____ (85)
b. Meeting with students in groups .... _____ (86)
c. Giving tests .... _____ (87)
d. Working with parents .... _____ (88)
e. Meeting with teachers .... _____ (89)
f. Writing transcripts for colleges and recommendations for jobs .... _____ (90)
g. Keeping the school records up-to-date .... _____ (91)
h. Attending meetings outside the school .... _____ (92)

In the spaces provided below, feel free to comment on the overall effectiveness of the guidance and counseling program at State College Area Senior High School.

Strong Points:

Weaknesses:

Suggested Improvements:

State College Area School District Counseling and Guidance Department
Junior High Guidance Awareness Survey

Junior high school presently attending _____ Grade_____

Sex (check one)   Female_____

Male_____

Directions: In this part of the survey, you are presented with a series of statements which are located in the middle of the page. On the right- and left-hand sides of these statements are columns of blanks under the headings "Yes" or "No." Each side represents a different question which is stated at the top of the columns. For every individual statement you should reply with either a "Yes" or "No" answer on each side.

Do you want your school counselor to help you by doing the following things?

Does your school counselor do these things?

Yes	No		Yes	No
(01) _____	(02) _____	a. Help you learn how to study.	(03) _____	(04) _____
(05) _____	(06) _____	b. Help you become acquainted with the school (the building, the rules, courses, etc.)	(07) _____	(08) _____
(09) _____	(10) _____	c. Help you plan your school program and courses.	(11) _____	(12) _____
(13) _____	(14) _____	d. Meet with you periodically to see how you are doing.	(15) _____	(16) _____
(17) _____	(18) _____	e. Help you to learn about different jobs (careers).	(19) _____	(20) _____
(21) _____	(22) _____	f. Help you learn how to get along better with others.	(23) _____	(24) _____
(25) _____	(26) _____	g. Help you with personal problems.	(27) _____	(28) _____
(29) _____	(30) _____	h. Help you find out how to get along better with teachers.	(31) _____	(32) _____
(33) _____	(34) _____	i. Keep your school records.	(35) _____	(36) _____
(37) _____	(38) _____	j. Give you standardized tests.	(39) _____	(40) _____
(41) _____	(42) _____	k. Interpret your standardized test results.	(43) _____	(44) _____
(45) _____	(46) _____	l. Help you become more aware of your abilities.	(47) _____	(48) _____
(49) _____	(50) _____	m. Help you become more aware of your interests.	(51) _____	(52) _____
(53) _____	(54) _____	n. Hold group meetings to discuss problems, school regulations, or other topics.	(55) _____	(56) _____
(57) _____	(58) _____	o. Be interested in what you have to say.	(59) _____	(60) _____
(61) _____	(62) _____	p. Be someone you can trust not to repeat what you told him/her.	(63) _____	(64) _____
(65) _____	(66) _____	q. Be available when you need him/her.	(67) _____	(68) _____

Directions: Below is a list of some things counselors do. Check the three you believe your counselor does most frequently.

69. Talking to students individually.   (69)_____
70. Talking with students in groups.   (70)_____
71. Giving tests.   (71)_____
72. Talking with parents.   (72)_____
73. Talking with teachers and administrators.   (73)_____
74. Keeping your school records up-to-date.   (74)_____

Directions: Use the remaining space on this survey (back side also) to answer the following questions.

a. What do you like best about the guidance and counseling services in your junior high school?

b. What do you like least about the guidance and counseling services in your junior high school?

State College Area School District Counseling and Guidance Department
Elementary Student Guidance Awareness Survey

Teacher's name _____
Counselor's name _____
School _____
How many years have you been at this
school? _____

Full year or grade in school   _____ (01)
(not including kindergarten)
Your Sex (check one)   Female   _____ (02)
                       Male   _____ (03)

Place a check (✓) in the blank which shows your answer to the question.

a. Do you know who _____ is? .... Yes _____ (04)
                                                                              No _____ (05)

b. Have you talked to _____ about anything? .... Yes _____ (06)
                                                                              No _____ (07)

c. Has _____ ever helped you solve a problem? .... Yes _____ (08)
                                                                              No _____ (09)

d. Has _____ ever talked to your class? .... Yes _____ (10)
                                                                              No _____ (11)

e. Do you think _____ could help you better by talking to
   your entire class? .... Yes _____ (12)
                                                                              No _____ (13)

f. Have you ever been in a group with _____ and several other students? .... Yes _____ (14)
                                                                              No _____ (15)

g. If you answered "Yes," did you like it? .... Yes _____ (16)
                                                                              No _____ (17)

h. What did you like or dislike about the group?

_____

_____

_____

i. Would you feel free to talk to _____ about
   something important to you? .... Yes _____ (18)
                                                                              No _____ (19)

j. What might keep you from talking with the counselor?

_____

_____

_____

k. Who has talked to you about jobs or careers you might want to do   a. Counselor   _____ (20)
   some day? (Check as many as you wish.)   b. Parent   _____ (21)
                                                                           c. Teacher   _____ (22)
                                                                           d. Friends   _____ (23)
                                                                           e. No one   _____ (24)

l. Who has talked to you about what you do best and what you like   a. Counselor   _____ (25)
   to do? (Check as many as you wish.)   b. Parent   _____ (26)
                                                                           c. Teacher   _____ (27)
                                                                           d. Friends   _____ (28)
                                                                           e. No one   _____ (29)

m. In what areas would you like _____ to be more helpful to you? (Check as many as you wish.)

    a. Helping me to solve problems .... _____ (30)

    b. Helping me to get along with other students .... _____ (31)

    c. Helping me to get along with teachers .... _____ (32)

    d. Helping me to get along at home .... _____ (33)

    e. Helping me to know how to work better at school .... _____ (34)

    f. Other .... _____ (35)

n. If you checked "Other," please explain:

_____

_____

_____

Erie Data Cards

INDIVIDUAL STUDENT COUNSELING	1

SCHOOL _____

COUNSELOR _____

0   Less than 10 minutes
1   10–19 minutes
2   20–29 minutes
3   30–39 minutes
4   40–49 minutes
5   50–59 minutes
6   60–69 minutes
7   70–79 minutes
8   80–89 minutes
9   90 or more

01   Attendance
02   Behavior
03   Career Counseling
04   Career Decision-Making
05   College Counseling
06   Drop-Out
07   Drug Counseling
08   Employment Counseling
09   Finances
10   Home Problems
11   Personal Social Adjustment
12   School Program Choice
13   Sex
14   Subject Change
15   Teacher-Student Problem
16   Value Counseling
17   Other

0   Problem Identified
1   Solution Implemented
2   Problem Solved

INDIVIDUAL STUDENT INFORMATION/SERVICE	2

SCHOOL _____

COUNSELOR _____

0   Less than 10 minutes
1   10–19 minutes
2   20–29 minutes
3   30–39 minutes
4   40–49 minutes
5   50–59 minutes
6   60–69 minutes
7   70–79 minutes
8   80–89 minutes
9   90 or more

01   Attendance
02   College Guidance
03   Discipline
04   Employment, Full Time
05   Employment, Part Time
06   Enrolling
07   Financial Aid, College
08   Financial Aid, Current
09   Free Lunch
10   Military Information
11   Occupational Information
12   Program Change
13   Program Information
14   Sick Calls
15   Summer School
16   Test Information
17   Test Interpretation
18   Transportation
19   Withdrawing
20   Work Permit
21   Other

Source: From the Erie, Pennsylvania, School District.

INDIVIDUAL ADULT CONFERENCE IN-SCHOOL	3

SCHOOL _____

COUNSELOR _____

0   Less than 10 minutes
1   10–19 minutes
2   20–29 minutes
3   30–39 minutes
4   40–49 minutes
5   50–59 minutes
6   60–69 minutes
7   70–79 minutes
8   80–89 minutes
9   90 or more

01   Administrator, Central Office
02   Administrator, Own School
03   Administrator, Other School
04   Business Representative
05   College Representative
06   Community Representative
07   Counselor Own School
08   Counselor Other School
09   Parent
10   Professional Non-School
11   Psychologist, School
12   Referral Agency
13   Social Worker
14   Teacher
15   Visiting Teacher
16   Other

ADULT GROUP AND OUT-OF-SCHOOL ACTIVITY	4

SCHOOL _____

COUNSELOR _____

0   Less than 10 minutes
1   10–19 minutes
2   20–29 minutes
3   30–39 minutes
4   40–49 minutes
5   50–59 minutes
6   60–69 minutes
7   70–79 minutes
8   80–89 minutes
9   90 or more

01   Case Conference
02   Meetings
03   Other Adult Groups
04   Case Conference
05   Classes Attended
06   Meetings
07   Other Adult Groups
08   Clerical Routine
09   Correspondence
10   Information, Looking Up
11   Recommendations, College
12   Recommendations, Job
13   Phone Calls
14   Transcripts
15   Other

_____ Units Counted

_____ Units Estimated

SOLITARY IN-SCHOOL ACTIVITY	5

SCHOOL _____
COUNSELOR _____

0   Less than 10 minutes
1   10–19 minutes
2   20–29 minutes
3   30–39 minutes
4   40–49 minutes
5   50–59 minutes
6   60–69 minutes
7   70–79 minutes
8   80–89 minutes
9   90 or more

01   Bulletins, Writing
02   Correspondence, Miscellaneous
03   Forms, Various
04   Information, Looking Up
05   Listing
06   Mail Handling
07   Program Changes
08   Recommendations, College
09   Recommendations, Job
10   Summons
11   Phone Calls, Parents
12   Phone Calls, School Personal
13   Transcripts
14   Trays, Checking

_____ Units Counted

_____ Units Estimated

STUDENT GROUP ACTIVITY	6

SCHOOL _____
COUNSELOR _____

0   Less than 10 minutes
1   10–19 minutes
2   20–29 minutes
3   30–39 minutes
4   40–49 minutes
5   50–59 minutes
6   60–69 minutes
7   70–79 minutes
8   80–89 minutes
9   90 or more

01   Class Visitation
02   Classroom Coverage
03   Group Counseling
04   Enrolling
05   Excuse from School
06   Free Lunch
07   Information, College
08   Information, General
09   Information, Occupational
10   Material Distribution
11   Information, Test
12   Monitoring Activities
13   Orientation
14   Program Choice
15   Tardiness
16   Testing
17   Test Interpretation
18   Transportation
19   Other

_____ Number of Students Served

SUBJECT INDEX